K

Psychoanalytic Theories

Perspectives from
Developmental Psychopathology

Psychoanalytic Theories

Perspectives from Developmental Psychopathology

PETER FONAGY PhD, FBA

and

MARY TARGET PhD

both of University College London

Brunner-Routledge
Taylor & Francis Group

Published in 2003 by
Brunner-Routledge
29 West 35th Street
New York, NY 10001
www.brunner-routledge.com

Distribution Center
Brunner-Routledge
10650 Toebben Drive
Independence, KY 41051
PH. 800-634-7064
FAX 800-248-4724

PSYCHOANALYTIC THEORIES

10 9 8 7 6 5 4 3 2 1

A CIP catalog Record for this book is available from the British Library.

⊖ The paper in this publication meets the requirements of the ANSI Standard
   Z39.48-1984 (Permanence of Paper)

Library of Congress Cataloging-in-Publication Data

Available from the publisher

Printed and bound in the UK by Athenaeum Press, Ltd.,
Gateshead, Tyne & Wear

ISBN: 0-415-93488-5

Contents

Chapter 5   107

Introduction to object relations theory

Chapter 6   118

The Klein-Bion model

Series foreword

After the first hundred years of its history, psychoanalysis has matured into a serious, independent intellectual tradition, which has notably retained its capacity to challenge established truths in most areas of our culture. The biological psychiatrist of today is called to task by psychoanalysis, as much as was the specialist in nervous diseases of Freud's time, in turn of the century Vienna. Today's cultural commentators, whether for or against psychoanalytic ideas, are forced to pay attention to considerations of unconscious motivation, defences, early childhood experience and the myriad other discoveries which psychoanalysts brought to 20th century culture. Above all, psychoanalytic ideas have spawned an approach to the treatment of mental disorders, psychodynamic psychotherapy, which has become the dominant tradition in most countries, at least in the Western world.

Little wonder that psychoanalytic thinking continues to face detractors, individuals who dispute its epistemology and its conceptual and clinical claims. While disappointing in one way, this is a sign that psychoanalysis may be unique in its capacity to challenge and provoke. Why should this be? Psychoanalysis is unrivalled in the depth of its questioning of human motivation, and whether its answers are right or wrong, the epistemology of psychoanalysis allows it to confront the most difficult problems of human experience. Paradoxically, our new understanding concerning the physical basis of our existence – our genes, nervous systems and endocrine functioning – rather than finally displacing psychoanalysis, has created a pressing need for a complementary discipline which considers the memories, desires and meanings which are beginning to be recognised as influencing human adaptation even at the biological level. How else, other than through the study of subjective experience, will we understand the expression of the individual's biological destiny, within the social environment?

It is not surprising, then, that psychoanalysis continues to attract some of the liveliest intellects in our culture. These individuals are by no means all psychoanalytic clinicians, or psychotherapists. They are distinguished scholars in an almost bewildering range of disciplines, from the study of mental disorders with their biological determinants to the disciplines of literature, art, philosophy and history. There will always be a need to explicate the meaning of experience. Psychoanalysis, with its commitment to understanding subjectivity, is in a premier position to fulfil this intellectual and human task. We are not surprised at the upsurge of interest in psychoanalytic studies in universities in many countries. The books in this series are aimed at addressing the same intellectual curiosity that has made these educational projects so successful.

We are proud that the Whurr Series in Psychoanalysis has been able to attract some of the most interesting and creative minds in the field. Our commitment is to no specific orientation, to no particular professional group, but to the intellectual challenge to explore the questions of meaning and interpretation systematically, and in a scholarly way. Nevertheless, we would be glad if this series particularly spoke to the psychotherapeutic community, to those individuals who use their own minds and humanity to help others in distress.

Our focus in this series is to communicate the intellectual excitement which we feel about the past, present and future of psychoanalytic ideas. We hope that our work with the authors and editors in the series will help to make these ideas accessible to an ever-increasing and worldwide group of students, scholars and practitioners.

Peter Fonagy
Mary Target
University College London
October 2002

Preface

This book is the end product of many years of thinking about the relationship between psychoanalysis and developmental psychology. Working at the Anna Freud Centre in London in the tradition established by Freud's daughter, we were acutely aware of just how fundamental developmental questions were to a psychoanalytic understanding of the mind, of abnormal behavior and of therapeutic intervention. The unfolding of a child's mental abilities is a process that presents challenges which, if unmet, can generate problems at later stages of childhood or in adult psychological functioning. Indeed within the developmental tradition all aspects of psychological function may be understood in terms of the vicissitudes of the topography of individual developmental paths. Distinguishing deviant paths from normal ones was one of Anna Freud's lasting achievements, but the developmental perspective actually serves to throw into relief all psychoanalytic formulations.

Anna Freud was pursuing the developmental tradition established by her father, who, borrowing from biology and especially from embryology, saw the mind's emergence from defined ontological stages as analogous to the stages of development of a fetus from fertilized ovum to newborn. Each major subsequent theoretical development within psychoanalysis includes a model of development and of how maturation or environmental experiences along the progress from infancy to adulthood can create risks for psychological dysfunction. Psychoanalytic models also invariably reach for developmental constructs to make sense of psychological abnormality that is beyond our common-sense understanding of how the mind functions. The discrepancy between a part of the mind which functions at a mature level and another which reflects more primitive modes of operation or understanding is perhaps the most common metaphor in psychoanalytic developmental theory. In many theories even the healing properties of psychotherapy are viewed within a developmental context, almost as if time could be turned back to allow the missed steps of early childhood to be taken.

This book, then, introduces psychoanalytic theories through the lens of developmental study. Development is a helpful backdrop because it enables us to bring what we know about both normal and abnormal child development to bear on psychoanalytic models of the mind. We have attempted to integrate or at least simultaneously consider findings from developmental studies and the major Anglo-American psychoanalytic traditions. The book assumes no previous knowledge of psychoanalytic perspectives. It is in fact intended for readers with an interest and perhaps a training in psychology, who would like to know more about different psychoanalytic models of personality development, and how these fit with the empirical evidence which may be available. As the reader will soon appreciate, the empirical evidence in relation to many psychoanalytic theories is tangential or thin, but we believe that it is nevertheless important to know where theories stand in relation to it.

Psychoanalytic models are relevant to the study of many fields outside the clinical practice of psychoanalysis. Thus, literature, history and in fact the action of non-psychoanalytic therapies such as cognitive-behavior therapy or drug treatments can be illuminated by an understanding of unconscious factors. Similarly, psychoanalytic models often help to explain behavior and relationships that are not at all psychotherapeutic in character: family relationships, group processes, organizations, political affiliations, and so on. This book aims to give a basic understanding of the models of mental function which generations of psychoanalytic clinicians have arrived at, mainly through their intensive study of private thoughts and feelings, and ways of relating, within intensive psychotherapy. The book considers the limitations of this approach at the same time as promoting its relevance. Some of the great minds of the last century built on Freud's ideas to understand the difficulties that people encounter in the course of development. Their models represent an extremely rich body of ideas that well repay detailed study. We hope that the summaries we provide will allow students and other interested readers to go some way along this path.

Acknowledgements

The authors would like to express their gratitude to several people who have helped to get this book written. The great burden of preparing the manuscript and references, and editing the evolving text, was carried at various times by Clare Welch and Kathy Leach. Extensive, thoughtful and most generous contributions to the preparation of various drafts of this work were also provided by Dr Anna Higgitt. The exceptional editorial gifts, scholarship and tactful constructive suggestions of Dr Elizabeth Allison were, as always, invaluable. Our friends Drs György Gergely and Efrain Bleiberg were responsible for important parts of the thinking in Chapter 12, and collaboration with each of them has been an inspiration as well as a great pleasure in recent years. The thoughtful comments and encouragement of three reviewers, Professors Stephen Frosh, Enrico Jones and Shmuel Erlich, were enormously helpful and much appreciated. One of the most experienced and wise scholars and editors in the field – Dr Elizabeth Spillius – gave an unexpectedly thorough read to the proofs. This allowed some invaluable final revisions. Above all, the superhuman forbearance of our publisher, Colin Whurr, as he encouraged and guided us at various stages of the project and patiently waited for the manuscript, went beyond words. At that point we did get it done, but we are very grateful to him for putting up with us. All the above helped well beyond the call of duty and the book belongs in large part to them. The errors that remain are our own.

CHAPTER 1

An introduction to this book and to the basic psychoanalytic model

1.1 Learning about psychoanalysis

This book is about psychoanalysis from the special angle of psychoanalytic developmental psychopathology. Developmental psychopathology is the study of the origins and course of individual patterns of maladaptation (Sroufe and Rutter, 1984). Psychoanalysis has contributed substantially to this field, and continues to do so. Psychoanalysis helps us to understand the psychological processes that underlie continuity and change in patterns of adaptation or maladaptation. How is it that some individuals emerge from a period of crisis stronger and richer for the experience, whereas others find it increasingly difficult to adapt and cope? Psychoanalytic theories see development as an active, dynamic process where individuals add meaning to their experience, and the meanings attributed to these alter their consequences. Individuals' biology shapes these experiences at the same time as being shaped by them. The psychoanalytic theories we are going to consider are all ambitious formulations, aiming to expand our understanding of this passage through life by adding explanations of unconscious meanings and influences.

The developmental approach to psychopathology is the traditional framework of psychoanalysis (see Tyson and Tyson, 1990); it aims to uncover the developmental stages and sequelae of different disorders of childhood and adulthood and factors that influence them (Sroufe, 1990; Sroufe, Egeland and Kreutzer, 1990). This book provides an extensive review of psychoanalytic theories, including classical and contemporary structural theories, developments of ego psychological models, and British and US object relational approaches. The discussion of each of these psychoanalytical schools aims to highlight the contributions each can make to developmental psychopathology, in terms of etiology, treatment and evidence. We argue that bringing together psychoanalysis and developmental psychopathology makes explicit what has been at the core of psychoanalytic theorizing and treatment, from Freud's day onward.

Given the vastness of the psychoanalytic literature we are not able to do full justice to any of the theories. We have not covered many important ideas originating in France, Germany, Italy, Latin America: our coverage is fullest in the Anglo-American psychoanalytic tradition. We have taken each theory and tried to highlight its developmental component, then turned to the ways in which the developmental ideas explain maladaptive pathways through life. Our focus tends to be on personality disorder as the clearest test of the adequacy of such explanations. With each theory we have looked for systematically collected data bearing on the ideas proposed. There are more psychoanalytic theories than we need. Although many overlap, there are also unique features to each body of theory. Choosing between them is a major challenge for psychoanalytic scholarship. The two criteria for selection are coherence and consistency with the known facts. We have attempted to apply both of these to the theories under consideration.

This book concerns ideas more than practice. Comparing the theories from the point of view of their clinical usefulness is obviously another criterion that we could have used (and others have used) to assess psychoanalytic models. The book, however, is aimed primarily at students of psychoanalytic theory, be these students striving to apply a psychoanalytic perspective to another discipline, or aiming to improve their ability to help distressed patients. Psychoanalysis as a discipline stretches far beyond psychoanalytic psychotherapy. The psychoanalytic understanding of the mind, particularly from a developmental perspective, is relevant to those working with cognitive behavioral techniques, or even with pharmacotherapy, as well as to those who offer classical psychoanalysis. Developmental psychoanalysis is an approach to the study of the mind, perhaps the richest and most productive of all the theoretical frames of reference now available. Some great minds of the century that has passed have built on Freud's ideas to understand the difficulties that people encounter in the course of development. Their models represent an extremely rich body of ideas that well repay detailed study. We hope that the summaries we provide will allow students to begin along this path.

1.2 The basic assumptions of psychoanalysis

The psychology that Freud discovered and elaborated has enjoyed considerable success as an explanatory framework. This is because its few basic assumptions and propositions are open to endless revision and refinement and, arguably, because the clinical procedure that provides its evidential base offers a unique perspective on the human mind. Most specific propositions that were briefly touched on above and are to be reviewed in this book are data-dependent, that is, they may be revised or even omitted without damaging the integrity of the psychoanalytic theoretical structure. However, all the theories to be discussed in this book share a common set of assumptions. The core assumptions of the basic psychoanalytic model (Sandler, 1962a; Sandler and Joffe, 1969) include: (a) *psychic determinism*, the conviction that cognitive, emotional and behavioral aspects of pathology have psychological causes (rather than just physical causality or random biological events); (b) the *pleasure–unpleasure principle*, namely that behavior may be seen as an effort to minimize psychic pain and maximize psychic pleasure and a sense of intrapsychic safety; (c) the *biological nature* of the organism drives its psychological adaptation; (d) a *dynamic unconscious*, where mental forces compete for expression, helps to determine which ideas and feelings may reach consciousness; and (e) the *genetic–developmental* proposition, which states that all behaviors are understandable as sequences of actions developing out of earlier (even earliest infantile) events. Let us elaborate these points.

(a) Psychoanalysts assume that mental disturbance is usefully studied at the level of psychological causation; that the representation of past experience, its interpretation and meaning, conscious or non-conscious, determines the individual's reaction to his or her external world and capacity to adapt to it. The emphasis on psychic causation does not imply either a lack of respect for or inadequate attention to other levels of analysis of psychiatric problems such as the biological, the family or broader social factors. Nevertheless, psychiatric problems, whether at the root genetic, constitutional or socially caused, are seen by the psychoanalyst as the meaningful consequence of the child's beliefs, thoughts and feelings and therefore accessible to psychotherapy. That a person's actions may be explained by his mental states (thoughts, feelings, beliefs and desires) is part of the commonsense psychology that we use without reflection (Churchland, Ramachandran, and Sejnowski, 1994). The extension of this model to unconsciously held beliefs and feelings may have been Freud's greatest single discovery (Hopkins, 1992; Wollheim, 1995).

(b) Complex *unconscious mental processes* are assumed to be responsible for both the content of conscious thinking and behavior. In particular, unconscious fantasies associated with wishes for instinctual gratification (past pleasure) or safety (Sandler, 1987b) motivate and determine behavior, affect regulation and the ability to cope with the social environment. Unconscious ideation is thought to generate emotional states which guide and organize mental functions.

(c) The experience of the self with others is internalized and leads to *representational structures of interpersonal interactions*. At the simplest level, they create expectations about the behavior of others but, more elaborately, they determine the 'shape' of the representations of self and other and, in combination, constitute the individual's internal world.

(d) It is assumed that psychic *conflict* is ubiquitous and that it causes the experience of unpleasure (or lack of safety). Intrapsychic conflict is inevitable, but some adverse childhood environments generate conflicts of overwhelming intensity. Children from such backgrounds cannot deal with later conflicts even within the normal range of experience. Trauma (such as death of a parent), abuse or long-term neglect thus undermine personality development by intensifying incompatible wishes or reducing the child's capacity to resolve conflict mentally.

(e) The child is predisposed to modify unconscious wishes unacceptable to conscious thought through a developmental hierarchy of *defense* mechanisms that work to avoid unpleasure. This hierarchy reflects the individual's degree of pathology; relying on early defenses is normally associated with more severe disturbances.

(f) Psychoanalysts assume that the patient's communication in a treatment context has meaning beyond that intended by the patient. They assume that defense mechanisms and other analogous mechanisms enable symptoms to carry *multiple meanings*, and to reflect the nature of internal representations of others and of their relationship to the individual. The analyst is able to bring the patient's attention to aspects of his or her behavior which are ego-dystonic and hard to understand. By making links, the analyst illustrates to the patient that his symptomatic behavior, while experienced as distressing, undesirable and perhaps irrational, may be seen as rational given the dual assumptions of unconscious mental experience and psychic causation.

(g) The relationship to the analyst is the focus of therapy. It provides a window on the patient's expectations of others and can become a vehicle for disowned aspects of the patient's thoughts and feelings. *Transference* displacement may include repudiated aspects of past relationships, or past fantasies about these, as well as conflictual aspects of current relationships to parents, siblings or other important figures (Tyson and Tyson, 1986). The patient's words and actions (re-enactments) affect the analyst, and through exploring the role he or she has been placed in by the patient, the analyst can better understand the patient's representations of role relationships and feelings about them.

(h) Modern psychoanalysis emphasizes the current state of the patient in relation to his or her environment, past relationships and adaptations to these. Psychoanalysts recognize that the therapy has an important holding or containing function in the patient's life, which goes beyond the specific impacts of interpretation and insight. The actual relationship with the analyst as a person creates the possibility of a reintegration or reorganization of the patient's internal world, which in turn facilitates his or her continued development. The establishment of an open, intense and safe relationship with another person may serve as the basis of new internalizations, bringing about a healthier resolution of past conflict and reparation of deficits.

1.3 The assumption of developmental continuity

A core assumption of psychoanalytic theory that is central to this book is the so-called genetic or *developmental point of view*, which psychoanalytic texts acknowledge to varying degrees. An essential idea running through all phases of Freud's thinking was the notion that pathology recapitulated ontogeny; that disorders of the mind could be best understood as residues of childhood experiences and primitive modes of mental functioning (see Freud and Breuer, 1895; Freud, 1905d; 1914; 1926). This implied that personality types and neurotic symptoms could be linked with specific developmental stages, and that symptoms could be understood in terms of fixations at and regressions to earlier periods of normal development. For example, Freud's theory of narcissism or self-development during infancy was invoked to explain adult psychosis, and conversely, his view of psychic life during infancy was constructed largely on the basis of observations of adult psychopathology. His notion of infantile grandiosity is derived from the grandiosity observed in many instances of psychosis. The presumed confusion, presumed hallucinatory experiences and lack of reality testing of Freud's infant seems to parallel psychotic experiences. For Freud, and almost all psychoanalysts who followed him, there is a tacit assumption of an isomorphism between pathology and development, which permits bi-directional causal inference between childhood and pathology. The assumption covers all psychopathology and all stages of development. For example, Freudian analysts explained neurotic pathology as a residue of oedipal concerns, dating mainly from the third to fifth year of life. Character disorder was attributed to residues from between the infantile and the oedipal, mostly from the second year of life.

Freud's (1905d) psycho-sexual theory of development was revolutionary in constructing an understanding of adult disturbances in terms of infantile and early childhood experience. Karl Abraham (1927) filled in the details of the model, identifying specific links between character formation, neurosis and psychosis on the one hand, and instinctual development on the other. Contemporary followers of Freud proposed alternative clinical foci, but all were based on developmental formulations: Alfred Adler's (1916) focus was on the child's feelings of inferiority as the root of the adult's striving for power and maturity; Sandor Ferenczi (1913) outlined the vicissitudes of the child's development of a sense of reality and the simultaneous sacrifice of fantasized omnipotence; Otto Rank's (1924) focus was at an even earlier stage, that of the birth trauma, which in his view underpinned all subsequent human conflicts, defenses and strivings. Even Carl Jung's (1913) model was developmental, if in a somewhat negative sense, in that he proposed that true maturity and mental health lay in the giving up of the 'child-self'.

More recent psychoanalytic theories continue to follow a developmental motif. Anna Freud (1936) provided a developmental model of ego defenses and later (1965) a comprehensive model of psychopathology based on the dimensions of normal and abnormal personality development. Melanie Klein (1935; 1936), influenced by Ferenczi and Abraham, was a pioneer in linking interpersonal relationships to instinctual developmental factors to provide a radically different perspective both on severe mental disorders and on child development. Meanwhile, in the US Heinz Hartmann (1939) with Kris and Loewenstein (1946) provided an alternative, equally developmentally oriented framework, focusing on the evolution of mental structures necessary for adaptation, and elaborated on the common developmental conflicts between mental structures in early childhood. Margaret Mahler (1979) and her colleagues (1975) provided psychoanalysts in the North American tradition with a dynamic map of the first three years of life, and ample opportunities for tracing the developmental origins of disorders. Fairbairn (1952a) traced the development of object seeking from immature to mature dependence; Jacobson (1964) explored the development of representations of self and other. Kernberg (1975) drew on previous work by Klein, Hartmann and Jacobson to furnish a developmental model of borderline and narcissistic disturbances; Kohut (1971; 1977) constructed a model of narcissistic disturbances based on presumed deficits of early parenting.

1.4 The developmental approach to psychopathology

The emerging field of developmental psychopathology (Garmezy and Rutter, 1983; Cicchetti, 1990a; Garmezy and Masten, 1994) has brought psychoanalysis and developmental psychology into close contact. Developmental psychopathology research has demonstrated that developmental continuity is an empirically elusive and conceptually complex problem (Kagan, 1987; Emde, 1988b), and cannot be simply assumed, as psychoanalysts are wont to do.

Recently, attempts to reconcile these empirical observations have reached toward the construct of mental representation, drawn from cognitive science (e.g. Mandler, 1985). Psychoanalytic theory in general (e.g. Jacobson, 1964) and psychoanalytic theories of object relations in particular (e.g. Bretherton, 1985; Sroufe, 1989; Westen, 1991b), concern themselves with the way the structural mechanisms of the mind underpin the process of internalization of experience and the creation of a psychological model of the interpersonal world. Increasingly, work in developmental psychiatry and psychology is focusing on the paths through which internal representations of early experiences with the primary figures of childhood come to have an impact upon the formation of later relationships. These may culminate in the types of relationship disorders and psychopathological conditions that appear across the lifespan (Emde, 1988a; Sroufe and Fleeson, 1988; Cicchetti, 1989; 1990a; Sameroff and Emde, 1989; Zigler, 1989).

1.5 General critiques of psychoanalytic theory

Few would question that psychoanalytic theory, and particularly Freud's ideas, have exerted a profound effect on twentieth-century thought; an equally small minority would consider its impact on the twenty-first century as assured. There have been numerous obituaries of psychodynamic thinking over the past decades (Grünbaum, 1984; Crews, 1995; Webster, 1995). Frederick Crews (1993) is perhaps representative of these critics. Crews asserts that psychoanalytic theory has no significant experimental or epidemiological support, that any body of knowledge built on Freud's dubious insights is likely to disappear into quicksand and that 'despite some well-intentioned efforts at reform a pseudoscience is what psychoanalysis has remained' (p. 55).

Attacks on Freud's corpus are by no means new. John Watson (1930) predicted that '20 years from now an analyst using Freudian concepts and Freudian terminology will be placed on the same plane as a phrenologist' (p. 27) and yet ushered in what is generally regarded as the heyday of psychoanalytic ideas. However, the pervasiveness and intensity of recent critiques cannot be shrugged off even by the most committed Freudians. As the psychoanalytic approach to developmental psychopathology moves into the new century, we believe it should deal with the challenges it faces and undertake a radical reappraisal of its epistemic framework. We believe that the psychoanalytic approach could make a timely and significant contribution to the progression of ideas in developmental psychopathology. In this section, we will consider some important limitations of current psychoanalytic ideas, which we believe psychoanalytic thinking should now address.

1.5.1 The evidential basis of theories

Most psychoanalytic theorizing has been done by clinicians who have not tested their conjectures empirically. Not surprisingly, therefore, the evidential basis of these theories is often unclear. For example, Melanie Klein asserted that the infant forms representations of the mother's breast and the father's penis. She would have been the first to admit that she had no direct evidence of this (see Spillius, 1994). Rather, in attempting to understand what adult patients say, Kleinian psychoanalysts find it helpful to assume the existence of such fantasies. In asking for additional evidence which triangulates with clinical material, we are not returning to operationalism, verificationism, or other discredited residues of logical positivism (see, for example, Leahey, 1980; Meehl, 1986). By restricting itself to a domain incompatible with controlled observations and testable hypotheses, psychoanalysis deprives itself of the interplay between data and theory that has contributed so much to the growth of twentieth-century science. In the absence of direct observations, psychoanalysts are frequently forced to fall back upon either the indirect evidence of clinical observation or an appeal to authority.

To accept clinical data as validating developmental hypotheses flies in the face not only of ferocious opposition from philosophers of science (e.g. Grünbaum, 1984; 1992), but also of common sense: to accept retrospective hypotheses requires the unlikely assumption that pathological states observed in the consulting room are isomorphic in their structure and function to early stages of development. The 'pathomorphic' (Klein, 1981) nature of psychoanalytic developmental theory biases psychoanalytic accounts toward abnormality. Thus developmental accounts will highlight aspects of development with connections to pathology. They will be far less illuminating about instances of psychological resilience despite intense trauma reported in anecdotal studies of famous individuals and clinical cases of adults maltreated as children, as well as in systematic studies of the impact of severe stress events on children (see Cicchetti et al., 1993).

Psychoanalytic ideas naturally reflect the clinical problems which preoccupied particular theoreticians. For example, Sullivan (1940; 1953) focused on the problem of social alienation and anomie as the core difficulty of the human condition, and postulated infantile anxiety, arising as a contagion from the mother, as the cause. Winnicott (1965a) conceived of inauthenticity and the false self as a core problem and focused on the failure of 'good enough' mothering and of the holding environment. Kohut's (1971; 1977) central clinical puzzle was how an enfeebled self develops and he emphasized the mother's capacity for empathic responsiveness. Melanie Klein's (1946) interests were in residues of primitive childhood thinking in adult pathology, and her developmental ideas centered on the persistence of an infantile psychotic core gaining dominance in the personality as a result of faulty internalizations. It is rarely clear whether each psychoanalytic approach is associated with a particular category of clinical cases or, as is more likely, theoreticians reconstruct their patients' histories in ways that fit the theory.

The validation of psychoanalytic theories poses a formidable challenge to the researcher. Most of the variables are private, complex, abstract and difficult to operationalize or test. Psychoanalytic accounts focus on very remote etiological variables, and even when constructs are apparently operationalizable (e.g. splits in the ego, masochism and omnipotence), they are rarely formulated with sufficient exactness to allow them to be disproved.

There is a further major logical problem with the reconstructionist stance. At the simplest level, clinical theories of development are based on the accounts of currently distressed people who attempt to recall events that occurred during early childhood, the most important phase of which was pre-verbal. Psychoanalysis has contributed significantly to our current sophistication about the distortion of memories of early experience (see Brewin, Andrews, and Gotlib, 1993). The clear danger is the circular assumption that something must have gone amiss during childhood, otherwise these individuals would not be in such difficulties. Thus most developmental theories make recourse to various errors of omission or commission on the part of the mother, many of which would be difficult to verify retrospectively. The converse is also true, that the presence of healthy responses in an otherwise disturbed individual, leads clinicians to postulate moderating factors such as the presence of 'a good object' in an otherwise devastated interpersonal environment. This confirmatory bias is inherent to enumerative inductivism, which clinical theories of development find hard to avoid (Cooper, 1985).

Clinical material has enormous value as an illustration of a theoretical model. It also helps to generate hypotheses for more formal investigation. Clinical insight, however, is unlikely to help resolve theoretical differences concerning developmentally remote variables that are considered to place an individual at risk of a disorder. One reason for this is that the observations of experienced clinicians do not always converge on common reconstructions. Clinical data offer a fertile ground for theory building, but not for distinguishing good theories from bad or better ones. The proliferation of clinical theories (over 400 psychotherapeutic approaches or 'schools') is the best evidence that clinical data are more suitable for generating theories than for evaluating them.

However, it should not be too readily assumed that the empirical data that are most useful in testing predictions and that allow optimal control of variables, minimize threats to validity and maximize the possibility of causal influence, are also most helpful in the construction of psychological theory. Westen (1990a; 1990b) points to the relative paucity of rich theories within current psychiatry and psychology which derive from controlled studies. Indeed, many psychological theories of psychopathology explicitly acknowledge their indebtedness to psychoanalytic ideas, which have inspired rich lines of empirical investigation, for example, Seligman's work on learned helplessness and depression (Seligman, 1975); Ainsworth et al.'s work on attachment (Ainsworth et al., 1978); Beck's schema theory of depression (Beck, 1967; 1976); and Slade's functional analysis of eating disorders (Slade, 1982).

The comparison of future psychoanalytic theories should move away from enumerative inductivism and develop closer links with data-gathering methods available in modern social science. To gather such data without obliterating the phenomena is an important challenge for the current generation of analysts.

1.5.2 The assumption of uniformity

Psychoanalytic developmental models aim at a level of abstraction where there is a one-to-one relationship between a particular pattern of abnormality and a particular developmental cause. Thus within any theory there is a single model for borderline personality disorder, narcissistic pathology, etc. Empirical studies, on the whole, are at odds with these accounts. For example, in eating disorder, where most psychoanalytic accounts involve specific pathology of early family relationships, empirical studies testify to the variations in parent–child interactions (see Kog and Vandereycken, 1985) and family dynamics (Grigg, Friesen and Sheppy, 1989), and there is no specific link to eating disorders (Yager, 1982; Strober and Humphrey, 1987; Stern et al., 1989).

There is a further sense in which uniformity is often inappropriately assumed by psychoanalytic theories, which may help to account for the point just made. Object relationships tend to be treated as a singular phenomenon which encompasses a number of subservient functions, e.g. empathy, understanding, the ability to maintain relationships, self and object representations etc. (see Kernberg, 1984). Current research is at odds with this kind of hierarchical model, and suggests the existence of a number of interlinked but independent mental functions that sustain social behavior and social cognition (see Fonagy, Edgcumbe et al., 1993). Westen (1991a; 1991b), for example, discusses four aspects of object relations: (1) the complexity of representations of people; (2) the affect tone of relationship paradigms; (3) the capacity for emotional investment; (4) the understanding of social causality. He offers empirical data to support the view that there is more or less developmental deficit on these dimensions in different pathologies. For example, borderline individuals show no deficit in the complexity of their representations of people, but show considerable pathology on the other dimensions. Too little is known about the common object relations abnormalities in specific disorders and the heterogeneity of individuals even within any of these major groupings.

Psychoanalysts should become less interested in global constructs and concern themselves far more with individual mental processes, their evolution, their vicissitudes and their role in pathological functioning. There may be a trade-off between apparent explanatory power and differentiation and exactitude. It seems to us, however, that if psychoanalysis is to survive, its preferred level of analysis will have to be groups of individuals (series of cases) rather than the single individual from whom generalizations to whole populations are made.

1.5.3 Alternative psychoanalytic accounts

There is a general failure amongst psychoanalytic writers to compare theoretical accounts of clinical observations (see Hamilton, 1993 for an exception). Instead, each framework is expanded to incorporate new data, making them unwieldy and difficult to contrast.

1.5.4 The stance toward the environment

Although recognizing that his patients' symptoms could be related to 'the purely human and social circumstances' of their lives (Freud, 1905a, p. 47), Freud increasingly sought to treat those symptoms as though they were entirely the work of endogenous processes. Although psychoanalytic accounts vary in terms of the relative emphasis given to the environment, they share a certain lack of sophistication in considering its influence. We have already touched on the exclusive focus on events within the earliest mother–infant relationship. Winnicott (1948) may well have been right to correct the Kleinian tendency to pathologize the infant and to attribute this pathology, more or less exclusively, to the baby's own drives. However, when he says that 'ordinary babies are not mad' (i.e. they are neither paranoid nor depressive), he acknowledges but one alternative to account for pathology: the mother. The work of Kohut, Adler, Modell, Masterson, Rinsley, and even Bowlby and Stern, has continued to focus on mothers' deficiencies as the cause of every variety of psychopathology. An extreme example of this was the unsuccessful attempt by some psychoanalysts to account for the most severe of mental disorders in terms of parental influences on the infant (for example the idea of the 'schizophrenogenic mother' (Fromm-Reichmann, 1948). More severe disorders were considered to be caused by either more severe parenting environments or environments of less severity but experienced at an earlier stage of life. Neither of these models fitted well with what was discovered about psychotic disorders such as schizophrenia (Willick, 2001).

Evidently, there is need for greater sophistication in thinking about the role of the environment. The influences between child and environment are reciprocal; constitutional and parental factors interact in the generation of risk (see, for example, Rutter, 1989a; 1993). A transactional approach suggests a poorness of fit model. For example, a temperamentally difficult child, born to parents disinclined to adopt a reflective, mentalizing stance toward the infant, may be at great risk, while neither factor alone might lead to difficulties.

Psychoanalytic views of environmental influences also lack sophistication in that, by and large, they ignore the wider cultural context. This may be a residue of the biological origin of psychoanalytic formulations (see Pine, 1985), and is by no means characteristic of all dynamic models (see, for example, Sullivan, 1953; Lasch, 1978). Some developmental phenomena may be so deeply biologically rooted that they are invariant cross-culturally (see Bowlby, 1969). Increasingly, however, evidence is accumulating that even the most basic psychological processes are accelerated or inhibited by cultural factors. Sissons Joshi and MacLean (1995) for example, found that in India, four-year-olds were fairly accurate when they were asked about a child concealing emotions from an adult in an appearance-reality task, whereas English children consistently failed. The authors attribute these differences to the greater respect and deference toward adults demanded of Indian children, especially girls. In view of the central role cultural factors play in the development of the self (see Mead, 1934) psychoanalysts may be ignoring their rootedness in Western culture at their peril. The individuated self, which is at the center of most psychoanalytic formulations, is also particularly Western in its orientation and contrasts with the relational self represented most strongly by non-Western cultures (see Sampson, 1988). The latter is characterized by more permeable and fluid self–other boundaries and by an emphasis on social control where this includes but reaches far beyond the person. The unit of identity for the relational self is not an internal representation of the other, or its abstraction or elaboration with an ego ideal, but rather the family or the community. It should be particularly noted that borderline personality disorder is a diagnosis most commonly applied to women (American Psychiatric Association, 1987). It is possible that, as a consequence of cultural forces or constitutional predisposition, women are less suited than men to the Western ideal of an individuated self (Gilligan, 1982; Lykes, 1985). Placing the individuated self at the peak of a developmental hierarchy risks ethnocentrism as well as pathologizing what may be an adaptive mode of functioning in some social contexts (see Heard and Linehan, 1993).

Findings from research on parent–child relationships in Japan and in the United States suggest that prolonging the symbiotic union between mother and infant does not undermine the individual's capacity to achieve autonomy (Rothbaum et al., 2000). The psychoanalytic literature (see below) is characterized by assumptions that there is a struggle between the desire for closeness and the desire for separation, and related to this, that conflicts between the needs of the self and of others are inevitable. Conflict is central to a Western (psychoanalytic) theory of development but it is not an essential part of a Japanese perception of childhood. The concept of self in psychoanalysis is almost by definition an independent entity, whereas within Japanese culture the self is conceived of as an interdependent structure (Markus, 1991). Western child-rearing practices appear to produce a separate self whose motivation for action is through expressiveness and exploration. Psychoanalysis with its value system rooted in autonomy and the achievement of self-determination by self-exploration through self-expression is perfectly consistent with these practices. By contrast, Asian child-care practices follow a path of 'symbiotic harmony' (Rothbaum et al., 2000) characterized by less encouragement of independence, more subtle directiveness and a far greater tolerance of closeness in infancy (Okimoto, 2001). The prototype of symbiotic harmony is the Japanese mother's extreme indulgence and the child's great dependence (*amae*) on the mother (Doi, 1973). Rather than struggling between closeness and separation, the struggle is rooted in a continual pull toward adapting the self to fit the needs of others. This view of childhood and selfhood is far less consistent with the model that psychoanalysts have considered universal. This does not mean that it cannot be understood in psychoanalytic terms, but psychoanalytic ideas will need to be broadened considerably in order to encompass the very different early environments which infants and children from other cultures experience.

1.5.5 Issues of gender: the feminist critique

Psychoanalytic developmental accounts have what many have seen as a gender bias. There are two aspects of this. Since the earliest work of Freud (1900) masculine development has invariably been more coherently described in psychoanalysis than its feminine counterpart (Orbach and Eichenbaum, 1982). In contrast, developmental models far more often implicate the mother than the father in pathological processes (e.g. Limentani, 1989). Although increasingly theory is written in terms of a 'caregiver' of either sex, it is not really known to what extent the actual gender affects pathological outcomes.

It is perhaps not surprising that Freud was unconcerned by the social inequalities his theories described. He maintained that the goal of achieving a society free of class division was founded on an illusion (Freud, 1933). He believed that people were never going to be able to live together without friction: to think that they might was to overlook 'the difficulties which the untameable character of human nature presents to every kind of social community' (Freud, 1933, p. 219). Some feminist writers have also seen Freud as over-influenced by the tendency of conservative Victorian patriarchs to see women as reproductive servants, or at idealized best, as civilizing and nurturing angels (e.g. Millett, 1971). Nevertheless, as Appignanesi and Forrester (2000) have pointed out, while it is excusable to be of one's historical time, to transform a time-bound prejudice into a model of the world in which women can only be failed men, and those who deviate from this model automatically become cases for psychoanalytic treatment, is unacceptable. Opposition to Freud's more polemical pronouncements about women grew, even in his lifetime, and several of the early pioneers of psychoanalysis risked 'excommunication' by challenging Freud's pronouncements about women. These included figures of real stature, such as Ernest Jones, Helene Deutsch, Melanie Klein and Jeanne Lampl de Groot.

It should be noted, however, that from the outset the feminist relation with psychoanalysis was marked by ambivalence, an ambivalence that indeed makes speaking of 'the' feminist critique, as if there were only one, highly problematic. Writers such as Klein chose to remain within the psychoanalytic institution despite their feminist criticisms of some of Freud's ideas because some of those who were also committed to feminist principles felt that psychoanalysis might even have something to contribute to their political agenda. The feminist writer Emma Goldman, for example, was impressed when she heard Freud lecturing in 1909 and shortly afterwards published an essay in which she indicated the affinity between psychoanalysis and feminism, which was due to the fact that psychoanalysis recognized that sexuality was pre-eminent in the make-up of women as well as men (Buhle, 1998). Despite its patriarchal tendencies, psychoanalysis gave articulation to female sexuality in a scientific and non-judgmental language free from the moralizing reflections of theological discourse. After Goldman's time, in the 1960s, women's liberation re-emerged in the context of a sexual revolution emphasizing freedom of sexual life, a radical ideology to which the psychoanalytic normalization of sexuality substantially contributed (e.g. Reich, 1925; 1933)

Despite this contribution to the sexual revolution, however, in the climate of increased gender awareness of the 1960s and 70s, Freud was initially represented as the main patriarchal apologist for male chauvinism. According to Kate Millett (1971), with the advent of psychoanalysis

> A new prophet arrived upon the scene to clothe the old doctrine of the separate spheres in the fashionable language of science ... Sigmund Freud was beyond question the strongest individual counter-revolutionary force in the ideology of sexual politics. (p. 178).

Millett saw the period of 1930–60 as that of the sexual counterrevolution whose political arm was Nazi Germany and the Soviet Union and whose ideological arm was psychoanalysis and sociological functionalism. Betty Friedan (1963) in *The Feminine Mystique* went further, suggesting that

> After the depression, after the war, Freudian psychology became much more than a science of human behavior, a therapy for the suffering. It became an all-embracing American ideology, a new religion ... Freudian and pseudo-Freudian theories, settled everywhere, like fine volcanic ash. (pp. 114–15)

feminist Critiques

The devastating critiques of writers like Millett and Friedan focused on (1) the phallocentric vision of the girl as a castrated, stunted man; (2) Freud's opinion of the superego (morality) of women as weak, dependent and never so inexorable as in men; (3) Freud's emphasis on the role of jealousy and envy in women's lives; (4) the depiction of the mature woman's sexuality as naturally passive and masochistic; (5) Freud's vision of women as ruled by their biological urges and thus further condemned to serve men; (6) Freud's misapprehension (definitively discredited by the research of Masters and Johnson) that mature women could experience a superior form of sexual pleasure attributable to 'vaginal orgasm' and by implication that women whose orgasm depended on the clitoris were in some way immature, neurotic, bitchy and/or masculine; (7) Freud's loss of belief in the reports of childhood sexual abuse by his women patients, leaving a complacent and complicit heritage for the then dominant mental health profession.

The publication of Juliet Mitchell's *Psychoanalysis and Feminism* (Mitchell, 1973) inaugurated the development of a more subtle and textured criticism of the limitations of Freud's (and psychoanalysis's) depiction of women than the sledgehammer approach taken by writers like Millett. For example, the notion of penis envy, initially unconditionally rejected as a pseudo-scientific myth, came to be seen as an accurate but misinterpreted observation. What women envied was not male anatomy, but the unjustifiable social superiority of the male gender. Envy of the penis could be symbolic of women's resentment of social emasculation, which Freud chose to overlook, preferring to focus on a superficial facet of this deep-rooted problem. Janine Chasseguet-Smirgel also suggested that female penis envy could be seen as manifesting the little girl's wish to establish an identity separate from that of her mother (Chasseguet-Smirgel, 1970). It should be acknowledged that unless Freud had drawn attention to penis envy, later feminist writers would not have been provoked into alternative explanations of it.

Toril Moi, following Cora Kaplan (Moi, 1985), has pointed out that Millett's attack on Freudian psychoanalysis depends for its effectiveness on seeing the sexual oppression to which it contributed as a conscious and deliberate plot against women by the ruling patriarchy. To argue this Millett has to suppress acknowledgement of one of Freud's key insights, that is, that conscious action is influenced by unconscious desire: thus, not all misogyny may be conscious, and women may unconsciously identify with the views and attitudes of their oppressors, internalizing them in a manner that complicates the oppressor/victim schema. Hence also conscious awareness of the workings of the ideology of male patriarchy, though necessary, is unlikely to be a sufficient condition of women's liberation. Mitchell (1973) pointed out that feminism needed psychoanalysis to develop a theory of sexual difference in a patriarchal society, to explain women's subordination by illuminating the underlying unconscious conflicts.

A further link, introduced to Anglo-American readers by Mitchell and others, was the superficially unlikely alliance between Lacanian psychoanalysis and feminism which initially developed in post-1968 France. Unlike Anglo-American feminists, who opened their engagement with Freud with a vigorous denunciation of his works, Moi notes that from the outset

> the French took it for granted that psychoanalysis could provide an emancipatory theory of the personal and a path to the exploration of the unconscious, both of vital importance to the analysis of the oppression of women in patriarchal society. (Moi, 1985, p. 96)

The particular interest of writers such as Julia Kristeva, Luce Irigaray and Hélène Cixous in the works of Jacques Lacan may seem surprising given that in contrast to the focus of the psychoanalysis of the English and British schools on the mother–infant relationship (see Chapter 5–8), Lacan's interpretation of Freud focuses on the essential role of the father and the 'phallic function' in the constitution and gendering of the human subject. The work of Cixous, Irigaray, Kristeva and others could be described as a response to Lacan's call for a 'return to Freud'; however, their conclusions about Freud did not always fall into line with Lacan's. For example, Luce Irigaray's subsequently published doctoral thesis *Speculum de l'autre femme* led to her immediate expulsion from Lacan's École Freudienne in 1974. Writers in the French feminist tradition have drawn on Lacan's interpretations of Freud despite reservations about their possible phallocentrism because Lacanian psychoanalysis is seen as offering particularly useful conceptual tools with which to analyze the misogyny of the Western philosophical tradition, whose pervasive influence affects psychoanalytic discourse along with every other. Superficially the feminist writings of the Continental tradition seem to be much less directly politically engaged than those of the Anglo-Americans. Their emphasis on philosophy is due to their tendency to see it as a master discourse underpinning the workings of all other kinds of discourse, including the political; thus, their concern with the philosophical should not be seen as a turn from politics, since in their view it is necessary to begin with philosophy to bring about change.

An account of the intricacies of Lacanian theory is beyond the scope of this book. However, among the reasons for the powerful attraction of feminist writers to Lacan are: (1) In his call for a 'return to Freud', Lacan represented himself as a subversive, even revolutionary figure, giving an account of a much less familiar and more unsettling Freud than the authorized version which in Lacan's view had become stagnant. This strategy suggested to feminists that it might be possible to rescue Freud from behind enemy lines and reinvent a less paternalistic figure who could help them. (2) Lacan's theory eschews all the biological aspects of Freud's work, rejecting them as tied up with outmoded nineteenth-century scientific theories. This makes it possible to rescue psychoanalytic accounts of female sexuality from accusations of essentialism justified by spurious biological arguments. (3) Lacan's account of the constitution of subjectivity does not describe it as a process of individuation or self-discovery, but understands the 'subject' primarily as one who is subjected: social, cultural, political and linguistic structures, which Lacan often gives the collective name of the 'symbolic order', and which are first represented to the child by the father's separation of the dyad of mother and child, assign the subject its place – a place in society is preordained for the child by the *nom-du-père* (Name of the Father). Thus, the assumption of an identity is above all an experience of alienation, since the symbolic order in terms of which this identity has to be articulated is beyond the subject's control (in Lacan's model, the infant's first achieves this identity-in-alienation in the 'mirror stage' at between six and 18 months, where the perception of the wholeness of the image in the mirror 'anticipates the mastery of his body that the infant has not yet objectively achieved' Benvenuto and Kennedy, 1986, p. 54). These ideas obviously invite explicit political application, and were very attractive to a group whose identity has historically not been self-determined (before the twentieth century, discourses on the nature of woman were almost exclusively male). (4) Lacan's account of the presymbolic, which he calls the 'imaginary order', describes it in terms of the infant's relation to his mother. In the imaginary order, the child is part of his mother and perceives no separation from her. Lacan emphasizes that the imaginary is not a stage which one passes through but another mode or 'order' of experience that persists in an uneasy relation with the symbolic throughout life. This state of primal unity has been appropriated for the feminist cause by writers such as Hélène Cixous, who see it as offering the possibility of resistance to the implicitly patriarchal structures of the symbolic; since the symbolic depends for its functioning on clear separations between signifiers, the imaginary in which all distinctions become blurred has the potential to undermine its functioning.

However, the temptation to stake out a feminist territory by identifying femininity with the presymbolic maternal imaginary runs the paradoxical risk of marginalizing women further, by denying them access to the symbolic order in which power games are played out. In the last decades of the twentieth century, feminist writers became increasingly critical of all attempts to describe the characteristics of femininity or female identity as such. If, historically, attempts to define woman's nature had been modes of resistance to change and served the function of putting her in her place, to continue to pursue this project, albeit with a revised political agenda, risked perpetuating the very structures feminists had set out to challenge. Significantly, the first articulation of this view came from the psychoanalyst Julia Kristeva, who suggests that 'the very dichotomy man/woman as an opposition between two rival entities may be understood as belonging to *metaphysics*' (Moi, 1985, p. 12). (It should be noted that to writers steeped in the Continental philosophical tradition, the word 'metaphysics' adumbrates political and ideological structures as well as philosophy.)

By contrast to the European feminist rapprochement with Freud via a return to a metaphoric reinterpretation of classical ideas, North American feminist analysts made their peace with him by using psychoanalytic tools to reject politically unsound dogma. For example, Nancy Chodorow (1989) argued that woman's mothering is one of the few universal and enduring elements of the sexual division of labor.

> Women's mothering ... creates heterosexual asymmetries which reproduce the family and marriage but leave women with needs that lead them to care for children, and men with capacities for participation in the alienated work world, it creates a psychology of male dominance and fear of women in men. (pp. 218–19)

The creation of gender identity is not via a biological self-discovery as Freud presumed but a psychological awareness of core gender identity which is most likely transmitted by the parents' expectations (Stoller, 1985). Chodorow (1978) fleshes out Freud's Oedipus complex which she regards as taking account only of the child's desires and fears in relation to the parents, omitting the parents' wishes and behavior toward the child. Object relations for Chodorow means patterns of family relationships. This is the advance which feminism requires. The evolution of sexual identity is a more complex affair in which the process of individuation and separation from the mothering figure (see Chapter 4) is harder for girls than for boys as the mother's femaleness constantly emphasizes difference and separateness in the case of boys while emphasizing sameness and regressive merging in the case of girls. Autonomy and a sense of self-in-relation is consequently more problematic for women than men (Gilligan, 1982). One of the conclusions that Chodorow came to was that the fear and loathing of mothers in Western culture together with all the fateful consequences of separate spheres would only be dissipated if men become mothers. As a consequence, non-gender specific parenting became the key item on the political agenda (Chodorow, 1989).

To summarize, then, although psychoanalysis is in many ways entangled with the patriarchal institutions and ways of thinking which twentieth-century feminism set out to challenge, it also offered a range of useful concepts that have begun to make it possible to think beyond these constrictions. The paradoxical attraction between feminism and psychoanalysis can be explained by the psychoanalytic commitment to breaking down or recasting destructive and damaging psychic constellations, an approach which, inspired by the famous feminist slogan 'The personal is political', feminists applied to sexual politics.

1.5.6 Lack of specificity

Most psychoanalytic models are non-specific in their explanation of different forms of pathology. Self-psychological accounts of severe disorders are a good example. All too often, when the issue of specificity is raised, theoreticians invoke constitutional differences (see, for example, Freud, 1908b, p. 187). Etiological models do not identify specific early and later variables that shape specific symptoms, or the interaction among contributing factors. As a result psychoanalytic formulations are poor at predicting specific disorders. For example, they are not well able to predict the decline in one form of pathology (e.g. conversion reaction), and the increase in others (e.g. eating disorders).

Even more striking is the lack of thorough understanding of the varying prevalence of disorders across the lifespan. We have little to say about the spontaneous improvement of borderline personality disorder over time (McGlashan, 1986; Stone, 1990) or why patients improve in the absence of therapeutic help. Why should there be far more pathology among boys than girls in early childhood and the reverse in adolescence (Goodman and Meltzer, 1999)? Many concepts referred to theoretically (e.g. narcissism) have multiple references, some pertaining to developmental course (e.g. inadequate experience of mirroring and soothing), some to covert mental states (e.g. a fragile sense of self), and some to manifest presentation (e.g. a grandiose view of the self; Westen, 1992).

Psychoanalytic theoreticians in the future will have to pay closer attention to this inclination to blur the edges of concepts to enhance their heuristic value in clinical work and elsewhere. Although there is a short-term gain, particularly through enhancing a professional group identity by enabling members to believe that they share ideas, in the long term such fuzziness impedes progress, and scientific debate is degraded by appeals to authority (e.g. that of Freud, or Kohut or other major theoreticians) rather than scrutiny of the ideas themselves.

1.5.7 The weakness of the developmental perspective

Most of the theories reviewed suffer from a surprisingly narrow view of development, evident in theories of the self (for a critical appraisal see Eagle, 1984; Stern, 1985) and object relations (Peterfreund, 1978). These critics have raised two closely related issues. The first pertains to unjustified confidence in tracing particular forms of psychopathology to specific phases (e.g. borderline disorder to the rapprochement sub-phase of separation and individuation). The second concerns the over-emphasis on early experience, which is frequently at odds with developmental data. Westen (1990a; 1990b) is particularly clear in his evidence that pathological processes of self-representation and object relationships actually characterize developmental phases far later than those that have traditionally concerned psychoanalytic theoreticians. The emphasis on deficits in pre-verbal periods is a particular problem for psychoanalytic theory because it places so many of the hypotheses beyond any realistic possibility of empirical testing. Freud (1911b; 1913a) himself apparently favored the idea that the libidinal fixations underlying the psychoses were to be found in the earliest stages of development, and certainly developmentally earlier than the neuroses. However, the presence of a regressive symptom or behavior does not necessarily indicate a developmental failure, because we are dealing with regression in the descriptive sense of 'childlike' rather than as an explanation.

Peterfreund (1978) criticized what he saw as a dominant tendency in psychoanalytic developmental theory to 'adultomorphize infancy', that is, the tendency to describe early stages of development in terms of hypotheses about later states of psychopathology. There is no doubt that if an adult behaved as an infant does, he or she could be described as being in a state of fusion, narcissism, omnipotence, autism, symbiosis, to have hallucinatory experiences, to be disoriented and to have delusions. The infant, however, has limited behavioral possibilities and to apply an adult-oriented system to describe his functioning inevitably leads to logically untenable accounts. Some of the 'regressive' manifestations associated with psychosis have no real counterpart in normal development. Stechler and Kaplan (1980) note that, as we cannot know what the infant experiences, it is hard to see how empirical evidence in support of psychoanalytic claims can ever be compiled (see also Wolff, 1996; Green, 2000c). Clinically-based developmental accounts also tend to mirror the meta-psychological commitment of the author to, for example, a drive versus an object relationship based theory (compare the accounts of Anna Freud and Melanie Klein). As psychoanalytic meta-psychology is anyway at best loosely coupled to clinical observations (Gill, 1976; Holt, 1976; Klein, 1976b; Schafer, 1976), it cannot provide an independent test of developmental theory.

In sum, finding what are presumed to be primitive modes of mental functioning in individuals with severe disorders, such as borderline personality disorder or schizophrenia, cannot be taken as evidence for the persistence or regressive recurrence of early pathogenic experiences. Yet, even if horizontal splitting (Kohut, 1971) or identity diffusion (Erikson, 1956; Kernberg, 1967) in some way represented early modes of thought, an issue that would be controversial in any case, their emergence in adult mental functioning could easily be related to that which occurred later than infancy trauma (Fonagy, 1996b). Recently, in a powerfully argued paper, Martin Willick (2001) provided a number of current examples from the literature that illustrate that this criticism applies not only to past psychoanalytic theory but also to some work being done today.

1.5.8 Trauma, reconstruction, memories and fantasies

The classical psychoanalytic view has emphasized the intrapsychic experience of the individual and is relatively uninterested in the 'real' world in which intrapsychic experience developed. There is a silent assumption that the maturational stages of drives are more important than so-called 'accidents' of the environment. In contrast many more recent theories, based on the study of adult pathology, see the *actual* behavior of the mother toward the young child as crucial in the reconstructed history (Sullivan, 1953; Bowlby, 1958; Winnicott, 1960b; Kohut, 1971). Are such reconstructions true?

There is a current controversy in psychoanalysis (reflecting a culture-wide debate) concerning the 'knowability' of early experience. Shengold (1989) links the controversy to the eighteenth-century debate initiated by George Berkeley concerning the knowability of reality beyond the mind and its ideas. In 1977 Florence Rush argued that Freud had both discovered and covered up the extent of childhood sexual abuse (Rush, 1977). Masson (1984) fueled the current debate with his oversimplified *Assault on Truth*, which denied the pathogenic power of fantasies, the cornerstone of most psychoanalytic contributions (Freud, 1905d). Masson (1984) chastises Freud for having defensively abandoned and deliberately withheld evidence supporting the seduction theory of the neurosis. In fact, Freud never 'suppressed' the seduction theory but amended it to make it correspond with the facts and brought it into relationship with the discovery of infantile sexuality and its potential for pathogenesis (Hanley, 1987). In 1906 Freud insisted that the 18 patients in 'The Aetiology of Hysteria' (Freud, 1906) had given him accurate accounts of having been seduced in childhood (p. 190). Freud reinforced his view of the pathogenic significance of actual seduction experience in the 'Introductory Lectures' (Freud, 1916-17, p. 370), 'On Female Sexuality' (Freud, 1931a, p. 232) and in 'Moses and Monotheism' (Freud, 1939, pp. 75-6).

In contrast, psychoanalysts adopting a hermeneutic approach (e.g. Steele, 1979; Spence, 1982) repudiate a therapeutic search for the 'real' past and embrace the criterion of internal coherence as the sole appropriate test of 'truth'. Spence (1982; 1984) insists that psychoanalysis cannot claim privileged knowledge of the past (Freud's notion that it could be uncovered by means of a quasi-archaeological endeavor). He argues that the encounter with the past in the therapeutic context is an act of creation of a 'plausible' coherent narrative of our patient's life. Spence (1982) gives a critical warning: 'Once stated, it (the narrative truth) becomes partially true, as it is repeated and extended, it becomes familiar; and as its familiarity adds to its plausibility, it becomes completely true' (p. 177).

This debate acquired recent impetus from the controversy over the so-called 'false memory syndrome', basically the inference by overzealous therapists that their patients had been seduced in childhood, leading to legal issues of culpability. It is difficult to resolve this argument within the domain of psychoanalysis, a discipline committed to blurring the distinction between external and internal reality, rather than (as the controversy demands) being definitive about the difference between them (Fonagy and Target, 1997). Psychoanalysts have, however, begun to respond to this challenge (e.g. Brenneis, 1994), and the role of memory in therapeutic action is becoming an issue of considerable importance (Fonagy, 1999b). Such attempts, however, all fail to address the core question of the status of internal versus external experience in the etiology of psychological disorder.

There can be no adequate resolution to this debate. Most clinicians working with adult victims of childhood abuse would concur with Shengold (1989) that

> Having had the actual sexual experience does not necessarily make one patient sicker than another who has only transferred onto the therapist the *fantasy* of sexual contact without acting out or repeating it; but the analyst who treats a patient will palpably sense the distinct quality conferred by the *actual* experience, and will feel its effect in the intensity of the patient's distrust, the corruptibility of the patient's superego, the depth of the expectation of repetition – and in other resistances that affect the viability of future treatment. (p. 40)

In most of the cases the quality of the patient's recall and the convergence of evidence leaves little room for doubt about whether abuse actually happened. In cases where doubt exists, both patient and analyst must tolerate it (Mollon, 1998). The search for meaning is a ubiquitous aspect of human personality, and the therapist must resist the temptation to give false meaning to current misery, anguish and dejection by 'discovering' a spurious historical account of early deprivation (Target, 1998).

1.6   An overview of psychoanalytic theories

Psychoanalytic theory is not a static body of knowledge; it is in a state of constant evolution. In the first half of the last century, Sigmund Freud (see Chapter 2) and his close followers worked to identify the roles of instinct in development and psychopathology (drive theory). Later, the focus evolved and shifted to the development and functions of the ego, more formally ego psychology (see Chapters 3 and 4), to a current interest in the early ← mother–infant dyad and its long-term effect on interpersonal relationships and their internal representation, embodied in object relations theories (see Chapters 5, 6, 7 and 8). Concurrently, a psychology of the self has evolved as part of most psychoanalytic theories. With its integration into mainstream theories there is a better conceptual basis for a comprehensive and phenomenological clinical theory (see Chapter 7 and 8). There has been a movement away from metapsychological constructs couched in a natural science framework, to a clinical theory closer to personal experience, whose core focus is the representational world and interpersonal relationships (see particularly Sandler and Rosenblatt, 1962b; Jacobson, 1964; and Chapter 9 and 10). Contemporary theories attempt to trace the sometimes highly ← elusive link between formative emotional relationships and the complex interactions they involve, and the formation of mental structures. *Contemporary* ←

Two factors have made this theoretical move possible: (1) observation-based psychoanalytic developmental theories (Freud, 1965; Mahler et al., 1975; Spillius, 1994); and (2) the growth of object relations theory which, within a developmental framework (see Pine, 1985), explores the evolution of a differentiated, integrated representational world that emerges within the context of a mother–infant matrix. Winnicott (1960c) termed this 'the holding environment'. At its broadest, object-relations theory concerns the development of schemata from a diffuse set of sensori-motor experiences in the infant, into a differentiated, consistent and relatively realistic representation of the self and object in interaction. This evolution is toward increasingly symbolic levels of representation, but with the general assumption that earlier levels of representations of interactions are retained in the mind and continue to exert powerful influences.

Psychoanalytic models have evolved through diverse attempts to explain why and how individuals in psychoanalytic treatment deviated from the normal path of development and came to experience major intrapsychic and interpersonal difficulties. Each model we will review focuses on particular developmental phases, and outlines a model of normal personality development derived from the analyst's clinical experience.

Freud was the first to give meaning to mental disorder by linking it to childhood experiences (Freud and Breuer, 1895), and to the vicissitudes of the developmental process (Freud, 1900). One of Freud's greatest contributions was undoubtedly the recognition of infantile sexuality (Green, 1985). Freud's discoveries radically altered our perception of the child from one of idealized innocence to that of a person, struggling to achieve control over his biological needs, and make them acceptable to society through the microcosm of his family (Freud, 1930). Freud's views will be described in greater detail in Chapter 2 of this book.

Ego psychologists balanced this view by focusing on the evolution of the child's adaptive capacities (Hartmann, 1939), which he brings to bear on his struggle with his biological needs. Hartmann's model (Hartmann, Kris, and Loewenstein, 1949) attempted to take a wider view of the developmental process, to link drives and ego functions, and show how very negative interpersonal experiences could jeopardize the evolution of the psychic structures essential to adaptation. He also showed that the reactivation of earlier structures (regression) was the most important component of psychopathology. Hartmann (1955, p. 221) was also among the first to indicate the complexity of the developmental process, stating that the reasons for the persistence of particular behavior are likely to differ from the reasons for its original appearance. Among the great contributions of ego psychologists are the identification of the ubiquity of intrapsychic conflict throughout development (Brenner, 1982), and the recognition that genetic endowment, as well as interpersonal experiences, may be critical in determining the child's developmental path. The latter idea has echoes in the epidemiological concept of resilience (Rutter and Quinton, 1984; Garmezy and Masten, 1991). The contributions of the ego psychological approach of the 1950s and 1960s North American psychoanalysis will be reviewed in Chapter 3.

Child analysts (e.g. Freud, 1965; Fraiberg, 1969; 1980) taught us that symptomatology is not fixed, but rather a dynamic state superimposed upon, and intertwined with, an underlying developmental process. Anna Freud's study of disturbed and healthy children under great social stress led her to formulate a relatively comprehensive developmental theory, where the child's emotional maturity could be mapped independently of diagnosable pathology. Particularly in her early work in the war nurseries (Freud, 1941–45), she identified many of the characteristics which later research linked to 'resilience' (Rutter, 1990). For example, her observations spoke eloquently of the social support which children could give one another in concentration camps, which could ensure their physical and psychological survival. More recent research on youngsters experiencing severe trauma have confirmed her assumption of the protective power of sound social support (Garmezy, 1983; MacFarlane, 1987; O'Grady and Metz, 1987; Werner, 1989). Anna Freud's work stayed so close to the external reality of the child that it lent itself to a number of important applications (Goldstein, Freud and Solnit, 1973; 1979).

Anna Freud was also a pioneer in identifying the importance of an equilibrium between developmental processes (Freud, 1965). Her work is particularly relevant in explaining why children, deprived of certain capacities by environment or constitution, are at greater risk of psychological disturbance. Epidemiological studies support this (Taylor, 1985; Yule and Rutter, 1985). Anna Freud was the first psychoanalyst to place the process and mechanisms of development at the centre-stage of psychoanalytic thinking. Her approach is truly one of developmental psychopathology, insofar as she defines abnormal functioning in terms of its deviation from normal development, while at the same time using the understanding gained from clinical cases to illuminate the progress of the normal child (Cicchetti, 1990a; Sroufe, 1990). It is a logical development of her work for us to begin to explore the nature of the therapeutic process, also in developmental terms. It is important to remind ourselves that sometimes we apply developmental notions to the therapeutic process metaphorically (Mayes and Spence, 1994), but essential components of treatment – particularly with children – and with personality disordered adults, inevitably involve the engagement of dormant developmental processes (Kennedy and Moran, 1991). Anna Freud's work and its relationship to developmental psychopathology will be the subject of the first half of Chapter 4.

Margaret Mahler, a pioneer of developmental observation in the United States, drew attention to the paradox of self-development, that a separate identity involves giving up a highly gratifying closeness with the caregiver. Her observations of the 'ambitendency' of children in their second year of life threw light on chronic problems of consolidating individuality. Mahler's framework highlights the importance of the caregiver in facilitating separation, and helps explain the difficulties experienced by children whose parents fail to perform a social referencing function for the child, which would help them to assess the realistic dangers of unfamiliar environments (Hornik and Gunnar, 1988; Feinman, 1991). A traumatized, troubled parent may hinder rather than help a child's adaptation (Terr, 1983). An abusive parent may provide no social referencing (Hesse and Cicchetti, 1982; Cicchetti, 1990b). The pathogenic potential of withdrawal of the mother, when confronted with the child's wish for separateness, was further elaborated by Masterson (1972) and Rinsley (1977), and helps to account for the transgenerational aspects of psychological disturbance (see Loranger, Oldham and Tullis, 1982; Baron et al., 1985; Links, Steiner and Huxley, 1988). The work of Mahler and her followers will be the subject of the second part of Chapter 4.

Joseph Sandler's development of Anna Freud's and Edith Jacobson's work in the UK, represents the best integration of the developmental perspective with psychoanalytic theory. His comprehensive psychoanalytic model has enabled developmental researchers (Emde, 1983; 1988a; 1988b; Stern, 1985) to integrate their findings with a psychoanalytic formulation, which clinicians were also able to use. At the core of Sandler's formulation lies the representational structure that contains both reality and distortion, and is the driving force of psychic life. A further important component of his model is the notion of the background of safety (Sandler, 1987b), closely tied to Bowlby's (1969) concept of a secure base. These and others of Sandler's developmental concepts will be reviewed in the final part of Chapter 4.

The focus of object relations theories on early development and infantile fantasy represented a shift in world view for psychoanalysis from a tragic to a somewhat more romantic world view (see for example Akhtar, 1992). The contrast between the classical and the object relations positions is described in Chapter 5 and the subsequent chapters elaborate on the major object relations theories. Melanie Klein and her followers, working in London, constructed a developmental model that at the time met great opposition because of the extravagant assumptions these clinicians were ready to make about the cognitive capacities of infants. Surprisingly, developmental research appears to be consistent with many of Klein's claims concerning perception of causality (Bower, 1989) and causal reasoning (Golinkoff et al., 1984). Kleinian developmental concepts have become popular because they provide powerful descriptions of the clinical interaction between (both child and adult) patient and analyst. For example, projective identification depicts the close control that primitive mental function can exert over the analyst's mind. Post-Kleinian psychoanalysts (Bion, 1962a; Rosenfeld, 1971b) were particularly helpful in underscoring the impact of emotional conflict on the development of cognitive capacities. The Klein-Bion model will be described in Chapter 6.

The early relationship with the caregiver emerged as a critical aspect of personality development from studies of severe character disorders by the object-relations school of psychoanalysts in Britain. W.R.D. Fairbairn's focus on the individual's need for the other (Fairbairn, 1952a) helped shift psychoanalytic attention from structure to content, and profoundly influenced both British and North American psychoanalytic thinking. As a result, the self as a central part of the psychoanalytic model emerged in the work of Balint (1937; 1968) and Winnicott (1971b). The concept of the caretaker or false self, a defensive structure created to master trauma in a context of total dependency, has become an essential developmental construct. Winnicott's (1965b) notions of primary maternal preoccupation, transitional phenomena, the holding environment, and the mirroring function of the caregiver, provided a clear research focus for developmentalists interested in individual differences in the development of self-structure. The significance of the parent–child relationship is consistently borne out by developmental studies of psychopathology. These studies in many respects support Winnicott's assertions concerning the traumatic effects of early maternal failure, particularly maternal depression (see Cummings and Davies, 1994) and the importance of maternal sensitivity for the establishment of a secure relationship (Ainsworth et al., 1978; Belsky, Rovine and Taylor, 1984; Grossmann et al., 1985; Bus and van IJzendoorn, 1992). The work of the British Independent school is reviewed in Chapter 7.

There have been many attempts by North American theorists to incorporate object-relations ideas into models which retain facets of structural theories. The work of two major figures is reviewed in Chapter 8. Kohut's self-psychology (Kohut, 1971; 1977; 1984; Kohut and Wolf, 1978) was based primarily on his experience of narcissistic individuals. His central developmental idea was the need for an understanding caregiver to counteract the infant's sense of helplessness in the face of his biological striving for mastery. Kohut emphasizes the need for such understanding objects throughout life and these notions are consistent with accumulating evidence for the powerful protective influence of social support across a wide range of epidemiological studies (Brown and Harris, 1978; Brown, Harris and Bifulco, 1986). Kohut also leans heavily on Winnicott and British object relations theorists, although his indebtedness is rarely acknowledged. The mirroring object becomes a 'selfobject', and the need for empathy drives development, which culminates in the attainment of a cohesive self. Drive theory becomes secondary to self theory, in that the failure to attain an integrated self-structure both leaves room for and in itself generates aggression and isolated sexual fixation. However, the self remains problematic as a construct; in Kohut's model, it is both the person (the patient) and the agent which is assumed to control the person (Stolorow, Brandschaft and Atwood, 1987). Nevertheless, Kohut's descriptions of the narcissistic personality have been powerful and influential examples of the use of developmental theory in psychoanalytic understanding. Moreover, Kohut's hypotheses concerning the profound and long-term consequences of a self 'enfeebled' by the failure of emotional attunement of the selfobject finds a powerful echo in the risk literature. The work of Cicchetti (1989; 1990a; 1990b) has shown a clear link between early trauma and disorganization and delay in self-development. Researchers working with maltreated infants and toddlers have noted striking attachment behaviors in such infants in spontaneous play as well as laboratory observations (Fraiberg, 1982; Carlsson et al., 1989; Crittenden and Ainsworth, 1989). The effectiveness of actions undertaken by the child is at the centre of Kohut's concept of self-esteem and is also the core of Bandura's notion of self-efficacy (Bandurs, 1982). Kohut's formulations were probably helpful in the operationalization of the concept of self-confidence (Garmezy,

1985; Rutter, 1990; Werner, 1990) although in some recent studies problem-solving skills and self-esteem appear to be independent indicators of resilience (Cowen et al., 1990).

An alternative integration of object relations ideas with North American ego psychology was offered by Otto Kernberg. Kernberg's contribution to the development of psychoanalytic thought is unparalleled in the recent history of the discipline. His systematic integration of structural theory and object relations theory (Kernberg, 1976b; 1982; 1987) is probably the most frequently used psychoanalytic model, particularly in relation to personality disorders. His model of psychopathology is developmental, in the sense that personality disturbance is seen to reflect the limited ability of the young child to address intrapsychic conflict. Neurotic object relations show much less defensive disintegration of the representation of self and objects into libidi-nally invested part-object relations. In personality disorder, part-object relations are formed under the impact of diffuse, overwhelming emotional states, which signal the activation of persecutory relations between self and object. Kernberg's models are particularly useful because of their level of detail and his determination to operationalize his ideas far more than has been traditional in psychoanalytic writing. It is not surprising, therefore, that a considerable amount of empirical work has been done directly to test his proposals (Westen, 1990b; Westen, 1990b; Westen and Cohen, 1993), and the clinical approach which he takes toward serious personality disturbance. Aspects of Kernberg's contribution will be reviewed in Chapter 8.

With the gradual demise of ego psychology in the US and the opening of psychoanalysis to psychologists and other non-medically qualified profes-sionals, a fresh intellectual approach to theory and technique gained ground in theoretical and technical discussions, rooted in the work of Harry Stack-Sullivan (Sullivan, 1953) and Clara Thompson (Thompson, 1964). The interpersonalist approach, represented by prolific contemporary writers such as Steve Mitchell, Lewis Aron, Jessica Benjamin, Philip Bromberg and many others, has revolutionized the role of the analyst in the therapeutic situation. Influenced by post-modernist ideas, this group of clinicians generally conceive the analytic relationship as far more of two equals rather than of patient and doctor. They recognize the fundamentally interpersonal character of the sense of self and thus the irreducibly dyadic quality of mental function. They consis-tently recognize the influence of the interpersonal nature of the mind on the process of therapy, and the active role which the analyst as a person plays in the treatment process. Particularly controversial is the insistence of many interper-sonalists that enactments by the analyst within the therapy are almost as inevitable as the patient's enactments in the transference. The contribution of this group of analysts will be the subject of Chapter 9.

Bowlby's (Bowlby, 1969; 1973; 1980) work on separation and loss also focused developmentalists' attention on the importance of the security (safety, sensitivity and predictability) of the earliest relationships. His cognitive-systems model of the internalization of interpersonal relationships (internal working models), consistent with object relations theory (Fairbairn, 1952a; Kernberg, 1975) and elaborated by other attachment theorists (Bretherton, 1985; Main, Kaplan and Cassidy, 1985; Crittenden, 1990), has been very influential. According to Bowlby, the child develops expectations regarding a caregiver's behavior and his or her own behavior. These expectations are based on the child's understanding of experiences of previous interaction, and organize the child's behavior with the attachment figure and (by extension) with others. The concept has had very broad application. Bowlby's developmental model highlights the transgenerational nature of internal working models: our view of ourselves depends upon the working model of relationships which characterized our caregivers. Empirical research on this intergenerational model is encouraging; an accumulating body of data confirms that there is intergenerational transmission of attachment security and insecurity (Main et al., 1985; Grossmann, 1989; see review by van IJzendoorn, 1995) and that parental mental representations shaping this process may be assessed before the birth of the first child (Fonagy et al., 1991; Benoit and Parker, 1994; Ward and Carlson, 1995; Steele, Steele and Fonagy, 1996). Psychoanalytic approaches based in developmental research, including attachment theory, will be introduced in Chapter 10. A number of theories have drawn deeply from the developmental research tradition, combining attachment theory ideas with psychoanalytic conceptions within general systems theory frames of reference. Some of these theories are covered in Chapter 11. For example, Daniel Stern's (1985) book represented a milestone in psychoanalytic theorization concerning development. His work is distinguished by being normative rather than pathomorphic, and prospective rather than retrospective. His focus is the reorganization of subjective perspectives on self and other as these occur with the emergence of new maturational capacities. Stern is the most sophisticated amongst psychoanalytic writers in dealing with several qualitatively different senses of self, each developmentally anchored. He is perhaps closest to Sandler in his psychoanalytic model of the mind, but his formulation of object relations also has much in common with those of Bowlby, Kohut and Kernberg. Many of Stern's suggestions have proved to be highly applicable clinically, including his notion of an early core self and the role of the schema-of-being-with the other. Other general systems theory interpretations of psychoanalysis originated in the work of practitioners of brief psychotherapy. Two particularly significant contributors are Mardi Horowitz (1988) and Anthony Ryle (Ryle, 1990). Both offer revisions of selected psychoanalytic concepts in the context of substantial revisions of classical techniques. Chapter 12 includes a description of our own work on self-development and the capacity for mentalization.

Early theories have not been supplanted by later formulations and most psychoanalytic writers assume that a number of explanatory frameworks are necessary to give a comprehensive account of the relationship of development and psychopathology (see Sandler, 1983). So-called neurotic psychopathology is presumed to originate in later childhood at a time when there is self–other differentiation and when the various agencies of the mind (id, ego, superego) have been firmly established. The structural frame of reference (Arlow and Brenner, 1964; Sandler, Dare and Holder, 1982) is most commonly used in developmental accounts of these disorders. Personality or character disorders (e.g. borderline personality disorder, narcissistic personality disorder, schizoid personality disorder, etc.), as well as most non-neurotic psychiatric disorders, are most commonly looked at in frameworks developed subsequent to structural theory. Here, a variety of theoretic frameworks are available, including the structural, most of which point to developmental pathology arising at a point in time when psychic structures are still in formation (see, for example Kohut, 1971; Modell, 1985). But do theories matter at all? Do they really influence the clinical work with patients? This is a difficult question to answer. Evidently, analysts from very different persuasions, with very different views of pathogenesis are convinced of the correctness of their formulations and are guided in their treatments by that conviction. Since we do not yet know what is truly mutative about psychotherapy, it might well be that for many patients the analyst's theory of their etiology is not so crucial. The complex relationship between clinical work and theoretical development will be considered in Chapter 13 alongside a brief review of evidence concerning the outcome of psychoanalysis.

We end the book by highlighting some limitations and strengths of the psychoanalytic approach. In Chapter 14 we shall consider some of the potential growth points of psychoanalytic ideas as well as some of the current challenges it faces. We will focus on the potential extraordinary consequences of the new discoveries about the brain and its genetic underpinnings for psychoanalysis at its interface with the neurosciences.

CHAPTER 2

Freud

2.1 Overview of Freud's model of development

In 1930 Watson, one of the first advocates of behaviorism, predicted that 'twenty years from now an analyst using Freudian concepts and Freudian terminology will be placed on the same plane as a phrenologist' (a person practicing the nineteenth-century art of telling people's characters by feeling bumps on their head, Watson, 1930, p. 27). But as Jahoda noted in her provocative address to the British Psychological Society in 1972, 'Freud won't go away', despite the disenchantment of the psychological community with many of his views. Jahoda attributes the inaccuracy of Watson's forecast to the fundamental psychological questions raised by Freud's ideas.

Freud (1895) initially believed that he had discovered the cause of neurosis in the event of childhood seduction. In this conception, the neurotic symptom represented the early trauma in a distorted form. For example, a child of eight with hysterical blindness might achieve relative internal safety by 'shutting his eyes' to the memory of having witnessed his mother's rape. This model posited no mental apparatus; rather, the symptom emerged through the physical conversion of energy. For example, he wrote in 1888: 'Where there is an accumulation of *physical* tension, we find anxiety neurosis' (quoted in A. Freud, 1954).

Freud's so-called abandonment of his seduction hypothesis in favor of his second model, which emphasized fantasy driven by the biological drive state, interrupted his career as a social theorist of development. It led Freud (1905d) to attempt to explain all actions in terms of the failure of the child's mental apparatus to deal adequately with the pressures of a maturationally predetermined sequence of drive states. Adult psychopathologies, as well as dreaming, jokes and parapraxes, were seen as the revisiting of unresolved childhood conflicts over sexuality (Freud, 1900; 1901; 1905b).

31

The influence of the social environment regained a prominent place in analytic theory with the third major shift in Freud's thinking (Freud, 1920; 1923; 1926). The compelling fit with clinical observational data in the dual instinct theory (Freud, 1920) enabled this new structural theory to survive long after Freud. For example, the significance for psychopathology of the child's struggle with innate destructive and self-destructive forces was finally fully recognized. At this time, Freud (1926) also revised his view of anxiety. Rather than an epiphenomenal experience associated with inhibited biological drives, he now saw it as a psychological state linked to the perception of internal (instinctual or moral) or external danger. The danger situation was specified as the fear of helplessness resulting from loss (loss of the mother, her esteem, loss of a body-part or loss of self-regard). This revision restored adaptation to the external world as an essential part of the psychoanalytic account, and recast the theory in more cognitive terms (Schafer, 1983). Freud nevertheless retained the concept of a more primitive form of anxiety which would arise in an involuntary, automatic way 'whenever a danger situation analogous to birth' occurred (S. Freud, 1926, p. 162). It is this automatic pervasive anxiety and the associated state of overwhelming helplessness which is warded off with the help of 'signal anxiety' which prompts the ego to limit the threat of a basic danger situation (see Yorke, Kennedy and Wiseberg, 1981).

This final revision in Freud's thinking provided a developmental framework based around the tripartite structural schema of id, ego and superego (Freud, 1923; 1933; 1940). The hypothesis that conflicts within the human mind are chiefly organized around three themes – (a) wish vs. moral injunction, (b) wish vs. reality and (c) internal reality vs. external reality – has had extraordinary explanatory power. In particular, the ego's capacity to create defenses became the cornerstone of psychoanalytic theorization and clinical work in the USA (Hartmann, Kris and Loewenstein, 1946) and Britain (Freud, 1936).

The limitations of Freud's developmental model are manifold. The subsequent elaboration of psychoanalytic theories is testament to cultural differences in psychological theory and the need of subsequent theorists to make their own contributions. Perhaps the most important post-Freudian contributions have been in the domains of the cultural and social context of development: the significance of early childhood experiences; the developmental significance of the real behavior of the real parents; the role of dependency, attachment and safety in development alongside the role of instinctual drives; the synthesizing function of the self; the importance of the non-conflictual aspects of development. Many of these shortcomings were pointed out by Freud's contemporaries, who frequently moved away from organized psychoanalysis under a cloud, at least as far as Freud was concerned. Their association with these themes may have delayed general consideration of their ideas within organized psychoanalysis. For example, Jung's rejection of libido theory drew attention away from his undoubted advances in the understanding of narcissism and his development of a theory of the self throughout the life-cycle (Jung, 1912; 1916; 1923).

2.1.1 First phase: the affect-trauma model

Freud's first major psychoanalytic proposal concerned the nature of hysteria (a condition in which the patient experiences physical symptoms, such as paralysis, in the absence of any organic cause). Together with Breuer, he built on the work of the French neurologist Charcot to demonstrate that the symptoms of the hysteric had psychological meaning and could not be attributed simply to the degeneration of the nervous system as had been previously thought (Breuer and Freud, 1895). Freud's model of neurosis at this time assumed that hysterics had experienced some major emotional trauma that had become repressed (forgotten) because it was unacceptable to the conscious mind. The emotions (affects) induced by the forgotten trauma continued to press for discharge (expression) into consciousness. Freud held that the patient's symptoms were caused by a breakthrough of this 'strangulated' affect. The exact nature of the symptoms could be understood by linking them with the forgotten traumatic event. The following real-life example demonstrates all the crucial components of the affect-trauma model of abnormal personality. A soldier developed a bizarre blindness for objects which were either about 15 or about 35 yards away from him. He recalled under hypnosis that his best friend had been shot when he was standing 15 yards away from him by a sniper who was some 35 yards distant. This memory had been unacceptable to his consciousness and needed to be repressed because he had felt responsible for his friend's death (he had not returned the sniper's fire to protect his friend).

Although the trauma could, as in this example, be a recent event, Freud believed that most involved childhood or early adolescent experiences that had aroused feelings which could not be fully expressed or resolved at the time: for example, sexual seductions in childhood were frequently recalled by his female hysterical patients during treatment. Freud's therapy involved helping them to release the pent-up emotion (catharsis) by bringing the repressed trauma back into consciousness (abreaction), largely through the use of hypnosis. Although Freud quickly abandoned this model, its impact on the mental health profession can be felt to this day. The searching for and 'successful' retrieval of early trauma remains an implicit objective of crude 'roadside' psychotherapy. Further, as part of his theory of traumatic neurosis, Freud developed a novel physiological model of the mind (Freud, 1895). Although Freud abandoned this attempt at providing a neurophysiological model, much of the project may be considered formative; the theory re-emerged in his later work in metaphors for psychological functions, rather than theoretical propositions concerning neurophysiological processes. Many of his ideas were also prescient, to be confirmed by neurobiological researchers of recent decades (e.g. Crick and Koch, 2000).

2.1.2 Second phase: the topographical model

By the turn of the century, Freud discovered that memories of childhood seduction and associated mental contents were not always accurate recollections, but sometimes fantasies relating to unconscious wishes (Freud, 1900). He began to focus on inborn drives as the motivating force of personality development and distortion of this development in psychopathology. As drives became his central concern, Freud's attention temporarily shifted from external events as causes of disorder to biological tension states activating (the term Freud used was translated as 'cathecting') ideas which pressed for discharge and gratification against the resistance of consciousness. Repressed wishes could find expression through dreams, albeit in an indirect form: thus the dream of a small child about losing a favorite pet might be an expression of an unconscious wish to 'lose' a sibling. Freud realized that the fulfilment of many of these wishes would be highly threatening and felt that this was one reason why so many dreams were associated with the experience of anxiety. Unconscious wishes may sometimes inadvertently receive direct expression in so-called slips of the tongue (Freud, 1901), as when an American woman senator talked in highly indignant terms about ideological repression in the United States 'for feminists, homosexuals and other perversions – I mean persuasions!'

2.1.2.1 The three systems of the mind

In constructing his psychological model of dreaming, Freud distinguished three layers of the mind. The deepest layer, the *system unconscious*, was thought to be made up of desires and impulses of a mostly sexual and sometimes destructive nature. The dominating concern of the system unconscious was the fulfilment of these desires or, as Freud called it, the 'pleasure principle' (Freud, 1911a).

The mode of thinking in the system unconscious (Freud, 1912b) was assumed by Freud to be fundamentally different from conscious thinking. Such 'primary process' thinking was assumed to be impulsive, disorganized, incomprehensible to rational thought, dominated by bizarre visual imagery and disregarding of time, order or logical consistency. Freud felt that dreams were to a large extent the product of these primary thought processes. Although frequently bizarre and usually baffling to conscious thought, dreams could be interpreted if the mechanisms of distortion were successfully unraveled. Freud reported a dream of seeing his sleeping mother being carried into the room by some bird-headed people. Freud interpreted the dream as a disguised expression of his sexual feeling for his mother; the word for bird (*vogel*) is similar to the German slang word for having sex (*vogeln*). Berger (1963) reported similar instances of play on words in dreams in an experimental study. In this study sleeping (and dreaming) subjects had the name of a close friend presented to them auditorily and, when awoken, were asked to recall their dreams. The subjects were not aware of having heard the stimuli, but nevertheless the names were often involved in the dreams indirectly, in puns (e.g. the name 'Gillian' was represented in the dream by a woman from Chile – a Chilean) or by association (e.g. the name 'Richard' giving rise to a dream of shopping in a store of that name).

Recent neurobiological work appeared to discredit Freud's theory of dreams as disguised wish fulfilments. An influential neurological theory by Hobson and McCarley (Hobson and McCarley, 1977), for example, suggests that rapid eye movement sleep which occurs mostly concurrently with dreaming in humans is the consequence of random firing in subcortical areas of the brain (the pons), which activates higher centres in a random way, perhaps with the neurological function of purging the memory system of surplus connections, in order to facilitate its daily restructuring of memory. However, elegant neuropsychological work by Mark Solms (1997a) (see Chapter 3, section 3.3 below) demonstrated that REM periods and the experience of dreaming were not necessarily associated to each other. Further, Solms reviewed literature which showed that dreaming was initiated in sub-cortical structures of the brain closely related to motivational systems. In fact, Solms's neuropsychological model based on findings from brain imaging and clinical lesion studies has a great deal in common with Freud's classical ideas. While this cannot be claimed as proof that Freud was right all along, recent discoveries about the brain have not in any way invalidated Freud's ideas from a century ago.

The *system pre-conscious* forms the middle layer within this topographical model and acts to censor forbidden wishes, only allowing access to consciousness if they are so distorted that their unconscious origins cannot be detected. The psychological phenomenon of perceptual defense can be explained in similar terms. Work in this field, summarized by Dixon (1981), demonstrated that some subjects have higher perceptual thresholds for distressing stimuli (such as the word 'cancer') than for neutral words. A number of experimental studies used the procedure of presenting neutral and emotional words to subjects, initially for such short durations that they were unaware of seeing the word. The exposure of the word is gradually increased until the subject is able to recognize it. These studies and others using more elaborate methodologies found that for some subjects emotional words needed to be presented for longer periods of time in order to be recognized. It is assumed that subjects perceive and evaluate the word pre-consciously but that because of its conflictual nature its entry into consciousness is hindered. This provides some evidence for Freud's suggestion that the motive for censorship is the avoidance of displeasure associated with conflictual ideas.

The uppermost layer of the mind is the *system conscious*, which is organized in terms of logic and reason, its main function being the handling of external reality, the avoidance of danger and the maintenance of civilized behavior. The conscious part of the mind is dominated by the 'secondary processes' or what Freud also called the 'reality principle'.

Freud redefined the notion of trauma in this model. Trauma was thought to occur if the conscious part of the mind was overwhelmed by irresistible urges to gratify unconscious wishes, followed by intolerable feelings of rejection or punishment.

2.1.2.2 Psychosexual development

In addition, Freud constructed a view of human life determined by primitive biological urges which the individual needs to master in the course of his or her development in order to conform to the demands of society. These urges or instincts are represented mentally in terms of wishes and are directed toward external *objects* for their satisfaction. He called them sexual instincts, although the word 'sexual' was used in an extended sense to mean something like 'physically pleasurable'.

Freud (1905d) identified three stages in the development of these infantile urges, distinguished on the basis of the zone of the body through which the sexual drive manifested itself at the time. The first phase, the oral, is dominated by instinctual pleasure obtained via sucking, eating, etc. After the age of two years, the focus of pleasure shifts to the anus (anal stage) and the child obtains pleasure from defecation. Between three and four years of age, the focus shifts yet again to the penis in boys and to the clitoris in girls (phallic stage). This stage is followed by a period of relative calm in psycho-sexual development (latency stage) which lasts until the onset of puberty. Sexuality returns in adolescence, and in normal development all previous stages of libidinal fixation come to be integrated within genital sexuality.

At each of these stages the child is faced with conflicts between instinctual desires and the conscious activities of the mind. Freud thought that the manner in which the child deals with such conflicts profoundly influences the future development of his or her personality. Stages where instinctual desires are either completely frustrated or too readily gratified may become points of 'fixation', to which the adult might well return if confronted by intolerable stresses in later life.

The *oral stage* (Abraham, 1927; Glover, 1924/1956) is commonly divided into two phases: the first, during which the baby sucks, and later an 'oral-sadistic' phase of biting. Two types of oral personality corresponding to these two phases, have been described. The first is dominated by passivity, relaxation and dependence, corresponding to a perpetuation of the baby's pleasure at being held by mother at the breast along with a confident belief that the milk will arrive. The second personality type, normally associated with the period of weaning, is characterized by activity and aggression, which can be seen as a perpetuation of the pleasure of biting.

These sources of pleasure can be observed to continue in individuals who are unable to resist using the oral channel for gratification: for example, individuals who persist in sucking their thumbs, chewing on pencils or pens, who talk all the time or console themselves by eating when unhappy. On the other hand, a person may try to fend off the desire to give in to these pleasures by manifesting extreme independence, impatience or cynicism. Fisher and Greenberg (1977) summarize the oral character as being preoccupied with issues of giving and taking, concern about independence and dependence, extremes of optimism and pessimism, unusual ambivalence, impatience and the continued use of the oral channel for gratification.

Several studies have examined whether these 'oral characteristics' do indeed appear together. Kline and Storey (1978; 1980) found evidence that the qualities of dependency, fluency, sociability and a liking for novelty and relaxation were associated with one another and corresponded well with psychoanalytic descriptions of the individual whose personality is most strongly affected by the first passive, receptive, sucking phase of the oral stage – oral optimism. They further found that the qualities of independence, verbal aggression, envy, coldness, hostility, malice and impatience were highly correlated, suggesting the oral pessimistic attitude of the infant disappointed and dissatisfied at the breast. Several researchers have produced some evidence for personality types that fit Freud's theory. The orientation toward seeking nurturance and contact with others (measured by personality tests, both projective and self-report, and by behavior such as help-seeking and touching) correlates with indexes of orality in the literal sense such as seeing breasts and mouths on the Rorschach projective test (Bornstein and Masling, 1985). Despite these encouraging findings, Howarth (1980; 1982) questioned the existence of these personality types and found that oral optimism was more simply accounted for as an aspect of sociability than as anything to do with psychoanalytic theory. Furthermore, there is almost no evidence to link these personality syndromes with particular patterns of breast-feeding experiences.

The second stage of instinctual development is linked to *anal pleasures* (Freud, 1908a; Jones, 1923) and the child's conflicts with the parents over potty-training. Anal fixation would occur if conflicts over anal matters were particularly intense, either because of especially strict toilet-training or because of exceptionally intense pleasure associated with this period. In Western society, anal pleasures, unlike oral ones, are socially unacceptable and are therefore rarely perpetuated into adult life. Thus fixation in the anal stage leads to the perpetuation of indirect expressions of anal erotic wishes or to attempts to defend against them. The intense struggle between child and caretaker over toilet-training is thought to be perpetuated in the character traits of obstinacy and stinginess: the child refusing to give up his or her valuable possessions (the faeces) at the say-so of his or her parents. The child will frequently feel the need to inhibit the wish to make a terrible mess. The defense against this wish is reflected in the opposite desire to be orderly, tidy and meticulous. The so-called anal (or obsessive-compulsive) character is therefore typified by orderliness, obstinacy, rigidity and a hatred of waste.

There is general agreement amongst reviewers that the major qualities that classical psychoanalysts ascribe to the anally oriented personality do tend to be found together (Fisher and Greenberg, 1977; 1996; Kline, 1981). Howarth (1982), despite his criticisms of the oral personality, accepted that there is a personality type epitomized by the neat, pedantic, clear, self-controlled and controlling individual who in a methodical and orderly way runs the bureaucracies of most nations. There is no evidence to suggest that individuals of this type received toilet-training that was in any way different from that of less obsessive-compulsive characters. Yet there is some, albeit dated, evidence which links measures of anxiety over bowel habits on the one hand to measures of orderliness, obstinacy and parsimony on the other. Rosenwald (1972), for example, demonstrated that the amount of anxiety experienced by persons about anal matters predicted how carefully they arranged magazines when requested to do so by the experimenter. Other studies found correlations between enjoyment of anal humour and questionnaire and behavioral measures of anality (O'Neill, Greenberg and Fisher, 1992).

It is unfortunate that psychological research effort has been devoted to the investigation of the above aspects of psychoanalytic theory because since the 1920s few psychoanalysts (including Freud himself) have taken this extremely simplistic view of character formation seriously. This, of course, does not mean that analysts have abandoned the concepts of psychosexual development, but the relationship between instinctual wishes and personality development is nowadays considered to be a great deal more complex than in Freud's first formulation.

The *phallic stage* is the third stage of psychosexual development. The so-called *Oedipus complex* arises in this stage. In the little boy, the phallic stage is thought to commence when, at the age of three to four years, his sexual interest comes to be focused on his penis and he becomes sexually interested in his mother. His masculinity is awakened, and this prompts him to seek to take over his father's role, pushing him aside. His aspirations are, of course, unrealistic, and this soon becomes apparent even to him. What is more, he fears that his father, whom he perceives as all-powerful and all-seeing, might discover his line of thinking and seek terrible vengeance by depriving him of that part of his body which is the current focus of his sexual interest. Under the imagined threat of castration, the boy decides to give up his interest in his mother and to deal with the threat by identifying with his father.

In girls, the Oedipus complex is complicated by two factors. First, girls are forced to change their object of primary affection from the mother to the father as they move into the phallic stage. (With boys, it is the mother who remains the primary object of affection throughout early childhood.) Secondly, the girl's turning toward father is prompted at least in part by her disappointment with mother for not having equipped her with a penis. The girl aims to have a penis at her command by seducing father, and later develops the fantasy of having his baby, which at an unconscious level she equates with a penis. In girls, the end of the Oedipus complex is not prompted by fear of physical injury but by fear of the loss of mother's love. The fear of retribution is less intense in girls than in boys, with the result that oedipal attitudes are less strongly repressed in women, the father frequently remaining a sexually attractive figure.

The fascinating illustrations from mythology and anthropology quoted by Freud (1913c) cannot be said to constitute scientific support for his formulations. There is scant evidence for the Oedipus complex in the experimental literature. Studies of children's attitudes to parents at the supposedly oedipal stage do not bear out the predicted shift in positive feelings from mother to father in boys and from mother to father and back in girls (Kagan and Lemkin, 1960). The finding that boys are more concerned about physical injury than girls is consistent with but cannot be held to prove the existence of castration anxiety (Pitcher and Prelinger, 1963). A study dating back half a century (Friedman, 1952), looked at the extent to which children produced positive or negative endings to stories. When the stem of the story concerned a child doing something nice with the opposite sex parent and then was joined by the same sex parent, the child typically produced a relatively sad ending to the story. However, when the stem described the interruption of the same pleasurable activity with the same sex parent by the opposite sex parent, children produced significantly more positive endings to the story. In an observational study parents of 3–6 year olds were asked to record the number of affectionate and aggressive acts performed by their child toward them over a week. In four-year-olds more affection was observed in relation to the opposite sex parent and more aggression in relation to the same sex parent, but this pattern was less evident by 5 and 6 years (Watson and Getz, 1990).

Investigations of penis envy have found no evidence that women assess their bodies as in any way inferior to those of men (Fisher, 1973); in fact, different lines of evidence suggest that on the whole women feel more comfortable, secure and confident about their bodies than men do. Referring to Freud's speculation that pregnancy is associated with a fantasy of possessing a penis, Greenberg and Fisher (1983) argued that women should experience pregnancy as a time of heightened 'phallic feelings'. Their measurement of phallic feelings was based on the number of penis-like objects women identified in shapeless inkblots. They found that women during pregnancy tended to report seeing more elongated objects (e.g. arrows, spears and rockets), more body protrusions (e.g. noses, tongues sticking out and fingers), more body attachments (e.g. horns, cigars and snorkels) and the like than they did either before or after pregnancy or than did non-pregnant women. The authors claim that this research supports Freud's suspicion that the penis assumes an important role in the unconscious psychic life of women. This kind of evidence is likely to meet with substantial and probably appropriate scepticism and even hostility. Evidence based on projective tests such as inkblot tests is frequently unreliable. A large number of alternative explanations could be put forward to account for the same data. Certainly, even within psychoanalysis, Freud's rather Victorian attitudes to women have not been accepted without criticism (Mitchell, 1973).

2.1.2.3 Theory of neurosis

Freud made an important distinction between neurotic symptoms and character traits. Whereas character (personality) traits owe their existence to successful defense against instinctual impulses, neurotic symptoms come into being as a result of the failure of repression (Freud, 1915c). In normal development, as the child progresses through the psychosexual stages, his or her instinctual strivings get closer and closer to adult genital sexuality. Particularly intense conflicts may result in the fixation of psychosexual energy (libido) at these earlier stages. If psychosexual development is seen as the onward marching of troops, then fixation resembles the establishment of garrisons at various points with a weakening of the onward marching force. During times of psychological stress the libido may regress to a point of libidinal fixation so that the person comes to be dominated by the associated infantile wishes. The problem is that whereas in infancy these wishes are normal, an adult or even an older child would be greatly disturbed by and thus would be struggling against intense oedipal, anal or oral wishes. The obsessional patient, for example, who washed his or her hands for an hour and a half after having gone to the toilet was seen by Freud as struggling with instinctual wishes characteristic of the anal stage. This symptom represented at one and the same time the wish to soil and the defense against it.

The idea that neurotics experience more intense pre-genital (oral, anal or phallic) impulses received some support from a study by Kline (1979). He demonstrated that a person's oral optimistic, oral pessimistic (first and second phases of oral stage) and anal fixation questionnaire scores taken together correlated with their overall degree of neuroticism.

An important development in this model concerned the role of *aggression*. In his early thinking, Freud was preoccupied with the problems of the psychosexual drives and saw aggression as a response to the frustration of these urges. The horrors of the First World War made a profound impression on him, and he began to be preoccupied with destructive urges. Gradually Freud (1915a; 1920) started to view aggression as an impulse every bit as important as sex and also an inherent quality of human nature. He postulated the existence of a second instinct, a death instinct, satisfied by destruction or dissolution. Aggression needs to be defended against and controlled in just the same way as the sexual urges. The so-called 'dual drive theory' had considerable explanatory potential. The apparently self-defeating behaviors of neurotic individuals could now be seen as a consequence of destructive wishes defensively directed against the person's own self. Further, the rigid manner with which certain individuals stuck to evidently self-destructive patterns of behavior could be explained in terms of the gratification of a pull toward annihilation.

The clinical implication of the shift from trauma theory to the drive model was that the aim of psychoanalysis shifted from concern with the uncovering of traumata to the integration of unacceptable unconscious wishes, the repression of which was considered the cause of the neurosis, into conscious thought.

2.1.3 Third phase: structural model

Freud gradually realized that his topographical model was too simplistic and unable to provide answers to a number of important questions, such as: where do we find a non-sexual instinct capable of repressing the sexual one, why do people feel guilt, and how does consciousness control impulses it is not yet aware of? It became clear to Freud that the unconscious cannot be equated with wishes, nor the conscious with forces of repression since the mechanism of repression is itself unconscious (Freud, 1923).

2.1.3.1 Structures of the mind

Freud rethought his model substantially (Freud, 1923) and conceived of three structures in the mind (enduring organizations which were nevertheless to some extent open to change). The first, entirely unconscious, structure, the *id*, was the reservoir of sexual and aggressive drives, as the system unconscious had been in the previous model. The id is a translation into English-Latin from the German *Es* meaning 'it'. The term in German carries childlike or primitive connotations.

The second structure, the *superego*, was seen as the organized psychic representation of childhood parental authority figures. The child's picture of the parents is naturally not realistic. The internalized authority figure was therefore held to be stricter and harsher than the parents were in reality. The superego becomes a vehicle for the ideals derived from parents and hence from society. It is the source of guilt, and as such is important in normal and pathological mental functioning. The superego is partly conscious but largely unconscious.

The third component of this model was the *ego*. Ego is the English translation from the German *Ich* (meaning 'I'), Freud's term for the part of the personality closest to what the individual recognizes as his self. The ego is largely unconscious. It has the role of mediating between the id and the superego. It was the ego's function to cope with the demands and restrictions of external reality and to mediate initially between the drives and reality and, later on, as a moral sense develops, between the drives and the superego. To achieve this the ego has a capacity for conscious perception and problem-solving to deal with external reality, and the mechanisms of defense are available to it to regulate internal forces. Although parts of the ego are conscious, much of its struggle with the internal demands placed upon it by the id and superego occurs unconsciously. The ego was not simply a group of mechanisms but a coherent structure whose task was to master the competing pressures of the id, superego and external reality.

Consciousness in the structural model was conceived of simply as a sense organ of the ego. In Freud's view, most sophisticated psychological processes could function outside consciousness. This is consistent with a viewpoint, now prevalent in cognitive and experimental psychology, that conscious experience is limited to the products of mental processes and that the processes themselves are beyond awareness (see Mandler, 1975).

Developmentally, the structural model assumes that the ego evolves from drive frustration. Id drives seek object contact to achieve gratification. When these objects are relinquished they are taken in through identification to form the basis of the ego. Freud (1923) recognized that the gratification of drives was not the only need of the human infant. The infant is forced to give up the early tie to the mother, and the fantasy of sexual relation with the parent of the opposite sex (the oedipal object) must similarly be relinquished. In Freud's view, this relinquishment could not take place unless the psychic energy attached to the mother could be transferred to an internal image of her with which the child identifies (Freud, 1914). In the oedipal period, sexual longing for the parent of the opposite sex is abandoned through an identification with the same sex parent or an identification with the opposite sex parent as a desperate way of denying the loss. Freud thought that gender identification and sexual orientation were both determined by the direction these identificatory processes took (Freud, 1924a). Thus the ego is formed out of frustrated id wishes and takes shape on the basis of the nature of the objects that reality forces the child to relinquish. The development of the superego is similarly thought to be based on the characteristics of the abandoned object-cathexes of the id. However, while the ego contains the cathexis, the superego is based on the defenses against the wishes derived from the id impulses. For example, the superego may turn id impulses into their opposites (a reaction formation), so that they become moral objections to the wishes in place of the wishes themselves. It is important to note the close link envisioned by Freud between the entire spectrum of mental functions and the drives, so that both the ego and the superego were seen as directly reflecting the object cathexes of early childhood.

While this model of the mind still saw the psyche as having a fundamentally biological origin, Freud once again shifted to attribute much more significance to external events and less to the sexual motive. Anxiety, guilt and the pain of loss were seen as very much more important in explaining abnormal behavior than were sexual drives. Defenses were no longer viewed as simple barriers against unconscious impulses but as ways of modifying and adapting unconscious impulses and also of protecting the ego from the external world. Anxiety, seen by Freud in the previous model as undischarged sexual energy, was here seen as a signal of danger arising within the ego whenever external demands or internal impulses represented a major threat (S. Freud, 1926). This might occur under a threat of loss of love or of enormous guilt as well as a threat of physical injury.

Freud conceived these three structures as metaphors, assisting him to conceptualize his clinical observations. He never postulated that anatomical structures corresponding to the id, ego or superego could be located. Some neurophysiologists have tried to do so, although none has succeeded (Hadley, 1983). However, there is some psychometric evidence to indicate that the distinction between the three mental structures drawn intuitively by Freud can be demonstrated empirically. In a large rating scale and questionnaire-based factor-analytic survey of motivational factors, Cattell (1957) and Pawlik and Cattell (1964) identified three dimensions of psychological functioning that arguably fitted in well with the id/ego/superego distinction. As it is unlikely that questionnaires can provide good access to an individual's unconscious functioning, and as the identification of dimensions in the statistical procedure of factor analysis is a fairly arbitrary affair, we do not regard such studies as confirmation of Freud's motivational system.

2.1.3.2 Defense mechanisms

The identification of defense mechanisms was one of Freud's early achievements, but it was not until the advent of the structural model that their function and organization could be adequately elaborated (Freud, 1936). Defenses are unconscious strategies serving to protect the individual from painful affect (anxiety or guilt). Such affect may arise: through conflict over impulses (ego versus superego, e.g. a prohibition against cheating in an exam) and external threat (ego versus reality, e.g. a violent disagreement between parents).

The first defense mechanism to be described by Freud was *repression*. This is the process by which an unacceptable impulse or idea is rendered unconscious. It has been suggested that repression is the primary form of defense and that other defenses are called into operation in response to its failure. *Projection* is the mechanism whereby unwanted ideas or impulses originating in the self are attributed to others. Thus, an active wish appears as a passively experienced outcome. In this way the object of aggression frequently comes to be feared.

Reaction formation is a mechanism that serves to deny impulses by intensifying their opposites. For instance, people disturbed by cruel impulses toward animals might join the RSPCA or the American Humane Association, channelling their energies into preserving rather than destroying life. The nature of their efforts may at times give us a clue to the character of the original impulse: an example of this is the ardent animal-lover who published a pamphlet describing fifteen ways of painlessly killing a rabbit.

Other defense mechanisms include *denial* (perceiving but refusing to acknowledge), *displacement* (the transfer of affect from one stimulus to another), *isolation* (when feelings are split off from thought), *suppression* (the conscious decision to avoid attending to a stimulus), *sublimation* (gratifying an impulse by giving it a socially acceptable aim), *regression* (reversion to a previously gratifying level of functioning), *acting out* (allowing one's actions to directly express an unconscious impulse) and *intellectualization* (separating a threatening impulse from its emotional context and placing it in a sometimes inappropriate rational framework).

The defense mechanisms have been the subject of intensive experimental research, although little that is conclusive has emerged. Repression, for example, has been studied in the laboratory, usually by creating anxiety in subjects associated with a particular type of material and seeing if the rate of forgetting is affected. In extensive reviews, Holmes (1974) and Pope and Hudson (1995) found no evidence of repression in these studies. In a classic study, Wilkinson and Cargill (1955), however, found that oedipal stories were recalled significantly less well than ones with a neutral theme. In his review, Kline (1981) felt this latter study was persuasive, as was the work of Levinger and Clark (1961), which demonstrated that words to which subjects had strong emotional responses were recalled less well than neutral words. The debate concerning recovered memories of sexual abuse (Mollon, 1998) brought the issue of repressed memories back into focus. Although agreement concerning the validity of motivated forgetting remains contro- versial (see, for example, Pope and Hudson, 1995), selective forgetting is now known to be a property of the memory system and the motivated distortion of recall has become a key tenet of cognitive behavioral accounts of psychopathology (Beck, 1976) as well as of psychoanalytic theories. As the neuropsychological mechanisms necessary for motivated influences on memory are increasingly accepted, the appropriate scientific question may not be whether repression exists but, more specifically, what its role is in psychological disturbance and treatment. Many psychoanalysts have taken the view that the recovery of memories in therapy is incidental to thera- peutic action (Spence, 1984; Fonagy, 1999b).

Unconscious processes are part of mental function. The so-called 'cognitive unconscious' (Kihlstrom, 1987) appears quite similar to Freud's concept of the preconscious. It is generally agreed that human memory includes two systems, one conscious and often labeled *explicit* and the other non-conscious, labeled *implicit*. The former involves conscious retrieval of information such as memories of childhood experiences. The latter is observable in an individual's behavior but cannot be voluntarily retrieved (Roediger, 1990; Schachter, 1992b). For example, experimental studies show that an experience that is not consciously registered and which resists conscious attempts at recall, nevertheless can and does influence an individual's behavior (Bowers and Schacter, 1990). Reading a word among many on a long list can bias the person's reading of an incomplete word (e.g. seeing but not registering the word 'assassin' predisposes the individual to see this in the word fragment A_A_IN rather than, say, 'Aladdin'). Freud's comparison of consciousness to the small fraction of the iceberg that sticks out of the sea indicates his recognition that the mind for the most part uses implicit non-conscious procedures to organize adaptation. Studies of brain- damaged patients with memory loss (amnesia) or split-brain patients demonstrate that Freud was right to assume that our behavior is often caused by complex thoughts of which we have no awareness (e.g. Gazzaniga, 1985; Bechara et al., 1995).

Interesting laboratory-based studies provide quite extensive evidence for unconscious motivational processes that influence or shape our attitudes. These are sometimes shown by studies of psychophysiological responses compared with conscious attitudes. For example, individuals whose conscious attitude to homosexuality was most negative showed the greatest sexual excitement when confronted with homosexual pornography (Adams, Wright and Lohr, 1996). This and other studies demonstrate that unconscious attitudes can have a measurable impact on performance, and that conscious attitudes do not predict involuntary behavior. A series of studies have demonstrated that a defensive disavowal of affect in experimental studies (claiming not to be emotionally aroused when one is) correlates with vulnerability to disease (Jensen, 1987; Weinberger, 1990). By contrast, writing about painful (e.g. shameful) experiences produces increases in immune functioning and physical health (Pennebaker, Mayne and Francis, 1997). Further evidence suggests excessive defensiveness predicts psychopathology. For example, defensive self-enhancement (narcissism) is found to be associated with fluctuating moods and being rated as deceitful and undependable (Colvin, Block and Funder, 1995). While demonstrating the existence of psychological mechanisms that may be called defenses, these studies do not bear on the theoretical and clinical role that Freud assigned to them.

2.1.3.3 The theory of neurosis

In the structural model, Freud conceived of the neurotic symptom as representing a combination of unacceptable impulses which threaten to overwhelm the ego and the defenses against them. The degree of health was a function of the ability of the ego to manage the press of drive-based wishes at the same time as addressing the constraints of reality (Freud, 1926). The degree to which the ego fails determines whether the person will fall ill. For example, if the ego is forced to use excessive repression, wishes will seek alternative expression and hysterical symptoms will be the consequence. Every symptom implies the ego's failure to balance the need for drive discharge with the constraints of superego strictures and external reality (Freud, 1933).

Anxiety, the hallmark of most neurotic reaction types, was seen by Freud (1926) as the ego signalling the imminent danger of being overwhelmed and mobilizing its defensive capabilities, in much the same way that a fire alarm set off at the first sign of smoke might be aimed at summoning the assistance of the fire brigade. Neurotic reaction types are distinguished by the manner in which the ego defends itself against the anxiety and guilt engendered by childhood impulses (Freud, 1931b). Thus, in phobias Freud saw the operation of the mechanisms of projection and displacement. A little boy projects his own envious and jealous anger onto his father because of his love and fear, and ends up by seeing him as murderously angry. Yet this also may become too painful and frightening to bear, and the fear is then displaced onto objects with whom he has less intimate ties: thus he may become terrified of burglars whom he fears might come to kill him during the night. The agoraphobic woman cannot leave the house because the incestuous wish concerning her father is projected and displaced onto males she might meet on the streets.

A paranoid person was thought to use reaction formation as a defense against conflictual homosexual impulses. 'I love him' turns into 'I hate him', which by projection becomes 'He hates me.' Experimental evidence from Zamansky (1958) showing that individuals with paranoia fixate longer on homosexual pictures than controls confirmed numerous clinical observations of intense conflict over homosexual impulses in such individuals.

In obsessive-compulsive neurosis, Freud thought individuals defended against aggressive impulses by reaction formation (Freud, 1933). Thus they might turn the feared wish to murder into endless concern over the safety of the person concerned. Sometimes the aggression was fended off by isolation, individuals continuing to experience the violent images consciously but feeling that they are bizarre, do not belong and are being thrust upon them from outside. The formulation of obsessional neurosis as due to underlying hostility is consistent with a study of Manchanda and colleagues (1979), who found increased hostility in obsessional neurotics on a questionnaire measure.

It was believed that depression involved dealing with ambivalent feelings by turning unconscious aggressive wishes against the self. Silverman (1983) reviewed studies appearing to provide evidence for psychoanalytic formulations of depression. In a number of studies it was demonstrated that the subliminal presentation of stimuli designed to stir up unconscious aggressive wishes (e.g. a picture of a snarling man holding a dagger) led to a worsening of depression on mood-rating scales.

As Freud increasingly came to see psychopathology as a result of conflict between competing psychological structures, so the emphasis in psychoanalytic clinical work shifted from an exclusive focus on drives to an equal emphasis on the forces which oppose them (Freud, 1937). Nevertheless, isolated studies appear to be consistent with Freud's so called 'hydraulic' model of motivation (the term hydraulic is used to signify the view that pressure effectively resisted or defended against in one part of the system is assumed to be a likely cause of difficulties elsewhere). For example, young female subjects asked to suppress negative emotion show greater physiological reactivity, which may be costly in the long term (Richards and Gross, 1999). While this kind of finding is not uncommon, there are other ways of accounting for them than in terms of a hydraulic model of motivation. Modern theorists would be more likely to conceptualize such results in terms of disconnections between the experiential and expressive components of emotion (Plutchik, 1993).

There is developmental evidence supporting the central role Freud gave to anxiety in the context of the structural model. Anxiety disorders in childhood and adolescence often precede and predict later disorders, particularly depressive disorders. Interviews of patients from retrospective studies suggest that the majority become anxious before they become depressed (Kovacs et al., 1989). Several prospective, longitudinal studies have also found that anxiety precedes depression in children, adolescents and young adults (Bresleau, Schultz and Peterson, 1995; Lewinsohn, Gotlib and Seeley, 1995; Cole et al., 1998). Even recurrent familial major depression in adulthood is mostly preceded by anxiety disorder in adolescence (Warner et al., 1999). Even if not all forms of depression are preceded by anxiety, the pattern occurs with sufficient frequency to underscore the fundamental nature of anxiety for psychological disorders. The opposite pattern of depression leading to anxiety has not emerged as a developmental phenomenon (Zahn-Waxler, Klimes-Dougan and Slattery, 2000).

2.1.4 Criticism and evaluation

Freud's corpus has often been the subject of both philosophical (epistemological) and psychological criticism (e.g. Eysenck, 1952; Popper, 1959; Wittgenstein, 1969; Grünbaum, 1984; Masson, 1984; Crews, 1995). A detailed review of these critiques is beyond our scope here, yet a selection of the major criticisms is important to restate as all the approaches to be reviewed in this book are based on Freud's work.

1. Freud *ignored spiritual values* and was strongly anti-religious.
2. He *neglected the social nature* of humankind and contributed little to our understanding of the psychology of groups and social systems.
3. He thought of human beings as striving to reduce the internal pressure created by drives and neglected drives such as *curiosity*, which push toward increases rather than decreases of internal tension, and are thus not consistent with his theory of motivation.
4. He told us little about the nature of what is perhaps most uniquely human: *consciousness*.
5. He was *unable to predict* the future path of an individual's development, and he only commented on a person's current life in terms of his or her past.
6. Freud *misunderstood women* and was excessively influenced by the prevailing culture of his time as far as his views of race, age, sexuality and politics were concerned.
7. He deliberately suppressed information concerning the traumatic origins of neurotic disorders.

8. Most criticisms concern the *data on which psychoanalysis is based* – the use of the then predominant clinical case study:
   (a) His initial discoveries were based on *introspection*, a tool which he himself later discredited.
   (b) His conclusions were based on a small *selected sample* of middle-class Viennese individuals.
   (c) His data consisted of his *biased recollections* of what patients said to him during clinical interviews, which he sometimes did not write down until long after the session had ended.
   (d) To the extent that he used parents' responses as confirmatory evidence of his interpretations, he may be accused of *influencing his patients* toward accepting his comments.
   (e) He rejected the use of more systematic methods of study.
   (f) It is claimed he sometimes falsified his data to fit his theories.
   (g) His claims for clinical effectiveness were exaggerated.
9. Equally important are the *inadequacies of formal aspects of his theorization*:
   (a) his terms are *ambiguous*, with changing meanings;
   (b) he uses many *metaphors*, and his tendency to *reify* these (pretend that the metaphors corresponded to real entities) sometimes led to major logical fallacies, such as appearing to talk about parts of a person's mind as if they were individuals;
   (c) many of Freud's metaphors were based in nineteenth-century physiology, which was increasingly perceived as constraining and inappropriate by twentieth-century psychology;
   (d) his theory *lacks parsimony* (more assumptions are made than are needed to account for the data);
   (e) the inadequacies of his theorization make the theory *difficult to test* using alternative methodology and, notwithstanding some brave attempts, these tests have by and large not been successful.

We shall return to the status of the evidence supporting psychoanalytic contentions in the later chapters. There can be no doubt, however, that these criticisms have some validity. As Westen (1998), in the best available review of the current empirical status of Freud's ideas, has pointed out: 'Many aspects of Freudian theory are indeed out of date, and they should be: Freud died in 1939, and he has been slow to undertake further revisions' (p. 333). Fisher and Greenberg (1996) have attempted to set out Freud's general theory of psychopathology in a propositional form. This summary makes problematic reading with much that now appears mechanistic, evolutionarily untenable, exclusively focused on sexuality and profoundly 'politically incorrect'. Yet puzzlingly, despite its obvious flaws, Freud's theory has remained amongst the most influential theories of personality in clinical practice. The key is perhaps to be found in the intuitive appeal of psychoanalytic ideas: they provide many clinicians with a framework within which to view aspects of their clients' behavior which would otherwise appear incomprehensible. Until another theory emerges that addresses the same range of experiences it is likely that a large number of clinicians will continue to treat Freud's ideas seriously despite the lack of scientific evidence.

The picture concerning developmental empirical evidence is not as bleak as many critics of Freud maintain (e.g. Crews, 1996). Westen (1998) demonstrated that there exists substantial empirical support for Freud's core construct: that human consciousness cannot account for its maladaptive actions. This and associated constructs are essential to all of modern psychoanalytic theory and will therefore be reviewed in more detail in various sections of the book. Here a brief summary should suffice.

There is good evidence for Freud's proposition that much of complex mental life is not conscious, that people can think, feel and experience motivational forces without being aware of them and can therefore also experience psychological problems which they find puzzling. Much current cognitive science research is focused on how memory can determine behavior implicitly, rather than through remembering a particular episode. We act in certain ways because of experience, despite our inability to recall those particular experiences (Schachter, 1992a; 1995; Squire and Kandel, 1999). More specifically, Freud's claim that unconsciously we are in some ways capable of more complex mental operations is supported by many research findings. For example, participants asked to compose a ballad after hearing a series of ballads could follow double the number of rules of ballads in their composition that they could consciously articulate (Rubin, Wallace and Houston, 1993).

Research on brain damage has provided ample evidence that processing relevant to emotional experience can take place outside awareness. For example, individuals with hemi-field neglect, who consistently ignore one half of the visual field, were presented with two pictures of a house. In one picture the house was depicted as on fire in the half of the visual field of which they had no awareness (Halligan and Marshall, 1991). The patients could not detect a difference between the house that was on fire and the house that was not. However, they invariably said they would prefer to live in the house that was not depicted as being on fire.

Social psychological investigations of prejudice serve as a good example of how unconscious processes can impact on everyday life. African Americans reliably report whether they experience an individual as racially prejudiced against blacks (Fazio et al., 1995). These reactions do not fit self-reported attitudes to ethnic minorities. However, individuals who are experienced by an African American as prejudiced appear to process negative information associated with an image of a black face faster and more accurately. Thus, even if the person is unaware of it, the presence of mental structures consistent with an attitude of prejudice is reliably sensed and is responded to by an observer.

Health psychology has provided evidence for the dynamic nature of unconscious affect. A review of risk factors for elevated blood pressure found that a defensive constriction of emotional experience was the best predictor of unexplained ('essential') hypertension amongst all the many personality variables that have been examined (Jorgensen et al., 1996). Writing about painful experiences and expressing unpleasant emotion leads not only to decreased arousal in the long run (Hughes, Uhlmann and Pennebaker, 1994) but also to increases in immune functioning (Pennebaker, 1997). Taken as a whole, studies such as these demonstrate that the kind of complex unconscious emotional processes which Freud described can be observed in the experimental laboratory as well as in the consulting room.

All Freud's models of the mind, but particularly his last, structural model, assumed mental conflict between incompatible unconscious ideas in order to understand sometimes seriously maladaptive neurotic behavior. Westen (1998) argues that a powerful cognitive-neuroscience model of conflicting ideas can be drawn from recent advances in artificial intelligence, namely models of parallel distributed processing (Rumelhart and McClelland, 1986). For example, self-serving biases (recalling one's past performance as having been better than it was, Morling and Epstein, 1997) might be interpreted as a compromise between two conflicting motivations, the motive for self-verification (confirm pre-existing views of oneself) and the motive for self-enhancement. The disposition of the ultimate neural processing system to generate a self-structure will automatically constitute a compromise between these two opposing motives simply because of the way parallel distributed networks function (Read, Vanman and Miller, 1997). Whether this is an accurate model or not, Westen argues that there is little that is inconsistent between Freud's century-old ideas and current models from artificial intelligence. In fact he makes a strong case that cognitive neuroscience would benefit from more serious consideration of affective and dynamic aspects of their complex information processing models.

A similar position has been adopted by a brilliant neuroscientist and Freud scholar, Mark Solms (Solms, 1997a; 1997b). He and his colleagues have reviewed the cognitive neuroscience literature and established many points of correspondence between Freud's ideas and positions independently created by neuroscientists. For example, Freud's theory of affect has many points of similarity with modern ideas such as those of Damasio (1999), LeDoux (1995, 1999) and Panksepp (1998; 2001). Although 'verifying' the psychoanalytic model via neuroscience research is an important ultimate goal, knowledge of brain/mind relations are not yet at the point where this is realistic. Solms and Nersessian (1999) appropriately point out that: 'A psychological model only becomes accessible to physical methods of investigation once the neural correlates of the component of the model have been identified' (p. 91). Although we now recognize many of the neural components, to date there is very little evidence concerning the developmental changes in neural substrates or psychobehavioral manifestations of specific emotion systems that might allow such direct translations (see Panksepp, 2001). Ultimately, Freud's model will be judged against the discoveries of neuroscience. In the meantime, consistency with experimental and developmental psychological observations is an appropriate criterion.

CHAPTER 3

The structural approach

3.1 The structural approach to development

Freud (1923) introduced the tripartite or structural model of the mind which described it as composed of instinctual derivatives (the id), an internalization of parental authority (the superego) and a structure independent of both these pressures, oriented toward internal and external adaptation (the ego). In 'Inhibitions, Symptoms and Anxiety' (1926) he added that innate features and the social environment both had important roles to play in the evolution of these structures and the primarily conflictual interactions between them. Freud's proposed sequence for the libidinal drive remained the cornerstone of developmental theory until the advent of ego psychology (Hartmann et al., 1946).

3.1.1 Hartmann's ego psychology model

Freud's model was refined and advanced in the ego psychology of Heinz Hartmann and his colleagues. Hartmann (1939) demonstrated the ways in which psychoanalysts frequently used the developmental point of view in an oversimplified and reductive way. His concept of the 'change of function' (Hartmann, 1939, p. 25) highlighted the fact that behavior originating at one point in development may serve an entirely different function later on. The internalization of parental injunction may, through reaction formation, lead the child to repudiate the anal wish to mess and soil, through excessive cleanliness and orderliness. The same behavior in the adult may serve quite different functions and is likely to be independent of the original drive; in other words, to have achieved 'secondary autonomy' (Hartmann, 1950). The failure to recognize this has been termed the 'genetic fallacy' (Hartmann, 1955, p. 221). Similarly, the persistence of dependent behavior in adulthood cannot be treated as if it were a simple repetition of the individual's early relationship with the mother. Adult behaviors are invariably seen as having

53

multiple functions (Waelder, 1930; Brenner, 1959; 1979), which are not reducible to their instinctual origins.

Hartmann's admonition continues to be relevant. The identification of what are presumed to be primitive modes of mental functioning in individuals with severe personality disorders (Kohut, 1977; Kernberg, 1984) is often regarded as evidence for the persistence or regressive recurrence of early pathogenic developmental experiences. Yet, even if splitting or identity diffusion were representative of early modes of thought (an issue that is in any case highly controversial, see Westen, 1990b), their re-emergence in adult mental functioning may be linked to later or continued trauma. The structural view of development, perhaps more than any other psychoanalytic developmental framework, attempts to take a holistic view of the developmental process, resisting the temptation to identify particular, especially early, critical periods (Tyson and Tyson, 1990).

Hartmann (1939) pointed out that some of the mechanisms used by the ego, such as perception, memory and motility, are not functions that evolve out of id frustration; rather, they appear to develop autonomously. He termed these 'apparatuses of primary ego autonomy', functions that become later integrated with the ego and are essential for its independent functioning, separate from the id and superego. Following Anna Freud (1936), Hartmann et al. (1946) postulated that the individual is endowed with an initial undifferentiated matrix from which both the id and the ego originate. Thus whereas in Freud's structural theory the ego (as we have seen) was dependent on the id, in Hartmann's ego psychology a substantial part of the mind (the psychic apparatus) operates in the 'conflict-free sphere'. Thus while at certain times fantasy is clearly best understood as a product of conflict between drives and the other psychic agencies, it is also a useful capacity for creative problem-solving and art (e.g. Kris, 1952).

The recognition of primary autonomy did not imply that Hartmann and his colleagues repudiated the link between drives and the structuring of the ego. In addition to the inborn motivation generated by primary autonomy of the ego, ego psychologists assume that drives play a crucial secondary role. They assume that the frustration of these drives contributes to the organization of the ego and leads to a secondary autonomy (Hartmann et al., 1949). Secondary autonomy is relative, never complete; the organized ego always remains linked to the id because the ego uses energy from the drives. Whereas Freud's emphasis was on libidinal cathexis, Hartmann claimed that aggressive impulses aimed at destroying the object were more dangerous and their neutralization consequently more vital. The successful neutralization or sublimation of aggression generates an ego structure that allows for good object relationships. If the neutralization of aggression is unsuccessful, psychological difficulties will result. For example, unneutralized aggression was thought potentially to attack a bodily organ, resulting in psychosomatic illness. At the extreme end of the developmental psychopathology spectrum, Hartmann (1953) argued that a complete failure to neutralize aggression forestalls the possibility of defense (counter-cathexis) and aggression overwhelms the organism, object relations become impossible and psychotic illness results.

Hartmann and colleagues also introduced the concept of an 'average expectable environment', which affirmed the importance of the actual parents, and outlined a scheme for the phase-specific maturation of autonomous, conflict-free ego functions. They thus allowed for both environmental and maturational influences upon personality development. They described the self as gradually becoming differentiated from the world during the first half of the first year, and the gradual evolution of the child's relationship to his or her own body and objects in the second half, as the influence of the reality principle is increasingly felt. In the second year, an ego–id differentiation phase was thought to emerge, marked by ambivalence, as the reality principle begins to assert its influence over the pleasure principle. The final phase is that of superego differentiation as a consequence of social influences, identification with parental values and the resolution of the oedipal conflict. Rapaport (1950), suggested a stage theory of the development of thinking which commences in hallucinatory wish fulfilment through the drive organization of memories, and moves through primitive modes of ideation and the conceptual organization of memories, until finally the capacity for abstract thought is attained.

Structural theorists see development as driven by a maturational pull, whereby independently emerging components and functions come to be linked, forming a coherently functioning organization (the ego) which is more complex than the sum of its parts (Hartmann, 1939; 1952). The system into which the defenses and adaptive functions of the ego were integrated is referred to as the 'synthetic function' of the ego. It is not simply an outgrowth of the id but an organized adaptive capacity that assures healthy functioning and has its own sources of growth. Stages of ego development represent nodal points at which 'fixation' may occur and to which, under the pressure of intense internal conflict, the individual may return. For example, obsessive-compulsive disorder is seen by structural theorists (Brenner, 1982; Arlow, 1985) as a regression to the phase of ego functioning, characteristic of the two-year-old (magical phenomenalism and repetitive, ritualistic behaviors). However, Kris (1952) emphasized that ego regressions should be considered part of normal development and may serve adaptive functions in, for example, artistic or scientific creativity (see also Blos, 1962, for an exposition of adaptive ego regression in adolescent development). Abrams (1977) pointed out that forward spurts of internal reorganization are frequently accompanied by 'backward slides', and the re-emergence of earlier structures in later developmental phases is a ubiquitous observation (Jones, 1922; Loewald, 1965; Brody and Axelrad, 1978; Neubauer, 1984). Sandler and Sandler (1992) go so far as to suggest that active inhibition of a natural regressive tendency is essential in order for the position of the individual to be maintained at a particular developmental phase.

David Rapaport (1951a; 1958) has given what is perhaps the clearest and most coherent statement of the classical ego psychological model of the mind. Rapaport conceived of the id as a constitutional given, whereas the ego was the 'created' personality. He claimed that the quality of the ego's healthy functioning, its adaptation to reality, was simply a function of the extent of its independence from the id. If the ego does not achieve independence, it will be unable to adapt to the demands of reality. Rapaport's view represented an advance in that his formulation truly frees psychoanalytic theory from its libidinal origins. The content of the intrapsychic conflict (oral, anal, phallic, oedipal) is hardly relevant. The same conflicts occur in healthy and disordered personalities. However, the ego which has been able to develop in a healthy way and has achieved autonomy from the id is better able to tackle these conflicts without symptomatic outcome. While broadly agreeing with Rapaport, Charles Brenner (1982), another giant of the ego psychology movement, pointed out that the distinctions between id and ego could never be as clear as suggested in Rapaport's writings since all mental phenomena were assumed to include a certain degree of compromise between ego and instinct. Only under conditions of conflict were ego and id clearly separable. Under normal circumstances, the ego worked hard to find ways for the id to achieve instinctual gratification and was obliged to negotiate the dangers that all id wishes inevitably generate.

Partly in response to the growth of object relations theory (see below), there has been a revival of the structural theory in psychoanalysis. Modern structural theory (see, for example, Boesky, 1989), retains Freud's (1923) tripartite model of id, ego and superego, but dispenses with concepts of psychic energy and other problematic notions. The theory takes as its central premise the ubiquity of internal psychic conflict (see Brenner, 1982), seeing this as an interaction between the three psychic agencies. Brenner suggests that all mental contents (thoughts, actions, plans, fantasies and symptoms) are compromise formations, multiply determined by components of conflict. The wish from the id conflicts with feelings of guilt, creating anxiety that is warded off by defense. The ego achieves a compromise by providing for instinctual gratification within the limits set by the intensity of guilt feelings and anxiety. Such compromises are achieved between the following components: (1) a drive derivative, an intense, personal and unique childhood wish for gratification; (2) unpleasure in the form of anxiety, or depressive affect, and associated fears of object loss, loss of love, or castration, linked with the drive derivative; (3) defense, which functions to minimize unpleasure; and (4) manifestations of superego functioning such as guilt, self-punishment, remorse and atonement. Self and object representations, in this scheme, are the result of compromise formations, which in their turn effect further compromises between the tendencies above. From a developmental standpoint, the interrelationships of these agencies are studied rather than either chronological age or libidinal phase. Similarly defense mechanisms are not a separate class of mechanisms as Anna Freud (1936) had assumed, but simply an ego function which, like all other such functions, has both an adaptive and a defensive role (Brenner, 1982). Healthy functioning in this context is the capacity to execute compromise formations (Arlow and Brenner, 1964; Brenner, 1994).

3.1.2 Psychic development within the structural model

3.1.2.1 Erikson

An important developmental schema was proposed by Eric Erikson (1950), whose primary concern was the interaction of social norms and biological drives in generating self and identity. His well-known description of eight developmental stages was based on biological events that disturb the equilibrium between drives and social adjustment. Personality would be arrested if the developmental challenge was not mastered through the evolution of new skills and attitudes. This would compromise later developmental stages. Erikson was remarkable amongst psychoanalysts for his attention to cultural and family factors and his extension of the developmental model to the entire life-cycle. His theory introduced plasticity to the psychoanalytical developmental model, as well as stressing the need for a coherent self-concept fulfilled in a supportive social milieu (see Jacobson, 1964; Schafer, 1968; Kohut, 1971; Stechler and Kaplan, 1980).

Erikson (1950; 1959) was the first to expand Freud's problematic erotogenic zone model, in his subtle concept of 'organ modes'. Prior to Erikson, it was assumed that activity associated with the pleasure inherent in each zone provided the basis for psychological modalities such as dependency and oral aggression, and for specific mechanisms such as incorporation and projection. Erikson's concept of organ modes extended the psychic function aspect of bodily fixation. In 1950 he wrote:

> in addition to the overwhelming need for food, a baby is, or soon becomes receptive in many other respects. As he is willing and able to suck on appropriate objects and to swallow whatever appropriate fluids they emit, he is soon also willing and able to 'take in' with his eyes whatever enters his visual field. His tactile senses, too, seem to 'take in' what feels good. (p. 57)

In this way he made a critical distinction between drive expression and mode of functioning, which opened up new vistas for the psychoanalytic understanding of human behavior.

The drive expression model binds understanding of social interaction to the gratification of biological needs. The notion of 'mode of functioning', on the other hand, frees us to think about *characteristic manners* of obtaining gratification or relating to objects at particular developmental stages. Erikson showed us how a person may find that a means of gratification, originally associated with a particular phase or erogenous zone, offers a useful way of expressing later wishes and conflicts. This enabled him to introduce a whole series of constructs, including identity, generativity, pseudo-speciation and basic trust. He expanded the drive model while remaining in a biological framework. His description of libido theory as tragedies and comedies taking place around the orifices of the body aptly summarizes Erikson's widening perspective enriched by anthropology and developmental study.

For Erikson, *basic trust* was the mode of functioning of the oral stage. The mouth was seen as the focus of a general approach to life – 'the *incorporative*' approach. Erikson stressed that these processes established interpersonal patterns which centered on the social modality of *taking*, and *holding onto* objects, physical and psychic. Erikson defines basic trust as a capacity 'to receive and accept what is given' (1950, p. 58).

By emphasizing the interactional psychosocial aspects of development, Erikson quietly altered the central position assigned to excitement in Freud's theory of psychosexual development. Although he accepted the libidinal phase model, and its timings, as givens, his formulation was one of the first to shift the emphasis from a mechanistic drive theory view, to the inherently interpersonal and transactional nature of the child–caregiver dyad as these are currently understood, related to the child's development of a sense of self.

Erikson became interested in the give and take between infant and caregiver at about the same time as John Bowlby (both Erikson and Bowlby began their work with Anna Freud, Bowlby in London in her Wartime Nurseries, Erikson in Vienna). Erikson saw early development as a continuous process, starting within the first few minutes of postnatal experience and extending throughout life, taking different forms at different times. His developmental stages did not end with adolescence but encompassed all phases of life, with characteristic changing emotional concerns. He was also unusual amongst classical analysts in taking social influences seriously. For many years, after Freud, Erikson was the most widely quoted psychoanalyst in textbooks of introductory psychology. Investigations of Eriksonian concepts of identity (Marcia, 1994), intimacy (Orlofsky, 1993), and generativity (Bradley, 1997) were considered by Westen (1998) to have been some of the most methodologically sound studies inspired by psycho-analytic theories of development.

Erikson's brilliant insight (1950), far ahead of his time, was that seemingly insignificant experiences would eventually become aggregated, leading to

> the firm establishment of enduring patterns for the balance of basic trust over basic mistrust ... [the] amount of trust derived from earliest infantile experience does not seem to depend on absolute quantities of food or demonstrations of love, but rather on the *quality* of the maternal relationship. (1959, p. 63)

3.1.2.2 Spitz

René Spitz (1959), one of the first 'empiricists' of the psychoanalytic tradition, formulated a general understanding of the developmental process in structural terms as early as 1936 (in an unpublished paper presented to the Vienna Psychoanalytic Society). He drew on Kurt Lewin's (1952) field theory as well as embryology (Spemann, 1938) and proposed that major shifts in psychological organization, marked by the emergence of new behaviors and new forms of affective expression, occur when functions are brought into new relation with one another and are linked into a coherent unit. He drew attention to the meaning of new forms of emotional expression such as the smiling response (2–3 months), initial differentiation of self and object, eight-month anxiety which indicates differentiation among objects, especially of the 'libidinal object proper' and the assertion of self in the 'no' gesture between 10 and 18 months. These 'psychic organizers' reflect the underlying advances in the formation of mental structure, each representing the integration of earlier behaviors into a new organization. The way in which these organizers herald dramatic changes in interpersonal interactions was elaborated in a highly influential series of papers by Robert Emde (1980a; 1980b; 1980c).

Spitz (1945; 1965) was also a pioneer in challenging what Greenberg and Mitchell (1983) have called the 'drive structural model' and in moving toward what they term the 'relational structural model'. He ascribed primary import-ance to the role of the mother and mother–infant interaction in a theory of developmental stages. He saw the parent as 'quickening' the development of the child's innate abilities and mediating all perception, behavior and knowledge.

Spitz (1957) saw self-regulation as an important function of the ego. Psychoanalytic observational studies repeatedly showed how constitutional, early environmental and interactional factors contribute to the structuring of the self-regulatory process leading to adaptation or maladaptation (Greenacre, 1952; Spitz, 1959; Weil, 1978). In particular, psychoanalysts have highlighted the role of affect in the development of self-regulation; the mother's emotional expression at first serves a 'soothing' or 'containing' function that facilitates the restoration of homeostasis and emotional equilibrium. Later, the infant uses the mother's emotional response as a signalling device to indicate safety. Later still, the infant internalizes the affective response and uses his own emotional reaction as a signal of safety or danger (Emde, 1980c; Call, 1984). It is quite broadly accepted within developmental theory that emotions serve as organizing, adaptive regulators of internal dynamic processes and interpersonal actions (Campos et al., 1983). Spitz was also remarkable in being one of the first psychoanalysts to note the presence of depression in young children (Spitz and Wolf, 1946). These descriptions suggested the presence of depression in children very early in life, at a time when most psychoanalysts still assumed that children did not have the psychological capabilities to experience sustained misery and despair (e.g. Sperling, 1959a).

3.1.2.3 Jacobson

Edith Jacobson (1964) reconstructed a wide variety of sequences over the lifespan on the basis of her experience of adult patients. She included the emergence of self and object representations in her theory and advanced the idea that the infant acquires self and object images with good (libidinal) or bad (aggressive) valences, depending on experiences of gratification or frustration with the caretaker. In order to clarify and distinguish among the concepts of ego, self and self-representation, she used the term 'self-representation' to stress the notion of the self and object as they were experienced, as distinguished from external objects. She saw the self as the totality of the bodily and psychic person, and defined self-representation as 'the unconscious, preconscious, conscious, intrapsychic representation of the bodily and mental self in the system ego' (p. 19). She assumed that early drive states shifted continuously from object to self with very weak boundaries between them. Distributional (good versus bad) and directional (self versus other) considerations were thought to shape all future growth as more stable self and object representations emerged.

Jacobson assumed that introjections and identificatory processes replaced the state of primitive fusion and that, through these, traits and actions of objects became internalized parts of self-images. She was particularly concerned with superego formation, which she saw as initially polarized between pleasure and unpleasure, then by issues of strength and weakness, and finally by the internalization of ethical considerations which regulated self-esteem as well as behavior. Jacobson applied her developmental perspective to a wide variety of disorders, most particularly to depression, which she associated with the gap between self-representation and ego ideal.

3.1.2.4 Loewald

Loewald (1951) was one of the first to argue that ego psychology had become reductive, obsessive and mechanistic, remote from human experience, and failed to address ego development that went beyond conflict and defense. He went back to id psychology (from ego psychology) and attempted to integrate drives and reality and drives and objects (Loewald, 1955). He sees the id as an organization related to reality and objects and drives as inherently related to and organized within object relations (Loewald, 1960). Loewald (1971a; 1973) proposes a developmental model that has at its centre a motive force toward 'integrative experience'; organizing activity defines the 'basic way of functioning of the psyche'. A number of classical concepts (internalization, symbolic representation, individuation) are reformulated as varieties of this inherent tendency toward disorganization and reorganization at a higher level. In Loewald's model drive, object, thought, action and mind are indivisible. His fundamental assumption is that all mental activity is relational (both interactional and intersubjective, see 1971a; Loewald, 1971b). Internalization (learning) is the basic psychological process which propels development (Loewald, 1973).

In several papers Loewald explains the centrality of oedipal experiences as a function of the emerging capacity for self-reflection (Loewald, 1979; 1985). The oedipal child is the inevitable product of growing awareness of self and other. The concept of the 'emerging core' refers to the individual's capacity for being 'separate', his ability to create and be responsible for a unique symbolic-representational personal experience, necessarily suffer guilt and atonement and therefore become able to 'join the moral order of the race'.

Loewald's model contains no reified structures (id, ego, etc.); Friedman (1986) notes that Loewald sees structures as processes. Wishes, thoughts and emotions are not treated in different frames of reference; each may evolve into more highly structured meaningful patterns. He sees this organizing activity as '*codetermined*' by other people: the meaning-generating mind works in a network of relationships. Loewald (1973, p. 70) sees separateness as the price of reflective self-awareness, which indicates the individual's capacity to accept responsibility for his fate.

Loewald's use of classical terminology is idiosyncratic (Fogel, 1989). He does not offer an alternative meta-psychology (Cooper, 1988) but suggests a basic psychoanalytic model which has internalization, understanding and interpretation at its core.

Settlage and colleagues (1988), propose a novel structural view of development across the lifespan. They consider that the stimulus for development is a disequilibrium of the previously adequate self-regulatory adaptive functioning, creating emotional stress. Such 'developmental challenges' may be caused by biological maturation, environmental demands, traumatic experiences or simply the perception of better possibilities for adaptation. The motivating tension can lead to regression, which may involve pathological solutions or developmental progression through conflict which is resolved by adaptive reorganization – in Piagetian (Piaget, 1967) terms, accommodation or assimilation self-regulated by means of equilibration. (Piaget's notion is prefigured in Freud's (1924b) notion of alloplastic and autoplastic adaptation. The former term refers to the individual's capacity to elicit responses and to relate to the external world in terms of needs and wishes. Freud saw this mode of adaptation as critical in ensuring the young child's capacity to elicit caring from others. Autoplastic adaptation is the capacity to change in response to perceived demands and implies compromise of internal need states and delay of immediate gratification. See also Ferenczi, 1930.) For example, pregnancy (Bibring et al., 1961) or parenthood (Benedek, 1959) may prompt psychic reorganization.

There are serious doubts about the viability of such a Piagetian, constructivist model of internalization. Developmentalists and cognitive scientists have demonstrated that Piaget's 'conflict-equilibration model' of cognitive development provides only a partial account of the establishment of more and more complex levels of structural representation (see for example Bryant, 1986). More recent developmental writings appear to favor a constitutional explanation of language acquisition, concept formation, object and event perception, thinking and reasoning and causal perception (Chomsky, 1968; Leslie, 1986; Meltzoff, 1990). These have more in common with Kleinian than with structural developmental theory.

The associationist learning theory account of development was criticized in the 1960s, on the grounds that it could not explain the internalization of highly complex and abstract structures that must underlie some cognitive capacities, such as language (Bever, 1968; Chomsky, 1968; Fodor, Bever and Garrett, 1974). This objection is equally applicable to some aspects of the structural theory of development (Gergely, 1991). The originators of the theory were increasingly forced to move away from the notion that ego capacities could be seen as evolving out of the 'taming of instinctual desires', and were forced to resort to a nativist account (see, for example, Rapaport, 1951b; 1958).

3.2 Structural model of developmental psychopathology

3.2.1 General features of the model

Within the structural model, neurosis and psychosis in adult life are seen as arising when an individual's urge for drive gratification reverts to a formerly outgrown infantile mode of satisfaction. Such regressions are brought about by psychic conflict that the ego cannot resolve. The id's regression and the associated revival of infantile urges intensifies the clash with parts of the personality that have maintained a mature level of functioning: intense internal conflict is the outcome. The ego's failure to manage such conflict – the intensification of guilt, the intensification of drive demands, and the greater inappropriateness of these demands in relation to the external world – leads to the formation of symptoms.

Symptoms are compromises, reflecting the ego's manifold attempts to restore equilibrium between the unacceptable drive representations and the opposing agencies of ego and superego. In other cases, the pathology may reflect the regression of the ego itself owing to psychological and organic causes. In psychosis, the ego is seen as being threatened by complete dissolution. Essential ego functions may resume modes of functioning characteristic of early childhood and come to be dominated by irrational, magical thoughts and uncontrolled impulses. Thus, whereas mental health is seen as the harmonious interaction between psychic agencies that function at age-appropriate levels, mental illness is seen as the failure of the ego's efforts. The pathogenic sequence is perceived as follows: (1) frustration; (2) regression; (3) internal incompatibility; (4) signal anxiety; (5) defense by regression; (6) return of the repressed; and (7) compromise and symptom formation.

Symptomatic disorders are not the only developmental consequences of childhood fixations. Within the classical structural model, inhibition is seen as a powerful, albeit potentially quite crippling, way of reducing conflict between the psychic agencies. At extreme levels, inhibitions are seen as characteristic of personality disorders (Freud, 1926). For example, an individual who avoids any kind of human contact that might stimulate drives and their associated affects may be seen as schizoid in personality type. Sexual impotence may be seen as the inhibition of the expression of the sexual drive. Inhibitions may apply to the ego (see A. Freud, 1936); an ego function that has become psychically painful may be abandoned. Ego restrictions of this kind would be exemplified by someone whose conflicts over competitiveness would cause them to withdraw from sports activities and invest their energies elsewhere, e.g. in writing. Restriction of affect may occur with individuals who experience emotion as highly threatening.

3.2.2 The structural model of the neurosis

The classical developmental model of the neurosis is well known and we will not elaborate it in detail here. Childhood sexual wishes arouse conscious repugnance when experienced in adulthood. They can reach awareness only when disguised. The neurotic compromise represents a disguised id derivative of childhood sexuality, the ego's defense, and signal anxiety marking the ego's experience of internal danger. It unifies the wish and the reaction against it in a part of the personality that is experienced as separate (ego dystonic). The subjective experience is of punishment, suffering and irritation which originates from, and is designed to placate, the superego.

Specific neurotic reactions reflect particular developmental fixations and characteristic modes of compromise formation. In conversion hysteria, the compromise achieves dramatic representation in somatic form and reflects an oral or phallic fixation. In obsessional neurosis, it is assumed that the ego binds anal sadistic and aggressive drive derivatives into forms of secondary process thinking (e.g. ruminations, obsessional doubts, etc.), but it is developmentally unable to neutralize these drive derivatives and therefore aggression and anal concerns will be transparent and arouse massive anxieties (see, for example, Fenichel, 1945; Glover, 1948). The process remains largely an internal one in that the neurotic compromise results in obsessions and is seen as located in the thought processes themselves. In phobias, the fear is externalized, but may reflect quite similar unconscious developmental concerns.

3.2.3 The structural theory of personality disorder

Whereas notions of neurotic pathology have, on the whole, evolved little since the structural theory of Freud, models of personality disorder have become 'paradigmatic' of various psychoanalytic models. As subsequent sections will illustrate, extremes of personality types, now embodied in the psychiatric diagnostic schemes as the second axis of psychiatric diagnosis (American Psychiatric Association, 1994), are formulated radically differently in different theoretical models according to the scheme of psychic structure and development which they propose. Classical psychoanalysis, as embodied in the structural model, offers a view of personality disorders, often formulated in contradistinction to more recent models, almost as if to demonstrate that these latter theories lack coherence and precision and that a revision of psychoanalytic theory is unnecessary. Abend and colleagues, for example, have examined post-Freudian contributions to the field of character neurosis, pessimistically pointing to conceptual ambiguities and problems of classification (Abend, Porder and Willick, 1983). Others oppose distinctions between severe personality disorders when these do not correspond to differences in terms of structural theory. Rangell (1982) for example goes so far as to say that the differentiation between borderline states and narcissistic disorders is a false one, and these groups should be brought together under the rubric of 'disturbed cases'.

Structural theory distinguishes those character disorders which dynamically resemble neurosis, and those which reflect a non-neurotic pattern based on structural deficit (see Waelder, 1960). The so-called character neurosis (a concept introduced by Alexander, 1930) is assumed to be dynamically similar to neurosis except that compromise formations are not split off from the ego and thus the symptoms are not experienced as ego alien or ego dystonic. Yorke, Wiseberg and Freeman (1989) refer to micro-structures of character neurosis which, like the micro-structures of id, ego and superego, become synthesized and durable. The obsessional character neurosis reflects this compromise between id derivatives, ego and superego, with the critical difference that the drive derivatives are better tolerated.

The notion of character neurosis is problematic. It suggests some kind of continuum between disorder and character type, the difference being chiefly in quantity rather than quality. There is good evidence that certain typical neurotic reactions may be found in non-clinical subjects, in character types, as well as in disorders. For example, Rachman and de Silva (1978) found that transient obsessions and compulsions occur within a fairly large proportion of the population, whereas the prevalence of the disorder is relatively low (American Psychiatric Association, 1994). There is some evidence to suggest that frank obsessions or compulsions correlate with obsessional traits, either concurrently or prior to the onset of symptoms (e.g. Flament and Rapaport, 1984). However, epidemiological studies indicate that only 15–20% of obsessive-compulsive disordered children develop obsessive character neurosis (Flament, Whitaker and Rapoport, 1988; Swedo et al., 1989) These findings suggest that the continuum model suggested by the notion of character neurosis may be inappropriate, and character pathology and neurotic symptomatology imply quite different underlying processes (see King and Noshpitz, 1990).

More severe personality disorders, e.g. narcissistic personality disorder, are regarded as a consequence of a developmental arrest, deviation or disharmony (see A. Freud, 1965). The structural view tends to see such cases in terms of faulty ego development (see Gitelson, 1955; Rangell, 1955; Frank, 1956). Important ego functions such as reality testing, anxiety tolerance and stable defenses are impaired, while others appear to retain their integrity, thus giving the patient a semblance of normality.

3.2.4 Model of borderline personality disorder

Individuals with borderline personality disorder were initially described in the psychoanalytic literature as frequently reacting adversely to classical psychoanalysis (Stern, 1938; Deutsch, 1942). The issue of modification of classical technique was raised at an early stage (Schmideberg, 1947). Knight (1953) was the first to propose a comprehensive developmental model of the disorder in terms of ego functions impaired by trauma. Among the ego functions he considered were: 'integration, concept formation, judgement, realistic planning, and defending against eruption into conscious thinking of id impulses and their fantasy elaborations' (p. 6). Erikson (1956; 1959) in his epigenetic sequence of identity formation described the syndrome of identity diffusion, reflecting deficiencies in the temporal continuity of self-experience, and in affiliation with a social group of reference. Jacobson (1953; 1954a; 1964) drew attention to how these individuals, at times, experience their mental functions and bodily organs not as belonging to them, but as objects which they wish to expel. They may also attach their mental and body self to external objects. She saw them as retaining an 'adolescent fluidity of moods' (1964, p. 159).

Abend, Porder and Willick (1983) and others, however, have questioned the usefulness of the term borderline, maintaining that profound ego weakness and identification with disturbed parents were the only character-istics to separate these patients from those with neurotic disorders. Otherwise their difficulties could be understood as reflecting a regressive defense against deeply disturbing oedipal issues.

3.2.5 Structural theory of antisocial personality disorder

Aichhorn (1925) was the first psychoanalyst to work seriously with delin-quent individuals, and his formulation was very influential. He posited a failure of progression from the pleasure principle to the reality principle in conjunction with a malformation of the superego in his developmental account of the disorder. He stressed deprivation as impeding the renunci-ation of the pleasure principle, and the internalization of poor parental norms as an explanation of superego dysfunction. Reich (1933) suggested that the ego kept the superego isolated at a distance and therefore unable to control impulses. Fenichel (1945) emphasized that the superego was not absent in these individuals, but pathological, not just isolated by the ego but also bribed. Johnson and Szurek (1952) suggested that superego lacunae (lack of superego in certain circumscribed areas) were at the root of the superego pathology. Such gaps in the superego were thought to occur because of the parents' unconscious wish to act out forbidden impulses; the child is unconsciously encouraged by the parents to act in amoral ways, but consciously discouraged from doing this. Lampl-de-Groot (1949) suggested that the balance of the superego and the ego ideal explained why certain individuals became neurotically depressed, while others became antisocial. The former corresponds to a severe superego and strong ego ideal, whereas the latter is a consequence of a menacing superego and a weak ego ideal. Singer (1975) proposed a tripartite model identifying: (1) drive disturbances (stealing as acquiring a bigger penis, to undo hidden feelings of being small, impotent, castrated and worthless); (2) disturbances of ego functions (heightened sensitivity to displeasure, disturbed reality testing, inability to delay action by fantasy); and (3) superego defects – the superego is corruptible (Alexander, 1930), isolated (Reich, 1933; Greenacre, 1945), and riddled with lacunae (Johnson and Szurek, 1952).

Many of these theoretical suggestions are hard to distinguish from clinical descriptions. For example, lack of guilt about antisocial behavior is part of a definition of anti- social personality (Hare and Cox, 1987). Other recent evidence, however, appears consistent with these classical writings. For example, in line with Reich's and Fenichel's suggestions, the presence of anxiety (autonomic reactivity) in antisocial youth reduces the risk of later criminal behavior (Raine, Venables and Williams, 1995). Interestingly, the closeness but opposition of depression and antisocial behavior, which was observed by Lampl-de-Groot, was supported by recent behavior genetics research. Depressive symptoms and antisocial behavior share common genetic influences. They could co-occur because of common genetic roots that increase vulnerability to both these types of problems (O'Connor et al., 1998).

3.2.6 Structural model of the psychoses

Hartmann (1953) suggested that the most important defect in schizophrenia was a failure in the process of neutralization. Neutralization, as we have seen, was considered by Hartmann to be rooted in the quality of the child's relations with the parent. However, he acknowledged that schizophrenia could come about as a consequence of organic impairments. He also cautioned against the 'genetic fallacy' whereby regressive symptoms are taken to be similar to early childhood states. Other psychoanalysts using the ego psychology approach (Jacobson, 1953; 1954a; Bak, 1954; 1971) believed that early ego development in schizophrenia was more disturbed than in illnesses considered less severe (e.g. perversions).

Thus psychotic symptoms are seen as regressions to very early, normal functioning. Severe ego impairments must be caused by some basic fault in laying down psychic structure during infancy. Greenacre (1953) stated it explicitly: 'the matrix of these severe disturbances lay in the disturbances in that period at the very dawn of the ego, roughly around six months and a little later' (p. 10). As we shall see, modern developmental observations are quite inconsistent with the notion of a 'normal' confusional state between self and object. Infants from birth can accurately identify their mothers and even imitate facial gestures (Meltzoff and Moore, 1997).

3.3 Criticism and evaluation

The notion of the *id* has changed in current structural theory (Arlow and Brenner, 1964; Schur, 1966; Hayman, 1969). Loewald (1971a; 1971b; 1978a;

1978b) is typical amongst contemporary structural theorists in interpreting Freud's concept not as a container of all biologically based intense physical desires, but rather as an organization related to reality and human figures. Instincts are no longer seen as firmly anchored to developmental stages (Greenacre, 1952), and the simplistic drive-reduction model has been abandoned by most theoreticians (Sandler, 1985). For example, we have suggested (Fonagy and Target, 1995) that the apparent centrality of bodily conflicts in many forms of psychological disturbance is misleading; frequently, it is the failure of the individual's capacity to resolve psychological conflict in the domain of ideas and wishes that causes them to be experienced somatically (rather than vice versa). Because the body is not an appropriate arena for the resolution of psychological conflict, conflict can become intensified at the level of drives or instincts – for example, through aggression.

The quasi-physiological character of the original model was intensely criticised in the 1970s and 1980s (Klein, 1976; Rosenblatt and Thickstun, 1977; Compton, 1981). Schafer (1974) criticizes the classical model on the grounds that it forces us to consider all forms of sexual pleasure, other than heterosexual genital sexuality, as arrested or deviant. Others see the primacy of sexuality in explanations of psychopathology as a misconception (Klein, 1981; Peterfreund, 1978). North American traditions have regarded Freud's biologism with distrust and disbelief. They increasingly prefer to emphasize both the immediate social world (see the description of the Interpersonal Schools in Chapter 9) and the autonomy of the self, even if that autonomy is an ever-receding personal and theoretical ideal (see Chapter 8). The tradition of individualism and self-help, of therapeutic optimism and the cult of self-esteem that have become such an integral part of psychoanalytic culture in the US finds a reflection in both major modifications to the structural model, and in new theories that in part precipitated and then gained strength from the demise of structural theory in the United States.

More recent reviews of drive theory have been more favorable. In the 1990s, the 'decade of the brain', much new information that appears surprisingly consistent with Freud's original ideas has emerged. Repeated exposure to drugs results in sensitization of a specific neural pathway in the brain (the dopaminergic ventral tegmental pathway) that forms the substrate for intense motivations (Berridge and Robinson, 1995). Howard Shevrin presented an important neuroscientific model linking the 'wanting system' identified as abnormally sensitized (over-sensitive) in drug-dependent individuals, with the ego psychological notion of psychic energy and drives (Shevrin, 1997). In a full treatment of this subject, he explored qualities of the 'wanting system' (peremptory in responding to arbitrary cues in the environment, irrational and unconscious) and a psychoanalytic conception of drive states, independent of affect states, unconscious, and characterized by cravings rather than the more tamed motivational derivatives of affect states experienced as part of formative affect relations.

A further indication that classical observations about drives might not have been so far off the mark as earlier critics have claimed comes from the work of Jaak Panksepp (1998). Shevrin (2001) has linked Panksepp's description of a 'SEEKING system' with a structural theory conception of drives. The same neural systems involved in 'the wanting system' are thought to be involved in the component of the SEEKING system that underpins *expectancy* states which motivate actions and without which the organism is reduced to inertia. Interestingly, Panksepp discusses the SEEKING system as characterized by 'psychic energization' (p. 145). External stimulation of the system will prompt an animal to explore very energetically. Anatomically this is the same system that rats will self-stimulate endlessly in order to achieve this state of expectance, without needing to fulfil the drive. Embodied in this system is a subjective state of pure anticipation, with no apparent object. It is indeed simply a state of wanting, which later, through processing in more advanced brain systems, acquires an object, and mental representation.

Neuropsychological work on dreams strengthens the argument for continued relevance of the drive model. Mark Solms (1997a; 2000) has successfully engaged those critics of drive-based dream theory who were willing to accept that dreaming was a subjective experience linked to a random brain activation process linked to rapid eye movement sleep (REM) (Hobson and McCarley, 1977). Solms's neuropsychological work linked with recent radiological and pharmacological findings suggests that the brainstem mechanisms that are known to control the REM state can only generate dreaming through the mediation of a second, probably dopaminergic, forebrain mechanism. The latter mechanism (and thus dreaming itself) can also be activated by a variety of non-REM triggers, such as dopamine agonists and antagonists with no concomitant change in REM. This implies that dreaming can be induced and modified by psychological states that correspond to other brain states, for example, focal forebrain stimulation and complex partial (forebrain) seizures during non-REM sleep, when the involvement of brainstem REM mechanisms is precluded. Likewise, dreaming is obliterated by focal lesions along a specific (probably dopaminergic) forebrain pathway, and these lesions do not have any appreciable effects on REM frequency, duration, and density.

These findings suggest that the forebrain mechanism is the final common path to dreaming and that the brainstem oscillator that controls the REM state is just one of the many arousal triggers that can activate the mechanism. The 'REM-on' mechanism (like its various NREM equivalents) therefore stands outside the dream process itself, which is mediated by an independent, forebrain 'dream-on' mechanism. Solms argues that the dopaminergic ventral tegmental pathways are the initiators of dreaming and the pathway from the ventral tegmental area connecting the amygdala, septal area, cingulate gyrus and the frontal cortex, is the final common path to dreaming. What Solms identifies as the neural system forming the substrate for the motivational impetus for dreaming is the same system that is sensitized by drug addiction. The activating systems for dreaming and craving are identical. The sensitization of this system by addictive substances appears to account for drug-related dreams long after behaviour of the drug dependent has ended (Johnson, 2001). Dreams are elaborated through other sections of the brain, they will begin to contain other concerns, motivations, and feelings. The origin of each and every dream is however in the neural structure that most closely fits Freud's concept of instinctual drive states, the ventral tegmental area.

CHAPTER 4

Modifications and developments of the structural model

4.1 Anna Freud's developmental model

The view that development is both cumulative and epigenetic (that is, that each developmental phase is constructed upon the previous one) is a fundamental tenet of all psychoanalytic developmental models. Anna Freud (1965) was one of the first to adopt a coherent developmental perspective on psychopathology, a precedent which is widely acknowledged by today's leading developmentalists (Emde, 1988b; Cicchetti, 1990a; Sroufe et al., 1990). She argued that psychological disorder could be most effectively studied in its process of developmental evolution, and that the profile among strands (lines) in development determined the risk of pathology for the individual child. Her theory was however a 'conflict theory' in the classical Freudian sense, in that she saw development as the child coming to terms with incompatibilities between two wishes, or with situations where unpleasant things are insisted on by someone whom the child wants to please, or where pain results from something from which the child expects pleasure. In all these, the child must come to terms with reality and find a compromise between diverse wishes, needs, perceptions or physical and social realities and object relationships. Thus, like Hartmann, Anna Freud moved away from the classical position that the only proper subject of analysis is the unconscious id, a position that she found restrictive, and emphasized the importance of analyzing the ego (Sandler and Freud, 1985). She emphasized the importance of analyzing issues that arise from demands to adjust to the outside world, as well as those that derive from the imperatives of id and superego.

Structures of the personality are expected to work in harmony in the absence of conflict, and under such circumstances the divisions of the personality may be hard to distinguish (Freud, 1936, pp. 5–8). The presence of conflict and the anxiety it generates call forth defenses from the ego and it is through these that the other psychic structures become more readily

71

apparent. The ego simply executes impulses that are not banned by the superego, without distortion. The listing and categorization of defenses became a significant concern for psychoanalysts and a group at Anna Freud's clinic (the Hampstead Clinic) chaired by Joseph Sandler attempted to clarify these ideas. Ultimately, the Hampstead Index Manual on Defence (Sandler, 1962a; Bolland and Sandler, 1965) was produced, but at the same time it was recognized that almost any ego function could serve a defensive function and thus any hope of providing an exhaustive list of defense mechanisms was illusory (Brenner, 1982). While Anna Freud recognized that any existing capacity could be used defensively (she called these acts 'defensive measures' as opposed to defense mechanisms), she also consistently claimed that defenses could be grouped according to the developmental maturity reflected by their operations (Sandler and Freud, 1985). For instance, while mastery is normally a pleasurable part of the child developing his capacity to exercise influence over his or her environment, it may be a compulsive, controlling, defensive way of counteracting a feeling of helplessness.

4.1.1 Developmental lines and other developmental concepts

The heart of Anna Freud's theory concerns child development. In the 1920s, Anna Freud's interest in child analysis (A. Freud, 1926) created an enthusiastic group around her who, as we shall see, carried her developmental orientation further in many directions. The group included Eric Erikson, Edith Jacobson and Margaret Mahler. Although a developmental interest was present from the very beginning, with her own intellectual progress, the developmental point of view increasingly permeated Anna Freud's theoretical position. Initially, Anna Freud's thinking about development was, in large measure, rooted in her father's view of instinctual drives. In Freud's description drives are characterized by a sense of pressure (the force of the drive) and aim (achievement of satisfaction), a somatic process that is the source, and an object that is the person through which the instinct can achieve its aim (S. Freud, 1915a). Anna Freud's theory preserved the link between drive satisfaction and an appropriate external object. In the Independent School the concern with drive satisfaction was replaced by pressures of relationships as principal motivators while Melanie Klein's theory retained instinctual gratification as the motivator but emphasized internal fantasy objects in place of external people. Anna Freud had an enduring interest in the role of the real parents in structuring the child's mind. Thus she took Freud's theory forward by identifying ways for the actual parent to contribute to the construction of the ego or the superego, but she always subordinated this process to the overriding principle of the search for drive satisfaction. The need to be looked after generates affectional bonds. For Anna Freud, the parents serve as models of ways of behaving, relating to others, modes of psychic defense, coping with problems or traumatic events. The process of internalization of the actual parent sets the course of ego development. Anna Freud saw object relations as a crucial aspect of development but not as a substitute for instinct theory or structural theory. The role of the object remains subservient to the drives. The parent is needed to protect the child from helplessness in the face of overwhelming inner experiences. Thus Anna Freud occupies a unique position between ego psychology and object relations theories of development. She considers relationships formative, but only as moderators of the maturational developmental process preordained by the unfolding of the drives.

Anna Freud (1962; 1963) provided a comprehensive developmental theory using the metaphor of developmental lines to stress the continuity and cumulative character of childhood development. Her idea was derived from her father's model of libidinal development, but her formulation stresses the interactions and interdependencies between maturational and environmental determinants in developmental steps. For example, aspects of the child's relationship to the mother may be described as a line moving from 'dependency to emotional self-reliance to adult object relationships', 'from sucking to rational eating', 'from wetting and soiling to bladder and bowel control', 'from irresponsibility to responsibility in body management'. Other lines, such as the movement from egocentrism to social partnership, are concerned with mastery of the environment. The entire profile of lines is examined as part of assessment (Yorke, 1980) and pathology is assessed in terms of large discrepancies among the lines and notable lags with respect to normal progress along each line.

The lines are intended to explore particular sequences of drive and structural development in some detail. They represent 'the results of interaction between drive and ego-superego development and their reaction to environmental influences' (Freud, 1965, p. 64). The lines place emphasis on observable behavior at the same time as specifying the internal psychic development necessary for the achievement of each step on each line. Developmental lines were not intended to substitute for metapsychology or to add an additional point of view to those of mental structure or economy or topography. Rather, they represent an attempt to address the great complexity of development through identifying specific sequences of progress (Neubauer, 1984).

In the initial presentation of this view, six developmental lines were considered, of which the one from dependency to emotional self-reliance and adult object relationship was considered the most 'basic' (p. 64). The line describes the changes at the level of observable mother–child relationships alongside the evolution of internal representations of objects that create templates for later relationships. Anna Freud identifies eight stages along this line starting with a biological unity between the mother–infant couple. Anna Freud suggests that in the first stage the baby has not yet discovered that the mother is not part of himself and is not under his control. Equally the mother experiences the baby as psychologically part of her, an experience that is only gradually given up as she begins to perceive the baby's individuality and difference from herself. Separation from mother in this phase is thought to give rise to 'separation anxiety proper' (p. 66). Anna Freud placed the development of attachment relationships rather late (in the second year of life) although she was thought to have revised her views in the light of her observation of normal infancy in the Hampstead Well Baby Clinic (Edgcumbe, 2000). She confuses matters somewhat by placing Margaret Mahler's autistic-symbiotic and separation-individuation phases within her first phase (Mahler et al., 1975). The first stage ends with the first year of life and this does not fit with Mahler's timetable.

The second stage is characterized by the need-fulfilling anaclitic relationship between the child and his object, based on the child's imperative body needs. It is thought to have a naturally fluctuating character as the need for the object increases with the arousal of drives but the importance of the object for the child is reduced when satisfaction has been reached. The child is thought to construct images of a good and a bad mother depending on the extent to which the child's needs were satisfied. Bad mother equals frustrating mother (Edgcumbe and Burgner, 1973). Stage 2 is considered by Anna Freud to start in the second half of the first year of life, but she was not specific about the chronology of these stages, considering them to be dependent on the child's personality and the circumstances of the mother–child relationship. However, the development of clear representations of the mother's mind as separate from the child's is assigned to this stage; thus Anna Freud sees breakdowns of the mother–child relationship in this stage as leading to breakdowns of individuation and distortions in the development of the self.

At the third stage the child achieves a consistent representation of the mother, which can be maintained irrespective of the satisfaction of drives. At this stage the child becomes able to form reciprocal relationships that can survive disappointments and frustrations. The stabilization of internal representations is thought to permit longer separations. Anna Freud sees early separations as undermining this process of generating object constancy, which in turn compromises the capacity to become separate.

Stage 4 is linked to what is colloquially known as the 'terrible twos', where the toddler's positive and negative feelings are focused on the same person and become visible. Ambivalence is normal at this stage, in consequence of the emergence of skills which permit the child to be independent and allow the mother to withdraw somewhat. The child is in conflict, wishing both to be independent and to retain the complete devotion of the mother. Anna Freud's view of aggression is linked to this stage. She considers it as an essential drive serving mastery and an important aspect of establishing object relationships, but when not balanced with libido (love and concern for the object) it becomes sadistic and destructive.

The fifth stage is object-centred, characterized by possessiveness of the parent of the opposite sex and jealousy and rivalry with the same sex parent. This so-called phallic-oedipal phase was considered by Anna Freud to be crucial in the generation of neurotic problems. The child needs to become fully aware of the separate existence of his object in order to be able to resolve conflicts over rivalry and possession. At this stage the child becomes aware that there are aspects of relationships between the parents from which he is excluded and that each parent sees his relationship with the other. This triangular relationship requires considerable maturity of the child's ego as well as sufficient development in the superego to generate anxiety and guilt about his incestuous wishes. Thus conflicts appropriate to this phase are in some sense an indication of healthy development whereas the absence of conflict indicates a developmental deficit that is likely to lead to non-neurotic forms of personality disorder. Lack of resolution of conflicts that emerge will create a vulnerability to neurotic problems.

In stage 6 the urgency of the child's drives is reduced and there is a transfer of libido from parents to peers and others in the child's social environment, e.g. teachers. The child's interests come to be sublimated and there is disillusion with the parents. Anna Freud sees this state as one of transfer of libido from parent to the community. Failure at this stage will lead to withdrawal from schoolwork and failure to integrate into the peer group. The next stage of pre-adolescent revolt for Anna Freud represents a regression from the reasonableness of latency children to a demanding, contrary, inconsiderate attitude characteristic of earlier stages. This regression is thought also to strengthen oral, anal and phallic drive components, reviving infantile fantasies and intensifying intrapsychic conflict. To help him deal with these conflicts the pre-adolescent may well withdraw from the parents in the hope of repudiating his infantile and incestuous fantasies. Yet even previously effective sublimations like this may fail and the pre-adolescent experiences increasing problems with schoolwork (Freud, 1949). Stage 8 is adolescence, which is seen by Anna Freud as representing the ego's struggle to master the upsurge of sexuality and aggression during this period. Development of the ego permits two new defense mechanisms to emerge: intellectualization and asceticism. They serve to defend the individual from the instinctual demands of the body. The individual at this stage is preoccupied with his internal struggle to transfer emotional investment from parents to new objects (Freud, 1958). A mourning for the lost parents of childhood has to take place before peer relationships and the change in relationship to the parents can be established. To withdraw libido from the parents the adolescent may engage in dramatic enactment, such as leaving home suddenly or making alliances with individuals or groups who are diametrically opposed to the parents' norms and values. Sometimes this may result in delinquent acts; at other times just uncooperativeness and hostility, or projecting these states onto the parents and perceiving them as hostile and persecuting. When the hostility is turned on the self the adolescent may be self-harming and suicidal, and such behaviors are indeed relatively more frequent for this age group (Diekstra, 1995). The withdrawal of libido from parents to the child's self explains the narcissistic grandiosity and omnipotence of adolescence. Anna Freud sees adolescence as a developmental disturbance where physical and psychological changes may upset a previously normal balance. There is a demand for academic and social achievement which may permanently injure the individual if this stage is poorly negotiated (Freud, 1969).

The developmental line from dependency to emotional self-reliance is the most important in that Anna Freud successfully pulls together a range of her ideas and describes a sequence of assumptions about the changing nature of relationships between childhood and adulthood. It should be noted that the stages of this and other lines are essentially descriptive and that they are dominated by theoretical concerns with bodily function, for example she has three lines all directly related to a movement toward body independence, sucking to eating, wetting and soiling to bladder and bowel control, and irresponsibility to responsibility in body management. In addition there is a line that traces the infant's play with his own and the mother's body to the use of toys and symbolic objects. Anna Freud added many more lines in later papers, for example, from physical to mental pathways of discharge, from animate to inanimate objects and from irresponsibility to guilt (Freud, 1974). In this last line she highlighted the stage of development before the full development of the superego and guilt, when children are unusually censorious with their peers. This occurs when the child has already developed an awareness of internal conflict but is as yet unwilling to accept the painful struggle within himself, so he externalizes repudiated wishes to other children in whom these can be condemned.

The notion of developmental lines is important for two reasons. First, it offers a way to evaluate the child's emotional maturity or immaturity alongside psychiatric symptoms. It could be considered as part of a second Axis of childhood diagnosis (American Psychiatric Association, 1994) with prognostic implications. It focuses the clinician on (a) the phase-appropriate developmental issues; (b) the meaning of the behavior in the context of the phase; and (c) the profile of adaptation shown by the child cutting across aspects of development. Secondly, unevenness of development may be regarded as a risk factor for psychiatric disturbance and thus developmental lines have etiological significance. A child's problem may be understood in terms of an arrest or regression in terms of a particular line of development (Freud, 1965). The clinical implication of Anna Freud's formulation is that in addressing a child's disturbance the psychoanalytic clinician should focus not only on the determinants of symptoms, but also on offering 'developmental help' to the child and restoring him or her to the 'path of normal development' (Freud, 1970b; 1976; 1983; Kennedy and Moran, 1991; Fonagy et al., 1993). In this spirit, a number of clinicians have proposed other lines of development relevant to clinical work. For example, Hansi Kennedy proposed a developmental line of insight that depends on the ego function of self-awareness (Kennedy, 1979). Insight in early childhood is used in the service of maintaining a comfortable inner state. Later on insight into others evolves but is rarely used for reflective self-awareness. Adolescents use insight both to understand self and others but cannot yet link past and present. Normal adults have also only limited self-awareness, which only comes to the fore when the need to resolve internal conflicts has already generated pathological results. There is a striking similarity between these concepts and the theory of mentalization outlined in Chapter 12.

4.1.2 Anna Freudian views of developmental psychopathology

4.1.2.1 General features of the model

Anna Freud (1955) early on noted the apparently reversible effect of even severe childhood trauma. She regarded the child as enormously resilient, with a self-righting capacity to return to the course of normal development after deviation. Her views foreshadowed more recent reconsideration of the supposedly inevitable pathogenic effects of chaotic environments and early deprivation (e.g. Emde, 1981; Anthony and Cohler, 1987). Rose Edgcumbe (2000) has recently provided a complex and sophisticated account of her ideas. Anna Freud was particularly sophisticated about the range of pathologies which emerged between neurotic and psychotic states – what appeared to her to be pre-neurotic non-conflictual disorders. With the benefit of a historical perspective, we may readily see the group of disorders she describes as ultimately analogous to disorders of personality in adults. Thus she identifies disturbances of narcissism, object relatedness, the absence of control over aggressive or self-destructive tendencies alongside a range of deficiencies of development (Freud, 1965, pp. 148–54). It should be emphasized that her concept of non-conflictual disorders was revolutionary and the linking of these pathologies to development prescient. Her developmental perspective, however, was never properly reconciled with structural theory.

Following Hartmann (1939), structural theorists have repeatedly stressed the ubiquity of conflict in development (Klein, 1976; Sander, 1983). The child is continually challenged by dissonance and incompatibility, and is seen as constitutionally capable of resolving conflict by environmental manipulation and the internalization of conflict, leading to internal compromises and the modification of psychic structure. Nagera (1966), strongly influenced by the work of Anna Freud (1965), termed these conflicts 'developmental' in order to stress the expectable and usually transitory nature of the tensions and sometimes symptoms that accompany forward movements between developmental stages. For example, the mother's phase-appropriate demands for bowel control may initially clash with the child's wishes, leading to temper tantrums that subside as the conflict is internalized and equilibrium is re-established. Developmental conflicts may be potentially resolvable or inherently insoluble (or divergent, see Kris, 1984). They are said to be divergent when opposing motivational forces direct the child toward two fundamentally incompatible but equally desirable courses of action such as masculinity and femininity, activity and passivity or dependence and autonomy. Divergent conflicts remain part of the ego and may be reactivated in specific social situations, e.g. in initiating sexual relationships.

In a major paper on the symptomatology of childhood, Anna Freud proposed a surprisingly phenomenologically oriented classification of childhood psychopathology based on understanding of unconscious mechanisms available to her at the time (Freud, 1970a). She suggested seven categories for psychological disorders. First, there is non-differentiation between somatic and psychic processes, where the mind–body axis remains more than usually open and somatic responses to experience fail to turn into emotional responses. Examples of these include eczema, asthma and migraine. Second, there are the compromises between psychic agencies that lead to phobias, hysteria and obsessional neurotic symptoms. Third, there are problems associated with a fragile border between ego and id that can lead to eruptions from the id manifesting as undefended enactments (delinquency, criminality) or eruptions of primary process thinking manifesting in problems of thinking or language. Fourth, she considered various forms of narcissistic disorder to be associated with changes in libido economy. Thus a shift of libido from mind to body might cause hypochondriacal symptoms. The withdrawal of object libido onto the self could cause disorders of self-esteem or self-centeredness. Fifth, learning failure and self-injurious behavior were considered by Anna Freud to be associated with changes in the quality or direction of aggression. Sixth, regression with whining, clinging or dependent behaviors, were seen by her to be ways of avoiding the conflicts of the phallic or oedipal phases. Finally, she envisioned difficulties due to organic causes and was quick to draw clinicians' attention to the ease with which these could be confused with inhibitions and other neurotic symptoms.

To date, Anna Freud's diagnostic system is an interesting alternative to purely phenomenological models. Naturally, it is hard for any psychoanalytic system based on clinical experience with a relatively small number of patients to compete with large-scale epidemiological studies (e.g. Rutter et al., 1976; Goodman and Meltzer, 1999). The categories identified by Anna Freud are quite similar to empirically derived clusters, perhaps with the major exception of Anna Freud grouping together all anxiety-related disorders into one neurotic category and her exclusion of depression as a significant problem in childhood.

4.1.2.2 An Anna Freudian model of anxiety

Anna Freud distinguished between fear of the internal world (impulses, wishes, feelings) and 'objective anxiety' such as fear of the real reactions of the child's parents or any other aspect of the external world (Sandler and Freud, 1985). In Report 12 of the summary of her wartime experiences in the Hampstead nurseries (Freud and Burlingham, 1944) she observed that the children's reactions to external threat were different from those of adults. For example, they were less likely to be traumatized by being bombed if they were with their mothers and if the mothers remained calm. There has been more recent support for this observation from an extremely careful study of children's reactions to Scud missile attacks in Israel (Laor et al., 1996). These workers found that children were far more likely to show prolonged symptoms of anxiety following the attack if the child's mother had also shown significant reactive symptoms.

Anna Freud understood that the danger of traumatization associated with external threats such as bombing was likely to increase when 'the destructiveness raging in the outer world may meet the very real aggressiveness which rages inside the child' (p. 161). In this context Freud and Burlingham offered a classification of traumatic anxiety that distinguished 'real anxiety', which they considered relatively rare, from four other types of anxieties related to various internal sources (anxiety caused by the threat of the arousal of destructiveness, anxiety which emerges because traumatic events come to represent superego strictures, anxiety that arises through the identification with the mother's anxiety, and anxiety where events trigger memory of traumatic loss).

Anna Freud suggested a developmental perspective to the emergence of anxiety problems in childhood (Freud, 1970a). The archaic fears of infancy, she believed, were likely to subside if the infant received enough reassurance, and if ego development allowed reality orientation to evolve fully. Separation anxiety, rooted in the fear of loss of the object, was thought to be associated with excessive separations or maternal unreliability. With the internalization of the object, as representative of the demand to control drives, a fear of the loss of the object's love ensues. While early fear of loss can manifest as fear of annihilation or total helplessness, fear of the loss of love also manifests as fear of punishment, fear of desertion or fear of natural disasters. This kind of fear may become excessive if internal conflicts or conflicts with parents are difficult to resolve. In the phallic phase, castration anxiety comes to dominate with fears of operations, robbers, ghosts, all of which are exacerbated by oedipal conflict. Anna Freud links the fear of shame and associated social anxieties to early school age and increasing contact with peers. When the superego fully develops, anxiety can turn into guilt. Anna Freud was convinced that the nature of the child's anxiety was a good indication of the nature of the child's development. The fate of these forms of anxiety, she felt, was dependent on the types of defenses the child was able to use. If these were not adequate, anxiety became overwhelming and the child could remain prone to panic states and anxiety attacks.

Yorke and his co-workers (Yorke, 1986; Yorke, Wiseberg and Freeman, 1989) have put forward a developmental model of anxiety which offers a good illustration of the 'Anna Freudian' approach. They propose that anxiety matures from a diffuse somatic excitation to signal anxiety as conceived by Freud (1926). At a stage when the infant is seen as part of an undifferentiated mother–baby unit (Spitz, 1965), the pathways between psyche and soma are assumed to remain open (Freud, 1974) so that psychic tension will be discharged somatically. The earliest forms of anxiety make maximal use of this somatic pathway. The night terrors experienced by some children are an example of reversion to a primitive form of anxiety still lacking in mental content (Fisher et al., 1970). As mentalization is established, but the ego's capacity to regulate affect is still limited, such somatic experiences give way to experiences of psychic panic or automatic anxiety (as seen in temper tantrums). The child may scream and seem bewildered and helpless because he cannot yet express himself adequately or understand his experience.

With the development of thought and language (what Freud (1933) called the capacity for 'trial action') the ego acquires the capacity to use 'trial affect', where anxiety is restricted to a signal level. Until this development, the preverbal child is easily plunged into complete helplessness that can be alleviated only by outside intervention from an auxiliary ego (the caregiver). The emergence of autonomous ego development allows for the restriction of anxiety by crude defensive measures such as denial or projection. The phallic and oedipal phases (3-5 years) are marked by a fear of helplessness, but the anxiety is not automatic even while it remains pervasive. With the achievement of the latency stage, anxiety becomes a signal that can prevent the arousal of pervasive anxiety with the use of increasingly mature defenses such as rationalization, intellectualization and humour. The supportive background of parents, teachers and peers, as well as social institutions, is essential to maintain the child's developmental progress at this stage. Biological maturation at puberty can lead to the re-emergence of basic anxiety and a shift back to pervasive or even automatic forms.

The assumption that pervasive panic and helplessness are the predominant modes of emotional expression during infancy and early childhood is not well supported by empirical evidence. As we will explain below (see for example Chapter 6, section 6.3 and Chapter 7, section 7.3), such a view may underestimate the constitutional capacities of infants and young children. Harris and Kavanaugh (1993) and Harris (1994) marshal a substantial body of observational and experimental data that illustrate the surprisingly rapid development of emotional processing in infants. They find little evidence to support the notion of primitive affects at early stages of development (see also Emde, 1980b; 1980c; Stern, 1985). Thus, infant research has suggested that the assumption of a primitive primary panic state is probably an inappropriate hypothetical construct of adult (or even child) psychoanalysis. Whereas far-fetched assumptions about infancy were common in classical theory and in other approaches (e.g. the Kleinian school), Anna Freud and her followers were consistently more concerned about consistency between observable phenomena and psychoanalytic claims.

4.1.2.3 The notion of developmental disharmonies

As we have seen, Anna Freud suggested that delays or failures in development could appear in relation to drives, ego or superego functioning. They could be the result of poor endowment or organic damage, inadequate care or lack of stimulation, internal conflicts or limitations in the parent's character. Traumatic experiences were seen as another potential cause of developmental failure. Development was not expected to proceed evenly across developmental lines. In three late papers Anna Freud advanced a unique developmental psychoanalytic orientation to psychopathology and treatment (A. Freud, 1974; 1978; 1981a). While accepting that metapsychology (and structural theory) was the crowning achievement of the psychoanalytic study of adults, a developmentally orientated psychoanalytic theory of child psychology was the domain of child psychoanalysis (Freud, 1978, p. 100). Anna Freud (1965) stressed that, for children, the required degree of inner equilibrium is very hard to establish, as the forces that determine the child's development are external as well as internal, and mostly outside the child's control. He needs to integrate his constitutional potential, the impact of the parental environment, and the vicissitudes of the gradual structuring of personality. When one or other of these aspects of development is distorted, disturbances of equilibrium are bound to occur.

Anna Freud proposed that discrepancies between the relative strengths of the psychic agencies result from constitutional and environmental factors and predispose to psychopathology. Normal development is threatened, for example, if parental support is withdrawn too early, leaving the child confronted with archaic fears of being alone or in darkness, which require the adult's participation as an auxiliary ego. If the ego matures too late, or if the parents are neglecting, the child may tend to regress to earlier, more intense forms of anxiety. Developmental pathology is, however, seen as separate from the symptomatic pathology of Hartmann's structural model. For example, classical interpretation is unlikely to be able to tackle the psychological difficulties faced by such a child (see Freud, 1974; 1983; Kennedy and Yorke, 1980) but treatment directed toward developmental progress may do so (Fonagy and Target, 1996c). Minor degrees of disharmony are ubiquitous (Yorke et al., 1989, p. 26). Gross disharmony, however, is seen as a 'fertile breeding ground' (Freud, 1981b, p. 109) for later neurosis and more severe psychopathology, and the major constituent of non-neurotic developmental disturbances of the personality (personality disorders).

Developmental disturbances could arise out of both internal and external stresses. An infant's sleep patterns may be incompatible with the environment. The child who struggles with the parents around issues of sleep may identify with the mother's handling and develop a hostile attitude to his own needs and wishes creating a predisposition to internalized conflicts. At this stage difficulties may be readily resolved by small changes in how the child is handled. A conflict with the parents about sleep at a later stage may be more complex. A toddler may be reluctant to go to sleep because he is anxious about regressing to the narcissistic state required in order to achieve a sleep state. The child may develop strategies for dealing with these anxieties (such as making excessive bedtime demands, thumb-sucking, or cuddling a soft toy). If the parents interfere with these strategies, the child's difficulties may be exaggerated and more chronic sleep disturbance may result where the attempt at coping with the developmental difficulty creates a more entrenched problem (e.g. a power struggle with the parents).

4.1.2.4 The Anna Freudian model of severe personality disorders

As Anna Freud's contribution to psychopathology principally concerned childhood, it is hardly surprising that her work does not touch on personality disorders, as currently conceived. However, many developmental lines envisioned by Anna Freud concerned ego and superego functions. These were considered to generate deficits that contributed to borderline, psychotic and other non-neurotic forms of adult psychopathology. A number of Anna Freud's close colleagues have stressed the relevance of developmental lines for an understanding of deficits in adult personality and functioning (Yorke, 1983;

Yorke et al., 1989). A key differentiation made by Anna Freud was between the inhibition of an impulse (a neurotic defense) and a restriction within the ego whereby the person gave up an entire area of psychic functioning, whether a cognitive capacity such as curiosity or imagination, or a social function, such as interpersonal relating. As early as 1936, Anna Freud discussed the concept of ego restriction but the concept was substantially elaborated later in her writings about developmental deficits. Anna Freud agrees with structural theorists that severe personality disorders reflect structural deficits in reality testing, development of defenses, anxiety tolerance, superego, strength, etc. She explains these as developmental deviations or disharmonies. For example, she suggests that the inadequate response by the mother to an infant's instinctual needs creates dangers and external conflict (Yorke et al., 1989). Such disharmony of need and environment will be most intensely felt when the developing structure is not yet ready to sustain the pressures caused by the resulting internal and external stresses. Ego development will suffer because the internalizing and identificatory processes will be specifically threatened. Object constancy, for example, may not develop if the early relationship with the mother is disrupted by trauma. The failure to achieve structured compromise produces the labile character of borderline personality disturbances. Narcissistic character disorder is seen as rooted in early emotional deprivation which compromises the process by which objects (representations of people) are invested with instinctual energy. The individual attempts to identify with the frustrating and disappointing object, providing a focus for libidinal cathexis that heightens egocentrism.

Since Anna Freud's death many psychoanalysts trained within her tradition have built on her areas of interest. The work of the Sandlers and Fonagy and Target's contributions are being covered separately, but other significant figures within what is now known as the Contemporary Freudian Group within the British Psycho-Analytic Society have developed important ideas about psychopathology and technique. Moses and Eglé Laufer carried out very extensive clinical research on adolescent breakdown and its treatment, elaborating a model focused on the role of sexuality in this crucial developmental stage (Laufer and Laufer, 1984). Following an Anna Freudian developmental approach, they studied both normal and deeply pathological adolescents. They noted that the 'turmoil' of the latter group was qualitatively different in those adolescents whose defense organization is incapable of warding off the regressive pull of pregenital wishes. They then experience their sexual body as the source as well as the representative of their abnormality. Laufer (1976) stressed the importance of a 'central masturbation fantasy', which is fixed by the Oedipus complex and contains regressive satisfactions of the main sexual identifications, but is particularly important, in his view, in adolescence. The core fantasy exists within a hierarchy of fantasies, and is assumed to have meaning and power beyond other fantasies. It is ultimately woven into the pathology of the person. Its pathological effects may contain, for example, a feeling of deadlock and lack of choice, which involves power, submission and passivity. The specific sexual contents are traced by Laufer to specific patterns of erotized childhood interactions. Such masturbation fantasies are idiosyncratic, i.e. specific to a given adolescent but not to adolescence; or as masturbatory fantasies and practices idiopathically related to individual childhood experiences. They experience the living out of the central masturbation fantasy mainly as being repetitively overwhelmed. These people usually reach a point in their adolescence at which they have a feeling of deadlock (which still contains the fight against giving in); subsequently they have a feeling of giving in, which is then followed by a feeling of surrender. For these adolescents, the predominant wishes remain pregenital, thus precluding the use of masturbation as a trial action; instead masturbation or sexual gratification from their bodies acts as a constant proof that they have surrendered. In these adolescents, the final sexual organization is established prematurely – prematurely either because the choices are nonexistent or because they view choice as an additional threat to an already precarious defense against further regression. What we see then, especially in young adulthood, is the pathological answer to the conflict that existed during adolescence; it is as if they have accepted that genitality, with regard to both object relationships and gratification, either cannot or must not be attained. Such an acceptance signifies the surrender of the body to the mother; it is as if such a young adult has given up genitality in order to avoid the attack from the oedipal parent, while at the same time offering his pregenital body to the mother who first cared for it.

Mervyn Glasser's (1986) notion of a 'core complex' includes an intense longing for indissoluble union with the object, which leaves the individual, at the same time, with a fear of being merged and annihilated. The core complex is a struggle between the wish to be 'enveloped' by the original object and the need for 'freedom' from the object. In a sexual perversion, such as cross-dressing, feelings of separation and abandonment are alleviated as the act serves to blot out the person's own identity and express the wish to be inside the mother's body. The subsequent undressing and shedding of the mother's identity might serve to free the patient from this union with the object and re-establish the sense of a separate identity. Glasser suggested that in perversion the father is emotionally, if not geographically, absent. A number of other analysts within this group have followed this interest in violence toward the self or others (Perelberg, 1999), and still others have focused on narcissistic and borderline states (Bateman, 1997). The group also has a continuing, lively interest in the analytic understanding of children and adolescents including a developmental approach to their treatment (e.g. Hurry, 1998).

4.1.3 Evaluation

Anna Freud, like all theorists whose work spans a number of decades, shifted her views considerably. She started by elaborating the role of the ego, suggesting that it was as important as the drives. Perhaps her interest in the ego generated an interest in the way personality development could be understood in the light of the unfolding of the ego's capacity in early life. It also generated an interest in the external world and the way life experiences impinged upon the individual as a function of his developmental state. It is not surprising that she independently identified the importance of the early mother–infant relationship and the impact of separation. In trying to understand the complex way in which evolving psychic structures interacted, she proposed the useful concept of developmental lines. This allowed her to retain the structural view of the mind and yet study the impact of interactions on the child's psychic functioning. Developmental lines broke down the large psychic units of agencies (id, ego, superego) into smaller units within which the minutiae of development could be explored. It is clear that the model suggested by Anna Freud, who should perhaps be described as a modern structural theorist, is fundamentally developmental, at least in that the individual is seen as capable of moving back along developmental lines if necessary to deal with some current, potentially overwhelming challenge, then move forward again. Within this framework there is no equation of behavior and pathology; a given behavior may reflect a temporary 'blip' rather than a true symptom. These ideas (mobility of function and the meaning of behavior) are key assumptions of broader developmental approaches to psychopathology (Garmezy and Masten, 1994; Cicchetti and Cohen, 1995b).

Developmental conflict should be differentiated from 'developmental interference' (Nagera, 1966) where environmental demands are so grossly out of keeping with the child's wishes that the consequent frustration and distress interferes with the child's forward movement. Developmental interference may result in the inhibition of entire psychological functions such as abstract thinking (Weil, 1978), body-integrity (Greenacre, 1952) and the capacity for mentalization (Fonagy et al., 1991). 'Infantile neurosis' (Nagera, 1966) implies that internalized conflict was not tackled successfully by the developing ego and the conflict of drive related wishes and internalized standards (superego) threatens the ego's sense of safety. Such infantile neurosis may be crippling, yet the underlying conflict may fall into the normal range, be resolved by further maturation of the mental structures, and motivate further adaptive efforts and independent psychological functioning.

Anna Freud's model is limited at times by its literal use of the structural model of drives (the balance between id, ego and superego, drive fixation etc.). She was unwilling to abandon what she perceived as the most scientific aspect of her father's contribution. Her use of metaphors as part of causal accounts risks reification, which others among her followers avoided through the development of less reductionist frameworks. Interestingly, her observational work during the war in the Hampstead Nurseries (1941–45) yielded many findings consistent with those of contemporary developmental research (e.g. the development of an attachment relationship during the first six months of life, the rise in ambivalence to the caregiver between six and 12 months, the parent's use of withdrawal of affection to socialize the child, the early sociability of the infant). Her later work was driven by theory and clinical observation of later developmental phases and makes little use of her early findings (Tyson and Tyson, 1990).

Because Anna Freud was clearer than many other psychoanalytic writers of that period, it is not surprising that many of her assumptions were quite directly challenged. For example, she, along with many other psychoanalysts of the time, assumed that adolescence was a stage of development which was normally associated with turmoil (Freud, 1958). Developmental research has revealed that adolescent turmoil is neither inevitable nor particularly benign; it signals underlying relationship problems (Rutter, 1989b). In the case of a number of major psychiatric issues, progress led to the abandonment of key psychoanalytic assumptions upon which Anna Freud's model rested. For example, she assumed that children did not have the ego- and cognitive developmental capacities to feel sustained guilt, misery and despair (i.e. those symptoms of distress that are part of the depressive experience). She favored the view that depression in children might be 'masked' or manifest as 'depressive equivalents', seen in somatic complaints or behavioral disturbances. It is now clear that children show the phenomena of depression, such as excessive guilt and other intropunitive emotions (Zahn-Waxler and Kochanska, 1990).

What makes Anna Freud's work unique is her commitment and that of her companion, Dorothy Burlingham, to the observational method. Those working in her nursery were asked, as part of their training, to provide literally hundreds of written observations. The observations formed the basis of detailed and sophisticated descriptions of the ways in which maturational and environmental factors combined in the course of development. Not only did she carry out observational studies, the first major one of which was the remarkable monograph on 'Infants without families' (A. Freud & Burlingham, 1944) but a number of follow-up studies were initiated in a research program streets ahead of its time (Kennedy, 1950; Bennett and Hellman, 1951; Burlingham, 1952; Hellman, 1962; Burlingham and Barron, 1963). Among the many discoveries of these early observational studies were descriptions of reactions to separation, showing not just the immediate distress but also the longest term disruptions to development.

Without the terminology, Freud and Burlingham described not just the basic components of attachment theory but also the impact of trauma and its psychic residue (post-traumatic stress disorder) (Freud and Burlingham, 1974). For example, Freud and Burlingham offer a classification of five types of anxiety a child may feel about air raids. In the fifth type of anxiety they illustrate how air raids may provoke a remembering and re-enacting of earlier traumatic experience (pp. 171–2). Other reports considered principles of education, comparisons of residential care and home environment, and most interestingly and innovatively observations of peer interactions. Reading these descriptions, it is an effort to bear in mind that Anna Freud and her colleagues were working with quite rudimentary theoretical tools yet the sensitivity of the observations is quite consistent with observational studies carried out much later with the advantage of object relations theory. For example, a five-year-old abruptly separated from parents is noted as saying: 'I am nobody, nothing' (p. 209). The observers are clearly sensitive to the immense impact on self-representation of the relational loss. The descriptions of separation are quite moving, even with the intervening distance of half a century and a considerable growth in our understanding.

Recently, Masten and Curtis (2000) drew attention to the two historically rich traditions of the study of the development of competence and psychopathology, both of which are present in the history of psychiatry and psychoanalysis but are not commonly integrated. Development of competence has remained the domain of developmental psychology while disturbance and dysfunction have been in the realm of child and adult psychiatry. Perhaps Anna Freud's corpus is a notable exception to this tendency to separate competence from pathology (Masten and Coatsworth, 1995). Her approach was consistent with the idea of developmental tasks most clearly elucidated by Erikson (see Chapter 3) as an index of individual adaptation. Outside the Anna Freudian tradition, failures of developmental tasks might often lead to referral to medical professionals which might often lead to a search for dysfunction, such as mental disorder. Anna Freud acknowledged that while developmental dimensions were by no means coterminous with psychological disturbance, the two had to be seen in interaction in order to understand the prospects of an individual child. It is now generally accepted that developmental achievements predict both risk for the onset of a mental disorder and the likely outcome of such disorder (Zigler and Glick, 1986). For example, the best predictor of adult mental health and adjustment is the presence of forms of competence and ego maturity, rather than the absence of problems (Kohlberg, Ricks and Snarey, 1984). In a highly sophisticated study of the development of depressive symptoms and social competence across time, it was demonstrated that while competence predicted changes in depression, depression did not predict future competence (Cole et al., 1996).

There is an even more general sense in which research on childhood problems has supported the Anna Freudian approach emphasizing individual pathways or lines of development. In recent years concerns have been raised about the limitations of analyzing individual life pathways using statistical approaches based on variables associated with later psychological disturbance. Such studies established more than a quarter of a century ago that no single family stressors were associated with increased likelihood of child behavior problems but rather, when two or more stressors were present, the risk of problems was found to increase several fold (Rutter et al., 1975). This finding, which is broadly consistent with Anna Freud's focus on the equilibrium of internal psychological forces that maintain development within the normal range, has been replicated across cultures (Sanson et al., 1991), over time (Sameroff and Seifer, 1990) and importantly with young children (Sameroff, 1998). Directly in line with Anna Freud's emphasis on individual developmental pathways, recent research on childhood psychopathology has made increasing use of so-called person-oriented statistical methods. These emphasize trajectories of similar groups of children rather than focusing on risk variables that yield little qualitative discrimination. For example, across several developmental studies of young children with early problems, it was demonstrated that those most likely to continue on a pathway toward behavioral problems in adolescence appeared to be those boys who experienced risks that cut across child, parenting, family and sociodemographic domains (Shaw, Winslow and Flanagan, 1999; Campbell, Shaw and Gilliom, 2000; Shaw et al., 2001). The studies suggest that in line with Anna Freud's assumptions, young children can overcome their difficulties if there are not other family problems, possibly because of a positive pull of development and the help which parents can give in restoring a child to a normal developmental path.

4.2 The Mahlerian model

4.2.1 Margaret Mahler's developmental model

Margaret Mahler (1968; 1975) offers a developmental model within which object relations and the self are seen as outgrowths of instinctual vicissitudes. She focuses on the growth from the unity of 'I' and 'not-I' to eventual separation and individuation. She asserts that the 'biological birth of the human infant and the psychological birth of the individual are not coincident in time' (Mahler et al., 1975, p. 3). Separation refers to the child's emergence from a symbiotic fusion with the mother, whereas 'individuation consists of those achievements marking the child's assumption of his own individual characteristics' (Mahler et al., 1975, p. 4).

Mahler's model assumes that the child develops from 'normal autism' through a 'symbiotic period' to the four subphases of the separation-individuation process (Mahler and Furer, 1968). Each step is strongly influenced by the nature of the mother–infant interaction, in particular by such factors as early symbiotic gratification and the emotional availability of the mother.

Mahler describes the infant's state in the first few weeks of life as *normal autism*. Mahler assumes that experiences are limited to 'deposits of memory traces of the two primordial qualities (pleasure – good versus painful – bad)' (Mahler and Furer, 1968, p. 8). The infant is thought to be surrounded by a 'quasi solid stimulus barrier', an 'autistic shell which (keeps) external stimuli out'. She suggested that pathological autism (as in the pervasive developmental disorder) was the basic defensive attitude of those children 'who cannot utilise the beacon of emotional orientation' and 'is an attempt at dedifferentiation and deanimation' (Mahler and Furer, 1968, p. 69). She also suggested that the so-called negative symptoms of schizophrenia (withdrawal, flatness of affect, etc.) were defensive. From the second month, the infant enters the *symbiotic phase*, marked by dim awareness of the need satisfying object. This is a state of undifferentiated fusion with the mother, in which the 'I' and 'not-I' are in a 'delusional, somato-psychic omnipotent fusion' with a common boundary based on the stimulus shield (Mahler et al., 1975, p. 45). For Mahler, this phase is

> an inferred intrapsychic state rather than an observable behavioral condition [which refers] to the character of the infant's primitive, cognitive affective life at a time when differentiation between self and mother has barely begun to take place. (Mahler and McDevitt, 1980, p.397).

Thus, during the first half of the first year Mahler's infant lives 'in a state of primitive hallucinatory disorientation' (Mahler et al., 1975, p. 42).

This is not unequivocally so. Mahler and Furer (1968) allude to 'mutual cueing', a circular interaction in which the infant adaptively alters its behavior in response to the mother's selective reactions to the cues with which the infant presents her. For each mother this results in the creation of 'her child'. It is only with attributes selectively evoked by the mother that the baby establishes a symbiotic dual-unity which is on the way to selfobject differentiation and reciprocal object relations (Mahler, 1967; Mahler et al., 1975). Lichtenstein's (1961; 1963) concept of 'identity theme' and Weil's (1970) 'basic core' concept are compatible ideas in that they also refer to this inevitable amalgamation of the self and the object wherein the developmental achievement of the self necessarily involves adaptation to the maternal object.

Mahler sees satisfactory symbiotic phase development as the source of benevolent feelings about the self and toward the object in that it contains the origins of infantile fantasies of omnipotence shared with the mother. If the mother's preoccupation with her infant is anxiety-ridden, inconsistent or hostile then the individuating child will not have a reliable frame of reference for checking back perceptually and emotionally to the symbiotic mother. However, Mahler (1963) recognizes the resilience of children and their capacity to extract benevolence from the mother even against considerable odds. A severely compromised symbiotic phase is, however, thought to leave permanent characterological scars in the form of fragmented identity, mindless hedonism, cognitive delay, more than average amounts of destructive aggression, and overall lack of affection (see Burland, 1986).

The separation–individuation process is thought to begin at four to five months, in the sub-phase of *differentiation* identified as hatching (differentiation of the body image) (Mahler et al., 1975) when the infant's pleasure in sensory perception can begin if his symbiotic gratification has been satisfactory. He turns away from the mother, thus beginning to differentiate himself from her. Playing peek-a-boo games may indicate a nascent reaction to, as well as adaptation to, the anxiety associated with the mother's occasional disappearance. Nine months to about 15–18 months is the second subphase of *practicing*. The child, practicing locomotion, is at the peak of his belief in his own magical omnipotence, derived from his sense of sharing his mother's magical powers. There is a 'love affair with the world' which has become his to explore although he returns to the mother for 'emotional refueling'. Of importance for identity formation is the stimulating effect of physical prowess 'for the establishment of body boundaries and a greater awareness of body parts and body self' (Mahler and McDevitt, 1980, p. 403). The toddler is elated with 'the escape from the tendency toward fusion with, or engulfment by, the mother' (pp. 403–5). Parens (1979) using Mahler's framework, points out that aggression begins to emerge in this sub-phase in the service of both separation and individuation, implying a departure from Freud's assumption of innate aggression.

The 'rapprochement' subphase is dated 15–18 to 24 months. The infant begins to have greater awareness of separateness, separation anxiety, and consequently an increased need to be with the mother. Mahler describes the child's behavior of shadowing the mother at the same time as darting away from her or clinging to her while pushing her away, and terms this 'ambitendency' (p. 95). The child expresses 'both the wish for reunion with the love object and his fear of engulfment by it' (Mahler et al., 1975, p. 77).

The handling of this subphase is thought to be critical for the child's future development. The mother must combine emotional availability with 'the gentle push' toward independence. If the balance of availability and push toward independence is weighted too much on either side, the infant may become desperately dependent and clingy and experience great difficulty in investing his environment with sufficient interest, and his pleasure and confidence in his own functioning will be impaired.

Settlage (1977) identifies the developmental tasks of the rapprochement subphase as: (1) mastery of intensified separation anxiety; (2) affirmation of basic trust; (3) gradual deflation of the sense of omnipotence of symbiotic unity; (4) compensation for the loss of omnipotence through increased sense of autonomy; (5) firming up of the core sense of self; (6) establishment of affect and drive regulation; (7) healing the tendency to maintain the relationship of the love object by normal splitting of the object into good and bad parts; and (8) replacing the splitting defense with repression.

The fourth subphase, the 'consolidation of individuality and the beginnings of emotional object constancy' (Mahler et al., 1975, p. 109) begins with the third year of life. The main task is the achievement of individuality and affective object constancy, which assumes that the cognitive symbolic inner representation of the object has been established (Mahler et al., 1975). There are other tasks which underscore the potentially lifelong character of this phase: the internalization of parental demands, unifying good and bad representations into an integrated whole, the establishment of gender identity and so forth.

4.2.2 Separation-individuation and psychopathology

Mahler (1974) described her work as enabling clinicians treating adults to make more accurate reconstructions of the pre-verbal period, thereby making patients more accessible to analytic interventions. Like Spitz, Mahler implicitly proposes an alternative model of psychopathology based on developmental imbalances in childhood. Several psychoanalytic workers have built on her conclusions in modifications of therapeutic technique toward addressing developmental deficits relatively directly through the relationship with the therapist (see Settlage, 1977; Blanck and Blanck, 1979; Pine, 1985; Kramer and Akhtar, 1988).

From her observational studies Mahler developed a view of narcissistic personalities as lacking in 'narcissistic libido' (healthy self-regard). She hypothesized that this was because the soothing ministrations of the mother during the symbiotic phase, and her emotional refueling of the child during the practicing subphase of separation-individuation, were deficient. The mother's failure to empathically support the child during the rapprochement subphase, when the child's ambitendency for autonomy and fusion is at its height, will lead to the collapse of the child's omnipotence. A fixation will occur and the renunciation of omnipotence and narcissistic enhancement from within (through autonomous activities) will be jeopardized. The self and object constancy necessary to negotiate the Oedipus complex success-fully will also be impaired. Such individuals will therefore have no clear image of themselves or their objects, may wish to avoid or control them, search for symbiosis with a perfect object, and will have difficulty in toler-ating criticisms, setbacks or ambivalence which challenges their view of the other.

The rapprochement subphase is seen by Mahlerians as 'the critical period' of character formation. Its crucial conflicts between separateness and closeness, autonomy and dependency, are repeated throughout devel-opment, particularly in periods accompanying illness, drug-induced states, etc. (Kramer and Akhtar, 1988). This part of Mahler's theory has been used extensively by those working with individuals with borderline personality disorder. Mahler et al. (1975) observed that some mothers responded to their returning infants in the rapprochement sub-phase with either aggression or withdrawal, and that the behavior of these infants was similar to that of borderline patients. Residues of rapprochement subphase conflicts are seen in this group in the form of persistent longings for, and dread of, fusion with the mother, and in continued splitting of self- and object- representations, which cumulatively prevent the establishment of object constancy and identity (Mahler, 1971; 1972; Mahler and Kaplan, 1977; Kramer, 1979). The search for an 'all-good' mother persists throughout life, and coercive clinging and negativistic withdrawal impede the establishment of 'optimal distance' (Bouvet, 1958).

Masterson (1972; 1976) elaborated Mahler's views of borderline pathology, enriching it with Bowlby's (1973) and Kernberg's (1976a; 1976b) perspectives. He suggested that the mother of the borderline individual was likely to have been borderline herself and thus encouraged symbiotic clinging and withdrew her love when the child strove toward independence. The father did not, or could not, perform his role of focusing the child's awareness toward reality. Masterson believes that borderline patients experience a deep conflict between the wish for independence and the threat of loss of love, and thus search for a clinging tie with a mother substitute. Such a tie will temporarily ensure a feeling of safety but any wish for self-assertiveness will present the individual with the terror of abandonment. A lifelong and vicious cycle of brief blissful unions, ruptures and emptiness and depression will ensue.

He discusses 'abandonment depression' as the consequence of the borderline child's quest for separation from the withdrawing or aggressive maternal object who in turn, for pathological reasons of her own, wishes to keep the child in a symbiotic relationship with her. He develops a fear that 'his very existence is dependent ultimately upon the presence of need grati-fying and life sustaining others' (Klein, 1989, p. 36). The withdrawing and rewarding object representations are kept rigidly separate to maintain the possibility of symbiotic union with the rewarding object and to ward off abandonment depression. Borderline individuals' dramatic responses to actual separation can thus be explained by their incomplete separation from their objects. The psychological experience of separation becomes equivalent to a loss of a part of the self. Borderline patients' common vigorous pursuit of their therapists at home, in their holidays or in other professional activity can be understood in this way. The self is experienced as needy, helpless and dependent, but rewarded for this stance by maintaining the love of the caregiver. The alternative is a loathsome, bad person who can drive others away by becoming independent and self-reliant. The clinging and demanding self masks the more competent, independent, real self (see Masterson, 1985; Masterson and Klein, 1989).

Rinsley (1977; 1978; 1982) further elaborated on Masterson's model based on the introjection of borderline interpersonal relationship patterns from a pathological primary object. Masterson and Rinsley (1975) suggest that a dual image of such objects exist in the borderline individual's mind: (1) the 'withdrawing object relations unit' which represents the critical withdrawing maternal image and associated anger and frustration and a self-representation as helpless and bad; (2) the 'rewarding object relations unit' which is made up of an image of the mother as approving, associated good feelings and an image of the self as compliant and passive. Rinsley (1977) suggests that the persistence of these structures into adulthood explains most features of borderline disorder including: splitting into 'good' and 'bad', part rather than whole object relations, inability to mourn, primitive ego and superego, stunted ego growth, hypersensitivity toward abandonment and the absence of normal phase-specificity of development.

Retrospective studies provide evidence which is consistent with Masterson and Rinsley's formulation. Loranger, Oldham and Tulis (1982) show that mentally ill relatives of borderline personalities are, in the main, themselves borderline (see also Baron et al., 1985; Links et al., 1988). Borderline patients appear to be more likely to have parents who have had mental illness, personality disorder, drug abuse and severe marital discord (Ogata, Silk, and Goodrich, 1990). Borderline patients have experienced more early separations, family breakdown, family violence, foster placements and physical and sexual abuse (Herman, Perry and van der Kolk, 1989; Links et al., 1988). Brown and Anderson (1991) found that an increase in the proportion of patients with borderline diagnosis was found with increasing severity of abuse. The prevalence of abuse is higher in this group than in ones with depressive pathology (Ogata et al., 1990a; 1990b), schizophrenia (Byrne et al., 1990), antisocial personality disorder (Zanarini, Gunderson and Frankenburg, 1990a; 1990b) or those with borderline traits (Links et al.,

1988). However, the key research question remains: what proportion of children who suffered physical or sexual abuse grow up into borderline individuals and what distinguishes them from those who do not? Clearly, many escape this fate. The pathways by which they achieve this need to be fully illuminated so that others can be helped to make this journey out of severe developmental psychopathology.

Empirical research supports the psychoanalytic view of the mistrustful, dark quality of depression in borderline as compared to non-borderline depressed patients. The former are far more preoccupied with concerns about loss, abandonment, alienation and desperation with respect to attachment figures (see Westen et al., 1992).

Burland (1986), using Mahler's framework, described an 'autistic character disorder' that resembles schizoid personality. He suggested that early, sustained and severe deprivation resulted in the incomplete psychological birth of the infant from the normal autistic phase. Because the gratifying symbiotic phase does not follow, the child fails to establish a libidinal object and subsequent sub-phases of separation-individuation are compromised. This developmental arrest manifests itself in poverty of affection and relationships, fragmented identity and mindless hedonism. Burland's description is based on severely deprived ghetto children and has greater ecological validity than many other psychoanalytic descriptions.

4.2.3 Empirical evidence for Mahler's developmental model

As we have seen, according to Mahler, during the first half of the first year, the infant is in a state of primary narcissism, his psychic functioning dominated by the pleasure principle. The structuring of the mind into id and ego, and the development of the oppositions of self and other, inner and outer, have not yet taken place. Evidence from infant research casts considerable doubt on this formulation.

Milton Klein (1981) was among the first of many to produce evidence suggesting that the state of 'normal autism' and non-differentiation between self and other may not be fit empirical observation. The new-born is sensitive to specific kinds of external stimuli such as the human face (Fantz, 1963), the human voice (Friedlander, 1970), and any stimulus over which they experience 'mastery' (Watson, 1979).

Bahrick and Watson (1985) demonstrated that the infant is able to differentiate degrees of contingency between his actions and events at three months of age. The famous study of the infant clearly taking pleasure in learning that the actions of moving his leg, or sucking on a specially modified dummy, results in the mobile above his head moving, illustrates that infants are interested in finding links between their actions and events they observe in their physical surroundings. Auditory learning occurs before birth, as the infant is sensitive to the stress pattern of the mother's voice immediately after birth (DeCasper and Fifer, 1980). There is also an innate coordination of perception and action, evidenced by the newborn's imitation of adult facial gestures based on a short-term memory system (Meltzoff and Moore, 1989). There is even evidence for long-term memory capacity at three to five months in motor recognition (Rovee-Collier, 1987). In sum, this and other evidence casts serious doubt on Mahler's notion of normal autism and selfobject merger (e.g. Lichtenberg, 1987).

Similarly, Mahler's notion of the lack of object permanence during the first year of life has been seriously questioned. Early evidence on the relative lateness of object permanence was based on the Piagetian manual search task (Piaget, 1954; Werner and Kaplan, 1963). Studies using occlusion tasks, with surprise as a dependent variable, have shown that infants are able to represent the continuous existence of a hidden object, and reason about its expectable 'behavior' (e.g. to reappear after a period of occlusion) as early as three months of age (Spelke, 1985; 1990). Thus physical objects are assumed by the infant to have cohesion, boundedness and rigidity.

Gergely (1991) and Stern (1993) both argue that the key feature of these early capacities is the infant's sensitivity to abstract, amodal properties and cross-modal invariances rather than modality-specific, physical features. The infant, perhaps from the earliest days, seeks perfect contingency with the physical world. This interest is not specific to a modality; the internal sensations associated with intensified sucking action translate readily into observed movement of a mobile, a desired sound or the appearance of an image. Thus the infant seems not to be a concrete experiencer of the physical world, as Mahler and classical psychoanalytical theory assume (see also Klein, 1935). Rather, the infant tries to identify aspects of the environment that specifically 'mold' to his needs and actions.

Mahler's developmental framework, however, may well be appropriate to the truly psychological world of the human infant. Fonagy, Moran and Target (1993) argue that whereas the infant is well aware of himself and the object in the physical domain, the same cannot be said of the infant's mental or psychological self which represent mental states of belief and desire. Whereas he may be fully aware of the cohesion and boundedness of the physical mother, he might well assume that psychological states extend beyond the physical boundaries. Full comprehension of mental states seems not to be acquired until considerably later. The nine-month-old infant does conceive of goals for physical objects (Gergely, Nadasdy, Csibra and Biro, 1995) but these are not differentiated between the animate and the inanimate world. Thus, a symbiotic inter-subjective unity may indeed characterize infancy and even early childhood, but solely at the level of mental representations of mental states.

Highly relevant to Mahler's model are studies where the extent of self-differentiation is examined in the context of aspects of psychological adaptation. Very significant work in this area has been performed by Sidney Blatt and colleagues at Yale University (e.g. Blatt and Blass, 1990; 1996). In a key paper, Blatt and Behrends (1987) argued that the pressure for individuation was only one half of a dialectic; the other, less explicitly acknowledged by Mahler, was the force toward relatedness. The balance between these two opposing needs represents psychological health and mature interpersonal relatedness. Psychopathology is an over-representation of one or other pole.

In line with these theoretical ideas, Blatt and co-workers established a method of assessing these two fundamental dimensions of self and object relatedness: (1) differentiation of self from other (based on Mahler's ideas) and (2) the establishment of increasingly mature levels of relating to others (Blatt and Blass, 1996; Diamond, Blatt, Stayner and Kaslow, 1991). The method involves eliciting brief narratives concerning the individual's thoughts and feelings about key relationships (mother, father self, therapist) from participants and coding these narratives using a manualized coding system. In general, higher ratings of differentiation-relatedness indicate that psychological development has progressed toward the emergence of (a) a consolidated, integrated and individualized sense of self-definition and (b) empathetically attuned, mutual relatedness in close relationships (Blatt, 1995; Blatt and Blass, 1996). In a study of adolescents treated in long-term in-patient psychotherapy, symptomatic improvement was found to be strongly associated with higher scores on this scale (Blatt, Stayner, Auerbach and Behrends, 1996; Blatt, Auerbach and Aryan, 1998). Further, over the course of long-term treatment there was an increase in differentiation-relatedness, from representations that were initially dominated by a lack of clear picture of the object and self as separate entities, to the emergence of object constancy with the beginning of an integration of positive and negative elements. Patients with greater therapeutic change had higher scores for their initial descriptions of their therapists than did patients with less therapeutic change. Initial differentiation-relatedness scores were usually higher for the description of the therapist than for mother, father and self-descriptions. Thus, in line with Margaret Mahler's ideas, patients making better use of therapy were also more capable at the start of their treatment of constructing more complex and nuanced representations of a new figure, the therapist, suggesting high levels of developmental attainment in separation-individuation.

4.2.4 Criticism and evaluation

Mahler's theory has been generally accepted by psychoanalysts (see Tyson and Tyson, 1990) because it dovetails with classical oedipal theory as well as being compatible with the theory of pre-genital drives (see Parens, 1980). Chief among its virtues is the way it has strengthened the tendency to reconstrue the psychoanalytic situation as a developmental one (see Loewald, 1960; Fleming, 1975; Settlage, 1980). It is thought that the psychoanalytic situation resolves separation-individuation conflicts with the analyst coming to be heard and experienced as 'a real person' in the interactions. It is now clear that Mahler's assumptions about severe forms of childhood psychosis, such as infantile autism or childhood schizophrenia, poorly fit her developmental model and seem unlikely to be explained by the notion of a developmental fixation in the symbiotic phase. While the most promising explanation for schizophrenia remains a neurodevelopmental one, with numerous indications of neurological, cognitive and behavioral dysfunctions long before the onset of the disorder, evidence points to the last months of gestation rather than the first months of life as a critical period for the vulnerability to potential causes of schizophrenia (Marenco and Weinberger, 2000). Evidence in favor of postnatal pathological processes is meagre. Similarly, the early emergence of symptoms characterizing autism is generally accepted but the resistance to social interaction is seen as an extreme form of a constitutional bias toward processing information from the physical rather than the interpersonal world (Baron-Cohen, 2000). Thus, while recent research confirms Mahler's theory that these serious disorders are evident from the first months of life, her implication that they are caused by the social events that take place in this period has not been substantiated.

Mahler's original contributions to the understanding of borderline personality disorder have been most lasting. Her view of these patients as fixated in a rapprochement, wishing to cling but fearing the loss of their fragile sense of self, wishing to be separate but also fearing to move away from the parental figure, have been crucial to both clinical intervention and theoretical understanding (see particularly Chapters 8 and 9). However, her theory is less helpful in understanding the high prevalence of childhood maltreatment in these patients' lives, particularly sexual abuse for which there is now overwhelming and high quality evidence (e.g. Jacobson and Rowe, 1999). There is also general scepticism, particularly from European psychoanalysts, about a psychoanalytic theory that can plausibly talk about a mother, no matter how early and how central, without a relationship to a father. This criticism of course could be even more forcefully raised against the British Independent school (see Chapter 7). It is claimed that in the unconscious there is no such thing as a two person (mother–baby) relationship. Wherever one finds the mother, one also inevitably finds a symbolic or imaginary paternal principle that has transformed the woman into a mother.

4.3 The work of Joseph Sandler

Sandler, a British psychoanalyst, was a student of Anna Freud's. His work is remarkable for perhaps coming closest to integrating the structural model with object relations theory (Greenberg and Mitchell, 1983). Notwithstanding his major contribution to modern psychoanalytic theory building, Sandler's work is rarely integrated into chapters or covered extensively in textbooks of psychoanalysis. The length and detail of the present coverage will redress this imbalance.

4.3.1 Advances in developmental theory

4.3.1.1 The representational world and the representation of affects

The most important new psychoanalytic concept that Sandler introduced is his frame of reference for the representational world (Sandler, 1960b; Sandler and Rosenblatt, 1962a). Sandler's concept is rooted in the work of Piaget (1936), Jacobson's (1954b) concept of self-representation, and Head's (1926) notion of body schema. Because the concept of mental representation has become central in cognitive science, years after Sandler's adoption of it, psychodynamically oriented psychologists, as well as psychoanalysts, use Sandler's notion to describe the internal representation of object relationships (e.g. Bowlby, 1980; Blatt and Behrends, 1987; Horowitz, 1991b).

Sandler's internal working model antedates but resembles Bowlby's influential formulation (see Chapter 10). Both view relationship representations as consisting 'in essence, of a set of expectations relating to the mother's appearance and activities' (Sandler, 1960b, p. 147). In Sandler's (1962b) conceptualization, representations of self and other have a 'shape'; they also add a critical emotional tone to the organization of sensations and perceptions of interpersonal experience. Once a self-representation is formed, object representations can be established. Sandler's metaphor links the representational model to structural theory: the ego is the theatre and representations are characters on the stage. We are aware of the characters enacting the drama but overlook the way the theatre works and stages the play.

Sandler introduced this idea to update and clarify many basic concepts in psychoanalysis (see below). For example, the process of introjection in early childhood duplicates parent representations but does not involve a change in self-representation. Incorporation, on the other hand, implies a change in self-representation to resemble the perceived object. Identification is a momentary fusion of self- and object representations that generally preserves their boundaries and separateness. An instinctual wish may be seen as a temporary modification in the representation of self or object; conflict can result in the exclusion of these representations from consciousness. Defenses rearrange the contents of the representational world (e.g. projection modifies the shape of the object representation to make it resemble the unconscious self-representation). Similarly, primary narcissism is the libidinal cathexis of the self-representation; object love is the transfer of this cathexis to the object representation. Secondary narcissism is the withdrawal of libidinal cathexis from the object representation now directed to the self-representation.

4.3.1.2 The concept of feeling states

In two papers with Joffe, on narcissism (Joffe and Sandler, 1967) and on sublimation (Sandler and Joffe, 1966), Sandler proposed placing feeling states rather than psychic energy at the center of the psychoanalytic theory of motivation. Joffe and Sandler questioned the appropriateness of libido theory as an explanation for narcissism, observing that secure individuals show love and concern for their objects while insecure ones show higher levels of self-interest and self-preoccupation. As an alternative, Joffe and Sandler offered the representational world frame of reference with its focus on the representation of feeling states and values. They suggested (Joffe and Sandler, 1967, p. 64) that disorders of narcissism arise out of the mental pain associated with the discrepancy between the mental representations of the actual self and of the ideal shape of the self. Problems of self-esteem are higher-order derivatives of the basic affect of pain. The pain is constantly present but may be made more bearable by psychic techniques, such as by seeking narcissistic supplies, overcompensating in fantasy, and identifying with idealized and omnipotent figures. If these adaptive maneuvers fail, a depressive reaction may develop. Feelings influence the values attached to mental representations; the value may be positive, negative, or both, but it is the feeling shape of the representations that is critical for narcissistic disorders.

In a 1959 presentation, Sandler (1960a) introduced the revolutionary concept of background of safety, within which the aim of the ego is to maximize safety or security rather than to avoid anxiety. Sandler (1989) opposed the safety and drive concepts, demonstrating that the urge to gain feelings of well-being and safety has to be stronger than instinctual gratification, in order to keep a check on the latter when its expression implies danger. Safety is the most radical example of the new motivational framework proposed by Sandler based on feeling states in place of drives.

Sandler (1972) did not 'get rid of the drives', rather, he argued that

> while drives, needs, emotional forces, and other influences arising from within the body are highly important in determining behavior, from the point of view of psychological functioning they exert their effect through changes in feeling (p. 296).

Sandler saw all conscious thinking as embedded within a matrix of feeling states that give direction to all adaptation. A key assumption was that feeling states represent a subjective state of self in relation to another person. Many creative contributors to the study of object relationships, particularly early mother–infant interactions, have made extensive use of Sandler's model (e.g. Emde, 1988a; Stern, 1985) as an alternative to poorly fitting drive theory accounts.

4.3.1.3 Actualization, role responsiveness and internal object relations

Sandler (1976b) showed how patients create role relationships to actualize an unconscious fantasy. They cast themselves and the analyst in a specific relationship that actualizes a variety of unconscious needs and defenses. The patients attempt to act on the external world to make it conform to an unconscious fantasy. Sandler (1976b) suggested that analysts should allow themselves a 'free-floating responsiveness', whereby they accept – at least in part – and reflect on the role assigned to them and put it to good use in understanding their patients. He cited the example of the woman whose unconscious fantasy was of soiling or wetting herself and having an adult around to clean her up. Over many sessions, she cried and asked for tissues. The analyst in this case was forced into the role of a parental introject. Countertransference then must be understood as part of this process, which extends beyond the clinical situation and reflects the normal functioning of the unconscious mind. Sandler's model thus anticipated by a couple of decades the emergence of the relational school of psychoanalysis (see Chapter 9).

This frame of reference offered an entirely new theory of internal object representations (Sandler and Sandler, 1978). Sandler showed how wishful fantasies are represented as interactions between self and object, the basic aim being to bring about a 'good' emotional state while distancing a bad one. Thus the object plays as important a role as the self in the mental representation that embodies the wish. Object relationships are thus fulfilments, not only of instinctual wishes, but also of the needs for safety, reassurance and affirmation. Such needs accompany the actualization of a wished-for childhood relationship, albeit heavily disguised at times. Overt relationships are derivatives of underlying wishful fantasy role relationships. As these representations are reinforced during the course of development, personality is formed and the individual becomes increasingly inflexible in the roles demanded of self and others. Character traits can thus be understood as well-established role responsiveness structures that serve to actualize a wished-for representation of a relationship, which in turn is a derivative of one existing in unconscious fantasy (Sandler, 1981).

The psychological structures that constitute the representation of these wished-for relationships are not conceived of as straightforward representations of the interaction between the child and the actual parent. Instead, the perception of these relationships is subject to defensive transformations, resulting from the ego's need to gratify yet defend against unconscious wishes. Thus the manifest relationship that emerges in the psychoanalytic setting (or in everyday encounters) is most frequently a heavily disguised version of the unconscious fantasy – originally represented in relationship terms – rather than a simple repetition of internalized patterns of interpersonal relations. Many 'dialogues', as Sandler (1990) termed them, between self and object are extremely painful yet, paradoxically, retained by patients. As Sandler (1990) pointed out, these dialogues provide a feeling of safety because they allow the patient to continue to experience the presence of the object. In fantasy the internal object can then continue to embody unacceptable aspects of self-representation, thus enhancing the experience of overall safety in the mental economy of affect.

4.3.1.4 The three-box model

Joseph and Anne-Marie Sandler (1984) proposed a coherent frame of reference that enabled two aspects of unconscious functioning to be distinguished. The first system or 'box' consists of

> those infantile reactions, infantile wishes or wishful fantasies that developed early in life and are the outcome of all the transformations that defensive activities and modifying processes have brought about during that period. (p. 418)

This system is the child within the adult, primitive in terms of mental structure but by no means restricted to sexual and aggressive impulses. Sandler and Sandler (1987) see the system as consisting of unconscious fantasies with wish-fulfilling, problem-solving, reassuring and defensive aspects. Indeed, it embodies the ego of the young child as well as the superego formation of the early years. From the point of view of cognitive sophistication, representations within this structure are less well elaborated and are dominated by childhood theories. Never directly accessible to consciousness, it is essentially unchangeable. However, the way the adult psyche accommodates to derivatives of this 'past unconscious' can change.

The second system or 'box' is also unconscious; representations within it may be more or less subject to censorship. Its label is 'the present unconscious' and it is equivalent to Freud's unconscious ego, but also contains unconscious representations normally assigned to the superego. It differs from the first system in that it is oriented to the present rather than the past. Conflict-solving compromises are created within it; the most important of these is the creation and modification of current unconscious fantasies and thoughts. Whereas events impinging on the first system may trigger past unconscious fantasy, the second system involves the constant modification of representations of self- and object interactions that are less peremptory and disruptive than the mental products of the first system. It is cognitively more involved and more closely linked with representations of the present-day reality. However, it shares the property of unconscious systems in tolerating contradictions. The nature of the second censorship, at the border between the second and third systems, differs qualitatively from that on the border of the first and second. Whereas the latter may be conceived of as analogous to Freud's repression barrier, the former is principally oriented toward avoiding shame, embarrassment and humiliation. The third system or box is conscious and only irrational to the degree that may be licensed by social convention.

Sandler's distinction between the three boxes of the mind has great clinical significance. The first box is a continuation of the past in the present. It is unaware of any need for adaptation because it is based on infantile aspects of the child's self. The second box, the present unconscious, consists of here-and-now adaptations to the conflicts and anxieties triggered in the first box. Material in this part of the mind is more likely to be accessible to interpretation – all the more so because the analyst can overcome the second censorship by providing an atmosphere of tolerance that weakens the inhibition based on shame, embarrassment and humiliation. Interpretations, even in the transference context, that attempt to access primitive fantasies immediately or to directly address the child within, without first addressing their derivatives in the second system, will inevitably muddle the two forms of the unconscious, reducing the impact of the intervention.

4.3.2 Sandler's models of psychological disorders

4.3.2.1 Neurotic disorders: obsession, depression and trauma

All Sandler's contributions to the understanding of psychological disturbance had a strong developmental orientation. Sandler and Joffe (1965b) understood obsessional phenomena in children by evoking the concept of 'the function of regression of aspects of the ego' (p. 145). The model suggested that particular modes of ego functioning may be associated with pleasure and feelings of safety, thus creating a pull to return to that mode of functioning in a manner analogous to drive regression. Obsessional children manifest 'a particular style of the perceptual and cognitive functions of the ego' that indicates its fixation in the second and third year of life (p. 436). In Sandler's papers on depression and individuation (Joffe and Sandler, 1965; Sandler and Joffe, 1965a), regression is described as a response to frustration and suffering that arises from the need to give up early magical and omnipotent ideal states in favor of reality; it functions as an attempt to stave off helplessness and possible depression.

In two papers, Sandler and Joffe (Joffe and Sandler, 1965; Sandler and Joffe, 1965a) reconsidered depression from a representational world perspective. With development, the ideal state moves away from magical and omnipotent experiences toward an appreciation of reality. Giving up ideal states may be analogous to the process of mourning rather than depression. However, ideal states of well-being involve mental object representations. Loss of the object may be usefully translated, then, to mean loss of a state of self for which the object was a vehicle. Depressive responses may follow when the individual fails to respond to psychic pain with an adequate discharge of aggression. The adaptive response is individuation, a process of working through that involves abandoning the pursuit of lost ideal states and adopting new ones that fit reality, as well as with internal states. This process occurs throughout life but is developmentally typical of particular stages determined by biology and culture.

The depressive response – capitulation in the face of pain – is the opposite of individuation. It is maladaptive in that although inhibition may dull psychic pain, 'it is not aimed at recovery' (Joffe and Sandler, 1965, p. 423). Sandler (1967) also revised the concept of trauma, prompted in part by the difficulty of defining it in absolute terms either as an intrapsychic experience of being overwhelmed or as a particular category of external events. In a theoretical advance that remains important today, he specified that the pathological impact of trauma does not depend on the child's initial experience of helplessness in the face of the event, but rather on the child's post-traumatic condition. He suggested that what may lead to traumatization (i.e. the clinical sequelae) is the continuing strain on the ego, determined principally by the degree of inner conflict that remains after the trauma, crippling personality growth and leading to the development of borderline, delinquent or psychotic pathology.

4.3.2.2 Primitive mechanisms: projective identification

Sandler did not write specifically about severe personality disorder, although it is simple enough to extend his theories in that direction. Particularly relevant are his ideas on primitive defense mechanisms, such as projective identification. Sandler's formulation of projective identification (see Sandler, 1987a) was a particularly useful attempt to link a dominant Kleinian notion to the sophisticated representational point of view now adopted by most theorists. Clinical observations in which the psychoanalyst appears to be experiencing a feeling more appropriately attributable to the patient were seen by Sandler as a wishful fantasy of the patient that included the analyst.

The fantasy involved modification of the representation of the object in the patient's mind so that it contains unwanted aspects of the self-representation. To actualize the fantasy, the patient attempts to modify (or control) the behavior of the analyst, so that it will conform with the distorted representation. Retaining selfobject boundaries is essential in order for the mechanism to fulfil its defensive function of getting rid of aspects of the self while maintaining the illusion of controlling them through control of the object.

This concept may be illustrated in the context of the transgenerational transmission of representations evident in mother–infant interaction (Fraiberg, Adelson and Shapiro, 1975; Sandler, 1994). The mother's interaction with her child is based on her representations of past attachment relationships. The mother may modify the representation of her child, making it identical to an unwanted aspect of herself. She may then manipulate the infant to behave consistently with her distorted representation. Naturally, this process works both ways; infants may distort their representation of their caregivers in order to deal with unmanageable affect, and provoke reactions in the adults that confirm the accuracy of their mental representation. The model is basically a dynamic one, in that what the child experiences as unmanageable is by no means absolute but, rather, depends to a large extent on the child's perception of what the caregiver finds unmanageable and unacceptable in him. Gradually, through this process, the child's self-representation may increasingly come to resemble the caregiver's representation of him. The dialectic process that occurs intra-psychically between self- and other representations (within the framework of the representation of the interactions between them) tends to develop an isomorphic set of representations in the two individuals.

4.3.3 Criticism and evaluation

Joseph Sandler was one of the most creative figures in bringing about what Ogden (1992) termed a 'quiet revolution' in psychoanalytic theory. His contributions form a coherent progression of thought on psychoanalysis and the analytic process, and he was a formative influence on psychoanalysis during the latter part of the last century. Sandler's contribution led psychoanalysis toward a psychology of feelings, internal representations and adaptation, closely tied to the analytic relationship. As well as contributing to our changing views of psychoanalytic theory, he has also influenced psychoanalytic technique. The 'three-box model' of psychic structure, emphasizing the importance of distinguishing present unconscious from past unconscious, has led to fruitful re-examination of further metapsychological and clinical concepts, including transference and countertransference. He sought to find the inherent linkages between apparently opposing ideas, and helped to close the gap between American ego psychologists, and British Kleinian and object relations theorists.

Sandler's overall approach to theorization colors the approach to theories taken in this book. Sandler pointed out that much of psychoanalytic theoretical development is preceded by the unconsciously constructed partial theories that evolve in the minds of practicing experienced analysts as they struggle to develop mental models of the minds of their patients. In his oft-cited paper (Sandler, 1983) on the relations between concept and practice in psychoanalysis, he pointed to the necessity for such proto-theories, as well as the simultaneous presence of incompatible preconscious theoretical constructions in the minds of many analysts. Evidence for such heterogeneity in mental models may be readily found in the multiplicity of meanings of psychoanalytic concepts, which cannot be determined without also considering their clinical context. The correspondence between 'official theory' and such tentative intuitions determines the likelihood of their emergence in consciousness.

Perhaps Sandler's most important contribution was his distinction between the experiential and the non-experiential realms. Whereas the former referred to Sandler and Joffe's representational model, the latter entailed mechanisms, structures and apparatuses. The non-experiential is inherently non-conscious, although it is not repressed or dynamically inhibited. The distinction between a fantasy (conscious or unconscious) and the organized function underpinning it (fantasizing) remains an evocative example. The model makes clear that experience is not the agent of change; rather, change is brought about by structures in the non-experiential realm, which cause corresponding changes in the experiential. Thus self-representation cannot be an agent, but it is an entity that will determine how mechanisms of the mind behave. This locates Sandler's model in a relatively clear position vis-à-vis Greenberg and Mitchell's (1983) dichotomy between drive and relational models. Sandler's model placed relational formulations within the framework of a structural psychology, albeit considerably modified from Freud, Hartmann, Kris, Loewenstein and Rapaport. While modifying structural theory, Sandler refused to abandon the ambition of psychoanalysis as a general psychology of structures and basic mental processes. In later papers, Sandler made extensive use of his important distinction. For example, in a paper on the structure of internal objects and internal object relationships, Sandler (1990) clarified his view of internal objects as 'structures' within the non-experiential realm, albeit constructed out of subjective experience, conscious or unconscious. Once created, such non-experiential structures can modify subjective experience, including the child's experience of the actual objects (people).

Sandler was one of an unfortunately relatively small number of psychoanalysts committed to the importance of research that complements clinical work. He saw psychoanalytic theory as a frame of reference to be applied to observations 'be it in diagnosis, therapy, education, or research' (Sandler, 1960b, p. 128; see also Sandler, 1962b). One such important development was Sandler's restatement of the model in terms of the child's representational world (Sandler and Rosenblatt, 1962a). With the collapse of associationist stimulus response psychology and the emergence of cognitive science, a real possibility for the integration of cognitive psychology and psychoanalysis presented itself (for some significant attempts to achieve this, see, for example, Foulkes, 1978; Erdelyi, 1985; Stern, 1985; Westen, 1991b; Bucci, 1997a). Sandler's formulations are consistent with modern cognitive psychology in that he describes how complex self- and object-representations are shaped by everyday emotional experiences, fantasies and memories of the individual alone and in interaction with others, and attributes a central role to them in the causation of behavior. The cognitive notion of mental representation is congenial to developmental and social psychologists working from a socio-cognitive perspective (see Fonagy and Higgitt, 1984; Sherman, Judd and Park, 1989; Westen, 1991a; 1991b).

While Sandler's contributions are evident to theoreticians and scholars, he has established no school that bears his name, nor are there a group of analysts who would claim to be 'Sandlerians'. Although this fact could be applauded as a measure of his avoidance of the psychoanalytic tradition of reliance on charismatic leadership that sometimes resembles a personality cult, it also indicates a number of limitations characterizing his work. While his theories were and are extensively used, those who use his ideas often do not know that they are doing so. There is no single idea that people link with his name (his ideas about countertransference and 'role-responsiveness' are perhaps an exception) and integrative summaries of his contribution are not often found in the literature. He advanced thinking by clarifying a range of psychoanalytic concepts, but was unable to excite psychoanalysts with the novelty of his contributions. His ideas were not unoriginal, but he never outlined a unique vision of particular clinical groups with sufficient clarity to capture the imagination of practicing clinicians. The subtleties of ideas interested him more than the broad brushstrokes of theory that he considered always to skirt unsustainable generalizations.

CHAPTER 5

Introduction to object relations theory

5.1 The definition of object relations theory

Object relations theory is far too diverse to have a single, agreed definition (Kramer and Akhtar, 1988). The term has been used to designate many ideas, of varying coherence and specificity. As object relations theories have come to dominate psychoanalysis, most theorists have appeared to aspire to this category, making a definition of the term even more problematic. Greenberg and Mitchell (1983), in their definitive review, use the term to include all theories 'concerned with exploring the relationship between real, external people and the internal images and residues of relations with them and the significance of these residues for psychic functioning' (p. 14). Strictly, this definition would not exclude structural theories, which is Greenberg and Mitchell's implicit aim. Lussier (1988) reminds us that authors such as Edith Jacobson (1954b), in writing about depression, use object relations concepts but remain rooted in a structural framework. Jacobson notes, for example, that the child will prefer to have a bad mother than no mother at all and may choose to destroy himself rather than kill that bad internal object. She also wrote that the child was frequently ready to sacrifice pleasure for the sake of security. As we have seen, the same may be said of the work of Mahler and that of the Sandlers. As Sprueill pointed out (1988), Freud saw objects in terms of drives, and it is almost impossible to imagine drives without objects.

Kernberg (1976a), in the foreword to a book by Volkan, offered a helpful clarification. He identifies three ways in which the term can be used: (1) to describe attempts to understand present interpersonal relations in terms of past ones, which would include the study of intrapsychic structures as deriving from fixation, modifying and reactivating earlier internalizations; (2) to mean a specialized approach within psychoanalytic metapsychology, describing the construction of mental representations of dyadic 'self' and 'object' relationships which are rooted in the original relation of the baby and mother, and the later development of this relation into dyadic, triadic and multiple internal and external interpersonal relationships in general; (3) in the most limited sense, to describe specific approaches of (a) the Kleinian school, (b) the British School of Independent Psychoanalysts, and (c) those theorists who have attempted to integrate the ideas of these schools into their own developmental theory. Kernberg's own theory best fits the second use of the term (e.g. Kernberg, 1984). In this book, we will use his third pragmatic definition, as object relationships concern structural theorists as much as the 'English' (Kleinian) and 'British' schools and their followers.

For the past quarter of a century there has been a genuine shift of interest associated with the rise of object relations theories. There is an implicit or explicit move away from the study of intrapsychic conflict, particularly conflicts relating to the sexual and aggressive drives, and the central organization of oedipal compromises and the complementary influences of biological and experiential forces in development (Rangell, 1985; Lussier, 1988; Spruiell, 1988). Regardless of particular theoretical models, psychoanalysis seems to have moved increasingly toward an experientially based perspective, emphasizing the individual's experience of being with others and with the analyst during analytic work (see, for example Gill and Hoffman, 1982; Schafer, 1983; Schwaber, 1983; Loewald, 1986). This approach inevitably emphasizes phenomenological constructs such as individuals' experiences of themselves (see Stolorow et al., 1987) and their experiences of psychic as opposed to external reality (see McLaughlin, 1981; Michels, 1985). The clinical emphasis upon experience inevitably drives theory away from a structural, mechanistic model toward what Mitchell (1988) broadly terms 'relational theory'. Patients in treatment express themselves in terms of relationships (Modell, 1990) and the move toward an object relations based metapsychology may thus be seen as led by an increasing demand on clinicians to explore clinical phenomena from the point of view of the patient.

Object relations theories vary along several dimensions. For example while some represent a move to replace drive theory approaches entirely (the interpersonal-relational schools would be an example of this trend, Mitchell and Black, 1995) others are built out of drive theory (e.g. Winnicott, 1962a), while others still derive drive theory from an object relations approach (e.g. Kernberg, 1982). Object relations theories also differ in the extent to which they depict a set of mechanisms to account for personality functioning. For example, in general systems theory approaches, the mental mechanism underpinning internalized relationship representations is at the heart of the theory (e.g. Stern, 1985) whereas in self-psychology models object relations are merely a route to a psychology of the self (e.g. Bacal, 1990).

Object relations theories share several assumptions. These include: (1) that severe pathology has pre-oedipal origins (i.e. the first three years of life); (2) that the pattern of relationships with objects becomes increasingly complex with development; (3) that the stages of this development represent a maturational sequence that exists across cultures, but that may nevertheless be distorted by pathological personal experiences; (4) that early patterns of object relations are repeated, and in some sense fixed throughout life; (5) that disturbances in these relations developmentally map onto pathology (see Westen, 1989); and (6) that patients' reactions to their therapists provide a window for examining healthy and pathological aspects of early relationship patterns.

However, psychoanalytic theories differ considerably in terms of the rigor with which the problem of object relationships is tackled. Friedman (1988) differentiates between hard and soft object relations theories. Hard theories, in which he includes the theories of Melanie Klein, Fairbairn and Kernberg, see much hate, anger and destruction, and dwell on obstacles, illness and confrontation, whereas soft object relations theorists (Balint, Winnicott and Kohut) deal with love, innocence, growth needs, fulfilment and progressive unfolding. Schafer (1994) has noted the current tendency in psychoanalytic thinking for theoretical minimalism. Friedman (1988) points out that object relations theories are more parsimonious in their assumptions than structural psychoanalytic theory. Spruiell (1988) regards all object relations theories as partial models, unable to encompass the broad developmental model, but his view is today a fairly isolated one.

Akhtar (1992) offers an extremely helpful overview of two contrasting approaches to object relations theory. He bases his distinction on Strenger's (1989) insightful model of the 'classic' and 'romantic' visions of man offered by psychoanalysts. The classic view, rooted in a Kantian philosophical tradition, holds that striving toward autonomy and the reign of reason is the essence of being human. By contrast, the romantic view, to be found in Rousseau and Goethe, values authenticity and spontaneity above reason and logic. In the classic view, man is seen as inherently limited but able to, in part, overcome his tragic flaws, to become 'fairly decent' (p. 320). The romantic view sees man as intrinsically good and capable, but vulnerable to restriction and injury by circumstance. The classic view corresponds to the tradition represented by Anna Freud, Melanie Klein, American ego psychologists, Kernberg, Horowitz and some exponents of the British object relations tradition. The romantic approach perhaps originates with the work of Ferenczi and is well represented in the work of Balint, Winnicott and Guntrip in the UK, and Modell and Adler in the United States. The first approach views psychopathology largely in terms of conflict; the second in terms of deficit. Acting out is seen as an inevitable consequence of deep-rooted pathology in the classical view, whilst the romantic view sees it as a manifestation of hope that the environment may reverse the damage done. The romantic psychoanalytic view is undoubtedly more optimistic, seeing man as full of potential and the infant as ready to actualize his destiny (Akhtar, 1989). In the classic psychoanalytic view, conflict is embedded in normal development. There is no escape from human weakness, aggression and destructiveness and life is a constant struggle against the reactivation of infantile conflicts. In the romantic view, there is primary love; in the classic view love is a developmental achievement that can never be totally free of early transference. Naturally, there are approaches that combine the classic and the romantic. Kohut and Kernberg propose models of development that are pure representatives of neither tradition.

In one sense object relations theory makes sense as a category of psycho-analytic propositions in opposition to classical Freudian theory and its subsequent elaborations by Loewald, Mahler, Sandler and others. They stand together against Freud's assumptions concerning the evolution of psychic structure as an intra-psychic process independent of the child's relationships. In particular, Freud's suggestion that the mind evolves in the wake of frustration of the child's drives allows for only one specific type of object relations (one where the child's needs are frustrated) to play a part in the creation of mental structures and functions. The fundamental difference between Freudian and object relations theory is the greater heterogeneity of possible relationship patterns that are considered pertinent to the development of mental structures.

Object relations theories assume that the child's mind is shaped by all early experiences with the caregiver. In particular, the notion of autonomous ego functions and the neutralization of drives in the service of ego development sits poorly with the work of most object relations theorists. The relational perspective implies dynamic tension throughout the course of development. There is no way to be free of the pressure of incompatible representations of self–other relationships. By contrast, object relations themselves are often, though not invariably, seen as independent of drives or physical gratification. Many theories, for example, attachment theory, assume an autonomous 'relationship drive' which forcibly brings the infant into contact with the caregiver independent of the gratification of primary needs. Other object relations theories such as the Kleinian retain Freudian notions of instinct but no longer consider its frustration as sufficient for the creation of mental structure. Mental structure is present as part of the child's constitution and relationship representations are initially driven and later come to control drives.

5.2 Compromises between classical and object relations approaches

By the mid-1980s object relations theory, in one of its many incarnations (see below), was the most widely accepted psychoanalytic model around the world. 'Home-grown' versions of the theory (Kohut, Kernberg) and British imports (Klein, Winnicott) replaced ego psychology in the United States; the British version of the theory came to hegemonize much of Europe while both North American and British theories in modified forms could be found in the vibrant Latin American psychoanalytic movement (e.g. Etchegoyen, 1991). However, by no means all psychoanalysts have accepted the shift of the basic psychoanalytic model from the classical Freudian structural model to object relations theory. In North America there are a number of psychoanalysts who remain fully committed to modifications of the structural approach as proposed for example by Brenner (1982; 1987; 1994). Other influential writers such as Harold Blum (1986; 1994), Vann Spruiell (1988), Len Shengold (1989) and the Tysons (Tyson and Tyson, 1990) have managed to retain a broadly ego psychological perspective while selectively adopting certain object relations ideas. However, none of these writers has wished to advance a psychoanalytic model that may serve as an alternative to object relations theory. Only writers in the interpersonalist tradition (to be reviewed in Chapter 9) have aspired to do this.

The sole geographical exception to the domination of object relations theory is the group of French-speaking countries, particularly France and French Canada. Here a specific version of Freudian theory has remained dominant throughout the last decades of the twentieth century. A review of French psychoanalytic ideas would require a separate book of its own (such as the Lebovici and Widlöcher 1980 volume summarizing postwar French psychoanalytic thinking). One justification for the limited coverage of the French school of psychoanalysis in the present volume is the limited interest of French theoreticians in a developmental perspective, which is the organizing theme of the present volume. Further, the present authors lack the knowledge and expertise to do justice to what is a theoretical tradition of equal weight to object relations theory. However, it would be even more negligent to give the reader no indication at all of the existence of a viable alternative frame of reference for psychoanalysis which emanates from the work of André Green (1986; 1995a; 1995b; 1997) and constitutes something of a compromise between the Freudian and object relations traditions.

5.2.1 A French approach to psychoanalytic theory: the example of the work of André Green

André Green might be described as a 'post-Lacanian' alongside other important French contributors such as Rosolato (1978), Laplanche (1989) and Anzieu (1993). Post-Lacanians stress the role of different types of signifiers that contribute to the complexity of the mind. Saussurean linguistics, which strongly influenced Lacan, distinguishes the signifier (the word) from the signified (the matrix of meaning to which the signifier refers). Different types of signifiers are thought to be associated with different representational systems in the mind. Green and other post-Lacanians assume that drives, affects, 'thing presentations' (concrete, directly experienced physical objects), word presentations, etc., may be distinguished in terms of the different kinds of signifiers (symbolic systems) they use in representation. Green (1999b) terms this the heterogeneity of the signifier. Patients' communications reveal an interplay of several channels of significations, some representative, some affective and others related to bodily states, acting out, reality statements, thought processes and so on. Green (2000a) argues that to understand the complexity, structure and function of meaning underlying discourse, it is essential to grasp the movement from one channel of communication to the next. He assumes the existence of mutually resonating chains of signifiers. An element of communication that is deeply felt is assumed to have what Green terms retroactive reverberation. That is, echoes are highlighted revealing how the power of their meaning can persist long after the discourse carrying them has died out.

Elsewhere, Green has described how free association gives access to a complex temporal structure that challenges the apparent linearity of discourse (Green, 2000b). Particular moments in discourse may often be understood only after the event. However, once pronounced the moment 'irradiates' the rest of the discourse. Something which has already been said can change its meaning in the light of the current moment (retroactive reverberation) but sometimes past utterances can work in a forward direction (heralding anticipation) to signify the first step of a sequence that is unpredictable but clearly linked to what was said earlier. Green, along with other French psychoanalysts, highlights the complex temporal structure of discourse and challenges the apparent linearity of temporality. Thus psychic causation is not just regressive (i.e. the problems of the individual are not invariably rooted in the past). Temporality is progressive as well as regressive and takes on a treelike structure, constantly producing unexpressed potentialities and potentialities generating retrospective echoes. Thus, in Green's view psychic organization never ceases to modify itself as time passes. Trauma is not in the past, but it may be in the present in interaction with the past. Green's theory builds extensively on Freud's suggestion of 'nachträglichkeit', translated into French as 'après-coup'. In the analytic process, as in the patient's mind, time is 'exploded'.

Green claims that our intuitive understanding of the present as caught between past and future is illusory. Memory traces may be recathected and experienced as new, or denial of time may arise as a consequence of 'the crazy fantasy that we can stop the march of time' (p. 18). The destructiveness aimed at the hated object also destroys its temporal context. Thus, somewhat paradoxically, it then survives in perpetuity, like the typical nightmare of the monster that cannot be killed and forever returns to haunt the dreamer. In neurotic symptoms, this aspect of the destruction of time causes the compulsive repetition of experiences without relief. Aspects of experience are bound together in time and it is these meanings which may be recognized and rediscovered later.

In order to achieve a reformulation of drive theory and bring it closer to object relations ideas, Green (1997) proposed the idea of 'an erotic chain'. Drives should not be seen simply as a motivating force contained within the id of the structural model (what French psychoanalysts tend to call 'the second topography'). Rather, Green suggests that sexuality unfolds through a series of formations. These formations are sequenced starting with the dynamic movements of the drive (primary process or defensive distortions), going on to actions that discharge the drive, followed by the experience of pleasure or unpleasure associated with the discharge, and then desire expressed in a state of waiting and search. At this stage, unconscious and conscious representations can feed the desire. A yet further stage of unfolding is the creation of conscious and unconscious fantasies that organize scenarios or wish fulfilment. Finally, the language of sublimations creates the infinite richness of the erotic and the amorous that defines adult sexuality. Thus, Green's model differs from that of Freud in that it unpacks the process of drive-based mental function into several levels of representational systems or signifiers. He criticizes object relations theorists and classical drive theorists for attempting to reduce sexuality to a single center of this chain. Thus Kleinians (see Chapter 6) are criticized for equating drives with unconscious fantasies, which is but one of the centers within this chain. He implicitly criticizes classical Freudians for focusing exclusively on the beginning of the chain. In his view the appropriate strategy must be to track the chain through its dynamic movements. Sexuality is conceived of as a process that makes use of and is related to the various formations of the psyche (ego, superego, etc.) as well as different kinds of defenses.

Green's suggestion appears at least superficially not dissimilar to the elaboration of the structural model proposed by Sandler and colleagues (Sandler and Joffe, 1969; Sandler and Sandler, 1983). Here too the drive model and object relations theory were effectively reconciled through distinguishing different levels of mental structures, with relationship representations characterizing only the upper levels. A key distinction between Sandler's and Green's models is to be found in the fundamentally developmental orientation of Sandler's thinking compared to Green's antipathy to the developmental approach. An interesting analogue to Green's model is the model of dreaming put forward by Mark Solms that is described in Chapter 3 (Solms, 2000). Solms's ventral-tegmental pathway hypothesis also assumes a neurological structure, which could be seen as underpinning the kind of layered, multiply encoded representational chain that Green suggests. Interestingly, Green is somewhat sceptical about the implications of neuroscience for psychoanalytic theorization (Green, 1999a).

Green's ideas have been popular partly because of their clear clinical relevance. He wrote eloquently concerning the work of the 'negative' particularly in relation to borderline psychopathology (Green, 1999c). A patient's negativistic expressions, such as 'I don't know', 'I can't remember', 'I am not sure', 'I can't hear what you are saying', when repetitive and prolonged, acquire the power to kill representation. In these cases the quality of elaboration or growth of ideas in free associations is missing. The patient's thinking is 'linear' with no apparent capacity to anticipate what is to follow. In a seminal paper (Green, 2000a), he argues that such use of language indicates that a kind of phobic avoidant functioning gets installed within the use of the representational systems that underpin communication. When connections between ideas are 'mutually potentiating' they are amplified when they come into contact and have to be kept separated. He suggests that severe psychological problems, beyond the neurotic, arise in situations where multiple traumas exist that bear on each other. Here again there is an important distinction from many object relations perspectives that show a tendency to reduce later trauma to earlier experience. For Green, it is the coming together of trauma at different levels that counts. Thus, while infantile sexual experience may be formative, severe traumatization can also occur if the mother of an adolescent boy destroys that young man's identity by introducing him to friends and acquaintances as her brother and occasionally as her husband. These experiences amplify earlier identity confusions between himself and his mother that perhaps first occurred in infancy. In Green's implicit 'developmental' model, such traumas do not exist in a developmental continuum but rather are forcefully separated by the mind and encysted to forestall catastrophic terrors associated with their coming together. He describes the avoidance of making such connections through negativity entailed in the destruction of the representational system as the 'central phobic position'.

Probably the most influential paper Green has published is that on 'The dead mother' (Green, 1983), in which he described a particular clinical phenomenon, assumed to be the result of an early history in which the child found that he had lost the mother's attention and investment, she had withdrawn into a depressed and emotionally deadened state, evocatively described as 'blank mourning' (this is part of the more general category of the negative, empty states of mind or 'psychic holes', referred to above). The child, particularly in the frequent case of an under-involved father, identifies with the mother who has decathected him. There follows a 'quest for lost meaning' (p. 152) which can produce either compulsive fantasy or compulsive thinking. One of these solutions may be an adaptive defense, a 'patched breast' (p. 152), but there will be constriction of the capacity for love, that space being largely occupied by identification with the 'dead mother's' preoccupation. There can be strong attachment to the analysis (more than to the analyst), felt as an intellectual quest, the consolidation of reality as a defense. Green describes technique with these patients as requiring avoidance of the classical psychoanalytic approach, the analysis giving an opportunity for live interaction, for the analysand to interest and enliven the analyst, as communicated through associations to the patient's words and to the vitality of his presence in the analyst's mind.

5.2.2 Criticism and evaluation

Green's writing on representational systems is enlightening and could be very usefully integrated into any of the object relations theories that we shall consider below. Green arguably rescued the most helpful aspect of Lacanian thinking: a deeper understanding of how discourse reveals both the contents and the mechanisms of the mind. His framing of the problems of severe personality disorders in terms of this mixture of classical metapsychology and sophisticated representational concepts may point the way to a completely independent tradition of psychoanalytic theorization with the potential to supersede object relations theories. His clinical descriptions are deeply evocative and have inspired many theoretical developments well beyond Green's own circle (e.g. Kohon, 1999). However, with regard to the theme of this book, the notion of development and the understanding of the interface of time with psychic structuralization, Green takes a very different route from the majority of the theorists whose work we discuss.

Green regards the developmental frame of reference as part of psychology rather than psychoanalysis (Green, 2000c). He argues that because infant observation is limited to the study of behavior rather than language, it should not be included in the purview of psychoanalysis. He considers intra-psychic processes to be the concern of psychoanalysis, but thinks that these are accessible solely through the clinical study of subjectivity (e.g. the hypothesized history behind the 'dead mother complex' is reconstructed from adult clinical work, observing actual children of depressed mothers would not be relevant). The division proposed is quite problematic as not only are most psychoanalytic theories built on developmental hypotheses, but for several decades cognitive psychology has been deeply concerned with psychological processes and for the last 20 years this concern has steadily extended to the study of unconscious cognitive functioning (e.g. Kihlstrom, 1987). The phenomena to which Green refers are not only in the psychoanalytic consulting room but also in the psychological 'laboratory'. For example, the suggestions that psychic experience of time is 'polychronous' and that trauma disorganizes temporality are both core observations (Terr, 1994; van der Kolk, 1996; DeBellis, 2001).

From a developmental standpoint we would insist, along with Winnicott, that 'time itself is very different according to the age at which it is experienced' (Winnicott, 1986, p. 5). Those of us who work with small children quickly discover that a child under four rarely has explicit memories of events. To create such memories they need to have developed an extensive repertoire of generic knowledge about the event structure of their lives and learn to talk about their memories having formulated them as narratives (Nelson, 1993a; 1993b; Fivush, Haden and Reese, 1996). This is not to say that they cannot 'remember', as self-evidently behavior is modified by specific experiences more or less from birth. However, it provides an explanation for Winnicott's observations in that the memory systems that ultimately create temporality are quite different in the early years.

What the small child retains is not a memory of specific experience as an episode in life. He has not lived long enough for life to have created the structures which could contextualize and give meaning to experience as belonging to a particular moment in the past differentiated from other moments. Rather, the memory is implicit, in the sense that it is encoded in a mental structure from which it may be retrieved without the experience of remembering (Schachter, 1992a; 1992b). Recovering past experience from this implicit part of memory is involuntary, non-conscious, and evident only through inference. Après-coup is perhaps in part the historicization of implicit memory in everyday life or in clinical psychoanalysis.

The infant and the small child retain experience in exactly such implicit memories that are stored separately in the brain. But, without the 'experience' of remembering, their sense of time is far more fluid. The memory that returns in après-coup is not for the most part a recollection of a specific experience, but of a type of interaction that has shaped individuals' expectations concerning their experience of being with the object.

Thus there is a fundamental point of disagreement between 'the French' and the general object relations position around their understanding of the developmental process. Green's concept of time and model of psychological disturbance are inconsistent with the fundamental assumptions of developmental psychopathology: the accumulation of risks for development from experience and the privileging of early experience as a primer of responses to later encounters. In one sense, as suggested elsewhere in this book (see Chapter 1, section 1.5.7), this is a welcome redressing of the balance. We shall see that some developmentally oriented object relations theories have made strong claims regarding the supposedly permanent effects of early adverse experiences, and also about the importance of critical periods in development that required experiences to occur during a narrow time frame if normal development was to proceed. These strong claims are perhaps not as well founded as object relations theoreticians had hoped, even in the light of recent neuroscience research (see for example Bruer, 1999). In the sections below we shall consider this issue in far greater detail and in relation to specific claims about 'developmental programming' made by psychoanalytic theories. However, in general it should be pointed out that while a simplistic interpretation of developmental influence is evidently inconsistent with the accumulated evidence, there are both conceptual and empirical reasons to favor models that consider early experiences to have determining effects upon later reactions, whether this is through the shaping of interpersonal expectations, distortions within the psychic apparatus or lasting neurological changes.

CHAPTER 6
The Klein-Bion model

6.1 The Kleinian model of development

6.1.1 General characteristics of the model

Melanie Klein's (1935; 1936; 1959) work combines the structural model with an interpersonal, object relations model of development. Until 1935 Klein was still working within the theoretical framework of Freud and Karl Abraham. Her papers on the depressive position (Klein, 1935; 1940), her paper on the paranoid-schizoid position (Klein, 1946) and her book *Envy and Gratitude* (Klein, 1957) established her as the leader of an original psychoanalytic tradition. There are several excellent introductions to the work of Klein; these include Segal (1974), Meltzer (1978), Caper (1988) and Hinshelwood (1989).

Klein started her work in the 1920s using Freud's model. Her studies of the origin of the superego led to her later formulations. She examined the growth of the ego and superego in terms of the early relationships between the child and the caregivers (the original conception of internal object relationships referred to the relationship between internal psychic structures). In her early work with children she was struck by the fact that the internal images of objects were much more ferocious and cruel than the actual parents appeared to be. She assumed that these internal figures were distorted by sadistic fantasies. She developed the conception of internal objects and the inner world, which was far from a replica of the external world, built up through the mechanisms of introjection and projection at work from the beginning of life. The study of early introjective and projective processes led to a reformulation of the developmental stages of the ego and the superego – for instance the enrichment of the ego by introjections and its impoverishment by projection into the superego.

Klein (1932) thought that mental structures arose out of a variety of internal objects whose character in unconscious phantasy changed as the child developed from infancy (Isaacs, 1943). The word 'phantasy' is

118

deliberately spelled with 'ph' rather than 'f' to underscore the qualitatively different nature of the unconscious psychological process envisioned by Klein, in contrast to that which we may extrapolate from our awareness of the creation of a conscious fantasy. The model is interpersonal (or 'relational': Mitchell, 1988) in that it relates the development of the ego and the internal objects to personal relationships (Klein, 1931). At every stage the infant's fantasies are modified by his actual experience of interaction with the environment, and the individual continues to use his actual (external) object world in the service of an internal, primarily defensive, system of relationships (Klein, 1935; 1948a; 1948b). Pivotal to an understanding of Klein's view of development is a perhaps uncritical acceptance of Freud's speculation about a death instinct (Freud, 1920), which Klein saw as a real psychological phenomenon present from birth, if not before, and a powerful determinant of the positions the psyche assumes in relation to the external world.

6.1.2 The two basic positions

In the Kleinian model the human psyche has two basic positions: the paranoid-schizoid and the depressive (Klein, 1935; 1946; 1952; Klein, Heimann, Issacs and Riviere, 1946). In the paranoid-schizoid position, the psyche relates to part rather than whole objects. Relationships to important objects such as the caregiver are split into relations to a persecutory and to an idealized object; the ego (the self) is similarly split. In the depressive position, the relation is to integrated parents, both loved and hated, and the ego is more integrated. The paranoid-schizoid superego is split between the excessively idealized ego ideal, experienced with narcissistic omnipotence, and the extremely persecutory superego of paranoid states. In the depressive position the superego is a hurt love object with human features.

The term 'position' is appropriate as it implies a particular constellation of object relationships, external and internal, fantasies, anxieties and defenses to which the individual is likely to return throughout life. They arise out of developmental stages – the paranoid-schizoid preceding the depressive – and maturity implies the predominant presence of the depressive position. Klein appears to have implicitly, although never explicitly, disregarded Freud's (1905d) notion of developmental stages and sees anal and phallic phantasies occurring alongside oral ones (Spillius, 1994). Klein and her followers unequivocally reject the notion that development is ever complete and that the fluctuation between these phases ever ceases (Klein, 1928, p. 214; 1945, p. 387).

The paranoid-schizoid position is the infant's earliest relationship with the external world and is dominated by innate internal representations (Klein, 1932, p. 195; 1959, p. 248). The baby's early efforts to organize internal and external perceptions are dominated by splitting. In this way he attributes all goodness, love and pleasure to an ideal object and all pain, distress and badness to a persecutory one. The model of this is the hungry infant who is unable to represent the breast as absent as this would assume the capacity for object constancy. He experiences in its place a gnawing sensation (hunger) which in phantasy becomes the thought of being, as it were, attacked from within by a bad internal breast. He experiences the absence of satisfaction as persecution. All good feelings of affection and desire are aimed at the idealized good object which the infant wishes to possess, take inside (introject) and experience as himself (identify with). Negative affect (hatred, disgust, etc.) is projected onto the persecutory object, since the infant wants to get rid of everything felt to be bad and disruptive. The infant's mental life is seen as extremely labile; good rapidly turns into bad, the bad gets worse and the good gets increasingly idealized. Each external object has at least one good and one bad representation, but both are just parts, not the whole object.

The depressive position is marked by the infant's capacity to perceive the mother as a whole object who accounts for both good and bad experiences, and reaching this position is seen by Klein (1935, p. 310) as the central process and achievement in the child's development. At this moment the infant realizes his own capacity to love and hate the parent. The discovery of this ambivalence, and of the absence and potential loss of the attacked object, opens the child to the experience of guilt about his hostility to a loved object. This is what Klein calls 'depressive anxiety' as distinct from the 'persecutory anxieties' of the earlier paranoid-schizoid position. Working through the depressive position brings with it reparative feelings (Klein, 1929; 1932; 1935; Riviere, 1936). The psychic pain associated with the integration is so great that it can lead to defenses characteristic of this position, including manic or obsessional reparation, and total denial of damage or contempt. Segal (1957) links the capacities for symbolization and sublimation to depressive reparation. Bion (1957) was the first to point out that the depressive position is never permanently achieved. In fact the very term 'position' suggests a permanence which this state of mind rarely has. It is now accepted that the mind cycles between the two (Ps↔D), as the achievement of D creates anxiety which can only be handled in the Ps state (by more primitive defenses such as splitting). As Kleinian theory has matured, the interest in a strictly development perspective has diminished. Bion's influence, in particular, has focused interest on the primitive mental mechanisms, whatever developmental stage has been reached.

As projections diminish in the depressive position, and the sense of both internal and external reality gains ascendance, the individual begins to gain an understanding of the nature of his own impulses and phantasies. Spillius (1993) suggested that the depressive position might be initiated by the child's perception of the parent as thinking and feeling (having a 'theory of mind' or mentalizing – see Fonagy, Steele, Moran et al., 1991; Morton and Frith, 1995). Mentalizing is closely related to Bion's (1962a; 1962b) notion of 'K', as getting to know oneself or the other person and the evasion of the process which he calls 'minus K'.

Modern Kleinian writers (see for example Quinodoz, 1991; Steiner, 1992) see the child's achievement of separateness and the perception of the object's independence as the critical aspect of the depressive position. This brings Kleinian developmental formulations closer to the Mahlerian model of separation-individuation. The emphasis on the object's separateness also links the concept of the depressive position to classical ideas about oedipal conflict. Once the object is perceived as a mentally independent entity, she is seen as having desires, wishes, loyalties and attachments of her own, which brings in concerns about her feelings about the 'third', for example, the father or new sibling (Britton, 1989; 1992; O'Shaughnessy, 1989).

6.1.3 The concept of projective identification and other developmental concepts

The concept of 'projective identification' is central to this model (Klein, 1946). Whereas in the classical theory of projection, impulses and wishes are seen as part of the object rather than the self, and identification implies attributing to the self qualities perceived in the object, projective identification involves externalizing 'segments of the ego' and attempting to gain control over these unwanted possessions via often highly manipulative behavior toward the object. Consequently, projective identification is a more interactive concept then either projection or identification. There is a much closer relation to the object, which now 'stands for' the projected aspects of the self (Greenberg and Mitchell, 1983, p. 128). The individual is seen as in part identifying with an aspect of the unacceptable impulses that were externalized and placed into the representation of the other. This applies equally to internal object relationships; thus, the superego not only contains the projected id impulses but also the projected parts of the ego itself. (This is why it is expected that the early superego will be experienced as physical (Riviere, 1936).) Herbert Rosenfeld (1952) described a florid schizophrenic patient who had three persecuting superegos – brown cow, yellow cow and wolf, which Rosenfeld saw as corresponding to his oral, urinary and anal impulses respectively.

The concept of projective identification was probably originally described by Tausk (1919). Melanie Klein (1957) defines projective identification as an unconscious infantile phantasy by means of which the infant is able to relocate his persecutory experiences, by separating (splitting) them from his self-representation and making them part of another object. Disowned unconscious feelings of rage or shame are firmly believed by the infant to exist within the mother. By acting in subtle but influential ways, he may achieve a confirming reaction of criticism or even persecution. Projective identification has explanatory power far beyond that of a mechanism of defense. The phantasy of magical control over an object may be achieved in this way. Projective identification is not a truly internal process. It involves the object, who may experience it as manipulation, seduction or a myriad of other forms of psychic influence. Spillius (1992) suggests the use of the term 'evocatory projective identification' to designate instances where the recipient of projective identification is put under pressure to have the feelings appropriate to the projector's phantasy. Bion's (1962a; 1962b; 1963) work suggests a distinction between normal projective identification where less pathological aspects of the self are externalized and which may underpin normal empathy and understanding, and more pathological projective identification which is linked to an absence of empathy and understanding. An extraordinary insight of Bion's is the recognition that projective identification is not a defense or a phantasy as Klein conceived but rather an interpersonal process – the self gets rid of distressing feelings by evoking the feeling in another self. The other person has to have a psychological experience that the self cannot afford to have. This phenomenon explains how projective identification can be used to communicate (Rosenfeld, 1987).

Bion (1959) pointed to the need for projective identification in infancy, a time when the baby is unable to absorb all his intense experiences. By projecting the unprocessed elements into another human mind (a container) that can accept and transform them into meanings, the baby's mind could cope. The mother's capacity to comfort her baby is thus a function of her ability to absorb his tension, to a point where he can internalize her as an object able to bear the original anxiety (Segal, 1981). The absence of a suitable container makes projective identification a pathogenic process of evacuation. The child is then left with overwhelming levels of anxiety and forced to deny reality, or even to become psychotic (Bion, 1962b). Bion (1962a; 1962b), underlined that the mother needs to 'contain' the baby mentally and respond to him emotionally and physically in a way that modulates unmanageable feelings and acknowledges his budding awareness of his own psychic states (his 'intentional stance', Dennett, 1983). She will 'reflect' to the baby her understanding of both his feelings and the cause of them. This goes beyond 'mirroring' (Meltzoff and Gopnik, 1993), as the mother not only reflects the baby's emotional state, but also her own capacity to deal with it, without being overwhelmed. We believe that this is the central aspect of Bion's containment concept (1962a; 1962b). The baby's emotional communications are 'reasonably calculated to arouse in the mother feelings of which the infant wishes to be rid' (Bion, 1962a; 1962b). Capable mothers experience and transform these feelings (Bion's 'beta elements') into a tolerable form, combining mirroring of intolerable affect with emotional signals, indicating that the affect is under control (Bion's 'alpha function'). The infant can cope with and re-internalize what was projected, thus creating a representation of these emotional experiences that is tolerable, in place of his original experience which was not. In time he internalizes the function of transformation and will have the capacity to regulate his own negative affective states. Because this process is non-verbal, the mother's physical availability to the baby is essential. This may be the socio-biological root of the infant's need for proximity to the mother's mind, and the basis of his vulnerability to adults who, incapable of understanding, provide inhumane care. The Freudian account of the mother as 'auxiliary ego' can also be thought to imply these 'containment' processes.

Bion linked the development of thought processes to the quality of containment. Thought arises out of the absence of the object to bridge the gap between need and action as Freud suggested, but only if there is sufficient tolerance for frustration (Bion, 1959). The latter capacity depends on the presence of a containing object. Bion calls this process 'learning from experience' (Bion, 1962a). If there is no containment the infant will avoid frustration by attacking the thoughts themselves as bad objects, together with the links between the thoughts, so that reality is destroyed or at least denied. The result is a fragmented thought process that can become psychotic, and a greatly intensified need for further projective identification and splitting to contain the frustration. Further, if the projective identification is not entirely successful and the object is incapable of containing the infant's anxiety, when the experience is re-introjected, the experience becomes attacking and starves the personality of its good qualities (Bion, 1957). If the baby cannot tolerate frustration he will avoid reality through the use of omnipotence and omniscience, which replace learning from experience.

Kleinian theorists use Freud's (1920) assumption of an 'aggressive drive' extensively. In her work with children, Klein (1932) was impressed that the children she analyzed had extremely ruthless sadistic phantasies, about which they usually felt very guilty and anxious (Spillius, 1994). Klein (1930; 1935) assumes that the baby's self is from the beginning constantly threatened with destruction from within by an aggressive drive. She follows Freud (1920) in seeing this as the inevitable result of the organism's wish to get rid of all excitation and reach the ultimate state of Nirvana. As libido was the energy of the life force, 'destrudo' was the energy of the death instinct. Klein (1948b, p. 29) believes that babies feel an unconscious fear of death from the beginning; this is the 'primary anxiety'. The mother's breast, her body and parental intercourse are the main targets for the projection in phantasy of the child's destructive impulses. Combined with fantasies deriving from frustration, and the wish to possess these sources of 'good' things, anxiety about his attacks on the mother's body means that it comes to feel dangerous and persecuting. The death instinct is seen by Klein (1946, pp. 4–5; 1958) as only partly projected onto the bad object; some of it is retained and continues to be felt, throughout life, as threatening annihilation from within.

Klein (1957) suggests that early, primitive *envy* represents a particularly malignant form of innate aggression. This is because unlike other forms that are turned against *bad* objects, already seen as persecutory, envy is hatred directed to the *good* object and arouses a premature expression of depressive anxiety about damage to the good object. The child resents the inevitable limitations of maternal care, cannot tolerate the mother's control over it and would prefer to destroy it rather then experience the frustration. This may interfere with the primal differentiation of 'good' and 'bad'. Envy is defended against by attacking the dependent libidinal self, in an effort to destroy the links to objects. The result is a primitive superego and the idealization of a disdainful self that is omnipotent, destructive and self-sufficient. Excessive envy is believed to interfere with working through the paranoid-schizoid position, and is seen as the developmental precursor of many forms of confusional states (J. Rosenfeld, 1950). For Herbert Rosenfeld (1978) the mother's failure to contain the baby's projection always leads to greater aggressiveness and envy, which in turn disrupts the normal splitting process, causing confusional states where love and hate can no longer be differentiated.

6.1.4 The place of experience in Klein's model

In Klein's model, parents have a corrective or mitigating influence which can modify the anxieties arising from the child's constitutional tendencies (Klein, 1932; 1935; 1960). In favorable circumstances, good experiences predominate over bad ones, and the idea of a good object is firmly established, as is the child's belief in his capacity to love. Klein's premise concerning the innateness of the earliest objects and their independence of actual experience may appear to belie this statement (Klein, 1952, p. 58; see for example Klein, p. 248; see also Sutherland, 1980, for a critical account). However, post-Kleinian psychoanalysts have successfully integrated environmental accounts with her ideas (see, for example, Bion, 1962a; Rosenfeld, 1965; Meltzer, 1974; Segal, 1981). Balint (1968) took Kleinian psychoanalysts to task for concentrating exclusively on what happens inside one person rather than essentially between two people. Bion (1970), through his interest in group psychology, was able to address this.

The actual state of the object while the child is in the depressive position is thought to be extremely important. If the mother appears to be damaged, the child's depressive anxiety, guilt and despair are increased. If she appears well and can empathize with her child about his aggressive feelings, his fear of them is decreased. The child identifies with the representation of the (internalized) good object and this strengthens the ego and promotes growth. The stronger ego is able to contain destructive ideas, so the child is less driven to project hatred and the power of the bad object diminishes. Gradual integration can now occur, and the child will approach the depressive position.

The child's capacity to cope with the pain and anxiety of the depressive position, seeing himself as destructive and envious, is thought to depend on external as well as constitutional factors. When the object cannot provide adequate containment, the ego remains weak; instead of genuine reparation, a fantasized or manic reparation takes place, or a regression to paranoid-schizoid defenses remains dominant. If the bad self and object are felt to be much stronger than the ideal one, the possibility of integration creates massive depressive anxiety, as it is felt that this will involve destroying the little good the child possesses. If fragmentation (splitting) predominates, integration is not possible and the personality will come to be dominated by bizarre objects that conglomerate.

In treatment, Kleinians prefer to work exclusively with interpretations, primarily transference interpretations aimed at the patient's current anxieties. They work analytically with very severe disorders, and stress early interpretation of negative transferences derived from the paranoid-schizoid position. Kleinians have contributed enormously to our understanding and use of projective and introjective aspects of the countertransference (Racker, 1968; Ogden, 1986; Spillius, 1988a; 1988c). Bion (1962a; 1962b) was a pioneer in this respect. For Bion, transference and countertransference are about the transfer of intolerable mental pain by projective identification, originally from baby to mother, then from patient to therapist.

6.1.5. The London Kleinians

Klein's theory, like Freud's, has been as much a source of inspiration as of admiration. The line of thinking started by Klein, Heimann, Isaacs, Rosenfeld, Segal and above all Bion, has continued to the present day, with active, creative theoretical contributions from a range of individuals working in London, whom Roy Shafer aptly named 'The Contemporary Kleinians of London' (Schafer, 1994b). This very creative group includes Betty Joseph, Irma Brenman Pick, Ron Britton, Michael Feldman, Ruth Malcolm, Edna O'Shaughnessy, Priscilla Roth, Elizabeth Spillius and John Steiner. The contribution this group has made cannot be adequately summarized in the space available. Fortunately, a recent volume edited by Bronstein (2001) offers an excellent, easily accessible sample of their work. More comprehensive presentations can be found in Spillius's two-volume compendium, *Melanie Klein Today* (Spillius, 1988).

While there is no definitive text that contains a singular body of contemporary Kleinian theory, this work shares certain assumptions, as follows. While continuing to uphold the traditional Kleinian distinction between paranoid-schizoid and depressive positions, these are no longer considered as developmental phases, but rather as prototypes of madness on the one hand and object-relatedness on the other. The external world is recognized as influencing personality, but in the clinical setting the patient's accounts of outside experiences are carefully scrutinized for what they reveal about unconscious phantasies. These accounts are considered in terms of playing out dramas from the internal world. The patient is seen as fluctuating between states of mind: the persecutory, disintegrative anxiety of the paranoid-schizoid position, and the devastating feelings of guilt of the depressive position. In the former, the person's destructiveness, envy and grandiosity are the focus, while in the latter anxieties concern loss of love, failures of understanding, the impact of one's own destructiveness and the fending off of resulting guilt. The classical concern with reconstructing early developmental history is abandoned. Particular emphasis is given to projective identification as a means of communication. The analysand allocates an aspect of his or her self to others in order to control them or perhaps protect them, but in any case to be rid of these disturbing parts of the self.

The focus of analysis is the totality of the relationship with the analyst (Joseph, 1985). Everything the patient says to the analyst is assumed, *a priori*, to imply something about the way the relationship is experienced unconsciously at that moment. This clinical approach is sometimes ridiculed, at times because of a superficial understanding of its rationale. The patient's account of external events, however grave, is seen as always having an implication for the experience of the analytic relationship, colored by unconscious phantasy and revealed just as radioactive dye reveals the functioning of internal organs in a scanner. This does not answer the critics who do not see the explication of these phantasies as the key to therapeutic success, but given that assumption the strategy makes sense.

An unremitting focus on the current mental state of the patient may at times be experienced as persecutory by patients with relatively severe psychopathology. This exclusive focus has been somewhat moderated in recent Kleinian writings. An important paper on this aspect of clinical work (O'Shaughnessy, 1992) suggested that this exclusive focus could itself become defensive. Another member of the group, John Steiner (1994), suggested varying the focus between the patient's state of mind and the presumed mental state of the analyst, with comments such as 'it seems to you that I feel...'.

6.2 Kleinian models of psychopathology

6.2.1 General models of pathology

Psychological illness indicates the predominance of the paranoid-schizoid position, whereas health implies the stabilization of the depressive framework, promoting development and maturity. 'Persecutory anxiety' arises when the 'bad object' is felt to threaten the ego. Excessive anxiety leads to fragmentation, giving rise to typical schizoid fears of annihilation and disintegration. Although this idea is implicitly present in Klein's early work (e.g. Klein, 1932, p. 215), its adoption reflects the influence of Fairbairn's work on ego splitting in the early 1940s (Fairbairn, 1944). Another feature of primitive anxiety is pathological projective identification (Bion, 1957), where part of the ego is fragmented and projected into the representation of the object. The object then becomes fragmented in turn. This gives rise to terrifying perceptions of what Bion calls 'bizarre objects', which contain projected fragments of the self and are imbued with hostility and anxiety. Segal (1985) cites the example of a psychotic patient who experienced the onset of a psychotic episode as his mind being invaded by millions of little computers which would destroy it. The experience was linked to an omnipotent fantasy, loosely based on reality, that through his work he would supply all British universities with computers, enabling him to dominate the whole of British university life. The computers represented fragments of his own personality invading the world (the infantile image of the object), which would splinter and dominate it, then reinvade him in the form of tiny bizarre ideas.

Bion (1962a; 1962b; 1967b) outlined the processes that can lead to pathology in the paranoid-schizoid position. He names two factors: (1) deficiencies in the mother's capacity for 'reverie' (see also Bion (1962a) on primary maternal preoccupation; Winnicott, 1962b)) and (2) overwhelming envy in the infant. The latter is better worked out in Kleinian theory than the former. In neurotic states, the transition between schizo-paranoid and depressive positions is partial; the superego contains both paranoid and depressive features, producing persecutory guilt, an unpleasant combination of the two positions. The most common anxiety is the fear of guilt and of the loss of the loved object. If the depressive position is not approached, there will be anxiety about fragmentation, annihilation and persecution, and the individual's reality sense will be grossly distorted by projections. This picture is more applicable to patients with severe personality disorders, such as borderline or narcissistic personalities.

6.2.2 Models of neurotic conditions

Klein viewed the intense anxiety aroused by sadistic infantile phantasies as the root of mental illness, either as direct cause (childhood psychosis) or through defense. Klein (1932, pp. 149–75) developed a new idea of obsessional neurosis as a defense against early psychotic anxiety, instead of a regression to the anal phase of libidinal development. The most common defenses in the paranoid position are projection, introjection, projective identification, splitting, omnipotence and denial (Klein, 1946). These defenses are marshalled to protect from annihilatory anxieties or their projected form, persecutory anxieties. In psychotic states the projection-introjection cycle fails and the projectively identified object enters the ego, creating a delusion of the mind and/or the body being under external control. In personality disorders there is a more powerful sense of a good object but the fragility of this structure will lead to the ego and superego coming to be organized around paranoid-schizoid defenses. This is why Klein views projective identification, for example, as so central in borderline conditions.

Neurotic patients still make use of paranoid position defenses although their personalities are not organized around these. In Klein's view neurosis is rooted in the psychotic anxieties of the paranoid and depressive positions. The good object acts as a counterbalance to envy and hate. However, neurotic problems are seen mainly as consequences of unresolved depressive anxiety. For example, if reparative efforts are felt to fail, a need for reparation may persist as perfectionism. Thus work inhibition can be seen as a fear of imperfection that results from the need for reassurance that the loved object has not been irreparably damaged. Similarly, obsessionality may be the result of needing the evidence of a perfect object to relieve the guilt that the possibility of imperfection so powerfully triggers. For the obsessional reparation cannot succeed. Depression arises because the experience of loss reminds the person of the damage they caused to the good object. If the infantile depressive position is not successfully resolved, loss in adulthood will lead the individual to feel that he has once again destroyed the loved object. He will then fear retaliation as well as punishment and persecution. Thus mourning becomes melancholia (Klein, 1940). Chronic depression arises when the person cannot escape the fear of injuring the loved object and therefore has to repress all aggressiveness, generating a relentless self-persecution. The turning of aggression upon the self is a compromise attempt at reparation – an attempt to protect the good object. Similarly an intense fear of separation, as is often the case in agoraphobia (Klein, 1937), can arise when the individual requires constant reassurance that the destruction of the loved object has not taken place. So difficulties associated with loss as well as separation are seen by Klein as originating in aggression toward the object and therefore linked to either persecutory or depressive anxiety. In general,

Klein regards the extent to which an individual is successful in overcoming the anxieties of the depressive position as the most critical feature of his or her emotional development, replacing the Oedipus complex as the central construct of pathogenesis.

6.2.3 Rosenfeld's developmental model of narcissism

Rosenfeld (Rosenfeld, 1964; 1971a; 1971b; 1971c) viewed narcissistic states as characterized by omnipotent object relations and defenses that deny the separateness and integrity of the object. The narcissistic character structure is a defense against envy and dependence (Rosenfeld, 1987). He stresses the destructiveness of the narcissist's relationship with others, his ruthless use of them and denial of his need for them. To recognize the object would mean recognizing the object's control over 'goodness', and his vulnerability to separation from it. The reliance on projection and projective identification is such that the distinction between self and object can become blurred. While the life of the borderline individual is dominated by this difficulty, one with narcissistic pathology uses splitting to create an illusion of the separation of self and other. Fusion is used by the narcissist as a defense against envy aroused by a sense of separateness from the object.

By introjective identification the narcissistic individual lays claim to the good part of the object, and in fantasy owns it. Projective identificatory processes help him deposit his own perceived inadequacies in others, whom he can then denigrate and devalue. Grandiosity, contempt and profound dependency are explained in terms of Melanie Klein's ideas concerning the notion of the manic defense (Klein, 1940). The narcissist's dependency makes him feel intolerably vulnerable to pain, which is unsuccessfully warded off through unprovoked attack on the good qualities of those whose dependability seems to mock his own feelings of helplessness and defectiveness. To deal with his envy, he devalues his objects. This denigration enables him to avoid recognizing in others a goodness which the person finds threatening to his own delusional state of self-idealization as the possessor of the 'good breast'. The failure of projective identification has led to an arrest in the development of the superego. The primitive superego attacks the dependent part of the self, and is projected out onto others leading to a persecutory fear that others are critical and attacking.

Thus there are two forms of narcissism: the destructive and the libidinal (Rosenfeld, 1971a). Libidinal (thin-skinned) narcissism is the idealization of one's self by the omnipotent introjection and/or projective identification of the good object. Destructive (thick-skinned) narcissism is the idealization of omnipotent destructive parts of the self that tolerates no dependency and derogates any suggestion of true affection. Thus whereas the thin-skinned narcissist seeks reassurance and is deeply dependent, the thick-skinned narcissist adopts a hostile, superior, isolationist posture. Segal (1983) takes issue with Rosenfeld, disputing the need to postulate libidinal narcissism: according to her all narcissism is rooted in excess aggression. She agrees however with Rosenfeld that the hostile, superior defensive structure mounted to avoid envy is the central problem of the narcissist.

If the destructive (non-libidinal, aggressive, envious) parts of the self are idealized, the individual will be tempted to try to destroy any love or goodness which is offered to him, in order to maintain the state of infantile omnipotence. In order to identify with the omnipotent destructive self, he will ferociously attack the sane and loving part of his mind and will, at times, feel completely barren and empty.

6.2.4 Models of borderline conditions

Melanie Klein considered that the fixation point for schizophrenia lay in the earliest months of infancy. Hanna Segal (1964) thought that the psychotic individual regresses to the earliest months of infancy, a phase of development that possessed features of the illness. She added:

> through a study of the case histories of schizophrenic and schizoid patients, and from observations of infants from birth, we are now increasingly able to diagnose schizoid features in early infancy and foresee future difficulties. (p. 55).

Although it is not clear what 'markers' Segal had in mind, in the modern neurodevelopmental model of schizophrenia it is increasingly accepted that neuro-behavioral dysfunctions do indeed antedate the emergence of full-blown psychosis. There appears to be a deficit in motor skills, particularly fine movements (Hans et al., 1999), walking and speaking delays (Jones et al., 1994). More controversial are observations of deficits in social behavior, but despite this there is indication that social withdrawal, anxiety, odd behavior and poor social relationships are commonly noted in children who later develop schizophrenic illnesses (Jones et al., 1994; Tyrka et al., 1995; Malmberg et al., 1998; Davidson et al., 1999).

Klein's (1948a; 1948b) ideas were vital to the understanding of borderline personality conditions. The paranoid-schizoid condition is the template for borderline personality functioning: (1) In object relationships splitting predominates over repression, and other people are either idealized or denigrated. There is no real knowledge of the other, and the inner world is populated by parts (or caricatures) of the object. (2) Since the depressive position is avoided and all badness is pushed into the object, no genuine sadness, mourning or guilt is felt. (3) Projective identification predominates; communication cannot be mutual, and the other person is manipulated, being forced to take on unacceptable aspects of the borderline individual's personality.

British followers of Melanie Klein (Klein, 1950; Bion, 1957; Segal, 1964) continue to stress that pathology inevitably arises from innate destructiveness, but the idea is now considerably expanded. More recent Kleinian thinking (see Spillius, 1988a, 1988b) concerns the defensive arrangements that many conditions linked to borderline pathology appear to share. The term organization (defensive organization – O'Shaughnessy, 1981; narcissistic organization – Rosenfeld, 1987; and Sohn, 1985; pathological organization – Steiner, 1987; 1992) refers to a relatively stable construction of impulses, anxieties and defenses that allows the individual to create a precious internal state, in which he is protected from the chaos of earlier developmental stages, but deprived of the more advanced modes of psychic functioning that would lead to intolerable depressive anxiety.

Spillius (1994) identifies two components to this idea: (1) the dominance of a bad self over the rest of the personality, indicating that masochistic, perverse, addictive elements are involved, not just aggression; (2) a structured pattern of defenses and impulses rooted somewhere between the paranoid-schizoid and depressive positions. The psychic defenses work together in a system that is extremely rigid but unstable. This system protects the individual from 'psychotic' confusion, but also makes change or therapeutic progress difficult and rarely entirely successful. The defenses may shift temporarily, but progress tends to be more apparent than real. It is as if the psychic structure itself comes to embody the destructive impulses that required it in the first place. Bion (1962a) provides one explanation for this: he suggests that the ego's identification with an object that is felt to be full of envy and hate results in an early disabling of the psychic processes needed for understanding cognitive and affective aspects of interpersonal relationships. Thus a state of quasi-deficit arises as the pathological resolution of intra-psychic conflicts. This is a powerful model with great explanatory potential that has been widely used by psychoanalytic thinkers from orientations other than the Kleinian (e.g. Bollas, 1987; Fonagy, 1991).

Splitting is both a cause and a consequence of the borderline person's difficulty in maintaining an ambivalent, balanced view of both self and object, which in Kleinian theory would require him to acknowledge his overwhelming destructive potential. Searles (1986) also stresses that splitting can prevent the formation of a memory of an object which would then have to be mourned. Splitting may also be part of a reaction to claustrophobic anxieties about being trapped inside the object, anxieties that develop due to ego boundary difficulties. These authors see the characteristic sadism and masochism of borderline patients as reflecting split aspects of the self. With more than one object at their disposal, borderline individuals may externalize their incapacity to integrate good and bad objects, by polarizing people working with them and constantly attacking the links between them (Main, 1957).

Rosenfeld (1978) suggested that the intensification of envy and aggression disrupted normal splitting. When intense affect is evoked the object and the ego are defensively split and fragmented, leading to a chaotic presentation of relationships imbued with intense affect. Because of the heavy reliance on projection and projective identification, the selfobject distinction becomes blurred. The anxiety-driven re-introjection of unwanted parts of the self is the core of a primitive superego structure. When this is projected in the course of treatment the patient can experience the therapist as hypercritical and hostile, thus provoking a counter-attack. There may be constant confusion between the identity of patient and analyst, with the analyst continually searching his or her subjective experience to identify the patient's projections so that these can be accepted, absorbed, put into words and re-introjected.

John Steiner has described a very specific type of defensive organization, which he considers characteristic of severe neurotic and borderline patients, that might account for the intractability of the treatment and the difficulties of making contact with them (Steiner, 1993). He uses the metaphor of 'psychic retreats' to describe the complex mental structure into which the patient can withdraw to avoid contact with both the analyst and with reality. He conceives of these organizations as a particular grouping of defenses linked with a set of closely-knit patterns of object relationships. The 'retreat' is from both depressive and paranoid positions, where the patient experiences himself as 'under the protection of a pathological organisation' (p.11). Because emerging from this position confronts the patient with either paranoid-schizoid or depressive anxieties, there is powerful apparent stability to the system. There can be an addiction-like perverse gratification to this, nevertheless the patient may come to analysis complaining of precisely the relationship patterns that are the components of the organization.

6.3 Evidence consistent with Kleinian formulations

Is there any evidence consistent with Klein's ideas? Her suggestions were always seen by some as speculative and improbable, 'adultomorphic'. How could babies have aggressive fantasies, fear retaliation, or feel jealous? At the time of Klein's writing there was little research to bear on this, but after thirty years of infant research some of Klein's 'extravagant' speculations about early childhood are now more imaginable.

Klein (1935) assumes that all infant experiences are personified, and classified on the basis of emotional states as either good or bad objects, and thus all internal privation (pain and hunger) is 'always felt as external frustration' (Klein, 1936, p. 46). Early affect-based categorization is consistent with modern semantic models based on 'family resemblance' (Rosch, 1978) and is seen in the inability of babies to use natural categories during much of the first year (Younger and Cohen, 1986). An intuitive emotion-centered primitive organization with sub-cortical or right-hemisphere neural representation has been much-discussed in the past years (Le Doux, Romanski and Xagoraris, 1989; Le Doux, 1994; Schore, 1997b). Gergely (1991) suggests that the baby may begin with multiple representations of the mother defined by the infant's current affective state, organized into positive and negative categories (see also Stern, 1994).

Early critics of Kleinian formulations focused on the assumption of unbelievably early higher-order cognitive and perceptual capacities (see King and Steiner, 1991 for a definitive account of the 'Controversial Discussions' which took place in the British Psycho-Analytical Society between 1941 and 1945). All these critiques confronted Kleinian claims with what 'common sense' about what babies can think; that is Kleinian theory was tested against 'folk psychology' or observation, rather than empirical research (see, e.g. Glover, 1945; Bibring, 1947; Joffe, 1969; Kernberg, 1969; Yorke, 1971). For example, projection in the paranoid-schizoid position assumes a differentiated sense of self and other, since without this it would be impossible to displace the source of bad feelings from the self onto another object. It also implies that the baby can blame his own feelings on the attributed attitude of the other, i.e. make a causal attribution.

Detailed documentation of the remarkably abstract and complex cognitive capacities of the human infant has been available for some time (e.g. Stone, Smith and Murphy, 1973; Watson, 1984; Stern, 1985; Meltzoff, 1990) . In particular the baby clearly does differentiate between self and other (e.g. Watson, 1991). For example, at five months a baby can differentiate a video image of his own legs moving from those of another baby's legs (Bahrick and Watson, 1985). However, the capacity for relatively complex tasks (for example the imitation of facial gestures, see Meltzoff and Moore, 1992) pretty much from birth, does not, of course, validate the strong claims made by Klein and her followers about causal reasoning. However, studies of the perception of causality in infancy (e.g. Bower, 1989) and causal reasoning (e.g. Golinkoff et al., 1984) suggest that there is an innate predisposition to impose at least a physical causal structure on perceptual experience. So Klein may well be correct that the infant sees the mother as having caused his feeling of frustration. But there is no evidence to support her implicit claim that the infant relates to the object as a psychological entity. Melanie Klein constantly attributed awareness of minds to the baby, which we now know the child is most unlikely to have until at least the second year (Baron-Cohen, Tager-Flusberg and Cohen, 2000). Fonagy, Moran and Target (1993) suggested that the infant's vulnerability in fact arises from his inability reliably to conceive of the other as a psychological, as opposed to a physical, being, and that Kleinian descriptions of the 'concrete' or 'non-symbolic' functioning of severely personality-disordered patients may be better understood as reflecting an inadequate understanding of the mental states of the self and other (but for opposing nativist views see Frith and Frith, 1999 or Leslie, 1994).

Kleinian and post-Kleinian assumptions about 'infantile part-object' representations such as breasts, penises, etc., seem to be inconsistent with the abstract, amodal nature of the infant's representations as revealed by laboratory studies (see Rochat, 1995). In an early study Meltzoff and Borton (1979) for example, showed three-week-old infants pacifiers of different shapes, one of which they were familiar with in a tactile modality, but neither of which they had seen before. The infant showed preference for looking at the pacifier that they had already experienced, which implies a cross-modal transfer of shape. It is hard to argue that infants have a realistic picture of sexual intercourse even if they were to witness the primal scene. Nevertheless, the emergent research-based model of the human mind is increasingly recognizing the importance of innate ideas, 'wired in' and selected by evolution, and in this context (e.g. Buss, 1995), it has to be said that some of Melanie Klein's ideas no longer seem as far-fetched as they did at first. None of this is proof of her ideas, but they cannot be dismissed as implausible given the directions in which developmental science is progressing.

6.4 Criticism and evaluation

Klein's ideas have provoked considerable controversy and ill-feeling. The concerns about attributing adult psychological capacities to infants have been considered above, but the question also arises as to why Klein dates pathology to such early stages (Bibring, 1947). The answer might be that the mental states of infancy are extremely hard to observe: the postulation of crucial pathogenic processes in infancy is extremely unlikely to be disproven. Psychoanalytic infant observation (Bick, 1964) also permits widely differing interpretations. However, evidence is accumulating that most of the important mental disorders of adulthood are indeed foreshadowed in infancy (e.g. Marenco and Weinberger, 2000). Further, early brain development is increasingly seen as pivotal in the evolution of psychological disturbance (Schore, 1997a). Whether there is evidence for the claims of pathological mental states in infancy, such as 'psychotic-like' anxieties (Klein, 1946), is more doubtful. The intensity of affect in infancy is totally disorganizing because the baby has little self-regulatory capacity. The psychotic adult also fails to regulate his affect. This does not prove a link between the two. The content of the emotion dysregulation in psychosis is most unlikely to resemble an infant's state. The content of the former involves myriads of representations acquired through childhood and adult life. The baby's dysregulation would probably have far less specific content and thus would be less identifiable as any specific affect, rather a general state of arousal which is gradually given shape by the mother's mirroring responses (Gergely and Watson, 1996).

There is considerable difficulty in the direct analogies proposed by Kleinian writers between infancy and psychotic states. Importantly, most psychiatrists would be quick to point out that the Kleinian use of the term psychotic does not at all match formal psychiatric descriptions. The cases they describe are, in fact, rarely frankly psychotic and are far more like schizoid personalities or other types of personality disorders (Willick, 2001). Of the classical Kleinian writers, only Herbert Rosenfeld reported on the treatment of unequivocally psychotic patients. The concept of 'projective identification' has been extensively criticized (see e.g. Meissner, 1980) but continues to be used because of its relevance to interpersonal, clinical phenomena (see Sandler, 1987c). Searles (1986), Giovacchini (1987) and many other North American analysts who are working with borderline patients use the construct in the broader sense of unconscious communication. It is appealing because it conveys the undoubted ability of these patients to 'get under the skin' of all those to whom they get close. Whether a psychologically extravagant concept such as projective identification is essential to describe these phenomena or whether a more parsimonious concept such as Sandler's (1976b) role responsiveness or King's (1978) reverse transference may be sufficient, is controversial. Undeniably, projective identification is the concept which has caught on and is used increasingly across many schools. The notion of the 'death instinct' is also disputed within current psychoanalytic theory, many finding it problematic and unnecessary (see e.g. Parens, 1979 for a comprehensive treatment). Envy may not be rooted in a biological predisposition but may instead be triggered by frustration, inconsistent mothering or the baby's difficulty in conceiving time and space (see Greenberg and Mitchell, 1983, p. 129). The clinical value of the concept is, however, hard to challenge, for instance in the common experience of patients who resent and fight all attempts to help.

Other criticisms address the 'fuzziness' (Greenberg and Mitchell, 1983, pp. 148-9) of Klein's descriptions (see Fairbairn, 1952a; Kernberg, 1980a for more rigorous formulations; Kernberg, 1980b; Modell, 1968). The emphasis on 'phantasy' as the building block of mental structure means that mental structuralization has been moved into the experiential realm (see Sandler and Joffe, 1969), rather than being seen as inaccessible to awareness. This carries the advantage of closeness to clinical experience, and rids theory of much reified pseudo-scientific terminology. However, it bypasses essential questions and findings about the mechanisms underpinning mental functions.

The attainment of the 'depressive position' illustrates some of the ambiguities of Kleinian terms. This change (whether or not seen as a stable developmental stage) clearly implies a qualitative shift in the perception of the object from part to whole. It is not clear, however, if it also implies (a) consciousness of conflicting feelings about the same person (e.g. love and hate); (b) the unconscious integration of various images with no necessary conscious correlate; (c) the ability to recognize that the same person can generate conflicting feelings, but that these do not necessarily 'belong' to that person, and so on. The developmental attainment of these capacities occurs at very different times. For example, children younger than five have great difficulty in recognizing mixed emotions (see Harter, 1977; 1986; Harris, 1989), but can represent the same person as sometimes angry and sometimes loving from the first year of life, without difficulties in object constancy (Stern, 1985). Grasping their own feelings about that person is, however, likely to be very partial until the development of some degree of reflective capacity toward the end of the second and beginning of the third year (Harris, 1989; 1994).

The work of Kleinian writers represents a major advance in clarifying the relationship between emotional development and psychological functioning. Many of their ideas have enriched the field of psychoanalytic theory and clinical practice well beyond their own School. Many remain to be operationalized for further study, but models such as Bion's (1962a; 1962b) container/contained (see page 122) have lessened the divide between the understanding of cognitive development and that of emotional disorder. This is essential to further advances in the field of developmental psychopathology.

CHAPTER 7

The 'Independent' school of British psychoanalysis

7.1 The developmental model of the British school

7.1.1 Overview of the British school

The Independent tradition is well-named. Unlike other psychoanalytic schools, it is the work of a number of individual analysts, has no single leader or theorist and therefore lacks the theoretical coherence of the tighter groups. Fairbairn (1954; 1963) and Guntrip (1961; 1969; 1975; 1978) were the systematic theory-builders, but major contributions came from Balint (1959; 1968), Winnicott (1953; 1958b), Khan (1963; 1974), Klauber (1966), Bollas (1987; 1989), and Klauber et al. (1987) who all explicitly refrained from establishing schools of disciples. There are some excellent overviews of their work (see e.g. Sutherland, 1980; Kohon, 1986; Hughes, 1989; Rayner, 1991).

The Independent Group of psychoanalysts of the British Psychoanalytical Society have made a major contribution to the exploration of earliest child development and the effects of the environment in facilitating or disrupting the child's move from total early dependence to mature independence. (The term British School is appropriately applied to them since Fairbairn was Scottish. The Kleinian group is, somewhat confusingly, sometimes referred to as the English School.) Fairbairn also changed our views of internalization processes, which he conceptualized as bipolar, comprising a fragment of the ego and an internal object (a part of the self-representation in a specific relation to an object representation).

The focus of the Independents on early development led them away from a libidinally driven, structural model to the development of a 'selfobject' theory. Although the theory remains dynamic in maintaining a focus on repudiated desires and wishes, different aspects of the ego, or parts of the self are now viewed as being in dynamic interaction with each other and with complementary internal and external objects. Fairbairn (1954; 1963) envisages the self as a crucial agent of motivation: there is no emotion without the self and no self without emotion (Rayner, 1991). Winnicott (1958b) described the intense desire to develop a sense of self and, conversely, how powerfully it may be hidden or falsified (see also Bollas, 1989, contributions on destiny and fate). Much of the more recent work of this group has been on technique and the patient's and analyst's experience of the analytic relationship (e.g. Casement, 1985, 1990; Bollas, 1987; Klauber, 1987; Stewart, 1989). As this important work is not within the focus of this book, it will not be reviewed here.

These ideas have permeated the psychoanalytic literature, radically altering dynamic developmental models of psychopathology. As the theory is largely unintegrated, we will present the ideas of some major thinkers separately.

7.1.2 The developmental contributions of the Independent Group

Balint (1937), influenced by the Budapest group of Ferenczi and Herman, took issue with Freud's (1914) concept of primary narcissism (that the infant's love of self, associated with autoerotism, invariably precedes object love). Balint proposed that a desire to be loved was primary, inborn. The baby assumes that the object is there as an undifferentiated part of the self to love him. This is a feeling of lack of differentiation from early objects that are not frustrating (Balint, 1968). The baby assumes that they exist *for him* and have no independent interest; the ego's attitude to them is *omnipotent*. Objects are experienced as loving insofar as they are available to him to control, preserving the illusion that they are in fact part of his self.

Serious trauma before the stable differentiation of self and objects creates a *basic fault* in the structure of the psyche, which Balint (1968) envisages not as a fracture, but as a basic misordering (equivalent to mismatched genetic coding on chromosomes). A person showing a basic fault has an underlying feeling that something is not right about him; he is not resentful about this, but invariably seeks a solution in the environment. The *basic fault* is seen as the developmental root of personality disorder.

With object differentiation, Balint (1959) identified two characteristic defenses in the child's management of anxiety: one is to love, even to be intensely dependent upon, the newly emerging objects (the *ocnophilic attitude*), the other is to dislike attachment to objects, but to love the *spaces* between them (the *philobatic attitude*). Instead of investing in objects the philobat invests in his own ego skills.

Fairbairn (1952a) was the most forthright of the object relations theorists: 'The libido is primarily object-seeking (rather than pleasure seeking as in classical theory)' p. 82. Pleasure is gained and anxiety is reduced by the quality of ego-object relation (internal or external) rather than in discharge of energy. Thus the baby stops crying when the image of the good breast is evoked by its sight or smell, not when it starts sucking. Careful reading of Fairbairn's (1952a) closely reasoned and intense book reveals that his implicit psychological model was far closer to general systems theory than to classical psychoanalytic formulations (for this kind of model see Chapter 12 and others, e.g. Rosenblatt and Thickstun, 1977; Peterfreund, 1980; Tyson and Tyson, 1990). The most important shift is from a psychoanalytic model mainly concerned with the unconscious and repression, to one focused around the notion of incompatible ideas. Insufficient intimacy with the primary object will give rise to 'splitting' in the self (the ego). Conflicting multiple ego-object systems are seen as the developmental roots of psychopathology. We have seen in the previous chapter how critical this idea became for Kleinian theorists, particularly in explaining serious mental disorder. Fairbairn's shift from explanations of psychopathology based on intersystemic conflict to one focused on the lack of integration of ideas was undoubtedly his greatest contribution to psychoanalysis. It forms the basis of most post-Freudian thinking and all object relations theories.

A contributor who made even more impact was Donald Winnicott. Winnicott (1965b) worked with infants and mothers as well as with severely personality disordered adults, and this is reflected in his psychoanalytic model of development. He saw the child as evolving from a unity of infant and mother, which has three functions that facilitate healthy development: holding-integration, handling-personalization and object-relating (Winnicott, 1962b; 1965a). The mother *holds* the infant, both actually and figuratively, and so gives cohesion to his or her sensorimotor elements. Her *primary maternal preoccupation* (a partial withdrawal from activities other than the baby and a state of heightened sensitivity to her own self, her body and the baby) helps the mother give the baby the 'illusion' that she responds accurately to his gestures because his wish creates her (and she is part of him).

Winnicott (1953) also introduced the idea of *transitional phenomena* in a study of how the infant uses the mother to facilitate independent functioning. A favorite blanket may help to soothe the infant because it is grasped in the moment when the infant fantasizes about breast feeding, it is associated with conjuring the mother (and the breast) up in her absence. The physical object (blanket, etc.) is both the infant (the 'me' aspect) and the mother (the 'not-me' aspect); it is transitional in facilitating the move from the omnipotence of relating to a subjectively created object, to relating to the 'real' mother who is part of external reality. Because the transitional object helps to bridge the gap between 'me and not-me' as the baby becomes aware of separation, the baby and his comforter may become inseparable, with the object crucially under the omnipotent control of the baby. Transitional objects are in the space between the self and external reality: a space in which (according to Winnicott) symbolization occurs, meaningful, affectionate, sharing-yet-separate companionship and love grow, where play and illusion are maintained in the spontaneous, creative activities of healthy people (Winnicott, 1971a).

The concept of the transitional object has been an influential but controversial one, with many commentators suggesting that Winnicott overstates his case (e.g. Elmhirst, 1980; Olinick, 1982). Others point out that transitional objects may be peculiar to Western, particularly white Anglo-Saxon, culture (see Gaddini and Gaddini, 1970; Litt, 1981) where physical contact with the mother is curtailed. However, the concept has been enthusiastically embraced by many analysts who have linked disturbances around transitional phenomena to a wide variety of disorders such as borderline personality disorder (Gunderson, Morris and Zanarini, 1985; Perry and Cooper, 1985; Giovacchini, 1987), schizophrenia (Searles, 1960), institutionalization (Provence and Ritvo, 1961), psychosomatic disorders (McDougall, 1974), fetishism (Sperling, 1959b; Greenacre, 1970), autism (Tustin, 1981), obsessional disorder (Solomon, 1962), learning difficulties and pervasive developmental disorders (Sherman and Hertzig, 1983). The very breadth of these applications argues for the concept having been over-extended.

Winnicott (1953; 1971a) describes how object relating arises from the experience of magical omnipotence. When selfobject differentiation is incomplete, object representations are best designated selfobjects. The infant's physical 'attacks' on the mother, and her survival of them, facilitate the development of the self and the mother's release from omnipotent control. The infant can perceive her as a *real or separate* other who can be used properly and not just omnipotently. Maternal holding is based on *comprehension*, holding in mind, of the infant's mental state. Winnicott (1967b) suggests that optimal development of self-esteem depends on the mother's capacity for affective *'mirroring'* of the infant. Failure and frustration are essential for ultimate adaptation in that they facilitate the break away from infantile omnipotence and give the mother an opportunity to *repair* the inevitable hurt by permitting *regression* to complete fusion.

Unlike Balint (1965), Winnicott does not assume that even early infancy is an idyllic era. The mother has to be *'good-enough'*, but her failure is inevitable and is the motivator of growth. Winnicott (1956b; 1956c) stresses that the baby must not be challenged too soon about the mother's 'realness' (her independent existence) and asked to negotiate the 'me and the not-me'. The baby's omnipotence gives rise to the ego nuclei, which will in time become integrated in the *real* experience of the *I* (the true self). Winnicott (1962b; 1965a) differentiates frustration of wishes from frustration of ego needs, where the child's knowing as opposed to willing is impinged upon or confused. This, he believes, leads to disintegration, disorientation, withdrawal and a sense of annihilation – a fragmentation of the continuity of being. Experience is traumatic if it is incomprehensible. Individuals who as adults live in fear of breakdown may have unconscious memories of such infantile experiences (Winnicott, 1973).

In Winnicott's view, the true self is rooted in the aggregation of sensori-motor aliveness which is assumed to characterize the newborn's mental world (Winnicott, 1965a). At this stage the self does not exist. Its development is built upon the emergence of differentiation of me from not me and the experience of the infant's own feelings and perceptions as distinct from those of others (Winnicott, 1962a). The ego has an inherent potential to experience a sense of continuity. When the child is allowed a basis for being, the basis for a sense of self follows (Winnicott, 1971b), developing between the baby and mother. We now know that an independent, but also important, primitive dyadic unit can exist with the father (Steele et al., 1996).

More central to Winnicott's ideas is that this potential for an experience of continuity of being must not be interfered with, because it allows the infant to bring forth what Winnicott calls his *creative gestures* or impulses (Winnicott, 1960b; 1965a). These are building blocks for his later uniqueness and creativity. Also central to his ideas is the radical claim (Winnicott, 1962a) that the strength or weakness of the child's ego is a function of the caregiver's capacity to respond appropriately to his initially absolute dependence. The baby's ego can only master and integrate the drives in so far as the mother can perceive and act on his rudimentary needs and intentions. Winnicott thus sees the stability and power of the infant's ego, before the separation of the mother from the self, as directly determined by the mother's ability to think about his mind.

'*Good-enough mothering*' ensures that the infant's ego becomes autonomous and no longer needs the mother's ego support; there is an inevitable detachment from the mother as part of the establishment of a separate personal self (Winnicott, 1960c, 1965a). Disruption of emotional homeostasis, such as distressed crying, is an indication of momentary discontinuity of being but is also a creative gesture of the ego. The integration of ego nuclei is through good-enough mothering, expressed through the 'holding' and 'handling' environments (Winnicott, 1962a).

The *holding environment* provides the setting for the integration of aggression and love, allowing toleration of ambivalence and the emergence of concern, followed by the acceptance of responsibility (Winnicott, 1963a). Elsewhere, Winnicott highlighted how the holding environment serves to shield the infant from unbearable mental experience, unthinkable or archaic anxiety, in the vulnerable passage from an unintegrated to an integrated state (Winnicott, 1962a). The experience of continuity of being is thus seen as dependent on three interacting factors: (a) a sense of safety in the inner world, (b) an ability to limit concern with external events, and (c) the generation of spontaneous creative gestures. This leads to Winnicott's often misunderstood, somewhat paradoxical assertion that relatedness comes from being alone in the presence of somebody else (Winnicott, 1958a). The true self can only evolve in the presence of an unobtrusive other who will not interrupt the continuity of experience of oneself. Here, Winnicott's view has much in common with Hegel's assertion that the self in its formation both loses itself in the other and also 'supersedes' the other 'for it does not see the other as an essential being but in the other sees its own self' (Hegel, 1807, p. 111). A natural evolution of the self occurs when the person looking after the child does not unnecessarily impinge on him, by substituting her own impulses while curtailing or redirecting the infant's creative gestures. The mother needs to maintain her own sense of well-being to act as a tension regulator for the infant. The lack of good-enough mothering distorts the ego's development, forestalling the establishment of an internal environment that could become the essence of the self.

An 'active and adaptive' *handling environment* contributes to the integration of bodily and mental states, establishing personalization. The handling of the baby is adaptive when he neither feels overwhelmed, nor experiences himself as a mere collection of organs and limbs surmounted by a wobbling head. The mother's sensitivity to the baby's moods is critical, as is the coherence lent to him by the goal orientedness of his physical being (activity as opposed to passivity). Winnicott viewed thumbsucking or smiling after a good feed as creative gestures, because they were within the infant's control. Daniel Stern (1985) explored these ideas most fully in his elaboration of the development of self-agency in the four to six month old, where proprioceptive feedback, the consequence of physical action, as well as the experience of forming plans were all seen as contributing to the continuity of the sense of self. If handled satisfactorily, the baby looks at the mother's face rather than breast, as his concerns with mind and meaning come to override his preoccupation with his physical needs.

Thus, Winnicott saw the following features of parenting as crucial: (a) non-intrusive caregiving, where the object may be gradually 'discovered' by the infant as a separate being, without threatening his tentative grasp on his experience of himself; (b) facilitation of the illusion that the object is a product of the baby's creative gestures, and therefore controlled and controllable; (c) an environment in which events only require responses for which ego support is available. The differentiation between me and not-me occurs when there is harmony between the mental states of the baby and caregiver, and between the baby's mental and physical state. The true self gradually emerges as an integration of experiences of creative, spontaneous interactions with other objects, interactions which are represented with vitality and detail, hence the phenomenal experience of realness or truth. In Winnicott's model the emergence of self represents the actualization of a potential which may be compromised by impingements from the environment, but which will otherwise be built out of its creative gestures.

If trauma occurs at the stage of absolute dependency, a self-defense in the form of a *caretaker self* may develop (Winnicott, 1960b; 1965a; 1971a). If the mother cannot 'comprehend' the infant through her gestures, he will be forced into compliance, alien to his true self. The infant may be taught to say 'ta' (colloquial English for thanks) but this will not bring with it the experience of gratitude (Winnicott, 1965b, p. 149). As the mother's gestures do not 'give meaning' to the infant's reactions, symbolic communication cannot be said to develop between them. The infant, and then the child, will have the capacity to 'go through the motions' of interpersonal relationships, but these encounters will be with the *false self*, which will serve to hide the true self (Winnicott, 1965b).

According to Winnicott (1965a) when impingements continue despite persistence by the infant, a number of reactions can arise: the self may be overwhelmed, it may anxiously anticipate further impingement, it may feel real only when in opposition to impingements, or finally it can acquiesce and hide its own gestures. In this latter case, Winnicott assumed that the self ends up mimicking its caretaking environment, resigned to the deficiency, setting aside creative gestures and perhaps forgetting they ever existed. Winnicott suggested that the infant compliantly relates to the caregiver's gestures as if they were his own, and this lies at the root of the *false self-structure*. The false self is marked by lack of spontaneity or originality. It follows from how false self-structure originates that such individuals later seek further impingements to recreate the experience of compliant relating and, with it, a sense of realness about their own existence.

Winnicott described how the false self may sometimes set itself up as real and generally convey this impression to others, but does so mechanically, lacking genuine links between internal states and actions. A self whose own creative gestures have not been recognized is an empty self which will either remain in archaic merger with the early object or look for powerful others to merge with, to fill itself with borrowed strength or ideals. Only when challenged by the need to act spontaneously as a whole person, particularly in intense relationships, will the limitations become evident. Change in these cases comes about when interactions, such as with the analyst, convince the hidden true self that its creative gestures will be permitted and its sense of existence affirmed within that relationship.

There may have been selectiveness in the response of the caregiver to specific aspects of the self. People whose identity is vested in intellectual functioning may have experienced environments which narrowly affirmed this area. A false self which organizes such a mind would be characterized by hard work leading to recognition, but might not own and enjoy success since this does not match the empty true self, split off from its intellectual functioning. A similar, partial false self-structure may arise when there is a wholesale identification with the object at the expense of the child's own creative solutions. This extreme conformity might break down when the person is separated from his context by, for instance, emigration, or family separation; all these stress the person's capacity for creative emotional solutions.

The false self serves to hide, and thus protect, the true self. The true self may emerge only in physical or psychological illness, where the pain associated with the original experience of impingement is recreated. Symptom formation may express the true self because historically this was how it could exist without being overwhelmed by the environment, while having creative gestures replaced or ignored. The false self seeks possible ways to express true experience. If it sees no opportunity for this without the danger of further exploitation, it may resort to the extreme gesture of suicide or some less direct form of self-destruction to protect the true self.

Winnicott also identified the kind of self which appears to be real, but is built on identification with early objects and thus lacks something uniquely its own. A similar type may be found amongst those who idealize their autonomy but the very exaggeration and rigidity of their self-sufficiency belies it. Yet others achieve an appearance of true self through a display of apparent connectedness with the other. But as the price of such connectedness is a submersion or enmeshment, where self and non-self are no longer clearly delineated; again we can see this as a manifestation of an inauthentic structure.

Winnicott added to our understanding of environmental influence, in distinguishing between deprivation and privation (Winnicott, 1963e; 1963f). Privation can only be experienced while the infant does not have an awareness of maternal care, in the phase of absolute dependence. Deprivation can only occur in the state of relative independence, once the baby is sufficiently aware of both his own needs and the object that he can perceive a need as unmet, or the other's care being lost (Winnicott, 1952). This distinction helps us to understand antisocial behavior where, in Winnicott's formulation, a certain degree of integration within the self has taken place but deprivation is sufficiently severe and chronic for the representation of the good-enough environment to be compromised (Winnicott, 1956a). In these cases there is no active discouragement of the expression of the true self, rather the child cannot cope with the failure or withdrawal of ego support and antisocial tendency develops to protect his sense of self.

Capacity for concern is limited because the self is reorganized at a more primitive level. Within Winnicott's model, the capacity for concern is achieved only toward the end of the second year of life when constructive and creative experiences of reparation lead the child to feel responsibility. Once concern has been established, the child can use constructive elements of his aggression in the service of work and play.

Khan (1963; 1974) helpfully elaborated the concept of trauma in the mother–infant relationship. He points out that single experiences are less 'traumatic' than repeated breaches in the protective shield provided by the mother from childhood to adolescence. These have the quality of strains, which do not so much distort the development of the ego as cumulatively create a vulnerability that weakens these individuals' capacities to cope with crises in adult life. This formulation is the converse of the modern under-standing of resilience developed within a secure and understanding infant–mother relationship (Fonagy et al., 1994).

Many psychoanalysts in North America, working with similar clinical problems to those encountered by Winnicott and other British Independent theorists, were profoundly influenced by their ideas. Modell (1975) attempted to integrate Winnicott's and Fairbairn's new ideas with ego psychology. He suggested that two classes of instincts should be considered: id instincts (libidinal and aggressive) and the newly recognized object-relations instincts. The latter might be considered the instincts of the ego, with no physiological basis, characterized by processes of interaction rather than discharge. They are gratified externally, by 'a fitting in of specific responses from other persons'. Modell (1975) suggests that 'affects are essen-tially object seeking'. Object relations provide a context in which the developing ego can master id instincts mainly by identification with good objects. Modell (1975) saw failure to tame the id as the major route to pathology, particularly to the failure to develop a coherent sense of self. The sense of disintegration is not a result of the intensity of the instincts; rather, id instincts are experienced more intensely by individuals with an incoherent sense of self, as are all anxiety provoking experiences which bring the non-cohesive self to the foreground. Unlike British theorists, Modell (1985) saw object relations theory as relevant only for a restricted group of patients, those with narcissistic personality problems (Modell, 1976).

The Independent tradition has a number of important modern champions, but interestingly few of these contributors have taken on Winnicott's developmental approach. Much of this work is summarized by Rayner (1991), and an important collection of Independent papers has been edited by Kohon (1986). Rayner (1991) summarizes the key aspects of the Independents' contributions under several headings. First, the conceptual importance of affects and their symbolization, as the central units of psychoanalysis were emphasized by both Pearl King (1978) and Adam Limentani (1977). Affects are seen as preliminary stages of deep thinking processes, where the emergence of symbolization of affects is seen as a vital aspect of healthy development (Rycroft, 1979). Milner (1969) explored artistic creativity as the symbolization of complex feeling states. A number of Independents have addressed the dialectic movement between merger and self–other differentiation, rooted in Winnicott's idea of transitional states, but possibly most thought-provokingly addressed in Matte Blanco's idea of symmetrization or homogenization. The central, and original, idea is the movement between separateness and unity (Matte Blanco, 1988). A key addition to classical Independent theory is the recognition of the formative aspects of late as well as early environment in the development of the self (Khan, 1963): the psychic structure is not completed in infancy.

7.2 British Independent contributions to developmental psychopathology

7.2.1 General views of psychopathology

Fairbairn's key contribution is the proposition that an early trauma of great severity is stored in memories which are 'frozen' or dissociated from a person's central ego or functional self (Fairbairn, 1944). This idea goes beyond the classical psychoanalytic notion of repression in the development of psychopathology. The classical model of pathogenesis (conflict → repression → reactivation of conflict → neurotic compromise) is still seen to apply to conflicts arising at the oedipal (3–4 year) level. The British Independents' models applies to disorders of the self, thought to arise out of traumatic events before that age. Although they apply particularly to narcissistic and borderline personality disorders, the notion of multiple self-representations is of more general importance. For example, the Independent approach to dream interpretation differs from the classical position, in that it sees dreams as communication patterns between different parts of the self (see Rycroft, 1966; 1979; Bollas, 1987).

Fairbairn illustrates the object relations view with a case of a woman suffering from nausea. The case reveals that the symptom was related to ideas about fellatio with the father, but it was also linked to the 'emotional badness' of the person of the father and the patient's wish to be rid of this view of him. The emphasis is on the explanatory power of the 'intentional stance' or whole person motive (Brentano, 1924). The explicit search for bodily sexual gratification may often be a pathological substitute for intimacy with a whole person, which feels inaccessible.

Fairbairn (1952a) sees the schizoid reaction of withdrawal from and primitive defense against the trauma of not being intimately known or loved as fundamental to all pathology. The environmental failure (the mother is unloving and the child's love for her is not recognized) leads the child to believe that his hate has destroyed the object. Note that for Melanie Klein the hate was primary and real, not secondary and assumed. Conversely, 'actual' early environmental failure and the need for therapeutic reconstruction is the focus of Fairbairn's, but not Melanie Klein's account (Padel, 1972).

Anxiety, like all pathological states, is rooted in the conflicts over infantile dependence. The regressive wish to be dependent carries with it the threat of loss of identity. The progressive goal of separation creates fear of being isolated and unsupported. Although a retreat to the home base might offer short-term relief, eventually it re-presents the anxiety over engulfment and loss of identity, and thus the conflict.

7.2.2 Schizoid and antisocial personality disorder

Winnicott (1965b) associated schizophrenia with total privation, that is the complete absence of good enough mothering, whereas severe personality disorder could be seen as the result of having had a 'good enough mother' who had been lost, and thus feeling forever deprived. Fairbairn (1954) agreed in seeing schizophrenia as characterized by complete maternal withdrawal leading to profound deprivation. It is assumed that the experience of privation makes the infant view his love as bad and destructive. This in turn makes him withdraw from emotional contact with the outer world, and ultimately creates a highly disturbed sense of external reality. Building on Wilfred Bion's ideas (Bion, 1955, 1962a), Rosenfeld (1965) argued that children who develop schizophrenia experience their mothers as having diminished tolerance of the projections of these infants. The mothers feel disturbed and persecuted and withdraw their feelings from the children.

Schizoid personality (Fairbairn, 1940; 1952a) arises out of the baby's feeling that love for the mother is destructive of her and therefore has to be inhibited along with all intimacy. In schizoid states, the ego is so split that the individual may be mystified about himself and is transiently disturbed about reality (finding the familiar in the unfamiliar and vice versa). These individuals resist perceiving others as whole persons and substitute bodily for emotional contacts. They hide their love and to protect themselves from others' love, they erect barriers, seeming indifferent, rude or even hateful. Intimate relationships can only be maintained by keeping part of the self uninvolved. Often, since the enjoyment of love is forbidden, they may give themselves over to the pleasure of hating and destruction. Fairbairn (1952a) differentiates depressive disorder from schizoid conditions in that it derives from later in infancy, and is rooted in the infant's feeling that his aggression was destructive toward the object and has to be defended against (e.g. turned against the self).

Winnicott (1960a) uses his formulation of the false self to elaborate a theory of antisocial behavior, particularly in children (Winnicott, 1956a). His framework differentiates two categories of reactions to environmental failure. On the one hand, internal and external impingements and the lack of a holding environment can lead to unfettered aggression, and antisocial behavior in which physical action discharges self-experience, a lack of concern for the other and a definition of the self in opposition to the environment. On the other hand, external impingements and the substitution of the gestures of the other for the gestures of the self engenders a false-self structure which performs and complies, may be true in highly selected aspects or based on wholesale identification with the object, but in either case, while superficially convincing, the self presented is fragile, vulnerable and phenomenologically empty. According to Winnicott, antisocial behavior begins due to the environment's failure to adjust to the child, but its continuation is ensured by its essentially 'reparative' function; it is an expression of hope, an attempt by the child to restore his situation to a pre-traumatic one. The child may steal to repossess love. For example, Winnicott (1963f) reported a case of an eight-year-old boy who had been caught stealing; Winnicott interpreted that he was searching for his 'good mother' from the time before she gave birth to his younger brother. The interpretation led to the end of the delinquent behavior.

With development, the original symbolic meaning of the antisocial act is lost and it is replaced by secondary gain (economic gain from stolen goods replaces the symbolic possession of love). In the case of destructive behavior, 'the child is seeking that amount of environmental stability which will stand the strain resulting from impulsive behavior' (p. 310).

Winnicott (1965a; 1967a) viewed the schizoid personality as a variety of 'false-self' organization. Beyond the over-compliant self lie deep anxieties about the cohesiveness of the self, a loss of relationship to the body and an absence of orientation. Winnicott (1965b, pp. 142–3) gives a sophisticated account of the concept of falseness in self-presentation, and does not see the false self as invariably pathological; in fact it may be an essential aspect of social adaptation, especially in a British culture. At the extreme, it is (like Fairbairn's picture of schizoid personality) only functional outside of intimate relationships, and when called upon within such relationships (for example, by an intensive psychotherapeutic encounter) it may 'break down', leaving an infantile and poorly developed sense of 'true self' unprotected. The 'false self' provides a mask behind which the 'true self' can secretly search for actualization. If the false self is challenged, suicide, the total destruction of the person, may be the only means left for the false self to protect the true self from annihilation.

Guntrip (1969) suggested that the propensity of schizoid individuals to withdraw from external relationships was rooted in early trauma from a hostile object or object hunger of such intensity that it is feared as devouring. Khan (1963; 1974) put forward a developmental model based on the notions of cumulative trauma from a mother failing in her protective function, and 'symbiotic omnipotence', whereby the mother through collusion maintains an exclusive closeness to the child, which actively discourages involvement with other objects. Khan also made a significant contribution to integrating Fairbairn's and Winnicott's views of this form of severe personality disturbance (Khan, 1974). His description of schizoid personality is very similar to Kernberg's structural theory based description in that it stresses poor affect tolerance, impulse control and failure to integrate aggression as its central features (Khan, 1963). Khan (1966) also goes further, identifying schizoid aspects of disorders which had classically been regarded as neurotic. For example, he describes phobias as the continued desire to cling to primary internal object representations, and argues that it is not the danger but the safety aspect of phobias which is critical – a formulation which is remarkably like certain behavioral formulations of agoraphobia (Rachman, 1984).

Christopher Bollas (1987; 1989) has described a number of character types, building on the work on Winnicott, Khan and others. An interesting example is the 'normotic' character who is abnormally normal, using a kind of manic defense to exclude inner life and emotional states, retaining an orientation exclusively to external reality. Bollas links this form of character to the 'anti-analysand' described by Joyce McDougall (1986).

7.2.3 Borderline personality disorder

Balint's (1968) notion of 'the basic fault' is important to the understanding of borderline psychopathology. He drew attention to the predominance of two- as opposed to three-person relationships, qualitative differences in the experience of oedipal feelings, the absence of conflict and the idiosyncratic use of language in borderline patients.

Winnicott did not put forward a comprehensive system of psychopathology but his view of psychopathology followed his developmental ideas so closely that it is almost possible to interchange his use of the words *patient* and *baby*. Impingements from an unfacilitating environment were thought to cause arrests in the maturational process. Premature awareness of the self–other distinction results in the eruption of annihilation anxiety, an 'unimaginable terror' or fear of falling apart (Winnicott, 1952). It should be noted that while in the context of theories closer to the Freudian paradigm these experiences would be seen as causing frustration and the stimulation of aggression, within the British Independent school the principal consequence is seen as a primitive anxiety that antedates the anxiety concerning death (Winnicott, 1956c, p. 303). The only modes of defense against these primitive anxieties are omnipotent fantasies which, once created, cannot be relinquished readily. The child will be forced to integrate all aspects of reality with these fantasies, reality will be brought into the sphere of omnipotence, and these are the developmental origins (according to Winnicott) of psychotic phenomena. Winnicott rejected the possibility of constitutional factors in psychosis. Since all states of frustration or tension may trigger annihilation anxiety, all disappointment must be magically relieved, fixating the personality at the level of magical thought. All reality that could pierce this fragile defense must then be brought into the sphere of omnipotence but this at the same time drives the child gradually closer and closer to frank psychosis (Winnicott, 1960c).

Winnicott considers borderline patients to have psychotic needs because they rely on omnipotent defenses to protect against annihilation anxiety. States of derealization or depersonalization similarly originate from the phase of absolute dependence and the absence of a definite sense of internal experience as belonging to oneself (Winnicott, 1962a). If the self is completely unintegrated, the likelihood of psychotic outcome is great. This would be the case if the impingement were severe. However, the clinical picture Winnicott describes in cases where a degree of integration was achieved and the omnipotent defense is stable, resembles borderline and narcissistic personality disorders (Winnicott, 1960c). Winnicott notes that these patients have no sense of others, including the therapist, having a life of their own. Their omnipotence is clear in their demand for the therapist to bring them home, offer them special fees, extra appointments, etc. They have no awareness that the other is separate and consequently feel no guilt if and when their anger or their rage injures. They may respond with violence or intense anger to threats to their omnipotence but appear to feel no remorse because they are fixed at a developmental phase prior to one where awareness of the other had a chance to develop. Winnicott's rationale for therapeutic intervention with such disturbances is for the therapist to assess the point of developmental arrest in such patients, to make an adaptation for the arrested need (Winnicott, 1959). Interpretations are frequently inadequate to this task. These are effective only when adapted to the patient's need. Thus, for example, interpretations might work by making patients feel that the analyst has the patient as the object of his concern (Winnicott, 1963b). Winnicott also identified that the therapist's failure of adaptation was not necessarily a disaster but also could be an opportunity for the patient to see, even if only briefly, that the therapist was not under the patient's omnipotent control (Winnicott, 1963c). Although rarely acknowledged, this insight of Winnicott's antedates a burgeoning literature on the paradoxical therapeutic properties of ruptures in the therapeutic alliance (Safran et al., 1990). In order for this process to occur, an unequivocal acknowledgement of failure on the part of the therapist is essential.

Winnicott sees certain behaviors that are typical of borderline cases in the context of deprivation rather than privation. For example, he sees problems of addiction to food, drugs, alcohol or sexual promiscuity as representing the mother and yet recognized by the addict as not being the mother. Similarly, Winnicott explains the need for the physical presence of the object as a result of impingement during the phase of dependence on a mother who is unable to shift from near-absolute adaptation to the lesser degree of adaptation necessary to help the baby to move into the next developmental phase (Winnicott, 1960b). The infant is sure enough of his internal experience to feel alive and whole in the mother's presence but not in her absence. Such individuals need to learn to be alone in the presence of the therapist (Winnicott, 1958a), as they were denied this essential experience and now often deny it to themselves. In such cases as these, Winnicott recommends the therapist should often allow the patient not to talk, not asking questions. By placing himself in the role of a transitional object, the therapist unblocks an arrested maturational process. The patient's expectations of special treatment are seen as an effort to lay claim to an object that was once possessed but has now been lost (Winnicott, 1963d). Winnicott recognizes that the borderline patient lives in an intermediate area of infancy, moving between merger and separation, absolute dependence and relative dependence. In this context Winnicott sees the setting of limits, as recommended, for example, by Kernberg (see Chapter 8), as anti-therapeutic in that the patient's desperate attempt to signal a need for help is quashed. Similarly, interpretations are de-emphasized; to the extent that they are part of the work, they concern the patient's unconscious object seeking and his or her use of objects. More importantly, the therapeutic space is used for the creation of transitional objects (Winnicott, 1971a).

Winnicott's ideas on borderline personality disorder were fragmented, described piecemeal rather than as a coherent set of propositions. André Green (1978) acknowledged Winnicott's contribution as being critical in making psychoanalysis relevant to borderline phenomena. Green (discussed already in the previous chapter) elucidated Winnicott's ideas suggesting that severe character pathology is associated with an arrest in the transitional phase, between the delusion of the 'subjective object' and the recognition of objective reality (Green, 1975). Green recognizes Winnicott's contribution in moving the analyst from a position of passive observer to 'an analytic object'. The analyst as new object was notable in the work of Hans Loewald (see Chapter 3). Green's formulation of borderline personality disorder is as an absence (Green, 1977), a lack of object representation resulting in a blankness. Green importantly asserts that the transference cannot be regarded as a repetition of early object relations with borderline individuals, but rather the absence needs to be transformed into a potentiality by the creation of an analytic object. The therapeutic challenge is in translating the language of action and somatization into words (Green, 1975). A similar suggestion was made by Margaret Little, an analysand of Winnicott's who suggested that borderline patients existed on an action level and therefore had to act because their somatic existence is disconnected from the linguistic or psychological level (Little, 1981). Earlier Masud Khan (1971) insisted that the borderline patient is unable to use the transitional space between reality and fantasy where cure by language can take place. They have to be helped to gain the ability to use analytic space through symbolic discourse rather than infusing it with action.

Modell (1963), following Winnicott's work in North America, suggested that borderline patients see their objects as having no independent psychological existence. Representations of real figures were irretrievably contaminated with mental processes subserving the self and came to be unduly influenced by 'processes arising within the individual' (p. 185). Modell (1963; 1968) was the first to describe this as the *transitional relatedness* of borderline patients. This refers to the use the infant makes of inanimate objects to obtain comfort in mother's absence. Borderline individuals frequently make use of inanimate objects in their adult lives to serve this purpose. Even more striking is their use of other people as if they were inanimate to serve a self-regulating, soothing function; used, as a toddler uses a teddy bear, in primitive, demanding and tenacious ways. Searles (1986) and Giovacchini (1987) see this as an indication that borderline patients may have been treated as transitional objects by their parents. Modell (1968) sees the borderline individual's image of himself as divided into a helpless infant and someone who is omnipotently giving or destructive. The lack of stability of their self and object representation leaves them with a 'harrowing dilemma' (p. 286) between extreme dependence and a terror of closeness.

In understanding narcissistic personality disorder, Modell (1975; 1984) used Winnicott's concept of mirroring, suggesting that narcissistic individuals have been traumatized by parents who fail in mirroring and validating their experience. He assumed that such children were frequently precocious in development and perceived that their parents had inadequate capacities for reality testing. They fall back on a compensatory self-structure in order to bypass having to rely on inadequate caregivers. Although in this way they are no longer dependent on parental figures whom they experience as unable to facilitate their development and they achieve a certain degree of reality testing for themselves, their 'self-sufficiency' is illusory and their autonomy is unreal. Psychoanalysis tackles this defensively invoked self-sufficiency in order to overcome it.

7.3 Evidence consistent and inconsistent with the 'Winnicottian' model of development and psychopathology

There is a remarkable correspondence between the personality types identified in Balint's model of ocnophilic and philobatic defenses and more recent empirical work on the typology of internal representational models of adult relationship patterns. This work emerged out of attachment theory (see Chapter 10), more specifically work with the Adult Attachment Interview (George, Kaplan and Main, 1985). The interview is designed to elicit the individual's account of his or her childhood attachment and separation experiences, and evaluations of the effects of those experiences on present functioning. Ratings of emotional and cognitive features of the individual's representational world as revealed in the transcripts constitute the basis of a four-way classification scheme (Main and Goldwyn, 1990; Bakermans-Kranenburg and van IJzendoorn, 1993;). (This is intended to represent adult correlates of the well-known four-way typology A/B/C/D of infant-caregiver attachments (after Ainsworth et al., 1978; Main and Solomon, 1986; Main and Hesse, 1990a).)

Secure ('F') individuals are neither ocnophilic or philobatic and are able to describe both pleasant and painful aspects of their lives without defensiveness, in a coherent manner which neither minimizes nor maximizes the emotional qualities and consequences of past relationship experiences. The *insecure-preoccupied* ('E') group appear to be entangled in their past experiences with attachment figures as ocnophilic individuals might be expected to be. By contrast the *'insecure-dismissing'* ('D') group may be described as philobats in that the typical interview is characterized by limited recall and a highly restricted range of affective responses to attachment experiences, denigration of past relationships and idealization of independence. The attachment theory categorization cannot verify Balint's classification, but it is interesting that the robust and valid attachment typology appears to overlap with Balint's tentative suggestions about the intrapsychic organization of relationship patterns.

Winnicott's dialectic view of the human infant was contrary to Freud's view that the infant begins life unable to differentiate self from the environment (Freud, 1911a). There is considerable contemporary support for Winnicott's perspective, with contemporary research offering plenty of evidence that the baby perceives himself as a separate physical entity moving in space among other physical objects (e.g. Neisser, 1995). Evidence from studies of visuospatial self-awareness demonstrate that infants from at least two months can use visual proprioceptive feedback to control their head posture, showing compensatory head movements when perceiving an object on a collision course (Dunkeld and Bower, 1980). John Watson proposed that the human infant is sensitive to aspects of the environment that are in perfect contingency with its motor responses because its motor responses naturally generate stimuli that are perfectly contingent (Watson, 1991, 1994). Contingency detection is thus self-detection, at least for the first months. In a classic study, three-month-old infants were shown to manifest preferential looking at a video monitor displaying the movements of their own legs while five-month-olds showed a preference for the monitor displaying non-contingent leg movements (Bahrick and Watson, 1985). This initial attention bias is consistent with the need for the infant to develop a primary representation of the bodily self (Watson, 1995). But this line of research has also provided consistent support for Winnicott's (1960b; 1962b) view, that a key feature of the infant's experience of his social world is his sense of control over the caregiver's contingent responses (Watson, 1972; Trevarthen, 1977; 1990). Two-month-olds can detect that their body's actions are capable of exercising control over aspects of the external world, such as the movement of a mobile, and will smile and coo when the contingently moving object is presented (Watson, 1972; Lewis, Allessandri and Sullivan, 1990). Whether infants have the fantasy that they 'create' mother or not, their sensitivity to aspects of the world that are contingent with their actions is consistent with Winnicott's speculations. It seems that infants are biologically prepared to attend to environmental events that respond to them, representing a biological path to social interactions in the course of which the infant can be reflected as a mental entity.

Also in line with Winnicott's assumptions about development is a large body of evidence that infants from the earliest orient actively toward people in general and facial displays capable of mirroring their internal states in particular. Thus they show neonatal imitation of facial gestures (Meltzoff and Moore, 1997). Infants are far from passive in the complex social exchanges between mother and child. The infant tries to ensure that mother maintains her interaction with him, to decrease the frequency of non-responsive or aversive gestures and to increase instances where she imitates his actions (e.g. Beebe, Lachmann, and Jaffe, 1997). There is general agreement that young infants engage in bi-directional affective interactions with their caregivers that are characterized by a 'protoconversational' structure including turn-taking. Gianino and Tronick (1988) have referred to the reciprocal pursuit of social aims as 'a mutual regulation model' (p. 47). The dominant biosocial view holds that mother and infant from the first months form an affective communicational system. For example, high correlations and contingencies have been demonstrated between maternal positive emotional expressions and infant social engagement (Cohn and Tronick, 1988). A great deal in this literature is consistent with Winnicott's claim that 'there is no such thing as a baby', only a dual unit of infant and mother where, for example, the mother and the infant mutually create the infant's moods (Tronick, 2001). The infant is thought to monitor and process the mother's affect to generate his or her own affective state which in turn, through a more complex representational structure, triggers mood states in the mother.

There has been considerable empirical research on the concept of transitional objects. The pervasiveness of comforting objects is well demonstrated, but there is no convincing evidence that the presence or absence of these implies either mental health or illness (Schaffer and Emerson, 1964; Ekecrantz and Rudhe, 1972; Sherman et al., 1981; Newson, Newson and Mahalski, 1982; Horton and Gewirtz, 1988). However, Free (1988) demonstrated that adolescents who recalled having a transitional object in childhood and those who currently used one were more likely to engage in creative activities such as dancing, poetry, etc.

Winnicott's views on the importance of sensitive maternal care in general and mirroring in particular are broadly supported by developmental research. For example, maternal sensitivity has been assessed in a wide variety of ways and found to be generally significantly correlated with good outcomes in relation to attachment security and other variables (Susman-Stillman et al., 1996; De Wolff and van IJzendoorn, 1997). More powerful support is provided by data that underscore the inherent limitations to maternal sensitivity consistent with Winnicott's 'good-enough' concept. While it is true that early caretaking tends to be prodigious in the service of the infant, the immaturity of the infant's resources and the magnitude of his needs outstrip even the most attentive provisions (Tronick and Cohn, 1989). Tronick and Cohn (1989) demonstrate that for a significant portion of time, infants experience negative affects, and that positive emotions such as joy are experienced a minority of the time. As we have seen, Winnicott does not assume that even early infancy is an idyllic era. He stated that the mother has to be 'good-enough', but that some failure is inevitable and motivates growth. Gianino and Tronick (Gianino and Tronick, 1988) found that the ratio of 'miscoordinated' states to coordinated, synchronous or matched interchanges between infant and mother is 70 to 30. Malatesta et al. (1989) report that moderate degrees of maternal involvement are preferable to high contingent responses. Research supports Winnicott's view that a moderate level of acceptance (Murphy and Moriarity, 1975) and maternal involvement (Belsky et al., 1984; Grolnick, Frodi and Bridges, 1984) is more beneficial to growth than perfect matching. Research has demonstrated that the infant may be more active in the process of repair than Winnicott perhaps assumed. Demos (1989) describes affective sequences of infant–mother interactions in the Boston University longitudinal study in which relations are at first good, then disrupted, and then followed by joint reparative actions in which the infant and caregiver restore good relations: 'The child learns that positive affect can be reliably re-established, that negative affect can be reliably endured or managed or gotten over, and that the child itself can be an active agent in causing things to happen' (Demos, 1989, p. 17).

Research in many respects supports Winnicott's assumptions concerning the traumatic effects of early maternal failure. Low levels of parental warmth and support, as well as parental rejection and hostility and family conflict, are known to be associated with depression in children and adolescents (e.g. McCauley, Pavidis and Kendall, 2000). Longitudinal research designs demonstrate the predictive power of observed parental characteristics such as hostility and low warmth on later depression even when levels of depression at the beginning of the observational study are controlled for (e.g. Ge, Best, Conger and Simons, 1996). Perhaps of special relevance to Winnicott are the negative consequences of maternal depression (Cummings and Davies, 1994). It has been evident for some time that the children of depressed parents are at increased risk for the development of psychopathology (Beardslee et al., 1983; Orvaschel, 1983; Welsh-Allis and Ye, 1988), particularly behavioral problems (Downey and Coyne, 1990; Fendrich, Warner and Weissman, 1990). Abnormalities in the infants appear early and manifest as difficult temperaments – exhibited as social unresponsiveness, low activity, excessive emotion, irritability and hypersensitivity (Sameroff, Seifer and Zax, 1982, Field, 1992; Murray and Cooper, 1997). Although it is possible that elevated risk for psychopathology and infant behavioral abnormalities are due to genetic factors (e.g. Kashani et al., 1981; Nolen-Hoeksema, 1987), or pre-natal or perinatal correlates of maternal depression such as elevated inter-uterine hormones, alcoholism or drug abuse (Zuckerman and Beardslee, 1987; Dodge, 1990; Field et al., 1990; Fergusson, Lynskey and Horwood, 1993), ample evidence suggests that less than optimal patterns of parent–child relations associated with maternal depression represent an important pathogen (Teti, Gelfand and Isabella, 1995; Lyons-Ruth et al., 1986; Tronick and Gianino, 1986). Laboratory studies of face-to-face interactions, involving simulated depressive behavior (negativity, intrusiveness and withdrawal) have been shown to elicit infant responses of anger, reduced activity, dysphoria and social withdrawal (Cohn and Tronick, 1983; Zekoski, O'Hara and Wils, 1987;

Field et al., 1990; Cohn and Campbell, 1992). Prolonged exposure to this pattern of interaction has been linked with the development of depressive behavioral styles observed in contexts outside mother–infant interactions (Field et al., 1988; Cohn, Campbell, Matias and Hopkins, 1990).

Insensitive parental behavior induces anger, distress, high activity, physiological arousal and other indicators of affective dysregulation (Field, 1987a; 1987b), Tronick (1989) speculates that parental insensitivity interferes with the child's emerging capacities to regulate emotion and arousal. Field (1989) demonstrated a relationship between maternal depression, aversive mother–child interactions in the infant's sympathetic arousal and lowered vagal tone, a finding which is consistent with the assumption that the infant's arousal system may become sensitized to all potentially stressful or challenging social impingements (see Cummings and Cicchetti, 1990; Cummings and Zahn-Waxler, 1992). Tronick and Gianino (1986) suggest that children of depressed parents may resort to social withdrawal to avoid the aversive state of dysregulation associated with insensitive or unresponsive parenting. These findings are consistent with Winnicott's identification of the incomprehensible caregiver who impinges on the child as the cause of later disturbance (Winnicott, 1960b; 1962a). More sophisticated developmental research, however, has revealed how early childhood development involves very different phases, with very distinct developmental needs from relationships (see Chapter 12 and 13).

Research does not, however, support Winnicott's exclusive concern with the infant–mother relationship. While there is good evidence that low levels of parental warmth and support, as well as parental rejection, hostility and family conflict are associated with a range of psychological problems in children (Ge, Conger and Simmons, 1996; Sheeber, Hops, Alpert et al., 1997), the evidence does not support the privileging of the mother–child relationship (see for example McCauley, Pavidis and Kendall, 2000 for research on childhood depression). Winnicott's assumption that the relationship between infant and mother provided the basis for all serious mental disorder flies in the face of accumulating evidence for the importance of genetic factors (Rutter, Silberg, O'Connor and Simonoff, 1999a; 1999b). While the data from behavior genetics studies should be considered in relation to all psychoanalytic theories (as well as other theories focused on early socialization), we shall consider these data here because Winnicott's description of the potential toxicities in the infant's psychosocial environment was highly influential. We shall return to the more general implications of behavior genetics for psychoanalysis in the final chapter of this book. There is very limited evidence that might unequivocally link early relationship experiences to the development of psychopathology. Most observed associations between parenting and disorder can be reinterpreted in terms of reverse causality: the child's disorder causes family dysfunction rather than the other way around. For example, hostile and critical parental attitudes, which we noted above are often associated with depression or conduct problems in longitudinal studies, are more commonly observed in children who have suffered from a psychological disorder for longer (Hooley and Richters, 1995), suggesting that the parents' exposure to psychopathology increases the likelihood of parental criticism, rather than the other way around.

Correlations between characteristics of early parenting and later child behavior, even in prospective studies, can be reinterpreted in a model in which the child's genetic characteristics are seen as determining the parent's response, rather than assuming that parenting influences the child. For example, the observed associations between parenting sensitivity and attachment classification may be driven by the behavior of the child and accounted for by the child's genetically determined predispositions (the so-called child to parent effects). It is also interesting that aspects of a family's experience of its own interactions are genetically determined. Thus, according to the findings of the Colorado Adoption Project, the parents' report of warmth and negativity in the family and the child's report of achievement orientation appear to be genetically determined, suggesting that aspects of the family environment are susceptible to the influence of the child's genetically rooted characteristics (Deater-Deckard, Fulker and Plomin, 1999). Parental warmth is influenced by the parents' genetic endowment, thus the association between warmth and lack of pathology may well be spurious (Losoya, Callor, Rowe and Goldsmith, 1997).

The relative contributions of genes and environment are estimated by examining the observed correlation between two siblings with the correlation that would be expected on the basis of the degree of genetic material the two have in common. Thus MZ twins who share all genetic material should resemble each other (correlate on a trait) about twice as much as DZ twins. Behavior genetic models of twin and adoption studies partition variability into genetic and environmental components by subtracting the proportion of variability on a specific trait accounted for by shared genes (h^2) from 100 ($E = 100 - h^2$). In most domains h^2 is 50–60% with less than half left to E. Two large-scale, high-quality, community-based studies, the Virginia Twin Study (Eaves et al., 1997; Hewitt et al., 1997) and the Non-shared Environment and Adolescent Development (NEAD) project (Reiss et al., 1995) have confirmed that most types of childhood psychopathology have quite substantial genetic components. For example, heritability estimates for ADHD range from 54% to 82% (Smalley, 1997; Nigg and Goldsmith, 1998). More or less the only psychological disorder of childhood with a negligible genetic component is separation anxiety (Topolski et al., 1997). Even for this disorder, heritability estimates for girls are substantial (31–74%), the low figures come from boys (0–19%).

Behavior genetics research revealed that influences that had previously been considered environmental were actually genetically mediated (Kendler et al., 1996). Apparently environmentally mediated family influences, such as children who are read to learning to read sooner than those who are not read to, are in fact mostly mediated by the shared genetic predisposition of caregiver and offspring, and are therefore in themselves unimportant (Rowe, 1994; Harris, 1998). In so far as behavior genetic studies showed family environment to matter, it was environment specific to each child within the same family (non-shared environment) that mattered (Plomin and Daniels, 1987). Environment may be partitioned into a shared and a non-shared component. If the trait under scrutiny has a shared environmental component, then both MZ and DZ twins would be significantly correlated on the trait, while if non-shared environmental factors are involved, then the siblings should not be correlated. Shared environmental influences may be estimated in adoption studies by comparing the correlation of adopted children and their adopted siblings with children in other households. If shared aspects of the environment such as parenting were indeed formative, then adopted siblings living in the same home should be significantly more alike than unrelated children across households. After the genetic and shared environmental components are estimated, what remains is the non-shared environment ($E_{us} = 100 - h^2 - E_s$). The non-shared environment appears to be the bulk of the environmental component – shared environment, an instance of which would be parental sensitivity, accounts for almost no variance (Plomin, 1994). Adopted children, it seems, are no more like their adopted siblings than unrelated children growing up in a different household (Plomin and Bergeman, 1991). Such findings are particularly striking in the case of twin studies where there are in-built controls for age, gender, temperament and birth order. This is important because the relatively weak observed effects of the shared environment have been used to suggest that environments generally assumed to be toxic by developmental psychopathology (such as high level of parental conflict, divorce, inconsistent discipline, parental psychiatric disturbance, multiple moves, death of the parent or even relative social disadvantage and neighborhood effects) are either of less importance than previously thought, or, more likely, are actually genetically mediated (Plomin, Chipuer and Neiderhiser, 1994). Plomin (1994) put this quite elegantly:

> So often we have assumed that the key influences on children's development are shared: their parents' personality and childhood experiences, the quality of their parents' marriage relationship, childrens' educational background, the neighbourhood in which they grow up, and their parents' attitude to school or to discipline. Yet to the extent that these influences are shared, they cannot account for the differences we observe in children's outcomes. (p. 23)

More or less the only disorders with a substantial shared environmental component are oppositional defiant disorder and conduct disorder (Thapar and McGuffin, 1996; Goldsmith, Buss and Lemery, 1997).

It has been argued that even non-shared environmental effects may be better understood as genetic in origin. Genetically influenced aspects of children's behavior may be responsible for provoking specific observed responses in parents and other people. This is sometimes termed evocative co-variance, when children with different genetic predispositions elicit complementary responses from the caregiver. Thus, the child's non-shared (specific) environment may have sometimes been erroneously attributed to parental behavior rather than to his or her genes (O'Connor, Deater-Deckard, Fulker et al., 1998). As much as 20% of the variability in how parents treat adolescents may be due to the genetic characteristics of the adolescent (O'Connor et al., 1995). There is evidence, for example, from studies of adopted children that authoritarian parenting may be elicited by the child's resistive or distractible behavior (Ge et al., 1996). The celebrated results of the NEAD study, showing that adolescents who seem to get more preferentially negative treatment from the parents relative to their twin siblings are at greater risk of developing depression and antisocial symptoms, while the more positively treated siblings are actually protected from those disorders (Reiss et al., 1995; Pike, Reiss, Hetherington and Plomin, 1996), may also be an instance of a pseudo-environmental effect. The correlation between parental conflict-negativity and adolescent disorder could also be accounted for by genetic factors in the adolescent (Neiderhiser et al., 1999).

Modern reviews of the controversy (see particularly Rutter, 2000) offer more sophisticated evaluations. For example, it is now clear that so-called shared environmental effects in behavior genetics studies have been exaggerated because they are estimated simply in terms of how alike or not siblings are. The importance of the influence of factors such as maternal warmth cannot be estimated in this way because the influence impacts on different members of the family in different ways: it will appear to be a non-shared environmental influence whereas it is actually shared. Further, most studies of the influence of early environment on development are based on twin and adoptive studies that sample environments of lower than average risk (Stoolmiller, 1999). There are further technical complications. For example, many studies drawing inferences about causation have conflated non-shared environmental variance with error variance, and other studies have assumed that identical and fraternal twins have 'equal environments'. It is quite likely that the critics have exaggerated their claims but nevertheless they have provided a valid challenge to psychosocial researchers (Rutter, 1999).

To summarize, evidence suggests that Winnicott overstated the case for environmental influences on normal and pathological development. While psychoanalysts prior to Winnicott and the British Independents have been inclined to environmentalism and preferred nurture to nature explanations of pathology, the Freudian heritage was one of great respect for constitutional factors and the role of genetics, for example, in symptom choice and vulnerability to environmental stress. While never totally rejecting the role of constitutional factors, in psychosis for example, Winnicott's theory emphasized the exclusive role of the early environment to a degree that has turned out to be clearly incompatible with the behavior genetics data.

7.4 Criticism and evaluation

It is complicated to evaluate the British Independent tradition simply because the contributors to this tradition have not adhered to any single set of principles that might be considered representative of the school. Thus any generalization about the group might be countered by writings from theorists that contradict the view. Certainly the views of Fairbairn and Winnicott, while consistent in terms of epistemology and broad developmental assumptions, actually have strikingly few specific points in common. Winnicott does not appear to privilege Fairbairn in terms of his citations and rarely uses him as a starting point for his arguments. He is far more likely to cite Freud, Klein and at times even Anna Freud. In fact one interesting characteristic of the Independent group is precisely that they frequently take their opposition to a piece of Kleinian or Freudian theory or practice as their starting point. This, in large measure, is the likely reason behind the lack of theoretical coherence within the group.

In favor of the approach, the originality and the liveliness of the contributors, both past and current should be acknowledged. The Independents ploughed a unique furrow in the international psychoanalytic movement. Their innovative approach led them to play a key role in freeing psychoanalytic theory from many of its most odious historical burdens (e.g. assumptions concerning homosexuality, gender bias, the pseudo-science of psychic energy theory) and moving it into the domain of a theory of unconscious aspects of the subjectivity of social relationships. Historically then the role of the school is immense, but how much can we still learn from their contributions today? The answer of course is that it depends on the theorist. Fairbairn was perhaps the most original and innovative of the Independents, but his work is rarely cited today. Of the modern Independents the work of Patrick Casement and Christopher Bollas has undoubted international significance, but few of the other members of this numerically large school are able to live up to the giants of their tradition. The freedom the tradition allowed itself to play with ideas and modes of therapy had its downside and created a number of casualties. It is our impression that controversies concerning boundary violations and improper practice are more frequent in followers of the technical experimenters, Balint and Winnicott, than others within the other two UK traditions of psychoanalysis (the Contemporary Freudian and London Kleinian).

In evaluating the theory it is best then to pick a historically representative contributor whose work is currently most influential. Given these criteria, the focus has to be on Winnicott's work. Winnicott's theory is without doubt the most thorough and coherent theory of developmental arrest available to psychoanalysis. While other theorists frequently compromise between the conflict and the developmental arrest models of psychopathology, or fail to spell out the clinical implications of arrest models in terms of offering developmental psychotherapeutic help, or offer such help but de-emphasize the role of arrest and deficit, Winnicott had the courage of his psychoanalytic convictions. Further, Winnicott was willing to see complexities and refused to succumb to the hegemony of omnibus theories of either Kleinian or Freudian kinds. He joined the Kleinian analysts in treating patients with severe disorders but did not abandon the Freudian tradition of privileging real experience over fantasy. He made technical innovations but stayed strictly within the psychoanalytic setting. He added action to the repertoire of psychoanalysts, but avoided being tainted with the brush of Franz Alexander's controversial corrective emotional experience concept by insisting that the latter was artificial although action as recommended by him was therapeutic, precisely because it adapted to a spontaneously expressed need of the patient. The implication of this approach has been to free the therapeutic situation to become a more flexible, less rigidly defined, analytic space within which the individual may as much create as discover a new sense of self. Winnicott contributed in major ways not just to the theory of normal and abnormal development but also to the developmental understanding of the therapeutic process.

The major weakness of Winnicott's theory, which actually runs across the entire British object-relations tradition, is what may be called a naive reconstruction of infancy in the adult mind. Although infant research confirms some speculation and informal observation, the developmental argument of a linear evolution from infancy to adulthood cannot be sustained. Human development is far too complex for infantile experiences to have direct links to adult pathology. In fact, to the extent that such research is available, longitudinal studies of infancy suggest that personality organization is subject to reorganization throughout development based on significant positive and negative influences (e.g. Emde and Spicer, 2000). The infantile experiences described by Winnicott and others are thus no less metaphorical and reductionistic than the ego psychological formulations they aimed to replace.

Winnicott's writing is characterized by gigantic inferential leaps made with scant regard for either evidence or common sense. For example, he was quite willing to contemplate the idea that patients on the couch were reliving the birth process. For Winnicott this was not simply a theoretical possibility. We know from Margaret Little's account of her analysis with Winnicott (Little, 1985) that Winnicott explained to her an attack of intense anxiety on the couch as an experience of reliving her birth. This evidently flies in the face of everything we know about the nature of the development of memory (Nelson and Bloom, 1998). The assumption that anyone can remember a birth experience, even somatically, is doubtful.

Winnicott's view influenced psychoanalysis in a subtle and profound way. For example, Kohut's advances of psychoanalytic theory, which will be covered in the next chapter, are almost entirely anticipated by Winnicott's work, although this is rarely acknowledged. Winnicott's influence has unhappily been epistemological as well as theoretical. His style of writing is highly evocative and his clinical examples are rich as well as persuasive. His writing is untroubled by considerations of parsimony, the need for unambiguous language or supportive evidence. While in Winnicott's hands this approach has been highly creative, in the hands of his followers evocative language can often disguise convoluted speculation and uninspired content.

A key contribution of the Independent Group is perhaps linked to its role as 'the witness' in the confrontation of Kleinian and Freudian ideologies. By and large, Independents have been consistently more reflective about the nature of their contribution to the debate than either of the other two Groups. This has led to thoughtful approaches to epistemology from Independent thinkers. A recent example is the work of David Tuckett (Tuckett, 1993; 2000b), who has systematically addressed the question of the evidence base of psychoanalytic argument. He has demonstrated that psychoanalytic knowledge is socially constructed, and psychoanalytic groups with different internal structures may bring more effective contributions at different phases of the development of knowledge. He argues that the London Kleinian Group, for example, is a strongly ordered group, whose ideas are relatively well-defined, and who operate with traditional charismatic and rule-governed structures of legitimation. By the same token, the Independent Group may be seen as relatively weakly ordered, in the sense that the ideas they share are quite general and difficult to specify. In such (weakly ordered) groups, which may characterize psychoanalysis as a whole, which have a combination of open-mindedness and lack of well-grounded ways of legitimating ideas, a negative Group identity may be created (e.g. non-Kleinian). Tuckett, however, emphasizes that weakly-ordered groups may be precursors to adaptation. The Independent Group has made a unique contribution to psychoanalytic ideas precisely through their open-mindedness, which has allowed them to integrate notions of early environmental influences on development with notions of psychic structure that have their roots in Kleinian thinking.

CHAPTER **8**

North American object relations theorists

8.1 Kohut's self-psychology

8.1.1 Developmental theory

Kohut's (Kohut, 1971; 1977; Goldberg, 1978; Kohut and Wolf, 1978; Mollon, 2001) theory emerged over the late sixties and early seventies. Like many psychoanalytic theories, it is not a singular coherent body of work. Initially, he applied his theory solely to narcissistic disorders, which he felt were the disorders between the neuroses and the psychoses. His theory concerned the development of the self and the application of the model to these disorders became known as self-psychology in the narrow sense. Self-psychology in the broad sense was an extension of the theory to the neuroses and the therapeutic process in general. To add to these complexities, his theory of self and self-development also changed in the course of this expansion. It is hard to create a definitive account of self-psychology. There is disagreement, for example, about whether Kohutian self-psychology is an object relations theory. Although some self-psychologists clearly see Kohut's work in this light (Bacal and Newman, 1990), others see it in the context of one person psychologies (i.e. an intra-psychic theory) (Wolf, 1988b).

Kohut's formulation is that narcissistic development proceeds along a path of its own and that parents serve as selfobjects. A selfobject (Kohut initially hyphenated the term but in later writing both he and his followers removed the hyphen) is defined as a person in the environment who performs particular functions for the self; these functions evoke the experience of selfhood (Wolf, 1988a). To begin with, empathic responses from the mirroring selfobject (assumed to be the mother) allow the unfolding of exhibitionism and grandiosity. This enables the child to build an idealized image of the parent with whom he wishes to merge. Frustration, when phase-appropriate and not too intense, permits a gradual modulation of infantile omnipotence through 'a transmuting internalization' of this mirroring function. Transmuting internalization of the selfobject leads gradually to consolidation of the *nuclear self* (Kohut and Wolf, 1978, pp. 83 and 416). The idealization of selfobjects, also through internalization, leads to the development of ideals. The internalizing of the mirroring function and idealized selfobject leads to the emergence of a 'bipolar self' with its ambitions and ideals and the natural talents available to it.

Kohut's theory of early development is fairly close to that of Freud (Freud, 1914; Kohut, 1971). Primary narcissism for both Freud and Kohut is defined by the libidinal investment of the self, a stage from which the infant emerges only when he begins to experience his supplies as coming from outside. The transfer of emotional investment to the parent results in idealization of her. As the Oedipus complex is resolved and the parental figure is re-internalized, the state of primary narcissism is restored. However, Kohut begins to differ from Freud by envisioning self-formation as beginning pre-psychologically (Kohut, 1977) simply because the infant is treated as if it was a self by an empathic caregiver. The psychologically life-sustaining function that the object performs is recognition through empathy of the self *in statu nascendi*. The empathic mother channels the innate potential for a self into a 'nuclear self' by selectively mobilizing aspects of the child's constitutional endowment by the mediation of empathy. The mother who treats the child as though the child has a self initiates the process of self-formation. The mother is thus the prototypical selfobject. It is parental failure to meet the child's narcissistic needs that leads to the emergence from primary narcissism. The grandiose or exhibitionistic self emerges as a defense against the awareness of vulnerability that is a direct consequence of the loss of primary narcissism. This grandiose exhibitionistic self relies on confirmation through an object who mirrors the child's need for admiration and approval. It is in this sense that Kohut considers the parent who provides such bolstering as performing a selfobject function. At these times, the child does not see the parent as separate or autonomous. At other times there is recognition of the parent as other, and the movement between these states generates an idealized parental imago. This idealized image of the parent is invested with narcissistic libido and becomes yet another way of experiencing a sense of well-being. Both the grandiose self and the idealized parental imago are transformations of primary narcissism – the first requiring the selfobject function of mirroring while the second requires the availability of the parent for idealization.

The idealized parental imago is gradually given up under the pressure of disappointments with the parent. The image of the parent is internalized as a set of ideals to which the child aspires. A structure is created through the simultaneous transformation and internalization of the idealized imago into ego ideal. Kohut labels this process transmuting internalization. The superego incorporates ego ideals. Because of their origin in primary narcissism, these ideals are central to well-being. Thus, the loss of superego approval can later lead to a profound loss of well-being.

Kohut does not provide a clear timetable for his model of development, although he implies that grandiosity changes into ambition with the help of the mother's mirroring between the second and fourth year. In this, his timetable of development is closer to Mahler's than to Winnicott's. Idealized goals appear from the fourth to sixth year, in line with classical Freudian superego development. For Kohut, narcissistic libido and object libido followed distinct developmental paths. The idealized parental imago, which contains the narcissistic investment, retains a drive-neutralizing capacity. It is not narcissism but object cathexis in Kohut's view that leads to the formation of the superego, whereas the idealization of the superego is a consequence of narcissistic investment (Kohut, 1966, p. 434). Thus a person whose internalization of the idealized parental imago was inadequate, may have a powerful and well-integrated superego that is, however, not idealized. Thus the narcissistic individual, as we shall see, can transgress superego demands without feeling bad.

Just as the idealized parental imago is transformed through internalization into ego ideals in the face of disappointment with the parental figure, so the child's grandiosity gradually diminishes in the face of parental responses that fail to satisfy his needs. Again, the process of transmuting internalization is at work, and if the grandiose needs are optimally frustrated, the internal structure of realistic ambition is generated. The self is thus made up of three basic constituents: striving for power and success (realistic ambition), idealized goals (the ego ideal), and talents and skills (Kohut and Wolf, 1978, p. 414). The individual's talents and skills are between the two poles of a 'bipolar' self where ambitions that drive the individual are at one pole and the loved ideals that they hope to achieve are at the other. In sum, in healthy development the infantile grandiose self and the idealized parental imago are transformed through transmuting internalizations into realistic ambitions and loved ideals.

Although the mirroring and idealized selfobjects come to be internalized, the 'self' continues to require selfobjects to varying degrees throughout life to help in the maintenance of self-cohesion (Kohut, 1984). According to Kohut, the development of the self requires 'empathic merger with the selfobject's mature self-organization and participation in the selfobject experience of an affect signal instead of affect spread' (Kohut, 1977, p. 87). Selfobjects are experienced as part of oneself whereas objects are the targets of desires, emanating from a more demarcated self-concept.

In Kohut's early work (1971) the self was seen as a component of the ego structure, though in his later writings (1977; 1984), it was regarded as a superordinate structure including drives and defenses. Kohut (1971; 1977;

1984) proposes that the main developmental achievement for any individual is the attainment of a cohesive self. He suggests that it is the 'enfeebled self' that turns defensively toward pleasure aims (drives) and then secondarily involves the ego in managing these aims (Kohut, 1977). Drives are breakdown products of disappointments to the self, usually involving failures in emotional attunement of the selfobject. A search for self-cohesion is the primary motivation for human behavior and is derived from inevitable denting of grandiosity and exhibitionistic needs (Kohut, 1971).

Kohut tried to redefine a number of aspects of structural psychoanalytic theory in terms of self-cohesion. For example, he differentiated between the anxiety related to danger situations, such as fear provoked when gratification of desires leads to self-reproach or possible rejection by the object, and the fear of disintegration of the self. Anxiety was primarily the self's experience of defect and a lack of cohesiveness and continuity.

In his later work, Kohut re-examined the Freudian concept of the Oedipus complex (Kohut, 1984) and identified a group of people for whom oedipal preoccupation is a defense against a fragmentary or devitalized self. He interpreted the Oedipus complex, as classically described, as the child's reaction to the parent's failure to enjoy and participate empathically in the child's growth. Unempathic parents are likely to react to their oedipal child with counter-hostility or counter-seduction, stimulating destructive aggression and isolated sexual fixation. This is a reversal of Freud's model, in that Kohut identifies castration anxiety and penis envy as imposed from outside, rather than as the result of constitutional predisposition. This is an illustration of Kohut's rejection of the classical theory of inborn drives: while dispositions to affection and assertiveness may be inborn, their transformation into sexual and aggressive drives occur only under pathogenic conditions. If the parents can empathize with the child's affectionate feelings for the parent of the opposite sex and assertive feelings toward the parent of the same sex, given affection and pride on the part of the parents, the child can integrate these affectionate and assertive strivings into his self-structure. The oedipal phase is thus no longer seen as the cornerstone of a mastery over drives, but rather as a phase in which affection and assertiveness strengthen self-structure. If the self is defective, affectionate and assertive feelings are not experienced joyfully but are split off into lust and hostility respectively. Oedipal conflicts are a product of a weak, defective self. Pathology ensues if the responses of the selfobject are not empathic but either excessively frustrating or stimulating. For example, the oedipal girl fears a seductive father and a hostile mother. If the parents are threatened by the child's assertiveness or intensification of a wish for greater closeness and respond by competitiveness or overstimulation then the child will suffer traumatic disappointment with the selfobjects of the oedipal phase, and the development of an affectionate and assertive self will be arrested. The joyful feelings are intensified, split off from the core of the self and transformed into gross sexuality and/or hostility. The child isolates the drives from the rest of the self. Thus, assertiveness becomes hostility and affection is sexualized. So, late in his career Kohut started to see the Oedipus complex as a highly pathological constellation, ultimately an effort to defend against 'disintegration anxiety' through the isolation of the drives. In the boy, castration anxiety is a symptom of the threatened self, not the source of all problems. The fear of the loss of the penis defends against the far more threatening loss of the integrity of the self.

Working from a Kohutian framework, Stolorow, Brandschaft and Atwood (1987) attempted to redefine the experiential nature of the self-concept. Stolorow and Atwood (1984) distinguished the self as an initiator of action from the self as an organizer of experience (a representational construct, Jacobson, 1964). They proposed the term 'self' as a specific concept, referring to the psychological structure through which self-experience gains continuity, cohesion and enduring organization. They see their experiential orientation as an empathic introspective perspective that focuses on the structuralization of experience, rather than the acquisition of abilities as judged by an external observer. Stolorow et al. (1987) criticized Kohut for confounding the self as structure with the person as agent. Kohut's view of the self as a superordinate structure with a mental apparatus, in their view, runs into the same problems of mechanistic thinking and reification which hindered ego psychology, as we have seen in Chapter 3. Kohut's motivational metaphor of a tension arc between idealizing and mirroring functions is just as distant from experience as the inter-agency conflict of the structural model. The disintegrating self is an experience and therefore cannot have 'disintegration products'. These concepts are reifications, residues from a mechanistic model. They move psychoanalysis back toward metapsychology and away from an experiential focus on the self.

A new suggestion emerged from this work (Stolorow, 1997; Stolorow et al., 1987; Stolorow and Atwood, 1989, 1991) that delineated psychoanalysis most clearly as the subject that gathers its data via empathy or the process of the meeting of two subjectivities. While the analyst may have his own viewpoint from which he or she interprets the patient's reality, this is no more 'objective' or privileged than the patient's view. Selfobjects are functions that help the self integrate affects into the organization of self-experience. They suggest four crucial selfobject functions, all of which serve to integrate the child's affects: (1) affect differentiation, (2) the synthesizing of affectively discrepant experience, (3) toleration of affects and the development of their use as signals, (4) the desomatization of affects, by which it becomes possible to think about them. The suggestion here is that the intersubjective experience of affects by the selfobject is as an organizing experience and prepares the self to cope with these emotions in later life.

8.1.2 Kohut's model of developmental psychopathology

8.1.2.1 General model of pathology

Kohut suggests that when parents consistently fail to provide for the child's narcissistic needs, the archaic grandiose self and the idealized parent imago may become hardened and fail to be integrated into later structures. They continue to exist within the individual's psychic organization and cause various forms of disturbance in his view of himself and his relationship with others. For example, intense or 'disintegration anxiety' reflects a threat of the idealized parent imago and the grandiose self to the self-organization: fear of losing the sense of who one is. In Kohut's framework this fear underlies all pathology, since it is so intolerable that the self will protect itself at all costs. The principle of primary self-preservation holds that the protection of the self is more important than any other concern including physical pain, sexual frustration or physical survival. Thus the severity of pathology is an indication of the stage at which self-development was arrested. The secondary conflicts that we observe in psychopathology can only occur because of structural weaknesses in the self.

In the Kohutian system there are three kinds of psychological disturbance (Kohut, 1984). (1) Psychoses are viewed as 'prepsychological states' where the arrest in development precedes awareness of selfobjects, precluding a cohesive sense of self or the capacity to relate, to use selfobjects or establish transferences. In Kohut's view, psychotics cannot be treated in psychoanalysis or psychological therapy as they lack a self-structure. (2) Some, but by no means all, personality disordered patients are viewed by Kohut as having a cohesive but enfeebled self, vulnerable to temporary fragmentation. This is most characteristic of narcissistic personality disorder, which Kohut strongly differentiates from borderline personality, regarding the latter as a successful defense against psychosis (Kohut, 1971). (3) By contrast, those with a neurotic pathology are not thought to suffer problems related to the robustness of their self-structure, but to have problems related to living up to their ideals.

Kohut and Wolf (Kohut and Wolf, 1978) described four types of self-pathology: (1) the understimulated self has inadequate selfobject responses in development, becomes bored, apathetic and seeks excitement by pathological means (e.g. promiscuity, addictions and perversions); (2) the selfobject's non-responsiveness can create fragmentation of the self, which has little contact with space and time and responds with bodily symptoms; (3) extreme lack of empathy or phase-inappropriate selfobject responses lead to an overstimulated self who receives no joy from success, because of archaic fantasies of greatness that cripple productivity; (4) the inability of childhood selfobjects to allow merger inhibits internalization of the self-soothing function, which leads to a sense of being overburdened by anxiety and negative, paranoid views of others. Thus pathology in the self is part of all forms of disturbance. We shall consider narcissistic disturbance first and other forms of disturbance separately, while recognizing that this distinction is not invariably maintained by Kohut.

8.1.2.2 Narcissistic personality disorder

Kohut (1971) offers no behavioral description of narcissistic personality disorder, seeing such a diagnosis as only possible in terms of the evolving transference relationship. If others are treated just to suit the patient's purpose rather than as full persons in their own right, the diagnosis might be warranted. Akhtar and Thompson (1982), however, summarize some of the behavioral features described in Kohut's writing (see Kohut, 1966; 1968; 1971): rage as a reaction to threats to self-esteem, the need for revenge to deal with narcissistic injury, difficulties in forming and maintaining relationships, perverse sexuality or a lack of sexual interest, lack of empathy, pathological lying, a limited capacity for humour toward the self, hypomanic states of exaltation, and over-concern with the body.

Kohut and Wolf (1978) describe five narcissistic personality types: (1) mirror-hungry personalities who compulsively need to evoke others' admiration to deal with a sense of worthlessness; (2) ideal-hungry personalities who search for others they can idealize to draw emotional sustenance; (3) alter-ego personalities who need a relationship that will conform to and confirm their own value system. These personality types are pathological only if they are extreme. Two other types invariably reflect deep defects in the self. These are: (4) merger-hungry personalities who need to control others to actualize their feeble inner structure in the outside world; (5) contact-shunning personalities who avoid others to control their desperate need for objects. The fourth of these categories seems to have much in common with borderline and the fifth with schizoid personality disorder although Kohut did not equate them in this way.

Kohut conceives of narcissistic personality as a form of developmental arrest. An individual's disappointment in his or her parents impinges on primary infantile narcissism and is fended off by the normal grandiose self. The latter, in contrast to Kernberg's formulation, is seen as a quasi-megalomanic self-image that helps the child to regain narcissistic equilibrium. The grandiose-exhibitionistic self, as we have seen in the description of normal development, will be gradually neutralized by the parents' age-specific mirroring responses. Similarly, the ideal parental images with which the young child wishes to merge are eventually modified as the child gradually internalizes disappointments with the parents, perceives their limitations, and integrates these into the child's own system of values and ideals. Parental failure causes an arrest in the movement from the grandiose exhibitionistic self to realistic ambition or the idealization of the parental imago to ego ideal.

A defect in the parental capacity to mirror the child's grandiosity leads to either a splitting off or a repression of the grandiose-exhibitionistic needs, which then cannot be moderated by reality through transmuting internalization. Thus, grandiosity remains out of touch with the reality-based self and does not come to be gradually integrated into it. In other words, the failure of empathic mirroring might disrupt the infant's contentment with his archaic grandiose self, and lead him to introject, as it were wholesale, the idealized but faulty parental image. Thus the self (in Winnicott's terms, the 'true self') fails to develop and the individual will only have access to a fragmented (part parent, part infantile) sense of self. His injured narcissism calls forth rage to protect the self and fantasies of grandiosity to cover its infantile vulnerability. Infantile narcissism is enhanced, rather than following the normal developmental process of gradual diminution.

Two types of problems are associated with the enhancement of infantile narcissism, depending on whether splitting or repression dominate. The repression of the grandiose self brings with it a general impoverishment, with low self-esteem, vague depression, and lack of initiative as the characteristic traits. When the grandiose self is split off, it manifests as a boastfulness, haughtiness, arrogance and a dismissing attitude that is out of touch with reality and split off from the rest of the psyche which is thus robbed of self-esteem. Whether the grandiosity is split off or repressed, self-esteem will be poor because of the depletion of narcissistically invested libido. Thus hypersensitivity to criticism is inevitable and the response of the psyche is defensive rage or deep shame – any limitation is experienced as a potential revelation of the deep inadequacy of the self. Besides the vulnerability to shame, hypochondriasis and propensity to self-consciousness are other expressions of repressed exhibitionistic needs. Further, the individual will continue to experience the need to be mirrored constantly in order to sustain the vulnerable nuclear self. The arrested grandiosity is not accessible to the rest of the psyche, so Kohut sees no contradiction between the arrogance of such individuals and their vulnerability to the mildest of slights.

Alternatively, the selfobject may fail the child in not providing a suitable object for idealization. If the parent is unable to help the child appreciate the parent's real limitations, or if the child was disappointed in a traumatic rather than a gradual way, the idealized parental imago will remain and the child will be left with an unattainable, unrealistic or partial system of values and ideas. Most dramatically, in the case of loss of the parent or other situations (such as maltreatment of the child) that force the relinquishing of the idealized parental image before the child is able to cope with this, the child is deprived of the opportunity to see the parent realistically. Thus the early idealization endures, may be repressed or split off, and will generate a deficit in self-structure. Other contexts where Kohut envisions this happening include the chronic unavailability of the parent, her sudden withdrawal, or persistent reluctance to allow the child to see her realistically. There is then a continual hunger for objects (an ideal-hungry personality is formed who seeks the object not for its qualities but rather to have the illusion of healing an internal defect). Thus, when the object is idealized it is experienced as part of the self. As object libido and narcissistic libido have separate developmental paths, superego formation may take place. However, as the sequence from the idealization of the object through transmuting internalization of the idealized parental imago to narcissistic investment in the superego does not take place, compliance with the superego gives rise to no pleasure. The person may be very moral but does not feel good as a result, and requires the actual approval of an esteemed figure in order for the experience of well-being to follow moral behavior.

Thus according to Kohut, the developmental response to a deficit in either the grandiose self or the idealized object is to erect a defensive exaggerated compensatory structure, strengthening the other pole of the self. This is a response in the normal range. If both poles of the self – the ego ideals and realistic ambitions – are damaged, severe narcissistic problems arise, according to Kohut, because the compensatory strategy cannot work. The arrest in self-development leads to grandiosity in place of realistic ambition and continuing dependency on idealized figures in place of an ego ideal or the idealization of the superego. Sexuality is subverted to narcissistic needs and the individual, through sexual fantasy or enactment, creates relationships with powerful idealized figures.

Thus in narcissistic personality disorder there is a defect in the self, predisposing the person to experiences of threatened fragmentation of the self and of empty depression. He can disguise these experiences by defensive and compensatory behavior, such as seeking adulation and excitement. Thus, in narcissistic personality disorder, this normal sequence is disrupted in the following ways: (1) The grandiose self persists in an unneutralized way because the child has not met with appropriate mirroring responses; (2) Patients in treatment are allowed to express both their idealization of the therapist and their own grandiosity without being met by confrontation or interpretation. The empathic stance taken by the therapist will re-activate the developmental process and through the inevitable and gradual disappointment of the patient, neutralization of both the grandiose self and of the idealization of the parent figure will be resumed.

Kohut assumes that, in Freud's time, children were largely over-stimulated whereas, in the late twentieth and early twenty-first century, children are reared in an under-stimulating, lonely psychological environment. He therefore argues that self-pathology is the dominant psychological illness of modern times.

8.1.2.3 Other disorders

Unlike many self-psychologists who followed him, Kohut did not reject the notion of the *structural neurosis* (Kohut, 1984). Both pathological narcissism and neurosis could be seen as the results of deficient selfobject function and the consequent defects in the self. The key difference is the developmental stage at which the defect starts. As we have seen, if the selfobject function is deficient in infancy, the nuclear self is itself enfeebled and disharmonious and pathological narcissism is the outcome. In the structural neurosis, there may also be lack of vitality and a failure of the nuclear self to reach its goals, but this is the result of the failure of mirroring of the selfobjects of the oedipal phase and the consequent absorption of energies in oedipal conflicts (in their turn consequences of the threat of assertiveness and affectionate impulses to the self).

For example, in *agoraphobia*, the breakdown of the self is caused by positive attitudes of assertiveness and affection not being appropriately mirrored and therefore being experienced as hostility and lust respectively. Normal affection for the father is converted into threatening sexual fantasies that are split off from the self. Perhaps, even earlier, the failure of the maternal selfobject has led to a deficit in self-soothing functions which turns anxiety into disintegration anxiety. The agoraphobic cannot leave the house without a maternal figure to soothe her. More generally, the neurotic symptom may be understood as an effort to bind or defend against the disintegration anxiety. The drive is the symptom and not the cause. This position is representative of Kohut's final fundamental stance that all psychopathology is rooted in disturbance in the structure of the self.

For Kohut, the self originates with the parental selfobjects dealing with the baby as if the baby had a self ('a virtual self'). Assertiveness is a healthy response protecting and maintaining the self. At its extreme, destructive rage is motivated by an experience of injury to the self (Kohut, 1972). In behavioral narcissistic disorders the patient attempts to fill the deficit in self-esteem with action, such as *delinquency, perversions or addictions* so that the weakness of the self is never experienced (Kohut and Wolf, 1978). Kohut's view of *violence* has been particularly influential (Kohut, 1972). The threat to the self and the sense of shame generate an overwhelming need to inflict injury on the shaming person, to avenge the wrong and thereby to repair the narcissistic injury. The violence might be triggered by a threat to the weakened self, either by unmet expectation of mirroring of the grandiose self or the frustration of the need for idealization. *Drug addiction* fills a missing gap in the psyche. It is assumed that the drug addict's primary object failed to perform the tension regulating function, which results in traumatic disappointment in the idealized object. The drug is used to fill the gap that the absence of the idealized object left behind. Similarly, *eating disorders* reflect the intensification and fragmentation of the oral drive in response to disruptions in the self. Overeating is an effort to experience the feeling of wholeness without relying on a failed and untrustworthy human environment (Kohut, 1977).

Kohut (1977) links *perversions* and other isolated manifestations of a sexual drive to prolonged empathic failures in the selfobject environment. The breakdown of self-assertiveness vis-à-vis the mirroring selfobject is seen in exhibitionism. Similarly, the breakdown of a healthy admiration for the idealized selfobject is manifested in voyeuristic preoccupation with the breast or the penis. In the case of fetishism, the object of the perversion is seen as the substitute for missing admiration and approval to nourish the grandiose self. These are all examples of narcissistic personality disorder based on failure of the self to develop fully, an aspect of human behavior which Kohut calls 'tragic man'. In Kohut's view, *schizoid personality* is a defensive organization motivated by the individual's preconscious awareness of the possibility of a narcissistic injury which could initiate an 'uncontrollable regression' (Kohut, 1971, p. 12). Consequently such individuals channel their libidinal resources into non-human interests.

A number of Kohutians consider the *borderline concept* to be, to some extent, an iatrogenic one, an indication of the failure of therapist empathy toward the patient's developmental needs (Kohut, 1984; Brandschaft and Stolorow, 1987). Kohut (1977; 1984) has put forward a trauma-arrest model that has numerous components relevant to borderline pathology (e.g., explanations of substance use, impulsiveness, identity problems, etc.). Although Kohut claimed to have no experience with this group and conflated it with psychosis, a number of North Americans including Buie and Adler (1982), Brandschaft and Stolorow (1987), Palombo (1987), Terman (1987) and Tolpin (1987) have elaborated his theories in relation to borderline pathology. Brandschaft and Stolorow (1987) building on their intersubjective approach, suggested that borderline pathology was codetermined by the intersubjective context. Recourse to terms like *borderline* occurs because therapists find it hard to appreciate the archaic intersubjective contexts from which such pathologies arise. Psychopathology is the operation of the patient's past structures of subjectivity in the present.

Buie and Adler (1982) address the self-pathology of borderline patients in terms of a disjointedness of thinking, feelings of loss of integration of body parts, a sense of losing functional control of the self and concerns about falling apart (p. 62). In addition, they share some less dramatic characteristics of self-pathology with borderline patients, including a feeling of unreality, a sense of dullness, depletion and emptiness (Adler, 1981, p. 46). Adler (1985), influenced by self-psychology, suggests that the fundamental developmental pathology of borderline patients is the failure to achieve an evocative memory of objects, resulting in an inability to hold onto selfobjects which might be soothing for the self. The result is inner emptiness, and without introjects the self cannot be adequately organized. When the borderline patient's intense relationships are threatened, by separation or otherwise, the patient faces an 'annihilatory panic' that in turn causes intense rage to protect the self. The loss of contact with soothing and supporting others leads to a collapse of the self and identity confusion because, as Kohut (1977) suggests, the self is built up and nourished through the 'transmuting internalization' of soothing and mirroring functions provided by early caregivers. Adler's emphasis on memory deficit may help explain why such patients, when in panic and rage, may fail to recognize their therapists emotionally even when aware they are physically present.

This theory, like all Kohutian developmental models of psychopathology, is thus essentially a deficiency theory: deficiency of necessary facilitating experiences leading to a primary psychic deficit, an inadequately developed sense of self. The characteristic manifestations of the borderline position may be understood as indications of the individual's tragic attempts to cope with the narrow confines of his or her intra-psychic world. The clear therapeutic implication is that effective intervention must focus on the nature of the individual's deficit, aiming at the provision of a therapeutic environment which may make good the early deprivation: in Kohutian terms, the provision of soothing and mirroring that leads to the restoration of the self achieved through mastery.

Kohut viewed clinical psychoanalysis as a means of helping the arrested self to complete its development. This process requires: (1) the therapeutic mobilization of the arrested self, (2) the use of the analyst as a selfobject, and (3) the transmuting internalization of this new selfobject into psychological structure. Thus, early interpretation of conflicts might forestall mobilization of the arrested self. Interpretations do not help by creating insight, but by giving the analyst an opportunity to be a mirroring selfobject. Failures of empathy in therapy might help by allowing the transmuting internalization of the selfobject. Interpretation is not used to make the unconscious conscious but to provide the frustration necessary for the resumption of transmuting internalization. The analyst functions in a similar manner to how parental selfobjects should have functioned and the extent that he succeeds in this difficult task determines the success of the treatment. The analytic stance is not one of alliance with the healthy part of the patient's personality against the self-destructive parts opposing the process of change; rather, the analyst aims to be empathic with the patient so that the patient's defensiveness will become unnecessary. This quite fundamental distinction follows from the fact that Kohut does not see the psyche as torn into warring factions: the analyst cannot collude with anti-therapeutic parts of the self. If the analytic relationship has become problematic, the analyst must have failed in the selfobject function (of empathy). Kohut's therapeutic strategy sets him apart from most of the other analytic approaches considered in this volume. Kohut is probably closest to Winnicott in suggesting that analysts should allow themselves to be used according to the patient's developmental needs of the moment. Analysis is the completion of the self, not the investigation of the unconscious.

The emphasis on empathic resonance as part of psychotherapy has been a common theme of self-psychology. Authors have given different slants in their conceptualization of the therapeutic process. Some consider 'affective attunement' to be the paradigmatic self-selfobject relationship that links mother–infant and therapist–patient relationships (Basch, 1985). Others stress that the acceptance by the therapist of the patient's childhood wishes as legitimate leads to growth and maturation (Ornstein and Ornstein, 1985). Yet others see interaction between analyst and patient in which the patient's needs are responded to in a new way, as a cohesion-fostering corrective emotional experience (Tolpin, 1983). These formulations all emphasize the mutative therapeutic aspect of the real relationship between patient and analyst. The shift is away from insight and interpretation and toward the experiential relational aspects. The most comprehensive explication of this comes from Bacal and Newman (1990) who suggested five selfobject functions within the therapist–patient interaction: affective attunement, validation, tension regulation, recognition of uniqueness and organization of the self. It is striking how close these suggestions are to technical recommendations by cognitive behavior therapists working with individuals with severe personality pathology (Linehan, 1993). Here, optimal responsiveness replaces optimal frustration as the guiding principle of therapy. Exploration is not a concern. Even clarification of emotions may invalidate the patient's experience. The analyst's role is to provide selfobject functions, not insight. Stolorow et al. (1987) go so far as to suggest that as the task of the analyst is to facilitate the unfolding of developmental strivings, the analyst should do whatever helps to achieve this. If abstinence is not helpful in this context then it should not be part of the analytic stance.

8.1.3 Evidence consistent with the concept of self-development and mastery

Kohut (1984) distinguished 'experience-near' from 'experience-distant' psychoanalytic propositions, on the basis of the clinician's intuitive grasp of the ideas. Experience-near theory is closer to the patient's subjectivity whilst experience-distant theory has an external frame of reference. In line with these suggestions, Kohut (1959; 1982) rejected the notion of psychoanalysis as a natural science, claiming that psychological knowledge, indisputably the core of psychoanalysis, could only be acquired by empathy and introspection and not by sensory observation. He argued for the elimination of concepts which – because of their clear behavioral reference – could, at least in principle, be externally verified (Kohut, 1982). Thus Kohut in principle rejected any evidence not gathered through empathic immersion in the patient's subjectivity.

There is only limited evidence to support the assumption that grandiosity is a normal stage of development. Kohut's evidence, such as it is, comes from his analysis of adult patients. Infancy research has shown mastery to be a significant feature of the baby's interaction. He smiles when alone as well as when in company (Trevarthen, 1990). De Casper and Carstens (1981) demonstrated that infants a few days old were able to elongate customary pauses between bursts of sucking in order to activate a recording of female singing. When in the next phase of the experiment their 'omnipotence' was lost and the singing was produced randomly, not contingent upon their sucking pauses, the infants' reactions were negative ('grimacing and vigorous crying', p. 32). As we saw in our discussion of the evidence supporting Winnicott's theories in Chapter 7, numerous studies have demonstrated that babies are highly sensitive to the contingent relations between their physical responses and consequent stimulus events. How do they perceive these contingencies so efficiently? Based on Watson's extensive studies (Watson, 1979; 1985; 1994), Gergely and Watson (Gergely and Watson, 1999) have recently proposed the existence of an innate *contingency detection module* that analyzes the probability structure of such relationships.

The suggestion, which fits well with Kohutian ideas, is that during the first 2–3 months the infant is particularly attuned to perfect contingencies. This helps the infant to identify a part of the world that is in perfect synchrony with his intentions and physical experience: his body. Sometime between three and five months the attention shifts to close but not perfect contingencies: the empathic mirroring selfobject. A number of other preferential-looking studies (Papousek and Papousek, 1974; Lewis and Brooks-Gunn, 1979; Rochat and Morgan, 1995; Schmuckler, 1996) in which the live image of the self was contrasted with the moving but noncontingent image of another baby indicate that 4–5-month-old infants differentiate self from other on the basis of response-stimulus contingencies and prefer to look at the *other*. Watson (1994) further hypothesized that around three months, due to maturational factors, the contingency detection mechanism is 'switched' from preferring perfect contingency to *high, but imperfect degrees of (social) contingencies* typically provided by the reactions of attachment figures attuned to the infants' affective-communicative displays. This maturational change orients the infant after three months of age away from self-exploration (perfect contingencies) and toward the *exploration and representation of the social world*. Related evidence on the development of affect representation links closely to Stolorow and colleagues' (Stolorow et al., 1987) speculations about emotional development. Gergely and Watson (1996; 1999) suggest that knowledge of emotions is acquired via the mother (selfobject), whose role it is to mirror the child's affect on her face and with her voice in such a way that the infant does not confuse this with the mother's emotion and recognizes it as a version of his internal state. The internalization of this image can then form a structure around which the child's representation of his own feelings will coalesce.

While there is good evidence for the interactional aspects of the selfobject theory, other aspects of Kohut's proposals have fared poorly in developmental research. The notion of infantile omnipotence is challenged by recent findings indicating that, on the majority of occasions, the infant cannot elicit synchronous behavior from the mother (Gianino and Tronick, 1988). In Stern's studies of mother–infant interaction there is a failure of mirroring every 19 seconds (Stern, 1995). This is not disastrous for Kohut's view, as he stresses that it is the inevitable shortcomings of maternal care rather than absolute perfection which lead to the development of healthy narcissism. The infant's subjective response, beyond observable emotional indicators, cannot be tested using current techniques. The identification of so-called 'mirroring cells' in the primate brain that are specifically activated when the rhesus monkey identifies itself in the world (see Schore, 1997b), is certainly consistent with self-psychology suggestions but falls far short of proof. Clinical and epidemiological evidence backs Kohut's suggestion that dangerous violent acts are the indirect consequences of narcissistic injury. Shame and humiliation appear to be very common triggers for violent acts, in studies by forensic psychotherapists (Gilligan, 1997).

There is important evidence for Kohut's views of the mother's role in imparting the skill of tension regulation to the infant. Modern research on arousal regulation (Posner and Rothbart, 2000; Rothbart, Ahadi and Evans, 2000) suggests that early parent–infant interaction sets limits on the efficiency of these mechanisms.

Elizabeth Meins and colleagues (Meins et al., 2001) provided a relatively direct test of Kohut's hypothesis that the mother talking to the infant as if it had a self would enhance self-development. They analyzed the content of speech of mothers with their six-month-old children and coded the number of comments the mother made on the baby's mental states (knowledge, desires, thought, interest), or comments about what the infant might think the mother thinks or his attempts to manipulate her ('are you just teasing me?'). The comments were further coded as appropriate if an observer of the sequence and context agreed with the mother's reading of the child's mental state, and did not see it as intrusive. The proportion of such 'appropriate mind-related comments' was highly significantly associated with attachment security in the child six months later, and this held even when traditional measures of maternal sensitivity were controlled for. Thus, it seems that Kohut was correct that treating the infant like a person directly facilitates self-formation.

The evidence concerning the child's need for unconditional admiration from his or her caretakers is, however, questionable (Gedo, 1980). There is certainly a powerful relationship between inconsistent, power-assertive or lax parental monitoring and antisocial behavior in children (Sanders and Dadds, 1992; Wasserman et al., 1996; Wootton et al., 1997; Kazdin and Wasser, 2000). Forehand, Lautenschlager, Faust and Graziano (1986) reported a direct link between parental depression, ineffective management techniques and childhood disobedience. Miller et al. (1989) report an interesting study of 4–5-year-old children and their mothers. Children who showed more sympathy in social situations had mothers who independently said that should their child hurt a peer, they would reason with him or her; the mother's effort to understand the child's motivation in stressful situations appears to have been conveyed to the child, an attempt to force the child to show concern appears to be counter-productive. However, concern for the other is by no means always the result of an empathic object. For example, toddlers whose mothers suffer from bipolar illness are especially likely to show empathic concern for distress (Zahn-Waxler et al., 1984) and are more likely to narrate stories that emphasize responsibility and involvement in other people's problems (Zahn-Waxler et al., 1990). Such children appear to show more prosocial behavior in response to the needs of their depressed mothers. Within Zahn-Waxler's model, this increased empathy may lead to pathological outcomes, possibly contributing to depression in childhood (Zahn-Waxler, Cole and Barrett, 1991).

Developmental research does not by and large confirm the existence of a narcissistic period in the first 2–3 years of life, superseded by the oedipal period, as Kohut (1977) suggests. Kohut (1984) is less specific about the developmental phase associated with normal narcissism and narcissistic pathology. There is plenty of evidence to suggest that egocentrism and excessive investment of the self do not normally end in the oedipal period (see Ford, 1979; Shantz, 1983; Westen, 1990a, 1990b). Rather, it persists throughout childhood and adolescence, with new forms of egocentrism simply replacing old ones. In general, the timetable for interpersonal awareness suggested by Kohut, but also by the intersubjectivists who built on his theoretical work, is not consistent with the cognitive achievements of infants. Gergely (2001) has powerfully argued that intersubjectivity could not meaningfully be part of the infant's capacities until the second or third year of life. Elsewhere, we have offered a complex developmental timetable of the emergence of agentive capacities and intersubjective awareness, which are not established until the third year and continue to evolve throughout childhood (Fonagy, Gergely, Jurist and Target, 2002).

The abandonment of egocentrism and the development of understanding of others' mental states are not all-or-nothing phenomena but occur piecemeal. This process may indeed start in early infancy through a biological preparedness to attend to people as entities (e.g. Nelson, 1987) and to see human causation as different from physical or mechanical causation (see Bertenthal et al., 1985). An understanding of others as having intentional subjective experiences is evident early in the second year from studies of joint perception (e.g. Butterworth, 1991), attention to emotional reactions (Adamson and Bakeman, 1985) and social referencing (Sorce et al., 1985). Three-year-olds appear to understand how desires are involved in emotions such as happiness (Wellman and Banerjee, 1991), and consider desires imputed to characters as potential explanations of their behavior (Bartsch and Wellman, 1989; Moses and Flavell, 1990). Only four-year-olds consistently demonstrate the capacity to consider the beliefs of the other (Perner, Leekam and Wimmer, 1987; Wellman and Bartsch, 1988). Understanding the point of view of the other by no means implies a willingness to act on this understanding under most circumstances. Research on childhood social interaction highlights the pragmatic self-interest of children, in both their friendship behavior (Shantz, 1983) and their morality (Rest, 1983). This complex developmental path implies that the development of normal narcissism is far more differentiated than is portrayed by Kohut and other self-psychologists.

Other emerging evidence is consistent with Kohut's emphasis on self-esteem as a central aspect of risk for psychological disturbances. For example, the seminal work of George Brown and Tirril Harris demonstrated the causal role of life events in triggering depression (Brown and Harris, 1989). This program of work has more recently demonstrated that life events that trigger feelings of humiliation and entrapment are most powerful in generating depression (Brown, Harris and Hepworth, 1995). Individuals with early adverse experiences that have served to undermine their self-esteem are most likely to respond with depression to negative life events (Brown, 1998). There is evidence from psychotherapy research that is consistent with the transmuting internalization model of therapeutic change. The therapeutic alliance (the therapeutic mobilization of the self) strongly predicts success (Horvath, Gaston and Luborsky, 1993; Svartberg and Stiles, 1994; Meissner, 1996). Even more pertinent to Kohut's formulation, it seems that breaks in the therapeutic alliance might be points that mark particularly rapid progress in psychotherapy (Safran and Muran, 2000). This appears to be consistent with Kohut's suggestion that occasional failures of empathy trigger transmuting internalizations.

Kohut's view of borderline psychopathology as a pre-psychotic condition has not been borne out by epidemiological or clinical evidence (Stone, Hurt and Stone, 1987; Berelowitz and Tarnopolsky, 1993; Gunderson and Sabo, 1993; Zanarini and Frankenburg, 1997). However, the link between grossly insensitive early caregiving and borderline personality disorder has been demonstrated in some well-designed prospective studies (Johnson, Cohen, Brown et al., 1999).

8.1.4 Critical appraisal of Kohut's model

Kohut's theory has generated a school of psychoanalysis, 'self-psychology'. This is not surprising given the richness of his theory and its capacity to explain a wide range of psychological problems. He brought a coherent theory of the development of the self into psychoanalysis, together with recognition of the need for object relationships for healthy self-esteem. Depression, hypochondriasis, delinquency, narcissistic personality disorder, eating disorders, perversions could all be explained in terms of an assumed depletion of the self. This would imply that all psychopathology, including anxiety problems and other neuroses, should be treated in the way self-psychology recommends narcissistic disorders need to be treated. Further, that the drive-ego model of structural neurosis can be dispensed with and replaced with the self-psychological view. Then, all pathology is arrested development, not conflict within the self. Defences are invariably self-preservative. To understand pathology we need to understand the relationship of the self to its selfobjects. To treat patients we need to accept that much of what classical theory considered as transference enactment or resistance is the expression of a legitimate need. Thus Kohut's theory is a dramatic reformulation, more fundamental than those previously suggested by psychoanalysts in the UK or US.

There are many critical reviews of Kohut's theory from within structural psychoanalytic models (see, e.g. Loewald, 1973; Wallerstein, 1981; Blum, 1982; Rangell, 1982; Rubovitz-Seitz, 1988; Stein, 1979). The critiques, in quite different ways, try to show that Kohut is 'unanalytic' (which means that his theory misses what is thought by the critics to be the essence of analysis). We will focus on a selection of the issues.

Schwartz (1978) sees Kohut's descriptions as over-inclusive. Fragmentations of the self lead to depressions, depersonalizations and disorganizing anxieties, as well as temporary or encapsulated psychotic states. By fitting all psychopathology into self-defects, Kohut has homogenized psychological disorder too much. Schizophrenia and borderline personality disorder are both seen as inaccessible to analysis because the borderline person is a schizophrenic able to cover his psychosis with defence. Homogenizing the treatable cases under the heading of defect of self is no better. It is unlikely that a treatment will be equally effective regardless of whether the patient has deeply narcissistic pathology or a phobia. However, linking depressive pathology to narcissism might be more helpful. The same problem (overextension) applies to technique. Kohut has only one stance with regard to the disgruntled and angry patient: find the analyst's empathic failure. Yet seeing angry attacks by the patient as invariably caused by the analyst and representing the patient's need to safeguard self-cohesion does not do justice to the many other factors that play a part, such as the need to foster disruption to avoid deeper anxieties, or the need to destroy a valued relationship before it is taken away by some other force.

Rothstein (1980) criticizes Kohut's failure to acknowledge the link between his ideas and structural theory: for example between Kohut's concept of fragmentation and Reich's (1960) construct of catastrophic feelings of annihilation; the emphasis on the therapist as a real person and the work of Alexander and French (1946), Stone (1954), Loewald (1960) and Klein (1976a; 1976b). To these can be added Kohut's scant references to the work of Winnicott: Kohut's view of pathology as arrested development has striking parallels with Winnicott's concept of psychopathology as blocked maturational processes.

Many have criticized Kohut's neglect of capacities other than the individual's relation to his or her grandiosity and exhibitionism, such as the capacities for intimacy and reciprocity. A major problem in Kohut's more recent formulation is the confusion between self and self-representation. The self is presented by Kohut in representational terms, yet he ascribes motivational properties to it (see Kohut, 1971). In this way, the self denotes most, if not all, of the personality and therefore becomes a superfluous term, much as the concept of ego was over-extended by ego psychologists (see, e.g. Schafer, 1976). Sandler's use of the term self (see Sandler, 1962a, 1987b) is logically coherent, because it is restricted to a mental model or representation that a person has formed of him- or herself, which is analogous to a representation someone else might form of him or her. Even greater confusion surrounds the notion of selfobjects. While Kohut insists that this is an intra-psychic concept, he sometimes clearly means external people. In his first book, selfobjects are linked to transitional phenomena (Winnicott, 1971c) and are thus clearly intrapsychic. Kohut considers pathogenic failures of selfobjects in the same paragraph as he discusses the patients' remembered relationship with his or her parents. Kohut then describes the mutative power of selfobjects in treatment. Here, selfobject is clearly an interpersonal construct and, given its centrality for Kohut, self-psychology would be an interpersonal, rather than object relations, theory.

To make matters even more complicated, in his last book Kohut (1984) wrote of activities such as reading or listening to music as selfobject functions. These functions of selfobjects bring them close to sublimatory functions of the autonomous ego (Hartmann, 1955). In an apparently helpful clarification, Wolf (1988b) pointed out that selfobject needs are concrete only in infancy. In later development they can be increasingly abstract with symbols or ideas serving selfobject functions. However, this extension of the selfobject concept carries a grave risk of circularity. Anything that makes a person feel good may be considered to have a selfobject function, and the only way we know if an activity or person has selfobject function is through observing its effects on well-being. Used this broadly the concept has no explanatory power.

There has been criticism of Kohut's model as 'parent-blaming'. Tyson and Tyson (1990) take issue with his emphasis on pathogenic parents, neglecting the infant's constitution and capacity to modify his own environment. At the root of his formulation of narcissistic personality and behavior disorders is the idea that these result from faulty selfobject responses to the narcissistic needs of the growing child between the phase of primary narcissism and the oedipal phase. This is a naïve environmentalist position, from the perspective of modern developmental psychopathology. Correlations between character-istics of early parenting and later child behavior can be reinterpreted given that any association may be attributable to the 50% of genetic overlap between a parent and a biological child. This has been termed *passive genotype-environment correlation*. Reiss and colleagues (Reiss et al., 2000), in a landmark investigation of genetic and environmental influences on adolescent development found that of 52 statistically significant associations between family relationship (e.g. parental warmth or sibling relationships) and measures of adjustment (e.g. depression and antisocial behavior), 44 showed genetic influences that accounted for more than half of the common variance. In almost half of the 52, little association between family relations and adolescent functioning remained once genetic influence was taken into consideration. Further, there is the so-called child-to-parent effect, where aspects of the family environment are shaped by the child's genetically rooted characteristics (best shown in adoption studies, e.g. Deater-Deckard et al., 1999).

Kohut's approach to the problem of narcissism is at odds with the tradi-tional psychoanalytic approaches that emphasize conflict and compromise. As we shall see, in Kernberg's model the grandiose self and primitive idealization are both seen as defenses (however pathological) against rage, envy, dependence or paranoid-schizoid anxieties. In the self-psychology frame of reference, pathological narcissism is part of a developmental arrest. Thus, notwithstanding its disadvantages in adulthood, the grandiosity and the idealization are appropriate in early childhood. That this is a fundamental divergence is evident in the different clinical approaches of these two great theoreticians. To Kohut, it appears to follow from a developmental arrest model that patients need the empathic understanding that they lacked in infancy and the analyst should make himself or herself available for the idealization that antedates transmuting internalization. Of course, Kernberg and other more conflict-oriented analysts would see this approach as deeply collusive with the pathological solutions patients have found to their conflict. Kohut's approach was obviously a reaction to what he perceived as the harsh stance of classical analysts to their patients. But by prescribing a single antidote (empathy) he probably obscures the distinction between patients who are responding to failures of empathy and those who bring pathological needs for disruption to the consulting room.

8.2 Kernberg's integration of the object relations and structural schools

8.2.1 Kernberg's developmental theory

Kernberg, an analyst with a Kleinian training, writing and practicing in the environment of ego psychology, achieved a remarkable level of integration between these two, quite possibly epistemologically inconsistent (Greenberg and Mitchell, 1983), developmental frameworks (see Kernberg, 1975; 1980a; 1980b; 1984; 1992). While Kernberg makes good use of Kleinian concepts (such as the model of early object relations and superego formation, aggression, envy, splitting, projective identification) in understanding severe psychopathology, he does not adopt the Kleinian model of development fully. In his theory, affects are the primary motivational system (Kernberg, 1982). The self-image is one of three components of the process of internalization (Kernberg, 1976b), the others being object representations and dispositions to affective states. Combinations of a self-representation, an object representation and an affect state linking them are the essential units of psychic structure. He sees affects as coming to be organized into libidinal and aggressive drives, always via interactions with a human object. To put this differently, Kernberg treats drives as hypothetical constructs manifested in mental representations and affects; these representations are of the self and object linked by some dominant affect state. The object is not just a vehicle for drive gratification, and the major psychic structures (id, ego, superego) are internalizations of object representations and selfobject relationships under the influence of various emotional states. The characteristics of internalization depend upon the affects that are active at the time. A superego may be harsh because of a prevailing affect of anger and criticism.

The psychological structure that is implied by this developmental model has a number of key aspects. (1) The infant is born with affect dispositions initially grouped into two classes: pleasure and unpleasure. Cognitive development yields increasingly complex affective states. (2) Affect is always embedded within a relationship between self and object images. The environment triggers the affect and the environment is the infant's perception of objects and experience of self. (3) Object relations units (selfobject-affect triads) are stored in affective memory and evolve into 'drives' in the context of the mother–infant relationship (as was originally suggested by Loewald, 1971a). Pleasurable affect evolves into libido and unpleasurable affect evolves into aggression, with affects retaining a role only as signals to the drive organization. (4) Drives are not assumed to be 'object seeking', as in Fairbairn's formulations, since they evidently switch objects through development and aggressive drives are only object seeking to the extent that they seek the object's destruction (Kernberg, 1976b). Thus in Kernberg's model of the mind, drives retain their traditional position as a primary motivator of behavior and are not replaced here by object relationship structures. (5) Development is the internalization of object relations units and the creation of defenses against these. The object relations units determine ego structure that in turn determines drive organization. Unlike in Kleinian theory, unconscious fantasies are not equated with psychic structure, object relations units generate structure but are not equivalent to it. (6) The unconscious, repressed part of the mind is made up of object relations units from which the child attempts to protect himself, using defenses of varying maturity.

There are three processes of internalization: introjection, identification and ego identity.

Introjection exists at the most basic level of the internalization process. It involves the reproduction of an interaction with the environment by means of the clustering of memory traces attached to the self or object image and the interactions of the two in their affective context. Whole interactions with the environment are taken into the psyche. This notion is based on the propositions of Spitz (1965) and Jacobson (Jacobson, 1964) that self and object images are not yet distinguishable during the earliest stages of interaction. We have already looked at the untenability of this assumption in the light of current infant research and the need for the proposition to be reformulated, perhaps in terms of awareness of the boundedness of mental functioning rather than a selfobject distinction.

The second internalization process is *identification*, which presumes the child's cognitive ability to recognize the variety of role dimensions that exist in interactions with others. Identification, for Kernberg (1976b; 1976c), involves the capacity of the self to model itself after the object, for instance at first in imitation of the mother. Kernberg sees such identifications as strongly influenced by fantasy and affect. The person's experiences of gratification and frustration influence affective states and determine the degree to which self-representation is flexible, true and complex.

Finally, *ego identity* is a term borrowed from Erikson (1956) to denote 'the overall organization of identifications and introjections under the guiding principle of the synthetic function of the ego' (Kernberg, 1976b, p. 32).

Kernberg's model of early development is based on reconstructions from the treatment of severely disturbed adults. These reconstructions are strongly influenced by Kleinian theory. Kernberg's model is less concerned with the child's real experience than with introjects and fantasies. Kernberg (1976b) is also strongly influenced by the work of Jacobson (1964) and proposes a three-stage developmental theory associated with a theory of character pathology based on developmental failure. Jacobson's model begins with an undifferentiated phase, out of which representations of self and object are gradually distilled. The second phase has representations of both but these are partial and organized into 'all good' and 'all bad' imagos. The third phase entails the integration of self and object images where these coalesce into mental structures that can become regulators because of their investment in object and self-representations. Kernberg (1980a) was also influenced by Margaret Mahler's model of the separation-individuation process which intervenes between the symbiotic and the oedipal stages of development.

The model has five, loosely developmentally specified, stages. In the first weeks of life, selfobject representations are undifferentiated. The differentiation occurs during the second stage, assumed to occur during the first half of the first year. During this time pleasurable and unpleasurable experiences are organized into good and bad selfobject representations respectively. A failure of selfobject differentiation makes the person vulnerable to psychotic states. The boundary between self and object must become established for the psyche to be experienced as separate from the environment. These first introjects cannot yet be integrated by the primitive ego, but later during this stage Kernberg assumes that the ego actively splits good and bad object images apart in order to 'protect' the good images from the destructive power of the bad ones.

In the third developmental stage, from the second half of the first year until approximately 18–36 months, self and object images become increasingly differentiated. Ego boundaries are now reasonably well established, so even if fusion of self and object images occurs in highly stressful situations for the infant, the boundaries are maintained. In the third year of life, the polarized good and bad representations gradually become integrated so that total object representations and total self representations are formed. This does not occur until the end of this crucial stage. The shift from splitting to self and object integration permits a corresponding movement from splitting as the principal mechanism of defense to repression. The root of severe character pathology in Kernberg's model is to be found in ego weakness following failure to achieve the ego integration that accompanies integration of good and bad parts of self and object representations. Replacing splitting by repression protects the individual from severe character pathology.

The fourth stage of Kernberg's model covers the oedipal period, in which libidinally and aggressively invested self-images coalesce into a coherent self-system. It is not until this stage that the tripartite structural model fully emerges. It seems very much as if, whereas the first three stages of Kernberg's model are based on a Kleinian meta-psychology, in the fourth stage a structural ego psychological model takes over. At this stage ego identity is established and self and object images are integrated to yield an ideal self and object representation. The integration of these ideal structures with the cruel and persecutory superego forerunners, present at the previous stage, moderated by actual parental prohibitions, gives rise to the superego as a psychic agency.

In the final stage of Kernberg's model, ego and superego integration are achieved. The gradual integration of the superego into the personality fosters ego identity. Effective interactions with others help to solidify this. Object images, if sufficiently well integrated, will facilitate smooth untroubled interactions with the social world, which Kernberg assumes to assist in the further consolidation of these internal representations. Kernberg's model pays more attention to the transactional aspects of development than most other psychoanalytic approaches.

8.2.2 Kernberg's model of developmental psychopathology

8.2.2.1 Kernberg's framework of pathology

Kernberg differs from other proponents of object relations theory such as Klein, Fairbairn or Mahler, in that he focuses less on when the currently dominant pathogenic conflicts and structural organization of the personality originated, and more on the current state of the patient's thinking. He accepts that subsequent development makes the establishment of one to one correspondence between current state and the past quite risky. He sidesteps the distinction between oedipal and pre-oedipal problems which characterizes much structural psychoanalytic writing. He believes that all levels of disturbance are more complex in severe personality disturbance, but all levels are involved across the entire spectrum of psychopathology. He distinguishes three groups of psychological problems that he considers accessible to psychological treatment. His focus on diagnosis sets him apart from other psychoanalysts who consider psychoanalytic treatment not to be particularly informed by categorizing individuals into groups. Kernberg (1984), however, views neurotic and milder character disorder problems as accessible to psychoanalysis, but thinks that more severe character problems are suited only to expressive psychotherapy.

Kernberg (1984) sees *neurotic pathology* as regression to a relatively integrated, although repressed, infantile self, connected to relatively integrated although also unconscious representations of the parental object. An integration of self- and object representations has been achieved and object relationships are stable. Pathology in these cases results from conflicts between the structures of ego and superego. Patients with a neurotic, rather than borderline, level of personality organization are able to integrate positive and negative representations of self and others. This is because they have passed through infantile and early childhood phases of development, where good and bad representations of self and others are combined across affective valences and a complex integrated representation of these, containing both loving and hostile elements, has evolved. These unconscious representations come to govern future object relationships in the therapeutic situation and elsewhere. Even such relatively integrated internal representations, however, contain selfobject dyadic configurations, dating to developmentally earlier stages than the integrated units of self or object, and reflect either a defensive or an impulsive aspect of early psychic conflict.

An individual is highly susceptible to anxiety when configurations of self and object representations are highly charged affectively, and are poorly differentiated. For example, a representation of the self as being weak and vulnerable may be coupled with an object representation of ruthless domination with a violent affective tone. When this configuration is activated in therapy or elsewhere, the individual may become highly anxious. The defensive side may emerge separately, triggered by activation of the impulse-based relationship pattern. Thus, for example, in a masochistic character structure, the experience of a good relationship may trigger an unconscious fantasy of sexual intimacy between the child and the parent and propel a critical nagging relationship pattern into consciousness, where the self is seen as criticized by the therapist or another figure (Kernberg, 1988, p. 487).

In the more severe character psychopathology, the primary defense is marked splitting. In an *intermediate group*, repression coexists with splitting. Inhibitions are weak and impulsivity is marked. Even though repression is used there is a much greater likelihood of rapid reversal, and alternation between moments where the patient's self-representation is activated while the object representation is externalized onto another figure, and other moments in which the individual identifies with the object representation, while externalizing the self-representation onto the other. In the example cited above, it is noteworthy that although an individual may feel criticized, the criticism can shift very quickly from the self onto the other so that now the critic is seen as the self who is hurt and mistreated, and the individual identifies with the critical stance. The idea of this oscillation of self and other can account for many instances where impulses appear to change into their opposite (active into passive, good into bad). The superego can be harsh and sadistic and exists alongside a very primitive ego ideal. The ego is neither well organized as a structure nor is it yet a stable system. There is a lack of superego integration, severe mood swings, contradictory feelings and behavior, a mixture of repression and other defenses, and mixed pregenital and genital aims in relationships at this intermediate level of personality functioning. This intermediate-neurotic level of character disorder includes passive-aggressive personalities, sadomasochistic personalities, as well as some infantile and narcissistic personalities

At very severe levels of *character pathology*, Kernberg (1984) identifies a defensive primitive dissociation or splitting of internalized object relations. This level of character pathology is marked by a lack of integration of self and object representations, projections of primitive superego nuclei, splitting, impulsivity, lack of empathy, and the unmodulated expression of libido and aggression. He sees such splitting as occurring in borderline personality organization, antisocial personalities, patients with multiple sexual deviations in narcissistic personalities, addictions, and even in analytically approachable psychosis.

The pathology in these 'low level' character disorders is defined by the failure to develop integrated representations of object relationships out of which a coherent ego and superego could emerge. Here, the tolerance of ambivalence that is characteristic of higher level neurotic object relationships is replaced by a defensive disintegration of the representation of self and objects into libidinally and aggressively invested part object relations. Instead of the more realistic and readily comprehensible relationship patterns of neurotic personalities, Kernberg finds highly unrealistic, sharply idealized or persecutory self and object representations. These cannot be traced back to actual or fantasized relationships in the past, as he believes they do not correspond to any real relationship.

What Kernberg sees as activated in these patients are, for example, highly idealized part-object relations formed under the impact of diffuse, overwhelming emotional states of an ecstatic nature, or equally overwhelming but terrifying and painful emotional states that signal the activation of aggressive or persecutory relations between self and the object. As the object relations are very poorly integrated, the reversals of the enactment of self and other representations may be very rapid. This can make relationships with such individuals confusing and even chaotic. For example, love and hate may exist in a dissociated way side by side; several object relations may be condensed into single images, etc. Kernberg identifies the central problems of borderline patients as the activation of primitive, overwhelming part-object relations that continuously alternate.

In contrast, the problem in the case of *psychosis* is the blurring of boundaries between self and object representations. Here, the confusion between self and object blurs the origin of the intolerable impulse, which is therefore reactivated without the protection of the defensive relationship pattern into which it was cast. Such patients will often be overwhelmed in any intimate relationship. Autistic psychosis may be linked to the first stage of development when self and object images are undifferentiated and the child is unable to form a symbiotic bond with the mother. In schizophrenia or psychotic depression the child is thought never to emerge from the symbiotic phase when the representations of self and object were merged. These kinds of pathologies have not been thoroughly examined by Kernberg whose focus has been on the third stage of his developmental sequence, the shift away from splitting and toward repression.

8.2.2.2 Kernberg's model of narcissistic personality disorder

Kernberg (1970) describes 'a narcissistic personality structure' in individuals who display an over-reliance on acclaim, grandiose fantasies, intense ambition and extreme self-absorption. He describes their behavior as superficially adaptive while showing a lack of empathy, a tendency to exploit others, feelings of emptiness, boredom and lack of enjoyment other than from admiration, and a general inability to love. Kernberg (1975) characterized the habitual defenses of such individuals as devaluation, omnipotence and withdrawal, particularly when trying to cope with, or mitigate, the envy of others. He noted that such individuals have a capacity for consistent work and success, but their activities are focused around opportunities for exhibitionism. He described this as a pseudo-sublimatory tendency, lacking in genuine commitment, corruptible and subject to shifts in order to win praise. Less well socially adjusted individuals may seek treatment because of a failure to establish long-term relationships and a general sense of aimlessness. Narcissistic pathology must, however, be distinguished from narcissistic defenses. In one sense all defenses are narcissistic in that one of their aims is to preserve self-esteem. Narcissistic personality structure, however, is more than this in that the libidinal investment in the self is equated with ideal qualities.

Notwithstanding this important clarification, somewhat confusingly, narcissistic problems are included by Kernberg at a number of levels of his schema. Pathological narcissism is placed on a spectrum from his stage 3 to stage 4 and some individuals are described as fluctuating between the stages. Some narcissistic individuals function at the borderline level and display major deficiencies of anxiety tolerance, impulse control and sublimation. In these individuals the narcissistic grandiose self is used as a defense against the underlying borderline personality organization. The grandiose self is a fusion of the ideal self, the ideal object, and the self-image. These people are distinguishable from other borderline individuals by their frequent explosions into narcissistic rage, and their inability to depend on other people, which contrasts markedly with the desperate clinging of other borderline people. For all these individuals, Kernberg (1975) notes that feelings of inferiority coexist with notions of grandiosity. He sees this as rooted in 'chronic intense envy and defenses against such envy, particularly devaluation, omnipotent control and narcissistic withdrawal' (p. 264). The envious attacks sooner or later encompass their own activities and achievements, and with the approaching of middle age their destructive self-devaluations may lead to a 'gradual deterioration of the patient's internal past' (Kernberg, 1980a, p. 138). Their omnipotent approach to reality may lead them to deny natural ageing and lead them to feel rivalry with young people (their children and colleagues), and full-blown mid-life crises, with major vocational shifts and inappropriate love relationships, may follow.

In pathological narcissism the needy parts of the person remain dissociated from experience. Unlike obsessional or hysterical personalities, which Kernberg sees as being organized around repression (Kernberg, 1984), narcissistic personalities are predominantly based around splitting yet have a cohesive, albeit highly pathological self. The grandiose self differentiates narcissistic personality from borderline disorder. At a higher level of narcissistic pathology are individuals who have particular talents, allowing considerable external gratification. Grandiose self-organization is made more stable by environmental support. Such individuals may have significant neurotic problems but normally do quite well with analytic help, although their character pathology may undermine engagement with the treatment process. At the other end of the spectrum are narcissistic individuals with antisocial tendencies. A further severe sub-type of narcissistic pathologies is 'malignant narcissism' where Kernberg assumes the patient has virtually no structured superego. These patients have the poorest prognosis in treatment.

There are some key features to Kernberg's understanding of narcissistic functioning. (1) The lack of realistic self-concept drives these patients to seek constant admiration, attention and affirmation. (2) The self-image is split into all good (grandiose) and all bad (devaluing) aspects, which alternate in consciousness. (3) There is an overriding need to gain external support for the grandiose self, which undermines the capacity for genuinely mutual relationships. Others who fail to support the grandiose self have to be devalued or attacked. (4) Narcissistic people often idealize others who possess qualities that they feel they lack. This is not genuine admiration, but the projection of the grandiose self onto the object, so that even idealized relationships will leave them feeling empty. (5) There is neither real empathy nor real attachment, since the object stands for the self and must be controlled to fit the projection; because most people cannot or do not want to fit the projection interpersonal relationships tend to fail. (6) Because the grandiose self captures the ego-ideal, the sadistic superego forerunners will not be integrated as a healthy superego, leaving narcissistic individuals vulnerable to sadistic self-attacks against which they defend by projection. Thus there may be some paranoia; there may also be sociopathy, because of the absence of an integrated superego. (7) In 'malignant narcissism' the idealized object images that are normally integrated into the superego are totally integrated into the grandiose self, and the sadistic superego forerunners can therefore express unmitigated aggression. They are integrated into a highly abnormal self-structure that defends against intense self-attacks by massive projection generating a paranoid experience of an exploitative, humiliating attack by the object. (8) Because the grandiose self is imbued with sadism there can be a tendency to take great sadistic pleasure in victories over others even when (for example, in treatment) the triumph heralds self-destruction.

Kernberg saw narcissistic pathology as rooted in experiences of a rejecting primary caregiver, who was cold but the only available source of comfort. The child inevitably falls back on the grandiose self. The child's rage in protecting this is projected onto the parents who are then perceived as even less likely to meet the child's needs, and the child is increasingly restricted to the grandiose self for soothing and comfort. The term 'grandiose self' is one also used by Kohut (1968), but in a different way from Kernberg. For Kernberg, this aspect of the self contains the admired aspects of the child, compensatory fantasies about being omnipotent, and the fantasy of a loving and understanding caregiver. It is not seen as a particular developmental phase which the individual needs to outgrow. The cold aggressiveness of the mother leads to envy and hatred in the child, which may be defended against by inciting envy in others. Kernberg has suggested that such children often do have some special attribute (such as attractiveness or talent) that is capable of activating envy. The intensity of envy and hatred make it hard for the person to depend on others and they may adopt a stance of arrogance. This has much in common with the thinking of the London Kleinian, Herbert Rosenfeld (1971a) who suggested that the grandiose self was an inherently aggressive structure which helped the individual to protect himself from a dependent libidinal self. The self-imposed privation leads to a self that is even more desperate and needy of sustenance from others yet feels empty and envies others all the more. This empty, hungry and enraged self lies at the core of the self-representation of the narcissistic individual.

In psychotherapy, the grandiose self increasingly emerges in the relationship. Interpretive exploration of it will give insight about the role of these distortions in maintaining self-esteem and self-continuity, in the context of helplessness and rage. Because the grandiose self appears to be so effective in defending against the borderline organization its distortions may be more difficult to resolve than the borderline problems themselves. In Kernberg's approach, in contrast to Kohut's, the grandiose self and accompanying ideal-ization can only be undone by interpretation. In treating such patients, the analysis must uncover their oral aggressiveness, persecutory anxiety, object hunger and fear of dependence. This is of course diametrically opposed to Kohut's clinical approach, which is seen by Kernberg as supportive psychotherapy, not psychoanalysis. The core of Kernberg's approach is inter-preting and working through the narcissistic resistances, a process that precedes the revelation of the borderline dynamics of pathological inter-nalized object relationships, the envy which generates its own resistances in the transference and countertransference.

8.2.2.3 Kernberg's model of borderline personality disorders

According to Kernberg, borderline is a level of psychic organization rather than a nosological entity. His criteria for the disorder include: (1) non-specific manifestations of ego weakness (poor affect tolerance, impulse control and sublimatory capacity), (2) primitive defenses including splitting, (3) identity diffusion, (4) intact reality testing but a propensity to shift toward dreamlike (primary process) thinking, (5) pathological internalized object relation-ships. There is some empirical evidence in support of Kernberg's criteria (see Kernberg, 1981). Ego weakness is seen as due to the split between good (libidinal) and bad (aggressive) self and object images that cannot be integrated into a structure able to regulate emotions and impulses: the ego.

For Kernberg (1967; 1977), the root cause of borderline states is the intensity of destructive and aggressive impulses, and the relative weakness of ego structures available to handle them. The aggressiveness may be inborn or due to severe trauma at this stage of development. In either case, the good introjects are repeatedly threatened with destruction by hostile images and impulses which are necessary to achieve stability. Kernberg sees the borderline individual as using developmentally early defenses in an attempt to separate contradictory images of self and others. This is necessary to protect positive images from being overwhelmed by negative ones. The wish to protect the object from destruction with only the most rudimentary psychic mechanisms available leads to the defensive fragmentation of self and object representations. Borderline symptoms therefore represent a continuation of an unresolved infantile conflict state.

As we have seen, the defenses of borderline individuals center on the splitting (defensive separating) of contradictory self and object representations in order to forestall the terror associated with ambivalence. Splitting causes others to be perceived as either 'all good' or 'all bad', with the result that attitudes to them may rapidly shift between extremes. Primitive idealization, also a consequence of splitting, protects the individual from 'all bad' objects by creating an omnipotent object in fantasy, which is the container of grandiose identifications. Later idealization is based on 'reaction-formation', which is motivated by the need to defend against the aggressive feelings. In primitive idealization there is no trace of aggression. There is, however, little regard for the object, however idealized, merely a need for it as a protection against the surrounding world of bad and dangerous representations (Kernberg, 1975, p. 30). Borderline individuals fail to achieve the main task of Stage 3 of development, to be able to blend the good and bad self- and object images into a single representation. The defenses remain primitive, since the integrated ego that normally emerges at the end of this stage is not there to manage affect and conflict. There is an ego-fixation in the splitting phase.

Kernberg sees projective identification as a by-product of the absence of selfobject differentiation; the individual using this defense is left with a sense of empathy with the object of projection, and a need to control him or her. The other primitive defensive organizations of this stage include projection, introjection and massive denial. The use of primitive denial ensures that the individual can ignore his 'good' feelings toward the object when 'bad' ones dominate his consciousness. Splitting also results in a 'diffuse sense of identity', which is characterized by a confused representation of the 'real' object, and an unintegrated primitive superego that sets unattainable ideals and internalized persecutory images. Since representations of the self are organized like those of others, splitting also leads to

> extreme and repetitive oscillation between contradictory self-concepts ... the patient, lacking in a stable sense of self or other, continually experiences the self in shifting positions with potentially sharp discontinuities – as victim or victimiser, as dominant or submissive, and so on. (Kernberg, Selzer, Koenigsberg et al., 1989, p. 28)

The integration of the ego is not achieved in the absence of repression and the emergence of the tripartite structure (id, ego, superego), and the result is non-specific weakness in the ego. This, in turn, creates vulnerability to instinctual tensions that cannot be effectively managed. Further, the normal conflicts between drives, superego and the environment cannot take place intrapsychically; the conflict becomes part of the person's actual relationship experiences.

Transient psychotic episodes can occur because of the ready fusion in self and object representations. The psychotic symptoms are transient because reality testing remains adequate. Kernberg does not share the self-psychological view that borderline individuals are pre-psychotic. Thus, while there may be massively distorted perceptions of people, due to denial, projection, splitting and projective identification, and the individual's sense of identity may be undermined by the fusion of self and object images under intense emotional pressure, nevertheless Kernberg sees the boundaries around physical reality as largely intact. His assumption is that, because the ego structure is based on pathological internalized object relations and primitive defenses dominate over mature ones, all symptoms of borderline personality organization may be explained in terms of a structural diagnosis. The advantage of the structural diagnosis is that it yields treatment-relevant information. The dominance of stage 3 over stage 4 structures indicates less intensive once or twice weekly psychotherapy, rather than 3–5 times weekly psychoanalysis.

The elegance of Kernberg's theory lies in bringing together the phenomenological (what Kernberg called experience-near) and metapsychological or structural (experience-distant) levels of description. Splitting describes how these individuals tend to manage their relationships. Idealization, devaluation and denial are at once indicators of the organization of intrapsychic relationship representations and tell-tale signs of the individual's failure to generate more advanced mental mechanisms. Thus, the signs of the disorder relate directly to the underlying meta-psychological dysfunction. The dramatic separation of good from bad representations is at once the indicator of a pathogenic process (a shift toward primary process thinking), the cause of the process (the failure to integrate internal representations that would lead to the structuralization of an ego) and the content of the process (pathological internalized object relationships). Kernberg goes beyond traditional ego psychology in that the explanation in terms of 'ego weakness' is no longer circular (see Chapter 3). Ego weakness is co-terminous with an active defensive process that leads to the split-ego organizations that cannot withstand close contact with bad object representations.

Kernberg (1987) illustrates how the self-destructiveness, self-mutilating behavior and suicidal gestures of the borderline individual tend to coincide with intense attacks of rage toward the object. They can re-establish control over the environment by evoking guilt feelings, or express unconscious guilt over the success of a deepening relationship. In some patients, self-harm occurs because the self-image becomes 'infiltrated' with aggression, so that their self-esteem increases and their grandiosity is confirmed by self-mutilation or masochistic sexual perversions. The therapist despairs at these patients' sense of triumph over pain and death. Therapeutic efforts seem futile to the patient, who unconsciously feels in control of death. Self-mutilation, such as cutting, may also protect from the identity diffusion (derealization) that is a constant threat to the fragmented internal world of the borderline individual. These processes would be challenging to understand without recognizing the excessively aggressive self and object representations unmitigated by positive contact. Such images are so painful that projecting them may feel like a matter of life or death. Projection, however, only makes the external world dangerous, so that it needs to be controlled by identification. The resulting weakening of ego boundaries generates the experience of selfobject fusion so characteristic of this condition. Omnipotence, the identification with the all-good self-image, can protect somewhat against this intense persecutory anxiety, as can devaluation which reduces fear of the object. When the attack turns against the self, the individual with borderline personality organization appears to feel in control. To withstand the harshness and painfulness of these attacks, the patient retreats into the ideal self-image and feels superior to ordinary human limitations. Because the rage of borderline patients lacks moderation, the attacks sometimes are exceedingly violent.

Kernberg (1970) groups together borderline and schizoid personality disorders, viewing both these as lower level character organizations (see also Kernberg, 1967). The overlap is to some extent substantiated by empirical investigations demonstrating co-morbidity between the two conditions (Plakun, Burkhardt and Muller, 1985), as well as overlaps in pathological psychic mechanisms (Grinker, Werble and Drye, 1968; Kernberg (1975; 1976b; 1984; 1989; Gunderson, 1985) believes that patients with antisocial personality disorder usually have underlying borderline personality organizations. Because superego integration is minimal at this level and sadistic forerunners are easily projected outwards, there is lack of guilt and of goals, inauthenticity and an intermittent capacity for sublimation. Antisocial behavior occurs in most severe personality disorders because of the common underlying personality organization (Kernberg, 1971). Superego pathology is particularly evident in an absence of loyalty, guilt, anticipatory anxiety and an incapacity to learn from prior experience. Kernberg (1989) also mentions the significant absence of self-reflection in these individuals.

Kernberg's treatment approach is well grounded in his theory and is carefully described in the manual of Transference Focused Psychotherapy, prepared by his research colleague, John Clarkin and the treatment research team he assembled (Clarkin, Kernberg and Yeomans, 1999). The expressive psychotherapy described in this manual (1) focuses on the patient's here-and-now affect (2) leading to the exploration of the activated selfobject representations (3) followed by the linking of split-off and contradictory selfobject representations using interpretations of the therapist–patient relationship. The manual specifies the treatment at three levels. (1) The strategies specify the overall goals of the treatment. (2) The level of tactics describes the therapist's decision points in every session. (3) Techniques refer to the moment to moment decisions in a session. At the level of strategies the therapist (a) defines the dominant object relations of the patient, (b) observes and interprets role reversals and (c) observes and interprets linkages between object relation dyads. The tactics of therapy cover a wide range of interventions including: (a) identifying affective turmoil, (b) naming the here-and-now object relations, (c) interpreting the dominant object relations, and (d) linking split-off object representations and affects.

8.2.3 Evidence consistent with Kernberg's formulations

On the whole, modern affect theories are consistent with Kernberg's formulations. The repetitive nature and the emotional salience of everyday social interactions are assumed to create affective biases which in turn become central organizing axes for personality over time (Izard, 1977; Malatesta et al., 1989). In line with Kernberg's speculations, affect theorists suggest that constitutional affect bias becomes consolidated through repetitions of discrete emotions and comes to be organized into rigid patterns. This may lead to specific forms of psychopathology. Thus, depression may be associated with a sadness bias while anxiety disorders are linked to an overrepresentation of self-object-affect triads linked to fear. Models based on these kinds of views need to be tested in longitudinal research focusing on the relationship of the child's initial, constitutional characteristics (e.g. stress reactivity seen in autonomic nervous system and hypothalamo-adrenal-pituitary axis arousal) and socialization experiences with parents that can shape particular affective biases implicated in particular disorders (Zahn-Waxler et al., 2000). Advances in research on emotions, however, suggests that an expanded conception of the structure and organization is required compared to Kernberg's formulations. For example, affective biases for depression are likely to involve worry, anxiety, guilt, shame, self-reproach, lack of pleasure, suppression of anger and hostility as well as some kind of empathic overarousal where the self becomes entangled with the problems of others. More complex models, positing configurations of emotion profiles, might be necessary to account for the very high levels of comorbidity of emotional disorders, for example, anxiety and depression (Angold, Costello, and Erkanli, 1999).

Some empirical work using projective techniques draws on Kernberg's theoretical model. Krohn's object representation scales for dreams (see Krohn and Mayman, 1974; Hatcher and Krohn, 1980) were constructed to assess levels of capacity for interpersonal relatedness. The aim of the measure is to examine the degree to which people are experienced as whole, consistent, alive and complex, as opposed to absent, desolate, fragmented and malignant. They are used primarily with Rorschach responses but can also be applied to early memories and dreams. There is a relationship between scores on this measure and general mental health (Grey and Davies, 1981) and the capacity to engage in psychotherapy (Hatcher and Krohn, 1980) as well as its outcome (Frieswyk and Colson, 1980).

A similar measure, also based on Rorschach protocols, was developed by Urist (1977) and Urist and Schill (1982). It draws on the work of Mahler and Kohut as well as Kernberg and identifies a seven-point continuum where a rating of one indicates reciprocity or mutuality, and seven indicates envelopment or incorporation. In between are points indicating collaboration, cooperation, simple interaction, analytic dependency, reflection mirroring and magical control coercion. The measure is correlated with outcome of psychotherapy (Kavanagh, 1985), and hospital treatment (Blatt, Ford, Berman et al., 1988), as well as the differential diagnosis of borderline personality disorder and schizophrenia (Spear and Sugarman, 1984).

Ryan's object relations scale (Ryan and Bell, 1984; Ryan and Cicchetti, 1985) also identifies borderline disorders and differentiates them from depressed or pathologically narcissistic states and neurotic disturbances in relatedness. Ryan and Cicchetti demonstrated an association between object relations and therapeutic alliance using the scale, while Ryan and Bell were able to predict the length of remission from hospital treatment for psychotic patients. Westen and his associates (Westen, Ludolph, Block et al., 1990; Westen, Ludolph, Lerner et al., 1990) developed a four-scale model for scoring object relations: complexity and differentiation of the representation of people, affective tonal relationships, capacity for emotional investment in relationships, and morals and understanding of social causality. The scale discriminates the borderline group of patients, demonstrating more malevolent representations, less emotional investment in relationships and values, and less accurate and logical attributions of causality. The complexity of the borderline representation was apparently greater than those of the other two groups.

These findings are, however, confounded with the issue of accuracy. Blatt, Brenneis, Schimek and Glick (1976) and Lerner and St Petr (1984) (see also Ritzler, Wyatt, Harder and Kaskey, 1980), using a different scoring system, also report patients showing higher developmental levels (levels of complexity) than normal, but questioned the accuracy and reality of their perceptions.

Perhaps the strongest support for Kernberg's model comes from the highly rigorous and imaginative work of Drew Westen (see Westen and Cohen, 1993). Westen and his colleagues designed a structured interview to elicit general characterization and specific memories of relationships with important others, and provide self-descriptions at increasing levels of abstraction. These workers give empirical backing to Kernberg's view of the transitory, split and poorly integrated quality of borderline self-representation. Such persons show little awareness of contradictions, egocentrism, an apparent lack of concern with the listener's perspective, poor differentiation between self and others, and extremely negative self-representations. In line with previous work (Bell, Billington and Cicchetti, 1988; Westen et al., 1990; Nigg et al., 1992), borderline individuals described relationship schemas with others that were generally malevolent, and in which the self and others usually took the roles of victim and victimizer. Self and other were often interchangeable (see Kernberg, 1984), the descriptions of roles reversing rapidly. The relationship schemas appear transitory, with the subject showing limited awareness of contradictions. The borderline patients' evaluations are all or nothing; for example, wishes or ideals are either totally achieved or not achieved at all. They are also unrealistic and confused about both feared and ideal self-representations. Their self-esteem dramatically fluctuates, particularly negatively. Their sense of self is disrupted by dissociative experiences (see Zanarini et al., 1990a). More generally, there is much support for Kernberg's concept of identity diffusion (Kernberg, 1975), seen in fluctuating investment in goals, values and relationships over time.

New evidence emerging from Kernberg's Personality Disorders Institute has confirmed many of his claims about the ego weakness of borderline patients. Clarkin and colleagues (see Clarkin, 2001) explored the capacity of borderline patients to exert effortful control. This is a temperamental ability to inhibit a dominant response in order to perform a subdominant response (Rothbart, Ahadi and Hershey, 1994). Effortful control (Rothbart et al., 2000) has three components (a) inhibitory control (e.g. 'I can easily resist talking out of turn, even when I'm excited and want to express an idea'), (b) activation control (e.g. 'I can keep performing a task even when I would rather not do it'), (c) attentional control (e.g. 'It is very hard for me to focus my attention when I am distressed'). BPD patients, as would be predicted by Kernberg's theory, are particularly high in negative affect (fear, sadness, discomfort and frustration) and low in effortful control. The findings suggest that the low capacity for effortful control (ego weakness) creates the risk for negative affect.

Executive functioning, the neuropsychological equivalent of effortful control, appears to be defective in BPD, but other aspects of attention and inhibitory processes (e.g. alerting and orienting) appear to be intact. The part of the brain responsible for these attentional processes (the anterior cingulate gyrus which controls limbic outflow) appears to be abnormal. The capacity to inhibit a dominant response in order to perform a subdominant response (measured by the Stroop test) is impaired in this group of patients when the material of the test is modified to be linked to current emotional concerns. An 'emotional Stroop' was found to produce effects in BPD compared to controls on fMRI in the Cornell laboratories. Other studies have also demonstrated cognitive dysfunctions in this group that might closely relate to their symptomatology. Memory and identity are intrinsically linked (Klein, 1970); an individual is by and large a memory of himself. Westen and Cohen (1993) demonstrate that the historical memory of borderline patients tends to have large gaps or discontinuities, and the self is represented as totally different during different time periods. These workers suggest that the social construction of identity may be disrupted in these patients by their failure to sustain long-term intimate relationships.

Kernberg often refers in his writings to the Menninger Psychotherapy Research Project (Kernberg et al., 1972). Kernberg's report of the project highlights evidence for the importance of expressive techniques in the treatment of individuals with severely borderline pathologies. Strictly speaking this is not a finding of the project. It is an informal observation of the differences between the treatments of patients who fared well and badly in this study. The study compared supportive techniques with psychoanalysis and did not have a treatment group who experienced expressive psychotherapy. In any case the long-term outcomes of the treatment trial turned out to be far more complex than they appeared in the 1960s and 1970s (Wallerstein, 1986; 1989; 1993). The majority of patients crossed over between treatments so the specific effects of psychoanalysis and supportive therapy are hard to determine. One general conclusion has been that supportive techniques on their own had surprisingly strong beneficial effects on these patients (particularly those with low ego strengths).

However, more recent evidence pertinent to Kernberg's therapeutic model is about to become available. A trial of Transference Focused Psychotherapy is under way that is contrasting the best available alternative treatment of BPD (Dialectical Behavior Therapy) with TFP. The full findings will not be known for some years but initial findings are encouraging. A pilot study of 17 patients with BPD showed substantial improvements over a year of therapy (Clarkin et al., 2001). This is the most serious attempt so far to demonstrate the effectiveness of a rigorously described and implemented outpatient treatment program for BPD.

8.2.4 Evaluation of Kernberg's model

Kernberg's work has been extremely influential in the United States, Europe and Latin America. He succeeded in systematizing psychoanalytic object relations theory into a unitary framework that is consistent with both classical and structural theory and with the work of British object relations theorists. The key elements of the integration are the contributions of Melanie Klein, Wilfred Bion, Edith Jacobson and Margaret Mahler. Perhaps even more important than the high level of theoretical integration arrived at was Kernberg's translation of object relations theory into a realistic clinical method, particularly well described for patients he designated as possessing a Borderline Personality Organization (BPO). Kernberg retained the technical stance of classical analysis: neutrality had a central place in his approach. When treating BPO patients, other object relations theorists, particularly Kohut and the British theorists (Winnicott, Fairbairn) recommend modifications to technique which bring the analyst as real person into the foreground. Kernberg's approach is more classical, expressive rather than supportive, but also more pragmatic than other theorists in the various object relations schools.

A valuable and rare aspect of Kernberg's approach is the emphasis on psychoanalytic diagnosis, with implications for treatment choice. Psychoanalysis is not regarded as the treatment of choice regardless of diagnosis, as most other clinical-theoretical approaches imply. Kernberg recommends psychoanalysis only if the patient's ego is strong enough to sustain the decomposition of the personality into its component object relations units and subsequent reintegration of them into a new structure. This is not the case for BPO, but is for psychoneurosis. Narcissistic personality disorder is somewhat ambiguous from this point of view as many patients fitting Kernberg's description are similar to BPO from a structural standpoint, yet Kernberg recommends psychoanalysis rather than expressive psychotherapy as the treatment of choice.

The integration is not perfect; for example, Kernberg leapt between drive theory and object relations approaches by using common terminology in the two frameworks (e.g. 'good' and 'bad' constellations of relations with objects). He made extensive use of affects as explanatory constructs, but his view of these fit poorly with classical (drive theory) formulations. Kernberg's bias was toward abandoning drive theory in favor of a relational approach (Greenberg and Mitchell, 1983). He achieved integration by radically altering the meaning of terms that have been part of the classical model, such as id, drives and objects. Kernberg's commitment to the concept of drives is rooted in his belief in the motivational force of aggression. Kernberg has, however, successfully distinguished instinctual acts and drives, the latter (as we have seen) being a maturational achievement based on the relatively effective integration of object relations representations. Aggression evidently fits Kernberg's description of an instinctual response but are these responses integrated into a drive as he suggests?

The Kernberg model might lose little of its power to explain pathology, and gain in coherence, if the concept of drive were abandoned. Aggression does not follow the cyclical nature of a biological impulse like sex, thirst and hunger. It is hard to see what the theory gains through the assumption of a mature biological destructive (and self-destructive) force. Kernberg's clinical examples and technical suggestions of work with hostility are open to interpretations in terms of solely object relations (say Fairbairnian) approaches and indeed clearly recommend an object relations (interpersonal) interpretative technique without reference to drive gratification or frustration. The distinction between instinctual acts and drives in Kernberg's framework also forces analysts to look at the hateful, hostile, destructive acts of borderline individuals as somehow developmentally earlier (instinctual and primitive) in contrast to the manifestation of the aggressive drive in assertiveness that is considered a sublimation of the primitive hatred. As we have noted, assertiveness, gratification from a sense of agency, is characteristic of the infant from the earliest times (three months) (e.g. Watson, 1995) and there is little evidence to support the notion of vengeful, cruel and annihilating states of mind characterizing early infancy (Stern et al., 1985; Stern, 1990, 1995).

Even if Kernberg's attempt at providing an integrated psychoanalytic model has not been an unqualified success, he has advanced the field dramatically in terms of providing operational definitions for many of the constructs that he uses. He has been commited to research throughout his career (Kernberg, 1974; 1989; 1993; Clarkin et al., 1999). His technical recommendations are clear and testable (Kernberg and Clarkin, 1993). His descriptions of psychopathology, particularly of personality disorder, can be tested against the operational criteria provided by the DSM (Miller, Luborsky, Barber and Docherty, 1993). His etiological hypotheses reflect the general weaknesses of psychoanalytic formulations (see below). His contribution is a landmark, not simply in terms of the advancement of psychoanalytic developmental formulations of severe personality disorders, but also because it brings about a major shift in the epistemic stance taken by psychoanalysts, from a clinical/hermeneutic toward an empirical perspective.

CHAPTER 9

The interpersonal-relational approach: from Sullivan to Mitchell

9.1 Overview of the relationist approach

The most rapidly evolving theoretical orientation within psychoanalysis in the last decade is the so-called interpersonal-relational approach. Many major figures are contributing to this orientation. Its hallmark is perhaps the assumption that the psychoanalytic encounter is co-constructed between two active participants, with the subjectivities of both patient and analyst generating the shape and substance of the dialogue. Many current major contributors are more or less committed to interpersonal-relational views, their works include McLaughlin (1991), Renik (1993), Hoffman (1994), Ogden (1994), Benjamin (1998), Bromberg (1998), other major contributors include Daniel Stern, Jay Greenberg, Lewis Aron, Stuart Pizer, Charles Spezzano, Edgar Levenson and Stephen Mitchell. Their views are all somewhat different, and there is no definitive interpersonal-relational view. We have singled out Stephen Mitchell for discussion here because his well-established and coherent corpus typifies the relational approach.

The key ideas of the so-called *Interpersonal School* of the 1940s and 1950s form the foundations of the interpersonal-relational approach. The major classical contributors included Harry Stack Sullivan, Erich Fromm, Frieda Fromm-Reichmann and Clara Thompson. Both Sullivan and Thompson were, in the 1930s, already demonstrating how to treat schizophrenic young men and schizoid young women patients from the perspective of interpersonal relations. Their approach was operationist (which could be called practical) and humanist, and explicitly excluded the libido metaphor. Sullivan never even tried to become a psychoanalyst, although he consistently acknowledged his debt to Sigmund Freud. It was probably Clara Thompson, originally a training analyst in the New York Psychoanalytic Society, who blended together Sullivan's '*Interpersonal Psychiatry*', Fromm's '*Humanistic Psychoanalysis*' and the Hungarian pioneer Ferenczi's clinical discoveries, to generate a novel and genuinely interpersonal approach to psychoanalysis (Thompson, 1964).

Many of Sullivan's ideas continue to be relevant. Among contemporary writers, perhaps Benjamin Wolstein's (1977; 1994) and Edgar Levenson's (1983; 1990) work should be mentioned as critical to any definition of the current interpersonal school. These authors remain more or less loyal to the Sullivanian tradition, and appear suspicious of the move toward integration with object relations theory, which is a key aspect of the relational approach. In recent years Sullivanian analysts have increasingly moved toward integrating Sullivan's thinking with contemporary systems of psychoanalytic thought, rather than attempting to maintain his ideas in pure form. This process of integration has been very productive for psychoanalytic thinking in its post-ego psychology phase.

A significant contribution to this integrationist trend, and the consequent shift toward a relational (rather than just interpersonal) school, was Greenberg and Mitchell's (1983) epic volume on object relations theories. This extraordinary volume reinterpreted many of Sullivan's and object relations ideas as 'relational' and contrasted them with classical, non-relational approaches, such as ego-psychology. By implicitly linking Sullivan's interpersonal theory to (British) object relations approaches, the book forged a close link between the increasingly powerful object relations schools and the interpersonalist tradition, which had until that time, been largely ignored by North American mainstream psychoanalysis and was practically unknown outside the US. Other thinkers who came to use a relational frame of reference arrived at this viewpoint from more traditional psychoanalytic backgrounds such as ego psychology (Renik, 1994) or individual approaches such as Gill's 'social model' (Gill and Hoffman, 1982; Gill, 1983).

One of the key innovations of the interpersonalists' approach is their replacement of the classic model of the psychoanalyst as observer with a model of the analyst as participant in a shared activity. There are numerous aspects of this shift in perspective. Interpersonalists supplement or replace notions of objective truth with subjectivity, the intrapsychic is replaced with the intersubjective; fantasy (poetics) gives way to pragmatics (descriptions of experience or of events); emphasis on the content of analytic interpretations shifts toward observation of the analytic process; the concepts of truth and distortion are supplemented with perspectivism; the search for strong theories gives way to attempts to avoid theoretical bias; and countertrans-ference-as-feeling is supplanted by countertransference-as-enactment.

In the meantime an influential stream of the North American psychoana-lytic establishment embraced a complete two-person, mutually participating interpersonal psychology with a very strong emphasis on the subjectivity of the here-and-now transference (e.g. Gill, 1994; Renik, 1996; Hoffman, 1998).

They are more often exclusively focused on the 'playground' of the therapeutic situation than traditional interpersonalists, such as Levenson (see below), who had always focused on the here-and-now encounter, but accompanied this with extra-transference interpretations. For many decades interpersonal psychoanalysts were considered not to be psychoanalysts at all. Only in the last two decades, as the psychoanalytic mainstream has so much weakened in the United States, have the contributions of the interpersonalist tradition come to be acknowledged. The idea of mutual participation in the transference has become part of the general psychoanalytic ethos. The ideal psychoanalyst was no longer a neutral observer, but the patient's collaborator engaged in a continuous negotiation about truth and reality – this dialogue being the only way of escaping preconception.

9.1.1 Sullivan's model of personality development and the interpersonalist approach

Historically, Sullivan's (1953) dissatisfaction with mainstream psychoanalysis is comparable to that of Fairbairn (1952b), not just in time but because of their shared central complaint that mainstream psychoanalysis overlooks the relationship-seeking aspect of human character. Sullivan went further than Fairbairn in cutting his ties with the Freudian approach, rejecting explanations for disorder in terms of intrapsychic mechanisms and adopting an exclusive focus on interpersonal relations. In Sullivan's view, nobody can be understood apart from his relationships with others: the way one is with others defines who one is. Intrapsychic concepts such as drives, defense mechanisms, or explanatory constructs such as structural conflicts between ego and id, id and superego, were seen by Sullivan as obscuring a person's problems by assuming a spurious divide between the person and his environment.

'All organisms live in continuous, communal existence with their necessary environment' (Sullivan, 1953, p. 31). The human environment, Sullivan stresses, includes continual interactions with others and, on a wider level, with the collective achievements of others (culture). It is folly to attempt to grasp the structure of any organism without considering the ecological niche it has adapted to fill. Sullivan portrayed the early interactions between the infant and its human environment as shaping an almost infinitely malleable potential to fit an interpersonal niche as closely as possible.

Sullivan's (1953) developmental model is rooted in the evolution of the capacity for relationships. The first stage of development was characterized by the relationship of 'maternal empathy'. For the infant's inherent biological and emotional needs to be satisfied, another person, the mother, who experiences the tensions created by unsatisfied needs in the infant as her own, must be present and thus acts upon them. This is experienced as 'tender behavior', and these interactions create a general need for tenderness which becomes a primary but non-biological need that can only be satisfied by the tender behavior of another. The nature of the interpersonal need changes with age. The early need for bodily contact (1st year) changes into a need for an audience for the child's actions (2nd through 4th year), to be followed by a need to learn to compete and compromise with others (5th through 8th year), and then a need for a good same sex friend through to puberty, which switches to a need to be intimate with a person of the opposite sex in adolescence. Thus, Sullivan completely rejects Freud's model of libidinal development in general and infantile sexuality in particular. 'Lust dynamism' is only a feature of adolescent development, and even here its capacity to disrupt depends on ongoing interpersonal experiences. If favorable, it becomes integrated with the need for intimacy.

Sullivan does not see sex as a drive to be tamed by development. Throughout, emotional needs predominate over biological ones. Anxiety, for example, indicates not frustrated drives, but the infant's sense of the anxiety his tension created in the mother. Anxiety has no identifiable object; it is 'caught' from the mother. It is interesting to note how closely Sullivan's formulation resembles models of the development of emotion understanding based on infant research (Gergely and Watson, 1996). In this latter formulation, the infant is seen as not having an inherent symbolic representation of its state of arousal; this arousal acquires meaning through the mother's response (mirroring) to the infant's state. If this is distorted in the direction of anxiety, the infant's experience of arousal might be biased in the same direction and the infant would have 'caught' the other's anxiety. The 'need for security' is the need to avoid anxiety (or fear of anxiety).

As in many object relations formulations, for Sullivan (1953) the extent of the mother's tenderness determines the degree and quality of integration in the infant's personality. When the child's needs produce anxiety in the caregiver, the child becomes anxious and the early relationship creates a tendency toward disintegration rather than integration. Sullivan, like 'English' (Kleinian) and 'British' (Independent) object relations theorists, noted the child's tendency to group all experiences with the caregiver ('prehensions') as either 'good mother' (non-anxious), or 'bad mother' (imbued with anxiety), experiences. Self and object experiences are not differentiated at this point, and the self emerges from this conglomerate affective image as the child discerns how he is generally responded to by the caretakers, responses which Sullivan (1953) termed 'reflected appraisals'. It is assumed that self-experiences inconsistent with others' appraisals are systemically excluded from the emerging sense of self. Maneuvers used by the child to avoid anxiety in the caregiver, that gain the caregiver's approval and increase tenderness, come to be organized as the 'good me', while behaviors that generate anxiety and therefore disapproval in the caregiver are organized into the 'bad me'. Sullivan conceived of a third category of experience, which produces such intense anxiety in the caretaker (and consequently in the child) that it cannot come into consciousness under any circumstances, as the 'not me' or 'dissociative' system. It is tempting to link this to the qualitatively different quality of attachment patterns observed in infants whose mothers respond to them by frightening or frightened behavior or even dissociation (Schuengel, Bakermans-Kranenburg and van IJzendoorn, 1999). Infants in this attachment category (the 'disorganized' category) are most likely to show later psychological disturbance (e.g. Lyons-Ruth, 1996b). More mature maneuvers to reduce anxiety (Sullivan called these 'security operations') are aimed at generating a sense of superiority (e.g. the illusion of power, stature, a sense of specialness). The self-system is a set of maneuvers from childhood that were aimed at reducing anxiety and preserving the shape of the self. These security operations come to be characteristic of a developing personality, and are thought to determine the kind of neurotic patterns that are likely to emerge in the course of later development.

Sullivan did not view anger or aggressiveness as inborn. Rage is the first response to punishment, but it is gradually replaced by anger as a more adaptive response. If anger is suppressed because it is punished, rage is more likely to re-emerge as tantrums or chronic resentment. 'Malevolent transformation' is the most debilitating form of distorted anger, when hostility replaces the need for tenderness. This is thought to occur when the child's request for tenderness is met by negativity; when the experience of anxiety and humiliation follows the expression of this need, a transformation will occur whereby the child will not only inhibit the need for tenderness but will refuse to allow anyone to act tenderly toward them. This will interfere profoundly with subsequent relationships.

Sullivan stressed that where there is conflict in the individual, it has been produced by conflictual, contradictory signals and values in the environment. Sullivan's (1964) definition of interpersonal situations privileges the dyadic: 'Configurations made up of two or more people, all but one of whom may be more or less completely illusory' (p. 33). This might seem confusing since 'interpersonal' (e.g. in comparison to 'intrapsychic') is ordinarily taken to refer to more than one person. The human environment, with which Sullivan insists the individual is in continual interchange, must involve at least one other in addition to the subject in question. The representational system created by the *real* interaction between the object and the child is then potentially used to distort further interpersonal encounters. Sullivan (1964) suggests that the 'correct view of personality [concerns] the doings of people, one with another, and with more or less personified others' (p. 33). The illusory others, by definition, are not derived from or generated in current interaction; the patient brings consolidations and transformations of real others in previous interactions to the current one. Past interactions are recorded, combined, reorganized, and re-experienced in complex relationships with real others in current interactions. Illusory personifications are shaped in early experience. Analysis offers insight into the way these models of relations with past others operate as an organizational grid through which present experience is filtered. Such insights enable the patient to discover potentially new experience in the present (Sullivan, 1964). It is quite likely that Piaget and other social scientists with structuralist views influenced Sullivan's model of parataxic distortions.

In general, psychopathology results when the satisfaction of (interpersonal) needs is disrupted by anxiety. As the source of anxiety is interpersonal, it is ultimately possible to trace all psychopathology back to a relationship that is dominated by anxiety. If the need for security dominates the possibility of need satisfaction, the personality is dysfunctional because it operates primarily out of the need for security rather than other developmentally appropriate emotional needs. The need for power, status and prestige will predominate. We can readily recognize aspects of narcissistic personality disorder in this description. In general, unfavorable early experiences were thought to generate attempts at warding off the possibility of anxiety (security operations), but if these were unsuccessful at protecting the individual from the experience of the 'bad me', low self-esteem could be expected to result. The 'bad me' generates anxiety, and low self-esteem inhibits the possibility of integrating situations capable of satisfying needs (e.g. falling in love). This is Sullivan's account of how psychopathology causes generalized impairment of personality function. The solutions sought are 'exploitative attitudes', whereby relationships are created in which the other is either explicitly or implicitly exploited. For example, masochism involves a 'substitutive process' where in place of explicitly exploiting the other, the person substitutes him or herself. Masochists may for example engage in relationships in which they are trapped into revealing private things, and thus experience chronic humiliation.

If the individual is unable to mount security operations against dissociative aspects of the personality, this leads to an experience where the 'not me' is personified, and can degenerate into a schizophrenic process. Sullivan termed this the 'paranoid transformation'. He firmly believed that like all other psychopathologies, schizophrenia was an understandable reaction to interpersonal anxiety (Sullivan, 1962). The anxiety was so devastating and so early in life that the dissociative component of the personality could not be warded off.

A curious feature of Sullivan's work is that he seems to feel obliged to create a frame of reference that would suffice as an alternative to the psychoanalytic. Awkward terms such as 'security operations', which add little to the concept of defense, are mobilized to create a boundary between Sullivanian and Freudian psychoanalysts. Similarly, parataxic distortion appears practically identical to the notion of internalized object relationships. His theory is an attempt to create a dynamic theory, without the notion of an unconscious, drives or internal object representations. In line with this wish to create a separate discipline, his conception of the goal of therapy was also improved interpersonal adaptation (Sullivan, 1956). Paradoxically, however, his route to achieving this was not via the deeper exploration of the therapeutic relationship, but rather by increasing the person's awareness of current relationships outside therapy. Sullivan's attitude to clinical work follows from his view that the past distorts interpersonal perception in the present. He describes a therapist who is to some degree committed to an intellectual effort of 'participant-observation'. Havens (1993) described this therapeutic attitude in detail. Sullivan thus intended to challenge the more traditional assumption that the psychiatrist gathers, and analyzes data from a more or less objective position. The work of the Sullivanian therapist is supposed to be one of active but engaged collaborative investigation: eliciting information from the patient and laboriously sorting out the past from the present, the illusory from the real, continually checking the data.

As participant observer, the analyst counteracts the patient's perception, rather than interpreting it. Sullivan (1954) described 'active techniques' that the therapist could use to show the patient that experiences that he felt to be shameful and anxiety-provoking were not construed in that way by the therapist. This approach seems quite close to Alexander and French's (1946) 'corrective emotional experience' idea. However, there is far more to the role: the therapist is a participant in order to understand. 'The events which contribute information', Sullivan (1964, p. 39) suggests, 'are events in which the psychiatrist participates; they are not events that he looks at from atop ivory towers.' Thus, the relationship-oriented aspect of Sullivan's clinical work was always coupled with a focus on helping patients gain awareness of relationship patterns. Even though Sullivan was often critical of interpretation, his interventions probably worked by increasing the patient's understanding of his way of relating, through experience of the transference relationship. Interestingly, Sullivan's attitude mirrors some of the discomfort felt by present-day interpersonal psychotherapists about being identified with traditional psychodynamic ideas (e.g. Klerman et al., 1984). However, the strongest evidence for the efficacy of psychodynamic therapy comes from studies of psychotherapy in the strictly interpersonalist tradition. The best controlled studies of relatively brief psychotherapy with mood disorders (Frank, Kupfer, Wagner et al., 1991; Shea et al., 1992; Shapiro et al., 1995), with adolescents (Mufson and Fairbanks, 1996), with eating disorders (Fairburn, 1994) and chronic users of health-care services (Guthrie et al., 1999) have all shown interpersonal therapy to be at least as effective as other brief therapies. Most studies that have looked at more classically psychoanalytic therapies have been less focused on particular clinical problems and have had less adequate experimental controls (Roth and Fonagy, 1996).

It was the New York psychoanalyst Thompson (1964) who brought psychoanalytic thinking into dialogue with interpersonalist thought. She argued that Sullivan's concept of parataxic distortion encompassed two different dimensions of Freud's clinical theory, both transference and character structure. They are means by which residues of the past are displaced into present situations ('transference' for Freud) and that displacement serves to organize the person's current experience and interactions with others ('character' in Freudian ego psychology). The reformulation of Sullivan's views by Thompson allowed interpersonalist analysts to define themselves, in contrast to their classical colleagues, as far more focused in the present. Interpersonalist psychoanalytic authors increasingly emphasized the embeddedness of the patient in the present (e.g. Levenson, 1983). Modern interpersonalists attempt to adapt the Sullivanian viewpoint to the clinical method using the patient–therapist relationship as the primary analytic instrument, while changing the primary analytic question from 'what does it mean?' to 'what is going on between us?'. Yet Sullivan's interest in the patient's behavior outside the session has not been lost (Levenson, 1987).

As we have seen, the interpersonal therapist aims to increase the patient's insight, not into his or her unconscious but into the therapeutic interaction. There is a parallel here with some general systems psychoanalytic theorists who see the residues of the past as procedures rather than as episodic memories. These theorists claim that the transference relationship is dominated by procedural memories, separated from past experiences that gave rise to them by neuropsychological as well as dynamic barriers (they represent different memory systems) (Amini et al., 1996; Migone and Liotti, 1998; Stern et al., 1998; Fonagy, 1999b). In both of these approaches, the meanings derived from reconstruction are seen as relatively incidental in the clinical process. What remains crucial is a clarification of the patient's ways of handling current anxieties and present experience.

9.1.2 Mitchell's relational model and the psychoanalytic relational school

Almost twenty years ago, Jay Greenberg and Stephen Mitchell (1983) performed a major service for the psychoanalytic community by bringing together, almost for the first time, an up-to-date synthesis of the work of major psychoanalytic thinkers. They also kick-started what might be termed the interpersonalist renaissance of psychoanalysis. By placing the interpersonal-relational approach in the context of other modern psychoanalytic contributions, they enabled the reader to see the work of Sullivan as just one example of the 'relational/structural' model, which they eloquently juxtaposed with the 'drive/structural' model. However, Greenberg and Mitchell's categorization of psychoanalytic theories into 'relational-structural' theories, that see man as an interpersonal being motivated to relate, and 'drive/structural' theories, where the propellant of human motivation is a biologically determined inherited tendency (the drives), never quite worked. There were too many examples where theorists attempted to be on both sides of the divide simultaneously (e.g. Kernberg, Sandler, Bowlby) and it is not clear (to these authors at least) that psychoanalytic models that admit both drives and that relationship-based motivators are necessarily any less coherent or empirically sound than those which (by Greenberg and Mitchell's criteria) are pure examples of either the drive or the relational model.

However, Stephen Mitchell's contribution was far greater than as the co-author of a scholarly integrative text. Following its publication, Mitchell established himself in a number of key books and papers as one of the two or three most significant psychoanalysts working in the US (Mitchell, 1988, 1993b; Mitchell and Black, 1995). His recent death at the age of 54 cut this creative life tragically short. Unlike many contributors to the field, Mitchell was invariably careful to offer his own relational contributions in the context of a detailed explication of other theories. For example, he placed sexuality (Mitchell, 1988) and aggression (Mitchell, 1993a) in the relational context, justifying a central place for both in human experience because they are powerful vehicles for establishing and maintaining relational dynamics. Similarly, he offered a relational perspective on therapeutic interaction in the context of a scholarly comparison of interpersonalist and Kleinian approaches (Mitchell, 1995). His paper on narcissism builds on the major perspectives current at the time (Mitchell, 1986). His final book (Mitchell, 2000) brings Loewald, Fairbairn, Bowlby, Winnicott and Sullivan together in a systematic statement of what constitutes relational psychoanalysis. Mitchell's contribution was essentially integrative. Other psychoanalysts who approach similar themes to Mitchell yet come from traditional object relations theory or even structural/drive theory approaches have become interested in relational ideas due to his inspirational writings.

Mitchell's contribution is relational in the sense that his central focus was the interpersonal nature of individual subjectivity. Mitchell (1988) put forward the radical proposition that psychic reality is a relational matrix, encompassing both the intrapsychic and interpersonal realms. A closely related perspective with roots in self-psychology is clearly elucidated by Stolorow and Atwood (1991):

> the concept of an isolated individual mind is a theoretical fiction or myth which reifies the subjective experience of individual distinctness ... The experience of distinctness requires a nexus of intersubjective relatedness that encourages and supports the process of self-delineation throughout the life cycle. (p. 193)

This perspective contrasts starkly with the traditional Freudian view (a view of the mind that Mitchell labels 'monadic'), which sees individuality as a compromise between the internal, biological and primitive on the one hand and the co-operative, organizational and mature on the other. For Mitchell, the relational is at the core of psychoanalysis – a core that he shows was present from its inception. The relational includes individuality, subjectivity and inter-subjectivity. It is human relating that achieves individuality and renders experience personal, unique and meaningful. The philosophical bases of this approach are shared by a number of psychoanalytic traditions. Marcia Cavell (1994), drawing on Wittgenstein, Davidson and others writes: 'subjectivity arises along with inter-subjectivity and is not the prior state' (p. 40).

Mitchell (1988) was critical of self-psychologists because he perceived their unit of analysis (the nuclear self) to be intrapsychic. He also criticized object relations theorists (such as Winnicott and Guntrip) who conceive of pathology in terms of developmental arrest, de-emphasizing the role of conflict and the relational nature of development. Mitchell built on the clinical implications of Sullivan's ideas, suggesting that the basic units of mind are relational configurations that are intrinsically in conflict. The subject matter of psychoanalytic theory and clinical work are the matrices of relational bonds within which personal meanings are embedded. Unlike Sullivan, Mitchell considered that such matrices constitute meaning: psycho-analysis is framed to elucidate meaning in the context of the patient-therapist interaction.

Relational theories, partly because of their historical origins, tend to repudiate the biological in thinking about motivation and human nature. The human adult self is not thought to be understandable in terms of other sorts of beings, animals or babies, but has its own distinctive nature. It is not motivated by 'special' drives, but is the agent of many kinds of activities, all of which contribute to the general project of creating, recreating and expressing itself within its relational context (see Mitchell, 1988). Whereas classical analytic theory stands or falls on its biological foundations (Sulloway, 1979), the heritage of interpersonal-relational theories is qualitatively different, more at home with post-modern deconstructive ideas than with

Sexuality

→ brain-behavior integration, and ultimately at odds with the reductionism of the biological context of attachment. Mitchell (1988) sees sexuality as a powerful biological and physiological force that emerges inevitably within a relational context, conditioned by an object world. The triggering, the experience and the memory of the sexual response are all shaped by the interpersonal context within which the sexual response arises and takes on psychological meaning. Sexuality is not seen as primarily a push from within, even if it is experienced in this way; it is better understood as a response, within a relational field, to an external or even internal object. This does not de-emphasize the biological, but posits a different understanding of how the sexual behavioral system relates to other systems.

Sexuality is seen as a genetically controlled physiological response which emerges within interpersonal contexts that are mutually regulatory, intersubjective, or relational. These contexts form the medium within which mind develops and operates: sexuality is formative to the extent that it is part of these contexts. Its power is not derived from organ pleasure but from its meaning in a relational matrix. A similar powerful relational argument was constructed for aggression (Mitchell, 1993a). Neither sexuality nor aggression is then a driving force of development or adaptation. Rather, sexual and aggressive responses are seen as understandable in the context of the individual's infantile and early childhood experiences that have 'taught him about the specific ways in which each of his object relationships will inevitably become painful, disappointing, suffocating, overly sexualized, and so on. There is no reason for him to believe that the relationship into which he is about to enter will be any different' (Ogden, 1989, pp. 181–2).

It should be noted that the majority of those pursuing an interpersonalist tradition do not accept Mitchell's work as representative of Sullivan's ideas or of the basic tenets of the interpersonalist tradition. For example, Levenson (1989) has attacked Mitchell's attempts to link object relations theory with the interpersonal viewpoint as unwarranted ecumenicalism that threatened to subvert the interpersonal point of view. One critical issue that separates the relational from the interpersonal model concerns assumptions about the nature and origins of psychic versus physical reality. Sullivan showed a keen interest in observable behavior. He was not a behaviorist, but he had a systematic interest in what actually happened between people. For Sullivan, this is 'the detailed inquiry' of finding out exactly who said what to whom. Thus many interpersonalists show a definite reluctance to privilege fantasy over actuality. This might be traced back to their critical attitude to Freud's rejection of his seduction hypothesis. Within Mitchell's relational approach, fantasy and actuality are not necessarily alternatives, they 'interpenetrate and potentially enrich each other' (Mitchell, 1998, p. 183). Reality is inevitably encountered through imagination and fantasy. By contrast, in Levenson's

(1981) view the crucial distinction is not between the interpersonal and the intrapsychic points of view but rather between the model that holds that 'reality is *behind* the appearance' (traditional psychoanalytic view) and that 'reality is *in* the appearance' (the interpersonal view). Fantasy, in Levenson's view, is the reaction to real interpersonal anxiety rather than driving the distortion of interpersonal perceptions. In Levenson's view, the classical model and Mitchell err in understanding fantasy as some kind of royal road to psychic reality, accessible via the interpretation of symbols and disguises. The patient's problems are not to be found in an intrapsychic reality that can be uncovered. Rather, they are the distortions produced by interpersonal anxiety in the real world.

Mitchell's view may be seen as a bridge between a hard interpersonalist and an equally hard classical analytic position. He acknowledges Hans Loewald (1974) as the originator of this non-conventional psychoanalytic understanding of the relationship between fantasy and reality. Loewald argued that reality testing was not simply the evaluation of ideas against external reality, it is also the 'experiential testing of fantasy – its potential and suitability for actualization' (p. 368). For life to be meaningful, vital and robust, fantasy and reality must not be too deeply separated from each other, as reality without fantasy is vapid and empty, and fantasy adrift from reality is not only lacking in relevance but also potentially threatening (Mitchell, 2000, p. 29).

Developmentally, in the beginning Mitchell assumes we discover ourselves in the context of a social, linguistic, relational matrix. The individual psyche is formed with subjectively experienced interior spaces. In Mitchell's relational perspective the human mind is seen as an interactive phenomenon, thus an individual human mind is a contradiction in terms. Subjectivity is invariably rooted in intersubjectivity and the self and the world outside is continually organized by the mind into recurring patterns. Subjective spaces are assumed to begin as 'microcosms of the relational field' (Mitchell, 2000 p. 57); i.e. interpersonal experiences are internalized and transformed into a distinctly personal experience. Naturally, the intrapsychic relational processes, once formed, serve to reshape interpersonal processes which, in turn, alter intrapsychic processes that will alter patterns of inter-action, perpetually transforming themselves and each other.

The organizational structures that organize experiences are developmentally specific to some degree, with organizational schemes emerging sequentially (although they are also thought to operate simultaneously in adulthood along the continuum from consciousness to the unconscious, in dialectical tension with each other throughout the life cycle). Ogden (1989) suggested that the organizational schemes could be grouped into (1) autistic-contiguous, (2) paranoid-schizoid and (3) historical modes which vary according to degrees of articulation of self–other boundaries, split versus whole object relations, quality of reality testing and awareness of the irreversibility of time. Mitchell (2000) identified an alternative grouping of four basic modes through which relationality operated: (1) *non-reflective, presymbolic behavior*, or what people actually do with each other that leads to the organization of relational fields around reciprocal influence and mutual regulation; (2) *affective permeability*, or the shared experience of intense affect across permeable boundaries; (3) the organization of experience into *self–other configurations*; (4) *intersubjectivity* or the mutual recognition of self-reflective agents.

It should be pointed out that Mitchell (2000) did not propose this scheme as a true developmental model. He clearly restricted the scope of his four modes of relational organization to a 'Procrustean conceptual scheme' (p. 59). This can be used, amongst other things, to place major psychoanalytic theoretical formulations into a scheme. Attachment theory (see Chapter 10) was originally particularly concerned with what mothers and infants actually did, particularly how maternal sensitivity to the child's cues could create expectations of other behavioral interactions (Mode 1). Mode 1 also includes recent work on the representations of interpersonal interactions into procedural aspects of memory, whether relegated to this by repression of trauma (Davies and Frawley, 1994) or constraints imposed by cognitive development (Stern, 1994; Stern et al., 1998). By contrast, theorists like Fairbairn and Kernberg focus on Mode 3, self–other configurations (in Fairbairn's case, libidinal and anti-libidinal egos in relation to objects). Of course both Kernberg and attachment theorists talk of other modes of operation but they consider self–other configurations and behavioral interactions respectively to be fundamental and the other modes to be derivative from these. Mode 2 experiences of affective permeability, where direct resonances emerge in interpersonal dyads, has been explored in the recent psychoanalytic literature where the analyst's own emotional experiences are seen as reflections of the patient's emotional turmoil (projective identification) (Ogden, 1979; Bollas, 1987; Bromberg, 1998; Davies, 1998).

Mode 4 theorizing on intersubjective dimensions of relationality has come from relationally oriented psychoanalytic feminists like Chodorow and Benjamin. For example, Benjamin (1988; 1995) is particularly concerned with the development of the sense of self as a personal subject-as-agent in relation to other such subjects. She naturally writes of behaviors, affects and other self–other configurations. Yet in her writings these are contextualized into dimensions on a trajectory through which intersubjectivity emerges. Benjamin (1988) introduced new themes into the analysis of feminine subjectivity with her focus on the question of power and domination in sexual relationships. Benjamin's starting point is that psychoanalysis should be able to conceptualize intersubjectivity by becoming a 'subject-subject' discipline rather than a 'subject-object' one. The latter form of discourse carries a constant risk of dichotomization, only one end of the pole can possibly attain agency. The subject and object become 'active' and 'passive', 'masculine' and 'feminine'. This discourse needs to be rewritten in 'subject–subject' terms so that agency can belong to both. She writes: 'Within the subject–object paradigm, in which there is always one subject, never two, it is necessary that whatever one side gains the other must lose' (Benjamin, 1998, p. 40) She suggested, in a Hegelian spirit, that the desire for recognition by the other is the principle which opens up the dyadic (mother–infant) relationship but also allows the closure of the relationship through fear and defense. It is the fear of and defense against this maternal image that leads to the ubiquity of masochism in female sexuality.

The pre-oedipal father performs a key function: 'beating back the mother, to defensively idealize someone other than the mother, and also to extend love to a second' (p. 61). Benjamin goes on to argue that the traditional opposition in psychoanalysis between pre-oedipal and oedipal has been part of a society-wide polarization of gender. Relational psychoanalytic theory, however, challenges this polarization or dichotomizing tendency. It offers a model of fluid and multiple identifications that cut across the traditional 'paternal' versus 'maternal' positions. In the traditional oedipal complementarity the other is repudiated so that the self can be sustained. In a more mature post-oedipal complementarity, elements of identification are brought together in a manner that does not place them into opposition; they are less threatening because they no longer cancel out the identity of either the self or the object. The idealization-denigration dichotomy is overcome. Gender becomes an arena of encounter between necessarily fragmentary subjects who nevertheless relate to one another as agents rather than as threats. The intersubjective relational emphasis is on connectedness, recognizing difference but not giving way to the temptation to discount the other once the difference has been identified.

9.1.3 Relational views of psychopathology and its treatment

Interpersonalists embrace Fairbairn's notion of attachment to 'bad' objects – objects that are unavailable or unsatisfying. Mitchell (1988) suggests that the absence of a sensitive object causes the child to precociously fulfil a missing parental function, and thus a worry-free surrender of self to desires is lost. As in Winnicott (1965b), the spontaneous gesture is seen as sacrificed because of adaptational needs that the infant should never have confronted. Conversely, the capacity to engage with feelings (negative and positive) may be seen as an opportunity for a worry-free surrender to the person's own experience, an opportunity which is opened by the assurance of sensitive objects. The absence of certain parental functions forecloses this possibility.

Sullivan, for example, considered that the degree of fear in acute schizophrenic episodes was rooted in the fears of infancy. He assumed that anxious mothers in some way imparted their anxieties to a psychologically vulnerable infant. This led to a self state of intolerable anxiety which Sullivan termed 'not me' anxiety. In some of his writings, Sullivan (1956) unequivocally blames the mother:

> let us talk about the extreme poverty of favorable opportunity that the schizophrenic has had for building a successful self-esteem system because, early in life, the idea was in way conveyed inescapably to him that he was relatively infrahuman. (pp. 163–4).

Another interpersonalist, Frieda Fromm-Reichman (1948), coined the term 'schizophrenogenic mother' to describe the rejecting mothering that she assumed psychotic individuals must have received. Similarly, Searles (1963) argued on the basis of psychotherapeutic experience with schizophrenic patients that countertransference experiences of anxiety, despair, feeling inhuman or crazy were communications by the patient of childhood experiences they had actually undergone with caregivers who had literally driven them crazy.

If sexual instincts are not the driving force of development, how do they become the focus of so much psychological disturbance? Mitchell (1988) argues that the biological power of sexuality and the relational requirement of another to fulfil sexual needs, makes sexuality a dangerous but powerful medium of interpersonal relating. It frequently renders the individual vulnerable to the other, who is desperately needed. Furthermore, because in most societies the body is accorded some privacy, the sexual body that is withheld and hidden lends itself to symbolization of the need for the object. When object seeking is felt to be a risky endeavor, sexuality becomes 'a search for symbolic reassurances and illusory guarantees' (Mitchell, 1988, p. 111). Sexual difficulties are sexualized expressions of relational conflicts. For example, if the search for the elusive object is concretely expressed by seeking genital contacts, compulsive promiscuity might be felt to satisfy the need.

Relational theorists tend to be equally critical of the developmental arrest model of psychopathology generally proposed by self-psychologists and object relations theorists. Mitchell (1988) for example, is critical of the notion that a baby arrested in infantile development lurks under the surface in adulthood. The babyish self is a strategy (a safety operation in Sullivan's model) that enables interaction with others, a consequence of ubiquitous relationship conflict, rather than an unconflicted arrested self that simply requires recognition and appropriate mirroring. Similarly, the childlike needs expressed by adult patients are not infantile needs but adult dependency needs accompanied by intense anxiety. Interpersonal needs are intense throughout the life-cycle; the notion of developmental arrest privileges the needs of the earliest periods of life at the risk of overlooking current relationship needs.

In general, psychopathology for relational theorists derives from the rigidity or tenacity with which specific relational configurations are held onto by the individual (e.g. Greenberg, 1991; Mitchell, 1988). Flexibility to experience different relationships in different ways comes close to the relational definition of mental health. So why would developmental patterns be so enduring? Mitchell (1988) argues that individuals cling to pathological patterns because these are the only relationships they know. The child learns what it needs to be like, to engage the parent with a minimum of anxiety, and these modes of engagement become relationship templates for subsequent encounters. Thus early patterns are adhered to because they were effective in avoiding anxiety, and if these are threatened the individual will fear isolation and loss of contact with the self. If there is conflict between specific relational configurations and the predominant self-shaping relational patterns, they will not be woven into the 'tapestry of the self' and will find hidden forms of expression, resulting in neurosis. Mitchell (1991) suggests that the aim of therapy is to help the patient develop a more adaptable self by trying to enter into the subjective world of the patient and becoming part of his relational world, while at the same time wondering with the analysand why his or her way of relating appears to be the only way that he or she can form a relationship with the analyst, and trying to broaden the structure of the analysand's relational world beyond the narrow confines of his or her childhood constraints.

A good example of the relational view of personality disorder can be found in Mitchell's discussion of narcissistic problems (Mitchell, 1988). Mitchell appears to take a position somewhere between that of Kernberg and Kohut. He acknowledges Kohut's insight into the child's need for narcissistic illusion of grandiosity, but criticizes him for ignoring the defensive nature of both grandiose and idealizing illusions. He takes a complementary position vis-à-vis Kernberg; he agrees in seeing the narcissistic illusion as defensive, but criticizes Kernberg for failing to integrate narcissism with normal development. He claims that in normal childhood the parent engages in play, indicating his or her knowledge that the narcissistic illusion must, at some stage be given up, yet also validating it by his or her joint pretend. We have advanced a similar view of dual psychic realities from a developmental psychopathology perspective (Fonagy and Target, 1996a; Target and Fonagy, 1996). Clinically, Mitchell advocates engaging the patient's grandiosity, while exploring why it appears to be the only way the patient has of relating to others, including the analyst. The combination of 'play' and interpretation creates the possibility of experiencing relationships with other dimensions.

Merton Gill (1982) came to a similar conclusion about the nature of therapeutic action based in part on empirical studies of recorded analytic sessions (Gill and Hoffman, 1982). Gill recommends that analysts should continue to interpret, but that the interpretations should emphasize the parallel between the material external to the therapy and the situation in the analysis. Gill does not regard the transference as the patient's distorted projection; rather it is a real social response to the actions of the analyst, and contains both transference and non-transference components. Thus transference is an interactional phenomenon, implying that the analyst must try to clearly delineate the real aspect of the relationship chiefly through the use of interpretation and insight (Gill, 1983).

At the more interpersonal end of the relational spectrum, the importance of the past is reduced in favor of privileging current critical social problems. The aim of therapy, according to Levenson (1990) for example, is the clarification of interpersonal patterns currently occurring outside the analytic setting, using the patient's behavior in the session as the material from which understanding may be generated (not as the basis upon which the patient's projections and other unrealistic perceptions can be explored). The therapeutic force is not interpretation, as the analyst's perception of reality has no privileged status (Levenson, 1982). The patient and analyst together form an interpersonal reality in which neither is the arbiter of truth, and both will inevitably become involved in enactment. Interpretation is participation, but analytic neutrality or silence would be equally so. If the analyst points out that the patient is sensitive, and the patient starts crying in response, the patient is being masochistic and the analyst (perhaps feeling benign or detached) is enacting a sadistic role. The analyst may carry this further and actually get angry with the patient. The sadomasochistic relationship is enacted. Change takes place not through interpretation but through expanded participation of the analyst in the patient's experiential world around the material, and through 'an interpersonal resonance' that is hard to define but that brings about an experience of 'reconfiguration' in the patient (Levenson, 1982, p. 99; 1990). This description appears quite close to the self-psychologists' concept of change following affect attunement (Kohut, 1984). In interpersonal theory it is claimed that as the patient's experiential world is enriched by the analyst's authentic engagement in this world, he or she gives up the wish not to change in favor of a wish to be his or her authentic self. Interpersonal analysis is not the talking cure but the experience cure; the analyst does not engage the patient's psychic reality but the patient's real world; the emphasis is not on interpretation and the addressing and meeting of the patient's childhood needs, but rather on authentic engagement with the patient.

The issue of authenticity is central to the interpersonalist/relational school. This is pointedly not considered a 'technique' such as 'corrective emotional experience' might be (Levenson, 1982). The interpersonal tradition, for decades alone among analytic approaches in maintaining a two-person point of view, focuses on analytic interaction and seeks to demystify the therapeutic process. In the dialectics that characterize the development of psychoanalytic ideas, the 'field theory' (Lewin, 1952) emphasis of the interpersonalists has been an antidote to the denial of the analyst's participation that for decades characterized the mainstream Freudian approach. From a clinical standpoint, one of the most striking contributions of interpersonalist/relational theory was that it provided an understanding of the ways in which the vicissitudes of actual early interpersonal experiences play themselves out in current relationships, including one that involves the analyst. The interpersonal emphasis on the analyst's authenticity has provided a breath of fresh 'air in the stultifying atmosphere created by the traditional demands to shoehorn the analyst's experience into an overly formal, mechanical, and ultimately deeply disingenuous analytic stance' (Mitchell, 1995, p. 86).

The participant observer concept was developed to challenge the more traditional assumption that the psychiatrist analyzes data from a more or less detached position. Sullivan repeatedly stresses the therapist's 'participation in the data', yet also emphasizes the therapist's control over the interview, the disastrousness of being surprised, and the usefulness of planned work. As Mitchell (1995) put it:

> One way to position Sullivan's epistemology in relation to more recent developments within the interpersonal tradition would be to say that Sullivan was halfway to Heisenberg. Sullivan put great emphasis on the importance of the analyst's participation in and impact upon what he is observing. However, unlike some later theorists, Sullivan believed that through self-awareness, the analyst was able to factor out that participation and apprehend reality in an objective, unmediated fashion. (p. 70)

Interpersonalist analysts have taken this point of view much further, distancing themselves from Freud's 'pre-Heisenbergian' epistemology. 'The analyst's point of view, even if arrived at through rational, self-reflective observation, cannot be separated from his forms of participation. Observation is never neutral. Observation is always contextual, based on assumptions, values, constructions of experience.' (Mitchell, 1995, p. 83) This was most eloquently expressed in Levenson's seminal work, *The Fallacy of Understanding*.

> Nothing ... can be understood out of its time and place, its nexus of relationships. It is an epistemological fallacy to think that we can stand outside of what we observe, or observe without distortion, what is alien to our experience. (Levenson, 1972, p. 8)

Relational theorists lead the way in highlighting the epistemological problems of assuming the accuracy of the analyst's perceptions. In fact there is quite broad-based agreement among relational and interpersonal theorists that the positivist epistemological position, which holds that objective reality is knowable in some privileged fashion by the analyst, is no longer tenable (Gill, 1983; Hoffman, 1990; 1991; 1994; Renik, 1993). Patient and analyst are co-participants in an interactional drama wherein they are continually constructing a shared interpersonal reality.

Mitchell (2000) pointed to the 'dramatically emancipatory tone' (p. 126) of relational literature on the countertransference, particularly where it concerned the analyst's passionate feelings about the patient. In classic times the analyst was best served by an attitude of pervasive and general restraint (Gill, 1994). The attitude conveyed by the concept of neutrality was negative, in that it proscribed responding to questions, expressing feelings, talking freely, or disclosing relevant personal experience. These developments are now generally accepted to have been to the 'good' in opening up useful clinical options and enhancing the integrity of the clinician (Mitchell, 2000). There has naturally been a reaction to this 'liberation movement' (e.g. Greenberg, 2000) with relational analysts portrayed as wild and revealing personal details in an unrestrained fashion. Although there is some evidence for this, reading of the relational literature reveals considerable emphasis upon disciplined self-reflection as a background for spontaneity in the analytic setting (e.g. Hoffman, 1998).

In a number of European traditions countertransference has become an all inclusive term. What is overlooked when the term is overextended to include all aspects of the analyst's participation in the interaction with the patient, what comes to be lost when countertransference is bandied about so loosely, is the analyst's subjectivity, that is, the unique way the person of the analyst – with his or her healthy and less healthy parts – contributes to the construction of the analytic process. By calling everything countertransference, we blur the distinction between what is prompted by the patient's material (countertransference) and what is mainly the analyst's (subjectivity). Lewis Aron (1996) has put this forcefully:

> referring to the analyst's total responsiveness as countertransference is a serious mistake. Thinking of the analyst's experience as 'counter' or responsive to the patient's transference encourages the belief that the analyst's experience is reactive rather than subjective.

Hoffman (1991) is perhaps most radical in claiming that even interperson-alists are implicitly positivistic when they aim to explore the patient's perceptions, because they are implying that they can get at something that is already there. He proposes to replace the positivist epistemology with a social-constructivist model, which demands that the analyst recognizes that intervention cannot capture a 'reality' and that any exploration might lead to something never before formulated, with the potential to impact on both the participants to the situation. This recognition will free the analyst to act in more open and authentic ways since he or she is no longer burdened by the myth of having to identify 'the correct' interpretation. What moves these interactions beyond an ordinary existential encounter is the analyst's constant self-reflective attempts to identify the nature of their involvement. By the same token, the interactions enable the patient to become aware that the patterns are relative rather than absolute; this constructivist attitude, when carried forward into the patient's life, may counteract the rigidity of the patient's patterns of relating (Hoffman, 1994).

There exists a range of different clinical approaches, all of which might be considered 'interpersonal/relational'. One litmus test of the 'genuine' inter-personal position has become countertransference disclosure, the analyst's description of his or her experience of the encounter. There is a range of views by current relational analysts but in most of these expressiveness appears to be balanced by considerations of restraint (Aron, 1996; Bromberg, 1998; Hoffman, 1998; Pizer, 1998; Maroda, 1999).

Among current authors, Ehrenberg is one of the most radical in her emphasis on countertransference disclosure. The relationship aspect of therapy for interactionist technique is perhaps most clearly formulated in Ehrenberg's concept of a meeting at the 'intimate edge' in relatedness (Ehrenberg, 1993). This is defined as the points of maximum closeness between individuals in a relationship over time without violation of the boundaries of either: it constitutes an interactive boundary between patient and analyst. Trying to achieve such a meeting in the therapeutic context brings into relief and opens for inquiry and exploration in the immediate interaction the obstacles, resistances to, and fears within the patient related to such a meeting. At the same time it facilitates clarification of individual boundaries, and allows for contact without violation of these boundaries. In this way, the therapeutic relationship becomes a medium for the patient's expanding self-awareness, greater intimate self-knowledge, and increasing self-definition. Ehrenberg places great emphasis on the use of countertrans-ference, and particularly on the analyst's disclosure of her own experience as the central vehicle for analytic exploration. Ehrenberg presents her approach as an antidote to fallacious claims to analytic objectivity. The patient is repeatedly confronted with 'what she did interpersonally', which places the focus on the 'intimate edge'. Ehrenberg makes 'the immediate interactive experience the crucible of the work and the arena for working through' (p. 6). At that edge, the analyst can be most authentically engaged, and here has the greatest opportunities for understanding and growth.

There have been other significant attempts from the relational standpoint at capturing the dialectic in the therapeutic relationship between the deep involvement of both participants on the one hand and critical differences in the manner of their involvement on the other. Some have contrasted the 'mutuality' of the analytic relationship with the 'asymmetry' of the roles of patient and analyst (Aron, 1996; Burke, 1992). Perhaps Ogden (1989) put it most clearly when he referred to the analytic situation as: 'intimacy in the context of formality' (p. 175). Mitchell (2000) points out that the responsibility of the analysand is to be responsive whilst the analyst is responsible for keeping the analytic relationship analytic. So whereas the analysand is asked to surrender to passions, as part of a constructive irresponsibility, the analyst may allow his or her feelings to emerge but never without taking into account the implication of these for the analytic process as a whole, as part of his duties of stewardship. Thus the emotional experience of the analyst can never be the same as that of the patient, particularly as feelings are more intense and the chances of compromising the analytic situation become greater. Mitchell's emphasis here is that although the emotional experience of the analyst may be real and intense it is also contextual. It is shaped by the analytic situation that makes certain feelings possible while precluding others. Importantly, he argues that neither restraint nor expressiveness can be considered an adequate guide to the handling of countertransference disclosures. 'Both restraint and spontaneity can be either thoughtful or thoughtless' (p. 146). Needless to say, simply stating this further ambiguity does not resolve the dilemma of many clinicians working in the field.

9.2 Evaluation of interpersonal/relational theory

9.2.1 Evaluation of the approach

While both object relations and interpersonal theories emphasize interpersonal relations, the former see this as the locus of pathology, whereas the latter see no other valid contexts for psychological issues of normal or abnormal development. Thus going beyond a simple change in emphasis, interpersonal-relational theories are *based* on interpersonal relations. Given their starting point these theories are less able to provide compelling models of development and pathology, as these are inherently intrapsychic constructs. It is impossible to talk of the process of the socialization of the child's mind if the mind is only considered to exist as an intrinsically social entity. Mitchell is undoubtedly more sensitive to the developmental point of view than most other interpersonalists, but even Mitchell's work ultimately focuses on the way current failures of relating create problems and may be adequately addressed in the present, rather than taking a developmental perspective. While Mitchell's last book went furthest in adopting a developmental relational perspective, according to the author's own admission this was largely derivative, leaning heavily on developmental formulations in other psychoanalytic theories, particularly attachment theory.

As the interpersonal-relational approach focuses on interpersonal patterns rather than psychiatric categories, it is unsurprising that its formulations tend to avoid labels such as depression, personality disorder or narcissism. The person is not seen as having problems, but as having problematic relationships. From an interpersonal-relational point of view diagnostic labels reify interpersonal problems and would distract from an appropriate therapeutic focus on relationship difficulties. These views have much in common with early behavioral scepticism about psychiatric diagnoses (e.g. Rachman and De Silva, 1978) and the concerns of some systemic family therapists (e.g. Minuchin, 1988). Some recent contributors have tried to integrate the psychiatric approach with the interpersonal school of psychoanalysis. For example, Lewis (1998) reviewed empirical research in three areas: studies of families and marriages, the role of adult relationships in undoing the adult consequences of destructive childhood experiences, and the relationship of marital variables and the onset and course of depressive disorder. Research results in all these areas are consistent with the relational assumption that current interpersonal relationships can determine the emergence and course of psychological disturbance.

Of course, the accumulating evidence for the biological/genetic (as opposed to psychosocial) causation of mental disorder is not consistent with a naïve interpersonalist tradition (e.g. Rutter et al., 1997; Reiss et al., 2000). However, most sophisticated behavior-genetic approaches to psychological disturbance consider the interactions of genes with the social environment to be the most important determinants (Kandel, 1998; 1999). So the mere fact that the interpersonalists have so far failed to integrate their ideas with the emerging biological frames of reference is perhaps regrettable but does not vitiate the approach.

There is certainly substantial developmental evidence that psychopathology is almost inevitably accompanied by relationship problems. For example, conduct disorder in children can be readily predicted from peer nominations of unpopularity (e.g. Stormshak et al., 1999). Peer relationships predict the course of psychological disturbance (e.g. Quinton et al., 1993). Even with very severe and enduring disorders such as schizophrenia, the quality of emotional interchange in the family (the absence of expressed negative emotion) can be critical in reducing the likelihood of relapse (Vaughn and Leff, 1981; Leff et al., 1982). Relationship problems are the most common type of life events that increase the risk for all kinds of disturbance (e.g. Tishler, McKenry and Morgan, 1981; Marttunen, 1994; Kendler and Karkowski-Shuman, 1997). There is a long and distinguished history of research linking life events to the onset of depression (Goodyer, 1995; Brown, 1998) and it is widely accepted that life events play a major role in precipitating the onset of episodes of major depression (Kessler, 1997). The general finding is that while most cases of depression seem to have been preceded by stressful life events in the few months beforehand, most life events do not lead to depression or other forms of disorder unless the individual also has a significant genetic vulnerability (Kendler et al., 1995; Kessler, 1997; Silberg, Rutter, Nealre and Eaves, 2001). More telling is the powerful protective effect that good interpersonal relations have in preventing psychological problems associated with various forms of risk (e.g. Berman and Jobes, 1995; Eggert, Thompson, Herting and Nicholas, 1995; Kellam and Van Horn, 1997). Several studies demonstrate the beneficial impact on antisocial individuals of a harmonious marriage (Laub, Nagin and Sampson, 1998; Zoccolillo et al., 1992). As mentioned above, the quality of research evidence supporting psychoanalytic therapies is undoubtedly strongest for interpersonal therapies (e.g. Fairburn, 1994; Shapiro et al., 1995; Mufson and Fairbanks, 1996; Guthrie et al., 1999). Thus, the empirical support for an interpersonal approach is strong, or at least stronger than is the case for most other psychoanalytic approaches, with the exception of the empirically based attachment theory (see Chapter 10).

It should be noted that theories considered under the interpersonal-relational heading are perhaps even more heterogeneous than those reviewed in previous chapters. Thus, generalizations about interpersonal-relational theories should always be qualified. For example, Mitchell's work is more deeply imbued with developmental concerns than other interpersonal theorists, and his ideas link closely to those of attachment theorists. His suggestions concerning the attachment to an established sense of self are particularly valuable. Other interpersonal theorists would see attachment theory as far too positivist and, (as other object relations theorists would agree) as social or interpersonal in the most superficial ways only.

The relative lack of emphasis on developmental and clinical theory inevitably leads to greater weight being placed on the theory of therapy. The novelty of the interpersonal-relational approach is certainly clearest here. Several important propositions have been advanced: (1) the analyst is always a participant and never an observer of the treatment process; (2) relationship experience rather than interpretation brings change in therapy; (3) hearing the analyst's interpretation is a relationship experience and may be an agent of change in patterns of relating; (4) enactment on the part of the analyst is inevitable; (5) the authenticity of the encounter between analyst and patient is critical and justifies a degree of self-disclosure on the part of the analyst; (6) neither analyst nor patient has privileged access to the truth about what happens between them (the so-called perspectivist position).

No single element on this list is unique to the interpersonal-relational approach, perhaps excepting the idea of the inevitability of self-disclosure on the part of the analyst. We have seen for example that Loewald (see Chapter 4) among the ego-psychologists, and Stolorow among the self-psychologists (see Chapter 8) have emphasized the interactional role of the analyst. Working in the analytic present rather than the historical past is of course also part of the Klein-Bion model (see Chapter 6). The inevitability of enactment in the course of treatments has been given serious consideration by both Bionian analysts (Joseph, 1989) and Joseph Sandler (Sandler, 1976b; 1987c). Nevertheless, the interpersonal-relational approach, by bringing these aspects together, opened up North American psychoanalytic thinking, which had been in the doldrums following the collapse of the ego-psychology hegemony. Perhaps object relations theory, both in its European and North American incarnations, lacked the radical quality required after the collapse of an all-embracing model that probably also served as a political system.

9.2.2 Critiques of relational thought

Relational theory flies in the face of many cherished assumptions of classical psychoanalytic theory (see Chapter 1). Relational theory is mute on the pre-experiential needs that motivate relationships. In this regard it is quite circular, specifying a universal perhaps biological need for relationships, evidence for which comes from observations of the human need for relationships. Thus, for example, Greenberg (1991) pointed out that relatedness was not autonomous but motivated by other needs, which are thinly disguised derivatives of the drive concept (in the case of self-psychology relatedness is motivated by the demand for self-structuralization and in the case of British object relations approaches by the relational basis of ego growth). We should note that while relational theorists dispense with the drive construct, followers of Klein, Winnicott or Kernberg stop short of this.

In doing away with the drive construct, relational theorists confine themselves to a model of development in which pathology can arise solely out of impingements upon a maturational pathway. Traditionally psycho-analysis is based around the idea of conflict inherent in the human condition, not simply through an environmental counterforce but also through the conflict between needs or between wishes. Kris (1984) made this point forcibly in his distinction between divergent and convergent conflicts. Conflict can thus occur in the absence of environmental impingement, as part of benign childcare.

It has also been claimed that relational theorists are inclined to emphasize the importance of relating at the expense of autonomy. In a series of seminal papers Blatt has argued that neither the drive for separateness nor the need for relatedness could be considered primary (e.g. Blatt and Blass, 1990; 1996). While Margaret Mahler and her followers arguably placed excessive emphasis on separateness and autonomy (Mahler et al., 1975), relational theorists perhaps give inadequate attention to this (Greenberg, 1991).

Many classical analysts find fault with the relational approach to the understanding of the patient's communications. Where is the unconscious? Where are the fantasies motivating the interpersonal behavior? These of course are fair questions. Yet, they also to some degree miss the point. Interestingly, even amongst the most severely classical of current psychoanalytic views, the modern Kleinian approaches, there has been an undeniable shift toward the interpersonal. For example, the distinguished Kleinian analyst, Betty Joseph's concept of the transference as a 'total situation' can be seen as an attempt at explicating the full complexity of the interpersonal encounter between analyst and patient (Joseph, 1985). Even earlier, Joseph Sandler (1976b) described role-responsiveness as the mechanism whereby the analyst inevitably finds himself or herself enacting a relationship pattern of significance for the patient. No doubt the theoretical accounts would differ (projective identification in Joseph's case and the externalization of unconscious expectations of the other's reaction in the case of Sandler), but the clinical focus would be identical in all these cases. It is harder to find common ground with interpersonalist 'hardliners' in their rejection of the notion of understanding in terms of meaning. Levenson (1990) accepts that the interpersonalist conceptualization of therapeutic change is obscure. Patterns of behavior may not be accessible to interpretation or understanding in terms of current fantasy or past experience. Yet there must be mental structures that maintain these interpersonal behaviors that change in the course of therapy, even if these exist at a procedural rather than episodic memory level (Fonagy and Target, 1997). The problem is not so much residues of the past, cluttering and distorting the present, but irrational attitudes in the present, interfering with more rational, healthier integrations. It is evidently insufficient or circular to explain why the person has sought help by referring to their social problems. The social problems may cause the distress but this does not illuminate the nature of the distress. For example, a child's referral may be prompted by the parents' marital disharmony, and helping the parents resolve their marital problems may indeed address the child's difficulties, but neither this diagnosis nor the treatment process would illuminate the child's experience. What is missing is an explanatory framework to understand the child's, or in general the patient's, subjective distress.

In Mitchell's construction of psychopathology the role of rigid adherence to past structures (attachment to 'bad' internal objects) plays a major role. It is unclear in this context whether the rigidity of the attachment or the nature of the past structure determines the severity of the pathology. Of course it could be both, but then in what proportion? Some obvious questions arise. It is undoubtedly useful to refocus the interest of the psychoanalyst from an exclusive concern with fantasy to one that incorporates the relationship problems and resources of the patient. However, if we are to use this as the guiding framework for intervention, for example, to determine if the patient is treatable, or what is the likelihood of success or the necessary 'clinical dose' of therapy, then we need a taxonomy of relationship problems to guide us in our clinical judgement. No such taxonomy is as yet available. The situation is in many respects analogous to the controversy in personality theory initiated by the behaviorist Mischel (1973) almost 30 years ago. The claim that personality was an artefact of observation, based on the misattribution of consistent behavior to personality traits rather than unchanging situations (the true determinants of behavior) eventually fell by the wayside because behaviorists could not replace the heuristic of a personality taxonomy with a convincing taxonomy of situations.

By emphasizing the equality, at least from an epistemological standpoint, of analyst and patient (the constructivist position) interpersonal-relational theorists present analysts with a conundrum. Analysts are supposed to focus on interpersonal reality even though they cannot claim to know it. They have no access to 'reality' yet their task is to focus on the patient's distortions of it. How? The rejection of positivism is of course only partial. Most relational analysts offer their perspective to the patient, however tentatively, and the social framework of the situation (they are the supposed experts, they are being paid, etc.) takes care of the rest. The theories often make reference to resistance. And of course relational analysts, like their classical fellows, cannot resist imposing their perspective on the clinical work of their colleagues (e.g. Levenson, 1989), thus by their deed contradicting the very assertion they set out to prove: that their view is no closer to the truth than any other. As soon as they hold one intervention to be better than another they need to provide criteria by which the quality of the view can be assessed. Constructivism is an idealization of the analytic relationship, just like the notion of neutrality it aims to replace. And it is in this context that the point of view is so valuable, as one pole of a dialectic.

There is much to be criticized about placing great weight on self-revelation by the analyst. While interpersonal-relational theorists have successfully established that psychoanalysis is an inherently interpersonal enterprise, they have failed to demonstrate that the interaction of two people on an equal footing is a valid form of therapy.

CHAPTER 10

Bowlby's attachment theory model

10.1 Introduction to psychoanalytic approaches based in developmental research

A range of psychoanalytic theories have profited from observations of infant behavior. As we have seen, ego psychological approaches, self-psychology, even the Kleinian approach, and particularly the British Independent tradition, inspired research on infancy based on observations from adult clinical work. By contrast, a far more restricted group of psychoanalytic theories were inspired by infancy research and some of their findings were then extended to the understanding of clinical psychotherapy with adult patients. Both these ways of proceeding have flaws. There are many contributors in this area and covering them all would require a book in itself. Included in those whose work we sadly cannot cover is a giant amongst these theoreticians: Robert Emde, who has done perhaps more than any other scientist to bring together thinking about early development, particularly on affect, and psychoanalytic and psychotherapeutic approaches (Emde, 1980b, 1980c, 1988a, 1988b, 1990; Emde and Robinson, 2000). Another major figure, from France, is Serge Lebovici whose work on infant psychopathology gave rise to a powerful international movement of infant mental health (Lebovici and Widlöcher, 1980; Lebovici, 1982; Lebovici and Weil-Halpern, 1989). Many others have assisted in the integration of early developmental research and psychoanalysis. A key figure promoting the developmental psychopathology approach in psychoanalytic theory is Donald Cohen, who as Director of the Yale Child Study Center was a powerful intellectual and political force behind developmental research-based theory-building (Mayes, Cohen and Klin, 1991; Mayes and Cohen, 1992; 1993; Cohen et al., 1994; Cicchetti and Cohen, 1995a; Cohen, 1995).

In this and the following two chapters, we will focus mainly on four approaches: first we shall consider John Bowlby's attachment theory model,

230

then the work of Daniel Stern and his colleagues, the development of cognitive-analytic therapy by Anthony Ryle, and finally our own line of work which has focused on the development of awareness of mental states in the self and others, rooted in early attachment relationships.

10.2 Bowlby's developmental model

Attachment theory is almost unique among psychoanalytic theories in bridging the gap between general psychology and clinical psychodynamic theory. John Bowlby's work on attachment theory started when, at the age of 21, he worked in a home for maladjusted boys. Bowlby's clinical experience with two boys, whose relationships with their mothers had been massively disrupted, made a profound impact on him. A retrospective study he carried out ten years later, examining the history of 44 juvenile thieves (Bowlby, 1944), formalized his view that the disruption of the early mother–child relationship should be seen as a key precursor of mental disorder. The one factor that distinguished the thieves from the clinic children was evidence of prolonged separation from parents, particularly striking among those whom he termed 'affectionless'. In the late 1940s Bowlby extended his interest in mother–infant relations by undertaking a review of research findings on the effects of institutionalization on young children (Bowlby, 1951). Children who had been seriously deprived of maternal care tended to develop the same symptoms as he had identified in his 'affectionless' young thieves. While giving central place to parenting in general and the infant–mother relationship in particular, the 1951 monograph was silent on the mechanisms by which maternal deprivation might be expected to generate adverse consequences. The maternal deprivation literature was itself wide-open to alternative interpretations, particularly ones that de-emphasized the mother–infant bond (e.g. Rutter, 1971). At about the same time, James Robertson, with Bowlby's encouragement, spent four years documenting on film the impact on 18–48 month olds of separation from the parents during admission to hospital or residential nursery (Robertson, 1962). Later, Christopher Heinicke more systematically collected observations that fully confirmed the Robertson material (Heinicke and Westheimer, 1966).

Bowlby was dissatisfied with prevailing views in the first half of the twentieth century concerning the origin of affectional bonds. Both psychoanalytic and Hullian learning theory stressed that the emotional bond to the primary caregiver was a secondary drive, based on feeding. Yet evidence was already available that in the animal kingdom at least, the young of the species could become attached to adults who did not feed them (Lorenz, 1935).

Bowlby (1958) was among the first to recognize that the human infant enters the world predisposed to participate in social interaction. Developmental psychology has made this discovery something of a truism (e.g. Watson, 1994; Meltzoff, 1995). Around the mid-point of the last century, however, Bowlby's determination to give central place to the infant's biological proclivity to form attachments to initiate, maintain and terminate interaction with the caregiver and use this person as a 'secure base' for exploration and self-enhancement, flew in the face of his psychoanalytic training.

Bowlby's critical contribution was his unwavering focus on the infant's need for an unbroken (secure) early attachment to the mother. He thought that the child who does not have this was likely to show signs of *partial deprivation* – an excessive need for love or for revenge, gross guilt and depression – or *complete deprivation* – listlessness, quiet unresponsiveness and retardation of development, and later in development signs of superficiality, want of real feeling, lack of concentration, deceit and compulsive thieving (Bowlby, 1951). Later (Bowlby, 1969; 1973), he placed these interactions into a framework of reactions to separation: protest → despair → detachment. Protest begins with the child perceiving a threat of separation and can proceed for up to a week. It is marked by crying, anger, attempts at escaping and searching for the parent. It lasts for as long as a week, and intensifies at night. Despair follows protest. Movement diminishes, crying becomes intermittent, the child appears sad, withdraws from contact, is more likely to be hostile to another child or a favorite object brought from home and appears to enter a phase of mourning the loss of the attachment figure (Bowlby, 1973). The final phase of detachment is marked by a more or less complete return of sociability. Attempts by other adults to offer care are no longer spurned, but the child who reaches this stage will behave in a markedly abnormal way upon reunion with the caregiver. In the Heinicke and Westheimer (1966) study of separations that ranged from 2 to 21 weeks, two of the children appeared not to recognize their mothers upon reunion, and eight turned or walked away. They alternately cried and looked expressionless. The detachment persisted to some degree following the reunion and alternated with clingy behavior suggesting intense fear of abandonment.

Bowlby's attachment theory, like classical psychoanalysis, has a biological focus (see especially Bowlby, 1969). Attachment readily reduces to a 'molecular' level of infant behaviors, such as smiling and vocalizing, that alert the caregiver to the child's interest in socializing, and bring him or her close to the child. Smiling and vocalizing are attachment behaviors, as is crying, which is experienced by most caregivers as aversive, and engage the caregiver in caretaking behaviors. Bowlby emphasized the survival value of attachment in enhancing safety through proximity to the caregiver in addition to feeding, learning about the environment and social interaction as well as protection from predators. It was the latter that Bowlby (1969) considered the biological function of attachment behavior. Attachment behaviors were seen as part of a behavioral system (a term Bowlby borrowed from ethology). This is key to understanding the heated nature of the controversy between psychoanalysis and attachment theory. A behavioral system involves inherent motivation. It is not reducible to another drive. It explains why feeding is not causally linked to attachment (Harlow, 1958) and why attachment can occur to abusive caretakers (Bowlby, 1956).

There is a subtle but important difference between Bowlby's formulations and those of object relations theorists (e.g. Fairbairn, 1952b) at this molecular behavioral level. The goal of the child is not the object, e.g. the mother. The goal that regulates the system is initially a physical state, the maintenance of a desired degree of proximity to her. This physical goal is later supplanted by the more psychological goal of a feeling of closeness to the caregiver. Because the goal is not an object but a state of being or feeling, the context in which the child lives, i.e. the response of the caregiver, will strongly influence the attachment system because, if the child perceives the attachment goal to have been attained, this will affect the system of behaviors.

Attachment theory from the beginning concerned more than attachment. In fact, as a developmental theory it only makes sense in the context of a number of key distinctions about what is *not* as well as what is attachment. The *exploratory behavioral system* is subtly interlinked with attachment, with the attachment figure providing the essential secure base from which to explore (Ainsworth, 1963). The child's exploratory behavior comes to an abrupt halt when the child finds the caregiver temporarily absent (Rajecki, Lamb and Obmascher, 1978). The absence of the attachment figure inhibits exploration. Thus secure attachment could be expected to be beneficial in terms of a range of cognitive and social capacities. By contrast, the *fear system* activates the attachment systems and the availability of the caregiver reduces the child's reaction to stimuli that would otherwise be perceived as dangerous (Bowlby, 1973). When the fear system is aroused by what Bowlby (1973) called 'natural' cues to danger (e.g. unfamiliarity, sudden noise, isolation), the child immediately seeks a source of protection and safety, the attachment figure. Thus separation involves two stressors: unprotected exposure and the sense of being cut off from the critical source of protection. Bowlby reserves the term anxiety for the situation where the fear system is aroused in the experienced absence of the attachment figure. The three behavioral systems, attachment, exploration and fear regulate the child's developmental adaptation; in combination they provide a means for the child to learn and develop without straying too far or remaining away too long (Ainsworth and Wittig, 1969).

In the second volume of the trilogy, Bowlby established the set goal of the attachment system as maintaining the caregiver's accessibility and responsiveness that he covered with a single term: 'availability' (Bowlby, 1973, p. 202). In fact it was not until the third section of the book that he addressed the critical role of appraisal in the operation of the attachment system. Here he asserts that availability means confident expectation, gained from 'tolerably accurately' (p. 202) represented experience over a significant time period, that the attachment figure will be available. The attachment behavioral system thus came to be underpinned by a set of cognitive mechanisms, discussed by Bowlby as representational models or following Craik (1943) as *internal working models*. Bowlby's views were actually quite 'Piagetian'. (The influence of Piaget on Bowlby is less frequently recognized than that of ethologists like Konrad Lorenz and Robert Hinde. Yet both Lorenz and Piaget attended the discussion groups that Bowlby organized at the World Health Organization in Geneva on parental care and personality development.)

Bowlby's original concept has been thoughtfully elaborated by some of the greatest minds in the attachment field (Main et al., 1985; Crittenden, 1990; Sroufe, 1990; 1996; Bretherton, 1991; Main, 1991; Bretherton and Munholland, 1999; 1994). It might be helpful to summarize the four representational systems that are implied in these reformulations: (1) expectations of interactive attributes of early caregivers created in the first year of life and subsequently elaborated; (2) event representations by which general and specific memories of attachment-related experiences are encoded and retrieved; (3) autobiographical memories by which specific events are conceptually connected because of their relation to a continuing personal narrative and developing self-understanding; (4) understanding of the psychological characteristics of other people and differentiating these from those of the self.

In the late 1970s Alan Sroufe and Everet Waters (Sroufe and Waters, 1977) redefined the set goal of the attachment system as 'felt security' rather than physical distance regulation. Thus internal cues such as mood, illness or even fantasy could be seen as relevant to the child's response to separation as well as external events and the social environmental context. Felt security as a concept extended the applicability of the concept of attachment from early childhood to older children and even adults (Cicchetti et al., 1990). Sroufe (1996) was able to reconceptualize attachment theory in terms of affect regulation. Securely attached individuals, who have internalized the capacities for self-regulation, are contrasted with those who precociously either down-regulate (avoidant) or up-regulate (resistant) affect. This is a substantial extension of the Bowlbian notion because the range of experiences that could contribute to felt security is in no way restricted to caregiver behavior. However, as Ainsworth (1990) pointed out, Bowlby's view may be reconciled with the notion of felt security, if the latter term is restricted to feelings that accompany appraisals of an attachment figure's current likely availability. Actual closeness of the attachment figure is frequently the means by which the child is able to feel secure (Ainsworth and Bowlby, 1991). Thus, the past influences expectations but does not determine these. Both older children and adults continue to monitor the accessibility and responsiveness of the attachment figure. Internalized aspects of the personality may be thought to interact with the quality of the current attachment relationships.

Potential external threats to availability take up a considerable portion of the 1973 book. Bowlby is impressed by symbolic communication of abandonment such as threats of suicide, threats of leaving or sending the child away. While such experiences are posited as 'actual', in this domain the reality of a threat and the child's psychic reality clearly overlap. Bowlby, for example, refers to metaphoric communications by the parent (e.g. 'you will be the death of me') interpreted concretely by the child as threatening availability. Domestic violence is a particularly potent source of developmental problems precisely because the fear of harm coming to the parent leads to anticipations of unavailability, confirmed by the inaccessibility of the mother at moments of acute marital conflict (Davies and Cummings, 1995, 1998). The consistent observation that open communication can reduce the extent to which disruptive events, such as parental anger, are perceived as threatening (Allen and Hauser, 1996; Allen, Hauser and Borman-Spurrell, 1996) implies a reduced role for fantasy as a source of bias in the appraisal of availability.

In his later works, Bowlby (1979; 1980; 1987) was increasingly influenced by cognitive psychology and particularly by the information processing model of neural and cognitive functioning. Just as cognitive psychologists defined representational models in terms of access to particular kinds of information and data, Bowlby suggested that different patterns of attachment reflect differences in the individual's degree of access to certain kinds of thoughts, feelings and memories. For example, avoidant insecure models of attachment permit only limited access to attachment related thoughts, feelings and memories whereas others provide exaggerated or distorted access to attachment relevant information. Thus for Bowlby cognitive as well as emotional access to attachment relevant information emerges as a function of the nature of the past relationship between infant and caregiver.

10.3 Other psychoanalytic views of Bowlby's theory

So how does attachment theory differ from more traditional psychoanalytic ideas (Rapaport and Gill, 1959)? The genetic or developmental viewpoint that Bowlby took forward involved the structural point of view, elaborated substantially in the context of modern cognitive psychology. The adaptive point of view also has a clear central place within the caregiver–child relationship. All three of these psychoanalytic principles are evidently at work in Bowlby's original formulations, and are still at work in more recent adaptations of attachment theory. However, two aspects were explicitly discarded. These were economic and the dynamic considerations. To most psychoanalysts of the 1950s and 1960s these features of psychoanalytic models were far more critical to the definition of the discipline than the first three. To make matters worse, Bowlby added a number of new perspectives to psychoanalytic thinking that at the time were hard to digest. These were: an ethological (what we now recognize as a socio-biological) perspective on mental function, an object-relations perspective with relationships rather than bodily drives as motivators, an epistemo-logical perspective that privileged the external environment, and a research perspective that challenged traditional clinical reports as the sole data source of psychoanalysis. It is hardly surprising that he was less than popular with his analytic colleagues.

In the early 1960s a number of major psychoanalytic figures turned on Bowlby following the publication of his article in the Psychoanalytic Study of the Child (Bowlby, 1960). Attachment theory was criticized as mechanistic, non-dynamic and involving basic misunderstandings of psychoanalytic theory (Freud, 1960; Schur, 1960; Spitz, 1960). Opposition to his views provided one small area of common ground for the followers of Anna Freud and Melanie Klein (Grosskurth, 1986), and for the next decades Bowlby was a relatively isolated figure in psychoanalysis. These critiques, which were added to by major figures such as Engel (1971), Rochlin (1971), Roiphe (1976) and Hanley (1978), raise a variety of issues but they boil down to relatively few simple disagreements. Bowlby is seen as having renounced drives, the Oedipus complex, unconscious processes, particularly uncon-scious phantasy, complex internalized motivational and conflict-resolving systems. He is further seen as having discarded the richness of human emotions, be these affects experienced by the ego and involving socialization or sources of pleasure rooted in the baby's body. Attachment theory is seen as ignoring biological vulnerabilities other than those rooted in the caregiver's behavior and as blaming all pathology on physical separation. Bowlby is accused of failing to consider the impact of the developmental state of the ego on the child's ability to make attachments and react to loss. He is also accused of ignoring negative attachment related to fear of the mother and trauma other than physical separation. Bowlby is seen to be reductionist in his emphasis on evolution at the expense of recognition of complex symbolic functioning.

A rapprochement has become possible because of a number of changes. These are: (1) A shift within attachment theory from a focus on behavior and environment to concern with internal representations in the infant and the parent. (2) Increasing concern within psychoanalysis with systematic observation and empirical research, together with a severe shortage of paradigms that are both scientifically acceptable (reliable and valid) and provide information of interest to psychoanalytic clinicians and theorists. (3) The breakdown of the theoretical hegemony that governed psychoanalysis in the United States (and to a lesser extent in Europe) that led to more plurality in theory, where clinical usefulness and intellectual appeal are the primary criteria for the acceptability of new ideas. (4) A growing recognition within attachment theory of 'paradigm boundedness', recognition of the limitations of a purely cognitive science approach in clinical work and a need for alternative theoretical frames of reference to enrich research and theory building of relevance to clinicians.

10.4 Empirical developments in attachment theory

In research-based psychoanalytic theories, unlike the theories discussed in previous sections, the developments of theory are not principally based on conceptual advances derived from clinical experience. Advances are made in both clinical and laboratory settings. We do not have space to offer a comprehensive summary of the findings of three decades of attachment research. Here we shall briefly overview selected findings that have contributed to the development of attachment theory and/or that are likely to have a bearing on its evolving relationship to psychoanalysis. For an excellent recent review of this work, the edited volume by Cassidy and Shaver (1999) represents a definitive summary.

10.4.1 Patterns of attachment in infancy

The second great pioneer of attachment theory, Mary Ainsworth (1969; 1985; Ainsworth et al., 1978), developed the well-known laboratory based procedure of the Strange Situation for observing infants' internal working models in action. When infants are briefly separated from their caregiver in a situation unfamiliar to them, they will show one of four patterns of behavior. Infants classified as *Secure* explore readily in the presence of the primary caregiver, are anxious in the presence of the stranger and avoid her, are distressed by their caregivers' brief absence, rapidly seek contact with the caregiver afterwards, and are reassured by this contact, returning to their exploration. Some infants, who appear to be made less anxious by separation, may not seek proximity with the caregiver following separation, and may not prefer her over the stranger; these infants are designated '*Anxious/Avoidant*'. A third category, '*Anxious/Resistant*' infants, show limited exploration and play, tend to be highly distressed by the separation, and have great difficulty in settling afterwards, showing struggling, stiffness, continued crying, or fuss in a passive way. The caregiver's presence or attempts at comforting fail to reassure, and the infant's anxiety and anger appear to prevent him from deriving comfort from proximity.

Secure infants' behavior is based on the experience of well co-ordinated, sensitive interactions where the caregiver is rarely over-arousing and is able to restabilize the child's disorganizing emotional responses. Therefore, they remain relatively organized in stressful situations. Negative emotions feel less threatening, and can be experienced as meaningful and communicative (Sroufe, 1979; 1996; Grossman, Grossmann and Schwan, 1986). Anxious/ Avoidantly attached children are presumed to have had experiences where their emotional arousal was not restabilized by the caregiver, or where they were over-aroused through intrusive parenting; therefore they *over-regulate* their affect and avoid situations that are likely to be distressing. Anxious/ Resistantly attached children *under-regulate*, heightening their expression of distress possibly in an effort to elicit the expected response of the caregiver. There is a low threshold for threat, and the child becomes preoccupied with having contact with the caregiver, but frustrated even when it is available (Sroufe, 1996).

A fourth group of infants who show seemingly undirected behavior are referred to as '*Disorganised/Disoriented*' (Main and Solomon, 1990). They show freezing, hand clapping, head-banging, the wish to escape the situation even in the presence of the caregiver (Lyons-Ruth and Jacobovitz, 1999; van IJzendoorn et al., 1999). It is generally held that for such infants the caregiver has served as a source of both fear and reassurance, and thus arousal of the attachment behavioral system produces strong conflicting motivations.

10.4.2 The attachment system as a determinant of interpersonal relationships

Prospective longitudinal research has demonstrated that children with a history of secure attachment are independently rated as more resilient, self-reliant, socially oriented (Waters, Wippman and Sroufe, 1979; Sroufe, 1983), empathic to distress (Kestenbaum, Farber and Sroufe, 1989), with deeper relationships and higher self-esteem (Sroufe, 1983; Sroufe et al., 1990).

Bowlby proposed that internal working models of the self and others provide prototypes for all later relationships. Such models are relatively stable across the lifespan (Collins and Read, 1994).

Because internal working models function outside of awareness, they are change resistant (Crittenden, 1990). The stability of attachment is demonstrated by longitudinal studies of infants assessed with the Strange Situation and followed up in adolescence or young adulthood with the *Adult Attachment Interview* (AAI) (George et al., 1985). This structured clinical instrument elicits narrative histories of childhood attachment relationships – the characteristics of early relationships, experiences of separation, illness, punishment, loss, maltreatment or abuse. The AAI scoring system (Main and Goldwyn, 1994) classifies individuals into *Secure/Autonomous, Insecure/Dismissing, Insecure/Preoccupied* or *Unresolved* with respect to loss or trauma, categories based on the structural qualities of narratives of early experiences. While autonomous individuals value attachment relationships, coherently integrate memories into a meaningful narrative and regard these as formative, insecure individuals are poor at integrating memories of experience with the meaning of that experience. Those *dismissing* of attachment show avoidance by denying memories, and by idealizing or devaluing (or both idealizing and devaluing) early relationships. *Preoccupied* individuals tend to be confused, angry or passive in relation to attachment figures, often still complaining of childhood slights, echoing the protests of the resistant infant. *Unresolved* individuals give indications of significant disorganization in their attachment relationship representation; this manifests in semantic or syntactic confusions in their narratives concerning childhood trauma or a recent loss.

Fourteen studies have so far demonstrated that the AAI administered to mother or father will predict not only the child's security of attachment to that parent but, even more remarkably, the precise attachment category which the child manifests in the Strange Situation (van IJzendoorn, 1995). Thus dismissing AAI interviews predict avoidant Strange Situation behavior while preoccupied interviews predict anxious-resistant infant attachment. Lack of resolution of mourning (unresolved interviews) predicts disorganization in infant attachment (see below). Temperament (child to parent effects) seems an inadequate account of the phenomena since the AAI of each parent, collected and coded before the birth of the child, predicts the attachment classification of the infant at 12 and 18 months (Fonagy, Steele and Steele, 1991; Steele, Steele and Fonagy, 1996).

Recent evidence by Slade and her colleagues provided an important clue about the puzzle of intergenerational transmission of attachment security. They demonstrated that autonomous (secure) mothers on the AAI represented their relationship with their toddlers in a more coherent way, conveying more joy and pleasure in the relationship, than did dismissing and preoccupied mothers (Slade et al., 1999). That the mother's representation of each child is the critical determinant of attachment status is consistent with the relatively low concordance in the attachment classification of siblings (van IJzendoorn et al., 2000). We believe that the parent's capacity to adopt the intentional stance toward a not yet intentional infant, to think about the infant in terms of thoughts, feelings and desires in the infant's mind and in their own mind in relation to the infant and his or her mental state, is the key mediator of the transmission of attachment and accounts for classical observations concerning the influence of caregiver sensitivity (Fonagy et al., 1991). Those with a strong capacity to reflect on their own and their caregiver's mental states in the context of the AAI were far more likely to have children securely attached to them – a finding which we have linked to the parent's capacity to foster the child's self-development (Fonagy et al., 1993). We have also found that mothers in a relatively high stress (deprived) group characterized by single-parent families, parental criminality, unemployment, overcrowding and psychiatric illness would be far more likely to have securely attached infants if their reflective function was high (Fonagy et al., 1994).

During the late 1970s and 1980s, attachment research came to be increasingly concerned with child maltreatment, physical and sexual abuse. The disorganized/disoriented classification of Strange Situation behavior marked by fear, freezing and disorientation (Main and Solomon, 1986) was linked to maltreatment of the child (e.g. Cicchetti and Barnett, 1991) and unresolved trauma in the history of the parent (Main and Hesse, 1990b). The frightened/frightening behavior of the parent is assumed to undermine the child's attachment organization (Main and Hesse, 1992). The attachment figure being at once the signal of safety and of danger can be readily seen to potentially undermine the entire attachment behavioral system. Childhood maltreatment accounts for some but not all attachment disorganization observed in infancy. The potential reasons for the disorganization of the attachment system were therefore extended to include experiences that were more subtle but nevertheless deeply unsettling from an infant's point of view. Moments of dissociation or strange, frightened expressions have been observed in parents of infants whose Strange Situation behavior was classified as disorganized (Schuengel, Bakermans-Kranenburg and van IJzendoorn, 1999; Schuengel, Bakermans-Kranenburg, van IJzendoorn and Blom, 1999). Infant disorganization has been linked to later psychopathology in a number of longitudinal investigations (Shaw, Owens, Vondra et al., 1996; Lyons-Ruth, 1996b), including dissociative symptoms in particular (Carlson, 1998). While attachment is still seen as all-pervasive, research and theory on attachment disorganization offers a more satisfactory theoretical link between early attachment experience and personality disturbance than has thus far been available and is therefore the cutting edge of current clinical attachment research (Lyons-Ruth and Jacobovitz, 1999; Solomon and George, 1999).

Evidence linking attachment in infancy with personality characteristics is stronger in some studies than in others. In a Minnesota Study, pre-schoolers with secure attachment histories were consistently rated by teachers as higher in self-esteem, emotional health, agency, compliance and positive affect and this persisted to age 10 (Elicker, Englund and Sroufe, 1992; Weinfield et al., 1999). The most recent findings from this cohort still show a prediction from infancy to adult measures of psychiatric morbidity with many potential confounding factors controlled for (Carlson, 1998; Weinfield et al., 1999). However, not all studies are able to replicate these findings (e.g. Feiring and Lewis, 1996). In contrast to Bowlby's prediction, the secure, avoidant and resistant classifications tend not to be strongly related to later measures of maladaptation; it is the disorganized/disoriented infant category which appears to have the strongest predictive significance for later psychological disturbance (Lyons-Ruth, Alpern and Repacholi, 1993; Lyons-Ruth, 1996a; Ogawa, Sroufe, Weinfield et al., 1997; Carlson, 1998).

More generally, associations between secure infant attachment and personality characteristics such as ego resilience appear in some samples and not others and the prediction of behavioral problems from insecurity when observed appears to be moderated by intervening experiences such as gender differences, environmental stress or the child's intellectual capacity (Erickson, Sroufe and Egeland, 1985; Fagot and Kavanagh, 1990; Lyons-Ruth et al., 1993). Evidence which suggests that attachment is the foundation for later adaptation is neither reliable nor consistent. It is precisely these kinds of gaps between theory and evidence which in our view should call attachment theorists' attention to the need to open dialogue with other theoretical approaches, including numerous psychoanalytic ideas.

10.5 Attachment and psychopathology

Numerous studies of low-risk samples failed to identify the simple relationship between insecure attachment in the first two years of life and emotional or behavioral problems in middle childhood (e.g. Feiring and Lewis, 1996). By contrast, studies with high-risk samples are more likely to find a relationship between insecure attachment in infancy and particularly externalizing problems in the school and pre-school years. For example, in a sample drawn from a high social risk population, children who showed early insecure relations were also consistently observed to be more prone to moodiness, poor peer relations and symptoms of depression and aggression, right up to pre-adolescence (Weinfield et al., 1999). Two recent follow-ups of this sample showed powerful prediction to psychopathology in adolescence. Anxiety disorder in adolescence was most likely to be associated with ambivalent attachment in infancy (Warren et al., 1997). Overall, avoidant infants showed the highest rate of disorders (70%) and resistant infants were no more likely to have diagnosable psychiatric disorder than secure ones. In the same sample, dissociative symptoms at 17 and 19 years were predictable from avoidant classification and disorganized behavior scores (Ogawa et al., 1997).

A number of studies (Lyons-Ruth et al., 1989; Lyons-Ruth, 1995; Shaw and Vondra, 1995; Shaw, Owens, Vondra et al., 1996) suggest that disorganized attachment is a vulnerability factor for later psychological disturbance in combination with other risk factors. A recent study with a large sample (n = 223) confirmed that those whose attachment classification was disorganized in infancy or atypical at age 24 months were most likely to be rated high on externalizing behavior at 3.5 years (Vondra, Shaw, Swearingen et al., 2001). In addition, a rich body of literature reviewed by Greenberg (1999) shows strong associations between concurrent measurement of attachment and psychopathology. However, cross-sectional investigations always leave open the possibility that non-secure attachment is but a further indication of the child's psychological disturbance.

There is general agreement that attachment security can serve as a protective factor against adult psychopathology, and that it is associated with a wide range of healthier personality variables such as lower anxiety (Collins and Read, 1990), less hostility and greater ego resilience (Kobak and Sceery, 1988), and greater ability to regulate affect through interpersonal relatedness (Simpson, Rholes and Nelligan, 1992; Vaillant, 1992). Insecure attachment appears to be a risk factor and is associated with such characteristics as a greater degree of depression (Armsden and Greenberg, 1987), anxiety, hostility and psychosomatic illness (Hazan and Shaver, 1990) and less ego resilience (Kobak and Sceery, 1988).

Five studies have linked attachment patterns and adult psychiatric illness (Dozier, Stovall and Albus, 1999). Psychiatric disorders are nearly always associated with insecure states of mind and unresolved status is highly over-represented in this group. In one longitudinal study (Allen et al., 1996), derogation and lack of resolution of abuse predicted criminal behavior and hard drug use in a high-risk sample. Although it has been suggested that a dismissing state of mind might be associated with antisocial personality disorder, eating disorders, substance abuse and dependence, and preoccupied states of mind would be linked with disorders that involve absorption in one's own feelings such as depression, anxiety and borderline personality disorder, the available studies do not support this kind of simplistic model (e.g. Fonagy et al., 1996). Eagle (1999) cites evidence that while preoccupied/enmeshed individuals experience more psychological distress, avoidantly attached individuals show a greater incidence of somatic symptoms and illnesses.

There are several problems with these kinds of studies. First, the co-morbidity of Axis I disorders, particularly in relatively severe clinical groups where co-morbidity is extremely high, preclude any simple links between attachment classification and a unique form of psychiatric morbidity. Secondly, the coding systems for establishing attachment classes are not truly independent of clinical conditions and some consistent associations might be simple cases of item overlap. (For example, if lack of ability to recall early (attachment) experience is a criterion for a dismissing attachment classification (Ds) and memory problems are part of the diagnostic criteria for major depression (MD), any association between Ds and MD could only be taken seriously if the memory deficit in relation to attachment was shown to be something beyond the general memory problems reported by MD patients.) Thirdly, the adult attachment coding systems were not developed with clinical groups in mind, and therefore it is not clear if or how the severity of psychiatric morbidity per se might distort the assignment of an attachment classification. Currently we are lacking the validity studies necessary to establish the usefulness of currently available attachment measures for categorization of psychopathology.

More recently a line of work linking attachment classification and treatment outcome has emerged where attachment classification is used as a predictor within specific diagnostic groups. Dismissing adults appear to be relatively resistant to treatment and within the context of therapy. Arguably, they deny their need for help in order to protect themselves from the possibility that the caregiver will be eventually unavailable. They might be rejecting of treatment, rarely asking for help (Dozier, 1990). Preoccupied adults have a more general inability to collaborate with and take in the therapist's words and support, but then become dependent and call therapists between hours (Dozier et al., 1991).

A synthetic view of this literature has been suggested by Sidney Blatt and colleagues (Blatt et al., 1995; Blatt and Blass, 1996; Blatt, Zuroff, Bondi et al., 1998). Blatt and his coworkers have proposed a dichotomy that overlaps in a highly informative way with the Bowlby-Ainsworth-Main categorization. They envision a dialectic between two developmental pressures that defines the evolving representations of self–other relationships: the needs for (a) a sense of relatedness, and (b) a sense of autonomous identity (Blatt and Blass, 1996). These developmental needs are thought to be in synergistic interaction throughout ontogeny and a lack of balance implies psychopathology. 'Anaclitic pathology' (an exaggerated need for relatedness – preoccupation/entanglement) is present in dependent, histrionic or borderline personality disorder. 'Introjective pathology' (an exaggerated quest for identity – dismissing or avoidant pathology) is thought to characterize schizoid, schizotypal, narcissistic, antisocial or avoidant individuals. John Gunderson (1996) writing about BPD from an attachment theory perspective, for example, identifies precisely the anaclitic pathology of these patients when pointing to their total incapacity to tolerate aloneness.

The person-centered approach of the attachment theory perspective thus has the potential greatly to deepen our understanding of psychiatric disturbance, as categorized by DSM-IV, by adding a dynamic developmental standpoint. For example, Blatt and colleagues, using the relatedness-autonomy dialectic, can differentiate two types of depression: a dependent (anaclitic) and a self-critical (introjective) type (Blatt and Bers, 1993). Thus depression in individuals with borderline personality disorder is characterized by emptiness, loneliness, desperation vis-à-vis attachment figures and labile, diffuse affectivity. For non-borderline individuals with major depression, these aspects correlate negatively with the severity of depression, whereas for borderline individuals, the same symptoms correlate almost perfectly with severity within the limits of the reliability of measurement (Westen et al., 1992; Rogers, Widiger and Krupp, 1995).

Response to treatment is powerfully predicted by this distinction. For example, in the NIMH trial of psychotherapy for depression (Elkin, 1994; Blatt et al., 1998), perfectionist individuals (introjective type), were unlikely to improve after the first few sessions, whereas patients with a high need for approval (anaclitic types) improved significantly in the second half of the treatment (Blatt et al., 1995). In general, it is possible that dismissing patients will tend to do poorly in most short-term treatments (Horowitz, Rosenberg and Bartholomew, 1996). The value of the psychoanalytic approach is highlighted by the fact that the majority of studies of depression neither explores nor differentiates between these groups, although the experience of psychological distress in the two groups is critically different. The person-centered attachment theory approach that takes the representational world as its focus can help to refine our predictions about psychological disturbance.

10.5.1 The disorganization of attachment

The most promising current area of attachment research is undoubtedly the study of disorganized/disoriented attachment behavior. Disorganized/disoriented attachment is marked in the Strange Situation by displays of contradictory behavior patterns sequentially or simultaneously: undirected, incomplete or interrupted movements, stereotypes, anomalous postures, freezing, fear of the parent or disoriented wandering (Main and Solomon, 1986; 1990). Main and Hesse's (1990b) now classical contribution linked disorganized attachment behavior to frightened or frightening caregiving: infants who could not find a solution to the paradox of fearing the figures from whom they wanted comfort (Main, 1995). In the intervening decade, a great deal has been learned about disorganized attachment. A meta-analysis of studies of disorganized attachment based on 2,000 mother–infant pairs (van IJzendoorn et al., 1999) estimated its prevalence at 14% in middle income samples and 24% in low income groups. Similarly, adolescent mothers tend to have an over-representation of disorganized infants (23%) as well as fewer secure (40% vs. 62%) and more avoidant (33% vs. 15%). The stability of the classification of disorganized attachment is fair (r = .36) (van IJzendoorn et al., 1999), with some indication that lack of stability may be accounted for by increases in the number of disorganized infants between 12 and 18 months (Barnett, Ganiban and Cicchetti, 1999; Vondra, Hommerding and Shaw, 1999).

Quite a lot is known about the causes of disorganized attachment. The prevalence of attachment disorganization is strongly associated with family risk factors such as maltreatment (Carlson, Cicchetti, Barnett and Braunwald, 1989), and major depressive disorder (Lyons-Ruth, Connell and Grunebaum, 1990; Teti et al., 1995). In addition, there is an extensively proven association between disorganization of attachment in the baby and unresolved mourning or abuse in the mother's Adult Attachment Interview (van IJzendoorn, 1995). Three studies have helped to clarify this superficially mysterious association between slips in the mother's narrative about past trauma, and bizarre behavior by the infant in the Strange Situation with her. Jacobovitz and colleagues reported a strong association between such slips in the AAI before the child was born and observations of frightened or frightening behavior toward the baby at eight months (Jacobovitz, Hazen and Riggs, 1997). These behaviors included extreme intrusiveness, baring teeth, entering apparently trancelike states, etc. If the trauma around which there was lack of resolution happened before the mother was aged 17, her frightened or frightening behavior was more evident. Interestingly, these unresolved mothers did not differ from the rest of the sample in terms of other measures of parenting such as sensitivity, warmth, etc.

In a similar study, Schuengel and colleagues found that mothers classified as unresolved and insecure displayed significantly more frightened or frightening behavior than those classified unresolved secure (Schuengel et al., 1999). Maternal frightened or frightening behavior predicted infant attachment disorganization, but the strongest predictor was maternal dissociated behavior. In an independent investigation, Lyons-Ruth and colleagues also found that frightened and frightening behavior predicted infant disorganization (Lyons-Ruth, Bronfman and Parsons, 1999), particularly when the mother strongly misinterpreted the baby's attachment cues and when the mother gave conflicting messages that both elicited and rejected attachment.

There is general agreement based on both cross-sectional and longitudinal investigations that disorganized infant attachment shifts into controlling attachment behavior in middle childhood (van IJzendoorn et al., 1999). Observational studies suggest that disorganized children are less competent in playing with other children and in conflict resolution (Wartner et al., 1994), and in consistency of interaction with different peers (Jacobovitz and Hazen, 1999).

10.5.2 Pathways from infancy to adult pathology

Attachment theory gives a model for the integration of early childhood experience with later development, particularly the emergence of psychopathology. As this brief review has demonstrated, there is considerable – although not overwhelming – evidence for the continuity of interpersonal experience. There are several research-based models to account for observed continuities.

The simplest model (Lamb et al., 1985; Lamb, 1987; Belsky, 1999; Thompson, 1999), is in terms of continuity not of mental structures, but merely of social environments, especially of the quality of care. Several large studies have shown that, at least for high levels of deprivation, early experience does not require continuity to have its impact (Chisolm, 1998; Marvin and Britner, 1999; O'Connor, Rutter and Kreppner, 2000).

A second mechanism that explains continuity involves the representation of relationships. In this framework, responsive parenting during infancy generates a working model of relationships in which positive expectations of intimacy and care from others are deeply encoded, affecting perception, cognition and motivation (Bretherton and Munholland, 1999). A growing literature of pervasive attributional biases (Crick and Dodge, 1994; Coie and Dodge, 1998; Matthys, Cuperus and van Engeland, 1999) is consistent with this view, and there is some direct support (Cassidy, Kirsh, Scolton and Parke, 1996).

A third explanation is at the level of continuity of neural organization and underlying gene expression. Myron Hofer's work with rodent pups has shown that the evolutionary value of staying close to and interacting with the mother goes way beyond protection, and involves many pathways for regulation of the infant's physiological and behavioral system (Hofer, 1995; Polan and Hofer, 1999). Hofer's reformulation provides a very different way of explaining the range of phenomena usually discussed under the heading of attachment. The traditional attachment model is clearly circular: separation disrupts a social bond, the existence of which is inferred from the separation response. In Hofer's model, what is lost in 'loss' is not mainly the bond but the opportunity to generate a higher-order regulatory mechanism. Attachment may mark changes in neural organizations that are involved in later psychological disturbance. For example, emotion regulation established in early childhood may substantially alter fear conditioning processes in the amygdala (LeDoux, 1995) or connections between the pre-frontal cortex and the limbic system (Schore, 1997a). Animal studies have offered good evidence of permanent changes to the stress mechanisms following adverse attachment experiences (Meaney et al., 1988; Plotsky and Meaney, 1993).

Animal models document the effects of early stress on a range of neurobiological systems including the hypothalamic-pituitary-adrenal axis, the dopaminergic, noradrenergic and serotonergic systems (Bremner and Vermetten, 2001). Additionally, adverse early experiences in non-human primates resulted in raised corticotrophin releasing factor in the cerebrospinal fluid as well as long-term effects on behaviors (Coplan et al., 1996). Animal models also show that certain interventions reduce the negative effects of early stress, indicating a degree of plasticity in the brain. Thus postnatal handling of rat pups has been shown to increase Type II glucocorticoid receptor binding that persisted throughout life along with increased feedback sensitivity to glucocorticoids (Meaney et al., 1988; Meaney, Aitken, Sharma and Sarrieau, 1989). This has been hypothesized to be due to a type of 'stress inoculation' from the mothers' repeated licking of the handled pups (Liu et al., 1997). Early stress has been found to be associated with lifelong increases in sensitivity of the noradrenergic system (Francis, Caldji, Champagne et al., 1999). As far as the serotonin system is concerned, a variety of stressors have been shown to result in increased turnover of serotonin in the medial pre-frontal cortex (Pei, Zetterstrom and Fillenz, 1990; Inoue, Tsuchiya and Koyama, 1994) and other areas including the locus ceruleus (Kaehler, Singewald, Sinner et al., 2000). Severe stress may result in damage in relation to the hippocampus (O'Brien, 1997). Thus, animal models offer a rich set of potential pathways that could mediate between early psychosocial experience, attachment and psychopathology.

The evidence from studies of clinical populations concerns relatively extreme environments. These results have on the whole been consistent with findings from the animal investigations, although human studies have just begun to consider the effects of early stress on brain structure and function (Rutter, 2000). Studies of adults with a history of childhood trauma have been consistent with long term changes in the HPA axis (Bremner et al.,

1997). Attachment security may have important biological associations and there is a complex relationship between the reactivity of the hypothalamic-pituitary-adrenal (HPA) axis and attachment. Several studies have demonstrated that insecurely attached infants, particularly those with disorganized patterns of attachment, have increased reactivity of the HPA axis (Spangler and Grossman, 1993; Nachmias et al., 1996). It may be argued that increased HPA activity is not part of an integrated physiological response such as the stress response, but rather it is an indication of the absence of the regulatory effect of the prior mother–infant interaction. Loss of the caregiver, at least within the animal model, reflects the withdrawal of a number of different regulatory processes that had been hidden within the attachment relationship. Experimental animal studies in which different elements of the interaction between mother and offspring are manipulated demonstrate that infant animals will show some of the HPA responses to separation but not others.

The implications for humans are naturally far from straightforward. Hofer (1996) argues that inadequate early care leads to disturbance because of the failure of the normal smooth modulation and co-ordination of physiological function, affect and behavior into a stable pattern. The major difference between human and animal models might be that whereas in infant animals the source of the regulation is probably at the level of behavioral interactions, in the case of mother–infant interaction this also occurs at the level of rapid interchanges of subjective expectations (cognitive representations or models of relationships). Facilitation from social support may operate through the regaining of interactional regulators. An examination of HPA reactivity to the stress of an unfamiliar situation, demonstrated that elevated cortisol response occurred only in inhibited toddlers with mothers to whom they were insecurely attached (Nachmias et al., 1996). Inhibited toddlers who were securely attached did not show these elevations, indicating that secure attachment may be a protective factor.

A fourth potential mediator of continuity is the isomorphism of behavioral disturbance and disturbed attachment behaviors. Greenberg (1999) suggests that disturbed behavior may also be viewed as an attachment strategy aimed to regulate the relationship with the parent. For example, oppositional behavior may regulate the caregiver's closeness and attention to the child. A pathway that up until now has received less attention concerns the capacity to direct and focus attention. This capacity has recently been shown to be related to many of the recognized sequelae of secure attachment, including social competence, empathy, sympathy, low levels of aggression and the development of conscience (Kochanska et al., 1998; Eisenberg, Fabes, Guthrie and Reiser, 2000; Eisenberg, Guthrie et al., 2000; Kochanska, Murray and Harlan, 2000). There is indirect evidence that the mother–infant relationship may be quite relevant to the quality of attentional effortful control (Rothbart and Bates, 1998). For example, mother–child dyads who were mutually responsive in infancy produced children who are more conscientious and better able to follow instructions (Kochanska and Murray, 2000). A further interesting study on a different sample showed that infants insecurely attached at 14 months had greater difficulties in regulating their emotions (Kochanska, 2001). The results clearly indicated that this was not associated with temperament variables. Controlling for the child's emotional reactions in several set situations at 9, 14 and 22 months, attachment classification at 14 months remained an excellent predictor of the child's emotionality (fearfulness, anger and more distress in situations designed to elicit pleasure). There may be many accounts of this but the powerful neurophysiological evidence that links attentional mechanisms involved in effortful control with the regulation of emotional reactions (Posner and Rothbart, 2000) suggests that one of the pathways that secure attachment follows is via superior mechanisms for the inhibition of dominant (immature) responses in favor of better socialized but non-dominant responses. Individuals whose mothers were able to model this capacity through early interactions remain more adept at this crucial task for the rest of their life.

Finally, mentalizing is a key human capacity, neuro-physiologically (Frith and Frith, 1999) and developmentally (Carlson and Moses, 2001). Secure attachment is strongly associated with the parent's capacity to mentalize (Fonagy, Steele, Moran et al., 1991), her understanding of the baby's behavior in terms of feelings and intentions (Meins et al., 2001), and his later capacity for representing such mental states. Thus, some of the general symbolic superiority of individuals with secure attachment histories (Thompson, 1999) is mediated by a readiness to think in mental state terms, a capacity which carries great advantage in relationships (Dennett and Haugeland, 1987; Bogdan, 1997; 2001).

10.6 Psychoanalytic advances in attachment theories

A number of major authors in attachment theory have been significantly influenced by psychoanalytic ideas and vice versa.

Karlen Lyons-Ruth has conducted ground-breaking research into the nature, causes and consequences of disorganized attachment in infancy (Lyons-Ruth, Bronfman and Atwood, 1999), and her relational diasthesis model is the only psychoanalytically inspired explanation currently available to account for these data (Lyons-Ruth, Bronfman and Atwood, 1999). The prediction of the model is that trauma will occur more frequently and will be harder to resolve in an already disorganized caregiving-attachment system.

Lyons-Ruth updates Bowlby by including both direct and later indirect disorganization as potential determinants of later outcome. There is preliminary data consistent with her model (Ogawa et al., 1997).

The model has many aspects that link research findings with psychoanalytic clinical work. Lyons-Ruth is part of a group of eminent researcher psychoanalysts working in Boston to understand the change process in psychoanalysis. This promises to deliver an integrated psychological model of the encoding of relationship experience as well as the mechanisms whereby these might be therapeutically altered (Lyons-Ruth, 1999). While the relational diathesis model is not yet fully integrated with psychoanalytic ideas, it is perhaps the most sophisticated attachment theory model to be advanced by a psychoanalytic researcher since John Bowlby.

Morris Eagle has focused on the integration of psychoanalysis and attachment theory, from the very broad standpoint of the problems for psychoanalytic theory in accepting the relational (object-relationship) perspective. From Eagle's point of view (1997; 1998; 1999), the most important contribution of attachment theory overlaps with that of object relations theory: the subjective experience in infancy of 'felt security', and its impact on later development. Eagle considers attachment theory to have been a 'reaction against and corrective to' (Eagle, 1997, p. 217) aspects of classical analytic theory, in particular Freudian and Kleinian theory. He emphasizes the radical difference between traditional psychoanalysis and attachment theory in relation to the role of external versus internal factors. He also vigorously challenges attachment theory from a psychoanalytic viewpoint. For instance, Eagle takes issue with Bowlby's assertion that IWMs reflect actual interactions with the caregiver (e.g. Eagle, 1999). Here Eagle is not making the common point that different infants could elicit different reactions from caregivers depending on their temperament (the so called child to parent effect), but rather that the same caregiver behavior might be experienced differently by different infants depending on their constitution. Unfortunately, while Eagle's logic is sound, modern genetics takes it to an infinite regress since constitution itself is dependent on experience (Kandel, 1998; 1999). Constitution is not an absolute, and it may indeed be Bowlby's IWMs which best predict whether a particular gene is expressed or not. However, this is a subtle point; Eagle's critique of attachment's theory's exaggerated claim to objectivity is well taken.

While Eagle is critical of attachment theory he also appreciates its strong points, particularly its empirical foundations. He is independent of the main line of research in attachment, and this lets him consider key concepts (such as the link between security and narrative coherence) in a very critical light. While Eagle is by no means a relational theorist (and was quite critical of that tradition in the past), his way of integrating psychoanalytic and attachment theories comes quite close to those of relational theorists such as Mitchell.

Jeremy Holmes's theoretical and clinical integration of psychoanalytic and attachment theory ideas is the fullest exposition to date of an 'attachment theory psychotherapy'. Holmes (2000) suggests that urgent tasks face psychoanalysis if it is to retain any place in science and medicine, and argues that attachment theory might be a useful ally. He points to the disagreement between attachment theorists and psychoanalysts regarding the mother infant relationship in the first few months of life. Attachment theorists stress the ways in which the mother and the infant seek each other out to relate to one another from the moment of birth. Mahler's classical account, by contrast (Mahler, 1975), holds that there is an undifferentiated symbiosis that covers the first few months. In Holmes's view, Myron Hofer's research (see above) shows that the mother's actions change the infant's physiology. Holmes suggests that affects are part of a human psychological immune system, which alerts the individual to danger. A secure relationship offers the emotional equivalent of the physical protection of the immune system. Trauma overwhelms and disrupts this. Holmes suggests that borderline personality disorder is the result of disturbance of the early mother–infant psycho-physiological regulatory system following early trauma, maternal depression or a similar experience.

Holmes places attachment theory at the heart of psychotherapy (Holmes, 1993a, 1993b). He profoundly disagrees with Bowlby's off-the-cuff comment that psychotherapy is merely about providing a secure base. Holmes (1998) defines three prototypical pathologies of narrative capacity: (a) clinging to rigid stories (dismissing), (b) being overwhelmed by un-storied experience (preoccupied) or (c) being unable to find narrative strong enough to contain traumatic pain (unresolved). These pathologies of narrative capacity have profound and distinct effects on the clinical process. The first category has inflexible versions of the patient's story which block the way, that need to be reworked and reassembled. By contrast, work with preoccupied adults involves the therapist finding a way of capturing the confusion of overwhelming feelings. Holmes proposes a specific therapeutic approach, BABI (Brief Attachment Based Intervention), which is a relatively well-structured intervention for moderately severe psychological disorders. It is time-limited with a strong emphasis on formulation, uses handouts, suggests homework between sessions and it is integrative in using Rogerian, dynamic and cognitive behavioral techniques.

Arietta Slade is another major figure linking clinical practice and attachment research (Slade, 1999a). Slade's view is not that attachment theory dictates a particular psychotherapeutic approach but rather that an understanding of the nature and dynamics of attachment informs clinical thinking (Slade, 1996; 2000; Slade et al., 1999). She demonstrates that listening for features such as changes in voice, lapses, irrelevances and more subtle disruptions of the organization of discourse in the attachment and clinical contexts are broadly the same. The therapist, by focusing on the failures of the narrative, is alert to issues where the patient is unable to mentalize an experience. Slade (2000) claims that such gaps in the narrative also offer hints about the nature of the experience of the patient as a child which might have generated the current deficits. Slade (1999; 2000) also considers the relevance of attachment theory and research for clinical work with children. Two issues are highlighted: First, for the child, attachment is not the past but the current context of treatment, defined by his or her own past experience and by the parents' attachment histories. Secondly, Slade has carried out important research on the mother's mental representation of the child, the extent to which this is determined by her own attachment experiences and to which it is modifiable in therapeutic work. The conception of a link between the mother's capacity to represent and recognize her child and the child's recognition of himself as a thinking and feeling person is at the heart of her clinical work.

Selma Fraiberg (1980) argued that disturbances between the infant and the parent in the first three years of life indicate unresolved conflicts that one or both of the babies' parents have in relation to important figures in their own childhood. In her paper, 'Ghost in the nursery', Fraiberg writes: 'We examine with the parents the past and the present in order to free them and their baby from old 'ghosts' that have invaded the nursery, and then we must make meaningful links between the past and the present through interpretations' (Fraiberg et al., 1975, p. 61). Attachment theory and this psychoanalytic infant–parent psychotherapy have recently been powerfully linked by Alicia Lieberman (1991). She recognized the resistances infant-parent therapists are likely to encounter in a direct approach (Lieberman and Pawl, 1993; Pawl and Lieberman, 1997). Her clinical approach is to focus on the feeling states involving salient current relationships and explore how these feeling states may also be present in relation to the baby (a vivid clinical example is provided in Silverman, Lieberman and Pekarsky, 1997).

In addition to insight-oriented interventions, Selma Fraiberg (1980) described three other therapeutic modalities in infant–mother psychotherapy. These were: brief crisis intervention, developmental guidance and supportive treatment. Fraiberg originally suggested that the baby was the appropriate focus of the transference. In the context of attachment theory this would be seen as the best opportunity for the observation of the mother's IWM of attachment relationships. The mother identifies with the baby and plays out residues of her own experience with her own mother. The immediacy of the experience arises through the simultaneous activation of the attachment and caregiving systems prompted by the birth of her child. As well as helping in understanding the parents' experience, the IWM concept is also used in the understanding of the infant's putative internal experience. Lieberman and her colleagues (Lieberman and Pawl, 1993; Lieberman and Zeanah, 1999) conceive of the infant's behavior in terms of defensive operations along the lines outlined by Ainsworth and colleagues (Ainsworth et al., 1978). Interestingly, the attachment classification of defensive behaviors is almost identical to the dramatic mechanisms of self-protection in the infants that Fraiberg observed in a clinic setting (Fraiberg, 1982). Although Fraiberg mentions Ainsworth in her paper, it seems she does this more to distinguish her ideas from attachment theory than to suggest an integration. Yet the theory she is committed to (modern ego-psychology) has no model for the psychic structure of infancy that could readily accommodate infantile defenses. Only object relations theories, particularly Kleinian developmental theory, equip the infant with sufficient mental structures to consider these as mechanisms of defense.

10.7 Evaluation of attachment theory and research

Bowlby's work was severely criticized by psychoanalysts committed to a drive discharge model for being insufficiently psychological (Freud, 1960; Schur, 1960) and assuming overly complex representational capacities for the infant (Spitz, 1960). This criticism was also leveled at Klein, and should be reevaluated in the light of recent research, as we have seen. Bowlby, on the other hand, was somewhat disingenuous in his critique of psychoanalysis, arguing that his proposal of a multi-track model of development, with a range of developmental pathways, was in contrast to psychoanalysis, which proposed a single possible developmental pathway, along which regression or fixation could occur. He ignored the work of analysts like Anna Freud and Eric Erikson who posited similar multi-track developmental networks. In essence Bowlby argued against a somewhat caricatured version of psychoanalysis, a position he retained to the end.

There has been little work on discontinuities in children's behavior in attachment theory terms, or on instances where experience appears to have little effect on the child's social development. Another limitation is that while psychoanalysis prioritized instincts and bodily processes rather than relationships in the creation of psychic organization, attachment theory has less to say about the bodily self or about sexuality. The attachment relationship may be critical in establishing an integrated sense of the physical and psychological self, also relevant to mature sexual relationships (Holmes, 1993a).

Overall, some of the early hopes of attachment theorists have been fulfilled by the three decades of research that have followed Ainsworth's and Bowlby's research. Attachment has been shown to be independent of temperament and maintained by processes that go way beyond stability of the environment. The determinants of security of attachment are increasingly well understood, and are closely related to the accurate perception of the infant as a psychological being. Secure attachment in infancy does not necessarily continue throughout life, but insecurity makes later security very unlikely. The attachment relationship with the caregiver is specific for both the child and the caregiver. Both can have different types of relationships with other members of the family. Yet the internal working model, assessed by the AAI, does predict the child's attachment class.

In terms of the long-term consequences of attachment classification from childhood, studies only partially confirm initial hopes of theorists and researchers. There can be little doubt that something is carried forward. Prediction from insecure-disorganized attachment is particularly powerful for various adverse outcomes, including psychiatric disorder. The pathways of association are by no means straightforward (Sroufe et al., 1999). For individuals with extremely harsh or chaotic early caregiving, the process of attentional, emotional and symbolic regulation might be derailed and the integration of self-states across behavioral states may never be fully achieved. Because early attachment disturbance makes itself felt as a dysfunction of self-organization (stress regulation, attention regulation and mentalization), and because these capacities are needed to deal with social stress, relationship disturbance in the early years together with additional social pressures does predict psychological disturbance.

CHAPTER 11

Schema theory and psychoanalysis

General systems theory, explicated by von Bertalanffy, removed the study of biological systems from the epistemological world of physics and created a frame of reference more appropriate for human behavior. 'In contrast to physical forces like gravity and electricity, the phenomena of life are found only in individual entities called organisms...[which] is a system, that is, a dynamic order of parts and processes standing in mutual interaction' (Bertalanffy, 1968, p.208). The mind is an open system, available to influence and modification from outside. Systems theory has been extensively applied to structural psychoanalytic formulations of development (e.g. Peterfreund, 1971; Basch, 1976; Noy, 1977; Rosenblatt and Thickstun, 1977; Boesky, 1988; Tyson and Tyson, 1990) as well as outside this framework (see e.g. Bowlby, 1980).

The motivation for adopting this model is primarily the reification and anthropomorphism of psychoanalytic metapsychological formulations and the inevitable logical contradictions they entail. Systems theory formulations of development address multiple components of developmental processes at several levels of abstraction simultaneously (Tyson and Tyson, 1990, p. 32). Bowlby's attachment theory, considered in the previous chapter, is a comprehensive implementation of general systems theory. Several other, more recent psychoanalytic accounts to some degree build on both attachment theory and general systems theory ideas and are also influenced by British object relations theory and cognitive science research. Some will be discussed in this chapter.

11.1 Horowitz's theory of personal schemas

Horowitz (1989; 1992) has offered a general systems theory reformulation of object relations, strongly influenced by Bowlby's (1980) notion of internal working models, Sandler's notion of role responsiveness (Sandler, 1976a; 1976b) and Kernberg's (1984) model of selfobject dyadic units, as well as by

255

current cognitive science. He proposes that the individual evolves multiple schemas of self and other, in one of two forms: as either person schemas or role-relationship models (RRMs). Person schemas combine hierarchically into more complex schemata of the self-in-relationship-with-the-other (see also Stern, below). Self-schemas integrate the individual's experiences and, ideally, present a stable image of the self. These RRMs are templates of relationships that can affect the formation of the concept of relationships as well as actual patterns of interpersonal transactions. RRMs are assumed to specify interaction patterns as sequences, much like scripts of plays, but in terms of expectations, wishes and appraisals of one person toward the other.

RRMs are organized into configurations (RRMCs) made up of RRMs, with a set of wishes, fears and defenses in relation to a specific theme. *Desired* RRMCs contain strong wishes and *dreaded* RRMCs are made up of feared RRMs. The derivatives of defensive operations are *compromise* RRMs that can be either adaptive (if successful) or problematic (if not), but in either case the affective valence of the RRM has been attenuated. A problematic RRMC will contain either negative affects or maladaptive traits, at a more manageable level than in dreaded RRMs. If the enactment of a desired RRM is blocked by the threat of a dreaded RRM, an attenuated solution to the desired RRM is found which provides a partial gratification of the wish. An RRMC may represent a firm linkage between RRMs so that a mental state organized by a desired RRM can trigger a mental state organized by a dreaded RRM. Such mental states may be represented by patterns of activation, such as those envisaged in parallel distributed computer models of neural activity.

Horowitz (1991a; 1991b) views anxiety as a mismatch between schemas and incoming information. If information is interpreted as suggesting a dreaded schema, anxiety will result. So if a wished-for RRM is a relationship with a powerful guiding figure, but this triggers with it a dreaded RRM of exploitation, the person will feel anxious when approached by a benign but powerful figure, because of the threat of exploitation. This may put control processes in place that increase the distance from this figure. Anticipation of the dreaded RRM is experienced as anxiety without the dreaded RRM ever being fully activated (coming into awareness). The control processes can, in the extreme, be severe enough to produce personality disorder, in this case perhaps of a schizoid or paranoid type.

In certain cases the dreaded RRM may be partly experienced, also leading to anxiety. A woman who loses her husband whom she felt was dependable but not loveable, may develop anxiety when she starts a relationship with another man for whom she has more intense feelings. The dreaded RRM is the experience of seeing herself as the unfaithful wife humiliating her dependable but unexciting husband (see Horowitz, 1991b). In post-traumatic stress disorder an experience is vividly encoded in memory. Because it is not integrated into the individual's prior integrated self-schema, it is liable to be activated as incoming information, and misinterpreted to imply the reoccurrence of the trauma. The trauma may also threaten to actualize a dreaded RRM, for example, of the self as weak and overwhelmed. The compromise state may be denial, depersonalization, restricted affect and hypervigilance (see Horowitz, 1986a; 1986b). In generalized anxiety disorder the dreaded RRM is seen as inescapable because either a compromise cannot be reached or the desired RRM contains some dreaded components. Horowitz's model is most extensively elaborated for the 12-session treatment of post-traumatic stress disorder (Horowitz, 1986a; 1991a), aimed at the realignment of RRMs.

Horowitz proposed a combination of Kernberg's and Kohut's ideas that integrated them into an information processing model, in order to account for narcissistic personality disorder. He viewed narcissistic individuals as having a cognitive distortion which forces them to integrate the meaning of events so as to aggrandize the self and to see it in as positive a way as possible. Their information processing is biased toward sources of praise and criticism. Further, an absence of cross-referential activity between meanings leads them to maintain incompatible psychological attitudes in separate clusters. They employ a shift in meaning of the information in order to prevent a reactive state of rage, depression or shame. Horowitz (1987) describes histrionic personalities as characterized by impressionistic distortions of incoming stimuli, rapid and short appraisal of meanings, and limited categories and availability of memory (see also, Gardner et al., 1959). Such individuals organize information about themselves as if they were passive, defective and childlike, and the ideal self is unintegrated and unstable. A general cognitive inhibition reduces the extent to which diverse representations may be integrated. The function of therapy is to reduce such inhibition.

Horowitz's model stands out among psychoanalytic formulations in offering a comprehensive framework specific to a range of psychiatric disorders at the same time as remaining open to research. Clinical judges can reliably assess roles, characteristics and traits of self and others, link them in wish-fear dilemmas, and assemble them into presumed RRMCs of particular patients in psychotherapy sessions (e.g. Horowitz and Eells, 1993). There is much in common between RRMC formulations and Luborsky's Core Conflictual Relationship Theme (CCRT) approach (Luborsky and Crits-Christoph, 1990; Luborsky, Barber and Beutler, 1993). There are no randomly controlled outcome studies on Horowitz's therapeutic strategies.

Horowitz's views link psychoanalysis more closely to cognitive accounts of psychopathology. There is an emphasis in these latter explanations on the unconscious determinants of behavior (see, for example Williams, Watts, MacLeod and Mathews, 1988; Mathews, 1990). They also stress pathological memory organization (e.g. Foa and Kozak, 1986), and the involuntary activation and processing of threat-cues without awareness (Mathews and MacLeod, 1986; McNally, Riemann and Kim, 1990). Although the model of the unconscious in cognitive psychology is very different from that of Freud and psychoanalysts, the mechanisms posited by Horowitz and those verified by cognitive theorists do share essential features. It is unclear whether Horowitz's framework will strengthen the empirical basis of psychoanalysis, or whether it is simply an implementation of connectionism, not significantly advancing either field (Fodor and Pylyshyn, 1988).

11.2 Stern's approach

Stern's first book (1985) represented a milestone in psychoanalytic theories of development. He challenges many previous ideas on developmental schemas. His work is unusual in that it is normative rather than patho-morphic, and prospective rather than retrospective. He focuses on the process of reorganization of subjective perspectives on self and other with the emergence of new maturational capacities. His model uses four different senses of self, each with an associated domain of relatedness. Stern (1985) suggested that every domain of self-experience begins at a particular age but then continues to influence experience throughout the lifespan. Importantly the self is seen as developing from within relationships. From birth to two months the infant's 'emerging self' begins. At this time the body acquires sensory data and the infant develops a sense of an emerging organi-zation concerning the world as directly experienced. After two months, for the next six months or so, the infant begins to evolve a sense of 'core self'. Stern assumes that the infant's sense of agency, the center of will, is a central feature of this phase. In addition, a sense of coherence concerning sensa-tions emanating from the body also dates back to this time. Stern also believes that the sense of self as continuous across time, in the form of a memory of self-experience, is a developmental achievement of a sense of core self. Rudimentary control of emotional experience is also arrived at by this time. What is not yet present is a subjective self. Stern suggests that it is not until the next stage, between 9 and 18 months, that there is a genuine sense of self and an experience of self with other. Signs of this develop-mental progress include conscious sharing of attention with another (as in pointing to a desired object). Not just an intentional focus but also inten-tions may be shared between self and other. Sharing also includes an awareness of emotion in the other and the sharing of emotion between child and caregiver is a new central feature of this stage. With the emergence of language a narrative self can come forth. From this point onwards the self will be defined by autobiographical narratives which nevertheless subsume and in important ways are conditioned by features of earlier stages of self-development.

Interestingly, increased understanding of the developmental changes that occur in neurological structures appears to point to a similar staging of self-development. Damasio's (1999) analysis of the neuroscience literature also suggested three forms of self and two forms of consciousness. His notion of the 'proto-self' is similar to Stern's emerging self in that it is seen as emerging from within deep structures within the brain that represent sensory information and from the body via a somato-sensory system generating direct experience, with both inner and outer worlds. Thus Stern's emerging self is comparable to Damasio's first-order neural maps. Second-order neural maps are generated by higher order circuits within the brain and entail the ways in which the proto-self is changed by its interaction with the world or with its own body. This second-order map compares the proto-self before and after the interaction. This neural structure is thus analogous to Stern's 'core self'; Siegel (2001) pointed out, 'this process of change defines the "core self"' (p. 75). Damasio claims that this leads to a heightened state of attention, that is at the core of consciousness. Core consciousness arises through the interaction with an object. The third phase of Damasio's model concerns extended consciousness, which according to Damasio involves third-order neural maps. These map on to Stern's 'subjective-self' notion, as Damasio describes them as neural representation of the changes in the core self over time.

Underlying the sense of subjective self are some clinically extremely relevant capacities. Their earliest manifestation may be the mental state of attention, which is evident in normal infants from about nine months of age in the monitoring of the gaze of the mother (Scaife and Bruner, 1975; Butterworth, 1991), and through gestures such as protodeclarative pointing (Bates et al., 1979). It is evident from gaze monitoring that infants apprehend the intentions and motives of others, as they appear not only to check where someone is looking but also, how the person is *evaluating* what he or she sees (the phenomena of social referencing, Sorce et al., 1985). Such emotional communication can be conveyed through the face or the voice by a parent or familiar caretaker, and it can regulate behavior toward an object, a location or a person (Boccia and Campos, 1989; Camras and Sachs, 1991).

Stern (1993) agrees with Sandler in focusing on the consciously or unconsciously experienced aspects of the representational world, not the non-experiential mental structures (or mental processes, see Fonagy, Moran, Edgcumbe et al., 1993) which underpin and create mental representations. He starts from the 'emergent moment', the subjective integration of all aspects of lived experience, emotions, behavior, sensations and all other aspects of the internal and external world. The emergent moment is seen as deriving from schematic representations of various types: event representations or scripts, semantic representations or conceptual schemas, perceptual schemas, and sensory-motor representations. He adds to these two further, clinically highly relevant, modes of representation: 'feeling shapes' and 'proto-narrative envelopes'. These schemata form a network which he terms 'the schema-of-a-way-of-being-with'.

Stern conceptualizes the 'schema-of-a-way-of-being-with' from the assumed subjective point of view of the infant who is in interaction with the caregiver. The infant's experiences across a number of domains are organized around a motive and a goal, and in this sense Stern echoes Freud's (1905d) original formulation of drives and object relationships in the *Three Essays*. The goals which organize these moments are not only biological, but include object relatedness, affect states, and states of self-esteem and safety, as well as physical gratification, be it of hunger, thirst, sexuality or aggression. The representation will contain a proto-plot with an agent, an action, instrumentality and context, which are all necessary elements for the comprehension of human behavior (see Bruner, 1990).

Stern (1993) offers a compelling example of a way-of-being with a depressed mother, and describes the baby trying repeatedly to recapture and reanimate her. He describes how depressed mothers, monitoring their own failure to stimulate, may make huge efforts to enliven their infant in an unspontaneous way, to which infants respond with what is probably an equally false response of enlivened interaction. This model maps very closely onto Sandler's model of projection and projective identification, and the two need to be combined to achieve a fully coherent account. The child identifies with the representation of the mother's distorted representation of him, communicated to him by projective identification, and this evolves into an expectation of 'a false way-of-being-with' the other.

The schemata of ways-of-being-with come closest to providing a neuropsychologically valid model of the representation of interpersonal experience. Certain features of the model are critical here. First, these schemata are emergent properties of the nervous system and the mind. Second, they make use of multiple, simultaneous representations of the lived experience. This is consistent with the clinical observation that even in pervasive brain injury, aspects of experience are retained. Third, they are based on prototypes, are less affected by single experiences and naturally aggregate common patterns of lived experience. Emergent moments are represented in the simultaneous activation of a set of nodes within a network, the strengthening of the connections between these nodes with each activation automatically constituting a 'learning process'. By conceptualizing schemas of way-of-being-with as networks, Stern links his model to that of the dominant model of cognitive science, parallel distributed processing (see Rumelhart and McClelland, 1986;

PDP is a currently popular computer simulation of learning processes, using a network of 'neurons'). Fourth, the model allows room for modification from inside, as well as outside. In postulating refiguration as a process whereby attention can scan representation, Stern offers a way in which internally generated activation (fantasy) may strengthen or alter experience. Fifth, in adopting Edelman's (1987) concept of neural Darwinism, Stern opens an important avenue for further work on the fate of representations which are not selected (see below).

The word 'shape' is used in different senses by Stern (1993) and by Sandler (1993). Whereas for Sandler, shape pertains to the gestalt experience of a mental representation (see also Werthheimer, 1945), for Stern shape primarily refers to a temporal patterning of arousal. Arousal amalgamates modalities of experience and in its purest form, may manifest as free-floating affect. In practice, affect cannot occur without cognition, but Stern's insistence upon the independence of these domains of representation is well taken. As clinicians, we are all familiar with the temporal feeling shape of sessions. Certain patients create clinical encounters where a range of affects follow one another in what appears to be a strictly ordered temporal sequence.

Taken together, the psychoanalytic propositions of Sandler and Stern have created a number of new bridges between clinically grounded psychoanalytic observations and progress in neuroscience. They offer the potential for dramatic revisions of psychoanalytic metapsychology. To take just one example, already touched upon: what was previously thought of as a qualitatively different structure of cognition, primary process thought, may simply be the activation of neural networks or representations selected out in the process of neural evolution. Pre-linguistic children are likely to organize their physical world in non-conceptual ways in some instances, according to the physical appearance of objects. Studies of language development (see for example Clark, 1983) show that the early use of language is frequently dominated by the physical appearance of objects (e.g. children frequently refer to all round objects with the same word). Such neural networks are selected out as the child understands more complex and conceptual relationships between these elements. In states of reverie, dreaming, or intense emotional arousal, these old 'vestigial' structures may become reactivated. Schemas may also lose out in the process of neural natural selection through the deliberate separation of frames or parts of a network which interfere with efficient adaptive neural functioning. Ideas that give rise to conflict and anxiety may thus be eliminated from neural nets. Schemas of ways-of-being-with, which have been eliminated in this way, may however re-emerge if other constraints on the system are temporarily lifted by dream sleep, by reverie, or by free association (Sandler and Joffe, 1967).

In a series of papers, Stern and his co-workers in Boston have described a radically new developmental understanding of psychoanalytic treatment (Stern, 1993; 1998; Stern et al., 1998). At the heart of this is the notion of implicit or procedural memory borrowed from cognitive science (Schachter, 1992b). Bob Clyman (1991) should be credited with bringing this idea to the attention of psychoanalysts and Crittenden (1990) with integrating the idea with attachment theory. The fundamental idea is that a component of personality is rooted in non-conscious schemata that define the 'how' rather than the 'what' of interpersonal behavior.

Over the past two decades, cognitive scientists have elaborated the notion of procedural memories based on the non-conscious, implicit use of past experience (e.g. Squire, 1987; Kihlstrom and Hoyt, 1990; Schachter, 1992b). There is general agreement that the memory system is at least of a dual nature with two relatively independent, neurologically and psychologically homogeneous systems underpinning it. In addition to autobiographical memory, which is at least in part accessible to awareness, an important component to memory is a non-voluntary system which is implicit, principally perceptual, non-declarative and non-reflective (Squire, 1987; Schachter, 1992b). Memory, in common parlance, involves an internal experience of recalling, and requires focal attention at the stage of encoding. This is declarative or explicit memory. It is developmentally unlikely to be as relevant to psychoanalysis as implicit memory which encodes relational and emotional experiences from the earliest days of life. It is likely that it is, at least in certain respects, more dominated by emotional and impressionistic information than its autobiographical counterpart (Pillemer and White, 1989; Tobias, Kihlstrom and Schacter, 1992; van der Kolk, 1994). It stores the 'how' of executing sequences of actions, motor skills being prototypical instances. The procedural knowledge that it contains is accessible only through performance. It is seen only when the individual engages in the operations into which knowledge is embedded. Given these features, the schematic representations postulated by attachment and object relations theorists are probably best construed as procedural memories, the function of which is to adapt social behavior to specific contexts.

The classification of patterns of attachment in infancy (Ainsworth et al., 1978) taps into procedural memory (Crittenden, 1990; Fonagy, 1995a). The strength of the Strange Situation (SSn) as a method of psychological assessment is to provide a powerful analogue of past situational contexts within which knowledge concerning the 'how' of behavior with a specific caregiver is accrued. In this sense attachment is a skill acquired in relation to a specific caregiver. Psychotherapists are familiar with exploring declarative memories. They then tend to derive a picture of an individual's relationship to others from invariant themes in the patient's narratives. Lester Luborsky's 'Core Conflictual Relationship Themes' (CCRT) technique (Luborsky and

Luborsky, 1995), for example, distinguishes three repeatedly emerging components: (a) the wish, (b) the response of the object, and (c) the response of the subject. By contrast Mary Main found it more appropriate to evaluate attachment security in adult narratives not from the content of childhood histories, but from the manner in which these stories were related (if secure, then coherent, reflective, balanced and detailed). In Mary Main's system, the quality of attachment relationships is assessed on the basis of the procedures used by an individual to create an attachment related narrative. The success of this instrument (van IJzendoorn, 1995) speaks volumes for the promise of a procedure-oriented psychodynamic approach.

Clinicians are also accustomed to working with procedural memory. Clinical sensitivity, in itself a skill represented as a set of procedures, is mostly astuteness about the multiple meanings encoded into a single verbal message using stress, speech pauses, intonation and other features of pragmatics, all expressions of procedurally stored knowledge. The innovative feature of the Stern model of 'now moments' is the emphasis on interpersonal factors in the generation of procedural aspects of personality functioning. Karlen Lyons-Ruth (1998) points out that the classical (problematic) notions of internalization poorly fit the acquisition of procedural knowledge. Both she and Tronick (1998) emphasize the two-person character of such information; awareness of the other is seen as a prerequisite for the articulation, differentiation and flexible use of these structures. Stern, as well as Tronick, highlights the dialectic roots of these structures, originating as they do in the recurrent rupture and repair cycles of mother–infant dialogue. As implicit relational knowledge structures arise out of developmental disequilibrium, it is to be expected that normally they are emotionally charged and that they retain a spontaneous quality. The concept of the implicit relational known is descriptively unconscious, unthought but not unknowable.

In Stern's (1998) description there is a further key concept, that of 'open space' which follows the developmental disequilibrium, if, in the 'now moment', two consciousnesses succeeded in encountering one another. In the 'open space' there is a certain disengagement born of confidence of the availability of the other, presumably affirmed by the marked presence of the other at the 'moment of meeting'. This idea, which is related to Donald Winnicott's description of the capacity to be alone (Winnicott, 1958a), is at the heart of the change process. Both participants are able to restructure their implicit relational systems in the light of their experience of the 'scaffolding' (Vygotsky, 1966) of the other's mental organization. The key assumptions of their model lead the authors inevitably to an interpersonalist psychology. Tronick's dual consciousness model is probably its clearest expression. 'I interact, therefore I am'. As the authors are well aware, they are contributing to a rich tradition, perhaps beginning with Hegel (1807), reinforced by Mead

(1934), Cooley (1964/1902), more recently by Davidson (1987) and in the psychoanalytic sphere by Cavell (1994). Yet Stern and his colleagues differ from modern psychoanalytic interpersonalists (see Fiscalini, Mann and Stern, 1995) in offering a coherent psychological model of intersubjectivity, complete with developmental roots and technical implications.

There are different ways of conceptualizing the therapeutic implications of the 'moments' model. The careful reader notes subtle differences between the authors in this regard. All the papers focus on micro-processes in therapy as the key to understanding psychic change but they differ somewhat in the degree to which they regard the traditional verbal articulation of the transference to be an additional potent force. The papers also express slightly different views on the importance of insight in addressing ruptures in the patient-analyst relationship. At the extreme, one may conclude from these papers that the classical understanding of the therapeutic relationship is a backdrop against which change of implicit relational structures can take place. The therapeutic properties of the setting, as traditionally conceived, are relegated to the status of benign conventions that serve to highlight deviations from the implicit rules of interaction. As Morgan (1998) puts it: 'It provides space for departure from these past expectancies with other people.' There is a dual message here: (1) the traditional parameters are required as an alternative to 'ordinary' relationships which entangle patients in their implicit relational structures rather than allowing them to take a distance from them; and (2) the traditional parameters provide for predictability of interpersonal behavior that is the material necessary, so to speak, for the relationship processes to work on.

The relegation of transference and its interpretation from a 'star' to a mere 'supporting role', may seem extravagant and even impious. Yet the facts support this claim. For instance, there are over 400 different schools of psychotherapy currently practiced (Kazdin, 2000). Therapists trained in these various orientations offer understanding to their clients which differs to the point of precluding common ground (Wallerstein, 1992). While most of these therapies have not been evaluated, many that have been subjected to controlled study appear to be similarly effective (Roth and Fonagy, 1996). It appears that the relationship component of therapy may be the effective ingredient since this is the main feature which the talking cures share.

Psychotherapy research has in fact thrown up a popular model that has many features in common with 'moment theory'. There is evidence to suggest that the extent to which ruptures to the therapeutic alliance are adequately addressed predicts well to the outcome of therapy (Safran et al., 1990; Horvath and Simmonds, 1991). The authors here appeal to the 'real relationship'. It is important that readers do not understand this phrase, as used elsewhere in the psychoanalytic literature, to mean the non-transferential aspects of the relationship. In these papers, real relationship refers to the non-conscious implicit relational mode or to use Stern's fortuitous phrase, 'a-way-of-being-with' or perhaps more exactly 'a style of relating'. The authors are careful to separate their comments from ones which could be made on the basis of the conscious, 'real' relationship. Stern points out that the aspects of relating the authors consider crucial to psychic change are always linked with 'feelings of authenticity', within unique experiences in the history of patient and therapist with each other, as opposed to other current or past relationships. The therapist is a new object whose involvement allows a departure from past expectancies with other people. Thus there is a dialectic with transference.

All this is captured in the notion of 'moments of meeting'. The trigger for these episodes are 'now moments' that contain an apparent rupture within periods of shared meaning referred to, a little disparagingly, as 'moving along'. Moments of meeting involve the intersubjective recognition of a shared subjective reality. Each partner contributes something unique and authentic. The spontaneity required places it by definition beyond both theory and technique, which are, for the most part, tied to explicit rather than implicit structures. The failure to seize the moment fails the patient: such opportunities are scarce given the fixed patterns of relatedness of many patients. The 'moment of meeting' can alter implicit relational knowing. This does not happen suddenly, as may be the case for intellectual insight (here the moment metaphor may be misleading), but gradually something shifts, which may be imperceptible to patient or analyst except perhaps for a sense of increased well-being in each other's company. Thus it is all but impossible to bring compelling clinical examples to illustrate the process, which has probably slowed the recognition of this phenomenon.

While it is undoubtedly helpful to explore psychotherapeutic progress from the point of view of implicit relational knowledge, the challenge to Stern and colleagues is the formal operationalization of these ideas. The group's analogies with infant observational paradigms (e.g. the 'still face') have inherent limitations which will only be overcome if an operational framework appropriate for adult psychoanalysis can be found. Probably many of the phenomena referred to could not readily be quantified without the use of tape-recording. Much progress has been made in this field over recent years (off-line computer analysis of psychotherapy discourse is now readily available, Bucci, 1997b). The authors need to identify reliable markers of change in procedural knowledge, and explore changes in these in relation to 'moments of meeting'.

At the conceptual level, more is required fully to map the distinctions between classical ideas of transference and the ideas of the Boston group (who recognize this need: Morgan, 1998). It is clear that a simple dichotomy between transference and implicit relational knowledge will not do. The problem lies in the loose definition of transference. By certain definitions of the term, all that happens between patient and analyst *is* transference. Most clinicians, however, see transference as the re-experiencing of a past relationship pattern with the analyst (Hamilton, 1996). Here, it is helpful to distinguish aspects of the therapeutic relationship motivated by old relationship schemata, re-activated by the analysis, from currently active relationship structures. Both include declarative and implicit knowledge structures.

What about technique? Here much more needs to be done, particularly in the current climate where the interpersonalist approach to psychotherapy has brought many innovations. The group makes it clear that they are not advocating dramatic technical innovation, and certainly not 'wild analysis'. This is reassuring for the classical therapist, but it cannot be correct. If the ideas proposed by the group have substance, it is most unlikely that exactly the same technical priorities drawn up for traditional theoretical frameworks and aims would best serve these new ideas. An exciting, new model of psychotherapeutic change is proposed, translated into a developmentally credible psychological model. If this set of ideas is intended simply to justify current methods of practice, it is of far less import than it would be if changes in technique followed from it, at least for certain groups of patients.

11.3 Ryle's cognitive analytic therapy: a full implementation of the procedural model of pathology and therapy

Relatively unknown in the US, but increasingly influential in the UK, is cognitive analytic therapy – a time-limited integrated psychotherapy (Ryle, 1982; 1990; 1995a). The procedural sequence model (PSM) is the framework used by Ryle to restate psychoanalytic ideas using cognitive language. This model provides the most comprehensive and complex implementation of the general procedural model that Stern and colleagues have outlined. It is not itself a psychoanalytic theory, but a collection of theoretical ideas and techniques that constitute a comprehensive clinical implementation of the work on schemata and procedural memory.

The model conceptualizes intentional acts as procedures entailing a series of steps, including appraisal of plans and predicted consequences, and the revision of aims and means following this evaluation. The therapeutic method is centered on reformulation. During the first month, patients monitor their symptoms, undesirable behaviors and mood shifts. Neurotic patterns are described in terms of three categories: dilemmas, traps and snags. These are described in the 'Psychotherapy File' given to patients at the end of the first session. They rate items within it to indicate how characteristic they are of them. These are then discussed together with Target

Problems and the dilemmas, traps and snags underlying them. Traps are things we cannot escape from such as 'trying to please'. Dilemmas are false choices about oneself or one's relation to others, for example, 'either I spoil myself and am greedy or I deny myself things and feel miserable' or 'either I am a brute or a martyr'. Snags are ways we stop ourselves from changing, for example, 'fear of the response of others'. The dilemmas, traps and snags characteristic of an individual are the Target Problem Procedures that are thought to underlie their central problems. 'TPs' and 'TPPs' form the agenda of the therapy. The remaining sessions (usually once a week over three months) are devoted to recognition of the TPPs using diaries and other self-monitoring devices as well as close monitoring of the client's behavior in the therapeutic situation. Modification of TPPs is principally achieved through behavioral techniques such as role-play as well as enhanced self-reflection. The explicit non-collusive relationship with the therapist is also thought to facilitate the development of new procedures.

Ryle (1985) incorporated object relations theory into CAT, introducing the notion of reciprocal role procedures. These are thought to develop on the basis of early object relationships, which are assumed to teach the child both what behavior is expected of him and what to expect of others. Self-management is learned through incorporating the parent's behavior into the child's repertoire. The emphasis in CAT is on early and profound deprivation as the cause of primitive defenses such as splitting, which characterizes individuals who cannot integrate their self-structure and seek confirmations from others for each of their split-off self states. Whereas neurotic clients restrict or distort their procedures, borderline personality disorder patients show dissociated self-states containing different procedures in each.

Thus CAT is a genuine integration of cognitive therapy (Beck, 1976) and object relations based psychodynamic therapy (Ogden, 1986). The approach to diagnosis has similarities to some we have considered above, particularly Luborsky and Horowitz. The therapeutic techniques suggested are different, and share much with schema oriented cognitive therapy where emotional problems are seen as the reactivation of schemas that have been dormant for many years (Beck and Freeman, 1990; Young, 1990; Bricker and Young, 1993). Ryle's integration also has much in common with other integrative models such as Gold and Wachtel's 'Cyclical Psychodynamics' which also emphasizes self-maintaining vicious cycles and intra- and inter-psychological processes and structured intervention techniques (Gold and Wachtel, 1993). Safran (1990a; 1990b) also links concepts of interpersonal schemata and the cognitive interpersonal cycle, and the therapy program focuses on challenging maladaptive interpersonal schemas. CAT, however, is more coherently integrated with traditional psychodynamic formulations than are these alternatives (Ryle, 1994).

The Procedural Sequence Object Relations Model (PSORM) illustrates the thoughtfulness of this integration. The Procedural Sequence Model identifies patterns which explain the persistence of neurotic behavior. For example, self-destructive acts may be attributed to a dilemma ('I must harm myself or harm others') or to a snag ('guilty and therefore self-punishing'). Patterns are maintained because of the connection between procedures. For example, the expectation of abandonment may generate a dilemma between being involved and thus risking abandonment and avoiding closeness. Being involved thus necessitates procedures for controlling emotionally significant others by compensatory procedures. A disorder or symptom such as bulimia may be seen as a compensatory procedure, a substitute for emotional emptiness. The PSORM postulates reciprocal role patterns that constitute a central core and are stated in terms of Inner Parent–Inner Child (IP–IC) relations. An example may be a powerfully rejecting Inner Parent relating to a submissive and needy Inner Child. The reciprocal nature of the role patterns encompass psychodynamic concepts such as identification, introjection and projection, internal objects and part-objects. Roles that are experienced as untenable are projected, that is, induced in the other, and can be replaced by symptomatic procedures or defensive ones. Procedures acquire their stability from confirming reciprocations that are generally readily elicited from others, thus leaving the central core repertoire unchanged. While Ryle and others writing from a CAT perspective are keen to acknowledge Soviet theoreticians such as Vygotsky, Bakhtin and Leonjew (e.g. Leiman, 1994), their views are very consistent with psychoanalysts writing in the interpersonalists' tradition (e.g. Mitchell, 1988).

The key difference between CAT and traditional psychodynamic therapy is the shift from interpretation to *description*. The CAT therapist describes the state of affairs, often in writing, which is then discussed and challenged in direct therapeutic conversations. Ryle rejects interpretation as inducing regression, reflecting an unbalanced power relationship and feeding the omnipotent fantasies of the therapist (Ryle, 1992; 1993). Ryle's approach lends more weight to conscious processes and his technique is based on insight and activating self-corrective mechanisms. It is striking that, notwithstanding the emphasis on such mature mental processes, Ryle and his colleagues report significant successes in the brief treatment of borderline personality disorder. In an ongoing study, BPD patients are offered up to 24 sessions of CAT and follow-up sessions at one, two, three and six months. There is a three month and one year follow-up. Initial results are promising (Ryle, 1995b; Ryle and Marlowe, 1995). Eight out of 13 patients no longer met BPD criteria four months after termination but seven were re-referred for a variety of other treatments. Five patients assessed at one year all showed continuing reductions in symptomatology and only one has remained in treatment.

A number of other outcome studies support the usefulness of CAT. A study of 48 outpatients randomly assigned to 12 sessions of CAT or Mann type brief therapy demonstrated the superiority of CAT on a Grid measure of change of construing problems (Brockman et al., 1987). Unfortunately the measure was neither standardized nor sufficiently independent from the treatment to justify firm conclusions. A study of poorly controlled diabetics randomized 32 patients to intensive education or CAT (Fosbury, 1994). At nine months follow-up CAT-treated patients had better diabetic control in terms of HbA1$_c$ levels. Other studies were either uncontrolled clinical reports (e.g. Cowmeadow, 1994; Duignan and Mitzman, 1994; Pollock and Kear-Colwell, 1994) or yielded insignificant differences between CAT and control treatments (e.g. the outpatient treatment of anorexia (Ryle, 1995b)). Thus the empirical basis of CAT cannot yet be considered well established (although relative to many other psychodynamic treatments its empirical status is highly favorable).

CHAPTER 12

Fonagy and Target's model of mentalization

On the basis of empirical observations and theoretical elaboration, Fonagy and Target have developed the argument that the capacity to understand interpersonal behaviour in terms of mental states is a key determinant of self-organization and affect regulation, and that it is acquired in the context of early attachment relationships. This capacity is referred to as mentalization, and operationalized for research as reflective function.

12.1 Fonagy and Target's developmental schema

Fonagy and Target have developed this psychoanalytic model with George Moran, Miriam and Howard Steele, Anna Higgitt, Gyorgy Gergely, Efrain Bleiberg and Elliot Jurist. It was first outlined in the context of a large empirical study, in which the security of infant attachment with each parent proved to be strongly predicted, not only by that parent's security of attachment during the pregnancy (Fonagy, Steele and Steele, 1991), but even more by the parents' capacity to understand their childhood relationship to their own parents in terms of states of mind (Fonagy, Steele, Moran et al., 1991).

We have tried to map the process by means of which the understanding of the self as a mental agent grows out of interpersonal experience, particularly primary object relationships (Fonagy et al., 2002). Mentalization involves both a self-reflective and an interpersonal component. In combination, these provide the child with a capacity to distinguish inner from outer reality, internal mental and emotional processes from interpersonal events. Both clinical and empirical evidence has been presented together with developmental observation to demonstrate that the baby's experience of himself as having a mind or psychological self is not a genetic given. It is a structure that evolves from infancy through childhood, and its development critically depends upon interaction with more mature minds, which are benign, reflective and sufficiently attuned.

Our understanding of mentalization is not just as a cognitive process, but developmentally begins with the 'discovery' of affects through the primary object relationships. Thus, we have focused on the concept of 'affect regulation', which is important in many spheres of theories of development and psychopathology (e.g. Clarkin and Lenzenweger, 1996). Affect regulation, the capacity to modulate emotional states, is closely related to mentalization, which plays a fundamental role in the unfolding of a sense of self and agency. In this account, affect regulation is a prelude to mentalization; yet, once mentalization occurs, the nature of affect regulation is transformed: not only does it allow adjustment of affect states, but more fundamentally it is used to regulate the self.

Jurist's concept of 'mentalized affectivity' (Fonagy et al., 2002) marks a mature capacity for the regulation of affect, and denotes the capacity to discover the subjective meanings of one's own feelings. Mentalized affectivity, we suggest, lies at the core of psychoanalytic treatment. It represents the experiential understanding of one's feelings in a way that extends well beyond intellectual understanding. It is in this realm that we encounter resistances and defenses, not just against specific emotional experiences, but against entire modes of psychological functioning; not just distortions of mental representations standing in the way of therapeutic progress but also inhibitions of mental functioning (Fonagy, Edgcumbe et al., 1993). Thus we can misunderstand what we feel, thinking that we feel one thing while truly feeling something else. More seriously, we can deprive ourselves of the entire experiential world of emotional richness. For example, the inability to imagine psychological and psychosocial causation may be the result of the pervasive inhibition and/or developmental malformation of the psychological processes that underpin these capacities.

This theory of affect regulation and mentalization is intended to enrich the arguments advanced by theorists such as Bowlby about the evolutionary function of attachment. We have argued that an evolutionary function of early object relations is to equip the very young child with an environment within which the understanding of mental states in others and the self can fully and safely develop.mentalization.

We have proposed two intimately connected developmental theories, both rooted in developmental psychology. Both concern the relationship between the acquisition of an understanding of the representational nature of minds on the one hand and affect regulation on the other. The social bio-feedback theory of parental affect mirroring, introduced and empirically tested by Gergely and Watson (Gergely and Watson, 1996), explores the way in which the infant's automatic emotion expression, and the mother's facial and vocal emotional displays in response, come to be linked in the baby's mind through a contingency detection mechanism identified by John Watson and colleagues (Watson, 1972; 1994; Bahrick and Watson, 1985). The forging of this link has two vital effects. First, the baby comes to associate the control he has over the parents' mirroring displays with the resulting improvement in his emotional state, leading, eventually, to an experience of the self as a regulating agent. Secondly, the establishment of a second order representation of affect states creates the basis for affect regulation and impulse control: affects can be manipulated and discharged internally as well as through action, they can also be experienced as something recognizable and hence shared. Affect expressions by the parent that are not contingent on the infant's affect will undermine the appropriate labeling of internal states which may, in turn, remain confusing, experienced as unsymbolized and hard to regulate.

For affect mirroring to serve as the basis of the development of a representational framework, the parent must indicate that her display is not for real, it is not an indication of how she *herself* feels. We have described this characteristic of the parent's mirroring behavior as its 'markedness'. An expression congruent with the baby's state, but lacking markedness, may overwhelm him. It is felt to be the parent's own real emotion, making his experience seem contagious, or universal, and thus more dangerous. In the short term, the baby's perception of a corresponding but realistic negative emotion is likely to escalate rather than regulate the infant's state, leading to cumulative traumatization rather than containment.

The distressed child looks, in the response of the parent, for a representation of his mental state that he may internalize and use as part of a higher order strategy of affect regulation. The secure caregiver soothes by combining mirroring with a display that is incompatible with the child's feelings (thus implying contact with distance and coping). This formulation of sensitivity has much in common with Bion's (Bion, 1962b) notion of the role of the mother's capacity to mentally 'contain' the affect state that feels intolerable to the baby, and respond in a manner that acknowledges the child's mental state, yet serves to modulate unmanageable feelings. Ratings of the quality of the reflective function of each parent during pregnancy were found independently to predict the child's later security of attachment in the London Parent–Child Project (Fonagy, Steele, Moran et al., 1992). The finding that the clarity and coherence of the mother's representation of the child mediates between the Adult Attachment Interview and mother's observed behavior is also consistent with this model (Slade et al., 1999).

There is general agreement that, as well as increasing attachment security in the child, the 'harmoniousness of the mother–child relationship contributes to the emergence of symbolic thought' (Werner and Kaplan,

1963; Mahler et al., 1975; Vygotsky, 1978; Bretherton, Bates, Benigni et al., 1979 p.224). Bowlby (1969) recognized the significance of the developmental step entailed in the emergence of 'the child's capacity both to conceive of his mother as having her own goals and interests separate from his own and to take them into account' (1969, p. 368). These writings have led to empirical tests. Moss, Parent and Gosselin (1995) reported that attachment security with mother was a good concurrent predictor of metacognitive capacity in the child in the domains of memory, comprehension and communication. The Separation Anxiety Test, a projective test of attachment security, predicts belief-desire reasoning capacity in 3½ to 6-year-old children when age, verbal ability and social maturity were all controlled for (Fonagy, Redfern and Charman, 1997). Furthermore, this can be predicted from attachment security in infancy: Eighty-two per cent of babies classified as secure with mother at 12 months passed the belief-desire reasoning task at 5½ years (Fonagy, 1997). In this task the child is asked what a character would feel, based on his or her knowledge of the character's belief. Forty-six per cent of those who had been classified as insecure failed. Infant-father attachment (at 18 months) also predicted the child's performance. This pattern has been partially replicated by Meins and colleagues (Meins et al., 1998).

Elsewhere we have considered several possible explanations of the empirical relationship between parental reflective function, infant security and child mentalizing capacity (Fonagy et al., 2002). We have argued that the evidence is best explained by the assumption that the acquisition of the theory of mind is part of an intersubjective process between the infant and caregiver (see Gopnik, 1993 for an elegant elaboration of such a model). In our view, the caregiver helps the child create mentalizing models, through complex linguistic and quasi-linguistic processes. She behaves toward the child in such a way that he gradually concludes that his own behavior may be best understood if he assumes that he has ideas and beliefs, feelings and wishes which determine his actions, and the reactions of others can be generalized to other similar beings. The mother approaches the crying baby with a question in her mind: 'Do you want your nappy changed?' 'Do you need a cuddle?' If sensitive, she is unlikely to address the situation without having the person in mind, so is unlikely to say to herself, 'Are you wet around your bottom?' or 'Have you been standing alone too long?' The sensitive caregiver can bridge the focus on physical reality and internal state, sufficiently for the child to identify contingencies between them. Ultimately, the child arrives at the conclusion that the caregiver's reaction to him makes sense given internal states of belief or desire within himself. Unconsciously and pervasively, the caregiver ascribes a mental state to the child with her behavior, treating the child as a mental agent. This is ultimately perceived by the child and used in the elaboration of mental models of causation, and permits the development of a core sense of selfhood organized along these lines. We assume that this is mostly a mundane process, and that it is preconscious to both infant and parent – inaccessible to reflection or modification. Parents, however, execute this natural human function in different ways. Some are alert to the earliest indications of intentionality, while others may need stronger indications before they can perceive the child's mental state and modify their behavior accordingly.

Our second theory concerns the nature of subjectivity before the child recognizes that internal states are representations of reality. We suggest that the very young child equates the internal world with the external (Fonagy and Target, 1996a; Target and Fonagy, 1996). What exists in the mind must exist out there and what exists out there must also exist in the mind. This 'psychic equivalence', as a mode of experiencing the internal world, can cause intense distress, since the projection of fantasy can be terrifying. The acquisition of a sense of pretend in relation to mental states is therefore essential. The repeated experience of affect-regulative mirroring helps the child to learn that feelings do not inevitably spill out into the world. They are decoupled from physical reality. We suggest that children whose parents provide more affect-congruent, contingent, and appropriately marked, mirroring displays facilitate this decoupling. By contrast, the displays of parents who (because of their own difficulties with emotion regulation) are readily overwhelmed by the infant's negative affect and produce a realistic unmarked emotion expression, disrupt the development of affect regulation. A major opportunity for learning about the difference between representational and actual mental states is lost. We have argued that the equation of external and internal continues to dominate the subjective world of individuals with severe personality disorders (Fonagy and Target, 2000).

In describing the normal development of reflective function in the child of two to five years (Fonagy and Target, 1996a; Target and Fonagy, 1996), we suggest that there is a transition from a split mode of experience to mentalization. We have advanced a number of propositions concerning the development of the psychological part of the self:

1. In early childhood, reflective function is characterized by two modes of relating internal experiences to the external situation: (a) in a serious frame of mind, the child expects the internal world in himself and others to correspond to external reality, and subjective experience will often be distorted to match information coming from outside (*'psychic equivalence mode'*), (e.g. Perner et al., 1987; Gopnik and Astington, 1988); and (b) while playing, the child knows that internal experience may not reflect external reality (e.g. Bartsch and Wellman, 1989; Dias and Harris,

1990), but then the internal state is thought to have no implications for the outside world ('*pretend mode*').

2. Normally at around four years old, the child integrates these modes to arrive at *mentalization*, or *reflective mode*, in which mental states can be experienced as representations. Inner and outer reality can then be seen as linked, yet differing in important ways, and no longer have to be either equated or dissociated from each other (Gopnik, 1993; Baron-Cohen, 1995).

3. Mentalization normally comes about through the child's experience of his mental states being reflected on, prototypically through secure play with a parent or older child, which facilitates integration of the pretend and psychic equivalence modes. This interpersonal process is perhaps an elaboration of the complex mirroring the parent offered earlier. In playfulness, the caregiver gives the child's ideas and feelings (when he is 'only pretending') a link with reality, by indicating an alternative perspective outside the child's mind. The parent or older child also shows that reality may be distorted by acting upon it in playful ways, and through this playfulness a pretend but real mental experience may be introduced.

4. In traumatized children, intense emotion, and associated conflict, may disrupt this integration, so that aspects of the pretend mode of functioning become part of a psychic equivalence manner of experiencing reality. For instance, where trauma has occurred within the family, the parent may not be able to 'play with' the most pressing aspects of the child's thoughts; these are often disturbing and unacceptable to the adult, just as they are to the child. The rigid and controlling behavior seen in preschool children with histories of disorganized attachment is thus seen as arising out of a partial failure on the part of the child to move beyond the mode of psychic equivalence in relation to specific ideas or feelings, so that he experiences them with the intensity that might be expected had they been current, external events.

The child's perception of mental states in himself and others thus depends on his observation of the mental world of his caregiver. He can perceive and conceive of his mental states to the extent that his parent's behavior implied them. This can happen through shared pretend playing with the child (empirically shown to be associated with early mentalization), and many ordinary interactions (such as conversations and peer interaction) will also involve shared thinking about an idea. Thus mental state concepts such as thinking are inherently intersubjective; shared experience is part of their very logic.

We know something about the impact of this on the child's developing sense of self. Avoidant infants respond to separation with minimal displays of distress while experiencing considerable physiological arousal (Spangler and Grossman, 1993). Crittenden (1988; Crittenden and DiLalla, 1988) reports that one-year-old maltreated children display falsely positive affect that does not match their true feelings. It seems that the internalization of the caregiver's defenses can lead not only to a failure to represent real emotional experience adequately, but also to the construction of an experience of self around this false internalization (Winnicott, 1965a).

Thus, the avoidant child learns to shun emotional states, while the resistant child focuses on his own distress to the exclusion of close intersubjective exchanges. Disorganized infants are a special category; hypervigilant of the caregiver's behavior, they use all cues available for prediction and may be acutely sensitized to intentional states. We have argued that in such children mentalization may be evident, but it does not have the positive role in self-organization that it does in secure children. What is most important for the development of mentalizing self-organization is the exploration of the mental state of the sensitive caregiver, which enables the child to find in his image of her mind a picture of himself motivated by beliefs, feelings and intentions. In contrast, what the disorganized child is scanning for so intently is not the representation of his own mental states in the mind of the other, but the mental states of that other which threaten to undermine his own self. They can constitute an alien presence within his self-representation, so unbearable that his attachment behavior becomes focused on re-externalizing these parts of the self onto attachment figures, rather than on the internalization of a capacity for containment of affects and other intentional states. There is considerable evidence to support the view that secure attachment enhances the development of the self, inner security, feeling of self-worth, self-reliance and personal power of the emerging self, as well as the development of autonomy (Matas, Arend and Sroufe, 1978; Londerville and Main, 1981; Gove, 1983 in Carlsson and Sroufe, 1995; Bates, Maslin and Frankel, 1985). Disorganized infants, even if perceptive, fail to integrate this emotional awareness with their self-organization.

There may be a number of linked reasons for this: (a) the child needs to use disproportionate resources to understand the parent's behavior, at the expense of reflecting on self-states; (b) the caregiver of the disorganized infant is likely to be less contingent in responding to the infant's self-state, and further to show systematic biases in her perception and reflection of his state; (c) the mental state of the caregiver of the disorganized infant may evoke intense anxiety through either frightening or fearful behavior toward the child, including inexplicable fear of the child himself.

These factors combine, perhaps, to make disorganized infants become keen readers of the caregiver's mind under certain circumstances, but (we suggest) poor readers of their own mental states. This model of the development of mentalizing capacity has considerable clinical implications. For example, in a study of attachment classification in patients with severe personality disorders (Fonagy et al., 1996), we found that the AAI narratives of borderline personality disordered patients had lower reflective function, coupled with histories of severe trauma which were apparently unresolved. Other findings suggested that, given a sensitive attachment relationship which provides the intersubjective basis for the development of mentalizing capacity, trauma (even if severe) was more likely to be resolved. Severe distortion of personality follows when abuse or neglect leads to a defensive inhibition of mentalization. Similarly, evidence is accumulating that amongst juvenile offenders, where histories of maltreatment are common, capacities for mentalization are severely restricted (Blair, 1995; Levinson and Fonagy, submitted).

Normal development is from fractionation toward integration, which involves the construction of specific co-ordinations amongst previously separate skills and provides the foundation for more complex, sophisticated control systems (Bidell and Fischer, 1994). Abnormalities of reflective function should not then be seen as either a consequence of 'arrest and fixation' at an early stage, or a 'regression' to that stage. Pathologies in the reflective function of the maltreated child may be expected to develop increased complexity with age and time, in a manner similar to other skills. The skill for limited reflectiveness developed by the child to withstand maltreatment is adaptive in that world, but produces complex and multiplying difficulties in other contexts (Noam, 1990). The ability to be reflective in general, but to restrict reflectiveness about the mental states of 'caregiving' others, or in later relationships that reactivate the same schemas, could be a result of natural fractionation, or of a purposeful (conscious or unconscious) attempt not to reflect in certain relationship domains. Here the unevenness is 'a developmental achievement', in that the person must actively maintain the separation of contexts that would naturally move toward integration. In attachment theory terms, the self is organized so that certain internal working models include a lot of reflectiveness – expectations about the mental states of self and other – while others seem impoverished, with minimal mentalizing skills. In the latter contexts the subject offers only stereotyped, concrete, low level descriptions. This does not imply developmental delay or regression, but a complex ability to co-ordinate two distinct levels of functioning. The abusive or emotionally depriving world within which they developed has demanded the sophisticated skills required for such an adaptation. Thus to talk of deficit or absence of a capacity in such individuals is an oversimplification. Measures of global abilities may not show differences between these individuals and others.

Maltreatment, or more broadly trauma, is seen as interacting with the domain- and situation-specific restrictions upon reflective function at two levels. First, maltreatment presents the young child with a powerful emotional disincentive for taking the perspective of others, because of the actual threat within the intentional stance of the abuser, as well as the constraints upon self-development imposed by the parent's failure to understand and acknowledge the child's budding intentionality. Secondly, the child is deprived of the later resilience provided by the capacity to understand a interpersonal situations (Fonagy et al., 1994). Thus individuals traumatized by their family environment are vulnerable in terms of the long-term impact of the trauma, their reduced capacity to cope with it, and their difficulty in finding better relationships later. Severe developmental psychopathology, ultimately entrenched personality disorder, can be the outcome. We have explored this outcome in several papers (Fonagy, 1991; Fonagy, Moran and Target, 1993; Fonagy et al., 1995; Fonagy and Target, 2000; Fonagy, Target and Gergely, 2000).

12.2 A model of developmental pathology in Fonagy and Target's framework

If secure attachment and mentalization come from successful containment, insecure attachment may be seen as the infant's identification with the parent's defensive behavior. Closeness to her is maintained at the cost of reflective function. A dismissing parent may altogether fail to mirror the child's distress because she avoids recognizing it, because of the painful experiences it unconsciously evokes, and/or because she distorts her image of his feelings. By contrast, the preoccupied caregiver may represent his state in an exaggerated way, or mixed with her own experience, so that the reflected experience is alarming or alien to the child. In either case, he internalizes the caregiver's attitude and 'this dysynchrony becomes the content of the experience of the self' (Crittenden, 1994, p. 89).

Affect mirroring can take pathological pathways, because the parent is overwhelmed by her own painful feelings in response to the infant's reaction, and presents an over-realistic emotionally arousing display. This not only undermines the infant's possibility of creating a secondary representation, but also the sense of a boundary between self and other – an internal experience suddenly becomes external. This corresponds to the clinical characterizations of projective identification, the habitual defense particularly associated with borderline personality disorder. Sustained experience of this kind might play an important role in establishing projective identification as the dominant form of emotional experience in the development of borderline personality organization (Kernberg, 1967). The emotional lability that is a hallmark of these patients is generally regarded as a clue to the nature of their disturbance (e.g. Rey, 1979). Their therapy rarely takes place without dramatic enactments, their own and sometimes their therapists', and their intense dependence on the therapist increases the difficulties of the treatment process.

A second type of deviant mirroring structure is one that we feel predisposes to narcissistic personality disorder rather than borderline states. When affect mirroring is marked but non-contingent, in that the infant's emotion is misperceived by the caretaker, the baby will still internalize the mirrored affect and map it onto his primary emotion state. As this mirrored state is incongruent with the infant's actual feelings, the secondary representation created will mislabel the primary emotional state. Over time, the ties between the underlying emotional state and the self-representation will weaken. The self will feel empty and false. Only when psychotherapy or other relationship experiences generate 'mentalized affectivity' will this fault line in the psychological self be bridged.

Another key concept in our description of deviant parental affect mirroring is that of the alien self. Where parental caregiving is highly insensitive and misattuned, we assume that a fault is created in the construction of the psychological self. As described, the infant, failing to find *himself* in the mother's mind, finds the mother instead (Winnicott, 1967b). He has to internalize the representation of the object's state of mind as a core part of himself. But in such cases the internalized other remains *alien* and unconnected to the structures of the constitutional self. In early development the 'alien self' is dealt with by externalization; thus, the young child showing disorganized attachment will frequently control and manipulate the parent's behavior. This is part of a projective identificatory process whereby he can experience his self as coherent and the alien part of his self-structure as outside his mind by perceiving these elements within someone else, often a parent. The disorganization of the self disorganizes attachment relationships by creating a constant need for this projective identification (the externalization of the alien self) in any close relationship.

The alien self is part of all of us, because transient neglect is part of ordinary caregiving; with the development of mentalization, and given a middle childhood relatively free of trauma, the gaps in the self corresponding to non-contingent parenting are covered over by the self-narratives which the reasonably functioning, mentalizing mind can create. The alien self is most pernicious when later experiences of trauma in the family or the peer group force the child to dissociate from pain by using the alien self to identify with the aggressor. In these cases the gaps come to be colonized by the image of the aggressor, and the child comes to experience himself as destructive and, in the extreme, monstrous. Thus we see inadequate early parenting as creating a vulnerability that may become destructive of development and seriously pathogenic if later experience is unfavorable, either in terms of failing to facilitate the later development of mentalization or explicitly calling for the use of the faults in self-development for defensive purposes. These factors interact: the likelihood of surviving psychological assault improves if mentalizing is freely available to interpret the perpetrator's behavior (Fonagy et al., 1994). However, brutalization in the context of attachment relationships generates intense shame. This, if coupled with a history of neglect and a consequent weakness in mentalization, becomes a likely trigger for violence against the self or others, because of the intensity of the humiliation experienced when the trauma cannot be processed and attenuated via mentalization. Unmentalized shame, which remains unmediated by any sense of distance between feelings and objective realities, is then experienced as the destruction of the self.

The defensive use of the alien part of the self is deeply pathogenic, although initially adaptive. It involves three important changes: (a) a further repudiation of mentalization, at least in attachment contexts, (b) disruption of the psychological self by the emergence of a torturing other within the self, and (c) dependence on the physical presence of the other as a vehicle for externalization. These features, in combination, account for many aspects of disordered functioning in borderline patients. Abused and traumatized individuals, unable to conceive of the mental states that could explain the actions of the abuser, voluntarily and defensively sacrifice their thinking about internal states. While able to think of mental states in self and other in the context of ordinary social relationships, they inevitably become conflicted and entangled once a relationship becomes emotionally intense, organized by mental structures that are involved in attachment relationships. The abandonment of mentalizing leaves them with an internal reality that is dominated by psychic equivalence. These individuals, like all other patients, organize the therapeutic relationship to conform to their unconscious expectations, except that for them these expectations have the full force of reality, and there is no sense of any alternative perspective. The inability to think about mental states removes the possibility of 'narrative smoothing' of the basic gaps in the self-structure, and the alien self emerges in a manner much clearer for the therapist to see and experience. Splitting becomes a dominant defense and projective identification (the externalization of the alien self) an essential part of survival. The vehicles for the projective identification must be present for the process of externalization to function, and dependency on these individuals turns into a dominant theme.

We have proposed that psychotherapy with individuals whose early experiences have led to a compromised mentalizing capacity should be focused on helping them to build this capacity. One way of conceptualizing the entire psychotherapeutic enterprise is as an activity that is specifically focused upon the rehabilitation of this function. This has close links with Bion's (1959) thinking about containment. So with some patients, particularly those at the borderline end of the spectrum, the therapist's task is similar to that of the parent who intuitively engages with the child's world of psychic equivalence to emphasize its representational character. Integrating the concrete and dissociated (pretend) modes of functioning is best achieved through focused work on the patient's current experience of the transference. Some enactments on the part of both therapist and patient are inevitable, since the patient cannot remain psychologically close to the therapist without externalizing the alien parts of the self. It is at these moments, when the therapist is enacting the split-off part of the patient's experience, that the patient's true self may be most accurately observed. Sadly, these are the hardest times for the therapist to communicate insight, given the intense emotional impact he is experiencing. Nevertheless, a determined focus on understanding the moment-to-moment changes in the patient's experience can be surprisingly effective (Bateman and Fonagy, 1999) and lasting (Bateman and Fonagy, 2001), even with severely impaired patients.

12.3 Evaluation of the mentalization model

One important concern with this model is its emphasis on relatively severe disorders of character rather than covering the entire spectrum of psychopathology. The model has less to say about what have traditionally been called neurotic disorders, and even within personality disorders it focuses on the more dramatic disturbances rather than those such as schizoid or avoidant disorders. Further, there is little that pertains to psychotic problems.

A second caution to note is that these ideas have a long history. Freud, ego psychologists and object relations theorists have written about what are generally referred to as problems of symbolization in various character disorders. When these views are carefully examined, it becomes clear that the dichotomy between symbolization and concreteness usually refers to the capacity for representing internal states. The advance we have made is to integrate the approach with developmental research and theory. The opposite criticism may also be made: It can be argued that the approach to mentalization here is overly cognitive, and pays too little attention to the emotional experiences of patients. The developmental formulations we have offered, even when directly addressing feelings, are mostly stated in terms of mental mechanisms, rather than necessarily speaking to the specific personal feelings of a patient. For instance, there is a downplaying of sexuality as the primary organizer of thoughts and feelings, rather sexual problems are sometimes understood as secondary to a failure at the level of mental mechanisms for the representation of internal states.

Related to this, it can be argued that the theory places too much emphasis on a single mechanism: reflective function, which may well not be necessary and is certainly not sufficient for a contented mental or interpersonal life.

Many people with very weak mentalization capacity manage relatively well, while others with strong skills in this domain are struggling. While we have argued that (a) mentalization is really required only in environments of high interpersonal stress, and that (b) some people who seem to be able to mentalize well but show poor functioning are showing partial or distorted reflective function capacity (see the discussion of the hypervigilance associated with disorganized attachment), the theory needs more refinement in these areas.

A further limitation of the theory, shared with many other object relations ideas, is that there is over-emphasis on the earliest years as formative, yet empirical evidence does not fully support this. Developmental psychopathology has shown that trauma in adolescence can cause loss of reflective function, just as can early maltreatment.

The critical weakness of the theory is also a strength: it moves away from many traditional psychoanalytic constructs. So, like Sandler's model, it is based on affects rather than drives, which antagonizes some psychoanalysts. However, the same feature allows us to create a stronger bridge between traditional psychoanalytic (intrapsychic) ideas and the newer interpersonalist framework. It is legitimate to ask whether this is a fully psychoanalytic model or an integrationist one (bringing psychoanalysis into relation with neighbouring disciplines). It is closely rooted in attachment theory, which some would not see as part of psychoanalysis, and we have deliberately maintained a close dialogue with developmental research in thinking about object relationships and the development of the self. It is for others to judge whether this is productive.

CHAPTER 13

On the practice of psychoanalytic theory

13.1 The relationship of theory and practice in psychoanalysis

Over recent decades psychoanalysts have witnessed an increasing fragmentation of theory, evident in the decline in citations of recent psychoanalytic articles in psychoanalytic journals (Fonagy, 1996a). This suggests that not only are readers of the social science and medical literature somewhat less interested in psychoanalysis, but analysts themselves are less interested in the ideas of other analytic groups. Arguably, the major psychoanalytic schools that emerged following Freud's death, and that organized the discipline over the last half of the twentieth century, are breaking apart. This fragmentation, euphemistically discussed as pluralism, could possibly spell the death of psychoanalysis. If present trends for theoretical schism continue, and psychodynamic writers come to share only history and terminology, the discipline might ultimately face theoretical entropy, with all writers jealously protecting their diminishing psychoanalytic patch.

Why might this happen? We suggest that a major problem with psychodynamic theory building lies in its relationship to clinical practice. Psychoanalysts have always argued, and we agree, that psychoanalytic treatment provides a unique window on human behavior and experience, which generates developmentally rich and clinically powerful accounts. The main function of theory for practitioners is in explaining clinical phenomena. The weakness of such clinical theories is their extensive reliance on induction. (There is some truth to the quip that psychoanalytic clinicians understand the word data to be a plural of the word anecdote.) A theory is used as a heuristic device rather than as a tool for deduction. The clinical usefulness and persuasiveness of inductive arguments can lead us, with the greatest of ease, to raise the status of 'clinical theories' to laws, gaining the impression as we do so that we have a tool for understanding that not only makes sense to us, but works for our patients and is furthermore scientific.

(In fact, most clinical laws are, in any case, only probabilistic (Ruben, 1993), therefore they could allow only inductive *statistical* explanations rather than deductive-nomological ones (see Carl Hempel's 1965 Covering-Role Model). While we know that child maltreatment can give rise to behavioral disturbance, this is by no means inevitably the case (e.g. Anthony and Cohler, 1987).)

There are at least four conditions that would need to be met for the accumulation of clinical observations to be a genuinely adequate basis for psychoanalytic theory. These are: (a) a clear logical tie between theory and technique, (b) deductive as well as inductive reasoning in relation to clinical material, (c) the unambiguous use of terms, and (d) a willingness to expose more clinical work to detailed scrutiny. The first of these is essential if we are to be able to separate technique and theory. If technique has a known and specifiable relationship with theory, then the inevitable contamination of observations by technique can be identified and studied. The second criterion, of deductive reasoning, must be satisfied if observations are to be capable of either proving or disproving theoretical models. The third criterion concerns the labeling of observations in such a way that these can be described, replicated and considered in relation to theoretical predictions. The final criterion would allow the data, clinical observations, to be selected and tested in relation to different theoretical perspectives. None of these criteria has yet been adequately met, and in the following sections we will discuss some implications of this situation.

13.1.1 Psychodynamic clinical practice is not logically deducible from any psychoanalytic clinical theory

It is our impression that clinical practice, at least psychoanalytic practice, is not logically deducible from available theory. There are several reasons for this.

First, psychoanalytic technique is known to have developed on a trial and error basis. Freud (1912c) willingly acknowledged this when he wrote: 'the technical rules which I am putting forward have been arrived at from my own experience in the course of many years, after unfortunate results had led me to abandon other methods' (p.111). For example, free association is acknowledged by Laplanche and Pontalis (1973) to have been 'found' (reached empirically) rather than deduced (p. 227). Similarly, Melanie Klein's (1927) and Anna Freud's (1926) discovery of play therapy could hardly be considered to have been driven by theory. Trial and error might, of course, be theoretically guided. If this were so, we would expect technique to have been logically derivable from theory, at least in some instances. Such claims are commonly made (Freud, 1904b, p. 252; Kohut, 1971, p. 264), but one example will have to suffice. Gedo (1979) boldly states that: 'principles of psychoanalytic practice ... [are] ... based on rational deductions from our most current conception of psychic functioning' (p. 16). In fact his book makes the claim that the unfavorable outcomes of developmental problems can be reversed 'only by dealing with those results of all antecedent developmental vicissitudes that later gave rise to maladaptation' (p. 21). What sounds like, and is claimed to be, 'a rational deduction' is in fact a hypothesis, emphatically stated to hide the absence of supporting argument. It is one thing to assume that development follows an epigenetic scheme but quite another that in therapy all earlier vicissitudes must be dealt with. There is no evidence for Gedo's claim, even from within the same self-psychological theoretical camp to which Gedo belongs (Kohut, 1984). The difference between Kohut's and Gedo's therapeutic approaches illustrates the absence of a deductive tie between the epigenetic model of self-psychology and the technical propositions which are claimed to relate to these. Kohut explicitly recommends that, under certain circumstances, developmental vicissitudes, such as narcissistic traumata, should be left alone (pp. 42–6).

The tendency to disguise the loose coupling of theory to practice by rhetoric is pernicious because it actually closes the door on imaginative clinical exploration, by fostering an illusion of theory-based certainty. The slow development of psychodynamic technique is, we believe, mainly due to the tendency of theorists to try to validate these hypotheses via congruence with certain accepted clinical practices. These practices are then claimed as uniquely effective and sacrosanct, at least until a new theory evolves.

Second, psychoanalysts do not understand, nor do they claim to, why or how their treatment works (see, for example Fenichel, 1941, p. 111; Fairbairn, 1958, p.385; Matte Blanco, 1975, p. 386; Modell, 1976, p. 285; Kohut, 1977, p. 105). Is this likely, if practice were logically entailed in theory? Surely a clear theoretical explanation for therapeutic action would follow. The nature of the therapeutic action of psychoanalysis is an inveterate theme for psychoanalytic conferences, started perhaps at the 14th International Psychoanalytic Association Congress in Marienbad (Glover et al., 1937) where Glover, Fenichel, Strachey, Nunberg and Bibring crossed swords. Since that time, at about ten-year intervals, alternating between the International and the American Psychoanalytic Association's meetings, there has been a symposium on this topic. At each of these meetings, speakers almost ritualistically assert that how analysis works 'is not adequately understood' (Fairbairn, 1958, p. 385). The state of epistemic affairs is well summarized in Matte Blanco's words: 'The fact is that nobody has, so far, succeeded in establishing with great precision what the factors are and how they combine with our understanding to produce the cure' (Matte Blanco, 1975, p. 386). (Discussing the therapeutic action of psychoanalysis assumes that we know what its effects are, that it *is*, indeed, therapeutic. While this is not generally doubted among psychoanalysts, we will return to this issue later.)

Third, as has already been suggested, psychoanalytic practice has changed little, if at all, since Freud's original description in a few brief papers before the First World War (Freud, 1912a; 1912c; 1913b). This state of affairs has been repeatedly acknowledged (Greenson, 1967, p. 3; Glover, 1968, p. 115). For example, Glover (1968) states: 'for certainly, and despite a multiplicity of articles on the subject of technique ... no very radical advances have been made in the therapeutic field' (p. 115). As traditionally psychoanalysts have not recorded their clinical work, such assertions are hard to prove (see below). However, the extensive supervision based on reported psychotherapeutic process, which forms the core part of psychoanalytic training, seeks to reinforce traditional technique, at least in the course of training. Over the same century, such enormous theoretical advances have taken place that it is hardly practical to try to summarize psychoanalytic theories. The discrepancy in the rates of progress between theory and practice is quite remarkable and would be hard to understand were it not for the relative independence of these two activities.

Fourth, the thorny issue of therapeutic effectiveness might also imply an independence of the theory and practice domains. There is only modest evidence to support the clinical claims of psychoanalysis as an effective treatment (Roth and Fonagy, 1996; Fonagy and Target, 1996b; Fonagy et al., 1999). There is much stronger support for many of its theoretical claims (e.g. Bucci, 1997b; Fonagy, Steele et al., 1993) including those related to treatment process (e.g. Luborsky and Luborsky, 1995). While lack of evidence for effectiveness does not imply lack of effectiveness, the discrepancy may also be explained by the assumption that practice is not entailed within theory. The evidence that exists is for a theory of mind with unconscious dynamic elements. Evidence is, however, lacking for the translation rules for moving from psychological theory to clinical practice. For example, work from our, and other, laboratories has provided good evidence for the psychoanalytic notion that the parent's childhood experience is transmitted to the next generation, partly determining the child's relationship to that parent (Fonagy, Steele et al., 1993). There is far less evidence to suggest that addressing the parent's past conflicts in psychotherapy helps her to establish secure attachment relationships with her children (van IJzendoorn, Juffer and Duyvesteyn, 1995).

Fifth, as has been implied, it has been impossible to achieve any kind of one-to-one mapping between therapeutic technique and theoretical framework. Interestingly, it is as easy to illustrate how the same theory can generate different techniques as how the same technique is justified by different theories. For example, Campbell (1982) demonstrated how clinicians with broadly similar theoretical orientations differed in the extent to which they adopted a position of technical neutrality or shared their thoughts and feelings with their patients or gratified their patients' primitive developmental needs. By contrast, it is equally striking how clinicians using very different theoretical frameworks can arrive at very similar treatment approaches. For example, Kernberg's (1989) work with borderline patients has much in common with those who practice using a Kleinian frame of reference (Steiner, 1993). Both these observations imply that practice is not logically entailed within theory.

Sixth, one may legitimately ask the question: what is psychoanalytic theory about if it is not about psychoanalytic practice? The answer is that it is predominantly about the elaboration of a psychological model and the way that this might be applied to the understanding of mental disorder, and to a lesser extent to other aspects of human behavior. (e.g. literature, the arts, history, etc.). Freud's corpus may be an eloquent example. His technical papers take up far less than a single one of the 23 volumes of his collected psychological writings. The value of theory for the psychoanalytic practitioner is in elaborating the meaning of behavior in mental state terms. How such elaboration is used, or indeed whether it is helpful when conveyed, is not deducible from the theory.

13.1.2 Inductive rather than deductive reasoning is used in relation to clinical material

The predominant theory-building strategy in clinical psychoanalysis is 'enumerative inductivism' (the accumulation of instances consistent with a premise). In treating a patient, we have access to a set of observations, based on assessment and the evolving treatment process. From this sample, certain observations are selected as telling, and from these the analyst draws conclusions about how the patient generally behaves and why he or she does so. The analyst will be predisposed to focus on those aspects of the patient's behavior and the relationship that make sense in terms of his favored theoretical constructs. Induction is thus made not just from the accumulation of observations about a particular individual, but also from formulations of past cases by other psychoanalysts in their 'clinical theories' (Klein, 1976a).

From a clinical point of view this is useful. To gather examples of the influence of an unconscious pattern prepares the ground for interpretations ('every time you are feeling such and such you do so and so') and helps the psychoanalyst to feel on firmer ground in working to elaborate a picture of the patient's internal world. The difficulty arises from our understanding, as clinicians, of the role of theory. We think that it lends credence to inductive observations because we assume that theories have been inferred from a very large number of observations, and subsequently tested against new, independent observations. What we can find ourselves doing instead, however, is piling induction on induction.

Thus, theory is intrinsically contaminated by the technique used to generate observations. As technique has evolved pragmatically and without a close or fully coherent connection to theory, theory will be shaped by what has been found clinically helpful, rather than practice being dictated by what is true about the mind. Thus, while theory is a vital adjunct to clinical practice, neither has been used in a way that would have helped to validate the other. To do this would require the careful monitoring of instances where a particular precondition was not followed by the theoretically expected outcome. Psychoanalysts are not alone with this problem. Not only most clinical thinking, but in fact all human reasoning shares this flaw. In the 1970s Peter Wason and Phil Johnson-Laird (Wason and Johnson-Laird, 1972), two eminent British cognitive psychologists, demonstrated a profound and ubiquitous vulnerability in human syllogistic reasoning. Given a premise such as 'if it rains (antecedent) the road is wet (consequent)', subjects are offered the choice of any of four example conditions to unequivocally test the premise: (a) it rains, (b) it does not rain, (c) the road is wet, (d) the road is not wet. Subjects tend to correctly select (a), often mistakenly select (c) and fail to select (d). (c) is irrelevant to testing the premise since a wide range of conditions not including the antecedent (rain) may have caused the consequent (wetness on the road). Negating the consequent (d), the road is not wet, *is* relevant to testing the premise, since if it had rained then the premise was clearly false. Even when specifically asked to evaluate the premise that B always follows A, we tend not to notice when A occurs without B. This is referred to as a failure *to negate the consequent*. We almost certainly miss many instances when the patient's reaction is not as we would have anticipated on the basis of a theoretical formulation, and we therefore do not use the disconfirmations to improve or discard psychoanalytic theories.

To take a simplistic example, signs of unconscious anger – displaced onto the self and away from someone ambivalently loved and now lost – are easily found in cases of depression, and Freud's description (1915b) continues to feel deeply true. But what of cases where we can see the inward direction of anger, but it does not lead to depression? Such cases could have been used to test and extend the psychoanalytic theory of depression. To ask clinicians (and this does not only apply to psychoanalysts) to note and act on such negative instances, however, seems to introduce something alien to the therapeutic process, setting therapeutic and research aims against each other. Despite some great exceptions such as Freud, the confirmatory bias identified by Wason, Johnson-Laird and their colleagues may be fatal, in most cases, to the popular notion of clinician as researcher.

This logical difficulty in choosing between theories is the main reason for their proliferation. As clinical observations are used inductively by theoreticians who are themselves clinicians, new psychodynamic theories readily emerge and obtain some confirmation. Even if the extent of confirmation is not great, the theories are likely to survive because positive instances are noticed and negative ones overlooked by those interested in the fate of the theory. New theories are felt to supplement rather than replace older ones (Sandler, 1983). Thus there are many partly incompatible formulations that need to be used together to provide comprehensive accounts. At any time psychoanalytic theory is like a family of ideas, with resemblances, relationships and feuds, and with new members expected to take their place alongside the rest and respect the authority of the ancestors, especially Freud. If a psychoanalytic approach is to survive, there must be ways of pruning this 'family tree', choosing between rival explanations so that the body of theory is strengthened rather than continuing to branch out.

13.1.3 The ambiguous use of terms

Perhaps in order to accommodate proliferating ideas, the definition of theoretical terms has been left vague (Sandler, 1983). This is neither unusual nor easily avoided. It is the way that human language and all human conceptual systems deal with the complexity of the phenomena we require them to signify (Wittgenstein, 1969; Rosch, 1978). However, the absence of operational definitions can encourage fragmentation, and can also obscure important differences between theoretical approaches.

We offer a small example of each, from our own research in child psychotherapy. In preparing a treatment manual for the study of outcome (Fonagy, Edgcumbe, Target et al., unpublished MS), we had to study the techniques and concepts used by psychotherapists with different theoretical orientations (following Anna Freud, Winnicott or Klein/Bion). While these clinicians were unable to agree on how to describe the rationale of their work, it became clear that in fact they were using different theoretical frameworks for a very similar technique, with similar aims. Equally, when we tried to achieve operational definitions for the categories in the Diagnostic Profile (Freud, 1965), an instrument developed by Anna Freud for formulating the nature of a child's psychopathology, and used by all those trained at her clinic, it emerged that the same words were being used in significantly different ways by different clinicians, who had always assumed that they were talking and writing about the same phenomena.

The validation of variables implicated by psychodynamic theories admittedly poses a formidable challenge. Most of the variables are private; many of them (for example, 'splits in the ego', masochism and omnipotence) are complex, abstract and difficult to operationalize or test precisely. Accounts of change focus on very remote variables. However, while the clarification of terms and concepts is laborious, it *is* possible (e.g. Sandler, 1962a). It is also vital if we are to find out where theoretical differences are real, and where they may only be imagined.

13.1.4 Allowing clinical observations to be shared and tested

Clinicians' narrative reports are necessarily selective in ways that undermine their scientific usefulness (Brown, Scheflin and Hammond, 1998). Psychoanalytic theory confirms that we cannot expect any participant in an interaction to be unbiased, to avoid errors, omissions and distortions. Far more important than bias, however, is that interactions are largely governed by non-conscious mechanisms, unavailable to introspection. There are quite dramatic illustrations of this, such as Krause's (1997) studies of facial expressions in face-to-face psychotherapy and Beebe et al.'s (1997) and Tronick's (1989) work on mother–infant interaction. The crucial information was never consciously known to the participants and could not have been reported, only observed.

There is a constant tension between making reliable, accessible observations, and a potentially fatal objection: that making recordings of analytic sessions available for study is an unacceptable intrusion, which would change the process beyond recognition. It is clear that we must do everything possible to gain informed consent to any procedure affecting clinical work, and to protect confidentiality. However, this is not an insuperable problem in other areas of psychotherapy research and need not be so in the future for psychoanalysis. We do not know to what extent audiotaping might interfere with key aspects of the psychoanalytic process. However, those clinicians who have experience of psychotherapy process research claim that even videotaping psychoanalysis does not need to distort the clinical work, as long as the patient's reactions are included in the material to be analyzed (Jones, 1993).

It seems to us that psychoanalysis needs to find a way of opening *some* work to outside observation, so that technique and theory, and the relationship between them, can be studied and evaluated. If psychoanalysis declares itself inaccessible to controlled observations and hypotheses testable by other researchers than the analyst, it will deprive itself of the interplay between data and theory. Without unbiased data, psychoanalysts fall back upon either the indirect evidence of clinical observation, or appeals to authority.

13.1.5 The nature of the relationship between theory and practice

Having claimed that in psychoanalytic work, practice is not logically entailed in theory, we would like briefly to consider the nature of the relationship between these two domains. Theory orients clinicians in their observation, description and explanation for clinical phenomena. It is inevitable that these will influence technique even though the relationship between the two is so loose. This relationship is particularly evident in psychoanalytic attempts to provide classification systems for psychological disorders (e.g. Freud, 1965; Kernberg, 1989). Here the categories are clearly theory driven. The most common use of theory is in providing models or analogies either to suggest or to rationalize therapeutic principles. Models (of development, of the mind and of disorder) are used to draw inferences to therapeutic interventions. These inferences are common sense arguments rather than deductions.

Psychoanalysts have often made the mistake of assuming that they were doing more than modeling – that their practice was theory based. There is a price to pay for such an assumption. When there is a pretence that practice is deduced from theory, the consequence may be the petrification of practice. In the absence of clear injunctions about the aspects of practice that are genuinely theory driven, it becomes difficult to know what aspects of practice may be altered without threatening the entire edifice. For example, if on the basis of Freud's structural model of the mind (Freud, 1923), it is suggested that psychic change may only be attained by either changes in the patient's defenses or their strengthening (Fenichel, 1945), then all interventions that do not entail one of these two modalities must be ruled out. This was the classical Anna Freudian position taken in relation to Melanie Klein's so-called deep or direct interpretations of unconscious wishes (King and Steiner, 1991). Yet the rationale for this technical stricture rests in the hydraulic metaphor of early Freudian thought and it is not truly entailed in the structural theory. This is not to say that the recommendation itself is not sensible (in fact, Kleinian clinicians have more recently moved away from the direct interpretations of unconscious desires). The burden of this argument is that the illusion of direct connection to theory, coupled with the weak links which exist between theory and practice may lead practitioners to be overly cautious about experimenting with new techniques since they cannot know what the theory does or does not permit.

There are clearly problems in psychoanalytic theories, which prevent a clear relationship to technique. As we have seen, uncertainty concerning the nature of the relationship may have been principally responsible for the slow progress of psychoanalytic therapy. If theory was de-coupled from practice, technique might progress on purely empirical grounds, on the basis of what is seen to work. If the theory is tightly linked to technique, advances in theorization should inevitably lead to practical gains. If, as we would maintain is the case in psychodynamic practice, the theory serves to justify practice through analogy (e.g. the developmental metaphor that the patient's therapy progresses analogously to the developmental process), then we must at all times be aware that what we are practicing is based on cumulative clinical experience and what we are theorizing may be at most a useful adjunct to clinical practice – but not its justification.

13.1.6 The generation of theory from psychodynamic work

So what has gone wrong with psychoanalytic theorization? The answer probably lies in the way in which psychoanalysts have used practice inductively, to generate theory.

The psychoanalyst is interesting in this context, partly because, in the absence of alternative (experimental) strategies for verifying theories, clinical work becomes the chief source of theory-building and partly because increasingly forceful critiques of psychoanalysis over the past half century highlight the dangers of its epistemology (Grünbaum, 1984; Crews, 1995).

There is no doubt that Freud created the basis for a brilliant clinical theory. As philosophers of mind have concluded, his insights have extended common sense or folk psychology to non-conscious mental functioning (Hopkins, 1992; Wollheim, 1995). Cognitive neuroscience has revealed that most of the work of the brain is non-conscious (Kihlstrom, 1987). Freud (1900; 1923), having recognized the importance of this fact in the development of psychopathology, advanced two radical propositions. First, mental problems may be understood in terms of non-conscious beliefs and feelings) (Freud and Breuer, 1895). Second, the effective treatment of these problems requires the individual to be made aware of these non-conscious mental states (Freud, 1909; 1916).

Freud's argument was absolutely sound. His fundamental error lay in being too specific about the contents of non-conscious conflicts of ideas (e.g. unconscious conflicts concerning toilet training) (Freud, 1905d; 1920; 1927). Anna Freud (1974) went further and tried to link types of childhood mental health problems and categories of unconscious conflict. Thus, she was persuaded by clinical experience that phobic disorders of childhood were linked to unresolved oedipal conflicts and obsessive-compulsive neurosis to the experience of potty training.

Of course, this simplistic implementation of a great theory had to be counter-productive. Many psychosocial experiences reach a common symptomatic end-point. Similarly, the same experience may antedate a variety of clinical manifestations (Cicchetti and Cohen, 1995b). Unfortunately, in over-specifying the theory, Freud laid psychoanalysis open to endless updating of aspects of theory that were never core to his ideas. For example, Melanie Klein was struck by the apparent destructiveness and cruelty shown by normal children (her own) (Klein et al., 1946). As the scientific methodology offering relatively firm data on infant mental states was not yet available, she felt free to attribute very complex ideation to the young infant without risk of contradiction (envy, projective identification and the depressive position). Others, whose interest was focused on later developmental periods (for example, Margaret Mahler – see Mahler et al., 1975), specified quite different central psychological conflicts (in this case, symbiosis, separation-individuation etc.).

We are not claiming that either of these, or the many hundreds of other (Kazdin, 1994), ideas concerning unconscious causes of conflict were wrong. It is very likely that both conflicts over destructive jealousy (envy) of a loved object, and the conflict between a desire for separateness and the wish to retain an illusion of union with the mother are important assumptions about mental states in understanding minds in distress. The problem is one of trying to claim exclusivity for these ideas. Here we are not pleading for an integrationist model (Goldfried and Newman, 1992). Rather, we are suggesting that Freud's original rich theorization is to blame for later clinicians conflating the framework of psychological mechanisms implied by the theory with the specific mental contents within this structural framework. Unconscious conflict is *core theory* and as such could, probably, be linked with recommendations about technique. Envy, oedipal rivalry, separation-individuation conflicts, narcissistic traumata are elaborations at a different level, clinical observation, and are therefore too confounded with practice to permit deductive inferences to clinical method.

Given the nature of human thinking and the inherent difficulty we all experience in syllogistic reasoning that involves the negation of the consequent (see above, and Johnson-Laird and Byrne, 1993), it is hardly surprising that psychoanalysts tended to favor the identification of examples that provided further evidence of their pre-conceptions. The predominant psychodynamic epistemic strategy, encapsulated in the clinical case report, became one of enumerative inductivism. As we have pointed out, this means that new theories are developed without discarding the old. Psychoanalysts got round the empirical problems created by partially incompatible formulations by loosening the definition of terms (Sandler, 1983). Disappointingly, yet inevitably, this has led to antagonism toward operationalization and an explicit preference for ambiguity. Equally predictable has been the multiplication of theories, rejection of parsimony as a criterion for eliminating competing ideas, the geographical specificity of particular theoretical traditions, the over-valuation of spoken and written rhetoric as criteria of validity, the polymorphous use of concepts and ultimately a theoretical edifice almost impossible to integrate.

13.2 Research on the outcome of psychoanalysis

In 1903, in his contribution to Loewenfeld's book on obsessional phenomena, Freud wrote: 'the number of persons suitable for psychoanalytic treatment is extraordinarily large and the extension which has come to our therapeutic powers from this method is...very considerable' (Freud,

1904a, p. 254). Earlier, in a series of three lectures on hysteria given in October 1905, he asserted: 'And I may say that the analytic method of psychotherapy is one that penetrates most deeply and carries farthest, the one by means of which the most effective transformations can be effected in patients' (Freud, 1905c, p. 260). His therapeutic optimism persisted for at least two decades. In 1917 he wrote: 'Through the overcoming of these resistances the patient's mental life is permanently changed, is raised to a higher level of development and remains protected against a fresh possibility of falling ill' (Freud, 1916–17, p. 451). Fifteen years later, however, his optimism had apparently wilted and he claimed 'never [to have] been a therapeutic enthusiast' (Freud, 1933, p. 151). In one of his last strictly psychoanalytic writings Freud (1937) decisively repudiated earlier statements on the prophylactic aspects of analysis. At this time he devastatingly stated:

> One has the impression that one ought not to be surprised if it should turn out in the end that the difference between a person who has not been analyzed and the behavior of a person after he has been analyzed is not so thorough-going as we aim at making it and as we expect and maintain it to be. (p. 228).

Recognizing the limited benefit which analysts are likely to observe following years of treatment, he added, 'It almost looks as if analysis were the third of those 'impossible' professions in which one can be sure beforehand of achieving unsatisfying results' (p. 248). (The other two are, of course, education and government.)

This was the state of affairs half a century ago. What hope is there in the era of empirically validated treatments (Lonigan, Elbert and Johnson, 1998), which prizes brief structured interventions, for a therapeutic approach that defines itself by freedom from constraint and preconception (Bion, 1967a), and counts treatment length not in terms of a handful of sessions but of a similar number of years? Can psychoanalysis ever demonstrate its effectiveness, let alone cost-effectiveness? After all, is psychoanalysis not a qualitatively different form of therapy, which requires a qualitatively different kind of metric to reflect its outcome? Symptom change as a sole indicator of therapeutic benefit must indeed be considered crude in relation to the complex interpersonal processes that evolve over the many hundreds of sessions of the average 3–5 times weekly psychoanalytic treatment. Little wonder that most psychoanalysts are sceptical about outcome investigations.

What is surprising, given this unpropitious backdrop, is that there is, in fact, some evidence for the effectiveness of psychoanalysis as a treatment for psychological disorder. Before summarizing this evidence, let us briefly outline the generally agreed hierarchy of research designs that tends to be applied to outcome studies in psychotherapy (Roth and Fonagy, 1996). Broadly, at the bottom of the hierarchy are case reports and case series studies, which at best establish a time-frame for change. Slightly above sit prospective pre-post studies, which can document the nature and extent of change. To be preferred are comparison studies where the effects of an intervention are contrasted with no treatment or 'treatment as usual'. The gold standard is the randomized controlled trial comparing the index treatment with another treatment of known effectiveness or a good placebo control. Most evidence for psychoanalysis is at the case study level. There are, however, exceptions.

13.2.1 The evidence base of psychoanalytic treatment

Psychoanalysts have been encouraged by the body of research that supports brief dynamic psychotherapy. A meta-analysis of 26 such studies has yielded effect sizes comparable to other approaches (Anderson and Lambert, 1995). It may even be slightly superior to some other therapies if long-term follow-up is included in the design. One of the best designed RCTs, the Sheffield Psychotherapy Project (Shapiro et al., 1995), found evidence for the effectiveness of a 16-session psychoanalytic treatment based on Hobson's (1985) model, in the treatment of major depression. There is evidence for the effectiveness of psychoanalytic therapy as an adjunct to drug dependence programs (Woody et al., 1995). There is ongoing work on a brief psychoanalytic treatment for panic disorder (Milrod et al., 1997). There is evidence for the use of brief psychoanalytic approaches in work with older people (Thompson, Gallagher and Breckenridge, 1987). There is evidence that psychotherapy can be used for people already suffering from physical illness and their condition, no matter how serious, improves. For example, weekly group psychotherapy can extend the life of women with metastatic breast cancer by 18 months (Speigel, Kraemer and Gottheil, 1989). Similar improvements were observed for lymphoma, leukaemia and melanoma (Speigel and Lazar, 1997).

There are also psychotherapy process studies that offer qualified support for psychoanalysis. For example, psychoanalytic interpretations given to clients that are judged to be accurate are reported to be associated with relatively good outcome (Crits-Christoph, Cooper and Luborsky, 1988; Joyce and Piper, 1993). There is even tentative evidence from the reanalysis of therapy tapes from the NIMH Treatment of Depression Collaborative Research Program that the more the process of a brief therapy (CBT, IPT) resembles that of a psychoanalytic approach, the more likely it is to be effective (Ablon and Jones, 1999).

Evidence is available to support therapeutic interventions which are clear derivatives of psychoanalysis. However, there is a certain degree of disingenuity in psychoanalysis embracing these investigations. Most analysts would consider that the aims and methods of short-term once a week psychotherapy are not comparable to 'full analysis'. What do we know about the value of intensive and long-term psychoanalytic treatment? Here the evidence base becomes somewhat patchy.

In an effectiveness study of psychoanalytic treatments conducted with 99 outpatients at the IPTAR Clinical Center (Freedman et al., 1999), there were incremental gains in patient-perceived outcomes when session frequency was increased from 1 to 2 or 3 weekly sessions. Twenty-four months of therapy was more effective than six months.

In another recent randomized controlled study (Bateman and Fonagy, 1999), patients with borderline personality disorder (BPD) were assigned to a psychoanalytically oriented day hospital treatment or treatment as usual, which in the vast majority of cases included a psychiatric day hospital. The psychoanalytic arm of the treatment included therapy groups three times a week as well as individual therapy once or twice a week over an 18 month period. There were considerable gains in this group relative to the controls in terms of suicidal and self-mutilating behavior, depressive and anxiety symptoms, and social and interpersonal functioning. These differences were not only maintained in the 18 months following discharge but increased, even though the day hospital group received less treatment than the control group (Bateman and Fonagy, 2001). A further controlled trial of intensive psychoanalytic treatment for children with chronically poorly controlled diabetes reported significant gains in diabetic control in the treated group that was maintained at one year follow-up (Moran et al., 1991). Experimental single-case studies carried out with the same population supported the causal relationship between interpretive work and improvement in diabetic control and physical growth (Fonagy and Moran, 1991). The work of Chris Heinicke also suggests that four or five times weekly sessions generated more marked improvements in children with specific emotional plus learning difficulties than a less intensive psychoanalytic intervention (Heinicke and Ramsey-Klee, 1986).

One of the most interesting studies to emerge recently was the Stockholm Outcome of Psychotherapy and Psychoanalysis Project (Sandell, 1999; Sandell et al., 2000). The study followed 756 persons who received national insurance funded treatment for up to three years in psychoanalysis or in psychoanalytic psychotherapy. The groups were matched on many clinical variables. Four or five times weekly analysis had similar outcomes at termination when compared with one to two sessions per week psychotherapy. However, in measurements of symptomatic outcome using the SCL-90, improvement on three year follow-up was substantially greater for individuals who received psychoanalysis than those in psychoanalytic psychotherapy. In fact, during the follow-up period, psychotherapy patients did not change, but those who had had psychoanalysis continued to improve, almost to a point where their scores were indistinguishable from those obtained from a non-clinical Swedish sample. While the results of the study are positive for psychoanalysis, certain of the findings are quite challenging. For example, those therapists whose attitude to clinical process most closely resembled that of a 'classical analyst' (neutrality and abstinence, exclusive orientation to insight) had psychotherapy clients with the worst outcomes.

Another large pre-post study of psychoanalytic treatments examined the clinical records of 763 children who were treated in psychoanalysis at the Anna Freud Centre (Fonagy and Target, 1996b). Children with certain disorders (e.g. depression, autism, conduct disorder) benefit relatively little from psychoanalysis or psychotherapy. Interestingly, children with complex emotional disorders (more than one disorder and poor social functioning) did surprisingly well in psychoanalysis, although they did poorly in once or twice a week psychoanalytic psychotherapy (Target and Fonagy, 1994a). Younger children derived the greatest benefit from intensive treatment. Adolescents appeared not to benefit from the increased frequency of sessions (Target and Fonagy, 1994b). The importance of the study is perhaps less in demonstrating that psychoanalysis is generally effective, but more in identifying groups for whom the additional effort involved in intensive treatment is essential, or others where it was not warranted.

Several prospective follow-along studies using a pre-post design have suggested substantial improvements in patients given psychoanalytic therapies for personality disorders (Stevenson and Meares, 1992; Høglend, 1993; Monsen et al., 1995a, 1995b;). However, these were all uncontrolled studies, with populations whose symptomatology is recognized to fluctuate substantially, and so the evidence can give us few reliable indications as to which particular subgroups may benefit from a psychoanalytic approach.

The Research Committee of the International Psychoanalytic Association has recently prepared a comprehensive review of North American and European outcome studies of psychoanalytic treatment (Fonagy et al., 1999). The committee concluded that existing studies failed to demonstrate unequivocally that psychoanalysis is more effective than either an alternative treatment or an active placebo, and identified a range of methodological and design problems in the fifty or so studies described in the report, including the absence of intent to treat controls, heterogeneous patient groups, lack of random assignments, the failure to use independently administered standardized measures of outcome, and so on. Nevertheless, the report is encouraging to psychoanalysts. Despite the limitations (shared by studies of most treatments), evidence across a significant number of pre-post investigations suggests that psychoanalysis appears to be consistently helpful to patients with milder (neurotic) disorders and somewhat less consistently so for other, more severe groups. Across a range of uncontrolled or poorly controlled cohort studies, mostly carried out in Europe, longer intensive treatments tended to have better outcomes than shorter, non-intensive treatments. The impact of psychoanalysis was apparent beyond symptomatology, in measures of work functioning and reductions in health care costs. Moreover, a number of studies testing psychoanalysis with 'state of the art' methodology are ongoing, and are likely to produce more compelling evidence over the next years. These include the Munich Psychotherapy of Depression Study, the Cornell Comparison of Transference Focused Psychotherapy (TFP) and Dialectical Behavior Therapy (DBT), the Munich-New York Collaborative Study of the Psychoanalytic Treatment of Borderline Personality Organization, the Helsinki Psychotherapy Study, and the Anna Freud Centre Prospective Study of Child Psychotherapy for Severe Emotional Disorder.

A pertinent, though curious, outcome statistic concerns the mortality rates of psychoanalysts compared with other people. A recent study (Jeffery, 2001) found that between 1953 and 1982 the mortality rate of male psychoanalysts was 48% lower than that of the male population at large. In other words, a career as a psychoanalyst in the United States ensures that in a given year one is half as likely to die as the average American male. Mortality rates are substantially lower for psychoanalysts than for other physicians, although being a psychiatrist, as all these analysts were, generally increases mortality relative to other medical specialties. Clearly the prosaic explanation is that the privileged longevity of psychoanalysts might be related to sedentary, low stress, relatively well-insulated professions. An alternative perspective suggested by Doidge (2001) is that psychoanalysis, which is a compulsory part of the training of these individuals, might in and of itself serve to lengthen life expectancy. In support of this view come findings from Germany of substantial decreases (up to one third) of medical visits for patients who have been in psychoanalytic treatment (Dührssen, 1972; Dossman, Kutter, Heinzel and Wurmser, 1997). In general, some of these German studies show improvements associated with psychoanalytic treatments in terms of decline of hospitalization (2/3), decline in lost working days (2/5) and medication use (1/3). Thus it is possible that full psychoanalysis in some as yet poorly understood manner modifies psychological structures which interface with stress regulating systems that in their turn are known to be linked to the functioning of immune system and ageing processes (Sapolsky, 1994).

While outcome data are clearly accumulatimg, and much of the data supports the claims made by psychoanalysts, it is undeniable that none of these studies captures the subjective experiences that are at the core of the analytic process. It seems that current research methodology is simply unequal to this task. Possibly with advances in neurosciences, and particularly the neuropsychology of emotion and cognition, objective indicators will be found for the experience of new understanding.

13.2.2 The need for a methodology

The development of research instruments is an essential part of this increasing methodological rigour. A significant gap in the field up until now, which has hindered the cumulative construction of a psychoanalytic knowledge base, is the absence of even a rudimentary system for describing clinical cases. This is an urgent need. A group of German psychoanalysts have already evolved operationalized psychodynamic diagnoses that could function in conjunction with or independently of DSM-IV (Cierpka et al., 1995; Arbeitkreis OPD, 1996). Other similarly operationalized nosologies are under development in Geneva, Barcelona and Stockholm. A comprehensive approach to the classification of predominant mechanisms of defense has also been undertaken in the United States (Crits-Christoph et al., 1988).

Measures are also required for the verification that psychoanalytic treatment has indeed taken place. This involves two challenges: first, the description of psychoanalytic treatment in a form that can be assessed, and secondly, a method of demonstrating therapist adherence and competence in the delivery of a specific treatment. To measure adherence we must use a manual. Yet with a few exceptions (Clarkin, Yeomans and Kernberg, 1998; Fonagy et al., unpublished MS), no one has tried to manualize psychoanalysis. The difficulties are obvious. Manuals usually describe brief treatments in a session-by-session sequence. They are most successful when treatments do not depend on the productivity of the patient, when the theoretical base provides a relatively unambiguous formulation of the disorder, and when treatment techniques may be directly linked to these formulations. In contrast, psychoanalysis is a long treatment that relies completely on the material brought by the patient, with techniques that are fairly easy to prescribe in the abstract, but which depend on the creativity and subjectivity of the analyst for their competent application. Moreover, as we have seen, it is impossible to achieve any kind of one-to-one mapping between psychoanalytic technique and a theoretical framework; psychoanalytic theory is largely not about clinical technique. Even when psychoanalysts are working within the same theoretical framework, they find it very difficult to arrive at a consensus as to the presence or absence of a psychoanalytic process.

The absence of an operationalized definition of what psychoanalysis is should not deter us; rather, this uncertainty necessitates a systematic examination of the psychoanalytic process. This research might ultimately identify the most generic critical components of the treatment, which could then be tested for effectiveness and ultimately cost-effectiveness. Several current research programs have the potential to systematize the psychoanalytic process in this manner. Krause (Anstadt et al., 1997; Krause, 1997) has studied reciprocal facial affect expression in the therapeutic dyad. Bucci

(1997b) has developed a coding system of referential activity, which involves the tracking of connections between nonverbal systems and the communicative verbal code (Bucci and Miller, 1993). Perhaps the most promising approach makes use of a relatively simple instrument called the Psychotherapy Process Q-set (Jones, Cumming and Pulos, 1993). This 100-item instrument provides a basic language for the description and classification of treatment processes in a form suitable for quantitative analysis. Entire therapeutic hours are rated by sorting the Q items, and statistical analysis is used to identify potential underlying structures of interaction. Time-series analysis is then used to assess changes by exploring the unfolding over time of different variables. This method has been effective in linking psychoanalytic concerns to biological variables during the analytic treatment of a diabetic adolescent (Moran and Fonagy, 1987).

A final empirical approach with potential is based on the assumption that a psychoanalytic process is effective, at least with certain groups of patients, because it engages modes of mental functioning that were defensively inhibited by the patient in the process of early adaptation to conflict-ridden environments (Fonagy, Moran, Edgcumbe et al., 1993). The capacity to represent mental states of self and other in the context of attachment relationships has been the focus of the work of this group (Fonagy, Steele, Moran et al., 1991; Fonagy, 1995b). An improvement in reflective (mentalizing) ability may be the long-term outcome of effective psychoanalytic treatment, and could be routinely monitored as an index of the psychoanalytic process. A number of European research groups are currently studying this approach.

However, while a wide range of measures is already potentially available to monitor the process of psychoanalytic therapy, many of these are too complex or cumbersome to be used routinely. Hence researchers are also working on instruments which would allow the easy collection of a minimal psychoanalytic data set, including measures of both process and outcome. For example, to measure therapeutic process, the European Psychoanalytic Collaborative Study on Process and Outcome has adapted a checklist (the Periodical Rating Scale, based on a scale developed at the Anna Freud Centre) that psychoanalysts complete monthly to indicate the manifest and latent content of sessions (Stoker, Beenen and the Dutch Psychoanalytic Institute, 1996). The checklist includes items related to the patient's general attitude, specific conscious and unconscious concerns, object relations, transference manifestations and reports of the analyst's style of intervention and the patient's reaction to these interventions. The checklist has been shown to have higher inter-rater reliability when used with transcribed sessions, and was shown to predict treatment outcome in a small-scale study of analyzes of young adults at the Anna Freud Centre. The report of anxiety, guilt, and idealization in the transference was associated with successful treatments, whereas reports of shame, humiliation and existential anxiety were associated with failed treatments.

A similar simplified approach could be taken to the measurement of psychoanalytic outcome. The minimum psychoanalytic data set could include baseline and annually collected outcomes data from analyst and patient; relatively simple outcome measures are already available for this. It is useful to have some measurement techniques that overlap with those employed by nonpsychoanalytic therapists. This is fairly easy in the symptom domain; self-report measures such as SCL-90-R (Derogatis, 1983) and the BDI (Beck et al., 1961) are commonly used in psychotherapy research. Similarly, the GAF ratings could readily represent the therapist's perspective. Barkham and colleagues (Barkham et al., 2001) have developed a new self-report questionnaire, with considerable promise for a simple generic measure of outcome, for the standard assessment of adult psychosocial treatments in the British healthcare system.

Measures already exist, therefore, which enable a rudimentary investigation of the outcome of psychoanalytic treatment. Baseline, annual and end of treatment information could be collected on all patients undertaking psychoanalysis under supervision. These data, if drawn from a substantial sample and if collected with reasonable rigour, could represent a first step toward answering key questions concerning the nature of the psychoanalytic process.

13.2.3 The hope of a future

There is no adequate excuse for the thin evidence base of psychoanalytic treatment. In the same breath that psychoanalysts often claim to be at the intellectual origin of other talking cures (e.g. systemic therapy, cognitive behavior therapy), they also seek shelter behind the relative immaturity of the discipline to explain the absence of evidence for its efficacy. Yet the evidence base of these 'derivatives' of psychoanalytic therapy has been far more firmly established than evidence for psychoanalysis itself. Of course, there are reasons for this – the long-term nature of the therapy, the subtlety and complexity of its procedures, the elusiveness of its self-declared outcome goals, and the incompatibility of direct observation with the need for absolute confidentiality. None of these is insuperable, however. For example, recording the analytic process appears to be possible without the destruction of the client's trust (Thomä and Kächele, 1987). Further, systematic observation can increase rigour, which may be a crucial common factor underlying many effective treatments (Fonagy, 1999a).

CHAPTER 14

Conclusions and future directions

As we have seen, the assumption of a correspondence between development and psychopathology is present in all psychoanalytic formulations. There are divergences in terms of the exact period of development involved in particular disorders, or the aspect of the developmental process underlying a particular pathology, but there is a shared assumption that the study of development and the study of pathology concern the same psychic processes. Here, we would like to tackle two aspects of this assumption.

First, it involves 'pars pro toto' reasoning. While there are analogies between aspects of mental functioning in psychosis and in early development (e.g. metanomic aspects of language use, absence of reflective capacity, idiosyncratic use of words, etc.), it is fallacious to argue that psychosis is the reactivation of infantile modes of functioning. As we have seen, there are important and striking differences between infantile modes of thought and the adult mind 'in regression' (viz. no evidence for hallucinatory processes, persecutory experiences, delusions of grandeur and so on in infancy). Even in the case of shared characteristics, later development must be assumed to substantively alter both the mechanism and function of the early structures assumed to be reactivated in severe psychopathology. It over-simplifies a very complex developmental process to ignore how an early deficit will have affected subsequent development. We should assume that 'primitive' aspects of severe psychopathologies probably have different functions in an adult mind from the ones they served in childhood.

Secondly, both structural and object relations accounts depend for their explanatory power on descriptions of the evolution of the ego, the self-structure and self–other differentiation in the context of primary object relationships in the first two or three years of life (Kohut, 1971; Kernberg, 1975; 1980a; Masterson, 1976). Mechanisms invoked to explain the phenomenology of severe disorders are all assumed to be rooted in early stages of development. However, as we have seen, many of these developmental models have little empirical support and some actually conflict with the empirical evidence that is available. Even if the pathology observed is analogous to an early mode of mental functioning, it is risky to link the etiology of the disorder to this phase of development (see Gunderson, 1984); later, or cumulative, trauma may well have led the individual to abandon more mature forms of functioning (which had developed adequately) and return to developmentally earlier forms of interaction.

For psychoanalysis to become a realistic developmental theory, it needs to evolve more concepts that pertain to later childhood, adolescent and adult development. Some developmental ideas generalize to the developmental process itself (for example, Klein's idea of the paranoid-schizoid and depressive positions, now seen as alternating throughout life, or Bowlby's construct of attachment that has now been tracked through the different phases of development). Beyond these generalizations, developmental understanding of later developmental phases will need to be improved to encompass the impact of environmental events and intrapsychic circumstances that continue profoundly to influence the trajectory of development beyond the first four years of life.

14.1 The promise of psychoanalysis

We intend here first to examine briefly whether psychoanalysis is compatible with new knowledge emerging from genetics and other related fields, and thus whether its discoveries could be integrated with the progress being made elsewhere. We then consider whether psychoanalysis has additional features that entitle it to exert a continuing influence within the fields of study of the mind.

14.1.1 The challenge of genetics

Over the last decade, it began to seem as if research in genetics had all but eliminated the place for a psychoanalytic account, and for any theory that advocated the key role of early family experience (see Scarr, 1992). There has been a claim that environmentally mediated family influences were inherited and therefore in themselves unimportant (Rowe, 1994; Kendler et al., 1996) and, further, that some genetically influenced aspects of children's behavior may have provoked the observed negative responses in parents and other people (O'Connor, Deater-Deckard et al., 1998). All estimates for the heritability of psychiatric disorders increase when lifetime risk, rather than point prevalence, is used as an index variable (Kendler et al., 1993). Generally, we saw a cultural shift, with both professionals and the lay public switching from a primarily psychosocial model of child and adult disturbance to a genetic-biological frame of reference that a priori excluded psychodynamic aspects.

A more balanced view of these genetic data was advanced by Michael Rutter and colleagues (Rutter et al., 1997), and this has reestablished the potential for psychoanalytic accounts. The main features of this view are outlined below.

Virtually all forms of psychopathology involve both gene-environment correlations and interactions. However, these correlations do not necessarily imply an etiological role for genetics. Individuals affect the environment and some gene-environment covariance may be due to person characteristics, irrespective of whether these person characteristics are genetic or environmental in origin (O'Connor, Deater-Deckard et al., 1998).

The notion of 'non-shared environment' (Plomin and Daniels, 1987) can help us to account for the ways in which children exposed to similar environments may develop differently, without necessarily having to supply a genetic explanation. First, key parameters within a shared environment differ in relation to a specific child, and secondly, genuinely shared environments are *experienced* differently by two children. Neither of these pathways to different outcomes necessarily involves genetic differences.

Neither twin studies nor adoption studies can provide firm indications of the relative importance of genes and environment. They provide estimates of individual difference within a population. For example, while height is clearly heritable, changes in average height over the past 100 years (in excess of one foot for males) reveal that much of the variability must be attributable to the environment. Secular trends over the past fifty years reveal a substantial increase in the prevalence of a number of childhood mental disorders (e.g. conduct disorder, suicidal behavior, depressive disorder and misuse of drugs: see Rutter and Smith, 1995). Twin studies, where children's ages are identical, exclude the critical environmental influences underlying such secular trends.

Heritability estimates are dependent on the samples studied. Samples are mostly biased, excluding environments most likely to be associated with personality disorders. Cultural factors are also mostly partialed out: if individuals from a variety of cultures were to be included in the same study, our estimates of the impact of shared environment on personality would be very different (Mandler, 1997).

Genetic effects may well be indirect as well as direct. Even a high genetic loading for a certain environmental hazard does not mean that the consequences would necessarily be genetically rather than environmentally mediated. For example, if child abuse were found to have a large genetic component, its toxic effects would still be via the destruction of trust in the abused child, rather than via a purely genetic process.

Studies that attempt to exclude direct and indirect genetic effects highlight the considerable influence of early experience. For example, a study of adult female twins demonstrated that a history of parental loss through separation, though not through death, was associated with adult vulnerability to depression and alcoholism (Kendler et al., 1996).

We believe that in general the challenge of genetics over the last decade has been helpful for the psychodynamic approach. It has served to balance the naïve environmentalism of the second half of this century which culminated, for example, in the overdiagnosis of post-traumatic stress disorder among victims of childhood maltreatment and gave rise to the unfortunate debate on false memories of abuse (Sandler and Fonagy, 1997). Psychodynamic theory has much to contribute to the integration of genetics into developmental science. The primary concern of psychoanalysis is with the interaction of multiple layers of representations in generating developmental outcomes (e.g. id, ego and superego, part and whole object representations). Data from genetics call for exactly such sophistication in understanding the way genes may or may not be expressed in particular individuals. For example, while risk factors operate in combination, there is substantial individual variability in response to stress and adversity. Much of this variability is poorly understood (Rutter, 1999), but it underscores the potential importance of intrapsychic variables. Whether or not the specific environmental factors trigger the expression of a gene may depend not only on the nature of those factors, but also on the way the child experiences them. This may in turn be a function of either genetic or environmental influences, or their interaction (Kandel, 1998). Thus intrapsychic representational processes are not just consequences of environmental and genetic effects – they may be their critical moderators. This has substantial clinical significance, since the understanding of an environment by the child is more readily modifiable than the environment itself, or the genes with which the environment interacts (Emde, 1988b). A psychodynamic, intrapsychic perspective may be helpful in considering, not just what precipitates a disorder, but also which processes influence the course of the disorder for better or worse.

14.1.2 Unconscious intentionality

The hallmark of psychoanalytic theory is the attention to dynamically unconscious mental processes and motivation in the explanation of complex and often paradoxical human behavior. We suggest that this knowledge could be integrated into the emerging sciences of the mind. Cognitive neuroscience has shown that most of the work of the brain is outside consciousness ('nonconscious') (Kihlstrom, 1987). This is now known to include not only memory acquired implicitly (see Milner, Squire and Kandel, 1998), but also implicit aspects of decision making, problem-solving and other cognitive tasks (e.g. Underwood, 1996).

Where the psychoanalytic position remains unique is in suggesting that motivational and affective processes that influence developmental processes may be unconscious. It is puzzling that this should be so, since the role of cognition in emotion and motivation is well established (Mandler, 1997) and therefore, almost by definition, affect and motivation should be part of the 'cognitive unconscious' (Kihlstrom, 1987). Neurological evidence has been accumulating to suggest that neural pathways for emotion entail two sets of structures. One is via the thalamus to the amygdala (which conveys primitive perceptual information with affective valence but without the involvement of consciousness), and the other involves the activation of cortical centers and deeper information processing prior to the activation of the amygdala (LeDoux, 1995). Patients with a variety of lesions who lose the capacity for conscious discrimination may retain the capacity to respond differentially at the emotional level (e.g. Bechara et al., 1995). There is evidence from non-neurological patients for unconscious affective preferences using low signal-to-noise ratio stimuli (e.g. Murphy, Monahan and Zajonc, 1995). Conditioned emotional responses may be elicited and even acquired (Wong et al., 1997) outside awareness. Unconscious attitudes, particularly racial prejudice, have been persuasively shown to influence not only the speed of information processing but also the reactions generated in independent observers (Fazio et al., 1995).

These and other findings, recently comprehensively summarized by Westen (1999), support the view that emotional processing occurs automatically, outside consciousness. Preliminary data also support the view that the unconscious processing of emotional information may be qualitatively different from its conscious processing, in terms of neural mechanisms (Morris, Ohman and Dolan, 1998), psychophysiological concomitants (Dozier and Kobak, 1992) and behavioral consequences (Greenwald and Banaji, 1995). To the extent that non-conscious factors have a role to play, then abnormalities in unconscious functioning, as postulated by psychoanalysis, continue to offer a highly significant contribution.

14.1.3 Unconscious motivation

Admitting that affects may not be conscious, is of course, not equivalent to stating that unconscious mental states motivate behavior. However, this is neither an extravagant assumption nor one unsupported by other sources of data. Westen (1999) pointed out that the assumption that human behavior is simultaneously motivated by multiple goals implies that the logical mechanism for organizing these must be outside consciousness, because of the excessive demands these would make on working memory. There is considerable evidence consistent with this view. For example, intending to carry out an action heightens activation of the information to be remembered even when the intention is no longer conscious, as evidenced by response latencies for recognizing to-be-remembered items from a list (Goschke and Kuhl, 1993). A range of studies have demonstrated that when people act on motives or preferences to which they have no access, they will find reasons for having done this which are both incorrect (Nisbett and Wilson, 1977) and likely to interfere with subsequent task performance (Wilson and Schooler, 1991).

The value of the concept of unconscious affect as motivation is strongest in explanations of psychological disturbance. Westen (1998) makes a strong case that the psychodynamic model is in line with contemporary connectionist or parallel distributed processing (PDP) models in cognitive science (Rumelhart and McClelland, 1986). Both psychodynamic and PDP models postulate multiple independent processing units which work alongside each other, at times in conflict, at times in collaboration, to generate both conscious and unconscious decisions. Within the PDP model, conflict is an 'emergent property' of the human nervous system. The constraints placed upon the system are both external (context-dependent) and internal (emotional and motivational). It follows from the independence of neural circuitry underlying the generation of individual mental states (beliefs, desires, fears, values) that these states may be opposed to one another. It further follows from developmental localizationist perspectives consistent with PDP (Kinsbourne and Hicks, 1979; Schore, 1999) that several neural processing nets emerge early and simultaneously in development to perform the same psychological function. This ensures plasticity and protects the organism from the consequences of brain injury.

In the course of development and the increasing involvement of specific brain locations with specific tasks, connections between some of these nets and processing units on the periphery of the evolving system (at greater cortical distance from the point of localization) will be increasingly marginalized (Edelman, 1992). As feedback to such systems is degraded by cortical distance, the processing characteristics of these vestigial systems will not be updated in line with neural nets that are closer to the focal area responsible for specific tasks. These vestigial nets will therefore remain archaic in their functioning. Thus conflict between the output of central and peripheral processing units, with processing characteristics reflecting varying levels of maturity, may be inevitable.

Consistent with the notion of relative independence of neural circuitry for a variety of emotional and motivational states, is the accumulating body of knowledge concerning the neural circuitry responsible for positive and negative affect states (Gray, 1990; Davidson, 1992). The complexity of interpersonal interactions, in terms of the concurrent presence of both positive and negative affect, has been demonstrated (Hartup and Stevens, 1997). The development of cognitive-emotional structures that resolve incompatibilities in emotional information processing represents a key developmental goal. For example, in the social referencing task, 12-month-olds respond with distress and confusion if they receive conflicting facial messages from their two parents (Hirshberg and Svejda, 1990). The failure to resolve conflict in relation to the anticipated behavior of the attachment figure is a key part of models of disorganized attachment (Main and Morgan, 1996; Lyons-Ruth and Jacobovitz, 1999). Psychoanalytic models of psychopathology mostly entail the notion of compromise formation (Brenner, 1982). Neo-Piagetian developmental theory (Fischer and Ayoub, 1994) also assumes that development is a step-wise integration of independently evolving cognitive capacities.

Thus, both neuropsychological and developmental models are consistent with psychoanalytic ideas concerning the coexistence of processing units from different developmental stages, the ubiquity of conflict between them, and the desirability of adaptive resolution of these conflicts as part of the developmental process. Psychoanalytic theories of conflict may have much to contribute to the study of development in the coming years.

14.1.4 Early childhood experience

Of greatest direct relevance to developmental psychopathology is the role of early childhood experience in determining adult personality. This has been a key tenet of all psychoanalytic propositions. The issue has been hotly debated within psychology (Rutter, 1999). Reviews in the 1980s concluded that there were few serious long-term sequelae of adverse childhood experiences that were clearly independent of later adversities (Rutter, 1981). Later research, however, demonstrated that early experiences did exert long-term effects (Sroufe et al., 1990), but these stemmed from (a) their contribution to the generation of further negative experiences (Sroufe and Fleeson, 1988), and (b) rendering these individuals more vulnerable to such experiences (Suess, Grossmann and Sroufe, 1992; Rutter et al., 1995). Psychodynamic theory might suggest that individuals with early adversity process their experiences differently and proactively create experiences compatible with past interactions (e.g. Caspi and Moffitt, 1995). There is evidence that individuals who have encountered early adversity are more likely to encounter both acute and chronic psychosocial adversities in adult life (e.g. Champion, Goodall and Rutter, 1995). While some of the early theories concerning the psychogenic causation of psychoses turned out to be extravagant and, by and large, unhelpful (Willick, 2001), the general emphasis on the importance of early experiences for healthy development have received good support from both psychological and neuroscience studies (Schore, 2001; Fonagy et al., 2002).

An alternative model of the relationship of early experience and a predisposition to psychopathology, fully consistent with Freud's ideas (Freud, 1915b), has emerged from the biological literature. Early stress (separation from its mother) in the life of a rodent pup led to enduring neuroendocrine abnormalities, whereas appropriate caregiving responses to the pup's distress led to a reduction in the pup's hypothalamic-pituitary-adrenal (HPA) response for the rest of the animal's life (Levine et al., 1967). Intervening research has demonstrated that responsive caregiving serves, in the long term, to reduce the pup's fearfulness and vulnerability to stress-related disease (Plotsky and Meaney, 1993; Liu et al., 1997). Other studies have demonstrated that early adverse life experiences in rats are associated with profound and persistent increases in gene expression for corticotrophin releasing factor (CRF), not only in the hypothalamus but also in limbic areas (Plotsky and Meaney, 1993; Nemeroff, 1996). Independently, it has been demonstrated that increased secretion of glucocorticoids over a prolonged period can lead to permanent damage to hippocampal neurons (McEwen and Sapolsky, 1995). These data provide an underpinning for the traditional psychoanalytic emphasis on the lifelong impact of very early attachment experiences.

Whether early environmental risk is carried forward primarily by the predisposition to select adverse environments (Quinton and Rutter, 1988; Farrington, Barnes and Lambert, 1996), by maladaptive affect regulation, by neuroendocrine abnormalities, or by some combination of the three, is not yet clear. However, all these models are consistent with psychoanalytical ideas (Kandel, 1999). In fact the psychological mechanisms implied may be the same regardless of the level of analysis (social or biological): such mechanisms might include unconscious biases in the processing of information, the absence of a capacity to plan (Quinton et al., 1993), or distorted models of relationship representation (Fonagy et al., 1996). There is accumulating evidence that prolonged early and severe privation, particularly the absence of an attachment relationship, may have irreversible effects (O'Connor et al., 2000). A counterpoint to these observations is other evidence of the possibility of change – so called 'turning point effects' (Caspi and Moffitt, 1993). There would be no point in practicing psychotherapy were it not for evidence that 'experiences in adult life make a decisive difference to people who have been placed at risk as a result of adverse experiences in childhood' (Rutter, 1999, p. 487). Research has demonstrated that the psychoanalytic focus on early experience is appropriate, and its depth-psychological perspective may illuminate outstanding questions.

14.1.5 Mental representations and object relationships

A key aspect of the psychoanalytic model of the mind, and the one where convergence with other measures is most marked (Westen, 1991b), is the emphasis on mental representations of relationships as mediators of self-organization and as determinants of the impact of the environment on the individual. These representational structures are thought to mediate the experience of abnormal development. The concept emerged originally in the context of object relations theory, as we have described. Numerous research methods have emerged to explore psychodynamic aspects of the child's representational world (e.g. Oppenheim, Emde and Warren, 1997; Toth et al., 1997; Macfie et al., 1999). There is accumulating evidence to suggest that children transform early interactions with primary caregivers into cognitive-affective schemas of self and other, which regulate and direct subsequent behavior (Bretherton and Munholland, 1999). These schemata not only bear the imprint of significant interactions, but also express the developmental level that dominates the individual's functioning (Westen, 1990b). According to psychoanalytic theory, beyond representing consensual reality, internal working models contain the unique constructions of each child. Representations are distorted by defenses (Newman, Duff and Baumeister, 1997) and impulses (Westen et al., 1997). These may be indications of a genetic predisposition or prior environmental experience. In either case, the child's distortion of the external world represents a significant challenge to studies aiming to find direct relationships between psychosocial adversity and psychopathology. Psychoanalytic object relations theory, with its focus on idiosyncratic distortions, may be able to make a significant contribution.

14.1.6 The particular strengths of psychoanalytic models

Some of the greatest minds ever to become interested in psychology and the mental disorders explored or adopted the frame of reference of psycho-analysis. They probably did so because it offered the richest set of ideas as elements for describing mental functioning. Here we will mention four features that continue to recommend the approach.

(a) *Generativity.* Many important psychological theories of psychopathology acknowledge that psychoanalytic ideas have inspired their lines of research (e.g. learned helplessness theory, schema theory, attachment theory, aggression and hostility as a cause of psychosomatic conditions, self-serving cognitive distortions based on defense mechanisms, and so on).

(b) *Unifying explanations.* Diverse symptoms and behavior can reflect a single hidden problem. For example, why are narcissistic individuals often forgetful of names, prejudiced, inconsiderate of others' time, vulnerable to slights and unable to remain in love? Psychoanalytic accounts, whether self-psychological or based on other object relations views, offer single explanations for such groups of phenomena.

(c) *A dynamic approach*: Development as a series of compromise formations. This gives depth, texture and complexity in line with new
knowledge emerging from both neuroscience and developmental
psychopathology. Many psychoanalytic accounts provide satisfying
functionalist explanations of observed patterns of behavior and the
observed characteristics of mental representation.

(d) *The mind as an instrument*. Theory is built from the sensitivity of the
therapist in generating models for understanding thoughts, feelings and
behavior beyond the normal range of conscious experience and common
sense psychology. Psychoanalytic listening, regardless of specific model,
perhaps equips clinicians to handle and make sense of particularly intense
and disturbing interactions. The resulting understanding is more complex
and psychologically deeper than other 'omnibus' theories of human
behavior (cognitive-behavioral, humanistic, systemic), even if psychoanalysis is therapeutically no more effective. This contains the appeal of
psychoanalytic ideas for many clinicians and others.

14.2 Concluding reflections

Psychoanalytic ideas remain radical and able to illuminate many aspects of
developmental psychopathology. Some future tasks for psychoanalytically
oriented clinician-researchers are: (a) To move away from enumerative inductivism, and make some use of the alternative data gathering methods
available in modern social and biological science. (b) To define psychoanalytic constructs and techniques more tightly. This must include not only
operational definitions but also the 'unpacking' of overarching concepts such
as object relationships, and the specification of predictions: what remote or
proximal variables account for specific symptoms, and what is the interaction among predisposing variables and other contributory factors? (c) To
develop a tradition of 'comparative psychoanalytic studies', where alternative psychoanalytic frameworks are considered side-by-side in relation to
the observations. This should be extended so that explanations from outside
psychoanalysis are considered, as they may suggest better or complementary
ways of understanding the data. In this context, achieving a standard of
reporting that allows for alternative ways of formulating a set of clinical
observations is essential (Michels, 2000; Tuckett, 2000a). (d) Related to the
above, to become more sophisticated in thinking about interactions between
the intrapsychic world and the environment (Rutter, 1993), and the
processes of risk and trauma. (e) To give greater consideration to the wider
social and cultural context within which object relations develop. (f) To
focus on the relevance of psychoanalytic theory and treatment to the
community at large. For example, psychoanalytic studies of intergenerational
trauma have focused on survivors of the Holocaust (Bergmann and Jucovy,

1982; Kogan, 1995). Yet we could also learn about this process from the study of other traumatized or persecuted groups (e.g. Belsky, 1993). (g) To throw away the shackles of an outdated, over-specified theory, and focus on the essential components of their psychological propositions.

On the other side, taking psychoanalytic ideas more seriously could have a very beneficial effect on epistemological and methodological aspects of developmental psychopathology. This particularly applies to the central notion that unconscious beliefs and affects influence behavior. A widening of focus could, for example, lead to a shift in emphasis from self-report to narrative data; to a closer examination of patterns of narration, as opposed to observations of narrative content; a greater concern with discordance and conflict amongst response systems, rather than a single minded search for congruence and consistency, and so on.

A fundamental task for psychoanalytic theorists is to recognize the weakness of the link between practice and theory, that changes of technique have no power to confirm or disconfirm cherished ideas and that practice may be radically changed with or without changes in theory. We could then see talented clinicians modifying technique while remaining faithful to the core assumptions of psychoanalysis. Thus, unconscious motivation and processes remain at the center, but advances in other fields might be able to optimize clinical effectiveness. However, a thorough familiarity with psychoanalytic ideas would remain essential to appreciate the complexity of the clinical encounter. The theories reviewed in this book have all made important contributions to the understanding of the personality and its disorders. Further progress in practice and theory requires that clinicians should be well versed in them if they are fully to grasp the clinical relationship at the heart of psychoanalytic ideas.

A psychoanalytic science should be seen as an integrative discipline, drawing on a range of scientific disciplines and other sources of information, focused on the struggles that subjective aspects of experience create for the person in the course of adaptive and maladaptive development. Psychoanalytic theory is very much alive, and its potential for enriching our understanding of developmental psychopathology has not been fully exploited in the century that has just closed.

References

Abend SM, Porder MS, Willick MS (1983) Borderline Patients: Psychoanalytic Perspectives. New York: International Universities Press.

Ablon JS, Jones EE (1999) Psychotherapy process in the National Institute of Mental Health Treatment of Depression Collaborative Research Program. Journal of Consulting and Clinical Psychology 67: 64-75.

Abraham K (1927) Selected Papers of Karl Abraham. New York: Brunner/Mazel, 1979.

Abrams S (1977) The genetic point of view: historical antecedents and developmental transformations. Journal of the American Psychoanalytic Association 25: 417-26.

Adams HE, Wright LW, Lohr BA (1996) Is homophobia associated with homosexual arousal? Journal of Abnormal Psychology 105(3): 440-5.

Adamson LB, Bakeman R (1985) Affect and attention: infants observed with mothers and peers. Child Development 56: 582-93.

Adler A (1916) The Neurotic Constitution. New York: Moffat Yard.

Adler G (1981) The borderline-narcissistic personality disorder continuum. American Journal of Psychiatry 138: 46-50.

Adler G (1985) Borderline Psychopathology and Its Treatment. New York: Jason Aronson.

Aichhorn A (1925) Wayward Youth. New York: Viking, 1935.

Ainsworth MDS (1963) The development of infant-mother interaction among the Ganda. In BM Foss (ed.), Determinants of Infant Behavior (Vol. 2, pp. 67-112). New York: Wiley.

Ainsworth MDS (1969) Object relations, dependency and attachment: a theoretical review of the infant-mother relationship. Child Development 40: 969-1025.

Ainsworth MDS (1985) Attachments across the lifespan. Bulletin of the New York Academy of Medicine 61: 792-812.

Ainsworth MDS (1990) Epilogue: some considerations regarding theory and assessment relevant to attachment beyond infancy. In MT Greenberg, D Cicchetti, EM Cummings (eds), Attachment in the Pre-School Years: Theory, Research and Intervention (pp. 463-88). Chicago, IL: University of Chicago Press.

Ainsworth MDS, Bowlby J (1991) An ethological approach to personality development. American Psychologist 46, 333-41.

Ainsworth MDS, Wittig, BA (1969) Attachment and exploratory behavior of one-year-olds in a Strange Situation. In BM Foss (ed.), Determinants of Infant Behavior (pp. 113-36). London: Methuen.

Ainsworth MDS, Blehar MC, Waters E, Wall S (1978) Patterns of Attachment: A Psychological Study of the Strange Situation. Hillsdale, NJ: Erlbaum.

Akhtar S (1989) Kohut and Kernberg: a critical comparison. In DW Detrick, SP Detrick (eds), Self Psychology: Comparisons and Contrasts (pp. 329-62). Hillsdale, NJ: Analytic Press.

Akhtar S (1992) Broken Structures: Severe Personality Disorders and Their Treatment. Northvale, NJ: Jason Aronson.

Akhtar S, Thomson JA (1982) Overview: narcissistic personality disorder. American Journal of Psychiatry 139: 12-20.

Alexander F (1930) The neurotic character. International Journal of Psycho-Analysis 11, 292-311.

Alexander F, French T (1946) The principle of corrective emotional experience: the case of Jean Valjean. In F Alexander, T French (eds), Psychoanalytic Theory, Principles and Application (pp. 66-70). New York: Ronald Press.

Allen JP, Hauser ST (1996) Autonomy and relatedness in adolescent–family interactions as predictors of young adults' states of mind regarding attachment. Development and Psychopathology 8: 793-809.

Allen JP, Hauser ST, Borman-Spurrell E (1996) Attachment theory as a framework for understanding sequelae of severe adolescent psychopathology: an 11-year follow-up study. Journal of Consulting and Clinical Psychology 64: 254-63.

American Psychiatric Association (1987) Diagnostic and Statistical Manual of Mental Disorders (DSM-III-R) (3rd edn, revised). Washington, DC: American Psychiatric Association.

American Psychiatric Association (1994) Diagnostic and Statistical Manual of Mental Disorders (DSM-IV) (4th edn). Washington, DC: American Psychiatric Association.

Amini F, Lewis T, Lannon R et al. (1996) Affect, attachment, memory: contributions towards a psychobiologic integration. Psychiatry 59: 213-39.

Anderson EM, Lambert MJ (1995) Short-term dynamically oriented psychotherapy: a review and meta-analysis. Clinical Psychology Review 15: 503-14.

Angold A, Costello EJ, Erkanli A (1999) Comorbidity. Journal of Child Psychology and Psychiatry 40: 57-87.

Anstadt T, Merten J., Ullrich B, Krause R (1997) Affective dyadic behavior, core conflictual relationship themes, and success of treatment. Psychotherapy Research 7: 397-419.

Anthony EJ, Cohler BJ (eds) (1987) The Invulnerable Child. New York: Guilford Press.

Anzieu D (1993) Autistic phenomena and the skin ego. Psychoanalytic Inquiry 13, 42-8.

Appignanesi L, Forrester J (2000) Freud's Women. London: Penguin.

Arbeitkreis OPD (ed.) (1996) Operationalisierte Psychodynamische Diagnostik: Grundlagen und Manual. Bern-Stuttgart: Hans Huber.

Arlow JA (1985) The structural hypothesis. In A Rothstein (ed.), Models of the Mind: Their Relationships to Clinical Work (pp. 21-34). New York: International Universities Press, Inc.

Arlow JA, Brenner C (1964) Psychoanalytic Concepts and the Structural Theory. New York: International University Press.

Armsden GC, Greenberg MT (1987) The inventory of parent and peer attachment: individual differences and their relationship to psychological well-being in adolescence. Journal of Youth and Adolescence 16: 427-54.

Aron L (1996) A Meeting of Minds: Mutuality in Psychoanalysis. New York: International Universities Press.

Bacal HA (1990) Does an object relations theory exist in self psychology? Psychoanalytic Inquiry 10: 197-220.

Bacal HA, Newman KM (1990) Theories of Object Relations: Bridges to Self Psychology (Personality, Psychopathology, and Psychotherapy). New York: Columbia University Press.

Bahrick LR, Watson JS (1985) Detection of intermodal proprioceptive-visual contingency as a potential basis of self-perception in infancy. Developmental Psychology 21: 963–73.

Bak R (1954) The schizophrenic defence against aggression. International Journal of Psycho-Analysis 35: 129–34.

Bak R (1971) Object relationships in schizophrenia and perversions. International Journal of Psycho-Analysis 52: 235–42.

Bakermans-Kranenburg MJ, van IJzendoorn, MH (1993) A psychometric study of the Adult Attachment Interview: reliability and discriminant validity. Developmental Psychology 29: 870–9.

Balint M (1937) Early developmental states of the ego, primary object of love, Primary Love and Psycho-analytic Technique (pp. 90–108). London: Tavistock, 1965.

Balint M (1959) Thrills and Regressions. London: Hogarth Press.

Balint M (1965) Primary Love and Psycho-analytic Technique. London: Tavistock.

Balint M (1968) The Basic Fault. London: Tavistock.

Bandura A (1982) Self-efficacy mechanism in human agency. American Psychologist 37: 122–47.

Barkham M, Margison F, Leach C, Lucock M, Mellor-Clark J, Evans C, Benson L, Connell J, Audin K (2001) Service profiling and outcomes benchmarking using the CORE-OM: towards practice-based evidence in the psychological therapies. Clinical Outcomes in Routine Evaluation-Outcome Measures. J Consult Clin Psychol 69(2): 184–96.

Barnett D, Ganiban J, Cicchetti D (1999) Maltreatment, emotional reactivity and the development of Type D attachments from 12 to 24 months of age. Monographs of the Society for Research in Child Development.

Baron J, Gruen R, Asnis L, Lord S (1985) Familial transmission of schizotypal and borderline personality disorders. American Journal of Psychiatry 142: 927–34.

Baron-Cohen S (1995) Mindblindness: An Essay on Autism and Theory of Mind. Cambridge, MA: Bradford, MIT Press.

Baron-Cohen S (2000) Autism: deficits in folk psychology exist alongside superiority in folk physics. In S Baron-Cohen, H Tager-Flusberg, DJ Cohen (eds), Understanding Other Minds: Perspectives from Autism and Developmental Cognitive Neuroscience (2nd edn, pp. 59–82). Oxford: Oxford University Press.

Baron-Cohen S, Tager-Flusberg H, Cohen DJ (eds) (2000) Understanding Other Minds: Perspectives from Autism and Developmental Cognitive Neuroscience. Oxford: Oxford University Press.

Bartsch K, Wellman HM (1989) Young children's attribution of action to beliefs and desires. Child Development 60: 946–64.

Basch MF (1985) Interpretation: toward a developmental model. In A Goldberg (ed.), Progress in Self Psychology, Vol. 1 (pp. 33–42). New York: Guilford Press.

Basch MF (1976) Psychoanalysis and communication science. Annals of Psychoanalysis 4: 385–421.

Bateman A (1997) The concept of enactment and 'thick-skinned' and 'thin-skinned' narcissism. International Journal of Psychoanalysis.

Bateman A, Fonagy P (1999) The effectiveness of partial hospitalization in the treatment of borderline personality disorder – a randomised controlled trial. American Journal of Psychiatry 156: 1563–69.

Bateman A, Fonagy P (2001) Treatment of borderline personality disorder with psychoanalytically oriented partial hospitalization: an 18-month follow-up. American Journal of Psychiatry 158(1): 36–42.

Bates E, Benigni L, Bretherton I, Camaioni L, Volterra V (1979) Cognition and communication from 9–13 months: correlational findings. In E Bates (ed.), The Emergence of Symbols: Cognition and Communication in Infancy. New York: Academic Press.

Bates J, Maslin C, Frankel K (1985) Attachment security, mother–child interactions, and temperament as predictors of behavior problem ratings at age three years. In I Bretherton, E Waters (eds), Growing Points in Attachment Theory and Research (pp. 167–93) Monographs of the Society for Research in Child Development, 50. (1-2, Serial No. 209).

Beardslee W, Bemporad J, Keller MB, Klerman GL (1983). Children of parents with a major affective disorder: a review. American Journal of Psychiatry 140: 825–32.

Bechara A, Tranel D, Damasio H, Adolphs R, Rockland C, Damasio A (1995) Double dissociation of conditioning and declarative knowledge relative to the amygdala and hippocampus in humans. Science 29: 1115–18.

Beck AT (1967) Depression: Causes and Treatment. Philadelphia: University of Pennsylvania Press.

Beck AT (1976) Cognitive Therapy and the Emotional Disorders. New York: International Universities Press/Meriden.

Beck AT, Freeman A (1990) Cognitive Therapy of Personality Disorders. New York: Guilford Press.

Beck AT, Ward CH, Mendelson M, Mock J, Erbaugh J (1961) An inventory for measuring depression. Archives of General Psychiatry 4: 561–71.

Beebe B, Lachmann F, Jaffe J (1997) Mother–infant interaction structures and presymbolic self and object representations. Psychoanalytic Dialogues 7: 113–82.

Bell MB, Billington R, Cicchetti D (1988) Do object relations deficits distinguish BPD from other diagnostic groups? Journal of Clinical Psychology 44: 511–16.

Belsky J (1993) Etiology of child maltreatment: a developmental-ecological analysis. Psychological Bulletin 114: 413–34.

Belsky J (1999) Interactional and contextual determinants of attachment security. In J Cassidy, PR Shaver (eds), Handbook of Attachment: Theory, Research and Clinical Applications (pp. 249–64). New York: Guilford.

Belsky J, Rovine M, Taylor DG (1984) The Pennsylvania Infant and Family Development Project. III: The origins of individual differences in mother–infant attachment: Maternal and infant contributions. Child Development 55: 718–28.

Benedek T (1959) Parenthood as a developmental phase. Journal of the American Psychoanalytic Association 7: 389–417.

Benjamin J (1988) The Bonds of Love: Psychoanalysis, Feminism and the Problem of Domination. London: Virago.

Benjamin J (1995) Like Subjects, Love Objects. New Haven, CT: Yale University Press.

Benjamin J (1998) The Shadow of the Other: Intersubjectivity and Gender in Psychoanalysis. New York: Routledge.

Bennett I, Hellman I (1951) Psychoanalytic material related to observations in early development. Psychoanalytic Study of the Child 6: 307–24.

Benoit D, Parker K (1994) Stability and transmission of attachment across three generations. Child Development 65: 1444–57.

Benvenuto B, Kennedy R (1986) The Works of Jacques Lacan: An Introduction. London: Free Association Books.

Berelowitz M, Tarnopolsky A (1993) The validity of borderline personality disorder: an updated review of recent research. In P Tyrer, G Stein (eds), Personality Disorder Reviewed. London: Gaskell, Royal College of Psychiatrists.

Berger RJ (1963) Experimental modification of dream content by meaningful verbal stimuli. British Journal of Psychiatry 109: 722–40.

Bergmann MS, Jucovy, ME (eds) (1982) Generations of the Holocaust. New York: Columbia University Press.

Berman AL, Jobes, DA (1995) Suicide prevention in adolescents (age 12–18): a population perspective. Suicide and Life-threatening Behavior 25: 143–54.

Berridge KC, Robinson T (1995) The mind of an addicted brain: neural sensitization of wanting versus liking. Current Directions in Psychological Science 4: 71–6.

Bertenthal BI, Proffit DR, Spetner NB, Thomas MA (1985) The development of infant sensitivity to biomechanical motions. Child Development 56: 531–43.

Bever T (1968) Associations to stimulus-response theories of language. In TR Dixon, DL Horton (eds), Verbal Behavior and General Behavior Theory. Englewood Cliffs, NJ: Prentice-Hall.

Bibring E (1947) The so-called English School of psychoanalysis. Psychoanalytic Quarterly 16: 69–93.

Bibring GL, Dwyer TF, Huntington DS, Vallenstein AF (1961) A study of the psychological processes in the pregnancy and earliest mother–child relationship. The Psychoanalytic Study of the Child 16: 9–72.

Bick E (1964) Notes on infant observation in psychoanalytic training. International Journal of Psycho-Analysis 45: 558–66.

Bidell TR, Fischer KW (1994) Developmental transitions in children's early on-line planning. In MM Haith, JB Benson, RJ Roberts, BF Pennington (eds), Development of Future-oriented Processes. Chicago, IL: University of Chicago Press.

Bion WR (1955) Language and the schizophrenic. In M Klein, P Heimann, R Money-Kyrle (eds), New Directions of Psychoanalysis (pp. 220–39). London: Tavistock Publications.

Bion WR (1957) Differentiation of the psychotic from the non-psychotic personalities. International Journal of Psychoanalysis 38: 266–75.

Bion WR (1959) Attacks on linking. International Journal of Psychoanalysis 40: 308–15.

Bion WR (1962a) Learning from Experience. London: Heinemann.

Bion WR (1962b). A theory of thinking. International Journal of Psychoanalysis 43, 306–10.

Bion WR (1963) Elements of Psycho-analysis. London: Heinemann.

Bion WR (1967a) Notes on memory and desire. Psychoanalytic Forum 2: 272–3, 279–80.

Bion WR (1967b) Second Thoughts. London: Heinemann.

Bion WR (1970) Attention and Interpretation. London: Tavistock.

Blair RJR (1995) A cognitive developmental approach to morality: investigating the psychopath. Cognition 57: 1–29.

Blanck G, Blanck R (1979) Ego Psychology, Vol. 2. Psychoanalytic Developmental Psychology. New York: Columbia University Press.

Blatt SJ (1995) Representational structures in psychopathology. In D Cicchetti, SL Toth (eds), Rochester Symposium on Developmental Psychopathology: Volume 6. Emotion, Cognition and Representation (pp. 1–33). Rochester, NY: University of Rochester Press.

Blatt, SJ, Behrends RS (1987) Internalization, separation-individuation, and the nature of therapeutic action. International Journal of Psycho-Analysis 68: 279-97.

Blatt SJ, Bers SA (1993) The sense of self in depression: a psychodynamic perspective. In ZV Segal, SJ Blatt (eds), Self Representation and Emotional Disorders: Cognitive and Psychodynamic Perspectives (pp. 171-210). New York: Guilford.

Blatt SJ, Blass RB (1990) Attachment and separateness: a dialectical model of the products and processes of development throughout the life cycle. Psychoanalytic Study of the Child 45: 107-27.

Blatt SJ, Blass RB (1996). Relatedness and self definition: a dialectic model of personality development. In GG Noam, KW Fischer (eds), Development and Vulnerabilities in Close Relationships (pp. 309-8). New York: Erlbaum.

Blatt SJ, Auerbach JS, Aryan M (1998) Representational structures and the therapeutic process. In RF Bornstein, JM Masling (eds), Empirical Studies of Psychoanalytic Theories: Vol. 8. Empirical Investigations of the Therapeutic Hour (pp. 63-107). Washington: The American Psychological Association.

Blatt SJ, Brenneis CB, Schimek JG, Glick M (1976) Normal development and psychopathological impairment of the concept of the object on the Rorschach. Journal of Abnormal Psychology 85, 364-73.

Blatt SJ, Quinlan DM, Pilkonis PA, Shea MT (1995) Impact of perfectionism and need for approval on the brief treatment of depression: The National Institute of Mental Health Treatment of Depression Collaborative Research Program revisited. Journal of Consulting and Clinical Psychology 63: 125-32.

Blatt SJ, Stayner D, Auerbach JS, Behrends RS (1996) Change in object and self representations in long-term, intensive, inpatient treatment of seriously disturbed adolescents and young adults. Psychiatry: Interpersonal and Biological Processes 59: 82-107.

Blatt SJ, Ford RQ, Berman W, Cook B, Meyer R (1988) The assessment of change during the intensive treatment of borderline and schizophrenic young adults. Psychoanalytic Psychology 5: 127-58.

Blatt SJ, Zuroff DC, Bondi CM, Sanislow CA, Pilkonis PA (1998) When and how perfectionism impedes the brief treatment of depression: further analyses of the National Institute of Mental Health treatment of depression collaborative research program. Journal of Consulting and Clinical Psychology 66: 423-8.

Blos P (1962) On Adolescence: A Psychoanalytic Interpretation. New York: Free Press.

Blum HP (1982). Theories of the self and psychoanalytic concepts: discussion. Journal of the American Psychoanalytic Association 30: 959-78.

Blum HP (ed.) (1986) Defense and Resistance: Historical Perspectives and Current Concepts. New York: International Universities Press.

Blum HP (1994) Reconstruction in Psychoanalysis. New York: International Universities Press.

Boccia M, Campos JJ (1989) Maternal emotional signals, social referencing, and infants' reactions to strangers. New Directions for Child Development 44: 24-9.

Boesky D (1988) The concept of psychic structure. Journal of the American Psychoanalytic Association 36 (Suppl.): 113-5.

Boesky D (1989) A discussion of evidential criteria for therapeutic change. In A Rothstein (ed.), How Does Treatment Help? Models of Therapeutic Action of Psychoanalytic Therapy (pp. 171-80). Madison, CT: International Universities Press.

Bogdan RJ (1997) Interpreting minds. Cambridge, MA: MIT Press.

Bogdan RJ (2001) Minding Minds. Cambridge, MA: MIT Press.

Bolland J, Sandler J (1965) The Hampstead Psychoanalytic Index. New York: International Universities Press.

Bollas C (1987) The Shadow of the Object: Psychoanalysis of the Unthought Known. New York: Columbia University Press.

Bollas C (1989) Forces of Destiny: Psychoanalysis and Human Idiom. London: Free Association Books.

Bornstein RF, Masling JM (1985) Orality and latency of volunteering to serve as experimental subjects: a replication. Journal of Personality Assessment 49: 306–10.

Bouvet M (1958) Technical variations and the concept of distance. International Journal of Psycho-Analysis 39: 211–21.

Bower TR (1989) The Rational Infant: Learning in Infancy. New York: WH Freeman.

Bowers KS, Schacter DL (1990) Implicit memory and test awareness. Journal of Experimental Psychology: Learning, Memory, and Cognition 16: 404–16.

Bowlby J (1944) Forty-four juvenile thieves: their characters and home life. International Journal of Psycho-Analysis 25: 19–52.

Bowlby J (1951) Maternal Care and Mental Health. WHO Monograph Series, No. 2. Geneva: WHO.

Bowlby J (1956) The growth of independence in the young child. Royal Society of Health Journal 76: 587–91.

Bowlby J (1958) The nature of the child's tie to his mother. International Journal of Psycho-Analysis 39: 350–73.

Bowlby J (1960) Grief and mourning in infancy and early childhood. Psychoanalytic Study of the Child 15: 3–39.

Bowlby J (1969) Attachment and Loss, Vol. 1: Attachment. London: Hogarth Press and the Institute of Psycho-Analysis.

Bowlby J (1973) Attachment and Loss, Vol. 2: Separation: Anxiety and Anger. London: Hogarth Press and Institute of Psycho-Analysis.

Bowlby J (1979) The making and breaking of affectional bonds. British Journal of Psychiatry 130: 201–10, 421–31.

Bowlby J (1980) Attachment and Loss, Vol. 3: Loss: Sadness and Depression. London: Hogarth Press and Institute of Psycho-Analysis.

Bowlby J (1987) Attachment. In R Gregory (ed.), The Oxford Companion to the Mind (pp. 57–8). Oxford: Oxford University Press.

Bradley C (1997) Generativity-stagnation: development of a status model. Developmental Review 17: 262–90.

Brandschaft B, Stolorow RD (1987) The borderline concept: an intersubjective view. In JS Grotstein, JA Lang (eds), The Borderline Patient: Emerging Concepts in Diagnosis, Psychodynamics and Treatment (pp. 103–26). Hillsdale, NJ: The Analytic Press.

Bremner JD, Vermetten E (2001) Stress and development: behavioral and biological consequences. Development and Psychopathology 13: 473–89.

Bremner JD, Licinio J, Darnell A, Krystal JH, Nemeroff CB, Owens M, Charney DF (1997). Elevated CSF corticotropin-releasing factor concentrations in posttraumatic stress disorder. American Journal of Psychiatry 154: 624–9.

Brenneis CB (1994) Belief and suggestion in the recovery of memories of childhood sexual abuse. Journal of the American Psychoanalytic Association 42: 1027–53.

Brenner C (1959) The masochistic character: genesis and treatment. Journal of the American Psychoanalytic Association 7: 197–226.

Brenner C (1979) The components of psychic conflict and its consequences in mental life. Psychoanalytic Quarterly 48: 547–67.

Brenner C (1982) The Mind in Conflict. New York: International Universities Press.

Brenner C (1987) Working through: 1914-1984. The Psychoanalytic Quarterly 56: 68-108.

Brenner C (1994) The mind as conflict and compromise formation. Journal of Clinical Psychoanalysis 3: 473-88.

Brentano F (1924) Psychologie vom Empirischen Standpunkt. Leipzig: O. Kraus.

Bresleau N, Schultz I, Peterson E (1995) Sex differences in depression: a role for pre-existing anxiety. Psychiatric Research 58: 1-12.

Bretherton I (1985) Attachment theory: retrospect and prospect. Monographs of the Society for Research in Child Development 50(1-2): 3-35.

Bretherton I (1991) Pouring new wine into old bottles: the social self as internal working model. In MR Gunnar, LA Sroufe (eds), Self Processes and Development: Minnesota Symposia on Child Psychology (Vol. 23, pp. 1-41). Hillsdale, NJ: Lawrence Erlbaum Associates.

Bretherton I, Bates E, Benigni L, Camaioni L, Volterra V (1979) Relationships between cognition, communication, and quality of attachment. In E Bates, L Benigni, I Bretherton et al. (eds), The Emergence of Symbols. (pp. 223-69). New York: Academic Press.

Bretherton K, Munholland KA (1999) Internal working models in attachment relationships: a construct revisited. In J Cassidy, PR Shaver (eds), Handbook of Attachment: Theory, Research and Clinical Applications (pp. 89-114). New York: Guilford.

Breuer J, Freud S (1895) Studies on Hysteria. London: Hogarth Press.

Brewin CR, Andrews B, Gotlib IH (1993) Psychopathology and early experience: a reappraisal of retrospective reports. Psychological Bulletin 113: 82-98.

Bricker DC, Young JE (1993) A Client's Guide to Schema-Focused Cognitive Therapy. New York: Cognitive Therapy Center of New York.

Britton R (1989) The missing link: parental sexuality in the Oedipus complex. In R Britton, M Feldman, E O'Shaughnessy, J Steiner (eds), The Oedipus Complex Today: Clinical Implications (pp. 83-102). London: Karnac.

Britton R (1992) The Oedipus situation and the depressive position. In R Anderson (ed.), Clinical Lectures on Klein and Bion (pp. 34-45). London: Routledge.

Brockman B, Poynton A, Ryle A, Watson JP (1987) Effectiveness of time-limited therapy carried out by trainees: comparison of two methods. British Journal of Psychiatry 151: 602-9.

Brody S, Axelrad S (1978) Mothers, Fathers, and Children: Explorations in the Formation of Character in the First Seven Years. New York: International University Press.

Bromberg PM (1998) Standing in the Spaces. Hillsdale, NJ: The Analytic Press.

Bronstein C (2001) Kleinian Theory: A Contemporary Perspective. London: Whurr Publishers.

Brown D, Scheflin AW, Hammond DC (1998) Memory, Trauma Treatment and the Law: An Essential Reference on Memory for Clinicians, Researchers, Attorneys, and Judges. New York, NY: WW Norton & Co.

Brown GR, Anderson B (1991) Psychiatric morbidity in adult inpatients with childhood histories of sexual and physical abuse. American Journal of Psychiatry 148: 55-61.

Brown GW (1998) Loss and depressive disorders. In BP Dohrenwend (ed.), Adversity, Stress and Psychopathology. New York: Oxford University Press.

Brown GW, Harris TO (1978) Social Origins of Depression: A Study of Psychiatric Disorders in Women. London: Tavistock.

Brown GW, Harris TO (1989) Life Events and Illness. London: Unwin Hyman.

Brown GW, Harris TO, Bifuloc A (1986) Long-term effects of early loss of parent. In M Rutter, CE Izard, PB Read (eds), Depression in Young People: Developmental and Clinical Perspectives (pp. 251-96). New York: Guilford.

Brown GW, Harris TO, Hepworth C (1995) Loss, humiliation and entrapment among women developing depression: a patient and non-patient comparison. Psychological Medicine 25, 7-21.

Bruer JT (1999) The Myth of the First Three Years: A New Understanding of Early Development and Lifelong Learning. New York: Free Press.

Bruner J (1990) Acts of Meaning. Cambridge: Harvard University Press.

Bryant P (1986) Theories about the causes of cognitive development. In PLC v Geert (ed.), Theory Building in Developmental Psychology. Amsterdam: Elsevier Science Publishers BV (North-Holland).

Bucci W (1997a) Patterns of discourse in 'good' and troubled hours: a multiple code theory. Journal of the American Psychoanalytic Association 45: 155-87.

Bucci W (1997b) Psychoanalysis and Cognitive Science: A Multiple Code Theory. New York: Guilford Press.

Bucci W, Miller N (1993) Primary process: a new formulation and an analogue measure. In N Miller, L Luborsky, J Barber, J Docherty (eds), Psychodynamic Treatment Research (pp. 381-406). New York: Basic Books.

Buhle MJ (1998) Feminism and Its Discontents: A Century of Struggle with Psychoanalysis. Cambridge, MA: Harvard University Press.

Buie DH, Adler G (1982) Definitive treatment of the borderline personality. International Journal of Psychoanalytic Psychotherapy 9: 51-87.

Burke W (1992) Countertransference disclosure and the asymmetry/mutuality dilemma. Psychoanalytic Dialogues 2: 241-71.

Burland JA (1986) The vicissitudes of maternal deprivation. In RF Lax (eds.), Self and Object Constancy: Clinical and Theoretical Perspectives (pp. 324-7). New York: Guilford Press.

Burlingham D (1952) Twins: A Study of Three Pairs of Identical Twins. New York: International Universities Press.

Burlingham D, Barron AT (1963) A study of identical twins: their analytic material compared with existing observation data of their early childhood. Psychoanalytic Study of the Child 18: 367-423.

Bus AG, van IJzendoorn, MH (1992) Patterns of attachment in frequently and infrequently reading mother–child dyads. Journal of Genetic Psychology 153: 395-403.

Buss DM (1995) Evolutionary psychology: a new paradigm for psychological science. Psychological Inquiry 6: 1-30.

Butterworth GE (1991) The ontogeny and phylogeny of joint visual attention. In A Whiten (ed.), Natural Theories of Mind. Oxford: Basil Blackwell.

Byrne CP, Velamoor VR, Cernovsky ZZ, Cortese L, Losztyn S (1990) A comparison of borderline and schizophrenic patients for childhood live events and parent-child relationships. Canadian Journal of Psychiatry, 35, 590-5.

Call JD (1984). From early patterns of communication to the grammar of experience and syntax in infancy. In JD Call, E Galenson, RL Tyson (eds), Frontiers of Infant Psychiatry (pp. 15-29). New York: Basic Books.

Campbell K (1982) The psychotherapy relationship with borderline personality disorder. Psychotherapy: Theory, Practice and Research 19: 166-93.

Campbell SB, Shaw DS, Gilliom M (2000) Early externalizing behavior problems: toddlers and preschoolers at risk of later maladjustment. Development and Psychopathology 12: 467–88.

Campos JJ, Barrett KC, Lamb ME, Goldsmith HH, Stenberg C (1983) Socioemotional development. In MM Haith, JJ Campos (eds), Infancy and Developmental Psychobiology (4th edn, Vol. 2, pp. 783–915). New York: Wiley.

Camras LA, Sachs VB (1991) Social referencing and caretaker expressive behavior in a day care setting. Infant Behavior and Development 14: 27–36.

Caper R (1988) Immaterial Facts. Northvale, NJ: Jason Aronson.

Carlson EA (1998) A prospective longitudinal study of attachment disorganization/disorientation. Child Development 69: 1107–28.

Carlson J, Cicchetti D, Barnett D, Braunwald KG (1989) Finding order in disorganization: lessons from research on maltreated infants' attachments to their caregivers. In D Cicchetti, V Carlson (eds), Child Maltreatment: Theory and Research on the Causes and Consequences of Child Abuse and Neglect (pp. 494–528). Cambridge: Cambridge University Press.

Carlson SM, Moses LJ (2001) Individual differences in inhibitory control and children's theory of mind. Child Development 72: 1032–53.

Carlsson E, Sroufe LA (1995) Contribution of attachment theory to developmental psychopathology. In D Cicchetti, DJ Cohen (eds), Developmental Psychopathology. Vol. 1: Theory and Methods (pp. 581–617). New York: Wiley.

Carlsson V, Cicchetti D, Barnett D, Braunwald K (1989) Disorganised/disoriented attachment relationships in maltreated infants. Developmental Psychology 25:525–31.

Casement P (1985) On Learning from the Patient. London: Tavistock.

Casement P (1990) Further Learning From the Patient: The Analytic Space and Progress. London: Routledge.

Caspi A, Moffitt T (1993). When do individual differences matter? A paradoxical theory of personality coherence. Psychological Inquiry 4, 247–71.

Caspi A, Moffitt T (1995) The continuity of maladaptive behavior: from description to understanding in the study of antisocial behavior. In D Cicchetti, D Cohen (eds), Developmental Psychopathology, Vol 2: Risk, Disorder, and Adaption (pp. 472–511). New York: Wiley.

Cassidy J, Shaver PR (eds) (1999) Handbook of Attachment: Theory, Research and Clinical Applications. New York: Guilford.

Cassidy J, Kirsh SJ, Scolton KL, Parke RD (1996). Attachment and representations of peer relationships. Developmental Psychology 32: 892–904.

Cattell RB (1957) Personality and Motivation Structure and Measurement. Yonkers, NY: New World.

Cavell M (1994) The Psychoanalytic Mind. Cambridge, MA: Harvard University Press.

Champion LA, Goodall GM, Rutter M (1995) Behavioral problems in childhood and stressors in early adult life: a 20 year follow-up of London school children. Psychological Medicine 25, 231–46.

Chasseguet-Smirgel J. (ed.) (1970) Female Sexuality. Ann Arbor, MI: University of Michigan Press.

Chisolm K (1998) A three year follow-up of attachment and indiscriminate friendliness in children adopted from Russian orphanages. Child Development 69: 1092–1106.

Chodorow N (1978) Reproduction of Mothering. Berkeley, CA: University of California Press.

Chodorow N (1989) Feminism and Psychoanalytic Theory. Cambridge: Polity Press.

Chomsky N (1968) Language and Mind. New York: Harcourt, Brace and World.

Churchland PS., Ramachandran VS, Sejnowski TJ (1994) A critique of pure vision. In C Koch, JL Davis (eds), Large-Scale Neuronal Theories of the Brain (pp. 23-60). Cambridge, MA: MIT Press.

Cicchetti D (1989) Developmental psychopathology: some thoughts on its evolution. Development and Psychopathology 1: 1-4.

Cicchetti D (1990a) An historical perspective on the discipline of developmental psychopathology. In J Rolf, A Masten, D Cicchetti, S Weintraub (eds), Risk Protective Factors in the Development of Psychopathology (pp. 2-28). New York: Cambridge University Press.

Cicchetti D (1990b) The organization and coherence of socioemotional, cognitive, and representational development: illustrations through a developmental psychopathology perspective on Down syndrome and child maltreatment. In R Thompson (ed.), Socioemotional Development. Nebraska Symposium on Motivation (pp. 259-79). Lincoln, NB: University of Nebraska Press.

Cicchetti D, Barnett D (1991) Attachment organization in preschool aged maltreated children. Development and Psychopathology 3: 397-411.

Cicchetti D, Cohen DJ (1995a) Developmental Psychopathology, Vols 1 and 2. New York: John Wiley & Sons.

Cicchetti D, Cohen DJ (1995b) Perspectives on developmental psychopathology. In D Cicchetti, DJ Cohen (eds), Developmental Psychopathology, Vol. 1: Theory and Methods (pp. 3-23). New York: John Wiley & Sons.

Cicchetti D, Cummings EM, Greenberg MT, Marvin RS (1990) An organizational perspective on attachment beyond infancy. In D Cicchetti, MT Greenberg, EM Cummings (eds), Attachment in the Preschool Years: Theory, Research, and Intervention (pp. 3-49). Chicago, IL: University of Chicago Press.

Cicchetti D, Rogosch FA, Lynch M, Holt AD (1993) Resilience in maltreated children: processes leading to adaptive outcome. Development and Psychopathology 5: 629-47.

Cierpka M, Bucheim P, Freyberger HJ et al. (1995). Die erste Version einer Operationalisierten Psychodynamischen Diagnostik (OPD-1). Psychotherapeutics 40: 69-78.

Clark HH (1983) Language use and language users. In G Lindzey, E Aronson (eds), Handbook of Social Psychology (pp. 179-231). Reading, MA: Addison-Wesley.

Clarkin J (2001). Borderline personality disorder, mind and brain: a psychoanalytic perspective. Paper presented at the Plenary Presentation, 7th IPA Research Training Program, London, 10 August 2001.

Clarkin JF, Lenzenweger MF (1996) Major Theories of Personality Disorder. New York: Guilford.

Clarkin JF, Kernberg OF, Yeomans F (1999) Transference-Focused Psychotherapy for Borderline Personality Disorder Patients. New York, NY: Guilford Press.

Clarkin JF, Yeomans F, Kernberg OF (1998) Psychodynamic Psychotherapy of Borderline Personality Organization: A Treatment Manual. New York: Wiley.

Clarkin JF, Foelsch PA, Levy KN, Hull JW, Delaney JC, Kernberg OF (2001). The development of a psychodynamic treatment for patients with borderline personality disorder: a preliminary study of behavioral change. Journal of Personality Disorders 15: 487-95.

Clyman RB (1991) The procedural organization of emotions: a contribution from cognitive science to the psychoanalytic theory of therapeutic action. Journal of the American Psychoanalytic Association 39 (Supplement): 349-82.

Cohen DJ (1995) Psychosocial therapies for children and adolescents: overview and future directions. Journal of Abnormal Child Psychology 23: 141–56.

Cohen DJ, Towbin KE, Mayes L, Volkmar F (1994) Developmental psychopathology of multiplex developmental disorder. In SL Friedman, HC Haywood (eds), Developmental Follow-Up: Concepts, Domains and Methods (pp. 155–82). New York: Academic Press.

Cohn JF, Campbell SB (1992) Influence of maternal depression on infant affect regulation. In D Cicchetti, S Toth (eds), Rochester Symposium on Developmental Psychopathology: Vol. 4. A Developmental Approach to Affective Disorders (pp. 103–30). Rochester, NY: University of Rochester Press.

Cohn JF, Tronick EZ (1983) Three-month-old infants' reaction to simulated maternal depression. Child Development 54: 185–90.

Cohn JF, Tronick EZ (1988) Mother–infant interaction: Influence is bidirectional and unrelated to periodic cycles in either partner's behavior. Developmental Psychology 24: 386–92.

Cohn JF, Campbell SB, Matias R, Hopkins J (1990) Face-to-face interactions of postpartum depressed and nondepressed mother–infant pairs at 2 months. Developmental Psychology 26: 15–23.

Coie JD, Dodge KA (1998) Aggression and antisocial behavior. In W Damon (ed.), Handbook of Child Psychology (5th ed.): Vol. 3. Social, Emotional, and Personality Development (pp. 779–862). New York: Wiley.

Cole DA, Martin JM, Powers B, Truglio R (1996). Modelling causal relations between academic and social competence and depression: A multitrait-multimethod longitudinal study. Journal of Abnormal Psychology 105: 505–14.

Cole DA, Peeke LG, Martin JM, Truglio R, Seroczynski AD (1998) A longitudinal look at the relation between depression and anxiety in children and adolescents. Journal of Consulting and Clinical Psychology 66: 451–60.

Collins NL, Read SJ (1990) Adult attachment, working models and relationship quality in dating couples. Journal of Personality and Social Psychology 58: 644–63.

Collins NR, Read SJ (1994) Representations of attachment: the structure and function of working models. In K Bartholomew, D Perlman (eds), Advances in Personal Relationships Vol 5: Attachment Process in Adulthood (pp. 53–90). London: Jessica Kingsley Publishers.

Colvin CR, Block J, Funder DC (1995) Overly positive self-evaluations and personality: negative implications for mental health. J Pers Soc Psychol, 68(6): 1152–62.

Compton A (1981) On the psychoanalytic theory of instinctual drives: Part IV, Instinctual drives and the ego-id-superego model. Psychoanalytic Quarterly 50: 363–92.

Cooley CH (1964) Human Nature and the Social Order (revised edition). New York: Shocken Books (original work published 1902).

Cooper AM (1985) A historical review of psychoanalytic paradigms. In A Rothstein (ed.), Models of the Mind: Their Relationships to Clinical Work (pp. 5–20). New York: International Universities Press.

Cooper AM (1988) Our changing views of the therapeutic action of psychoanalysis: comparing Strachey and Loewald. Psychoanalytic Quarterly 57: 15–27.

Coplan JD, Andrews MW, Rosenblum LA, Owens MJ, Friedman S, Gorman JM, Nemeroff CB (1996) Persistent elevations of cerebrospinal fluid concentrations of corticotropin-releasing factor in adult nonhuman primates exposed to early life stressors: Implications for the pathophysiology of mood and anxiety disorders. Proceedings of the National Academy of Sciences 93: 1619–23.

Cowen EL, Wyman PA, Work WC, Parker GR (1990) The Rochester Child Resilience Project: overview and summary of first year findings. Development and Psychopathology 2: 193-212.

Cowmeadow P (1994) Deliberate self-harm and cognitive analytic therapy. International Journal of Short-Term Therapy 9: 135-50.

Craik K (1943) The Nature of Explanation. Cambridge: Cambridge University Press.

Crews F (1993) The Unknown Freud. New York Review of Books, November 18

Crews F (1995) The Memory Wars: Freud's Legacy in Dispute. London: Granta Books.

Crews F (1996) The verdict on Freud. Psychological Science 7:63-7.

Crick F, Koch C (2000) The unconscious homunculus. Neuro-psychoanalysis 2(1):3-11.

Crick NR, Dodge KA (1994) A review and reformulation of social information-processing mechanisms in children's social adjustment. Psychological Bulletin 115: 74-101.

Crits-Christoph P, Cooper A, Luborsky L. (1988). The accuracy of therapists' interpretations and the outcome of dynamic psychotherapy. Journal of Consulting and Clinical Psychology 56: 490-5.

Crittenden PM (1988) Relationships at risk. In J Belsky, T Nezworski (eds), Clinical Implications of Attachment (pp. 136-74). Hillsdale, NJ: Erlbaum.

Crittenden PM (1990) Internal representational models of attachment relationships. Infant Mental Health Journal 11: 259-77.

Crittenden PM (1994) Peering into the black box: an exploratory treatise on the development of self in young children. In D Cicchetti, SL Toth (eds), Disorders and Dysfunctions of the Self. Rochester Symposium on Developmental Psychopathology, Vol 5 (pp. 79-148). Rochester, NY: University of Rochester Press.

Crittenden PM, Ainsworth MDS (1989) Childhood maltreatment and attachment theory. In D Cicchetti, V Carlson (eds), Childhood Maltreatment: Theory and Research on the Causes and Consequences of Child Abuse and Neglect (pp. 432-63). Cambridge: Cambridge University Press.

Crittenden PM, DiLalla D (1988) Compulsive compliance: the development of an inhibitory coping strategy in infancy. Journal of Abnormal Child Psychology 16: 585-99.

Cummings EM, Cicchetti D (1990) Towards a transactional model of relations between attachment and depression. In D Cicchetti, MT Greenberg, EM Cummings (eds), Attachment in the Preschool Years: Theory, Research, and Intervention (pp. 339-72). Chicago, IL: University of Chicago Press.

Cummings EM, Davies PT (1994) Maternal depression and child development. Journal of Child Psychology and Psychiatry 35: 73-112.

Cummings EM, Zahn-Waxler C (1992) Emotions and the socialization of aggression: adults' angry behavior and children's arousal and aggression. In A Fraczek, H Zumkley (eds), Socialization and Aggression (pp. 61-84). New York and Heidelberg: Springer.

Damasio A (1999) The Feeling of What Happens: Body and Emotion in the Making of Consciousness. New York: Harcourt Brace.

Davidson D (1987) Knowing one's own mind. Proceedings and Addresses of the American Philosophical Association 60: 441-57.

Davidson M, Reichenberg A, Rabinowitz J, Weiser M, Kaplan Z, Mark M (1999) Behavioral and intellectual markers for schizophrenia in apparently healthy male adolescents. American Journal of Psychiatry 156: 1328-35.

Davidson R (1992) Emotion and affective style: hemispheric substrates. Psychological Science 3: 39-43.

Davies JM (1998) Between the disclosure and foreclosure of erotic transference-counter-transference: can psychoanalysis find a place for adult sexuality? Psychoanalytic Dialogues 8: 747–66.

Davies JM, Frawley MG (1994) Treating the Adult Survivor of Childhood Sexual Abuse: A Psychoanalytic Perspective. New York: Basic Books.

Davies PT, Cummings EM (1995) Marital conflict and child adjustment: an emotional security hypothesis. Psychological Bulletin 116: 387–411.

Davies PT, Cummings EM (1998) Exploring children's security as a mediator of the link between marital relations and child adjustment. Child Development 69: 124–39.

Deater-Deckard K, Fulker DW, Plomin R (1999) A genetic study of the family environment in the transition to early adolescence. Journal of Child Psychology and Psychiatry 40: 769–95.

DeBellis MD (2001) Developmental traumatology: the psychobiological development of maltreated children and its implications for research, treatment, and policy. Development and Psychopathology 13: 539–64.

DeCasper AJ, Carstens AA (1981) Contingencies of stimulation: effects on learning and emotion in neonates. Infant Behavior and Development 4: 19–35.

DeCasper AJ, Fifer WP (1980) Of human bonding: newborns prefer their mothers' voices. Science 208: 1174–76.

Demos EV (1989) Resiliency in infancy. In TF Dugan, R Coles (eds), The Child in Our Times (pp. 3–22). New York: Brunner-Mazel.

Dennett DC (1983) Styles of mental representation, Proceedings of the Aristotelian Society (pp. 213–26). London: Aristotelian Society.

Dennett DC, Haugeland JC (1987) Intentionality. In RL Gregory (ed.), The Oxford Companion to the Mind. Oxford: Oxford University Press.

Derogatis LR (1983) SCL-90-R: Administration, Scoring and Procedures – Manual II. Baltimore, MD: Clinical Psychometrics Research Inc.

Deutsch H (1942) Some forms of emotional disturbance and their relationship to schizophrenia. Psychoanalytic Quarterly 11: 301–21.

De Wolff MS, van IJzendoorn MH (1997) Sensitivity and attachment: a meta-analysis on parental antecedents of infant attachment. Child Development 68: 571–91.

Diamond A, Blatt SJ, Stayner D, Kaslow N (1991) Self-other Differentiation of Object Representations. Unpublished research manual: Yale University.

Dias MG, Harris PL (1990) The influence of the imagination on reasoning by young children. British Journal of Developmental Psychology 8: 305–18.

Diekstra RFW (1995) Depression and suicidal behaviors in adolescence: sociocultural and time trends. In M Rutter (ed.), Psychosocial Disturbances in Young People. Cambridge: Cambridge University Press.

Dixon NF (1981) Preconscious Processing. Chichester: Wiley.

Dodge K (1990) Developmental psychopathology in children of depressed mothers. Developmental Psychology 26: 3–6.

Doi T (1973) Anatomy of Dependence. Tokyo: Kodansha International Press.

Doidge N (2001) Introduction to Jeffery: why psychoanalysts have low mortality rates. Journal of the American Psychoanalytic Association 49: 97–102.

Dossman R, Kutter P, Heinzel R, Wurmser, L. (1997). The long-term benefits of intensive psychotherapy: a view from Germany. Psychoanalytic Inquiry, Special Supplement, Extended Dynamic Psychotherapy: Making the Case in the Era of Managed Care.

Downey G, Coyne JC (1990). Children of depressed parents: an integrative review. Psychological Bulletin 108: 50–76.

Dozier M (1990) Attachment organization and treatment use for adults with serious psychopathological disorders. Development and Psychopathology 2: 47–60.

Dozier M, Kobak R (1992) Psychophysiology in attachment interviews: converging evidence for deactivating strategies. Child Development 63:1473–80.

Dozier, M, Stovall KC, Albus KE (1999) Attachment and psychopathology in adulthood. In J Cassidy, PR Shaver (eds), Handbook of Attachment: Theory, Research and Clinical Applications (pp. 497–519). New York: Guilford.

Dozier M, Stevenson AI, Lee SW, Velligan DI (1991) Attachment organization and familiar overinvolvement for adults with serious psychopathological disorders. Development and Psychopathology 3: 475–89.

Dührssen A (1972) Analytische Psychotherapie in Theorie, Praxis und Ergebnissen. Göttingen: Vandenhoek and Ruprecht.

Duignan I, Mitzman SF (1994) Measuring individual change in patients receiving time-limited cognitive analytic therapy. International Journal of Time-Limited Psychotherapy 9: 151–60.

Dunkeld J, Bower TG (1980) Infant response to impending optical collision. Perception 9: 549–54.

Eagle MN (1984) Recent Developments in Psychoanalysis: A Critical Evaluation. Cambridge, MA: Harvard University Press.

Eagle MN (1997) Attachment and psychoanalysis. British Journal of Medical Psychology 70: 217–29.

Eagle MN (1998) The relationship between attachment theory and psychoanalysis. Paper presented at the Annual American Psychological Association Convention, Washington, DC.

Eagle MN (1999) Attachment research and theory and psychoanalysis. Paper presented at the Psychoanalytic Association of New York, November 15 1999.

Eaves LJ, Silberg JL, Meyer JM, Maes HH, Simonoff E, Pickles A, Rutter M, Neale MC, Reynolds CA, Erikson MT, Heath AC, Loeber R, Truett KR, Hewitt JK (1997). Genetics and developmental psychopathology: 2. The main effects of genes and environment on behavioral problems in the Virginia Twin Study of Adolescent Behavioral Development. J Child Psychol Psychiatry 38(8): 965–80.

Edelman GM (1987). Neural Darwinism: The Theory of Neuronal Group Selection. New York: Basic Books.

Edelman GM (1992) Bright Air, Brilliant Fire. New York: Basic Books.

Edgcumbe R (2000) Anna Freud: A View of Development, Disturbance and Therapeutic Techniques. London: Routledge.

Edgcumbe R, Burgner M (1973) Some problems in the conceptualisation of early object relationships: Part I: The concepts of need satisfaction and need-satisfying relationships. Psychoanalytic Study of the Child 27: 283–314.

Eggert LL, Thompson EA, Herting JR, Nicholas LJ (1995) Reducing suicide potential among high-risk youth: tests of a school-based prevention program. Suicide and Life-Threatening Behavior 25: 276–96.

Ehrenberg D (1993) The Intimate Edge. New York: Norton.

Eisenberg N, Fabes RA, Guthrie IK, Reiser M (2000) Dispositional emotionality and regulation: their role in predicting quality of social functioning. Journal of Personality and Social Psychology 78: 136–57.

Eisenberg N, Guthrie IK, Fabes RA, Shephard SA, Losoya SH, Murphy BC, Jones S, Poulin R, Reiser M (2000) Prediction of elementary school children's externalizing problem behaviors from attentional and behavioral regulation and negative emotionality. Child Development 71: 1367–82.

Ekecrantz L, Rudhe L (1972) Transitional phenomena: frequency, forms and functions of specially loved objects. Acta Psychiatry Scandinavia 48: 261-73.

Elicker J, Englund M, Sroufe LA (1992) Predicting peer competence and peer relationships in childhood from early parent–child relationships. In R Parke, G Ladd (eds), Family–Peer Relationships: Modes of Linkage (pp. 77-106). Hillsdale, NJ: Erlbaum.

Elkin I (1994) The NIMH treatment of depression collaborative research program: where we began and where we are. In AE Bergin, SL Garfield (eds), Handbook of Psychotherapy and Behavior Change (pp. 114-39). New York: Wiley.

Elmhirst S (1980) Transitional objects in transition. International Journal of Psycho-Analysis 61: 367-73.

Emde RN (1980a) Emotional availability: a reciprocal reward system for infants and parents with implications for prevention of psychosocial disorders. In PM Taylor, F Orlando (eds), Parent–Infant Relationships (pp. 87-115). New York: Grune & Stratton.

Emde RN (1980b) Toward a psychoanalytic theory of affect: Part 1, The organizational model and its propositions. In SI Greenspan, GH Pollock (eds), The Course of Life: Infancy and Early Childhood (pp. 63-83). Washington, DC: DHSS.

Emde RN (1980c) Toward a psychoanalytic theory of affect: Part II, Emerging models of emotional development in infancy. In SI Greenspan, GH Pollock (eds), The Course of Life: Infancy and Early Childhood (pp. 85-112). Washington, DC: DHSS.

Emde RN (1981) Changing models of infancy and the nature of early development: remodelling the foundation. Journal of the American Psychoanalytic Association 29: 179-219.

Emde RN (1983) Pre-representational self and its affective core. The Psychoanalytic Study of the Child 38: 165-92.

Emde RN (1988a) Development terminable and interminable II. Recent psychoanalytic theory and therapeutic considerations. International Journal of Psycho-Analysis 69: 283-6.

Emde RN (1988b) Development terminable and interminable. I. Innate and motivational factors from infancy. International Journal of Psycho-Analysis 69: 23-42.

Emde RN (1990) Mobilizing fundamental modes of development: empathic availability and therapeutic action. Journal of the American Psychoanalytic Association 38: 881-913.

Emde RN, Robinson JA (2000) Guiding principles for a theory of early intervention: a developmental-psychoanalytic perspective. In SJ Meisels, JP Shonkoff (eds), Handbook of Early Childhood Intervention, 2nd edn. New York: Cambridge University Press.

Emde RN, Spicer P (2000) Experience in the midst of variation: new horizons for development and psychopathology. Development and Psychopathology 12(3): 313-32.

Engel GL (1971) Attachment behavior, object relations and the dynamic point of view: a critical review of Bowlby's Attachment and Loss. International Journal of Psycho-Analysis 52:183-96.

Erdelyi MH (1985) Psychoanalysis: Freud's Cognitive Psychology. New York: WH Freeman.

Erickson MF, Sroufe LA, Egeland B (1985) The relationship between quality of attachment and behavior problems in preschool in a high-risk sample. Monographs of the Society for Research in Child Development 50(1-2): 147-66.

Erikson EH (1950) Childhood and Society. New York: Norton.

Erikson EH (1956) The problem of ego identity. Identity and the Life Cycle (pp. 104–64). New York: International Universities Press, 1959.

Erikson EH (1959) Identity and the Life Cycle. New York: International Universities Press.

Etchegoyen H (1991) The Fundamentals of Psychoanalytic Technique. London: Karnac.

Eysenck HJ (1952) The effects of psychotherapy: an evaluation. Journal of Consulting Psychology 16: 319–24.

Fagot BI, Kavanagh K (1990) The prediction of antisocial behavior from avoidant attachment classifications. Child Development 61: 864–73.

Fairbairn WRD (1940) Schizoid factors in the personality. An Object-Relations Theory of the Personality. New York: Basic Books, 1952.

Fairbairn WRD (1944) Endopsychic structure considered in terms of object-relationships. International Journal of Psycho-Analysis 25: 60–93.

Fairbairn WRD (1952a) An Object-Relations Theory of the Personality. New York: Basic Books, 1954.

Fairbairn WRD (1952b) Psychoanalytic Studies of the Personality. London: Tavistock.

Fairbairn WRD (1954) Observations on the nature of hysterical states. British Journal of Medical Psychology 29: 112–27.

Fairbairn WRD (1958) On the nature and aims of psychoanalytical treatment. International Journal of Psycho-Analysis 39: 374–85.

Fairbairn WRD (1963) Synopsis of an object-relations theory of the personality. International Journal of Psycho-Analysis 44: 224–5.

Fairburn CG (1994) Interpersonal psychotherapy for bulimia nervosa. In GL Klerman, MM Weissman (eds), New Application of Interpersonal Psychotherapy (pp. 353–78). New York: Guilford Press.

Fantz R (1963) Pattern vision in newborn infants. Science 140: 296–7.

Farrington DP, Barnes GC, Lambert S (1996) The concentration of offending in families. Legal and Criminological Psychology, 1, 47–63.

Fazio R, Jackson JR, Dunton B, Williams CJ (1995) Variability in automatic activation as an unobtrusive measure of racial attitudes: a bona fide pipeline? Journal of Personality and Social Psychology 69: 1013–27.

Feinman S (1991) Social Referencing and the Social Construction of Reality in Infancy. New York: Plenum Press.

Feiring C, Lewis M (1996) Finality in the eye of the beholder: multiple sources, multiple time points, multiple paths. Development and Psychopathology 8: 721–33.

Fendrich M, Warner V, Weissman MM (1990) Family risk factors, parental depression, and psychopathology in offspring. Developmental Psychology 26: 40–50.

Fenichel O (1941) Problems of Psychoanalytic Technique. New York: Psychoanalytic Quarterly.

Fenichel O (1945) The Psychoanalytic Theory of Neurosis. New York and London: Norton and Routledge.

Ferenczi S (1913) Stages in the development of the sense of reality. First Contributions to Psycho-Analysis (pp. 213–44). London: Karnac Books, 1980.

Ferenczi S (1930) Notes and Fragments, II. New York: Basic Books, 1952.

Fergusson DM, Lynskey MT, Horwood LJ (1993) The effect of maternal depression on maternal ratings of child behavior. Journal of Abnormal Child Psychology 21:245–69.

Field T (1987a) Affective and interactive disturbances in infants. In JD Osofsky (ed.), Handbook of Infant Development (Vol. 2, pp. 972–1005). New York: John Wiley.

Field T (1987b) Interaction and attachment in normal and atypical infants. Journal of Consulting and Clinical Psychology 55: 853–9.

Field T (1989) Maternal depression effects on infant interaction and attachment behavior. In D Cicchetti (ed.), Rochester Symposium on Developmental Psychopathology, Vol.1: The Emergence of a Discipline (pp. 139–63). Hillsdale, NJ: Erlbaum.

Field T (1992) Infants of depressed mothers. Development and Psychopathology 4:49–6.

Field T, Healy B, Goldstein S, Guthertz M (1990) Behavior-state matching and synchrony in mother-infant interactions of nondepressed vs. depressed dyads. Developmental Psychology 26: 7–14.

Field T, Healy B, Goldstein S, Perry S, Bendell D, Schanberg S, Zimmerman E, Kuhn C (1988) Infants of depressed mothers show 'depressed' behavior even with nondepressed adults. Child Development 59: 1569–79.

Fiscalini J, Mann CH, Stern DB (1995) Handbook of Interpersonal Psychoanalysis. Hillsdale, NJ: The Analytic Press.

Fischer KW, Ayoub C (1994) Affective splitting and dissociation in normal and maltreated children: developmental pathways for self in relationships. In D Cicchetti, SL Toth (eds), Rochester Symposium on Developmental Psychopathology: Vol. 5. Disorders and Dysfunctions of the Self (pp. 149–222). Rochester, NY: University of Rochester Press.

Fisher C, Byrne J, Edwards A, Karn E (1970) The psychophysiological study of nightmares. Journal of the American Psychoanalytic Association 18: 747–82.

Fisher S (1973) The Female Orgasm. New York: Basic Books.

Fisher S, Greenberg R (1977) The Scientific Credibility of Freud's Theories and Therapy. Brighton: Harvester Press.

Fisher S, Greenberg R (1996) Freud Scientifically Reappraised: Testing the Theories and Therapy. New York: John Wiley & Sons, Inc.

Fivush R, Haden C, Reese E (1996) Autobiographical knowledge and autobiographical memories. In DC Rubin (ed.), Remembering our Past: Studies in Autobiographical Memory (pp. 341–59). New York: Cambridge University Press.

Flament MF, Rapaport JL (1984) Childhood obsessive compulsive disorders. In TR Insel (ed.), New Findings in Obsessive Compulsive Disorder (pp. 24–43). Washington, DC: American Psychiatric Press.

Flament MF, Whitaker A, Rapaport JL (1988) Obsessive compulsive disorder in adolescence: an epidemiological study. Journal of the American Academy of Child and Adolescent Psychiatry 27: 764–71.

Fleming J (1975) Some observations on object constancy in the psychoanalysis of adults. Journal of the American Psychoanalytic Association 23: 743–59.

Foa EB, Kozak MJ (1986) Emotional processing of fear: exposure to corrective information. Psychological Bulletin 99: 20–35.

Fodor JA, Pylyshyn ZW (1988). Connectionism and cognitive architecture: a critical analysis. Cognition 28: 3–71.

Fodor JA, Bever T, Garrett MF (1974) The Psychology of Language. New York: McGraw-Hill.

Fogel GI (1989) The authentic function of psychoanalytic theory: an overview of the contributions of Hans Loewald. Psychoanalytic Quarterly 58: 419–51.

Fonagy P (1991) Thinking about thinking: some clinical and theoretical considerations in the treatment of a borderline patient. International Journal of Psycho-Analysis 72:1–18.

Fonagy P (1995a) Mental representations from an intergenerational cognitive science perspective. Infant Mental Health Journal 15: 57–68.

Fonagy P (1995b) Playing with reality: the development of psychic reality and its malfunction in borderline patients. International Journal of Psycho-Analysis 76: 39–44.

Fonagy P. (1996a) The future of an empirical psychoanalysis. British Journal of Psychotherapy 13: 106–18.

Fonagy P (1996b) Irrelevance of infant observations. Journal of the American Psychoanalytic Association 44: 404–22.

Fonagy P (1997) Attachment and theory of mind: overlapping constructs? Association for Child Psychology and Psychiatry Occasional Papers 14: 31–40.

Fonagy P (1999a) Achieving evidence-based psychotherapy practice: a psychodynamic perspective on the general acceptance of treatment manuals. Clinical Psychology: Science and Practice 6: 442–4.

Fonagy P (1999b) Memory and therapeutic action (guest editorial). International Journal of Psycho-Analysis 80: 215–23.

Fonagy P, Higgitt A (1984) Personality Theory and Clinical Practice. London and New York: Methuen.

Fonagy P, Moran GS (1991) Studies of the efficacy of child psychoanalysis. Journal of Consulting and Clinical Psychology 58: 684–95.

Fonagy P, Target M (1995) Understanding the violent patient: the use of the body and the role of the father. International Journal of Psycho-Analysis 76: 487–502.

Fonagy P, Target M (1996a) Playing with reality: I. Theory of mind and the normal development of psychic reality. International Journal of Psycho-Analysis 77: 217–33.

Fonagy P, Target M (1996b) Predictors of outcome in child psychoanalysis: a retrospective study of 763 cases at the Anna Freud Centre. Journal of the American Psychoanalytic Association 44: 27–77.

Fonagy P, Target M (1996c) Psychodynamic developmental therapy for children: a contemporary application of child psychoanalysis. In ED Hibbs, PS Jensen (eds), Psychosocial Treatment Research with Children and Adolescents. Washington, DC: National Institutes of Health and the American Psychological Association.

Fonagy P, Target M (1997) Perspectives on the recovered memories debate. In J Sandler, P Fonagy (eds), Recovered Memories of Abuse: True or False? (pp. 183–216). London: Karnac Books.

Fonagy P, Target M (2000) Playing with reality III: The persistence of dual psychic reality in borderline patients. International Journal of Psychoanalysis 81(5): 853–74.

Fonagy P, Moran GS, Target M (1993) Aggression and the psychological self. International Journal of Psycho-Analysis 74: 471–85.

Fonagy P, Redfern S, Charman T (1997) The relationship between belief-desire reasoning and a projective measure of attachment security (SAT). British Journal of Developmental Psychology 15, 51–61.

Fonagy P, Steele H, Steele M (1991) Maternal representations of attachment during pregnancy predict the organization of infant–mother attachment at one year of age. Child Development 62: 891–905.

Fonagy P, Target M, Gergely G (2000) Attachment and borderline personality disorder: a theory and some evidence. Psychiatric Clinics of North America 23: 103–22.

Fonagy P, Gergely G, Jurist E, Target M (2002). Affect Regulation and Mentalization: Developmental, Clinical and Theoretical Perspectives. New York: Other Press.

Fonagy P, Edgcumbe R, Moran GS, Kennedy H, Target M (1993) The roles of mental representations and mental processes in therapeutic action. The Psychoanalytic Study of the Child 48: 9–48.

Fonagy P, Edgcumbe R, Target M, Miller J, Moran G (unpublished manuscript). Contemporary Psychodynamic Child Therapy: Theory and Technique.

Fonagy P, Miller J, Edgcumbe R, Target M, Kennedy H (1993) The Hampstead Manual of Psychodynamic Therapy for Children.

Fonagy P, Moran GS, Edgcumbe R, Kennedy H, Target M (1993). The roles of mental representations and mental processes in therapeutic action. The Psychoanalytic Study of the Child 48: 9–48.

Fonagy P, Steele H, Moran GS, Steele M, Higgitt A (1991) The capacity for understanding mental states: the reflective self in parent and child and its significance for security of attachment. Infant Mental Health Journal 13: 200–17.

Fonagy P, Steele M, Moran GS, Steele M, Higgitt A (1992) The integration of psychoanalytic theory and work on attachment: the issue of intergenerational psychic processes. In D Stern, M Ammaniti (eds), Attaccamento e Psiconalis (pp. 19–30). Bari, Italy: Laterza.

Fonagy P, Steele M, Moran GS, Steele M, Higgitt A (1993) Measuring the ghost in the nursery: an empirical study of the relation between parents' mental representations of childhood experiences and their infants' security of attachment. Journal of the American Psychoanalytic Association 41: 957–89.

Fonagy P, Steele M, Steele H, Higgitt A, Target M (1994). Theory and practice of resilience. Journal of Child Psychology and Psychiatry 35: 231–57.

Fonagy P, Kachele H, Krause R, Jones E, Perron R, Lopez L (1999) An Open Door Review of Outcome Studies in Psychoanalysis. London: International Psychoanalytical Association.

Fonagy P, Steele M, Steele H, Leigh T, Kennedy R, Mattoon G Target M (1995) Attachment, the reflective self, and borderline states: the predictive specificity of the Adult Attachment Interview and pathological emotional development. In S Goldberg, R Muir, J Kerr (eds), Attachment Theory: Social, Developmental and Clinical Perspectives (pp. 233–78). New York: Analytic Press.

Fonagy P, Leigh T, Steele M, Steele H, Kenndy R, Mattoon G, Target M, Gerber A (1996). The relation of attachment status, psychiatric classification, and response to psychotherapy. Journal of Consulting and Clinical Psychology 64: 22–31.

Ford ME (1979) The construct validity of egocentrism. Psychological Bulletin 86: 1169–89.

Forehand R, Lautenschlager GJ, Faust J, Graziano WG (1986) Parent perceptions and parent-child interactions in clinic-referred children: a preliminary investigation of the effects of maternal depressive moods. Behavior Research and Therapy 24: 73–5.

Fosbury JA (1994). Cognitive analytic therapy with poorly controlled type I diabetic patients. Paper presented at the European Association for the Study of Diabetes, Dusseldorf, Germany, September 27– October 1.

Foulkes D (1978) A Grammar of Dreams. New York: Basic Books.

Fraiberg S (1969) Libidinal object constancy and mental representation. The Psychoanalytic Study of the Child 24: 9–47.

Fraiberg S (1980) Clinical Studies in Infant Mental Health. New York: Basic Books.

Fraiberg S (1982) Pathological defenses in infancy. Psychoanalytic Quarterly 51: 612–35.

Fraiberg SH, Adelson E, Shapiro V (1975) Ghosts in the nursery: a psychoanalytic approach to the problem of impaired infant-mother relationships. Journal of the American Academy Child Psychiatry 14: 387-422.

Francis DD, Caldji C, Champagne F, Plotsky PM, Meaney MJ (1999) The role of corticotropine-releasing factor-norepinephrine systems in mediating the effects of early experience on the development of behavioral and endocrine responses to stress. Biological Psychiatry 46: 1153-66.

Frank E, Kupfer DJ, Wagner EF, McEachrn AB, Cornes C (1991) Efficacy of interpersonal therapy as a maintenance treatment of recurrent depression. Archives of General Psychiatry 48: 1053-59.

Frank J (1956) Contribution to scientific proceedings, reported by LL Robbins. Journal of the American Psychoanalytic Association 4: 561-2.

Free K (1988) Transitional object attachment and creative activity in adolescence. In PC Horton, H Gewirtz, KJ Kreutter (eds), The Solace Paradigm: An Eclectic Search for Psychological Immunity (pp. 145-58). Madison, CT: International Universities Press.

Freedman N, Hoffenberg JD, Vorus N, Frosch A (1999) The effectiveness of psychoanalytic psychotherapy: the role of treatment duration, frequency of sessions, and the therapeutic relationship. Journal of the American Psychoanalytic Association 47: 741-72.

Freud A (1926) Four lectures on child analysis, The Writings of Anna Freud, Vol. 1 (pp. 3-69). New York: International Universities Press.

Freud A (1936) The Ego and the Mechanisms of Defence. New York: International Universities Press, 1946.

Freud A (1941-45) Reports on the Hampstead Nurseries. The Writings of Anna Freud. New York: International Universities Press, 1974.

Freud A (1949) On certain difficulties in the pre-adolescent's relation to his parents. The Writings of Anna Freud (Vol. 4, pp. 489-97). New York: International Universities Press.

Freud A (1954) The widening scope of indications for psychoanalysis: discussion. Journal of the American Psychoanalytical Association 2: 607-20.

Freud A (1955) The concept of the rejecting mother. The Writings of Anna Freud (pp. 586-602). New York: International University Press, 1968.

Freud A (1958) Adolescence. The Psychoanalytic Study of the Child 13: 255-78.

Freud A (1960) Discussion of Dr. Bowlby's paper (Grief and mourning in infancy and early childhood), The Writings of Anna Freud (pp. 167-86). New York: International University Press, 1969.

Freud A (1962) Assessment of childhood disturbances. The Psychoanalytic Study of the Child 17: 149-58.

Freud A (1963) The concept of developmental lines. The Psychoanalytic Study of the Child 18: 245-65.

Freud A (1965) Normality and Pathology in Childhood. Harmondsworth: Penguin Books.

Freud A (1969) Adolescence as a developmental disturbance. The Writings of Anna Freud (Vol. 7, pp. 39-47). New York: International Universities Press.

Freud A (1970a) The symptomatology of childhood: a preliminary attempt at classification. The Writings of Anna Freud: Vol 7 Psychoanalytic Psychology of Normal Development 1970-1980 (pp. 157-88). London: Hogarth Press and the Institute of Psychoanalysis.

Freud A (1970b) The Writings of Anna Freud: Vol 8 Psychoanalytic Psychology of Normal Development 1970-1980. London: Hogarth Press and the Institute of Psychoanalysis.

Freud A (1974) A psychoanalytic view of developmental psychopathology. The Writings of Anna Freud, 8 (pp. 119-36). New York: International Universities Press, 1981.

Freud A (1976) Changes in Psychoanalytic Practice and Experience. New York: International University Press, 1981.

Freud A (1978) The principal task of child analysis. The Writings of Anna Freud (Vol. 8, pp. 96-109). New York: International Universities Press, 1981.

Freud A (1981a) Child analysis as the study of mental growth, normal and abnormal. The Writings of Anna Freud (Vol. 8, pp. 315-30). New York: International Universities Press, 1981.

Freud A (1981b) The concept of developmental lines: their diagnostic significance. The Psychoanalytic Study of the Child 36: 129-36.

Freud A (1983) Problems of pathogenesis: introduction to the discussion. The Psychoanalytic Study of the Child 38: 383-8.

Freud A, Burlingham D (1944) Infants without Families. New York: International Universities Press.

Freud A, Burlingham D (1974) Reports on the Hampstead nurseries. Infants without Families and Reports on the Hampstead Nurseries 1939-1945 (pp. 3-540). London: Hogarth.

Freud S (1895) Project for a scientific psychology. In J Strachey (ed.), The Standard Edition of the Complete Psychological Works of Sigmund Freud (Vol. 1, pp. 281-93). London: Hogarth Press.

Freud S (1900) The interpretation of dreams. In J Strachey (ed.), The Standard Edition of the Complete Psychological Works of Sigmund Freud (Vol. 4, 5, pp. 1-715). London: Hogarth Press.

Freud S (1901) The psychopathology of everyday life. In J Strachey (ed.), The Standard Edition of the Complete Psychological Works of Sigmund Freud (Vol. 6, pp. 1-190). London: Hogarth Press.

Freud S (1904a) Freud's psycho-analytic procedure. In J Strachey (ed.), The Standard Edition of the Complete Psychological Works of Sigmund Freud (Vol. 7, pp. 247-54). London: Hogarth Press.

Freud S (1904b) Freud's psychoanalytic procedure. In J Strachey (ed.), The Standard Edition of the Complete Psychological Works of Sigmund Freud (Vol. 7, pp. 247-54). London: Hogarth Press.

Freud S (1905a) Fragment of an analysis of a case of hysteria. In J Strachey (ed.), The Standard Edition of the Complete Psychological Works of Sigmund Freud (Vol. 7, pp. 7-122). London, UK: Hogarth Press.

Freud S (1905b) Jokes and their relation to the unconscious. In J Strachey (ed.), The Standard Edition of the Complete Psychological Works of Sigmund Freud (Vol. 8, pp. 1-236). London: Hogarth Press.

Freud S (1905c) On psychotherapy. In J Strachey (ed.), The Standard Edition of the Complete Psychological Works of Sigmund Freud (Vol. 7, pp. 255-68). London: Hogarth Press.

Freud S (1905d) Three essays on the theory of sexuality. In J Strachey (ed.), The Standard Edition of the Complete Psychological Works of Sigmund Freud (Vol. 7, pp. 123-230). London: Hogarth Press.

Freud S (1906) My views on the part played by sexuality in the aetiology of the neuroses. In J Strachey (ed.), The Standard Edition of the Complete Psychological Works of Sigmund Freud (Vol. 7, pp. 269–80). London: Hogarth Press.

Freud S (1908a) Character and anal eroticism. In J Strachey (ed.), Standard Edition of the Complete Works of Sigmund Freud (Vol. 9 pp. 167–175). London: Hogarth Press.

Freud S (1908b). 'Civilized' sexual morality and modern nervous illness. In J Strachey (ed.), The Standard Edition of the Complete Psychological Works of Sigmund Freud (Vol. 9, pp. 177-204). London: Hogarth Press.

Freud S (1909) Analysis of a phobia in a five-year-old boy. In J Strachey (ed.), The Standard Edition of the Complete Psychological Works of Sigmund Freud (Vol. 10, pp. 1–147). London: Hogarth Press.

Freud S (1911a). Formulations on the two principles of mental functioning. In J Strachey (ed.), The Standard Edition of the Complete Psychological Works of Sigmund Freud (pp. 67-104). London: Hogarth Press.

Freud S (1911b) Psycho-Analytic notes upon an autobiographical account of a case of paranoia (Dementia Paranoides). In J Strachey (ed.), The Standard Edition of the Complete Psychological Works of Sigmund Freud (Vol. 12 pp. 3–82). London: Hogarth Press.

Freud S (1912a) The dynamics of transference. In J Strachey (ed.), The Standard Edition of the Complete Psychological Works of Sigmund Freud (Vol 12 pp. 97–109). London: Hogarth Press and the Institute of Psycho-Analysis.

Freud S (1912b) A note on the unconscious in psycho-analysis. In J Strachey (ed.), The Standard Edition of the Complete Psychological Works of Sigmund Freud (Vol. 12, pp. 257-66). London: Hogarth Press and the Institute of Psycho-Analysis.

Freud S (1912c) Recommendations to physicians practising psychoanalysis. In J Strachey (ed.), The Standard Edition of the Complete Psychological Works of Sigmund Freud (Vol. 12, pp. 109-20). London: Hogarth Press.

Freud S (1913a) The disposition to obsessional neurosis. In J Strachey (ed.), The Standard Edition of the Complete Psychological Works of Sigmund Freud (Vol. 12 pp. 317-326). London: Hogarth Press.

Freud S (1913b) On beginning treatment. In J Strachey (ed.), The Standard Edition of the Complete Psychological Works of Sigmund Freud (Vol. 12, pp. 121-44). London: Hogarth Press.

Freud S (1913c) Totem and taboo. In J Strachey (ed.), The Standard Edition of the Complete Psychological Works of Sigmund Freud (Vol. 13 pp. 1-161). London: Hogarth Press.

Freud S (1914) On narcissism: an introduction. In J Strachey (ed.), The Standard Edition of the Complete Psychological Works of Sigmund Freud (Vol. 14, pp. 67-104). London: Hogarth Press.

Freud S (1915a) Instincts and their vicissitudes. In J Strachey (ed.), The Standard Edition of the Complete Psychological Works of Sigmund Freud (Vol. 14, pp. 109-40). London: Hogarth Press.

Freud S (1915b) Mourning and melancholia. In J Strachey (ed.), The Standard Edition of the Complete Psychological Works of Sigmund Freud (Vol. 14, pp. 237-258). London: Hogarth Press.

Freud S (1915c) Repression. In J Strachey (ed.), The Standard Edition of the Complete Psychological Works of Sigmund Freud (Vol. 14, pp. 143-58).

Freud S (1916) Introductory lectures on psycho-analysis. In J Strachey (ed.), The Standard Edition of the Complete Psychological Works of Sigmund Freud (Vols 15, 16, pp. 13-477). London: Hogarth Press.

Freud S (1916-17) Analytic therapy. Lecture XXVIII in introductory lectures on psycho-analysis. In J Strachey (ed.), The Standard Edition of the Complete Psychological Works of Sigmund Freud (Vol. 17, pp. 448-63). London: Hogarth.

Freud S (1920) Beyond the pleasure principle. In J Strachey (ed.), The Standard Edition of the Complete Psychological Works of Sigmund Freud (Vol. 18, pp. 1-64). London: Hogarth Press.

Freud S (1923) The ego and the id. In J Strachey (ed.), The Standard Edition of the Complete Psychological Works of Sigmund Freud (Vol. 19, pp. 1-59). London: Hogarth Press.

Freud S (1924a) The dissolution of the Oedipus complex. In J Strachey (ed.), The Standard Edition of the Complete Psychological Works of Sigmund Freud (Vol. 19, pp. 173-82). London: Hogarth Press.

Freud S (1924b) The loss of reality in neurosis and psychosis. In J Strachey (ed.), The Standard Edition of the Complete Psychological Works of Sigmund Freud (Vol. 19, pp. 183-90). London: Hogarth Press.

Freud S (1926) Inhibitions, symptoms and anxiety. In J Strachey (ed.), The Standard Edition of the Complete Psychological Works of Sigmund Freud (Vol. 20, pp. 77-172). London: Hogarth Press.

Freud S (1927) Fetishism. In J Strachey (ed.), The Standard Edition of the Complete Psychological Works of Sigmund Freud (Vol. 21, pp. 152-7). London: Hogarth Press.

Freud S (1930) Civilization and its discontents. In J Strachey (ed.), The Standard Edition of the Complete Psychological Works of Sigmund Freud (Vol. 21, pp. 57-146). London: Hogarth Press.

Freud S (1931a) Female sexuality. In J Strachey (ed.), The Standard Edition of the Complete Psychological Works of Sigmund Freud (Vol. 21, pp. 221-46). London: Hogarth Press.

Freud S (1931b) Libidinal types. In J Strachey (ed.), The Standard Edition of the Complete Psychological Works of Sigmund Freud (Vol. 21, pp. 215-20). London: Hogarth Press.

Freud S (1933) New introductory lectures on psychoanalysis. In J Strachey (ed.), The Standard Edition of the Complete Psychological Works of Sigmund Freud (Vol. 22, pp. 1-182). London: Hogarth Press.

Freud S (1937) Analysis terminable and interminable. In J Strachey (ed.), The Standard Edition of the Complete Psychological Works of Sigmund Freud (Vol. 23, pp. 209-53). London: Hogarth Press.

Freud S (1939) Moses and monotheism. In J Strachey (ed.), The Standard Edition of the Complete Psychological Works of Sigmund Freud (Vol. 23, pp. 3-137). London: Hogarth Press.

Freud S (1940) Splitting of the ego in the process of defense. In J Strachey (ed.), The Standard Edition of the complete Psychological Works of Sigmund Freud (Vol. 23, pp. 275-78). London: Hogarth Press.

Freud S, Breuer J (1895) Studies on hysteria. In J Strachey (ed.), The Standard Edition of the Complete Psychological Works of Sigmund Freud (Vol. 2, pp. 1-305). London: Hogarth Press.

Friedan B (1963) The Feminine Mystique. New York: Norton.

Friedlander BZ (1970) Receptive language development in infancy. Merrill-Palmer Quarterly 16: 7-51.

Friedman L (1986) An Appreciation of Hans Loewald's 'On the Therapeutic Action of Psychoanalysis'.

Friedman L (1988) The clinical polarity of object relations concepts. Psychoanalytic Quarterly 57: 667–91.

Friedman SM (1952) An empirical study of the castration and Oedipus complexes. Genetic Psychology Monographs 46: 61–130.

Frieswyk S, Colson D (1980) Prognostic considerations in the hospital treatment of borderline states: the perspective of object relations theory and the Rorschach. In J Kwawer (ed.), Borderline Phenomena and the Rorschach Test (pp. 229–56). New York: International Universities Press.

Frith CD, Frith U (1999) Interacting minds – a biological basis. Science 286(5445): 1692–95.

Fromm-Reichmann F (1948) Notes on the development of treatment of schizophrenics by psychoanalytic psychotherapy. Psychiatry 11: 263–73.

Gaddini R, Gaddini E (1970) Transitional objects and the process of individuation: a study in three different social groups. Journal of the American Academy of Child Psychiatry 9: 347–65.

Gardner RW, Holzman PS, Klein GS, Linton HB, Spence DP (1959) Cognitive Control: A Study of Individual Consistencies in Cognitive Behavior. New York: International Universities Press.

Garmezy N (1983) Stressors of childhood. In N Garmezy, M Rutter (eds), Stress, Coping, and Development in Children (pp. 43–84). Baltimore, MD: John Hopkins University Press.

Garmezy N (1985) Stress-resistant children: the search for protective factors. In JE Stevenson (ed.), Recent Research in Developmental Psychopathology. Journal of Child Psychology and Psychiatry Book. Oxford: Pergamon Press.

Garmezy N, Masten A (1991) The protective role of competence indicators in children at risk. In EM Cummings, AL Greene, KK Karraker (eds), Life-span Developmental Psychology: Perspectives on Stress and Coping (pp. 151–74). Hillsdale, NJ: Erlbaum.

Garmezy N, Masten A (1994) Chronic adversities. In M Rutter, E Taylor, L Hersov (eds), Child and Adolescent Psychiatry: Modern Approaches (pp. 191–208). Oxford: Blackwell Scientific Publications.

Garmezy N, Rutter M (1983) Stress, Coping, and Development in Children. New York: McGraw-Hill.

Gazzaniga MS (1985) The Social Brain: Discovering the Networks of the Mind. New York: Basic Books.

Ge X, Conger RD, Simmons RL (1996) Parenting behaviors and the occurrence and co-occurrence of adolescent symptoms and conduct problems. Developmental Psychology 32: 717–31.

Ge X, Best K, Conger RD, Simons RL (1996) Parenting behaviors and the occurrence and co-occurrence of adolescent symptoms and conduct problems. Developmental Psychology 32: 717–31.

Ge X, Conger RD, Cadoret R, Neiderhiser J, Yates W (1996) The developmental interface between nature and nurture: a mutual influence model of child antisocial behavior and parent behavior. Developmental Psychology 32: 574–89.

Gedo JE (1979) Beyond Interpretation. New York: International Universities Press.

Gedo JE (1980) Reflections on some current controversies in psychoanalysis. Journal of the American Psychoanalytic Association 28: 363–83.

George C, Kaplan N, Main M (1985) The Adult Attachment Interview. Unpublished manuscript, Department of Psychology, University of California at Berkeley.

Gergely G (1991) Developmental reconstructions: infancy from the point of view of psychoanalysis and developmental psychology. Psychoanalysis and Contemporary Thought 14: 3–55.

Gergely G (2001) The development of understanding of self and agency. In U Goshwami (ed.), Handbook of Childhood Cognitive Development. Oxford: Blackwell.

Gergely G, Watson J (1996) The social biofeedback model of parental affect-mirroring. International Journal of Psycho-Analysis 77: 1181–1212.

Gergely G, Watson J (1999) Early social-emotional development: contingency perception and the social biofeedback model. In P Rochat (ed.), Early Social Cognition: Understanding Others in the First Months of Life (pp. 101–37). Hillsdale, NJ: Erlbaum.

Gergely G, Nadasdy Z, Csibra G, Biro S (1995) Taking the intentional stance at 12 months of age. Cognition 56: 165–93.

Gianino AF, Tronick EZ (1988) The mutual regulation model: the infant's self and interactive regulation and coping and defensive capacities. In TM Field, PM McCabe, N Schneiderman (eds), Stress and Coping Across Development (pp. 47–68). Hillsdale, NJ: Erlbaum.

Gill MM (1976) Metapsychology is not psychology. In MM Gill, PS Holzman (eds), Psychology versus Metapsychology: Essays in Memory of George S. Klein. New York: International Universities Press.

Gill MM (1982) Analysis of Transference, Vol I: Theory and Technique. New York: International Universities Press.

Gill MM (1983) The interpersonal paradigm and the degree of the therapist's involvement. Contemporary Psychoanalysis 19: 200–37.

Gill MM (1994) Psychoanalysis in Transition: A Personal View. Hillsdale, NJ: Analytic Press.

Gill MM, Hoffman I (1982) A method for studying the analysis of aspects of the patient's experience of the relationship in psychoanalysis and psychotherapy. Journal of the American Psychoanalytic Association 30: 137–67.

Gilligan C (1982) In a Different Voice: Psychological Theory and Women's Development. Cambridge, MA: Harvard University Press.

Gilligan J (1997) Violence: Our Deadliest Epidemic and Its Causes. New York: Grosset/Putnam.

Giovacchini P (1987) The 'unreasonable' patient and the psychotic transference. In JS Grotstein, MF Solomon, JA Lang (eds), The Borderline Patient: Emerging Concepts in Diagnosis, Psychodynamics and Treatment (pp. 59–68). Hillsdale, NJ: The Analytic Press.

Gitelson M (1955) Contribution to scientific proceedings, reported by L Rangell. Journal of the American Psychoanalytic Association 3: 294–5.

Glasser M (1986) Identification and its vicissitudes as observed in the perversions. Int J Psychoanal 67 (Pt 1): 9–17.

Glover E (1924/1956) Notes on oral character formation. In E Glover (ed.), On the Oral Development of the Mind. London: Mayo.

Glover E (1945) Examination of the Klein system of child psychology. The Psychoanalytic Study of the Child 1: 75–118.

Glover E (1948) Psycho-Analysis. London and New York: Staples.

Glover E (1968) The Birth of the Ego. New York: International Universities Press.

Glover E, Fenichel O, Strachey J, Bergler E, Nunberg H, Bibring E (1937) Symposium on the theory of the therapeutic results of psycho-analysis. International Journal of Psycho-Analysis 18: 125–84.

References 339

Gold JR, Wachtel PL (1993) Cyclical psychodynamics. In J Stricker, JR Gold (eds), Comprehensive Handbook of Psychotherapy Integration (pp. 59–72). New York: Plenum Press.

Goldberg A (1978) Self Psychology: A Casebook. New York: International Universities Press.

Goldfried MR, Newman CF (1992) A history of psychotherapy integration. In JC Norcross, MR Goldfried (eds.), Handbook of Psychotherapy Integration (pp. 44–91). New York: Basic Books.

Goldsmith HH, Buss KA, Lemery KS (1997) Toddler and childhood temperament: expanded content, stronger genetic evidence, new evidence for the importance of environment. Developmental Psychopathology 33: 891–905.

Goldstein J, Freud A, Solnit AJ (1973) Beyond the Best Interests of the Child. New York: Free Press, 1979.

Goldstein J, Freud A, Solnit AJ (1979) Before the Best Interests of the Child. New York: Free Press.

Golinkoff RM, Hardig CB, Carlson V, Sexton ME (1984) The infant's perception of causal events: the distinction between animate and inanimate objects. In LP Lipsitt, C Rovee-Collier (eds), Advances in Infancy Research. Norwood, NJ: Ablex.

Goodman R, Meltzer H (1999) The Development and Well-being of Children and Adolescents in Great Britain. London: Office of National Statistics.

Goodyer IM (1995) Life events and difficulties: their nature and effects. In IM Goodyer (ed.), The Depressed Child and Adolescent: Developmental and Clinical Perspectives (pp. 171–93). Cambridge: Cambridge University Press.

Gopnik A (1993) How we know our minds: the illusion of first-person knowledge of intentionality. Behavioral and Brain Sciences 16: 1–14, 29–113.

Gopnik A, Astington JW (1988) Children's understanding of representational change and its relation to the understanding of false belief and the appearance–reality distinction. Child Development 59: 26–37.

Goschke T, Kuhl J (1993) Representations of intentions: persisting activation in memory. Journal of Experimental Psychology: Learning, Memory and Cognition 19: 1211–26.

Gray JA (1990) Brain systems that mediate both emotion and cognition. Cognition and Emotion 4: 269–88.

Green A (1975) The analyst, symbolisation and absence in the analytic setting: on changes in analytic practice and analytic experience. International Journal of Psycho-Analysis 56: 1–22.

Green A (1977) The borderline concept. A conceptual framework for the understanding of borderline patients: suggested hypotheses. In P Hartcollis (ed.), Borderline Personality Disorders (pp. 15–46). New York: International Universities Press.

Green A (1978) Potential space in psychoanalysis. In S Grolnick, L Barkin (eds), Between Reality and Fantasy (pp. 167–90). New York: Jason Aronson.

Green A (1983) The dead mother. In A Green (ed.), On Private Madness. London: Karnac.

Green A (1986) On Private Madness. London: Hogarth.

Green A (1995a) Has sexuality anything to do with psychoanalysis? International Journal of Psycho-Analysis 76: 871–83.

Green A (1995b) Propédeutique. Paris: Champvallon.

Green A (1997) Les chaînes d'Eros. Actualité. Paris: Odile Jacob.

Green A (1999a) Consilience and Rigour. Neuro-Psychoanalysis 1: 40–4.

Green A (1999b) The Fabric of Affect and Psychoanalytic Discourse. London: Routledge, Kegan & Paul.

Green A (1999c) The Work of the Negative. London: Free Association.

Green A (2000a) The central phobic position: a new formulation of free association. International Journal of Psycho-Analysis 81: 429–51.

Green A (2000b) Le temps éclaté. Paris: Minuit.

Green A (2000c) Science and science fiction in infant research. In J Sandler, A-M Sandler, R Davies (eds), Clinical and Observational Psychoanalytic Research: Roots of a Controversy (pp. 41–73). London: Karnac Books.

Green R (1985) Atypical psychosexual development. In M Rutter, L Hersov (eds), Child and Adolescent Psychiatry: Modern Approaches (pp. 638–49). Oxford: Blackwell Scientific Publications.

Greenacre P (1945) Conscience in the psychopath. American Journal of Orthopsychiatry 15: 495–509.

Greenacre P (1952) Pregenital patterning. International Journal of Psycho-Analysis 33: 410–15.

Greenacre P (ed.) (1953) Affective Disorders. New York: International Universities Press.

Greenacre P (1970) The transitional object and the fetish with special reference to the role of illusion. International Journal of Psycho-Analysis 51: 447–56.

Greenberg J (1991) Oedipus and Beyond: A Clinical Theory. Cambridge, MA: Harvard University Press.

Greenberg J (2000) The analytic participation: a new look. Journal of the American Psychoanalytic Association 49: 359–380.

Greenberg JR, Mitchell SA (1983) Object Relations in Psychoanalytic Theory. Cambridge, MA: Harvard University Press.

Greenberg MT (1999) Attachment and psychopathology in childhood. In J Cassidy, PR Shaver (eds), Handbook of Attachment: Theory, Research, and Clinical Applications (pp. 469–96). New York: Guilford.

Greenberg RP, Fisher S (1983) Freud and the female reproductive process: tests and issues. In J Masling (ed.), Empirical Studies of Psychoanalytic Theory. Hillsdale, NJ: Analytic Press.

Greenson RR (1967) The Technique and Practice of Psychoanalysis. New York: International Universities Press.

Greenwald AG, Banaj M (1995) Implicit social cognition: attitudes, self-esteem, and stereotypes. Psychological Review 102: 4–27.

Grey A, Davies M (1981) Mental health as level of interpersonal maturity. Journal of the American Academy of Psychoanalysis 9: 601–14.

Grigg DN, Friesen JD, Sheppy MI (1989) Family patterns associated with anorexia nervosa. Journal of Marital and Family Therapy 15: 29–42.

Grinker R, Werble B, Drye RC (1968) The Borderline Syndrome: A Behavioral Study of Ego Functions. New York: Basic Books.

Grolnick W, Frodi A, Bridges L (1984) Maternal control style and the mastery motivation one-year olds. Infant Mental Health Journal 5: 72–8.

Grosskurth P (1986) Melanie Klein: Her World and Her Work. New York: Knopf.

Grossmann K (1989) Avoidance as a Communicative Strategy in Attachment Relationships. Lugano, Switzerland, September 20–24.

Grossmann K, Grossmann KE, Spangler G, Suess G, Unzer L (1985) Maternal sensitivity and newborn orienting responses as related to quality of attachment in Northern Germany. In I Bretherton, E Waters (eds), Growing Points in Attachment Theory and Research. Monographs of the Society for Research in Child Development (Vol. 50 (1-2, Serial No. 209), pp. 233–56).

Grossman KE, Grossmann K, Schwan A (1986) Capturing the wider view of attachment: a reanalysis of Ainsworth's Strange Situation. In CE Izard, PB Read (eds), Measuring Emotions in Infants and Children (Vol. 2, pp. 124–71). New York: Cambridge University Press.

Grünbaum A (1984) The Foundations of Psychoanalysis: A Philosophical Critique. Berkeley, CA: University of California Press.

Grünbaum A (1992) In defense of secular humanism. Free Inquiry 12: 30–9.

Gunderson JG (1985) Borderline Personality Disorder. Washington, DC: American Psychiatric Press.

Gunderson JG (1996) The borderline patient's intolerance of aloneness: insecure attachments and therapist availability. American Journal of Psychiatry 153(6): 752–8.

Gunderson JG, Sabo A (1993) The phenomenal and conceptual interface between borderline personality disorder and PTSD. American Journal of Psychiatry 150: 19–27.

Gunderson JG, Morris H, Zanarini M (1985) Transitional objects and borderline patients. In TH McGlashan (ed.), The Borderline: Current Empirical Research. Washington, DC: American Psychiatric Press.

Guntrip H (1961) Personality Structure and Human Interaction. New York: International University Press.

Guntrip H (1969) Schizoid Phenomena, Object Relations and the Self. New York: International Universities Press.

Guntrip H (1975) My experience of analysis with Fairbairn and Winnicott. International Review of Psychoanalysis 2: 145–56.

Guntrip H (1978) Psycho-analysis and some scientific and philosophical critics. British Journal of Medical Psychology 51: 207–24.

Guthrie E, Moorey J, Margison F, Barker H, Palmer S, McGrath G, Tomenson B, Creed F (1999) Cost-effectiveness of brief psychodynamic-interpersonal therapy in high utilizers of psychiatric services. Archives of General Psychiatry 56(6): 519–26.

Hadley JL (1983) The representational system: a bridging concept for psychoanalysis and neurophysiology. International Review of Psychoanalysis 10: 13–30.

Halligan PW, Marshall JC (1991) Left neglect for near but not far space in man. Nature 350: 498–500.

Hamilton V (1993) Truth and reality in psychoanalytic discourse. International Journal of Psycho-Analysis 74: 63–79.

Hamilton V (1996) The Analyst's Preconscious. Hillsdale, NJ: The Analytic Press.

Hanley C (1978) A critical consideration of Bowlby's ethological theory of anxiety. Psychoanalytic Quarterly 47: 364–80.

Hanley C (1987) Review. The assault on truth: Freud's suppression of the seduction theory. International Journal of Psycho-Analysis 67: 517–21.

Hans SL, Marcus J, Neuchterlein KH, Asarnow RF, Styr B, Auerbach JG (1999) Neurobehavioral deficits in adolescence in children at risk for schizophrenia: The Jerusalem Infant Development Study. Archives of General Psychiatry 56: 741–8.

Hare RD, Cox DN (1987) Clinical and empirical conceptions of psychopathy, and the selection of subjects for research. In RD Hare, D Schalling (eds), Psychopathic Behavior: Approaches to Research (pp. 1–21). Toronto, Ontario: John Wiley & Sons.

Harlow HF (1958) The nature of love. American Psychologist 13: 673–8.

Harris JR (1998) The Nurture Assumption: Why Children Turn Out the Way They Do. Parents Matter Less than You Think and Peers Matter More. New York: Free Press.

Harris PL (1989) Children and Emotion: The Development of Psychological Understanding. Oxford: Basil Blackwell.

Harris PL (1994) The child's understanding of emotion: developmental change and the family environment. Journal of Child Psychology and Psychiatry 35: 3–28.

Harris PL, Kavanaugh RD (1993) Young children's understanding of pretence. Society for Research in Child Development Monographs (Serial No. 237).

Harter S (1977) A cognitive-developmental approach to children's expression of conflicting feelings and a technique to facilitate such expression in play therapy. Journal of Consulting and Clinical Psychology 45: 417-32.

Harter S (1986) Cognitive-developmental processes in the integration of concepts about emotions and the self. Social Cognition 4: 119–51.

Hartmann H (1939) Ego Psychology and the Problem of Adaptation. New York: International Universities Press, 1958.

Hartmann H (1950) Comments on the Psychoanalytic Theory of the Ego. New York: International University Press, 1964.

Hartmann H (1952) The mutual influences in the development of ego and id. Essays on Ego Psychology (pp. 155–82). New York: International University Press, 1964.

Hartmann H (1953) Contribution to the metapsychology of schizophrenia. The Psychoanalytic Study of the Child 8: 177–98.

Hartmann H (1955) Notes on the theory of sublimation. Essays on Ego Psychology (pp. 215–40). New York: International University Press, 1964.

Hartmann H, Kris E, Loewenstein R (1946) Comments on the formation of psychic structure. The Psychoanalytic Study of the Child 2: 11–38.

Hartmann H, Kris H, Loewenstein R (1949) Notes on the theory of aggression. Psychoanalytic Study of the Child 3–4: 9–36.

Hartup WW, Stevens N (1997 Friendships and adaptation in the life course. Psychological Bulletin, 121, 355–70.

Hatcher R, Krohn A (1980) Level of object representation and capacity for intense psychotherapy in neurotics and borderlines. In J Kwawer, P Lerner, A Sugarman (eds), Borderline Phenomena and the Rorschach Test. New York: International Universities Press.

Havens L (1993) Participant Observation: The psychotherapy schools in action. New York: Jason Aronson.

Hayman A (1969) What do we mean by 'id'? Journal of the American Psychoanalytic Association 17: 353–80.

Hazan C, Shaver PR (1990) Love and work: an attachment theoretical perspective. Journal of Personality and Social Psychology 59: 270–80.

Head H (1926) Aphasia and Kindred Disorders of Speech. New York: Macmillan.

Heard HL, Linehan MM (1993) Problems of self and borderline personality disorder: a dialectical behavioral analysis. In ZV Segal, SJ Blatt (eds), The Self in Emotional Distress: Cognitive and Psychodynamic Perspectives (pp. 301-25). New York and London: Guilford Press.

Hegel G (1807) The Phenomenology of Spirit. Oxford: Oxford University Press.

Heinicke CM, Ramsey-Klee DM (1986) Outcome of child psychotherapy as a function of frequency of sessions. Journal of the American Academy of Child Psychiatry 25: 247-53.

Heinicke CM, Westheimer IJ (1966) Brief Separations. New York: International Universities Press.

Hellman I (1962) Hampstead nursery follow-up studies: I. Sudden separation. Psychoanalytic Study of the Child 17: 159–74.

Hempel C (1965) Aspects of Scientific Explanation. New York: Lasalle.

Herman JL, Perry C, van der Kolk, BA (1989). Childhood trauma in borderline personality disorder. American Journal of Psychiatry 146: 490–5.

Hesse P, Cicchetti D (1982) Perspectives on an integrated theory of emotional development. New Directions for Child Development 16: 3–48.

Hewitt JK, Silberg JL, Rutter M, Simonoff E, Meyer JM, Maes H, Pickles A, Neale MC, Loeber R, Erickson MT, Kendler KS, Heath AC, Truett KR, Reynolds CA, Eaves LJ (1997) Genetics and developmental psychopathology: 1. Phenotypic assessment in the Virginia Twin Study of Adolescent Behavioral Development. J Child Psychol Psychiatry 38(8): 943–63.

Hinshelwood R (1989) A Dictionary of Kleinian Thought. London: Free Association Books.

Hirshberg L, Svejda M (1990) When infants look to their parents: II. Twelve-month-olds' response to conflicting parental emotional signals. Child Development 61: 1187–91.

Hobson JA, McCarley RW (1977) The brain as a dream state generator: an activation-synthesis hypothesis of the dream process. American Journal of Psychiatry 134: 1335–48.

Hobson RF (1985) Forms of Feeling: The Heart of Psychotherapy. New York: Basic Books.

Hofer MA (1995) Hidden regulators: implications for a new understanding of attachment, separation and loss. In S Goldberg, R Muir, J Kerr (eds), Attachment Theory: Social, Developmental, and Clinical Perspectives (pp. 203–30). Hillsdale, NJ: The Analytic Press, Inc.

Hofer MA (1996) On the nature and consequences of early loss. Psychosomatic Medicine 58: 570–81.

Hoffman IZ (1990) In the eye of the beholder: a reply to Levenson. Contemporary Psychoanalysis 26: 291–304.

Hoffman IZ (1991) Discussion: toward a social constructivist view of the psychoanalytic situation. Psychoanalytic Dialogues 1: 74–103.

Hoffman IZ (1994) Dialectic thinking and therapeutic action in the psychoanalytic process. Psychoanalytic Quarterly 63: 187–218.

Hoffman IZ (1998) Ritual and Spontaneity in the Psychoanalytic Process. Hillsdale, NJ: The Analytic Press.

Høglend P (1993) Personality disorders and long-term outcome after brief psychodynamic psychotherapy. Journal of Personality Disorders 7: 168–81.

Holmes DS (1974) Investigations of repression: differential recall of material experimentally or naturally associated with ego threat. Psychological Bulletin 81: 632–53.

Holmes J (1993a) Attachment theory: a biological basis for psychotherapy? British Journal of Psychiatry 163: 430–8.

Holmes J (1993b) John Bowlby and Attachment Theory. London: Routledge.

Holmes J (1998) Defensive and creative uses of narrative in psychotherapy: an attachment perspective. In G Roberts, J Holmes (eds), Narrative and Psychotherapy and Psychiatry (pp. 49–68). Oxford: Oxford University Press.

Holmes J (2000) Attachment theory and psychoanalysis: a rapprochement. British Journal of Psychotherapy 17: 157–80.

Holt RR (1976) Drive or Wish: A Reconsideration of the Psychoanalytic Theory of Motivation.

Hooley JM, Richters JE (1995) Expressed emotion: a developmental perspective. In D Cicchetti, SL Toth (eds), Emotion, Cognition and Representation (Vol. VI). Rochester, NY: University of Rochester Press.

Hopkins J (1992) Psychoanalysis, interpretation, and science. In J Hopkins, A Saville (eds), Psychoanalysis, Mind and Art: Perspectives on Richard Wollheim (pp. 3–34). Oxford: Blackwell.

Hornik R, Gunnar MR (1988) A descriptive analysis of infant social referencing. Child Development 59: 626–34.

Horowitz LM, Rosenberg SE, Bartholomew K (1996) Interpersonal problems, attachment styles and outcome in brief dynamic psychotherapy. Journal of Consulting and Clinical Psychology 61: 549–60.

Horowitz MJ (1986a) Stress Response Syndromes. Northvale, NJ: Jason Aronson.

Horowitz MJ (1986b) Stress-response syndromes: a review of post-traumatic and adjustment disorders. Hospital and Community Psychiatry 37: 241–9.

Horowitz MJ (1987) States of Mind: Configurational Analysis of Individual Psychology (Vol. 2). New York: Plenum.

Horowitz MJ (1988) Introduction to Psychodynamics: A New Synthesis. New York: Basic Books.

Horowitz MJ (1989) Nuances of Technique in Dynamic Psychotherapy. Northvale, NJ: Jason Aronson Inc.

Horowitz MJ (1991a) Emotionality and schematic control processes. In MJ Horowitz (ed.), Person Schemas and Maladaptive Interpersonal Patterns (pp. 413–23). Chicago, IL: University of Chicago Press.

Horowitz MJ (1991b) Person schemas. In MJ Horowitz (ed.), Person Schemas and Maladaptive Interpersonal Patterns (pp. 13–31). Chicago, IL: University of Chicago Press.

Horowitz MJ (1992) Person Schemas and Maladaptive Interpersonal Patterns. Chicago, IL: University of Chicago Press.

Horowitz MJ, Eells TD (1993) Case formulations using role-relationship model configurations: a reliability study. Psychotherapy Research 3: 57–68.

Horton PC, Gewirtz H (1988) Acquisition and termination of first solacing objects in males, females, and in a clinic and nonclinic population: implications for psychological immunity. In PC Horton, H Gewirtz, KJ Kreutter (eds), The Solace Paradigm: An Eclectic Search for Psychological Immunity (pp. 159–84). Madison, CT: International Universities Press, Inc.

Horvath AO, Simmonds BD (1991) Relation between working alliance and outcome in psychotherapy: a meta-analysis. Journal of Consulting and Clinical Psychology 38: 139–49.

Horvath AO, Gaston L, Luborsky L (1993) The therapeutic alliance and its measures. In NE Miller, L Luborsky, JP Barber, JP Docherty (eds), Psychodynamic Treatment Research: A Handbook for Clinical Practice (pp. 247–73). New York: Basic Books.

Howarth E (1980) A test of some old concepts by means of some new scales. Psychological Reports 47: 1039–42.

Howarth E (1982) Factor analytic examination of Kline's scales for psychoanalytic concepts. Personality and Individual Differences 3: 89–92.

Hughes C, Uhlmann C, Pennebaker J (1994) The body's response to processing emotional trauma: linking verbal text with automatic activity. Journal of Personality 62: 565–85.

Hughes J (1989) Reshaping the Psychoanalytic Domain. Berkeley, CA: University of California Press.

Hurry A. (ed.) (1998) Psychoanalysis and Developmental Theory. London: Karnac.

Inoue T, Tsuchiya K, Koyama T (1994) Regional changes in dopamine and serotonin activation with various intensity of physical and psychological stress in the rat brain. Pharmacology, Biochemistry and Behavior 49: 911-20.

Isaacs S (1943) The nature and function of phantasy. In M Klein, P Heimann, S Isaacs, J Riviere (eds), Developments in Psycho-Analysis (pp. 67-121). London: Hogarth Press (1952).

Izard CE (1977) Human Emotions. New York: Plenum Press.

Jacobovitz D, Hazen N (1999) Developmental pathways from infant disorganization to childhood peer relationships. In J Solomon, C George (eds), Attachment Disorganization (pp. 127-59). New York: Guilford Press.

Jacobovitz D, Hazen N, Riggs S (1997) Disorganized mental processes in mothers, frightening/frightened caregiving and disoriented/disorganized behavior in infancy. Paper presented at the Biennial Meeting of the Society for Research in Child Development, Washington, DC.

Jacobson E (1953) Contribution to the metapsychology of cyclothymic depression. In P Greenacre (ed.), Affective Disorders: Psychoanalytic Contributions to Their Study (pp. 49-83). New York: International Universities Press.

Jacobson E (1954a) Contribution to the metapsychology of psychotic identifications. Journal of the American Psychoanalytic Association 2: 239-62.

Jacobson E (1954b) The self and the object world: vicissitudes of their infantile cathexes and their influence on ideational affective development. The Psychoanalytic Study of the Child 9: 75-127.

Jacobson E (1964) The Self and the Object World. New York: International Universities Press.

Jacobson KC, Rowe DC (1999). Genetic and environmental influences on the relationships between family connectedness, school connectedness, and adolescent depressed mood: sex differences. Dev Psychol 35(4): 926-39.

Jahoda M (1972) Social psychology and psychoanalysis: a mutual challenge. Bulletin of British Psychological Society 25: 269-74.

Jeffery EH (2001) The mortality of psychoanalysts. Journal of the American Psychoanalytic Association 49: 103-11.

Jensen MR (1987) Psychobiological factors predicting the course of breast cancer. Journal of Personality 55: 317-42.

Joffe WG (1969) A critical review of the status of the envy concept. International Journal of Psychoanalysis 50: 533-45.

Joffe WG, Sandler J (1965) Notes on pain, depression, and individuation. Psychoanalytic Study of the Child 20: 394-424.

Joffe WG, Sandler J (1967) Some conceptual problems involved in the consideration of disorders of narcissism. Journal of Child Psychotherapy 2: 56-66.

Johnson AM, Szurek SA (1952) The genesis of antisocial acting out in children and adults. Psychoanalytic Quarterly 21: 323-43.

Johnson B (2001) Drug dreams: a neuropsychoanalytic hypothesis. Journal of the American Psychoanalytic Association 49: 75-96.

Johnson JG, Cohen P, Brown J et al. (1999). Childhood maltreatment increases risk for personality disorders during early adulthood. Archives of General Psychiatry 56: 600-5.

Johnson-Laird PN, Byrne RM (1993) Precis of deduction. Behavioral and Brain Sciences 16: 323-80.

Jones E (1922) Some problems of adolescence, Papers on Psycho-Analysis (pp. 389-406). Boston: Beacon Press, 1961.

Jones E (1923) Anal erotic character traits. In E Jones (ed.), Papers on Psychoanalysis. London: Baillière Tindall.

Jones EE (1993) How will psychoanalysis study itself? Journal of the American Psychoanalytic Association 41: 91-108.

Jones EE, Cumming JD, Pulos S (1993) Tracing clinical themes across phases of treatment by a Q-set. In N Miller, L Luborsky, J Barber, J Docherty (eds), Psychodynamic Treatment Research: A Handbook of Clinical Practice (pp. 14-36). New York: Basic Books.

Jones P, Rodgers B, Murray R, Marmot M (1994) Child developmental risk factors for adult schizophrenia in the British 1946 Birth Cohort. Lancet 344: 1398-1402.

Jorgensen RS, Johnson BT, Kolodziej ME, Schreer GE (1996) Elevated blood pressure and personality: a meta-analytic review. Psychological Bulletin 120: 293-320.

Joseph B (1985) Transference: the total situation. International Journal of Psychoanalysis 66: 447-54.

Joseph B (1989) Psychic Equilibrium and Psychic Change. London: Routledge.

Joyce AS, Piper WE (1993) The immediate impact of transference interpretation in short-term individual psychotherapy. American Journal of Psychotherapy 47: 508-26.

Jung CG (1912) Wandlungen und Symbole der Libido. Leipzig and Vienna: Deuticke.

Jung CG (1913) Psychology of the Unconscious. New York: Dodd, Mead, 1949.

Jung CG (1916) Psychology of the Unconscious. London: Routledge & Kegan Paul.

Jung CG (1923) Psychological Types. London: Routledge & Kegan Paul.

Kaehler ST, Singewald N, Sinner C, Thurner C, Phillipu A (2000) Conditioned fear and inescapable shock modify the release of serotonin in the locus coeruleus. Brain Research 859: 249-54.

Kagan J (1987) Psychological Research on the Human Infant: An Evaluative Summary. New York: Wiley.

Kagan J, Lemkin J (1960) The child's differential perception of parental attributes. Journal of Abnormal and Social Psychology 61:440-7.

Kandel ER (1998) A new intellectual framework for psychiatry. American Journal of Psychiatry, 155, 457-69.

Kandel ER (1999) Biology and the future of psychoanalysis: a new intellectual framework for psychiatry revisited. American Journal of Psychiatry 156: 505-24.

Kashani J, Husain A, Shekim W, Hodges K, Cytryn L, McKnew DH (1981). Current perspectives on childhood depression: an overview. American Journal of Psychiatry 38: 143-53.

Kavanagh G (1985) Changes in patients' object representations during psychoanalysis and psychoanalytic psychotherapy. Bulletin Menninger Clinic 49: 546-64.

Kazdin AE (1994) Psychotherapy for children and adolescents. In AE Bergin, SL Garfield (eds), Handbook of Psychotherapy and Behavior Change (4th edn, pp. 543-94). New York: Wiley.

Kazdin AE (2000) Psychotherapy for Children and Adolescents: Directions for Research and Practice. Oxford: Oxford University Press.

Kazdin AE, Wasser G (2000) Therapeutic changes in children, parents and families resulting from treatment of children with conduct problems. Journal of the American Academy of Child and Adolescent Psychiatry 39(4): 414-20.

Kellam SG, Van Horn YV (1997) Life course development, community epidemiology, and preventive trials: a scientific structure for prevention research. American Journal of Community Psychology 25: 177-88.

Kendler KS, Karkowski-Shuman L (1997) Stressful life events and genetic liability to major depression: genetic control of exposure to the environment? Psychological Medicine 27: 549-64.

Kendler KS, Neale MC, Kessler RC, Heath AC, Eaves LJ (1993) A longitudinal twin study of personality and major depression in women. Archives of General Psychiatry 50: 853-62.

Kendler KS, Kessler RC, Walters EE, MacClean C, Neale MC, Heath A, Eaves LJ (1995) Stressful life events, genetic liability and onset of an episode of major depression in women. American Journal of Psychiatry 152: 833-42.

Kendler KS, Neale MC, Prescott CA, Kessler RC, Heath AC, Corey LA, Eaves LJ (1996) Childhood parental loss and alcoholism in women: a causal analysis using a twin-family design. Psychological Medicine 26: 79-95.

Kennedy H (1950) Cover memories in formation. Psychoanalytic Study of the Child 5: 275-84.

Kennedy H (1979) The role of insight in child analysis. Journal of the American Psychoanalytic Association, Supplement 27: 9-28.

Kennedy H, Moran G (1991) Reflections on the aims of child psychoanalysis. The Psychoanalytic Study of the Child 46: 181-98.

Kennedy H, Yorke C (1980) Childhood neurosis v. developmental deviations: two clinical case histories. Dialogue: A Journal of Psychoanalytic Perspectives 4: 20-33.

Kernberg OF (1967) Borderline personality organization. Journal of the American Psychoanalytic Association 15: 641-85.

Kernberg OF (1969) A contribution to the ego-psychological critique of the Kleinian school. International Journal of Psycho-Analysis 50: 317-33.

Kernberg OF (1970) A psychoanalytic classification of character pathology. Journal of the American Psychoanalytic Association 18: 800-22.

Kernberg OF (1971) Prognostic considerations regarding borderline personality organization. Journal of the American Psychoanalytic Association, 19, 595-635.

Kernberg OF (1974). Toward an integrative theory of hospital treatment, Object Relations Theory and Clinical Psychoanalysis. New York: Jason Aronson.

Kernberg OF (1975). Borderline Conditions and Pathological Narcissism. New York: Jason Aronson.

Kernberg OF (1976a). Foreword. In V.D.Volkan (ed.), Primitive Internalized Object Relations (pp. xiii-xvii). New York: International Universities Press.

Kernberg OF (1976b). Object Relations Theory and Clinical Psychoanalysis. New York: Aronson.

Kernberg OF (1976c). Technical considerations in the treatment of borderline personality organisation. Journal of the American Psychoanalytic Association, 24, 795-829.

Kernberg OF (1977). The structural diagnosis of borderline personality organization. In P.Hartocollis (ed.), Borderline personality disorders: The concept, the syndrome, the patient (pp. 87-121). New York: International Universities Press.

Kernberg OF (1980a). Internal World and External Reality: Object Relations Theory Applied. New York: Aronson.

Kernberg OF (1980b). Some implications of object relations theory for psychoanalytic technique. In H.Blum (ed.), Psychoanalytic Explorations of Technique: Discourse on the Theory of Therapy (pp. 207-239). New York: International University Press.

Kernberg OF (1981) Structural interviewing. Psychiatric Clinics of North America 4: 169-95.

Kernberg OF (1982) Self, ego, affects and drives. Journal of the American Psychoanalytic Association 30: 893–917.

Kernberg OF (1984) Severe Personality Disorders: Psychotherapeutic Strategies. New Haven, CT: Yale University Press.

Kernberg OF (1987) Borderline personality disorder: a psychodynamic approach. Journal of Personality Disorders 1: 344–6.

Kernberg OF (1988) Object relations theory in clinical practice. Psychoanalytic Quarterly 57: 481–504.

Kernberg OF (1989) The narcissistic personality disorder and the differential diagnosis of antisocial behavior. Psychiatric Clinics of North America 12: 553–70.

Kernberg OF (1992) Aggression in Personality Disorders and Perversions. New Haven and London: Yale University Press.

Kernberg OF (1993) The current status of psychoanalysis. Journal of the American Psychoanalytic Association 41: 45–62.

Kernberg OF et al. (1972) Psychotherapy and psychoanalysis: final report of the Menninger Foundation Psychotherapy Research Project. Bulletin Menninger Clinic 36: 3–275.

Kernberg OF, Clarkin JF (1993) Developing a disorder-specific manual: the treatment of borderline character disorder. In NE Miller, JP Barber, JP Docherty (eds), Psychodynamic Treatment Research: A Handbook for Clinical Practice (pp. 227–46). New York: Basic Books.

Kernberg OF, Selzer MA, Koenigsberg HW, Carr AC, Appelbaum AH (1989) Psychodynamic Psychotherapy of Borderline Patients. New York: Basic Books.

Kessler RC (1997) The effects of stressful life events on depression. Annual Review of Psychology 48: 191–214.

Kestenbaum R, Farber E, Sroufe LA (1989) Individual differences in empathy among preschoolers' concurrent and predictive validity. In N Eisenberg (ed.), Empathy and Related Emotional Responses: New Directions for Child Development (pp. 51–6). San Francisco, CA: Jossey-Bass.

Khan M (1963b) The concept of cumulative trauma. The Psychoanalytic Study of the Child 18: 283–306.

Khan M (1966) The role of phobic and counter-phobic mechanisms and a separation anxiety in the schizoid character formation. International Journal of Psycho-Analysis 47: 306–13.

Khan M (1971) Infantile neurosis as a false self organization. The Privacy of the Self (1974) (pp. 219–33). New York: International Universities Press.

Khan M (1974) The Privacy of the Self. London: Hogarth Press.

Kihlstrom JF (1987) The cognitive unconscious. Science 237: 1445–52.

Kihlstrom JF, Hoyt IP (1990) Repression, dissociation, and hypnosis. In JL Singer (ed.), Repression and Dissociation (pp. 181–208). Chicago, IL: University of Chicago Press.

King P (1978) Affective response of the analyst to the patient's communications. International Journal of Psycho-Analysis 59: 329–34.

King P, Steiner R (1991) The Freud-Klein Controversies: 1941–45. London: Routledge.

King R, Noshpitz JD (1990) Pathways of Growth: Essentials of Child Psychiatry, Vol.2, Psychopathology. New York: John Wiley & Sons.

Kinsbourne M, Hicks RE (1979) Mapping cerebral functional space: competition and collaboration in human performance. In M Kinsbourne (ed.), Asymmetrical function of the brain (pp. 267–73). Cambridge: Cambridge University Press.

Klauber J (1966) An attempt to differentiate a typical form of transference in neurotic depression. International Journal of Psycho-Analysis 47: 539–45.

Klauber J (1987) Illusion and Spontaneity in Psycho-Analysis: Free Association Books.

Klein GS (1970). Perception, Motives and Personality. New York: Knopf.

Klein GS (1976a) Freud's two theories of sexuality. Psychological Issues, Monograph 36: 14–70.

Klein GS (1976b) Psychoanalytic Theory: An Exploration of Essentials. New York: International Universities Press.

Klein M (1927) Symposium on child analysis. Love, Guilt and Reparation: The Writings of Melanie Klein, Vol. I (pp. 139–69). London: Hogarth Press (1975).

Klein M (1928) Early stages of the Oedipus conflict. Love, Guilt and Reparation (1975, pp. 186–98). London: Hogarth (1975).

Klein M (1929) Infantile anxiety-situations reflected in a work of art and in the creative impulse. Contributions to Psychoanalysis, 1921–1945 (pp. 227–35). New York: McGraw-Hill, 1964.

Klein M (1930) The importance of symbol-formation in the development of the ego. Contributions to Psychoanalysis, 1921–1945. New York: McGraw-Hill, 1964.

Klein M (1931) A contribution to the theory of intellectual inhibitions. Contributions to Psychoanalysis, 1921–1945. New York: McGraw-Hill, 1964.

Klein M (1932) The Psycho-Analysis of Children. London: Hogarth Press.

Klein M (1935) A contribution to the psychogenesis of manic-depressive states. Love, Guilt and Reparation: The Writings of Melanie Klein, Vol. I (pp. 236–89). London: Hogarth Press (1975).

Klein M (1936) The psychotherapy of the psychoses. Contributions to psychoanalysis, 1921–1945. New York: McGraw-Hill, 1964.

Klein M (1937) Love, guilt and reparation. Love, Guilt and Reparation: The Writings of Melanie Klein Vol. I (pp. 306–43). New York: Macmillan, 1984.

Klein M (1940) Mourning and its relation to manic-depressive states. Love, Guilt and Reparation: The Writings of Melanie Klein Vol. I (pp. 344–69). New York: Macmillan, 1984.

Klein M (1945) The Oedipus complex in the light of early anxieties. Love, Guilt and Reparation: The Writings of Melanie Klein, Vol. I (pp. 370–419). London: Hogarth Press, 1985.

Klein M (1946) Notes on some schizoid mechanisms. In M Klein, P Heimann, S Isaacs, J Riviere (eds), Developments in Psychoanalysis (pp. 292–320). London: Hogarth Press.

Klein M (1948a) Contributions to Psycho-Analysis, 1921–1945. London: Hogarth Press.

Klein M (1948b) On the theory of anxiety and guilt. Envy and Gratitude and Other Works, 1946–1963. New York: Delacorte Press, 1975.

Klein M (1950) Contributions to Psycho-Analysis, 1921–1945. London: Hogarth Press, 1977.

Klein M (1952) The mutual influences in the development of ego and id. Envy and Gratitude and other Works, 1946–1963. New York: Delacorte Press, 1975.

Klein M (1957) Envy and gratitude. The Writings of Melanie Klein (Vol. 3, pp. 176–235). London: Hogarth Press.

Klein M (1958) On the development of mental functioning. The Writings of Melanie Klein, Vol. 3, Envy and Gratitude and other Works (pp. 236–46). London: Hogarth Press, 1975.

Klein M (1959) Our adult world and its roots in infancy. In R Money-Kyrle (ed.), The Writings of Melanie Klein (Vol. 3, pp. 247-63). London: Hogarth Press, 1975.

Klein M (1960) The narrative of a child analysis. The Writings of Melanie Klein. London: Hogarth Press.

Klein M, Heimann P, Issacs S, Riviere J (eds) (1946) Developments in Psychoanalysis. London: Hogarth Press.

Klein Milton (1981) On Mahler's autistic and symbiotic phases: an exposition and evolution. Psychoanal.Contemp.Thought 4: 69-105.

Klein R (1989) Introduction to the disorders of the self. In JF Masterson, R Klein (eds), Psychotherapy of the Disorders of the Self (pp. 30-46). New York: Brunner/Mazel.

Klerman GL, Weissman MM, Rounsaville BJ, Chevron ES (1984) Interpersonal Psychotherapy of Depression. New York: Basic Books.

Kline P (1979) Psychosexual personality traits, fixation and neuroticism. British Journal of Medical Psychology 52: 393-5.

Kline P (1981) Fact and Fantasy in Freudian Theory (2nd edn). London: Methuen.

Kline P, Storey R (1978) The dynamic personality: what does it measure? British Journal of Psychology 68: 375-83.

Kline P, Storey R (1980) The aetiology of the oral character. Journal of Genetic Psychology 136: 85-94.

Knight R (1953) Borderline states. Bulletin of the Menninger Clinic 17: 1-12.

Kobak R, Sceery A (1988) Attachment in late adolescence: working models, affect regulation and perceptions of self and others. Child Development 59: 135-46.

Kochanska G (2001) Emotional development in children with different attachment histories: the first three years. Child Development 72: 474-90.

Kochanska G, Murray KT (2000) Mother-child mutually responsive orientation and conscience development: from toddler to early school age. Child Development 71: 417-31.

Kochanska G, Coy KC, Tjebkes TL, Husarek SJ (1998) Individual differences in emotionality in infancy. Child Development 69: 375-90.

Kochanska G, Murray K, Harlan E (2000) Effortful control in early childhood: continuity and change, antecedents, and implications for social development. Developmental Psychology 36: 220-32.

Kog E, Vandereycken W (1985) Family characteristics of anorexia nervosa and bulimia: a review of the research literature. Clin. Psychol. Rev. 5: 159-80.

Kogan I (1995) The Cry of Mute Children: A Psychoanalytic Perspective of the Second Generation of the Holocaust. London: Free Association Books.

Kohlberg L, Ricks D, Snarey J (1984) Childhood development as a predictor of adaptation in adulthood. Genetic Psychology Monographs 110: 91-172.

Kohon G (1986) The British School of Psycho-analysis: The Independent Tradition. London: Free Association Books.

Kohon G (ed.) (1999) The Dead Mother: The Work of André Green. London: Routledge.

Kohut H (1959) Introspection, empathy, and psychoanalysis: an examination of the relationship between mode of observation and theory. Journal of the American Psychoanalytic Association 7: 459-83.

Kohut H (1966) Forms and transformations of narcissism. Journal of the American Psychoanalytic Association 14: 243-72.

Kohut H (1968) The psychoanalytic treatment of narcissistic personality disorders. The Psychoanalytic Study of the Child 23: 86-113.

Kohut H (1971) The Analysis of the Self. New York: International Universities Press.

Kohut H (1972) Thoughts on narcissism and narcissistic rage. The Psychoanalytic Study of the Child 27: 360–400.

Kohut H (1977) The Restoration of the Self. New York: International Universities Press.

Kohut H (1982) Introspection, empathy and the semi-circle of mental health. International Journal of Psychoanalysis 63: 395–407.

Kohut H (1984) How Does Analysis Cure? Chicago, IL: University of Chicago Press.

Kohut H, Wolf ES (1978) The disorders of the self and their treatment: an outline. International Journal of Psycho-Analysis 59: 413–26.

Kovacs M, Gatsonis C, Paulauskas SL, Richards C (1989) Depressive disorders in childhood IV. A longitudinal study of comorbidity with and risk for anxiety disorders. Archives of General Psychiatry 46: 776–82.

Kramer S (1979) The technical significance and application of Mahler's separation-individuation theory. Journal of the American Psychoanalytic Association 27: 241–62.

Kramer S, Akhtar S (1988) The developmental context of internalized preoedipal object relations: clinical applications of Mahler's theory of symbiosis and separation-individuation. Psychoanalytic Quarterly 57: 547–76.

Krause R (1997) Allgemeine Psychoanalytische Krankheitslehre. Grundlagen. Stuttgart: Kohlhammer.

Kris AO (1984) The conflicts of ambivalence. The Psychoanalytic Study of the Child 39: 213–34.

Kris E (1952) Psychoanalytic Explorations in Art. New York: International University Press.

Krohn A, Mayman M (1974) Object representations in dreams and projective tests. Bulletin of the Menninger Clinic 38: 445–66.

Lamb M (1987) Predictive implications of individual differences in attachment. Journal of Consulting Clinical Psychology 55: 817–24.

Lamb ME, Thompson RA, Gardner W, Charnov E (1985) Infant–Mother Attachment: The Origins and Developmental Significance of Individual Differences in Strange Situation Behavior. Hillsdale, NJ: Erlbaum.

Lampl-de-Groot J (1949) Neurotics, delinquents and ideal formation. In KR Eissler (ed.), Searchlights on Delinquency (pp. 225–45). New York: International Universities Press.

Laor N, Wolmer L, Mayes L et al. (1996) Israeli preschoolers under Scud missile attacks. a developmental perspective on risk modifying factors. Archives of General Psychiatry 53: 416–23.

Laplanche J (1989) New Foundations for Psychoanalysis (D Macey, trans.). Oxford: Blackwell.

Laplanche J, Pontalis JB (1973) The Language of Psychoanalysis. New York: Norton.

Lasch C (1978) The Culture of Narcissism: American Life in an Age of Diminishing Expectations. New York: Norton.

Laub JH, Nagin DS, Sampson RJ (1998) Trajectories of change in criminal offending: good marriages and the desistance process. American Sociological Review 63: 225–38.

Laufer M (1976) The central masturbation fantasy, the final sexual organization, and adolescence. Psychoanal. Study Child 31: 297–316.

Laufer M, Laufer E (1984) Adolescence and Developmental Breakdown. New Haven, CT: Yale University Press.

Leahey TH (1980) The myth of operationism. J.Mind and Behavior 1:127–43.

Lebovici S (1982) The origins and development of the Oedipus complex. International Journal of Psycho-Analysis 63: 201–15.

Lebovici S, Weil-Halpern F (1989) Psychopathologie du Bébé. Paris: Presses Universitaires de France.

Lebovici S, Widlöcher, D. (1980). Psychoanalysis in France. New York: International Universities Press Inc.

LeDoux JE (1995) Emotion: clues from the brain. Annual Review of Psychology 46: 209–35.

LeDoux JE (1999) Commentary on Psychoanalytic theory: clues from the brain. Neuro-psychoanalysis 1: 44–9.

LeDoux JE, Romanski L, Xagoraris A (1989) Indelibility of subcortical emotional memories. Journal of Cognitive Neuroscience 1: 238–43.

Leff J, Kuipers L, Berkowitz R et al. (1982) A controlled trial of social intervention in the families of schizophrenia patients. British Journal of Psychiatry 141: 121–34.

Leiman M (1994) The development of Cognitive Analytic Therapy. International Journal of Short Term Psychotherapy 9: 67–82.

Lerner HD, St Petr S (1984) Patterns of object relations in neurotic, borderline, and schizophrenic patients. Psychiatry 47: 77–92.

Leslie AM (1986) Getting development off the ground: modularity and the infant's perception of causality. In PLC v Geert (ed.), Theory Building in Developmental Psychology. Amsterdam: Elsevier Science Publishers BV (North Holland).

Leslie AM (1994) TOMM, ToBy, and agency: core architecture and domain specificity. In L Hirschfeld, S Gelman (eds), Mapping the Mind: Domain Specificity in Cognition and Culture (pp. 119–48). New York: Cambridge University Press.

Levenson E (1972) The Fallacy of Understanding. New York: Basic Books.

Levenson E (1981) Facts or fantasies: on the nature of psychoanalytic data. Contemporary Psychoanalysis 17: 486–500.

Levenson E (1982) Language and healing. In S Slipp (ed.), Curative Factors in Dynamic Psychotherapy (pp. 91–103). New York: McGraw Hill.

Levenson E (1983) The Ambiguity of Change. New York: Basic Books.

Levenson E (1987) An interpersonal perspective. Psychoanalytic Inquiry 7, 207–14.

Levenson E (1989) Whatever happened to the cat? Contemporary Psychoanalysis 25: 537–53.

Levenson EA (1990) The Purloined Self. New York: Contemporary Psychoanalysis Books.

Levine S, Haltmeyer GC, Kaas GG, Penenberg VH (1967) Physiological and behavioral effects of infantile stimulation. Physiology and Behavior 2: 55–63.

Levinger G, Clark J (1961) Emotional factors in the forgetting of word associations. Journal of Abnormal and Social Psychology 62: 99–105.

Levinson A, Fonagy P (submitted) Attachment classification in prisoners and psychiatric patients.

Lewin K (1952) Field Theory and Social Science. London: Tavistock Publications.

Lewinsohn PM, Gotlib IH, Seeley JR (1995) Adolescent psychopathology: IV. Specificity of psychosocial risk factors for depression and substance abuse in older adolescents. Journal of the American Academy of Child and Adolescent Psychiatry 34: 1221–9.

Lewis JM (1998) For better or worse: interpersonal relationships and individual outcome. American Journal of Psychiatry 155: 582–9.

Lewis M, Allessandri SM, Sullivan MW (1990) Violation of expectancy, loss of control and anger expressions in young infants. Developmental Psychology 26(5): 745–51.

Lewis M, Brooks-Gunn J (1979) Social Cognition and the Acquisition of Self. New York: Plenum Press.

Lichtenberg JD (1987) Infant studies and clinical work with adults. Psycho-Analytic Inquiry 7: 311-30.

Lichtenstein H (1961) Identity and sexuality: a study of their interrelationship in man. Journal of the American Psychoanalytic Association 9: 179-260.

Lichtenstein H (1963) The dilemma of human identity: notes on self-transformation, self-observation, and metamorphosis. Journal of the American Psychoanalytic Association 11: 173-223.

Lieberman AF (1991) Attachment theory and infant-parent psychotherapy: some conceptual, clinical and research issues. In D Cicchetti, S Toth (eds), Rochester Symposium on Developmental Psychopathology: Vol. 3. Models and Integrations (pp. 261-88). Hillsdale, NJ: Erlbaum.

Lieberman AF, Pawl J (1993) Infant-parent psychotherapy. In CH Zeanah (ed.), Handbook of Infant Mental Health (pp. 427-42). New York: Guilford Press.

Lieberman AF, Zeanah CH (1999) Contributions of attachment theory to infant-parent psychotherapy and other interventions with infants and young children. In J Cassidy, PR Shaver (eds), Handbook of Attachment: Theory, Research and Clinical Applications (pp. 555-74). New York: Guilford.

Limentani A (1977) Affects and the psychoanalytic situation. International Journal of Psycho-Analysis 58: 171-97.

Limentani A (1989) Between Freud and Klein. London: Free Association.

Linehan MM (1993) The Skills Training Manual for Treating Borderline Personality Disorder. New York: Guilford Press.

Links PS, Steiner M, Huxley G (1988) The occurrence of borderline personality disorder in the families of borderline patients. Journal of the Personality Disorders 2: 14-20.

Litt C (1981) Children's attachment to transitional objects: a study of two pediatric populations. American Journal of Orthopsychiatry 51: 131-9.

Little M (1981) Transference Neurosis and Transference Psychosis. New York: Jason Aronson.

Little M (1985) Winnicott working in areas where psychotic anxieties predominate. Free Associations 3: 9-42.

Liu D, Diorio J, Tannenbaum B, Caldji C, Francis D, Freedman A, Sharma S, Pearson D, Plotsky PM, Meany MJ (1997) Maternal care, hippocampal glucocorticoid receptors, and hypothalamic-pituitary-adrenal responses to stress. Science 277: 1659-62.

Loewald HW (1951) Ego and reality. Papers on Psychoanalysis (pp. 3-20). New Haven, CT: Yale University Press, 1980.

Loewald HW (1955) Hypnoid state, repression, abreaction, and recollection. Papers on Psychoanalysis (pp. 33-42). New Haven, CT: Yale University Press, 1980.

Loewald HW (1960) On the therapeutic action of psycho-analysis. International Journal of Psycho-Analysis 41: 16-33.

Loewald HW (1965) Some considerations on repetition and repetition compulsion. Papers on Psychoanalysis (pp. 21-32). New Haven, CT: Yale University Press, 1980.

Loewald HW (1971a) On motivation and instinct theory. Papers on Psychoanalysis (pp. 102-37). New Haven, CT: Yale University Press, 1980.

Loewald HW (1971b) The transference neurosis: comments on the concept and the phenomenon. Papers on Psychoanalysis (pp. 302-14). New Haven, CT: Yale University Press, 1980.

Loewald HW (1973) On internalization. Papers on Psychoanalysis (pp. 69-86). New Haven, CT: Yale University Press.

Loewald HW (1974) Psychoanalysis as an art and the fantasy character of the analytic situation. Papers on Psychoanalysis (pp. 352-71). New Haven, CT: Yale University Press, 1980.

Loewald HW (1978a) Instinct theory, object relations and psychic structure formation. Journal of the American Psychoanalytic Association 26: 453-506.

Loewald HW (1978b) Instinct theory, object relations, and psychic structure formation. Papers on Psychoanalysis (pp. 384-404). New Haven, CT: Yale University Press, 1980.

Loewald HW (1979) The waning of the Oedipus complex. Papers on Psychoanalysis (pp. 384-404). New Haven, CT: Yale University Press, 1980.

Loewald HW (1985) Oedipus complex and development of self. Psychoanalytic Quarterly 54: 435-43.

Loewald HW (1986). Transference-countertransference. Journal of the American Psychoanalytic Association, 34, 275-288.

Londerville S, Main M (1981) Security of attachment, compliance, and maternal training methods in the second year of life. Developmental Psychology 17: 238-99.

Lonigan CJ, Elbert JC, Johnson SB (1998) Empirically supported psychosocial interventions for children: an overview. Journal of Clinical Child Psychology 27: 138-45.

Loranger A, Oldham J, Tullis E (1982) Familial transmission of DSM-III borderline personality disorder. Archives of General Psychiatry 39: 795-9.

Lorenz K (1935) Der Kumpan in der Umvelt des Vogels [Companionship in Bird Life]. In CH Schiller (ed.), Instinctive Behavior (pp. 83-128). New York: International Universities Press.

Losoya SH, Callor S, Rowe DC, Goldsmith HH (1997) Origins of familial similarity in parenting: a study of twins and adoptive siblings. Developmental Psychopathology 33: 1012-23.

Luborsky L, Crits-Christoph P (1990) Understanding Transference: The CCRT Method. New York: Basic Books.

Luborsky L, Luborsky E (1995) The era of measures of transference: the CCRT and other measures. In T Shapiro, R Emde (eds), Research in Psychoanalysis: Process, Development, Outcome (pp. 329-51).

Luborsky L, Barber J, Beutler L (1993) Introduction to special section: a briefing on curative factors in dynamic psychotherapy. Journal of Consulting and Clinical Psychology 61: 539-41.

Lussier A (1988) The limitations of the object relations model. Psychoanalytic Quarterly 57: 528-46.

Lykes MB (1985) Gender and individualistic vs. collectivist bases for notions about the self, Journal of Personality 53: 356-383.

Lyons-Ruth K (1995) Broadening our conceptual frameworks: can we re-introduce relational strategies and implicit representational systems to the study of psychopathology. Developmental Psychology 31: 432-6.

Lyons-Ruth K (1996a) Attachment relationships among children with aggressive behavior problems: the role of disorganized early attachment patterns. Journal of Consulting and Clinical Psychology 64: 32-40.

Lyons-Ruth K (1996b) Attachment relationships among children with aggressive behavior problems: the role of disorganized early attachment patterns. Journal of Consulting and Clinical Psychology 64: 64-73.

Lyons-Ruth K (1998) Implicit relational knowing: its role in development and psychoanalytic treatment. Infant Mental Health Journal 7: 127-31.

Lyons-Ruth K (1999) The two person unconscious: intersubjective dialogue, enactive relational representation and the emergence of new forms of relational organisation. Psychoanalytic Inquiry 19(4): 576–617.

Lyons-Ruth K, Jacobovitz D (1999) Attachment disorganization: unresolved loss, relational violence and lapses in behavioral and attentional strategies. In J Cassidy, PR Shaver (eds), Handbook of Attachment Theory and Research (pp. 520–54). New York: Guilford.

Lyons-Ruth K, Alpern L, Repacholi B (1993) Disorganized infant attachment classification and maternal psychosocial problems as predictors of hostile-aggressive behavior in the preschool classroom. Child Development 64: 572–85.

Lyons-Ruth K, Bronfman E, Atwood G (1999) A relational diathesis model of hostile-helpless states of mind: expressions in mother–infant interaction. In J Solomon, C George (eds), Attachment Disorganization (pp. 33–70). New York: Guilford Press.

Lyons-Ruth K, Bronfman E, Parsons E (1999) Atypical attachment in infancy and early childhood among children at developmental risk. IV. Maternal frightened, frightening, or atypical behavior and disorganized infant attachment patterns. In J Vondra, D Barnett (eds), Typical Patterns of Infant Attachment: Theory, Research and Current Directions (Vol. 64, pp. 67–96): Monographs of the Society for Research in Child Development.

Lyons-Ruth K, Connell DB, Grunebaum HU (1990) Infants at social risk: maternal depression and family support services as mediators of infant development and security of attachment. Child Development 61: 85–98.

Lyons-Ruth K, Zoll D, Connell D, Grunebaum HU (1986) The depressed mother and her one-year-old infant: environment, interaction, attachment and infant development. In EZ Tronick, T Field (eds), Maternal Depression and Infant Disturbance. (pp. 61–82). San Francisco: Jossey-Bass.

Lyons-Ruth K, Zoll D, Connell DB, Grunebaum HU (1989) Family deviance and family disruption in childhood: associations with maternal behavior and infant maltreatment during the first two years of life. Development and Psychopathology 1: 219–36.

McCauley E, Pavidis K, Kendall K (2000) Developmental precursors of depression. In I Goodyear (ed.), The Depressed Child and Adolescent: Developmental and Clinical Perspectives. New York: Cambridge University Press.

McDougall J (1974) The psycho-soma and the psychoanalytic process. International Review of Psycho-Analysis 1: 437–60.

McDougall J (1986) Theater of the Mind. New York: Basic Books.

McEwen BS, Sapolsky RM (1995) Stress and cognitive function. Current Opinion in Neurobiology 5:205–16.

MacFarlane AC (1987) Post-traumatic phenomena in a longitudinal study of children following a natural disaster. Journal of the American Academy of Child and Adolescent Psychiatry 28:764–9.

Macfie J, Toth SL, Rogosch FA, Robinson J, Emde RN, Cicchetti D (1999) Effect of maltreatment on preschoolers' narrative representations of responses to relieve distress and of role reversal. Developmental Psychology 35: 460–5.

McGlashan T (1986) The Chestnut Lodge follow-up study III: Long-term outcome of borderline personalities. Archives of General Psychiatry 43: 20–30.

McLaughlin JT (1981) Transference, psychic reality and countertransference. Psychoanalytic Quarterly 50: 639–64.

McLaughlin JT (1991) Clinical and theoretical aspects of enactment. Journal of the American Psychoanalytic Association 39: 595–614.

McNally RJ, Riemann BC, Kim E (1990) Selective processing of threat cues in panic disorder. Behavior Research and Therapy 28: 407-12.

Mahler MS (1963) Thoughts about development and individuation. The Psychoanalytic Study of the Child 18: 307-24.

Mahler MS (1967) On human symbiosis and the vicissitudes of individuation. Journal of the American Psychoanalytic Association 15: 740-63.

Mahler MS (1968) On Human Symbiosis and the Vicissitudes of Individuation. New York: International Universities Press.

Mahler MS (1971) A study of separation-individuation process and its possible application to borderline phenomena in the psychoanalytic situation. The Psychoanalytic Study of the Child 26: 403-24.

Mahler MS (1972) On the first three subphases of the separation-individuation process. International Journal of Psycho-Analysis 53: 333-8.

Mahler MS (1974) Symbiosis and individuation: the psychological birth of the human infant, The Selected Papers of Margaret S. Mahler. New York: Jason Aronson.

Mahler MS (1975) On human symbiosis and the vicissitudes of individuation. Journal of the American Psychoanalytic Association 23: 740-63.

Mahler MS (1979) The Selected Papers of Margaret S. Mahler. New York: Aronson.

Mahler MS, Furer M (1968) On Human Symbiosis and the Vicissitudes of Individuation, Vol. 1: Infantile Psychosis. New York: International University Press.

Mahler MS, Kaplan L (1977) Developmental aspects in the assessment of narcissistic and so-called borderline personalities. In P Hartocollis (ed.), Borderline Personality Disorders: The Concept, the Syndrome, the Patient (pp. 71-86). New York International Universities Press.

Mahler MS, McDevitt JF (1980) The separation-individuation process and identity formation. In SI Greenspan, GH Pollock (eds), Infancy and Early Childhood, Vol. 1 of The Course of Life, Psychoanalytic Contributions toward Understanding Personality Development (pp. 395-406). Washington, DC: Publication No. (ADM) 80-786. National Institute Mental Health.

Mahler MS, Pine F, Bergman A (1975) The Psychological Birth of the Human Infant: Symbiosis and Individuation. New York: Basic Books.

Main M (1991) Metacognitive knowledge, metacognitive monitoring, and singular (coherent) vs. multiple (incoherent) model of attachment: findings and directions for future research. In CM Parkes, J Stevenson-Hinde, P Marris (eds), Attachment Across the Life Cycle (pp. 127-59). London: Tavistock/Routledge.

Main M. (1995) Recent studies in attachment: overview, with selected implications for clinical work. In S Goldberg, R Muir, J Kerr (eds), Attachment Theory: Social, Developmental, and Clinical Perspectives. (pp. 407-74). Hillsdale, NJ: Analytic Press, Inc.

Main M, Goldwyn R (1990) Adult attachment rating and classification systems. In M Main (ed.), A Typology of Human Attachment Organization Assessed in Discourse, Drawings and Interviews. New York: Cambridge University Press.

Main M, Goldwyn R (1994) Adult Attachment Rating and Classification System, Manual in Draft, Version 6.0. Unpublished manuscript: University of California at Berkeley.

Main M, Hesse E (1990a) Adult lack of resolution of attachment-related trauma related to infant disorganized/disoriented behavior in the Ainsworth Strange Situation: linking parental states of mind to infant behavior in a stressful situation. In MT Greenberg, D Cicchetti, M Cummings (eds), Attachment in the Preschool Years: Theory, Research and Intervention (pp. 339-426). Chicago, IL: University of Chicago Press.

Main M, Hesse E (1990b) Parents' unresolved traumatic experiences are related to infant disorganized attachment status: Is frightened and/or frightening parental behavior the linking mechanism? In M Greenberg, D Cicchetti, EM Cummings (eds), Attachment in the Preschool Years: Theory, Research and Intervention (pp. 161-82). Chicago, IL: University of Chicago Press.

Main M, Hesse E (1992) Disorganized/disoriented infant behavior in the Strange Situation, lapses in the monitoring of reasoning and discourse during the parent's Adult Attachment Interview, and dissociative states. In M Ammaniti, D Stern (eds), Attachment and Psychoanalysis (pp. 86-140). Rome: Gius, Latereza & Figli.

Main M, Morgan H (1996) Disorganization and disorientation in infant Strange Situation behavior: phenotypic resemblance to dissociative states. In LK Michelson, WJ Ray (eds), Handbook of Dissociation: Theoretical, Empirical, and Clinical Perspectives (pp. 107-38). New York, NY: Plenum Press.

Main M, Solomon J (1986) Discovery of an insecure-disorganized/disoriented attachment pattern. In TB Brazelton, MW Yogman (eds), Affective Development in Infancy (pp. 95-124). Norwood NJ: Ablex.

Main M, Solomon J (1990) Procedures for identifying infants as disorganized/disoriented during the Ainsworth Strange Situation. In M Greenberg, D Cicchetti, EM Cummings (eds), Attachment during the Preschool Years: Theory, Research and Intervention (pp. 121-60). Chicago, IL: University of Chicago Press.

Main M, Kaplan N, Cassidy J (1985) Security in infancy, childhood and adulthood: a move to the level of representation. In I Bretherton, E Waters (eds), Growing Points of Attachment Theory and Research. Monographs of the Society for Research in Child Development (Vol. 50, pp. 66-104). Chicago, IL: Chicago University Press.

Main T (1957) The ailment. British Journal of Medical Psychology 30: 129-45.

Malatesta CZ, Culver C, Tesman JR, Shepard B (1989) The development of emotion expression during the first two years of life. Monographs of the Society for Research in Child Development 54: 1-104.

Malmberg A, Lewis G, David A, Allebeck P (1998). Premorbid adjustment and personality in people with schizophrenia. British Journal of Psychiatry 172: 308-13.

Manchanda R, Sethi BB, Gupta SC (1979) Hostility and guilt in obsessional neuroses. British Journal of Psychiatry 135, 52-4.

Mandler G (1975) Mind and Emotion. New York: Wiley & Sons.

Mandler G (1985) Cognitive Psychology. An Essay in Cognitive Science. Hillsdale, NJ: Lawrence Erlbaum Associates.

Mandler G (1997) Human Nature Explored. New York: Oxford University Press.

Marcia JE (1994) The empirical study of ego identity. In HA Bosma, TLG Graafsma, HD Grotevant, DJ de Levita (eds), Identity and Development: An Interdisciplinary Approach (pp. 67-80). Thousand Oaks, CA.: Sage.

Marenco S, Weinberger DR (2000) The neurodevelopmental hypothesis of schizophrenia: following a trail of evidence from cradle to grave. Dev Psychopathol 12(3): 501-27.

Markus H (1991) Culture and self: implications for cognition, emotion, and motivation. Psychological Review 98: 224-53.

Maroda K (1999) Seduction, Surrender, and Transformation. Hillsdale, NJ: The Analytic Press.

Marttunen M (1994) Psychosocial maladjustment, mental disorders and stressful life events precede adolescent suicide. Psychiatrica Fennica 25: 39-51.

Marvin RS, Britner PA (1999) Normative development: the ontogeny of attachment. In J Cassidy, PR Shaver (eds), Handbook of Attachment: Theory, Research and Clinical Applications (pp. 44-67). New York: Guilford.

Masson J (1984) The Assault on Truth: Freud's Suppression of the Seduction Theory. New York: Farrar, Straus & Giroux.

Masten AS, Coatsworth JD (1995) Competence, resilience and psychopathology. In D Cicchetti, DJ Cohen (eds), Developmental Psychopathology. Vol. 2: Risk, Disorder and Adaptation (pp. 715-52). New York: John Wiley.

Masten AS, Curtis WJ (2000) Integrating competence and psychopathology: pathways towards a comprehensive science of adaptation and development. Development and Psychopathology 12: 529-50.

Masterson JF (1972) Treatment of the Borderline Adolescent: A Developmental Approach. New York: Wiley Interscience.

Masterson JF (1976) Psychotherapy of the Borderline Adult: A Developmental Approach. New York: Brunner/Mazel.

Masterson JF (1985) The Real Self: A Developmental, Self, and Object Relations Approach. New York: Brunner/Mazel.

Masterson JF, Klein R (1989) Psychotherapy of the Disorders of the Self: The Masterson Approach. New York: Brunner/Mazel.

Masterson JF, Rinsley D (1975) The borderline syndrome: the role of the mother in the genesis and psychic structure of the borderline personality. International Journal of Psycho-Anal 56: 163-77.

Matas L, Arend RA, Sroufe LA (1978) Continuity of adaptation in the second year: the relationship between quality of attachment and later competence. Child Development 49: 547-56.

Mathews A (1990) Why worry? The cognitive function of anxiety. Behavior Research and Therapy 28: 455-68.

Mathews A, MacLeod C (1986) Discrimination of threat cues without awareness in anxiety states. Journal of Abnormal Psychology 95: 131-8.

Matte Blanco I (1975) The Unconscious as Infinite Sets. London: Duckworth.

Matte Blanco I (1988) Thinking, Feeling and Being. London: Routledge.

Matthys W, Cuperus JM, van Engeland H (1999) Deficient social problem-solving in boys with ODD/CD, with ADHD, and with both disorders. Journal of the American Academy of Child and Adolescent Psychiatry 38: 311-21.

Mayes LC, Cohen DJ (1992) The development of a capacity for imagination in early childhood. Psychoanalytic Study of the Child 47: 23-48.

Mayes LC, Cohen DJ (1993) Playing and therapeutic action in child analysis. International Journal of Psycho-Analysis 74: 1235-44.

Mayes LC, Spence DP (1994) Understanding therapeutic action in the analytic situation: a second look at the developmental metaphor. Journal of the American Psychoanalytic Association 42: 789-816.

Mayes LC, Cohen DJ, Klin A (1991) Experiencing self and others: a psychoanalytic perspective on theory of mind and autism. In H Tager-Flusberg, S Baron-Cohen, D Cohen (eds), Understanding Other Minds: Perspectives from Autism. Oxford: Oxford University Press.

Mead GH (1934) Mind, Self and Society. Chicago, IL: University of Chicago Press.

Meaney MJ, Aitken D, Bhatnager S et al. (1988). Effect of neonatal handling on age-related impairments associated with the hippocampus. Science 239: 766.

Meaney MJ, Aitken DH, Sharma S, Sarrieau A (1989) Neonatal handling alters adrenocortical negative feedback sensitivity and hippocampal type II glucocorticoid receptor binding in the rat. Neuroendocrinology 50: 597-604.

Meehl PE (1986) Diagnostic taxa as open concepts: metatheoretical and statistical questions about reliability and construct validity in the grand strategy of nosological revision. In T Millon, GL Klerman (eds), Contemporary Directions in Psychopathology: Toward DSM IV (pp. 215-31). New York: Guilford Press.

Meins E, Fernyhough C, Russel J, Clark-Carter D (1998) Security of attachment as a predictor of symbolic and mentalising abilities: a longitudinal study. Social Development 7: 1-24.

Meins E, Ferryhough C, Fradley E, Tuckey M (2001) Rethinking maternal sensitivity: mothers' comments on infants mental processes predict security of attachment at 12 months. Journal of Child Psychology and Psychiatry 42: 637-48.

Meissner WW (1980) A note on projective identification. Journal of the American Psychoanalytic Association 28: 43-67.

Meissner WW (1996) The Therapeutic Alliance. New Haven, CT: Yale University Press.

Meltzer D (1974) Mutism in infantile autism, schizophrenia and manic-depressive states. International Journal of Psycho-Analysis 55: 397-404.

Meltzer D (1978) The Kleinian Development. Strathtay: Clunie Press.

Meltzoff AN (1990) Foundations for developing a concept of self: the role of imitation in relating self to other and the value of social mirroring, social modeling and self practice in infancy. In D Cicchetti, M Beeghly (eds), The Self in Transition: Infancy to Childhood. Chicago, IL: University of Chicago Press.

Meltzoff AN (1995) Understanding the intentions of others: re-enactment of intended acts by 18-month-old children. Developmental Psychology 31: 838-50.

Meltzoff AN, Borton W (1979) Intermodal matching by human neonates. Nature 282: 403-4.

Meltzoff AN, Gopnik A (1993) The role of imitation in understanding persons and developing a theory of mind. In S Baron-Cohen, H Tager-Flusberg, D Cohen (eds), Understanding Other Minds: Perspectives from Autism (pp. 335-66). New York: Oxford University Press, Inc.

Meltzoff AN, Moore MK (1989) Imitation in newborn infants: exploring the range of gestures imitated and the underlying mechanisms. Developmental Psychology 25:954-62.

Meltzoff AN, Moore MK (1992) Perception, action and cognition in early infancy. Annals of Paediatrics 32: 63-77.

Meltzoff AN, Moore MK (1997) Explaining facial imitation: theoretical model. Early Development and Parenting 6: 179-92.

Michels R (1985) Perspectives on the nature of psychic reality: panel introduction. Journal of the American Psychoanalytic Association 33: 515-25.

Michels R (2000) The case history. Journal of the American Psychoanalytic Association 48: 355-66, 417-20.

Migone P, Liotti G (1998) Psychoanalysis and cognitive-evolutionary psychology: as attempt at integration. International Journal of Psychoanalysis 79: 1071-95.

Miller NE, Luborsky L, Barber JP, Docherty JP (1993) Psychodynamic Treatment Research: A Handbook for Clinical Practice. New York: Basic Books.

Miller PA, Eisenberg N, Fabes RA et al. (1989) Mothers' emotional arousal as a moderator in the socialization of children's empathy. In N Eisenberg (ed.), Empathy and Related Emotional Responses: New Directions for Child Development. San Francisco, CA: Jossey-Bass.

Millett K (1971) Sexual Politics. London: Rupert Hart-Davies.

Milner B, Squire LR, Kandel ER (1998) Cognitive neuroscience and the study of memory. Neuron Rev 20: 445–68.

Milner M (1969) The Hands of the Living God. London: Hogarth Press.

Milrod B, Busch F, Cooper A, Shapiro T (1997) Manual for Panic-Focused Psychodynamic Psychotherapy. Washington, DC: American Psychiatric Press.

Minuchin P (1988) Relationships within the family: a systems perspective on development. In RA Hinde, J Stevenson-Hinde (eds), Relationships within Families: Mutual Influences (pp. 7–26). Oxford: Clarendon Press.

Mischel W (1973) Toward a cognitive social learning reconceptualization of personality. Psychological Review 80: 252–83.

Mitchell J (1973) Psychoanalysis and Feminism. Harmondsworth: Penguin.

Mitchell SA (1986) The Wings of Icarus: illusion and the problem of narcissism. Contemporary Psychoanalysis 22: 107–32.

Mitchell SA (1988) Relational Concepts in Psychoanalysis: An Integration. Cambridge, MA: Harvard University Press.

Mitchell SA (1991) Contemporary perspectives on the self: toward an integration. Psychoanlytic Dialogues 1: 121–47.

Mitchell SA (1993a) Aggression and the endangered self. Psychoanalytic Quarterly 62: 351–82.

Mitchell SA (1993b) Hope and Dread in Psychoanalysis. New York: Basic Books.

Mitchell SA (1995) Interaction in the Kleinian and interpersonal traditions. Contemporary Psychoanalysis 31: 65–91.

Mitchell SA (1998) Attachment theory and the psychoanalytic tradition: reflections on human relationality. British Journal of Psychotherapy 15: 177–93.

Mitchell SA (2000) Relationality: From Attachment to Intersubjectivity. Hillsdale, NJ: Analytic Press.

Mitchell SA, Black M (1995) Freud and Beyond. New York: Basic Books.

Modell AH (1963) Primitive object relationships and the predisposition to schizophrenia. International Journal of Psycho-Analysis 44: 282–92.

Modell AH (1968) Object Love and Reality. New York: International Universities Press.

Modell AH (1975) A narcissistic defense against affects and the illusion of self-sufficiency. International Journal of Psycho-Analysis 56: 275–82.

Modell AH (1976) 'The holding environment' and the therapeutic action of psychoanalysis. Journal of the American Psychoanalytic Association 24: 285–307.

Modell AH (1984) Psychoanalysis in a New Context. New York: International Universities Press.

Modell AH (1985) Object relations theory. In A Rothstein (ed.), Models of the Mind: Their Relationships to Clinical Work (pp. 85–100). New York: International Universities Press.

Modell AH (1990) Other Times, Other Realities. Cambridge, MA: Harvard University Press.

Moi T (1985) Sexual/Textual Politics. London: Routledge.

Mollon P (1998) Remembering Trauma: A Psychotherapist's Guide to Memory and Illusion. Chichester: Wiley.

Mollon P (2001) Releasing the Self: The Healing Legacy of Heinz Kohut. London: Whurr.

Monsen J, Odland T, Faugli A, Daae E, Eilerstein DE (1995a) Personality disorders and psychosocial changes after intensive psychotherapy: a prospective follow-up study of an outpatient psychotherapy project, 5 years after the end of treatment. Scandinavian Journal of Psychology 36: 256–68.

Monsen J, Odland T, Faugli A, Daae E, Eilerstein DE (1995b) Personality disorders: changes and stability after intensive psychotherapy focussing on affect consciousness. Psychotherapy Research 5: 33–48.

Moran GS, Fonagy P (1987) Psycho-analysis and diabetes: an exploration of single case study methodology. British Journal of Medical Psychology 60: 370–8.

Moran GS, Fonagy P, Kurtz A, Bolton A, Brook C (1991) A controlled study of the psycho-analytic treatment of brittle diabetes. Journal of the American Academy of Child and Adolescent Psychiatry 30: 926–35.

Morgan AC (1998) Moving along to things left undone. Infant Mental Health Journal 19:324–32.

Morling B, Epstein S (1997) Compromises produced by the dialectic between self-verification and self-enhancement. Journal of Personality and Social Psychology 73: 1268–83.

Morris JS, Ohman A, Dolan RJ (1998) Conscious and unconscious emotional learning in the human amygdala. Nature 393: 467–70.

Morton J, Frith U (1995) Causal modeling: a structural approach to developmental psychology. In D Cicchetti, DJ Cohen (eds), Developmental Psychopathology. Vol. 1: Theory and Methods (pp. 357–90). New York: John Wiley.

Moses LJ, Flavell JH (1990) Inferring false beliefs from actions and reactions. Child Development 61: 929–45.

Moss E, Parent S, Gosselin C (1995) Attachment and theory of mind: cognitive and metacognitive correlates of attachment during the preschool period. Paper presented at the biennial meeting of the Society for Research in Child Development, Indianapolis, IN, March–April.

Mufson L, Fairbanks J (1996) Interpersonal psychotherapy for depressed adolescents: a one-year naturalistic follow-up study. Journal of the American Academy of Child and Adolescent Psychiatry 35: 1145–55.

Murphy LG, Moriarity AE (1975) Vulnerability, Coping and Growth. New Haven, CT: Yale University Press.

Murphy ST, Monahan JL, Zajonc R (1995) Additivity of nonconscious affect: combined effects of priming and exposure. Journal of Personality and Social Psychology 69: 589–602.

Murray L, Cooper PJ (1997) The role of infant and maternal factors in postpartum depression, mother–infant interactions and infant outcome. In L Murray, PJ Cooper (eds), Postpartum Depression and Child Development (pp. 111–35). New York: Guilford Press.

Nachmias M, Gunnar MR, Mangelsdorf S, Parritz RH, Buss K (1996) Behavioral inhibition and stress reactivity: moderating role of attachment security. Child Development 67: 508–22.

Nagera H (1966) Early Childhood Disturbances, the Infantile Neurosis, and the Adulthood Disturbances. New York: International University Press.

Neiderhiser JM, Reiss D, Hetherington EM, Plomin R (1999) Relationships between parenting and adolescent adjustment over time: genetic and environmental contributions. Development and Psychopathology 35: 680–92.

Neisser U (1995) Criteria for an ecological self. In P Rochat (ed.), The Self in Infancy: Theory and Research. Advances in Psychology 112. (pp. 17–34). Amsterdam, Netherlands: North-Holland/Elsevier Science Publishers.

Nelson CA, Bloom RE (1998) Child development and neuroscience. Child Development 68: 970-87.

Nelson K (1993a) Explaining the emergence of autobiographical memory in early childhood. In A Collins, SE Gathercole, MA Conway, PE Morris (eds), Theories of Memory (pp. 355-85). Hove: Erlbaum.

Nelson K (1993b) The psychological and social origins of autobiographical memory. Psychological Science 4: 7-14.

Nelson LA (1987) The recognition of facial expressions in the first two years of life: mechanisms of development. Child Development 58: 889-909.

Nemeroff CB (1996) The corticotropin-releasing factor (CRF) hypothesis of depression: new findings and new directions. Molecular Psychiatry 1: 326-42.

Neubauer PB (1984) Anna Freud's concept of developmental lines. The Psychoanalytic Study of the Child 39:15-27.

Newman LS, Duff K, Baumeister R (1997) A new look at defensive projection: thought suppression, accessibility, and biased person perception. Journal of Personality and Social Psychology 72: 980-1001.

Newson J, Newson E, Mahalski P (1982) Persistent infant comfort habits and their sequelae at 11 and 16 years. Journal of Child Psychology and Psychiatry 23: 421-36.

Nigg JT, Lohr NE, Westen D, Gold L, Silk KR (1992) Malevolent object representations in borderline personality disorder and major depression. Journal of Abnormal Psychology 101: 61-7.

Nigg JT, Goldsmith HH (1998) Developmental psychopathology, personality, and temperament: reflections on recent behavioral genetics research. Human Biology 70: 387-412.

Nisbett RE, Wilson TD (1977) Telling more than we can know: verbal reports on mental processes. Psychological Review 84, 231-59.

Noam GG (1990) Beyond Freud and Piaget: biographical world – interpersonal self. In TE Wren (ed.), The Moral Domain (pp. 360-99). Cambridge, MA: MIT Press.

Nolen-Hoeksema, S. (1987) Sex differences in unipolar depression: evidence and theory. Psychological Bulletin 101: 259-82.

Noy P (1977) Metapsychology as a multimodel system. International Review of Psychoanalysis 4: 1-12.

O'Brien JT (1997) The 'glucocorticoid cascade' hypothesis in man: prolonged stress may cause permanent brain damage. British Journal of Psychiatry 170:199-201.

O'Connor TG, Rutter M, Kreppner J (2000) The effects of global severe privation of cognitive competence: extension and longitudinal follow-up. Child Development 71(2): 376-90.

O'Connor TG, Deater-Deckard K, Fulker D, Rutter M, Plomin R (1998) Genotype-environment correlations in late childhood and early adolescence: antisocial behavioral problems and coercive parenting. Developmental Psychology 34: 970-81.

O'Connor TG, McGuire S, Reiss D, Hetherington EM (1998) Co-occurrence of depressive symptoms and antisocial behavior in adolescence: a common genetic liability. Journal of Abnormal Psychology 107: 27-37.

O'Connor TG, Hetherington EM, Reiss D, Plomin R (1995) A twin-sibling study of observed parent-adolescent interactions. Child Dev 66(3): 812-29.

Ogata SN, Silk KR, Goodrich S (1990a) The childhood experience of the borderline patient. In P Links (ed.), Family Environment and Borderline Personality Disorder (pp. 87-103). Washington, DC: American Psychiatric Press.

Ogata SN, Silk KR, Goodrich S, Lohr NE, Westen D, Hill E (1990a) Childhood abuse and clinical symptoms in borderline patients. American Journal of Psychiatry 147: 1008–1013.

Ogata SN, Silk KR, Goodrich, S, Lohr NE, Westen D, Hill E (1990b) Childhood sexual and physical abuse in adult patients with borderline personality disorder. American Journal of Psychiatry 147: 1008–13.

Ogawa JR, Sroufe LA, Weinfield NS, Carlson EA, Egeland B (1997) Development and the fragmented self: longitudinal study of dissociative symptomatology in a nonclinical sample. Development and Psychopathology 9: 855–79.

Ogden T (1979) On projective identification. International Journal of Psycho-Analysis 60: 357–73.

Ogden T (1986) The Matrix of the Mind: Object Relations and the Psychoanalytic Dialogue. New York: Aronson.

Ogden T (1989) The Primitive Edge of Experience. New York: Aronson.

Ogden T (1992) The dialectically constituted/decentred subject of psychoanalysis II. The contributions of Klein and Winnicott. International Journal of Psycho-Analysis 73: 613–26.

Ogden T (1994) The analytic third: working with intersubjective clinical facts. International Journal of Psychoanalysis 75: 3–19.

O'Grady D, Metz JR (1987) Resilience in children at high risk for psychological disorder. Journal of Pediatric Psychology 12: 3–23.

Okimoto JT (2001) The appeal cycle in three cultures: an exploratory comparison of child development. Journal of the American Psychoanalytic Association 49(1): 187–215.

Olinick S (1982) Meanings beyond words: psychoanalytic perceptions of silence and communication, happiness, sexual love and death. International Review of Psycho-Analysis 9: 461–72.

O'Neill RM, Greenberg RP, Fisher S (1992) Humor and anality. Humour 5:283–91.

Oppenheim D, Emde R, Warren S (1997) Children's narrative representations of mothers: their development and associations with child and mother adaptation. Child Development 68:127–38.

Orbach S, Eichenbaum L (1982) Outside In … Inside Out: Women's Psychology: A Feminist Psychoanalytic Approach. London: Penguin.

Orlofsky J (1993) Intimacy status: theory and research. In JE Marcia, AS Waterman, DR Matteson et al. (eds), Ego Identity: A Handbook for Psychosocial Research. New York: Springer-Verlag.

Ornstein P, Ornstein A (1985) Clinical understanding and explaining: the empathic vantage point. In A Goldberg (ed.), Progress in Self Psychology, Vol. 1 (pp. 43–61). New York: Guilford Press.

Orvaschel H (1983) Maternal depression and child dysfunction. In BB Lahey, AE Kazdin (ed.), Advances in Clinical Child Psychology (pp. 169–97). New York: Plenum Press.

O'Shaughnessy E (1981) A clinical study of a defensive organisation. International Journal of Psycho-Analysis 62: 359–69.

O'Shaughnessy E (1989) The invisible Oedipus complex. In J Steiner (ed.), The Oedipus Complex Today (pp. 129–50). London: Karnac Books.

O'Shaughnessy E (1992) Enclaves and excursions. International Journal of Psychoanalysis 73: 603–11.

Padel JH (1972) The contribution of WRD Fairbairn. Bulletin of the European Psycho-Analytical Federation 2: 13–26.

Palombo J (1987) Selfobject transference in the treatment of borderline neurocognitively impaired children. In JS Grotstein, JA Lang (eds), The Borderline Patient: Emerging Concepts in Diagnosis, Psychodynamics and Treatment Vol 1 (pp. 317–46). Hillsdale, NJ: Atlantic Press.

Panel (1937) Symposium on the theory of the therapeutic results of psycho-analysis. International Journal of Psycho-analysis 18: 125–84.

Panksepp J (1998) Affective Neuroscience: The Foundations of Human and Animal Emotions. Oxford: Oxford University Press.

Panksepp J (2001) The long term psychobiological consequences of infant emotions: prescriptions for the twenty-first century. Infant Mental Health Journal 22:132–73.

Papousek H, Papousek M (1974) Mirror-image and self recognition in young human infants: a new method of experimental analysis. Developmental Psychobiology 7: 149–57.

Parens H (1979) The Development of Aggression in Early Childhood. New York: Aronson.

Parens H (1980) An exploration of the relations of instinctual drives and the symbiosis/separation-individuation process. Journal of the American Psychoanalytic Association 28: 89–114.

Pawl J, Lieberman AF (1997) Infant–parent psychotherapy. In J Noshpitz (ed.), Handbook of Child and Adolescent Psychiatry (Vol. 1, pp. 339–51). New York: Basic Books.

Pawlik K, Cattell RB (1964) Third-order factors in objective personality tests. British Journal of Psychology 55: 1–18.

Pei Q, Zetterstrom T, Fillenz M (1990) Tail pinch induces changes in the turnover and release of dopamine and 5-hydroxytrptamine in different brain regions of the rat. Neuroscience 35: 133–8.

Pennebaker JW (1997) Opening Up: The Healing Power of Expressing Emotions. New York: Guilford Press.

Pennebaker JW, Mayne TJ, Francis ME (1997) Linguistic predictors of adaptive bereavement. J Pers Soc Psychol 72(4): 863–71.

Perelberg RJ (ed.) (1999) Psychoanalytic Understanding of Violence and Suicide. London: Routledge.

Perner J, Leekam S, Wimmer H (1987) Three-year-olds' difficulty in understanding false belief: cognitive limitation, lack of knowledge, or pragmatic misunderstanding? British Journal of Developmental Psychology 5: 125–37.

Perry J, Cooper S (1985) Psychodynamics, symptoms, and outcome in borderline and antisocial personality disorders and bipolar type II affective disorder. In TH McGlashan (ed.), The Borderline: Current Empirical Research. Washington, DC: American Psychiatric Press.

Peterfreund E (1971) Information, Systems, and Psychoanalysis: An Evolutionary Biological Approach to Psychoanalytic Theory. New York: International University Press.

Peterfreund E (1978) Some critical comments on psychoanalytic conceptualizations of infancy. International Journal of Psycho-Analysis 59: 427–41.

Peterfreund E (1980) On information and systems models for psychoanalysis. International Review of Psycho-Analysis 7: 327–45.

Piaget J (1936) The Origins of Intelligence in Children. New York: International Universities Press, 1952.

Piaget J (1954) The Construction of Reality in the Child. New York: Basic Books.

Piaget J (1967) Biology and Knowledge. Chicago: University of Chicago Press, 1972.

Pike A, Reiss D, Hetherington EM, Plomin R (1996) Using MZ differences in the search for nonshared environmental effects. J Child Psychol Psychiatry 37(6):695–704.

Pillemer DB, White SH (1989) Childhood events recalled by children and adults. In HV Reese (ed.), Advances in Child Development and Behavior, Volume 26 (pp. 297–340). New York: Academic Press.

Pine F (1985) Developmental Theory and Clinical Process. New Haven, CT: Yale University Press.

Pitcher EG, Prelinger E (1963) Children Tell Stories: An Analysis of Fantasy. New York: International Universities Press.

Pizer S (1998) Building Bridges: The Negotiation of Paradox in Psychoanalysis. Hillsdale, NJ: The Analytic Press.

Plakun EM, Burkhardt PE, Muller JP (1985) Fourteen-year follow-up of borderline and schizotypal personality disorders. Comprehensive Psychiatry 26: 448–55.

Plomin R (1994) Genetics and Experience: The Interplay Between Nature and Nurture. Thousand Oaks, CA: Sage Publications Inc.

Plomin R, Bergeman CS (1991) The nature of nurture: genetic influences on 'environmental' measures. Behavior and Brain Sciences 14: 373–86.

Plomin R, Daniels D (1987) Why are children in the same family so different from one another? Behavioral and Brain Sciences 10: 1–16.

Plomin R, Chipuer HM, Neiderhiser JM (1994) Behavioral genetic evidence for the importance of non-shared environment. In EM Hetherington, D Reiss, R Plomin (eds), Separate Social Worlds of Siblings (pp. 1–31). Hillsdale, NJ: Erlbaum.

Plotsky PM, Meaney MJ (1993) Early, postnatal experience alters hypothalamic corticotropin-releasing factor (CRF) mRNA, median eminence CRF content and stress-induced release in adult rats. Brain Research. Molecular Brain Research 18: 195–200.

Plutchik R (1993) Emotions and their vicissitudes: emotions and psychopathology. In M Lewis, JM Haviland (eds), Handbook of Emotions (pp. 53–66). New York: Guilford Press.

Polan HJ, Hofer M (1999) Psychobiological origins of infant attachment and separation responses. In J Cassidy, PR Shaver (eds), Handbook of Attachment: Theory, Research and Clinical Applications (pp. 162–80). New York: Guilford.

Pollock PH, Kear-Colwell JJ (1994) Women who stab: a personal construct analysis of sexual victimisation and offending behavior. British Journal of Medical Psychology 67: 13–22.

Pope HG, Hudson JI (1995) Can memories of childhood sexual abuse be repressed? Psychological Medicine 25: 121–6.

Popper K (1959) The Logic of Scientific Discovery. London: Routledge & Kegan Paul, 1992.

Posner MI, Rothbart MK (2000) Developing mechanisms of self-regulation. Development and Psychopathology 12: 427–41.

Provence S, Ritvo S (1961) Effects of deprivation on institutionalized infants: disturbances in development of relationships to inanimate objects. The Psychoanalytic Study of the Child 16: 189–204.

Quinodoz JM (1991) Accepting fusion to get over it. Review Français de Psychoanalyse 55: 1697–1700.

Quinton D, Pickles A, Maughan B, Rutter M. (1993) Partners, peers, and pathways: assortative pairing and continuities in conduct disorder. Special issue: Milestones in the development of resilience. Development and Psychopathology 5: 763–83.

Quinton D, Rutter M (1988) Preventing Breakdown: The Making and Breaking of Intergenerational Links. Aldershot, Hants: Avebury.

Rachman S (1984) Agoraphobia: a safety-signal perspective. Behavioral Research and Therapy 22: 59–70.

Rachman S, De Silva P (1978) Abnormal and normal obsessions. Behavior Research and Therapy 16: 233–48.

Racker H (1968) Transference and Countertransference. London: Hogarth Press.

Raine A, Venables PH, Williams M (1995) High autonomic arousal and orienting at age 15 years as protective factors against crime development at age 29 years. American Journal of Psychiatry 152: 1595–1600.

Rajecki DW, Lamb M, Obmascher P (1978) Toward a general theory of infantile attachment: a comparative review of aspects of the social bond. The Behavioral and Brain Sciences 3: 417–64.

Rangell L (1955) The borderline case. Journal of the American Psychoanalytic Association 3: 285–98.

Rangell L (1982) The self in psychoanalytic theory. Journal of the American Psychoanalytic Association 30: 863–91.

Rangell L (1985) On the theory of theory in psychoanalysis and the relation of theory to psychoanalytic therapy. Journal of the American Psychoanalytic Association 33: 59–92.

Rank O (1924) The Trauma of Birth. New York: Harcourt, Brace, 1929.

Rapaport D (1950) On the psychoanalytic theory of thinking. International Journal of Psycho-Analysis 31: 161–70.

Rapaport D (1951a) The autonomy of the ego. Bulletin of the Menninger Clinic 15: 113–23.

Rapaport D (1951b) Toward a theory of thinking. In D Rapaport (ed.), Organization and Pathology of Thought (pp. 689–730). New York: Columbia University Press.

Rapaport D (1958) The theory of ego autonomy: a generalization. Bulletin of the Menninger Clinic 22: 13–35.

Rapaport D, Gill MM (1959) The points of view and assumptions of metapsychology. International Journal of Psycho-Analysis 40:153–62.

Rayner E (1991) The Independent Mind in British Psychoanalysis. London: Free Association Books.

Read SJ, Vanman EJ, Miller LC (1997) Conectionism, parallel constraint satisfaction processes, and Gestalt principles: (Re)introducing cognitive dynamics to social psychology. Personality and Social Psychology Review 1: 26–53.

Reich A (1960) Empathy and countertransference, Psychoanalytic Contributions (pp. 344–60). New York: International University Press, 1973.

Reich W (1925) The impulsive character. In W Reich (ed.), Early Writings, Vol. 1. New York: Farrar, Strauss.

Reich W (1933) Character Analysis (VR Carfagno, trans.) (3rd edn). New York: Farrar, Strauss & Giroux (1972).

Reiss D, Hetherington EM, Plomin R et al. (1995) Genetic questions for environmental studies: differential parenting and psychopathology in adolescence. Archives of General Psychiatry 52: 925–36.

Reiss D, Neiderhiser J, Hetherington EM, Plomin R (2000) The Relationship Code: Deciphering Genetic and Social Patterns in Adolescent Development. Cambridge, MA: Harvard University Press.

Renik O (1993) Analytic interaction: conceptualizing technique in the light of the analyst's irreducible subjectivity. Psychoanalytic Quarterly 62: 553–71.

Renik O (1994) Publication of clinical facts. International Journal of Psycho-Analysis 75: 1245-50.

Renik O (1996) The perils of analytic neutrality. Psychoanalytic Quarterly 65: 495-517.

Rest JR (1983) Morality. In JH Flavell, EM Markman (eds), Handbook of Child Psychology, Vol. 3, Cognitive Development (pp. 556-629). New York: Wiley.

Rey JH (1979) Schizoid phenomena in the borderline. In A Capponi (ed.), Advances in the Psychotherapy of the Borderline Patient (pp. 449-84). New York: Jason Aronson.

Richards JM, Gross J (1999) Composure at any cost? The cognitive consequences of emotion supression. Personality and Social Psychology Bulletin 35: 1033-44.

Rinsley DB (1977) An object relations view of borderline personality. In P Hartocollis (ed.), Borderline Personality Disorders: The Concept, the Syndrome, the Patient (pp. 47-70). New York: International Universities Press.

Rinsley DB (1978) Borderline psychopathology: a review of etiology dynamics and treatment. International Review of Psycho-Analysis 5: 45-54.

Rinsley DB (1982) Borderline and Other Self Disorders: A Developmental and Object Relations Perspective. New York: Jason Aronson.

Ritzler B, Wyatt D, Harder D, Kaskey M (1980) Psychotic patterns of the concept of the object on the Rorschach. Journal of Abnormal Psychology 89: 46-55.

Riviere J (1936) On the genesis of psychical conflict in early infancy. International Journal of Psycho-Analysis 55: 397-404.

Robertson J (1962) Hospitals and Children: A Parent's Eye View. New York: Gollancz.

Rochat P (1995) Early objectification of the self. In P Rochat (ed.), The Self in Infancy: Theory and Research. Advances in Psychology 112 (pp. 53-71). Amsterdam, Netherlands: North-Holland/Elsevier Science Publishers.

Rochat P, Morgan R (1995) Spatial determinants in the perception of self-produced leg movements in 3- to 5-month-old infants. Developmental Psychology 31: 626-36.

Rochlin G (1971) Review of Bowlby J Attachment and Loss: Attachment. Psychoanalytic Quarterly 50: 504-6.

Roediger HL (1990) Implicit memory: retention without remembering. American Psychologist 45: 1043-56.

Rogers JH, Widiger T, Krupp A (1995) Aspects of depression associated with borderline personality disorder. American Journal of Psychiatry 152, 168-270.

Roiphe H (1976) Review of J Bowlby, Attachment and Loss. II: Separation, Anxiety and Anger. Psychoanalytic Quarterly 65: 307-9.

Rosch E (1978) Principles of categorization. In E Rosch, BB Floyd (eds), Cognition and Categorization (pp. 28-49). Hillsdale, NJ: Lawrence Erlbaum.

Rosenblatt AD, Thickstun JT (1977). Modern Psychoanalytic Concepts in a General Psychology. Part 1: General Concepts and Principles. Part 2: Motivation. New York: International Universities Press.

Rosenfeld H (1952) Notes on the psycho-analysis of the superego conflict in an acute schizophrenic patient. International Journal of Psycho-Analysis 33: 111-31.

Rosenfeld H (1964) On the psychopathology of narcissism: a clinical approach. International Journal of Psycho-Analysis 45: 332-7.

Rosenfeld H (1965) Psychotic States: A Psychoanalytic Approach. New York: International Universities Press.

Rosenfeld H (1971a) A clinical approach to the psychoanalytic theory of the life and death instincts: an investigation into the aggressive aspects of narcissism. International Journal of Psychoanalysis 52: 169-78.

Rosenfeld H (1971b) Contribution to the psychopathology of psychotic states: the importance of projective identification in the ego structure and object relations of the psychotic patient. In EB Spillius (ed.), Melanie Klein Today (pp. 117–37). London: Routledge, 1988.

Rosenfeld H (1971c) Theory of life and death instincts: aggressive aspects of narcissism. International Journal of Psycho-Analysis 52: 169–83.

Rosenfeld H (1978) Notes on the psychopathology and psychoanalytic treatment of some borderline patients. International Journal of Psychoanalysis 59: 215–21.

Rosenfeld H (1987) Impasse and Interpretation. London: Tavistock Publications.

Rosenfeld HJ (1950) Notes on the psychopathology of confusional states in chronic schizophrenias. International Journal of Psychoanalysis 31: 132–7.

Rosenwald CC (1972) Effectiveness of defences against anal impulse arousal. Journal of Consulting and Clinical Psychology 39: 292–8.

Rosolato G (1978) Symbol formation. International Journal of Psycho-Analysis 59: 303–13.

Roth A, Fonagy P (1996) What Works for Whom? A Critical Review of Psychotherapy Research. New York: Guilford Press.

Rothbart MK, Ahadi SA, Evans DE (2000) Temperament and personality: origins and outcomes. Journal of Personality and Social Psychology 78: 122–35.

Rothbart MK, Ahadi SA, Hershey KL (1994) Temperament and social behavior in childhood. Merrill-Palmer Quarterly 40: 21–39.

Rothbart MK, Bates JE (1998) Temperament. In N Eisenberg (ed.), Handbook of Child Psychology: Vol. 3. Social, Emotional, and Personality Development (5th edn., pp. 105–76). New York: Wiley.

Rothbaum F, Pott M, Azuma H, Miyake K, Weisz J (2000) The development of close relationships in Japan and the United States: paths of symbiotic harmony and generative tension. Child Development 71: 1121–42.

Rothstein A (1980) Toward a critique of the psychology of the self. Psychoanalytic Quarterly 49: 423–55.

Rovee-Collier CK (1987) Learning and memory in infancy. In JD Osofsky (ed.), Handbook of Infant Development (2nd edn). New York: Wiley.

Rowe D (1994) The Limits of Family Influence: Genes, Experience and Behavior. New York: Guilford Press.

Ruben D (ed.) (1993) Explanation. Oxford: Oxford University Press.

Rubin D, Wallace W, Houston B (1993) The beginnings of expertise for ballads. Cognitive Science 17: 435–62.

Rubovitz-Seitz P (1988) Kohut's method of interpretation: a critique. Journal of the American Psychoanalytic Association 36: 933–60.

Rumelhart DE, McClelland JL (1986) Parallel Distributed Processing. Cambridge, MA: MIT Press.

Rush F (1977) Freud and the sexual abuse of children. Chrysalis 1: 31–45.

Rutter M (1971) Maternal Deprivation Reassessed. Harmondsworth, Middlesex: Penguin.

Rutter M (1981) Maternal Deprivation Reassessed (2nd edn). Harmondsworth, Middlesex: Penguin.

Rutter M (1989a) Epidemiological approaches to developmental psychopathology. Archives of General Psychiatry 45: 486–500.

Rutter M (1989b) Isle of Wight revisited: twenty-five years of child psychiatric epidemiology. Journal of the American Academy of Child and Adolescent Psychiatry 28: 633–53.

Rutter M (1990) Psychosocial resilience and protective mechanisms. In J Rolf, AS Masten, D Cicchetti, S Weintraub (eds), Risk and Protective Factors in the Development of Psychopathology (pp. 181-214). New York: Cambridge University Press.

Rutter M (1993) Developmental psychopathology as a research perspective. In D Magnusson, P Casaer (eds), Longitudinal Research on Individual Development: Present Status and Future Perspectives (pp. 127-52). New York: Cambridge University Press.

Rutter M (1999) Psychosocial adversity and child psychopathology. British Journal of Psychiatry 174: 480-93.

Rutter M (2000) Psychosocial influences: critiques, findings and research needs. Development and Psychopathology 12: 375-405.

Rutter M, Champion L, Quinton D, Maughan B, Pickles A (1995) Understanding individual differences in environmental risk exposure. In P Moen, GH Elder Jr, K Luscher (eds), Examining Lives in Context: Perspectives on the Ecology of Human Development (pp. 61-93). Washinton, DC: American Psychological Association.

Rutter M, Dunn J, Plomin R, Simonoff E, Pickles A, Maughan B, Ormel J, Meyer J, Eaves L (1997) Integrating nature and nurture: Implications of person-environment correlations and interactions for developmental psychology. Development and Psychopathology 9: 335-64.

Rutter M, Quinton D (1984) Long-term follow-up of women institutionalized in childhood: factors promoting good functioning in adult life. British Journal of Developmental Psychology 18: 225-34.

Rutter M, Silberg J, O'Connor T, Simonoff E (1999a) Genetics and child psychiatry: I Advances in quantitative and molecular genetics. J Child Psychol Psychiatry 40(1): 3-18.

Rutter M, Silberg J, O'Connor T, Simonoff E (1999b) Genetics and child psychiatry: II Empirical research findings. J Child Psychol Psychiatry 40(1): 19-55.

Rutter M, Smith DJ (eds) (1995) Psychosocial Disorders in Young People. Time Trends and Their Causes. Chichester: John Wiley & Sons.

Rutter M, Tizard J, Yule W et al. (1976) Isle of Wight Studies 1964-1974. Psychological Medicine 6: 313-32.

Rutter M, Yule B, Quinton D et al. (1975) Attainment and adjustment in two geographical areas: 3. Some factors accounting for area differences. British Journal of Psychiatry 126: 520-33.

Ryan ER, Bell MD (1984) Changes in object relations from psychosis to recovery. Journal of Abnormal Psychology 93: 209-15.

Ryan ER, Cicchetti DV (1985) Predicting the quality of alliance in the initial psychotherapy interview. Journal of Nervous and Mental Disease 12: 717-25.

Rycroft C (1966) Psycho-Analysis Observed. London: Constable.

Rycroft C (1979) The Innocence of Dreams. London: Hogarth.

Ryle A (1982) Psychotherapy: A Cognitive Integration of Theory and Practice. London: Academic Press.

Ryle A (1985) Cognitive theory, object relations and the self. British Journal of Medical Psychology 58: 1-7.

Ryle A (1990) Cognitive Analytic Therapy: Active Participation in change. Chichester: Wiley.

Ryle A (1992) Critique of a Kleinian case presentation. British Journal of Medical Psychology 65: 309–17.

Ryle A (1993) Addiction to the death instinct? a critical review of Joseph's paper 'Addiction to near death'. British Journal of Psychotherapy 10: 88-92 (with response by Ann Scott, 93–6).

Ryle A (1994) Psychoanalysis and cognitive analytic therapy. British Journal of Psychotherapy 10: 402–5.

Ryle A (ed.) (1995a) Cognitive Analytic Therapy: Developments in Theory and Practice. Chichester: Wiley.

Ryle A (1995b) Research relating to CAT. In A Ryle (ed.), Cognitive Analytic Therapy: Developments in Theory and Practice (pp. 175–89). Chichester: Wiley.

Ryle A, Marlowe MJ (1995) Cognitive analytic therapy of borderline personality disorder: theory and practice and the clinical and research uses of the self states sequential diagram. International Journal of Short Term Psychotherapy 10(1): 21–34.

Safran JD (1990a) Towards a refinement of cognitive analytic therapy in the light of interpersonal theory: practice. Clin. Psychol. Rev. 10: 107–21.

Safran JD (1990b) Towards a refinement of cognitive analytic therapy in the light of interpersonal theory: theory. Clin. Psychol. Rev. 10: 87–105.

Safran JD, Muran JC (2000) Negotiating the Therapeutic Alliance. New York: Guilford Press.

Safran JD, Crocker P, McMain S, Murray P (1990) The therapeutic alliance rupture as a therapy event for empirical investigation. Psychotherapy 27: 154–65.

Sameroff AJ (1998) Understanding the social context of early psychopathology. In J Noshpitz (ed.), Handbook of Child and Adolescent Psychiatry. New York: Basic Books.

Sameroff AJ, Emde R (1989) Relationship Disturbances in Early Childhood. New York: Basic Books.

Sameroff AJ, Seifer R (1990) Early contributors to developmental risk. In J Rolf, N Garmezy (eds), Risk and Protective Factors in the Development of Psychopathology. New York: Cambridge University Press.

Sameroff AJ, Seifer R, Zax M (1982) Early Development of Children at Risk for Emotional Disorder. Monographs of the Society for Research in Child Development 47(7). Chicago, IL: University of Chicago Press.

Sampson, EE (1988) The debate on individualism: indigenous psychologies of the individual and their role in personal and societal functioning. American Psychologist 43: 15–22.

Sandell R (1999) Long-term findings of the Stockholm Outcome of Psychotherapy and Psychoanalysis Project (STOPPP). Paper presented at a conference on Psychoanalytic Long-Term Treatments: A Challenge for Clinical and Empirical Research in Psychoanalysis, Hamburg, Germany.

Sandell R, Blomberg J, Lazar A, Carlsson J, Broberg J, Rand H (2000) Varieties of long-term outcome among patients in psychoanalysis and long-term psychotherapy: a review of findings in the Stockholm outcome of psychoanalysis and psychotherapy project (STOPP). International Journal of Psychoanalysis 81(5): 921–43.

Sander LW (1983) Polarity, paradox, and the organizing process in. In JD Call, E Galenson, RL Tyson (eds), Frontiers of Infant Psychiatry (pp. 333–46). New York: Basic Books.

Sanders MR, Dadds MR (1992) Children's and parents' cognitions about family interaction: an evaluation of video-mediated recall and thought listing procedures in the assessment of conduct-disordered children. Journal of Clinical Child Psychology 21: 371–9.

Sandler J (1960a) The background of safety. International Journal of Psycho-Analysis 41: 191–8.

Sandler J (1960b) On the concept of superego. The Psychoanalytic Study of the Child 15, 128–62.

Sandler J (1962a) The Hampstead Index as an Instrument of Psychoanalytic Research. International Journal of Psycho-Analysis 43: 287–91.

Sandler J (1962b) Psychology and Psychoanalysis. British Journal of Medical Psychology 35: 91–100.

Sandler J (1967) Trauma, strain, and development. In SS Furst (ed.), Psychic Trauma. New York/London: Basic Books.

Sandler J (1972) The role of affects in psychoanalytic theory. In J Sandler (ed.), From Safety to Superego: Selected Papers of Joseph Sandler (pp. 285–300). New York: Guilford Press.

Sandler J (1976a) Actualisation and object relationships. Journal of the Philadelphia Association of Psychoanalysis 3: 59–70.

Sandler J (1976b) Countertransference and role-responsiveness. International Review of Psycho-Analysis 3: 43–7.

Sandler J (1981) Character traits and object relationships. Psychoanalytic Quarterly 50: 694–708.

Sandler J (1983) Reflections on some relations between psychoanalytic concepts and psychoanalytic practice. International Journal of Psycho-Analysis 64: 35–45.

Sandler J (1985) Towards a reconsideration of the psychoanalytic theory of motivation. Bulletin of the Anna Freud Centre 8: 223–43.

Sandler J (1987a) The concept of projective identification. In J Sandler (ed.), Projection, Identification, Projection Identification (pp. 13–26). Madison, CT: International Universities Press.

Sandler J (1987b) From Safety to the Superego: Selected Papers of Joseph Sandler. New York: Guilford Press.

Sandler J (1987c) Projection, Identification, Projective Identification. London: Karnac Books.

Sandler J (1989) Toward a reconsideration of the psychoanalytic theory of motivation. In AM Cooper, OF Kernberg, ES Person (eds), Psychoanalysis: Toward the Second Century (pp. 91–110). New Haven, CT: Yale University Press.

Sandler J (1990) On the structure of internal objects and internal object relationships. Psychoanalytic Inquiry 10(2): 163–81.

Sandler J (1993) Communication from patient to analyst: not everything is projective identification. British Psycho-Analytical Society Bulletin 29: 8–16.

Sandler J (1994) Fantasy, defense, and the representational world. Fifth World Congress of the World Association for Infant Psychiatry and Allied Disciplines (1992, Chicago, IL). Infant Mental Health Journal 15(1) Spec. Issue: 26–35.

Sandler J, Fonagy P (eds) (1997) Recovered Memories of Abuse: True or False? London: Karnac Books.

Sandler J, Freud A (1985) The Analysis of Defence: The Ego and the Mechanisnms of Defence Revisited. New York: International Universities Press.

Sandler J, Joffe WG (1965a) Notes on childhood depression. International Journal of Psycho-Analysis 46: 88–96.

Sandler J, Joffe WG (1965b) Notes on obsessional manifestations in children. Psychoanalytic Study of the Child 20: 425–38.

Sandler J, Joffe WG (1966) On skill and sublimation. Journal of American Psychoanalytic Association 14: 335-55.

Sandler J, Joffe WG (1967) The tendency to persistence in psychological function and development, with special reference to fixation and regression. Bulletin of the Menninger Clinic 31: 257-71.

Sandler J, Joffe WG (1969) Towards a basic psychoanalytic model. International Journal of Psycho-Analysis 50: 79-90.

Sandler J, Rosenblatt B (1962a) The concept of the representational world. The Psychoanalytic Study of the Child 17: 128-45.

Sandler J, Rosenblatt B (1962b) The representational world. In J Sandler (ed.), From Safety to Superego. Selected Papers of Joseph Sandler (pp. 58-72). London: Karnac Books, 1987.

Sandler J, Sandler A-M (1978) On the development of object relationships and affects. International Journal of Psycho-Analysis 59: 285-96.

Sandler J, Sandler A-M (1983) The 'second censorship', the 'three-box model', and some technical implications. International Journal of Psychoanalysis 64: 413-26.

Sandler J, Sandler A-M (1984) The past unconscious, the present unconscious, and interpretation of the transference. Psychoanalytic Inquiry 4: 367-99.

Sandler J, Sandler A-M (1987) The past unconscious, the present unconscious and the vicissitudes of guilt. International Journal of Psychoanalysis 68: 331-41.

Sandler J, Sandler A-M (1992) Psychoanalytic technique and theory of psychic change. Bulletin of the Anna Freud Centre 15: 35-51.

Sandler J, Dare C, Holder A (1982) Frames of reference in psychoanalytic psychology: XII. The characteristics of the structural frame of reference. British Journal of Medical Psychology 55: 203-7.

Sanson A, Oberklaid F, Pedlow R, Prior M (1991) Risk indicators: assessment of infancy predictors of pre-school behavioral maladjustment. Journal of Child Psychology and Psychiatry 32: 609-26.

Sapolsky RM (1994) Why Zebras Don't Get Ulcers: A Guide to Stress, Stress-related Disease and Coping. New York: WH Freeman.

Scaife M, Bruner J (1975) The capacity for joint visual attention in the infant. Nature 253: 265-6.

Scarr S (1992) Developmental theories for the 1990s: development and individual differences. Child Development 63: 1-19.

Schachter DL (1992a) Priming and multiple memory systems: perceptual mechanisms of implicit memory. Journal of Cognitive Neuroscience 4: 244-56.

Schachter DL (1992b) Understanding implicit memory: a cognitive neuroscience approach. American Psychologist 47: 559-69.

Schachter DL (1995) Implicit memory: a new frontier for cognitive neuroscience. In MS Gazzaniga (ed.), The Cognitive Neurosciences (pp. 815-24). Cambridge, MA: MIT Press.

Schafer R (1968) Aspects of Internalisation. New York: International Universities Press.

Schafer R (1974) Problems in Freud's psychology of women. Journal of the American Psychoanalytic Association 22: 459-85.

Schafer R (1976) A New Language for Psychoanalysis. New Haven, CT: Yale University Press.

Schafer R (1983) The Analytic Attitude. New York: Basic Books.

Schafer R (1994a) The conceptualisation of clinical facts. International Journal of Psycho-Analysis 75: 1023-30.

Schafer R (1994b) The Contemporary Kleinians of London. Psychoanalytic Quarterly 63: 409-32.

Schaffer HR, Emerson PE (1964) Patterns of response to physical contact in early human development. Journal of Child Psychology and Psychiatry 5:1-13.

Schmideberg M (1947) The treatment of psychopathic and borderline patients. American Journal of Psychotherapy 1: 45-71.

Schmuckler MA (1996) Visual-proprioceptive intermodal perception in infancy. Infant Behavior and Development 19: 221-32.

Schore AN (1997a) Early organization of the nonlinear right brain and development of a predisposition to psychiatric disorders. Development and Psychopathology 9: 595-631.

Schore AN (1997b) Neurobiology and psychoanalysis. In M Moscowitz, Mark C, Kaye C, Ellman S (eds.), The Neurobiological and Developmental Basis of Psychotherapeutic Intervention. Northville, NJ: Jason Aronson.

Schore AN (1999) Commentary on Freud's affect theory in light of contemporary neuro-science. Neuro-Psychoanalysis 1: 49-55.

Schore AN (2001) Contributions from the decade of the brain to infant mental health: an overview. Infant Mental Health Journal 22: 1-6.

Schuengel C, Bakermans-Kranenburg M, van IJzendoorn M (1999) Frightening maternal behavior linking unresolved loss and disorganised infant attachment. Journal of Consulting and Clinical Psychology 67: 54-63.

Schuengel C, Bakermans-Kranenburg MJ, van IJzendoorn MH, Bom M (1999) Unresolved loss and infant disorganisation: links to frightening maternal behavior. In J Solomon, C George (eds), Attachment Disorganization (pp. 71-94). New York: Guilford Press.

Schur M (1960). Discussion of Dr. John Bowlby's paper. The Psychoanalytic Study of the Child, 15, 63-84.

Schur M (1966) The Id and the Regulatory Principles of Mental Functioning. New York: International Universities Press.

Schwaber E (1983) Psychoanalytic listening and psychic reality. International Review of Psycho-Analysis 10: 379-92.

Schwartz L (1978) Review of 'The Restoration of the Self' by Heinz Kohut. Psychoanalytic Quarterly 47: 436-43.

Searles HF (1960) The Nonhuman Environment. New York: International Universities Press.

Searles HF (1963) Transference psychosis in psychotherapy of chronic schizophrenia. Collected Papers on Schizophrenia and Related Subjects (pp. 654-716). New York: International Universities Press, 1965.

Searles HF (1986) My Work with Borderline Patients. Northvale, NJ: Aronson.

Segal H (1957) Notes on symbol formation. International Journal of Psycho-Analysis 38: 391-7.

Segal H (1964) Introduction to the Work of Melanie Klein. New York: Basic Books.

Segal H (1974) An Introduction to the Work of Melanie Klein. London: Hogarth.

Segal H (1981) The Work of Hanna Segal. New York: Jason Aronson.

Segal H (1983) Some clinical implications of Melanie Klein's work: emergence from narcissism. International Journal of Psycho-Analysis 64: 269-76.

Segal H (1985) The Klein-Bion model. In A Rothstein (ed.), Models of the Mind: Their Relationships to Clinical Work (ed.) (pp. 35–48). New York: International Universities Press, Inc.

Seligman MEP (1975) Helplessness. San Francisco, CA: Freeman.

Settlage CF (1977) The psychoanalytic understanding of narcissistic and borderline personality disorders: advances in developmental theory. Journal of the American Psychoanalytic Association 25: 805–33.

Settlage CF (1980) Psychoanalytic developmental thinking in current and historical perspective. Psychoanalysis and Contemporary Thought 3: 139–70.

Settlage CF, Curtis Z, Lozoff, M, Silberschatz G, Simburg E (1988) Conceptualizing adult development. Journal of the American Psychoanalytic Association 6:347–70.

Shantz CU (1983) Social cognition. In JH Flavell, EM Markman (eds), Handbook of Child Psychology, Vol. 3, Cognitive Developments. New York: Wiley.

Shapiro, DA, Rees A, Barkham M, Hardy G, Reynolds S, Startup M (1995) Effects of treatment duration and severity of depression on the maintenance of gains after cognitive-behavioral and psychodynamic-interpersonal psychotherapy. Journal of Consulting and Clinical Psychology 63: 378–87.

Shaw DS, Vondra JI (1995) Infant attachment security and maternal predictors of early behavior problems: a longitudinal study of low-income families. Journal of Abnormal Child Psychology 23: 335–57.

Shaw DS, Gilliom M, Ingoldsby EM, Schonberg MA (2001) Developmental trajectories of early conduct problems from ages 2 to 10. Symposium on: Developmental Trajectories in Antisocial Behavior from Infancy to Adolescence. Paper presented at the Biennial Meeting of the Society for Research in Child Development, April 19–22, 2001, Minneapolis, MN.

Shaw DS, Owens EB, Vondra JI, Keenan K, Winslow EB (1996) Early risk factors and pathways in the development of early disruptive behavior problems. Development and Psychopathology 8: 679–99.

Shaw DS, Winslow EB, Flanagan C (1999) A prospective study of the effects of marital status and family relations on young children's adjustment among African American and Caucasian families. Child Development 70: 742–55.

Shea MT, Elkin I, Imber SD, Sotsky SM, Watkins JT, Collins JF, Pilkonis PA, Beckham E, Glass DR, Dolan RT, Parloff MB (1992) Course of depressive symptoms over follow-up: findings from the NIMH treatment of depression collaborative research programme. Archives of General Psychiatry 49: 782–7.

Sheeber L, Hops H, Alpert A, Davies B, Andrews J (1997) Family support and conflict: prospective relations to adolescent depression. Journal of Abnormal Child Psychology 25: 333–44.

Shengold L (1989) Soul Murder: The Effects of Childhood Abuse and Deprivation. New York: Ballantine Books.

Sherman M, Hertzig M (1983) Treasured object use – a cognitive and developmental marker. Journal of the American Academy Child Psychiatry 22: 541–4.

Sherman M, Hertzig M, Austrian R, Shapiro T (1981) Treasured objects in school-aged children. Pediatrics 68: 379–86.

Sherman S, Judd CM, Park B (1989) Social cognition. Annual Review of Psychology 40: 281–326.

Shevrin H (1997) Psychoanalysis as the patient: high in feeling, low in energy. Jounal of the American Psychoanalytic Association 45: 841–64.

Shevrin H (2001) Drug dreams: an introduction. Journal of the American Psychoanalytic Association 49: 69–71.

Siegel DJ (2001) Toward an interpersonal neurobiology of the developing mind: attachment relationships, 'mindsight' and neural integration. Infant Mental Health Journal 22: 67–94.

Silberg J, Rutter M, Nealre K, Eaves LJ (2001) Genetic moderation of environmental risk for depression and anxiety in adolescent girls. British Journal of Psychiatry 179: 116–21.

Silverman LH (1983) The subliminal psychodynamic activation method: overview and comprehensive listing of studies. In J Masling (ed.), Empirical Studies of Psychoanalytic Theories. Hillsdale, NJ: Analytic Press.

Silverman R, Lieberman AF, Pekarsky JH (1997) Anxiety disorders. In AF Lieberman, S Wieder, E Fenichel (eds), Casebook of the Zero to Three Diagnostic Classification of Mental Health and Developmental Disorders of Infancy and Early Childhood (pp. 47–59). Arlington, Virginia: Zero to Three.

Simpson JA, Rholes WS, Nelligan JS (1992) Support seeking and support giving within couples in an anxiety provoking situation: the role of attachment styles. Journal of Personality and Social Psychology 60: 434–46.

Singer M (1975) The borderline delinquent: the interlocking of intrapsychic and interactional determinants. International Review of Psycho-Analysis 2: 429–40.

Sissons Joshi M, MacLean M (1995) Indian and English children's understanding of the distinction between real and apparent emotion. Child Development 65: 1372–84 .

Slade A (1996) A view from attachment theory and research. Journal of Clinical Psychoanalysis 5: 112–23.

Slade A (1999a) Attachment theory and research: implications for the theory and practice of individual psychotherapy with adults. In J Cassidy, PR Shaver (eds), Handbook of Attachment: Theory, Research and Clinical Applications (pp. 575–94). New York: Guilford.

Slade A (1999b) Representation, symbolization and affect regulation in the concomitant treatment of a mother and child: attachment theory and child psychotherapy. Psychoanalytic Inquiry 19: 824–57.

Slade A (2000) The development and organisation of attachment: implications for psychoanalysis. Journal of the American Psychoanalytic Association 48: 1147–74.

Slade A, Belsky J, Aber JL, Phelps JL (1999) Mothers' representations of their relationships with their toddlers: links to adult attachment and observed mothering. Developmental Psychology 35(3): 611–19.

Slade P (1982) Towards a functional analysis of anorexia nervosa and bulimia nervosa. British Journal of Clinical Psychology 21: 167–79.

Smalley SL (1997) Genetic influences in childhood-onset psychiatric disorders: autism and attention-deficit/hyperactivity disorder. American Journal of Human Genetics 60: 1276–82.

Sohn L (1985) Narcissistic organisation, projective identification and the formation of the identificate. International Journal of Psychoanalysis 66: 201–13.

Solms M (1997a) The Neuropsychology of Dreams: A Clinico-Anatomical Study. Mahwah, NJ: Erlbaum.

Solms M (1997b) What is consciousness? Journal of the American Psychoanalytic Association 45: 681–703.

Solms M (2000) Dreaming and REM sleeping are controlled by different brain mechanisms. Behavior and Brain Sciences 23: 843–50; 904–1121.

Solms M, Nersessian E (1999) Freud's theory of affect. Neuro-psychoanalysis 1: 5–14.

Solomon J, George C (1999) Attachment Disorganization. New York: Guilford.

Solomon JD (1962) The fixed idea as an internalized transitional object. American Journal of Psychotherapy 16:632–44.

Sorce J, Emde R, Campos J, Klinnert MO (eds) (1985) Maternal emotional signalling: its effect on the visual cliff behavior of 1 year olds. Developmental Psychology 21: 195.

Spangler G, Grossman KE (1993) Biobehavioral organization in securely and insecurely attached infants. Child Development 64: 1439–50.

Spear W, Sugarman A (1984) Dimensions of internalized object relations in borderline and schizophrenic patieints. Psychoanalytic Psychology 1: 113–29.

Speigel D, Lazar SG (1997) The need for psychotherapy in the medically ill. Psychoanalytic Inquiry, Special Supplement, Extended Dynamic Psychotherapy: Making the Case in the Era of Managed Care.

Speigel D, Kraemer H, Gottheil E (1989) Effective psychosocial treatment on survival of patients with metastatic breast cancer. Lancet 2: 888–91.

Spelke ES (1985) Preferential looking methods as tools for the study of cognition in infancy. In G Gottlieb, N Krasnegor (eds), Measurement of Audition and Vision in the First Year of Post-Natal Life (pp. 323–63). Hillsdale, NJ: Lawrence Erlbaum.

Spelke ES (1990) Principles of object perception. Cognitive Science 14:29–56.

Spemann H (1938) Embryonic Development and Induction. New Haven, CT: Yale University Press.

Spence DP (1982) Narrative Truth and Historical Truth. Meaning and Interpretation in Psychoanalysis. New York/London: Norton.

Spence DP (1984) Narrative Truth and Historical Truth. New York: Norton.

Sperling M (1959a) Equivalents of depression in children. Journal of the Hillside Hospital 8: 138–48.

Sperling M (1959b) A study of deviate sexual behavior in children by the method of simultaneous analysis of mother and child. In L Jessnor, E Davenstad (eds), Dynamic Psychopathology in Childhood. New York: Grune & Stratton.

Spillius EB (1988a) General Introduction. In EB Spillius (ed.), Melanie Klein Today: Developments in Theory and Practice. Vol. 1: Mainly Theory. London: Routledge.

Spillius EB (1988b) Melanie Klein Today: Developments in Theory and Practice. Vol. I: Mainly Theory. Vol. II: Mainly Practice. London: Routledge.

Spillius EB (1988c) Vol. 1. Mainly theory; Vol. 2. Mainly practice. In EB Spillius (ed.), Melanie Klein Today: Developments in Theory and Practice. London: Routledge.

Spillius EB (1992) Clinical experiences of projective identification. In R Anderson (ed.), Clinical Lectures on Klein and Bion (pp. 59–73). London: Routledge.

Spillius EB (1993) Developments in Kleinian thought: overview and personal view. British Psycho-Anal.Society Bulletin 29: 1–19.

Spillius EB (1994). Developments in Kleinian thought: overview and personal view. Psychoanalytic Inquiry 14: 324–64.

Spitz RA (1945) Hospitalism: an inquiry into the genesis of psychiatric conditions in early childhood. The Psychoanalytic Study of the Child 1: 53–73.

Spitz RA (1957) No and Yes: On the Genesis of Human Communication. New York: International Universities Press.

Spitz RA (1959) A Genetic Field Theory of Ego Formation: Its Implications for Pathology. New York: International University Press.

Spitz RA (1960) Discussion of Dr. John Bowlby's paper. The Psychoanalytic Study of the Child 15: 85-94.

Spitz RA (1965) The First Year of Life. New York: International University Press.

Spitz RA, Wolf R (1946). Anaclitic depression. Psychoanalytic Study of the Child 5: 113-17.

Spruiell V (1988) The indivisibility of Freudian object relations and drive theories. Psychoanalytic Quarterly 57, 597-625.

Squire LR (1987) Memory and Brain. New York: Oxford University Press.

Squire LS, Kandel ER (1999) Memory: From Molecules to Memory. New York: Freeman Press.

Sroufe LA (1979) Socioemotional development. In J Osofsky (ed.), Handbook of Infant Development (pp. 462-516). New York: Wiley.

Sroufe LA (1983) Infant-Caregiver Attachment and Patterns of Adaptation in Preschool: The Roots of Maladaption and competence (Vol. 16). Hillsdale, NJ: Erlbaum.

Sroufe LA (1989) Pathways to adaptation and maladaptation: psychopathology as a developmental deviation. In D Cicchetti (ed.), Rochester Symposium on Developmental Psychopathology: The Emergence of a Discipline (pp. 13-40). Hillsdale, NJ: Erlbaum.

Sroufe LA (1990) An organizational perspective on the self. In D Cicchetti, M Beeghly (eds), The Self in Transition: Infancy to Childhood (pp. 281-307). Chicago, IL: University of Chicago Press.

Sroufe LA (1996) Emotional Development: The Organization of Emotional Life in the Early Years. New York: Cambridge University Press.

Sroufe LA, Fleeson J (1988) The coherence of family relationships. In RA Hinde, J Stevenson-Hinde (eds), Relationships within Families: Mutual Influences (pp. 27-47). Oxford: Clarendon Press.

Sroufe LA, Rutter M (1984) The domain of developmental psychopathology. Child Development 83: 173-89.

Sroufe LA, Waters E (1977) Attachment as an organizational construct. Child Development 48: 1184-99.

Sroufe LA, Egeland B, Kreutzer, T. (1990) The fate of early experience following developmental change: longitudinal approaches to individual adaptation in childhood. Child Development 61: 1363-73.

Sroufe LA, Carlson E, Levy AK, Egeland B (1999) Implications of attachment theory for developemntal psychopathology. Development and Psychopathology 11: 1-13.

Stechler G, Kaplan S (1980) The development of the sense of self: a psychoanalytic perspective. The Psychoanalytic Study of the Child 35: 85-105.

Steele H, Steele M, Fonagy P (1996) Associations among attachment classifications of mothers, fathers, and their infants: evidence for a relationship-specific perspective. Child Development 67, 541-55.

Steele RS (1979) Psychoanalysis and hermeneutics. International Review of Psycho-Analysis 6: 389-411.

Stein MH (1979) Book review: The Restoration of the Self by Heinz Kohut. Journal of the American Psychoanalytic Association 27: 665-80.

Steiner J (1987) The interplay between pathological organisations and the paranoid-schizoid and depressive positions. International Journal of Psychoanalysis 68: 69-80.

Steiner J (1992a) The equilibrium between the paranoid-schizoid and the depressive positions. In R Anderson (ed.), Clinical Lectures on Klein and Bion (pp. 46-58). London: Routledge.

Steiner J (1993) Psychic Retreats: Pathological Organisations in Psychotic, Neurotic and Borderline Patients. London: Routledge.

Steiner J (1994) Patient-centred and analyst-centred interpretations: some implications of 'containment' and 'counter-transference'. Psychoanalytic Inquiry 14: 406–422.

Stern A (1938) Psychoanalytic investigation and therapy in borderline group of neuroses. Psychoanalytic Quarterly 7: 467–89.

Stern DN (1985) The Interpersonal World of the Infant: A View from Psychoanalysis and Developmental Psychology. New York: Basic Books.

Stern DN (1990) Joy and Satisfaction in Infancy. New Haven, CT: Yale University Press.

Stern DN (1993) Acting versus remembering and transference love and infantile love. In E Person, A Hagelin, P Fonagy (eds), On Freud's 'Observations on Transference-Love'. New Haven, CT: Yale University Press.

Stern DN (1994) One way to build a clinically relevant baby. Infant Mental Health Journal 15: 36–54.

Stern DN (1995) The Motherhood Constellation: A Unified View of Parent-Infant Psychotherapy. New York: BasicBooks.

Stern DN (1998) The process of therapeutic change involving implicit knowledge: some implications of developmental observations for adult psychotherapy. Infant Mental Health Journal 19: 300–8.

Stern DN, Hofer L, Haft W, Dore J (1985) Affect attunement: the sharing of feeling states between mother and infant by means of inter-modal fluency. In TM Fields and NA Fox (eds), Social Perception in Infants. Norwood, NJ: Ablex.

Stern DN, Sander L, Nahum J, Harrison A, Lyons-Ruth K, Morgan A, Brusch Weiler Stern N, Tronick E (1998). Non-interpretive mechanisms in psychoanalytic therapy: the 'something more' than interpretation. International Journal of Psycho-Analysis 79(5): 903–21.

Stern SL, Dixon KN, Jones D, Lake M, Nemzer E, Sansone R (1989) Family environment in anorexia nervosa and bulimia. International Journal of the Eating Disorders 8: 25–31.

Stevenson J, Meares R (1992) An outcome study of psychotherapy for patients with borderline personality disorder. American Journal of Psychiatry 149: 358–62.

Stewart H (1989) Technique at the basic fault: regression. International Journal of Psycho-Analysis 70: 221–30.

Stoker J, Beenen F, Dutch Psychoanalytic Institute (1996) Outline of a quality monitoring and checking system for longterm (4 or 5 times a week) psychoanalytic treatment. Paper presented at the Stuttgart Kolleg, February 1996.

Stoller RJ (1985) Presentations of Gender. New Haven, CT and London: Yale University Press.

Stolorow RD (1997) Review of 'A dynamic systems approach to the development of cognition and action'. International Journal of Psycho-Analysis 78: 620–3.

Stolorow RD, Atwood G (1984) Psychoanalytic phenomenology: toward science of human experience. Psychoanalytic Inquiry 4: 87–104.

Stolorow RD, Atwood G (1989) The unconscious and unconscious fantasy: an inter-subjective-developmental perspective. Psychoanalytic Inquiry 9: 364–74.

Stolorow RD, Atwood G (1991) The mind and the body. Psychoanalytic Dialogues 1: 190–202.

Stolorow RD, Brandschaft B, Atwood G (1987) Psychoanalytic Treatment: An Intersubjective Approach. Hillsdale, NJ: Analytic Press.

Stone L (1954) The widening scope of indications for psychoanalysis. Journal of the American Psychoanalytical Association 2: 567–94.

Stone LJ, Smith HT, Murphy LB (1973) The Competent Infant. New York: Basic Books.

Stone MH (1990) The Fate of Borderline Patients: Successful Outcome and Psychiatric Practice. New York: Guilford Press.

Stone MH, Hurt SW, Stone DK (1987) The PI 500: long-term follow-up of borderline inpatients meeting DSM-III criteria: I. Global outcome. Journal of Personality Disorders 1: 291–8.

Stoolmiller M (1999) Implications of the restricted range of family environments for estimates of heritability and nonshared environment in behavior-genetic adoption studies. Psychological Bulletin 125: 392–409.

Stormshak EA, Bierman KL, Bruschi C et al. and Conduct Problems Prevention Research Group (1999) The relation between behavior problems and peer preference in different classroom contexts. Child Development 70: 169–82.

Strenger C (1989) The classic and romantic visions in psychoanalysis. International Journal of Psycho-Analysis 70: 595–610.

Strober M, Humphrey LL (1987) Familial contributions to the etiology and course of anorexia nervosa and bulimia. Journal of Consulting and Clinical Psychology 55: 654–9.

Suess GJ, Grossmann K, Sroufe LA (1992) Effects of infant attachment to mother and father on quality of adaptation in preschool: from dyadic to individual organisation of self. International Journal of Behavioral Development 15: 43–65.

Sullivan HS (1940) Conceptions of Modern Psychiatry. New York: Norton.

Sullivan HS (1953) The Interpersonal Theory of Psychiatry. New York: Norton.

Sullivan HS (1954) The Psychiatric Interview. New York: Norton.

Sullivan HS (1956) Clinical Studies in Psychiatry. New York: Norton.

Sullivan HS (1962) Schizophrenia as a Human Process. New York: Norton.

Sullivan HS (1964) The Fusion of Psychiatry and Social Science. New York: Norton.

Sulloway FJ (1979) Freud: Biologist of the Mind. New York: Basic Books.

Susman-Stillman A, Kalkoske M, Egeland B, Waldman I (1996) Infant temperament and maternal sensitivity as predictors of attachment security. Infant Behavior and Development 19: 33–47.

Sutherland JD (1980) The British object-relations theorists: Balint, Fairbairn, Guntrip. Journal of the American Psychoanalytic Association 28: 829–60.

Svartberg M, Stiles TC (1994) Therapeutic alliance, therapist competence, and client change in short-term anxiety-provoking psychotherapy. Psychotherapy Research 4: 20–33.

Swedo SC, Rapoport JL, Leonard HI, Lenane M (1989) Obsessive-compulsive disorder in children and adolescents: clinical phenomonology of 70 consecutive cases. Archives of General Psychiatry 46: 335–41.

Target M (1998) The recovered memories debate. International Journal of Psychoanalysis 79: 1015–28.

Target M, Fonagy P (1994a) The efficacy of psychoanalysis for children with emotional disorders. Journal of the American Academy of Child and Adolescent Psychiatry 33: 361–71.

Target M, Fonagy P (1994b) The efficacy of psychoanalysis for children: developmental considerations. Journal of the American Academy of Child and Adolescent Psychiatry 33: 1134–44.

Target M, Fonagy P (1996) Playing with reality II: the development of psychic reality from a theoretical perspective. International Journal of Psycho-Analysis 77: 459-79.

Tausk V (1919) On the origin of the 'influencing machine' in schizophrenia. Psychoanalytic Quarterly 2: 519-56 (1933).

Taylor DC (1985) Psychological aspects of chronic sickness. In M Rutter, L Hersov (eds), Child and Adolescent Psychiatry: Modern Approaches (pp. 614-24). Oxford: Blackwell Scientific Publications.

Terman DM (1987) The borderline concept: a critical appraisal and some alternative suggestions. In JS Grotstein, JA Lang (eds), The Borderline Patient: Emerging Concepts in Diagnosis, Psychodynamics and Treatment. Hillsdale, NJ: The Analytic Press.

Terr LC (1983) Chowchilla revisited: the effects of psychic trauma four years after a school-bus kidnapping. American Journal of Psychiatry 140: 1543-50.

Terr LC (1994) Unchained Memories: True Stories of Traumatic Memories, Lost and Found. New York: Basic Books.

Teti D, Gelfand D, Isabella R (1995) Maternal depression and the quality of early attachment: an examination of infants, preschoolers and their mothers. Developmental Psychology 31: 364-76.

Thapar A, McGuffin P (1996) A twin study of antisocial and neurotic symptoms in childhood. Psychological Medicine 26: 1111-18.

Thomä, H., Kächele H (1987). Psychoanalytic Practice. I: Principles. New York: Springer-Verlag.

Thompson C (1964) Transference and character analysis. In M Green (ed.), Interpersonal Psychoanalysis (pp. 22-31). New York: Basic Books.

Thompson LW, Gallagher D, Breckenridge JS (1987) Comparative effectiveness of psychotherapies for depressed elders. Journal of Consulting and Clinical Psychology 55: 385-90.

Thompson RA (1999) Early attachment and later development. In J Cassidy, PR Shaver (eds), Handbook of Attachment: Theory, Research and Clinical Applications (pp. 265-86). New York: Guilford.

Tishler CL, McKenry PC, Morgan KC (1981) Adolescent suicide attempts: some significant factors. Suicide and Life Threatening Behavior 11(2): 86-92.

Tobias BA, Kihlstrom JF, Schacter DL (1992) Emotion and implicit memory. In S Christianson (ed.), The Handbook of Emotion and Memory: Research and Theory (pp. 67-92). Hillsdale, NJ: Erlbaum.

Tolpin M (1983) Corrective emotional experience: a self-psychological reevaluation. In A Goldberg (ed.), The Future of Psychoanalysis (pp. 255-71). New York: International Universities Press.

Tolpin M (1987) Injured self-cohesion: developmental, clinical and theoretical perspectives. In JS Grotstein, JA Lang (eds), The Borderline Patient: Emerging Concepts in Diagnosis, Psychodynamics and Treatment (pp. 233-49). Hillsdale, NJ: Atlantic Press.

Topolski TD, Hewitt JK, Eaves LJ, Silberg JL, Meyer JM, Rutter M, Pickles A, Simonoff E (1997) Genetic and environmental influences on child reports of manifest anxiety and symptoms of separation anxiety and overanxious disorders: a community-based twin study. Behav Genet 27(1): 15-28.

Toth SL, Cicchetti D, Macfie J, Emde, RN (1997) Representations of self and other in the narratives of neglected, physically abused, and sexually abused preschoolers. Development and Psychopathology 9: 781-96.

Trevarthen C (1977) Descriptive analyses of infant communicative behavior. In HR Schaffer (ed.), Studies in Mother–Infant Interaction. London: Academic Press.

Trevarthen C (1990) Intuitive emotions: their changing role in communication between mother and infant. In M Ammaniti, N Dazzi (eds), Affetti: Natura e sviluppo delle relazione interpersonali (pp. 97–139). Roma-Bari: Laterza.

Tronick EZ (1989) Emotions and emotional communication in infants. American Psychologist 44: 112–19.

Tronick EZ (1998) Dyadically expanded states of consciousness and the process of therapeutic change. Infant Mental Health Journal 19: 290–9.

Tronick EZ (2001) Emotional connection and dyadic consciousness in infant–mother and patient–therapist interactions: commentary on paper by Frank M Lachman. Psychoanalytic Dialogue 11: 187–95.

Tronick EZ, Cohn JF (1989) Infant–mother face-to-face interaction: age and gender differences in coordination and the occurrence of miscoordination. Child Development 60: 85–92.

Tronick EZ, Gianino AF (1986) The transmission of maternal disturbance to the infant. In EZ Tronick, T Field (eds), Maternal Depression and Infant Disturbance (pp. 5–11). San Francisco, CA: Jossey Bass.

Tuckett D (1993) Some thoughts on the presentation and discussion of the clinical material of psychoanalysis. International Journal of Psycho-Analysis 74 (Pt 6), 1175–89.

Tuckett D (2000a) Comments on Michels's 'The case history'. Journal of the American Psychoanalytic Association 48: 403–11.

Tuckett D (2000b) Theoretical pluralism and the construction of psychoanalytic knowledge. In J Sandler, R Michels, P Fonagy (eds), Changing Ideas in a Changing World: The Revolution in Psychoanalysis. Essays in Honour of Arnold Cooper (pp. 237–46). New York: Karnac.

Tustin F (1981) Autistic States in Children. London: Routledge & Kegan Paul.

Tyrka AR, Cannon TD, Haslam N, Mednick SA, Schulsinger F, Schulsinger H, Parnas J (1995) The latent structure of schizoptypy: 1. Premorbid indicators of a taxon of individuals at risk for schizophrenia spectrum disorders. Journal of Abnormal Psychology 104: 173–83.

Tyson P, Tyson RL (1990) Psychoanalytic Theories of Development: An Integration. New Haven, CT and London: Yale University Press.

Tyson RL, Tyson P (1986) The concept of transference in child psychoanalysis. Journal of the American Academy of Child Psychiatry 25: 30–9.

Underwood G (ed.) (1996) Implicit Cognition. New York: Oxford University Press.

Urist J (1977) The Rorschach test and the assessment of object relations. J.Personality Assessment 41: 3–9.

Urist J, Schill M (1982) Validity of the Rorschach mutuality of autonomy scale: a replication using excerpted responses. J.Personality Assessment 46: 450–4.

Vaillant GE (1992) Ego Mechanisms of Defense: A Guide for Clinicians and Researchers. Washington, DC: American Psychiatric Association Press.

van der Kolk BA (1994) The body keeps the score: memory and the evolving psychobiology of post-traumatic stress. Harvard Review of Psychiatry 1: 253–65.

van der Kolk BA (1996) Trauma and memory. In BA van der Kolk, AC McFarlane, L Weisaeth (eds), Traumatic Stress. New York: Guilford.

van IJzendoorn MH (1995) Adult attachment representations, parental responsiveness, and infant attachment: a meta-analysis on the predictive validity of the Adult Attachment Interview. Psychological Bulletin 117: 387–403.

van IJzendoorn MH, Juffer F, Duyvesteyn MGC (1995) Breaking the intergenerational cycle of insecure attachment: a review of the effects of attachment-based interventions on maternal sensitivity and infant security. Journal of Child Psychology and Psychiatry 36: 225–48.

van IJzendoorn M, Scheungel C, Bakermanns-Kranenburg MJ (1999) Disorganized attachment in early childhood: meta-analysis of precursors, concomitants and sequelae. Development and Psychopathology 22: 225–49.

van IJzendoorn MH, Moran G, Belsky J, Pederson D, Bakermans-Kranenburg MJ, Kneppers K (2000) The similarity of siblings attachments to their mothers. Child Development 71: 1086–98.

Vaughn CE, Leff JP (1981) Patterns of emotional response in relatives of schizophrenic patients. Schizophrenia Bulletin 7: 43–4.

van Bertalanffy L (1968) General System Theory: Foundations, Development, Applications. New York: George Braziller.

Vondra JI, Hommerding KD, Shaw DS (1999) Atypical attachment in infancy and early childhood among children at developmental risk. VI. Stability and change in infant attachment in a low-income sample. Monographs of the Society for Research in Child Development 64:, 119–44.

Vondra JI, Shaw DS, Swearingen L, Cohen M, Owens EB (2001) Attachment stability and emotional and behavioral regulation from infancy to preschool age. Development and Psychopathology 13: 13–33.

Vygotsky LS (1966) Development of the Higher Mental Functions. Cambridge, MA: MIT Press.

Vygotsky LS (1978) Mind in Society: The Development of Higher Psychological Processes. Cambridge, MA: Harvard University Press.

Waelder R (1930) The principle of multiple function: observations on over-determination. In SA Guttman (ed.), Psychoanalysis: Observation, Theory, Application (pp. 68–83). New York: International University Press, 1976.

Waelder R (1960) Basic Theory of Psychoanalysis. New York: International Universities Press.

Wallerstein RS (1981) The bipolar self: discussion of alternate perspectives. Journal of American Psychoanalytic Association 29: 377–94.

Wallerstein RS (1986) Forty-two Lives in Treatment: A Study of Psychoanalysis and Psychotherapy. New York: Guilford Press.

Wallerstein RS (1989) The psychotherapy research project of the Menninger Foundation: an overview. Journal of Consulting and Clinical Psychology 57: 195–205.

Wallerstein RS (ed.) (1992) The Common Ground of Psychoanalysis. Northvale, NJ: Jason Aronson.

Wallerstein RS (1993). The effectiveness of psychotherapy and psychoanalysis. In T Shapiro, R Emde (eds), Research in Psychoanalysis: Process, Development, Outcome (pp. 299–312). New York: International University Press.

Ward MJ, Carlson EA (1995) Associations among Adult Attachment representations, maternal sensitivity, and infant–mother attachment in a sample of adolescent mothers. Child Development 66: 69–79.

Warner V, Weissman MM, Mufson L, Wickramaratne PJ (1999) Grandparents, parents and grandchildren at high risk for depression: a three generation study. Journal of the American Academy of Child and Adolescent Psychiatry 38: 289–96.

Warren SL, Huston L, Egeland B, Sroufe LA (1997) Child and adolescent anxiety disorders and early attachment. Journal of the American Academy of Child and Adolescent Psychiatry 36: 637–44.

Wartner UG, Grossman K, Fremmer-Bombrik E, Suess G (1994) Attachment patterns at age six in South Germany: predictability from infancy and implications for pre-school behavior. Child Development 65: 1014–27.

Wason PC, Johnson-Laird PN (1972) Psychology of Reasoning: Structure and Content. Cambridge, MA: Harvard University Press.

Wasserman GA, Miller LS, Pinner E, Jaramillo B (1996) Parenting predictors of early conduct problems in urban, high-risk boys. Journal of the American Academy of Child and Adolescent Psychiatry 35: 1227–36.

Waters E, Wippman J, Sroufe LA (1979) Attachment, positive affect, and competence in the peer group: two studies in construct validation. Child Development 50: 821–9.

Watson JB (1930) Behaviorism (rev. edn). New York: Norton.

Watson JS (1972) Smiling, cooing, and 'the game'. Merrill-Palmer Quarterly 18: 323–39.

Watson JS (1979) Perception of contingency as a determinant of social responsiveness. In EB Thoman (ed.), The Origins of Social Responsiveness (pp. 33–64). New York: Lawrence Erlbaum.

Watson JS (1984). Bases of causal inference in infancy: time, space, and sensory relations. In LP Lipsitt, C Rovee-Collier (eds), Advances in Infancy Research. Norwood, NJ: Ablex.

Watson JS (1985) Contingency perception in early social development. In TM Field, NA Fox (eds), Social Perception in Infants (pp. 157–76). Norwood, NJ: Ablex.

Watson JS (1991) Detection of Self: The Perfect Algorithm, Sonoma State University, Sonoma, CA.

Watson JS (1994) Detection of self: the perfect algorithm. In S Parker, R Mitchell, M Boccia (eds), Self-Awareness in Animals and Humans: Developmental Perspectives (pp. 131–49). Cambridge: Cambridge University Press.

Watson JS (1995) Self-orientation in early infancy: the general role of contingency and the specific case of reaching to the mouth. In P Rochat (ed.), The Self in Infancy: Theory and Research (pp. 375–93). Amsterdam: Elsevier.

Watson MW, Getz K (1990) The relationship between Oedipal behaviors and children's family role concepts. Merrill-Palmer Quarterly 36: 487–505.

Webster R (1995) Why Freud Was Wrong: Sin, Science and Psychoanalysis. London: HarperCollins.

Weil AP (1970) The basic core. The Psychoanalytic Study of the Child 25: 442–60.

Weil AP (1978) Maturational variations and genetic-dynamic issues. Journal of the American Psychoanalytic Association 26: 461–91.

Weinberger DA (1990) The construct validity of the repressive coping style. In JL Singer (ed.), Repression and Dissociationi. Chicago, IL: University of Chicago Press.

Weinfield NS, Sroufe LA, Egeland B, Carlson AE (1999) The nature of individual differences in infant-caregiver attachment. In J Cassidy, PR Shaver (eds), Handbook of Attachment: Theory, Research and Clinical Applications (pp. 68–88). New York: Guilford.

Wellman HM, Banerjee M (1991) Mind and emotion: children's understanding of the emotional consequences of beliefs and desires. British Journal of Developmental Psychology 9: 191–214.

Wellman HM, Bartsch K (1988) Young children's reasoning about beliefs. Cognition 30, 239–77.

Welsh-Allis G, Ye W (1988) Psychopathology in children of parents with recurrent depression. Journal of Abnormal Child Psychology 16: 17–28.

Werner EE (1989) Children of the garden island. Scientific American 260(4): 106–11.

Werner EE (1990) Protective factors and individual resilience. In SJ Meisels, M Shonkoff (eds), Handbook of Early Childhood Intervention (pp. 97–116). New York: Cambridge University Press.

Werner H, Kaplan B (1963) Symbol Formation. New York: Wiley.

Werthheimer M (1945) Productive Thinking. New York: Harper & Brothers.

Westen D (1989) Are 'primitive' object relations really preoedipal? Amer.J.Orthopsychiat. 59: 331–45.

Westen D (1990a) The relations among narcissism, egocentrism, self-concept, and self-esteem. Psycho-Analysis and Contemporary Thought, 13, 185–241.

Westen D (1990b) Towards a revised theory of borderline object relations: contributions of empirical research. International Journal Psycho-Analysis 71: 661–94.

Westen D (1991a) Cognitive-behavioral interventions in the psychoanalytic psychotherapy of borderline personality disorders. Clin. Psychol. Rev. 11: 211–30.

Westen D (1991b) Social cognition and object relations. Psychological Bulletin 109: 429–55.

Westen D (1992) The cognitive self and the psychoanalytic self: can we put our selves together? Psychological Inquiry 3: 1–13.

Westen D (1998) The scientific legacy of Sigmund Freud: toward a psychodynamically informed psychological science. Psychological Bulletin 124(3): 333–71.

Westen D (1999) The scientific status of unconscious processes: is Freud really dead? Journal of the American Psychoanalytic Association 47(4): 1061–1106.

Westen D, Cohen RP (1993) The self in borderline personality disorder: a psychodynamic perspective. In ZV Segal, SJ Blatt (eds), The Self in Emotional Distress: Cognitive and Psychodynamic Perspectives (pp. 334–60). New York and London: Guilford Press.

Westen D, Lohr N, Silk K, Gold L, Kerber K (1990) Object relations and social cognition in borderlines, major depressives, and normals: A TAT analysis. Psychological Assessment: A Journal of Consulting and Clinical Psychology 2: 355–64.

Westen D, Ludolph P, Block MJ, Wixom J, Wiss C. (1990) Developmental history and object relations in psychiatrically disturbed adolescent girls. American Journal of Psychiatry 147: 1061–8.

Westen D, Ludolph P, Lerner H, Ruffins S, Wiss FC (1990) Object relations in borderline adolescents. J.Acad.Child and Adolesc.Psychiatry 29: 338–48.

Westen D, Muderrisoglu S, Fowler C, Shedler J, Koren D (1997) Affect regulation and affective experience: individual differences, group differences, and measurement using a Q-sort procedure. Journal of Consulting and Clinical Psychology 65: 429–39.

Westen D, Moses MJ, Silk KR, Lohr NE, Cohen R, Sega H (1992) Quality of depressive experience in borderline personality disorder and major depression: when depression is not just depression. Journal of Personality Disorders, 6: 383–92.

Wilkinson FR, Cargill DW (1955) Repression elicited by story material based on the Oedipus complex. Journal of Social Psychology 42: 209–14.

Williams JMG, Watts FN, MacLeod C, Mathews A (1988) Cognitive Psychology and Emotional Disorders. Chichester: Wiley.

Willick MS (2001) Psychoanalysis and schizophrenia: a cautionary tale. Journal of the American Psychoanalytic Association 49: 27–56.

Wilson TD, Schooler JW (1991) Thinking too much: introspection can reduce the quality of preferences and decisions. Journal of Personality and Social Psychology 60: 181–92.

Winnicott DW (1948) Paediatrics and psychiatry. In DW Winnicott (ed.), Collected Papers (pp. 157–73). New York: Basic Books, 1958.

Winnicott DW (1952) Psychoses and child care. Through Paediatrics to Psychoanalysis (pp. 229–42). New York: Basic Books, 1975.

Winnicott DW (1953) Transitional objects and transitional phenomena. International Journal of Psycho-Analysis 34: 1–9.

Winnicott DW (1956a) The antisocial tendency. In DW Winnicott (ed.), Collected Papers: Through Paediatrics to Psycho-analysis. London: Tavistock, 1958.

Winnicott DW (1956b) Mirror role of mother and family in child development. In DW Winnicott (ed.), Playing and reality (pp. 111-118). London: Tavistock.

Winnicott DW (1956c) Primary maternal preoccupation. In DW Winnicott (ed.), Collected Papers: Through Paediatrics to Psycho-analysis (pp. 300–5). London: Tavistock, 1958.

Winnicott DW (1958a) The capacity to be alone. The Maturational Processes and the Facilitating Environment (pp. 29–36). New York: International Universities Press, 1965.

Winnicott DW (1958b) Collected Papers: Through Paediatrics to Psycho-analysis. London: Tavistock.

Winnicott DW (1959) Classification: is there a psycho-analytic contribution to psychiatric classification? The Maturational Processes and the Facilitating Environment. New York: International Universities Press, 1965.

Winnicott DW (1960a) Ego distortion in terms of true and false self. In DW Winnicott (ed.), The Maturational Processes and the Facilitating Environment (pp. 140–52). New York: International Universities Press, 1965.

Winnicott DW (1960b) The theory of the parent-infant relationship. International Journal of Psycho-Analysis 41: 585–95.

Winnicott DW (1960c) The theory of the parent-infant relationship. In DW Winnicott (ed.), The Maturational Process and the Facilitating Environment (pp. 37–55). New York: International Universities Press.

Winnicott DW (1962a) Ego integration in child development. In DW Winnicott (ed.), The Maturational Processes and the Facilitating Environment (pp. 56–63). London: Hogarth Press, 1965.

Winnicott DW (1962b) The theory of the parent–infant relationship: further remarks. International Journal of Psycho-Analysis 43: 238–45.

Winnicott DW (1963a) Communicating and not communicating leading to a study of certain opposites. In DW Winnicott (ed.), The Maturational Processes and the Facilitating Environment (pp. 179–92). New York: International Universities Press, 1965.

Winnicott DW (1963b) Dependence in infant care, in child care, and in the psycho-analytic setting. In DW Winnicott (ed.), The Maturational Processes and the Facilitating Environment (pp. 171–8). New York: International Universities Press, 1965.

Winnicott DW (1963c) The development of the capacity for concern. In DW Winnicott (ed.), The Maturational Processes and the Facilitating Environment (pp. 73–82). New York: International Universities Press, 1965.

Winnicott DW (1963d) From dependence toward independence in the development of the individual. In DW Winnicott (ed.), The Maturational Processes and the Facilitating Environment (pp. 83–92). New York: International Universities Press, 1965.

Winnicott DW (1963e) Morals and education. In DW Winnicott (ed.), The Maturational Processes and the Facilitating Environment. New York: International Universities Press, 1965.

Winnicott DW (1963f) Psychotherapy of character disorders. In DW Winnicott (ed.), The Maturational Processes and the Facilitating Environment. London: Hogarth Press, 1965.

Winnicott DW (1965a) Ego distortion in terms of true and false self. In DW Winnicott (ed.), The Maturational Process and the Facilitating Environment (pp. 140–52). New York: International Universities Press.

Winnicott DW (1965b) The Maturational Process and the Facilitating Environment. London: Hogarth Press.

Winnicott DW (1967a) The location of cultural experience. Playing and Reality (pp. 95–103). London: Tavistock Publications.

Winnicott DW (1967b) Mirror-role of the mother and family in child development. In P Lomas (ed.), The Predicament of the Family: A Psycho-Analytical Symposium (pp. 26–33). London: Hogarth Press.

Winnicott DW (1971a) Playing and Reality. London: Tavistock.

Winnicott DW (1971b) Playing: creative activity and the search for the self. In Playing and Reality (pp. 62–75). New York: Basic Books.

Winnicott DW (1971c) Transitional objects and transitional phenomena. In DW Winnicott (ed.), Playing and Reality (pp. 1–25). London: Tavistock.

Winnicott DW (1973) Fear of breakdown. International Review of Psycho-Analysis 1: 103–7.

Winnicott DW (1986) Home Is Where We Start From. New York: WW Norton & Co.

Wittgenstein L (1969) The Blue and Brown Books. Oxford: Blackwell.

Wolf ES (1988a) Case discussion and position statement. Psychoanalytic Inquiry 8: 546–51.

Wolf ES (1988b) Treating the Self. New York: Guilford.

Wolff PH (1996) The irrelevance of infant observations for psychoanalysis. Journal of the American Psychoanalytic Association 44: 369–92.

Wollheim R (1995) The Mind and Its Depths. Cambridge, MA: Harvard University Press.

Wolstein B (1977) Psychology, metapsychology, and the evolving American school. Contemporary Psychoanalysis 13: 128–54.

Wolstein B (1994) The evolving newness of interpersonal psychoanalysis: from the vantage point of immediate experience. Contemporary Psychoanalysis 30: 473–98.

Wong P, Bernat E, Bunce S, Shevrin H (1997) Brain indices of nonconscious associative learning. Consciousness and Cognition 6: 519–44.

Woody GE, McLellan AT, Luborsky L, O'Brien CP (1995) Psychotherapy in community methadone programs: a validation study. American Journal of Psychiatry 192: 1302–8.

Wootton JM, Frick PJ, Shelton KK, Silverthorn P (1997) Ineffective parenting and childhood conduct problems: the moderating role of callous-unemotional traits. Journal of Consulting and Clinical Psychology 65: 301–8.

Yager J (1982) Family issues in the pathogenesis of anorexia nervosa. Psychosomatic Medicine 44: 43–60.

Yorke CSB (1971) Some suggestions for a critique of Kleinian psychology. The Psychoanalytic Study of the Child 26: 129–55.

Yorke CSB (1980) The contributions of the diagnostic profile and the assessment of developmental lines to child psychiatry. Psychiat.Clinics N. America 3: 593–603.

Yorke CSB (1983) Anna Freud and the psychoanalytic study and treatment of adults. International Journal of Psycho-Analysis 64: 391–400.

Yorke CSB (1986) Reflections on the problem of psychic trauma. The Psychoanalytic Study of the Child 41: 221–36.

Yorke CSB, Kennedy H, Wiseberg S (1981) Some clinical and theoretical aspects of two developmental lines. The Course of Life (pp. 619–37). Adelphi, MD: US Dept. of Health.

Yorke CSB, Wiseberg S, Freeman T (1989) Development and Psychopathology: Studies in Psychoanalytic Psychiatry. New Haven, CT and London: Yale University Press.

Young JE (1990) Cognitive Therapy for Personality Disorders: A Schema-Focused Approach. Sarasota, FL: Professional Resource Exchange.

Younger BA, Cohen LB (1986) Developmental change in infants' perception of correlations among attributes. Child Development 57: 803–15.

Yule W, Rutter M (1985) Reading and other learning difficulties. In M Rutter, L Hersov (eds), Child and Adolescent Psychiatry: Modern Approaches (pp. 444–64). Oxford: Blackwell Scientific Publications.

Zahn-Waxler C, Kochanska G (1990) The development of guilt. In R Thompson (ed.), Nebraska Symposium on Motivation: Vol 36. Socioemotional development (pp. 183–258). Lincoln, NB: University of Nebraska Press.

Zahn-Waxler C, Cole P, Barrett KC (1991) Guilt and empathy: sex differences and implications for the development of depression. In J Garber, K Dodge (eds), The Development of Emotion Regulation and Dysregulation (pp. 243–72). Cambridge: Cambridge University Press.

Zahn-Waxler C, Cummings EM, McKnew D, Radke-Yarrow M (1984) Altruism, aggression and social interactions in young children with a manic-depressive parent. Child Development 55: 112–22.

Zahn-Waxler C, Ianotti RJ, Cummings EM, Denham S (1990) Antecedents of problem behavior in children of depressed mothers. Development and Psychopathology 2: 271–92.

Zahn-Waxler C, Klimes-Dougan B, Slattery MJ (2000) Internalizing problems of childhood and adolescence: prospects, pitfalls, and progress in understanding the development of anxiety and depression. Development and Psychopathology 12: 443–66.

Zamansky HS (1958) An investigation of the psychoanalytic theory of paranoid delusions. Journal of Personality 26: 410–25.

Zanarini MC, Frankenburg FR (1997) Pathways to the development of borderline personality disorder. Journal of Personality Disorders 11: 93–104.

Zanarini MC, Gunderson JG, Frankenburg FR (1990a) Cognitive features of borderline personality disorder. American Journal of Psychiatry 147: 57–63.

Zanarini M, Gunderson JG, Frankenburg FR (1990b) Discriminating borderline personality disorder from other Axis II disorders. American Journal Psychiatry 147: 161–7.

Zekoski EM, O'Hara MW, Wils KE (1987) The effects of maternal mood on mother–infant interaction. Journal of Abnormal Child Psychology 15: 361–78.

Zigler E (1989) Foreword. In D Cicchetti (ed.), Rochester Symposium on Developmental Psychopathology, Vol. 1: The Emergence of a Discipline (pp. ix–xii). Hillsdale, NJ: Erlbaum.

Zigler E, Glick M (1986) A Developmental Approach to Adult Psychopathology. New York: John Wiley & Sons.

Zoccolillo M, Pickles A, Quinton D, Rutter M (1992) The outcome of childhood conduct disorder: implications for defining adult personality disorder and conduct disorder. Psychological Medicine 22: 971–86.

Zuckerman BS, Beardslee WR (1987) Maternal depression: a concern for pediatricians. Pediatrics 79: 110–17.

Index

402 Psychoanalytic Theories: Perspectives from Developmental Psychopathology